The Papers of
Howard Washington Thurman

Volume 4

The Papers of

Howard Washington Thurman

VOLUME 4

The Soundless Passion of a Single Mind,
June 1949–December 1962

Senior Editor   Walter Earl Fluker
Associate Editor   Peter Eisenstadt
Managing Editor   Silvia P. Glick
Senior Advisory Editor   Luther E. Smith, Jr.

The University of South Carolina Press

Published by the University of South Carolina Press
Columbia, South Carolina 29208

www.sc.edu/uscpress

Manufactured in the United States of America

28 27 26 25 24 23 22 21 20 19 18 17
10 9 8 7 6 5 4 3 2 1

Library of Congress Cataloging-in-Publication Data
can be found at http://catalog.loc.gov/.

ISBN 978-1-61117-804-3 (cloth)

This book was printed on recycled paper with
30 percent postconsumer waste content.

This volume would not have been possible without the generous
material and financial support of the following contributors:
    The Lilly Endowment Inc.
    The Louisville Institute
    The Henry Luce Foundation
    The National Endowment for the Humanities
    The National Historical Publications and Records Commission
    The Pew Charitable Trusts

CONTENTS

List of Illustrations *ix*
Acknowledgments *xi*
List of Abbreviations *xv*
Biographical Essay *xvii*
Editorial Statement *li*
Howard Thurman Chronology *lvii*

22 June 1949	From Emily Worthy *1*
21 August 1949	"The Quest for Peace" *2*
November 1949	From Sue Bailey Thurman to Howard, Madaline, and Olive *9*
January 1950	To Friend *12*
3 May 1950	To Fellowship Church Family *17*
28 September 1950	To Mary McLeod Bethune *18*
14 November 1950	"The Power of the Spirit and the Powers of This World" *21*
1 March 1951	From Roland Hayes *30*
27 April 1951	To Dr. and Mrs. George Collins *32*
19 May 1951	To Dr. Willard Johnson *34*
21 May 1951	To John Overholt *35*
29 January 1952	Gene K. Walker to Spingarn Medal Co. *38*
26 April 1952	To Carlton E. Byrne *40*
26 June 1952	To Gail Hudson *43*
1 August 1952	To Walter G. Muelder *45*
20 December 1952	To Harold C. Case *46*
8 January 1953	To Gene K. Walker *47*
16 January 1953	From Walter G. Muelder *49*
26 January 1953	From Harold C. Case *52*
31 January 1953	To the Board of Trustees of Fellowship Church *53*
6 February 1953	To Harold C. Case *56*
7 March 1953	To Harold C. Case *57*

9 March 1953   To the Board of Trustees and Members of the
               Fellowship Church *60*

11 March 1953 To Coleman Jennings *61*

12 March 1953 From Joseph Van Pelt *63*

21 March 1953 To Arthur U. Crosby *64*

23 March 1953 From Jannette E. Newhall *65*

18 April 1953 To A. J. Muste *66*

23 April 1953 From Cardella Clifton and Family *67*

19 May 1953   To the Board of Trustees of Fellowship Church *67*

21 September 1953 To Benjamin E. Mays *73*

19 January 1954 To Dryden Phelps *74*

28 February 1954 "Horn of the Wild Oxen" *77*

16 May 1954   "Be Ye Not Overcome by Evil" *81*

21 June 1954   Annual Report, Dean of the Chapel *85*

25 August 1954 From Roland Hayes *94*

28 November 1954 From Sidney Dimond *95*

1 December 1954 From Albert W. Dent *96*

14 December 1954 To Albert W. Dent *98*

1955   "Limitation of Intake" *99*

2 January 1955 "He Looked for a City" *105*

18 January 1955 From Mary McLeod Bethune *108*

18 January 1955 To Melvin Watson *111*

February 1955 "Freedom under God" *112*

24 March 1955 To Dorothy Henderson *120*

23 April 1955 To Dryden Phelps *121*

23 May 1955   Eulogy for Mary McLeod Bethune *123*

19 November 1955 Speech at Lambda Kappa Mu Human Relations
               Award Dinner *131*

1956   "Habakkuk Exposition" *136*

7 January 1956 From Henry Bollman *150*

14 March 1956 To Martin Luther King, Jr. *151*

16 March 1956 From Martin Luther King, Jr. *153*

17 April 1956 From James Earl Massey *154*

25 April 1956 To C. H. Winecoff *158*

29 April 1956 "Chapel Committee Meeting" *158*

9 July 1956   Harold C. Case to Margaret Harding *164*

July 1956   To Harold C. Case *165*

28 March 1957 To John Overholt *167*

May 1957   "The Christian Minister and the Desegregation
               Decision" *170*

5 May 1957   "The Gothic Principle" *178*

6 May 1957 "The Responsibility of the Professional to Society" 182
6 September 1957 From Walter N. Pahnke 193
4 October 1957 From Harold C. Case 198
15 October 1957 To Harold C. Case 198
1958 "The New Heaven and the New Earth" 201
19 March 1958 To Clarence R. Johnson 207
18 May 1958 "Faith the Tutor" 209
6 July 1958 "The American Dream" 215
23 July 1958 To Harold C. Case 221
20 October 1958 To Martin Luther King, Jr. 222
26 October 1958 "The Third Component" 224
8 November 1958 From Martin Luther King, Jr. 231
19 November 1958 To Martin Luther King, Jr. 233
28 November 1958 To Harold C. Case 234
24 February 1959 To George Britton 237
3 March 1959 To Zalman M. Schachter 240
11 March 1959 To Arthur L. James 242
24 April 1959 From Richard Nixon 244
24 April 1959 To Harold C. Case 246
31 May 1959 From Clarence Proctor 248
12 June 1959 To Clarence Proctor 249
15 June 1959 To M. H. Fleming 250
22 June 1959 From Martin Luther King, Jr. 251
11 September 1959 To Martin Luther King, Jr. 252
30 September 1959 From Martin Luther King, Jr. 253
20 November 1959 "We Believe [Love Its Own Reward]" 254
26 December 1959 From Francis Geddes 257
1960 Letter in Support of United World Federalists 259
23 January 1960 To William J. Trent, Jr. 260
25 January 1960 To Francis Geddes 262
18 February 1960 From Charles V. Hamilton 264
May 1960 To Francis Geddes 265
3 August 1960 From Francis Geddes 266
15 August 1960 To Friends of the International Fellowship Community 268
16 August 1960 To Francis Geddes 276
Fall 1960 "Windbreak . . . Against Existence" 281
29 September 1960 To the Chairman and Board of Directors of Fellowship Church 285
23 October 1960 "An Imperative to Understanding" 288

31 October 1960   To Lloyd Smith *294*
17 November 1960   To E. B. Thompson *296*
1961   "Two Options" *297*
16 March 1961   To J. Wendell Yeo *300*
25 May 1961   From William Holmes Borders *304*
31 August 1961   From Adam C. Powell, Jr. *306*
8 September 1961   To Adam C. Powell, Jr. *307*
19 September 1961   To James Van Pelt *307*
14 January 1962   "Albert Schweitzer" *309*
24 January 1962   To Gilbert Ambrose *314*
13 February 1962   To A. J. Muste *316*
2 March 1962   "Howard University and the Frontiers of Human Freedom" *317*
6 March 1962   To James M. Nabrit, Jr. *323*
11 July 1962   Drafts of Telegrams to John F. Kennedy, Robert F. Kennedy, and Laurie Pritchett *326*
16 October 1962   "Worship and Word" *327*
29 October 1962   From Timothy Leary *333*

Appendix
8 August 1963   Text of Telegram to Shirley Katzander on the Good Friday Experiment *335*
Index *337*

List of Illustrations

Howard Thurman, 1965 *xxi*
Letter from Sue Bailey Thurman to Howard, Madaline, and Olive *11*
George Makechnie and Howard and Sue Bailey Thurman at Howard
    Thurman's retirement event *91*
Howard Thurman with Huston C. Smith *119*
Howard Thurman with a copy of *The Growing Edge* *193*
Howard and Sue Bailey Thurman with Harold and Phyllis Case *199*
Howard Thurman with Anne Thurman at her graduation from Boston
    University School of Law *209*
Howard Thurman with George Makechnie at wedding *238*
Commemoration of Phillis Wheatley at Marsh Chapel *245*
Liturgical dance at Marsh Chapel *255*
Howard and Sue Bailey Thurman with Daniel Marsh and
    George Makechnie *301*
Howard and Sue Bailey Thurman with African students at Boston
    University *315*
Howard Thurman, seated *333*

Acknowledgments

Howard Thurman often spoke of the solitary discipline of single-mindedness—the utter abandonment of psychological, social, and cultural entrapments that block our visions of the good; and the total commitment of our powers to make real that which we envision as the deep intent and purpose of our lives. Stated more eloquently, he wrote, "The time and place of a man's life on earth are the time and place of his body, but the meaning and significance of his life are as vast and far-reaching as his gifts, his times, and the passionate commitment of all his powers can make it" (*With Head and Heart*, 208).

Volume 4 of *The Papers of Howard Washington Thurman*, covering the years 1949–62, is titled *The Soundless Passion of a Single Mind*. The phrase "the soundless passion of a single mind" is from the poem "The Stream: Verses on Singleness of Mind, Written among the Black Mountains," by Charles Langbridge Morgan, and was a favorite line of Thurman's often used by him as a sermon title. The title speaks to Thurman's commitment to create an interreligious, interracial fellowship in the heart of American life at a time when the nation was transitioning from the bloodbath of World War II, struggling with the perennial questions of race and ethnicity, and addressing the rising global challenges to colonialism and to its domestic American counterpart in the modern civil rights movement. Thurman's vision of "a friendly world under friendly skies" found alternately hospitable and frustrating conditions at Boston University after his ecclesiological experiment at the Fellowship Church from 1944 to 1953. Volume 4 begins in the latter years of Fellowship Church and weaves together the tapestry of the period to unveil the larger portrait of Howard Thurman as dean of Marsh Chapel and professor of spiritual resources at Boston University School of Theology.

My work as editor and director of the Howard Thurman Papers Project resonates deeply with the kind of passionate commitment that characterized Howard Thurman's unwavering vision. My special thanks are extended to the other members of our editorial team, Peter Eisenstadt and Silvia P. Glick, whose expertise, intelligence, and commitment to this documentary edition have been invaluable. I am grateful to Luther E. Smith, my longtime colleague and senior advisory editor of the project, and to Julian Cook, who has provided critical support as a research assistant.

We extend our thanks to the Lilly Endowment, Inc., for continuing to be a steadfast partner, having given the largest percentage of support to date for our work. Christopher Coble, vice president for religion, has been especially generous in the production of this volume and the next. In addition we are deeply indebted to the National Endowment for the Humanities (NEH) for the funding provided under its "We the People" program, an initiative supporting projects that help advance knowledge of the principles that define America; this program funded the Howard Thurman Papers Project in 2009 and 2010 and most recently for 2014–16. Special thanks are extended to Lydia Medici, our NEH program analyst in the Division of Research Programs, and to Peter Scott, our NEH grants administrator, for their support, encouragement, and enthusiasm for our work.

The Thurman family has been supportive of the project from its beginning. The ongoing support of Howard Thurman's grandson, Anton Wong, and of Thurman's granddaughter, Suzanne Chiarenza, has been invaluable to our success.

During our work on Thurman's years at Boston University, the editors were reminded of the close relationship between Howard Thurman and the late George Makechnie, in whose honor we publish this volume. Makechnie held many roles at Boston University, including that of dean of the College of Health & Rehabilitation Sciences: Sargent College. Makechnie, a longtime friend and colleague of Thurman, was among the first to welcome the Thurmans upon their arrival at Boston University in 1953 and contributed more than any single person at Boston University to insure Thurman's legacy, founding the Howard Thurman Center for Common Ground in 1986 and writing *Howard Thurman: His Enduring Dream* (1988). Makechnie and his family were prominently featured in J. Anthony Lukacs's prizewinning study of the Boston integration struggles, *Common Ground* (1985), its title borrowed from one of Thurman's books. The title was a tribute to the influence of Thurman on the Makechnies. Upon receiving the Howard Thurman Oikoumene Award in 1999 at Morehouse College, Makechnie stated, "At the time of my official retirement in 1972, Howard wrote and humbly I share his words: 'From you I have learned much. The most precious gift you have given me is yourself—in such an offering the miracle appeared, you somehow managed to give me to myself, greatly enriched, and spiritually glorified. Thank you and thank God!' More appropriately these should have been my words to him" ("Remembering Dr. Howard Thurman," 1999).

Since 2010 Boston University School of Theology has provided the most fitting setting for the continuing work of the project. From 1953 to 1963 Thurman served as the university's dean of Marsh Chapel, the first African American to occupy such a position at a majority-white university. The years 1962–65 were spent by Thurman in what was called the "wider ministry" and as an at-large minister, as noted in this volume's biographical essay. Thurman's early years at Boston University coincided with the matriculation of a young theologian and soon-to-be pastor who would shape the moral and legal landscape of twentieth-century America, Dr. Martin Luther King, Jr. This volume contains correspondence between Thurman and King that highlights the depth of the friendship between these two men.

Our home at the School of Theology owes a great debt to the generous hospitality and graciousness of spirit embodied in Dean Mary Elizabeth Moore and the faculty, staff, and students who are part of a long and cherished tradition of producing prophetic leaders for the church and the world. The project has also greatly benefited from its close relationship with the Special Collections at Boston University, renamed in 2003 the Howard Gotlieb Archival Research Center to honor its founder. Howard Gotlieb, now deceased, and his entire staff provided assistance to the project and granted those involved access to Thurman's papers, along with the authority to catalog the bulk of the papers, which had not yet been organized. Vita Paladino, the present director of the Gotlieb Center, has been a great source of inspiration and support. Kenneth Elmore, dean of students, and Katherine Kennedy, the present director of the Thurman Center, deserve mention for their excellent work on diversity and student programming that marks the life of the center.

Many individuals, institutions, and organizations contributed to this volume through their generosity in granting permission to publish documents. We are grateful to the following rights holders for permission to publish correspondence and previously published writings: the Estate of Howard Thurman; the Trustees of Boston University; the Church for the Fellowship of All Peoples, San Francisco; James Earl Massey; Francis Geddes; Adam Clayton Powell III; Afrika Hayes-Lambe; Pamela Norstrom; Joan D. Dimond; Walter J. Dent; Annette Bollman Morey; Kristin Kreamer; the Richard Nixon Foundation; Clarence Proctor; *Bostonia*; Charles V. Hamilton; Harriet O. St. Amant; Elinor Maria Benson; and the Futique Trust/Timothy Leary Estate.

Numerous institutions have assisted us in our work. For invaluable contributions to the present volume, we with gratitude acknowledge the following institutions for providing access to their collections: the Eleanor Roosevelt Papers, Franklin Delano Roosevelt Library, Hyde Park, New York; the Collections of the Department of History, Presbyterian Church (U.S.A.), Philadelphia, Pennsylvania; the Moorland-Spingarn Research Center, Howard University Archives, Washington, D.C.; the Stuart A. Rose Manuscript, Archives, and Rare Book Library of Emory University, Atlanta, Georgia; the Fellowship Church of All Peoples, San Francisco, California; and the John Swomley Papers, Swarthmore College Archives, Swarthmore, Pennsylvania.

Mentors and friends such as Clayborne Carson, James Earl Massey, Randall K. Burkett, and Edward K. Kaplan have encouraged our work through the various

xiv ACKNOWLEDGMENTS

stages of the project's development. Sadly, one of the initial Howard Thurman Papers Project advisory board members and an ardent supporter of Thurman's legacy, Vincent Harding, passed away on 19 May 2014. Others who have worked with the project over time include Catherine Tumber, Quinton Dixie, Kai Jackson-Issa, Alton Pollard, Clarissa Myrick-Harris, Alma Jean-Billingsea, Michael Joseph Brown, Jamison Collier, Onaje Woodbine, Julian Cook, and Derrick Muwina.

Finally, I thank my wife, Sharon Watson Fluker, whose love and support sustain me and enable me to continue this work.

List of Abbreviations

Collections and Repositories

FC   Church for the Fellowship of All Peoples, San Francisco, California
JSP-SWA   John Swomley Papers, Swarthmore College, Swarthmore, Pennsylvania

Abbreviations Used in Source Notes

The following abbreviations describe the documents upon which the transcriptions were based.

Script

A   Autograph (manuscript in author's hand)
H   Handwritten (manuscript in hand other than author's)
P   Printed
T   Typed

Format

At   Audio tape
D   Document
Fm   Form
L   Letter or memo
Ph   Photo
W   Wire or telegram

Version

c   Copy (carbon)
d   Draft
f   Fragment

Signature

I   Initialed
S   Signed
Sr   Signed with representation of author

ABBREVIATIONS USED IN ENDNOTES

PHWT   *The Papers of Howard Washington Thurman*
WHAH   *With Head and Heart* (the autobiography of Howard Thurman)

Biographical Essay

"I am 52 years old, which means that according to the classical American time-table, I have 13 years of active work," Howard Thurman wrote to the trustees of the Church for the Fellowship of All Peoples in San Francisco in January 1953. He continued, "This gives me no sense of urgency but it does point up the fact that if my life is to be spent to the fullest advantage on behalf of what seems to me to be the great hope for mankind, it is important to work on its behalf where there is the maximum possibility of contagion."[1]

Contagion, for Thurman, was a central religious value. It reflected the ability to spread one's message and one's example, like spores floating through air, falling on receptive, fertile ground. In many ways this brand of spiritual fertility had been his life's mission from the time that as a teenager in Florida he decided to dedicate himself to a religious vocation. In the decade from 1944 to 1953 he came as close as he ever would to realizing his dream of creating a genuinely interracial and interreligious community. However, there was a gap between Thurman's grand ambitions for the Fellowship Church and the less than ideal ways in which they were realized. As much as he loved the church and its members, Thurman would from time to time privately decry what he saw as some of its limitations: the inevitable pettiness and squabbling; the localism of some of its members who insisted that it was just another neighborhood church; the instability of its leadership; and chronic financial woes. Perhaps what troubled him most was a feeling that by his very success and the inherent charisma of his ministry, the Fellowship Church was becoming the church of Howard Thurman, and as such, a church that would have difficulty surviving the day when he would have to step down from its leadership.[2]

Beyond all of these issues, Thurman worried that the Fellowship Church had limited his possibility for contagion. By 1953 it was clear that the Fellowship Church had not—and would not—become the catalyst of a national movement of similar churches, as he often had hoped. He was preaching to more or less the same group of people week in and week out. He missed the sort of deep mentorship that is an integral part of teaching advanced divinity students, and he felt to some extent cut off from the rising generation of black students, particularly black divinity students. Although Thurman did not seek to leave the Fellowship

Church, when the right position came along, he made his decision fairly quickly with regret and sadness but without much hesitation.

The offer made in 1953 to Thurman was impressive. Not only would he become the first tenured black professor at Boston University School of Theology, but he would also become dean of the chapel. As one of the university's nine deans, he would be "the coordinator of all religious affairs at the university, assisting the deans and student councils of the several colleges and schools in planning programs and assemblies of religious nature and be the adviser to numerous interfaith, interdenominational and denominational organizations on campus." Thurman wrote to the church trustees that for "one of America's great universities" to give this level of responsibility to a black academic was a "completely unprecedented step in American education," one that made "a limitless contribution to intergroup relations at this fateful moment in the history of America and the world."[3]

Thurman had been a frequent visitor to Boston University and the Boston area. As early as March 1933 he spoke at the School of Education on "The Tragedy of Dull-Mindedness."[4] He was back at Boston University—at the School of Theology—the following year, in October 1934, speaking on "Preaching the Kingdom of God to the Disinherited," which was published the following summer under the title "Good News for the Underprivileged."[5] He made frequent return visits, and even after his move to San Francisco in 1944 he usually included a stop in the area on his annual preaching tour to the East, with Wellesley College and Dana Hall School, both in Wellesley, as favored destinations. In April 1947 he delivered the Ingersoll Lecture at Harvard University.

In many ways the position at Boston University School of Theology struck Thurman as a combination of the best aspects of both Howard University and the Fellowship Church. He would be teaching again at a graduate school of theology, offering his brand of spiritual contagion to a group of young, unfinished minds. But unlike at Howard University, he would be teaching a racially diverse group of students. Boston University had a long and distinguished history of educating and graduating blacks. The School of Theology had granted a Ph.D. to an African American, J. W. E. Bowen, as early as 1887.[6] Few mainstream universities in the 1950s had comparable success in offering advanced theological training to African Americans. The university's historian, Kathleen Kilgore, wrote, "By the time Howard Thurman arrived in the early 1950s, the University had, for the first time in its history, not just a few but a substantial number of black students."[7]

The faculty of Boston University School of Theology was forthright in its commitments to social change. Its dean from 1945 to 1971, Walter G. Muelder, was only one of the many faculty members with a reputation for outspokenness on questions of war and peace, capitalism and labor, and civil rights.[8] For

Muelder's efforts, his leadership and the School of Theology were tarred by the *Reader's Digest* in February 1950 as examples of "Methodism's Pink Fringe." Among the reasons the *Reader's Digest* provided for accusing Muelder of "giving aid and comfort to Communists" was his insistence on the religious importance of "racial brotherhood."[9] In Boston, Thurman would join one of the largest and most distinguished theological faculties in the country. If at Howard University the School of Theology was something of a despised stepchild, at Boston University the situation was reversed. Theological education had been central to the mission of Boston University (which began as the Methodist General Biblical Institute in Concord, New Hampshire) since its creation in 1869, and the school soon evolved into one of the preeminent Methodist-sponsored institutions of higher learning in the country.

Like many institutions of higher learning in the postwar years, Boston University was rapidly expanding. From 1925 to 1951, under the presidency of Daniel L. Marsh (1880–1968)—a Methodist minister and 1908 graduate of the Boston University School of Theology—the university underwent a considerable expansion. After the war the university moved to a new, sprawling urban campus along Commonwealth Avenue near the Charles River, across from Cambridge. The School of Theology was moved to its new neo-Gothic home on Commonwealth Avenue in 1948. In 1950 the new university chapel opened next to the School of Theology; it was designed in a medieval style by the prominent architect Ralph Adams Cram and was named after the university's longtime president.[10] Marsh Chapel, as its eponym wrote, was a place that "confers spirituality and permanence on the fleeting objects of sense"; it would be Thurman's spiritual home for over a decade.[11] Daniel Marsh would become Thurman's firm admirer and wrote him in 1961, "What you say about your 'ministry of Marsh Chapel,' & about 'the great challenge which Marsh Chapel represents to' you makes me thank God that you are where you are. You have risen to the comprehension of the task & the opportunity confronting you. God bless you with durable success."[12]

Although Marsh was determined to maintain the Methodist heritage of Boston University, by the time he was succeeded in 1951 by Harold Case—who, like all previous presidents of the university, was a Methodist minister—the student body was no longer primarily Methodist and the university indeed was no longer a majority-Protestant institution. Probably no more than 40 percent of the students were Protestant, with the remainder being either Jewish or Roman Catholic.[13] However, despite their large numbers, non-Protestant religious groups lacked official status. The first Catholic mass on the campus was celebrated only in 1952, and Hillel House, for Jewish students, opened the following year. Thurman's arrival was in part an attempt by Case and Muelder to diversify the School of Theology beyond its inbred, denominational origins. As late as

1945 the faculty was made up entirely of Methodists, all of whom save one were School of Theology alumni. Since becoming dean, Muelder had made a special effort to hire non-Methodists, and Thurman was the most visible such appointment yet.

Thurman was joining a faculty with a distinctive theology. The School of Theology and the university's philosophy department were the centers of personalism, or what became widely known as "Boston personalism," which has been described as the "most coherent school of American liberal theology."[14] Personalism's progenitor was Borden Parker Bowne (1847–1910), who taught at Boston University from 1876 until his death. By the time Thurman arrived at Boston University, the local brand of personalism was well into its third generation of advocates, its local ubiquity aided by the School of Theology's usual practice of hiring its own graduates. In the years just prior to Thurman's arrival, the most prominent exponent of personalism was the philosophy professor Edgar S. Brightman, who was Thurman's longtime friend. He passed away in late February 1953 but not before hearing of Thurman's appointment. Brightman's congratulations were extended posthumously via a colleague.[15]

Personalism remained a dominant philosophical and theological current at Boston University throughout Thurman's years there, with L. Harold DeWolf, Paul Deats, Peter Bertocci, and Dean Muelder among its leading exponents. Personalism is difficult to define succinctly, but its adherents assert that personality is the primary metaphysical reality. Brightman claimed that personalism is "the thesis that the universe is a society of persons under the leadership of a Supreme Creative Person who gives meaning and immanent cooperation to all that is finite."[16] It occupied the broad middle ground in liberal Protestantism for most of the twentieth century, combining an idealistic metaphysics with a pluralistic and nondogmatic theology. If personalists rejected atheism and agnosticism, they also had little patience with Christian orthodoxy or Niebuhrian neo-orthodoxy, and they joined a vibrant concern for recognizing and maximizing personality in the social realm to a deep appreciation for the abiding mysteries of divine presence and personality. Racial justice in America was a key element of the Boston personalists' social agenda.[17]

Thurman never thought of himself as a personalist, in part because of his general disinterest in formal philosophy and theology, but he had for many decades made use of the language of theological personalism. As early as 1924 he decried "any attitude . . . which strangles personality and inhibits its highest growth and development." The following year he listed as a paramount obligation of the Christian the recognition of "the sacredness of human personality,"[18] and he wrote eight years later that "to say 'I affirm my faith in God with my entire personality' is one of the supreme affirmations of the human spirit."[19] He would often write that the greatest evil of the Jim Crow system was its denial to

Howard Thurman, 1965. From the
Bailey Thurman Family Papers;
the Stuart A. Rose Manuscript,
Archives, and Rare Book Library,
Emory University.

African Americans of, as he wrote in 1940, their "persona."[20] In *Disciplines of the Spirit,* a book that was the product of his years at Boston University, he wrote, "Deny personality to human beings and the ethical demand no longer obtains. Much of the evil in human life and society is rationalized in this way."[21] Nonetheless, if Thurman shared much with the tradition of Boston personalism, he viewed it as a supportive, sympathetic outsider.

Although Thurman's personal religious beliefs were certainly congruent with the dominant views at the School of Theology, he was hired primarily because of his abilities as a charismatic preacher and a shaper of religious communities and—not coincidentally—because of his long friendship with the university's president, Harold Case, an acquaintance of some twenty years standing. Case was a 1927 graduate of the Boston University School of Theology, and before his return to Boston in 1951, he had worked extensively as a congregational pastor serving congregations in suburban Chicago; Topeka, Kansas (not far from his hometown of Cottonwood Falls); Scranton, Pennsylvania; and after 1945 Pasadena, California, where he served the First Methodist Church, one of the largest Methodist churches in the country with over thirty-five hundred members. When both men were on the West Coast, Thurman was a frequent visitor to

Case's church, and their admiration was mutual. Thurman wrote to a Southern California correspondent in 1946, "You are quite fortunate to be under the contagious ministry of Harold Case. He and Mrs. Case are two very extraordinary people for whom I have a profound and pointed admiration."[22]

Case and Thurman were already friends when at the end of 1937 during a speaking engagement at a Methodist conference in St. Louis, Thurman was barred from the hotel's dining room. Although he fulfilled his speaking obligation, Thurman was in a bitter, angry mood when, as early in the evening as he could, he retreated to the train station to sleep off his anger in a Pullman coach. When he arrived at the train, Case and his wife Phyllis were waiting for him. After expressing their regrets, Harold Case said, "Our main purpose for meeting you here is to say that if the time ever comes when we can take some firm, even dramatic action to show that the incident that happened here is not our desire or in keeping with the true genius of the Methodist Church, I want you to know that you can depend on us to do it."[23] In 1953 the moment had arrived.

Case's immediate reason for hiring Thurman was that the chapel was, as Thurman later wrote, "nearly moribund;"[24] the congregation consisted of a "few professors and elderly residents of the Bay State Road area."[25] Thurman was encouraged to create at Boston University a religious community like Fellowship Church. This would be a "community church at the university, membership of which would come from the university family and the community of Boston. This would be a non-creedal, non-sectarian, interracial, interfaith and intercultural religious fellowship."[26]

Thurman would create this new community, he told the trustees of the Fellowship Church, from the university's thirty thousand students—including the four hundred plus students at the School of Theology—who came from more than 230 universities and colleges in the United States and from twenty-five foreign countries. This was the interracial diversity of the Fellowship Church amplified and magnified manyfold, creating a new religious community that might "touch at every step of the way hundreds of young people who themselves will be going to the ends of the earth to take up their responsibilities as members of communities. Conceivably, this means the widest possible dissemination of the ideas in which I believe, in the very nature of the operation itself."[27]

Although President Case was the prime mover in the effort to obtain Thurman's services for Boston University, Thurman had many other supporters at the university. These included Brightman, who had been a national member of the Fellowship Church since 1946,[28] and Dean Muelder, whose suggestion to Thurman in a July 1952 letter probably began the process of wooing Thurman to Boston.[29] Another Thurman supporter was Allan Knight Chalmers (1897–1972), who upon joining the School of Theology faculty in 1948 discussed with Muelder the possibility of Thurman coming to the university—Muelder had already considered it—and he also discussed it with Case when he arrived in 1951. When news of Thurman's new position became public, Chalmers wrote Thurman, "No words can quite express my joy in your coming to Boston."[30]

However, not everyone at Boston University shared Chalmers's enthusiasm. Case's plan to hire Thurman was not without its critics. Thurman wrote in his autobiography that "there had been much opposition to my appointment and ministry both on racial and theological grounds," which he had learned about only much later. It was, Thurman felt, to Case's "everlasting credit" that he never revealed to Thurman "even a hint of the pressure to which he was subjected."[31] Even so, Thurman, sensitive in such matters, must have felt the coolness and reserve with which he was greeted in some quarters. He wrote that an unnamed but clearly high-ranking and still influential "greatly revered retired administrator" at Boston University told him that "when Harold Case announced that he had invited you here as dean of the chapel, I did everything I could to oppose your coming." He told Thurman this only after being won over to his side, telling him at the same time that he had been deeply moved by one of Thurman's services: "I want you to know that few times in my life have I had this kind of profound religious experience."[32]

Thurman had his own doubts about accepting the Boston University position. He told Case that "if I come, I think all of you will have a brand-new experience; you will have to learn to work in tandem with a black man" and promised that "there will be times when this will cause you discomfort."[33] Thurman worried how, as a non-Methodist determined to preach his unconventional brand of Christianity, his message would be received. He worried about what he was leaving behind and how he left it, whether his voice would be heard on a large urban campus, and about the problems of relocating his family to a city that was not renowned for its commitment to racial harmony. He worried about a return to the stifling hierarchies, petty jealousies, and endless scrutiny that were the inevitable consequences of being a visible figure at a major university, here compounded by being a black man amid an overwhelmingly white faculty. But doubts and fears along with hopes and dreams are all part of starting a new job, and Thurman felt up to the challenge.

Thurman's decision to accept the Boston position brought him unparalleled national publicity. The black press, as might be expected, was often effusive. The *Amsterdam News* lauded his appointment as befitting "one of the most beloved Christian ministers—a minister's minister—known as scholar, philosopher, poet, preacher and ambassador between diverse peoples."[34] The appointment prompted the *New York Times* to take serious note of Thurman for the first time, with a short article about Thurman and his new position beneath his photograph.[35]

In April 1953 *Life* magazine hailed Thurman as one of a dozen "Great Preachers" who were bringing "America back to the churches." He was the only African American included in the group, which included Norman Vincent Peale, Fulton J. Sheen, and Billy Graham, among other religious celebrities. The caption beneath Thurman's photograph read as follows: "Dr. Thurman, 54, pressed pants to get through school. In 1944 he became pastor of the Fellowship Church in San Francisco, which, composed of whites, Negroes, and Orientals, was an experiment in 'total Christianity.' Under Dr. Thurman the 'experiment' has been successful. He preaches to, not at, his audience, giving ideas to wrestle with, thoughts to meditate upon. This month he accepted Boston University's offer to become university preacher and professor in the School of Theology."[36]

That October in the *Atlantic Monthly* the writer and journalist Jean Burden[37] published a lengthy profile of Thurman, hailing him as a "prophet" who was one "of the champions of the disinherited," standing "for justice in an unjust society," and a "mystic, scholar, poet" as well.[38] The article was a short biography of Thurman with some details, provided by the subject, not available elsewhere, such as his love of Latin, which he learned "with the enthusiasm that most boys apply to marbles and baseball," while he studied "Shakespeare and the librettos of all of the operas." He told Burden of his determination at an early age to become a minister: "When I was born, God must have put a live coal in my heart, for I was His man and there was no escape." The article discussed Thurman's formative experiences at Rochester Theological Seminary, the early stages of his career, the trip to India, the experience at Khyber Pass, and the history of the Fellowship Church. The article concluded with Thurman, "a mystic in the most practical down-to-earth sense," telling of what he tried to accomplish at the Fellowship Church and by extension, Burden suggested, his hopes for Boston University: "Whenever man has the scent of the eternal unity in his spirit, he hunts for it in his home, in his work, among his friends, in his pleasures and in all the levels of his function. It is my simple faith that this is the kind of universe that sustains this kind of adventure. And what we are fumbling towards now. . . . Tomorrow will be the way of life for everybody!" (ellipsis in original).

Thurman started at Marsh Chapel by sweeping away the old ways of doing things. At his first service on 20 September 1953, worshippers were greeted with a new order of service, which Thurman later noted was "based upon the religious theory upon which the chapel would proceed under my leadership."[39] Some traditionalists were no doubt startled. Thurman dropped the Lord's Prayer, the Affirmation of Faith, and the Act of Common Prayer from the service. In their place, in a service largely stripped of particular or parochially Christian elements, was an extended "Period of Meditation." This did not mean that the service was entirely de-Christianized by Thurman. His initial Marsh Chapel sermon was on a familiar Thurman topic, the temptations of Jesus. The program for this initial service included Thurman's statement of his intentions for the chapel: "This Sunday morning worship service is so designed as to address itself to the deepest needs and aspirations of the human spirit. In so doing it does not seek to undermine whatever may be the religious context which gives meaning and richness to your particular life; but rather to deepen the authentic lines along which your quest for spiritual reality has led you. It is our hope that you will come to regard the Chapel not only as a place of stimulation, challenge, and dedication, but also as a symbol of the intent of the University to recognize religion as fundamental to the human enterprise."[40]

Thurman soon made Marsh Chapel into a new spiritual home, and as with every other step in his career, he quickly found a large and appreciative audience for his message, an audience that was composed of Boston University students and faculty, with some regular attendees from elsewhere in the Boston area. As F. Thomas Trotter, who was the Protestant chaplain at Boston University at the time of Thurman's arrival, recalled, "When Howard arrived, the tempo picked up. Marsh Chapel became a church."[41] Thurman soon had a regular congregation of about 225, which increased to about 300 by his last full year as an active minister (1961–62), and he often filled the 500-seat chapel to capacity.[42] The congregation was generally about two-thirds white and one-third minority.[43]

Hubert E. Jones attended Thurman's services while a graduate student at Boston University; he later became dean of the School of Social Work. Jones stated, "With my mind's eye I can see him in the pulpit of Marsh Chapel. He was an immense presence—awesome, not just in preaching, but in a way that would lead one into personal meditation."[44] This was a common sentiment. Joan Diver, George Makechnie's daughter, who as a young girl regularly attended services at Marsh Chapel, remembered Thurman speaking "in a thunderous roar or a barely audible whisper" and recalled that using "his full range of voice he would repeatedly urge each of us gathered to seek, find, and affirm our innermost 'center.'"[45] Since Marsh Chapel services were broadcast weekly over the radio, Thurman's message found a larger audience than his immediate auditors. In 1956 a radio listener, Henry Bollman, having just heard Thurman's sermon, wrote him conveying his "appreciation of [Thurman's] profound understanding of the meaning of God's peace." A student of Hinduism, Bollman wrote, "Until I heard you today, I have never heard a Christian preacher who could be put on the same level of spiritual understanding as the great Swamis of India."[46] From 1958 until he left Boston in the summer of 1965, Thurman also appeared weekly on a local television program, "We Believe," to which he provided a fifteen-minute meditation each Friday morning.[47]

Most of Thurman's auditors were from the immediate Boston University community. An example was Barbara Jordan, a student at the Boston University School of Law from 1956 to 1959 and later a notable congresswoman from Texas, who said, "I went to Chapel practically every Sunday. The minister there,

Howard Thurman, was outstanding. . . . His sermons were focused upon the present time that all of us were having difficulty coming to grips with. . . . I saved every chapel program. [They] contained a message that was always something moving and meaningful."[48]

Martin Luther King, Jr. was another Boston University student who sometimes heard Thurman preach at Marsh Chapel. The two men overlapped only one year at the university; King's final year in Boston, when he had already finished his course work and was concentrating on writing his dissertation, was Thurman's first. Thurman later wrote of King, with an excess of modesty, "I suppose I am one of the few members of the Graduate School of Theology at Boston University that while he was there had no influence on his life."[49] But King had known Thurman and known about Thurman his entire life. In 1929, when King was born in Atlanta, Thurman was teaching at Morehouse, where Martin Luther King, Sr., class of 1930, was completing his studies. Another connection was that Thurman's future wife, Sue Bailey, had been the roommate of King's mother, Alberta Williams, at Spelman Seminary—a high school—in 1920–21. Although it cannot be firmly documented, there were likely occasions when King's and Thurman's paths crossed before 1953. We know that when King arrived at Boston University he was a close reader of Thurman's work, especially *Jesus and the Disinherited*.[50] In all, Thurman concluded, "my life from one point of view is one which has been a part of the general and the specific context in which he [King] lived and thought and worked."[51]

However, Thurman had yet to take in the full measure of King during the year they were both in Boston—or perhaps King had not yet fully matured into the leader he would become. The two men were not close in Boston. In December 1954, when Thurman was asked about the suitability of King for the position of dean of the chapel at Dillard University, he recommended someone else.[52] Their time together, in Thurman's remembering, was limited to watching the World Series in the fall of 1953, when both men no doubt rooted for the Brooklyn Dodgers against the still all-white—and eventually victorious—New York Yankees. Sue Bailey Thurman seems to have established a closer connection to both King and his new bride, Coretta Scott King. Efforts by Sue Bailey Thurman to persuade King to spend the summer of 1954 as an assistant pastor at the Fellowship Church were cut short when he accepted the call to Dexter Avenue Baptist Church in Montgomery, Alabama, for the fall of 1954.[53]

If Thurman was not yet paying close attention to Martin Luther King, Jr., the reverse was not true. As King's roommate that year, Philip Lenud, told a researcher, King sometimes attended Marsh Chapel, listened carefully, and shook "his head in amazement at Thurman's deep wisdom."[54] That King was an avid student of Thurman's sermons was demonstrated by the number of times references to them, explicit or implicit, came up in King's early preaching. On at least eight occasions between 1953 and 1959, King made use of sermon material from Thurman, and there were three allusions to Thurman in King's first sermon collection, *Strength to Love* (1963).[55] A comparison of the itineraries of the two men shows that there were nineteen Sundays in the 1953–54 academic year when King was in Boston and Thurman was preaching in Marsh Chapel.[56]

As important as Thurman's duties were at Marsh Chapel, they were only the beginning of his responsibilities. In 1957 Harold Case called Thurman Boston University's "senior religious officer" who "has given intellectual significance to the quest for spiritual values among students, faculty and staff, and community members" and helped coordinate the United Ministry to Students to "provide the best total leadership for a healthy religious climate on the campus."[57]

Thurman's presence at Boston University was felt in many ways and in many places. He spoke at meetings and convocations of numerous campus groups— twelve in his first year, among them the nursing school, the medical school, and the Hillel organization. He had a special affinity for speaking to health care professionals. This was perhaps because, as noted by Patricia K. Donahue—who regularly heard him preach at Marsh Chapel and would later become chief of pediatric surgery at Massachusetts General Hospital—"Howard Thurman has taught and exemplified in the face of deprivation, pain, and sorrow, that instead of anger and despair there should be searching, seeking, understanding, calm, and love."[58]

Thurman's reputation as a spiritual counselor preceded him to Boston, and counseling soon became one of his major responsibilities. After his first year at Boston University, he estimated that in this capacity he met with an average of eleven persons a week. Thurman counseled "undergraduates, faculty members, graduate students and persons from the wider university community" in sessions sometimes lasting over an hour each.[59] The demand for his counseling services, he wrote the following year, in 1955, "has been in excess of the time and the availability of the Dean of the Chapel." Thurman noted that to "the degree in which the Sunday services meet the spiritual needs of the congregation, the demand for personal interviews increases. . . . an increased demand has come from individuals throughout the university. This is very gratifying."[60]

Thurman also filled the role of host at Boston University, along with his wife, Sue Bailey Thurman. The Thurmans gave receptions for students, faculty, and visiting guests at their apartment at 184 Bay Street Road, close to the center of the university, holding gatherings as often as one to three times a week. Thurman reported that in the 1955–56 academic year, he and Sue entertained over eight hundred persons in their apartment.[61] Over his years as dean of the chapel, the gatherings ranged in size from six to sixty-five (the monthly reception for the chapel choir), with the Thurmans providing refreshments or meals for the visitors.[62] The Thurmans, as they had at Howard University, had an open-door policy at their residence for those in need of friendship and nurturance. At Christmas they opened their home to students who stayed on campus over the break, and the Thurmans served them a festive breakfast, with Howard, whose love of cooking was inherited from his mother, preparing his special version of Chicken à la King, described as being "loaded with meat and vegetables, with spices and seasonings sprinkled as only his fertile imagination could concoct."[63] All of this was in addition to his teaching responsibilities as professor of spiritual resources.

Rather than teach formal theology courses, Thurman's instruction at Boston University was directed toward helping "men and women who were going into the ministry to acquaint themselves with their own inner life." His teaching distilled a lifetime's thought about spirituality and mysticism and the challenge of how to impart to others something private and basically incommunicable, something that "could be caught, but I did not think it could be taught."[64] Despite this difficulty, he became renowned as a teacher of spirituality. In his first semester at Boston University, he took over part of a course in homiletics, a subject that he thought usually did not rise much above a collection of useful pointers on public speaking. He had his students spend half the semester just reading the Bible aloud, trying to communicate its moods, trying to get students to listen to the Bible in a new way detached from its surface meanings.[65]

The main course that Thurman offered at the School of Theology was the two-semester Spiritual Disciplines and Resources, which he taught every year from 1953 to 1962. The first semester was a study of religious experience focusing on the Christian tradition, with a reading list that included Quakers (Douglas Steere), existential Protestants (Søren Kierkegaard), the Catholic-inspired mysticism of Evelyn Underhill and Simone Weil, and the Zen Buddhism of D. T. Suzuki.[66] The second semester was a "study of suffering, tragedy, and love as the disciplines of the spirit through which an individual may be ushered into the Presence of God."[67] As always for Thurman, the struggle with these questions was to examine the most cloistered and secret parts of the soul and to confront one's specific social and political reality. The substance of the course was reflected in his 1963 book, *Disciplines of the Spirit,* which was dedicated "to the students in my course on Spiritual Disciplines and Resources, 1953–1962." The contents of the volume were "winnowed out of the collective quest in which several generations of students and I have engaged."[68] Its five chapters—1) "Commitment," 2) "Growing in Wisdom and Stature," 3) "Suffering," 4) "Prayer," and 5) "Reconciliation"— touched on many matters. The volume ended with a condemnation of segregation as a "disease of the human spirit and the body politic" and an acknowledgment of the necessity of human love—to "deny it is to perish."[69]

If the students in Spiritual Disciplines and Resources obtained an overview of Thurman's religious and social views, this was almost incidental to the main purpose of the course, an attempt by Thurman to help his students try to "clear away whatever may block our awareness of that which is God in us"[70] and to move toward an intense prayerfulness less as a heightened state of consciousness and more as a habitual way of being. Thurman employed many techniques toward this goal. His lectures were often preceded by extended periods of silence; there were guided meditations, times for contemplation, and spontaneous responses to particular icons, symbols, ideas, poems, or religious figures. One of Thurman's favorite exercises was to go to the blackboard and have the students contemplate and respond to a single, charged word.

The course also had a number of "laboratory" sessions, which regularly met for an hour and a half at 6:30 in the morning. In an example of a typical assignment for a laboratory session, students were asked to read Psalm 139, Thurman's favorite, before the 6:30 A.M. meeting every day for a week. The class started with Thurman reading the psalm, with each member of the class instructed to "open his mind to the music of the words, to the general atmosphere which listening to the psalm generated in the mind" without paying attention to its meaning or ideas. Thurman then played a piece of slow, meditative music, such as the music of J. S. Bach, the prelude to Richard Wagner's quasi-Christian opera *Parsifal,* or Max Bruch's orchestral setting of the traditional Yom Kippur chant, Kol Nidre.[71] Each member of the class was then asked to select "a sentence, a phrase, a word, or an idea to which individual attention could be given for purposes of reflection, thought, meditation, or prayer" and to contemplate this silently for forty minutes. The session ended at 8:00 A.M., with the final verse of the psalm—"see if there be any wicked way in me, and lead me in the way everlasting"—as a benediction.[72] For one participant, Zalman Schachter-Shalomi, the purpose of this exercise was to "translate an experience of one sense to another: ... we would read a psalm several times and then listen to a beautiful meditative Bach composition—in order to 'hear' the psalm's meaning in the sounds of the music. In this way, we refined and became better able to experience the divine around us."[73]

Zalman Schachter-Shalomi's participation in the class was a notable example of the success Thurman was having in using his teaching at Boston University as a source of interreligious spirituality, a resource that each participant could apply to his own faith tradition. After escaping Nazi-occupied Europe, Schachter—he added the Shalomi in the 1970s—studied with the Lubavitcher Hasidim in Brooklyn but eventually came to find their brand of strict orthodoxy too narrow and confining, and he entered the path that took him to Boston University. However, after signing up for Spiritual Disciplines and Resources, he immediately got cold feet, wondering what he had to gain from a course taught by a Protestant instructor in a Methodist university on something as personal and religion-specific as "spiritual resources." When he went to see Thurman about his concerns, Thurman "put down his coffee mug. His graceful hands went back and forth, as though mirroring my dilemma. Finally, Howard Thurman looked right at me and said, 'Don't you believe in the Ruach Hakodesh [holy spirit]?'" For Schachter, hearing "a non-Jew speak these Hebrew words so eloquently shattered my composure." Schachter got up and left hurriedly, still uncertain whether to take the course. After he decided to enroll, he found Spiritual Disciplines and Resources to be "a tremendous learning experience," one that played a major role in his spiritual development. Schachter-Shalomi, who in the 1960s was one of the founders of the Jewish renewal or "havurah" movement, an effort to respiritualize the practice of Judaism, always counted Thurman as one of his most important mentors, and the two would remain close friends.[74]

Thurman was always a magnet for spiritual explorers, especially those who, like Schachter-Shalomi, preferred journeys to places uncharted. It was another student friendship and mentorship during Thurman's Boston University years that would lead to involvement in what was likely the most controversial incident in his entire career, the Good Friday Experiment on 20 April 1962 at Marsh Chapel, a test of the spiritual potential of psychedelic drugs. Thurman's personal involvement was peripheral, but through his friendship with and mentoring of one of the two coleaders of the experiment, Walter Pahnke, he helped to shape its goals and broader religious context.[75]

Given Pahnke's interests in psychiatry and religion, it is not surprising that his attention turned to the potential spiritual properties of psychotropic substances. This was a subject of growing attention in the 1950s, fueled in the general culture by the greater availability of psychedelic drugs such as mescaline, psilocybin, and LSD—all legal substances at the time, as they would be at the time of the Good Friday Experiment—and heralded by Aldous Huxley's *The Doors of Perception* (1954), his account of his mescaline experiences, and similar works.[76] By 1959 Thurman was familiar with this literature, likely through Pahnke, and he was sharing his excitement about the spiritual potential of psychedelics with his friends. Coleman Jennings wrote to Thurman late that year, returning to him "the copy of the fascinating articles about the marvels of LSD. It is something I would like to follow up on, for it seems to have limitless possibilities."[77]

At some point Pahnke's path crossed that of Timothy Leary (1920–96), who in 1959 joined the Harvard psychology department, where he would spend four stormy years. Within a few years of being fired by Harvard for his unorthodox experiments with psychedelic substances, Leary would become perhaps the leading luminary of the counterculture of the 1960s, his name a byword for excessive drug use. In 1962 he would, with Pahnke, be the coleader of the Good Friday Experiment. In the fall of 1960 Leary along with Richard Alpert, who later achieved his own countercultural fame as Baba Ram Dass, created the Harvard Psilocybin Project—subsequently informally renamed the Harvard Psychedelic Project—to test the therapeutic and spiritual properties of psilocybin and other psychedelics. By the beginning of 1962 Leary had gathered around him, in his words, an "informal group of ministers, theologians, academic hustlers, and religious psychologists in the Harvard environment [that] began meeting at least once a month" to discuss—and for many in the group, to test—psychedelic drugs and their possible spiritual significance.[78]

Walter Pahnke was a part of this group, and he proposed a double-blind experiment to test the spiritual properties of psilocybin. Known as the Good Friday Experiment, it was the subject of Pahnke's 1963 Harvard dissertation.[79] Pahnke wanted to test whether psychedelic drugs could induce spiritual experiences on a group of subjects who would be open to mystical or religious experiences, such as divinity students, and to do so in a familiar religious context that might prompt or inspire such a response, as in a chapel on one of the holiest days of the Christian year. Leary approved of Pahnke's ambitions but disliked his effort to bring a modicum of scientific rigor to psychedelic testing, and in the words of Leary's biographer, he "did everything he could to stand in his [Pahnke's] way."[80] The two men had fierce fights on whether to include a control group that would take a nonpsychedelic substance and whether the guides—the facilitators of the experiment—would also participate in the drug taking. Pahnke won the former argument while Leary won on the latter point, but Pahnke refused to take any psychedelic substance during the experiment and would not do so until he completed his dissertation, out of fear of compromising his objectivity.

According to Leary's account, when Pahnke told him of his plans, Pahnke said that he had "already spoken with Dean Thurmond [sic], and he'll let us use the small chapel,"[81] and no doubt something similar to this occurred. Leary was increasingly under fire at Harvard, especially for what was deemed the lack of adequate scientific controls on his distribution of hallucinogens. By the end of 1961 his ability to distribute and experiment with psychedelic drugs under Harvard auspices was severely curtailed. Leary had considerable difficulty in obtaining psilocybin since Harvard was limiting his access to it, and he legally obtained it only the night before from a psychiatrist in Worcester, Massachusetts. The Good Friday Experiment would be Leary's last major drug trial at Harvard, and in many ways it was the culminating episode in the first phase of the effort to demonstrate the broader social and spiritual utility of psychedelics.

On the morning of Good Friday in 1962, the twenty men in the experiment—divinity students from Andover-Newton Seminary and Harvard Divinity School who were largely recruited by Walter Huston Clark, a professor at Andover-Newton—along with ten trained guides, which included Leary and Pahnke, gathered in the basement chapel and several other adjacent rooms.[82] The study participants were given crushed powder in envelopes around 10:00 A.M. In the double-blind experiment, fifteen were given 30 milligrams of psilocybin. The other half were given nicotinic acid, a nonpsychedelic stimulant. Shortly before noon the main service started upstairs, and those involved in the Good Friday Experiment went into Robinson Chapel, which Thurman had set up in 1954 to provide a quiet space for meditation and reflection and into which the service would be piped. Playing the service into Robinson Chapel was a common practice and was not set up solely for the Good Friday Experiment. Shortly before the beginning of the main Good Friday service upstairs, Thurman addressed the participants in the experiment. Pahnke wrote that "the minister welcomed everyone in the chapel before he went upstairs to start the service,"[83] and according to another account, Thurman asked the participants to "maintain a reverent silence."[84] The basement chapel was locked and guarded, and there was no contact between the study participants and the worshippers at the main Good Friday service in Marsh Chapel.

Thurman's Good Friday services at Marsh Chapel were unlike any other that he conducted during the year, in their length of about two and a half hours and in their atmosphere of quiet, somber solemnity. The service in 1962, like its predecessors, retold the life of Jesus, with soft organ music and with Thurman reading from the Gospels—the Woman at the Well, the Temptations of Jesus, the Beatitudes. At the climax of the service, Thurman read Edna St. Vincent Millay's poem "Conscientious Objector," which begins, "I Shall die / but that is all I shall do for Death"; gave a reading of the Seven Last Words; and offered meditations on the cross and on death. After a soloist sang the spiritual "Were You There When They Crucified My Lord?," the service slowly drew to a close.[85]

In the basement chapel, the reactions of those who had taken psilocybin were intense. Some remembered Thurman's readings as being "enormously powerful." On hearing Thurman's recitation of the Millay poem, one participant who took psilocybin had the sensation of his "insides being clawed out" and then realized that indeed he had "died" and that his ego had "to die in order to live in freedom. I had to die in order to become who I could be. I did make a choice, in that willingness to die."[86] Another remembered kneeling to pray and "entering into the fullness of all being."[87] Also given psilocybin was Huston Smith, a well-known professor of philosophy and religious studies. He remembered the Good Friday Experiment as one of the central religious moments of his life, his first direct personal encounter with God. He wrote that Thurman "was a remarkable man, both spiritually and in his ability to inspire people," but he "didn't remember the contents of [Thurman's] words, only their moving impact," which convinced him that in some way he was in God's immediate presence, hearing the songs of angels.[88]

Others had more disturbing reactions. One of those given nicotinic acid remembered, "It was the stupidest thing you ever saw in your life. Guys were crawling around you on the floor on their hands and knees."[89] Some experienced "bad trips." One participant imagined he was a fish; another thought that he was a snake and started writhing on the floor.[90] Others remembered reactions of paranoia on being prevented from leaving the ground-floor chapel area.[91] The scariest response occurred after Thurman told his listeners that "you have to tell people that there is a man on the cross": one participant bolted from the chapel and ran out to Commonwealth Avenue to tell the administrators of Boston University just that. He had to be restrained by the experiment's supervisors. In his dissertation, largely based on the detailed reports and questionnaires that the participants filled out, Pahnke concluded that the subjects who received psilocybin "experienced phenomena which were indistinguishable from, if not identical with, certain categories defined by our typology of mysticism."[92] A follow-up study conducted by Rick Doblin in 1991 took some issue with Pahnke's methodology and argued that his dissertation underplayed the bad and not-so-good trips of several participants, but he concurred with Pahnke, on the basis of retrospective interviews, that with one exception, all of the psilocybin participants felt that "their original experience . . . had genuinely mystical elements" and that it made "a uniquely valuable contribution to their spiritual lives."[93]

Thurman's reaction to the Good Friday Experiment is unclear. He did not mention the event in his autobiography nor in his extant correspondence save one exception—that instance being in August 1963, when the *Reporter* printed a lengthy article by Noah Gordon, "The Hallucinogenic Drug Cult," which included a subheading, "The Miracle of Marsh Chapel." In an angry response to the magazine editor, Thurman insisted that the chapel had no involvement with the procuring of drugs used, which was undoubtedly the case, and that the chapel's involvement was limited to "the use of the facilities of rooms on the ground floor."[94] Leary wrote to Thurman in October 1962 on his ongoing work with Pahnke, mentioning that "as you know the Good Friday experiment has turned out to be a ringing success—spiritually (for the subjects) and scientifically."[95] If Thurman's contact with Leary likely ended with the latter's departure from Harvard, his friendship with the Pahnkes, Walter and Eva, continued without interruption. At Pahnke's funeral in 1971—he died, much too soon, in a scuba diving accident—a special prayer composed by Thurman for the occasion was read.

In the end Thurman respected and remained interested in Pahnke's work but probably found it to be, as a means of spiritual or mystical insight, superfluous. According to the Thurman scholar Luther Smith, Thurman, when asked in a public discussion about the Good Friday Experiment, said something to the effect that "it just may be that one comes to the encounter with God through a chemical that God has made to be part of a plant. But I believe this is the most expensive way to arrive at such an encounter."[96] Beyond its notoriety, the Good Friday Experiment is an important example of Thurman's encouragement of the exploration of the mystical experience, to its furthest and most unconventional reaches.

Thurman's grandest ambition for his role as dean of the chapel at Boston University was to create a new type of religious organization, one for which there were few if any precedents. Thurman envisioned a formal community of worshippers connected to a university chapel, shaped by its members, part of Boston University, but not limited or constrained by this connection. Creating a chapel fellowship had been Thurman's fondest wish since he first considered moving to Boston. His failure to realize this would sour and ultimately shorten his formal association to Boston University.

Thurman wanted a chaplaincy that would function as the spiritual hub of a great university, fed by and reflecting the inspiration and vitality of young people, with their quests, uncertainties, and energies, as he had tried to create at Rankin Chapel at Howard University. In addition he wanted to create the sort of religious community he had created at Fellowship Church: an interracial, international, and interreligious fellowship using worship to bridge human division and separateness, a fellowship that was equally at home with the interiority of private religious experience and worship and the public demands of social witness and action.

This had been Thurman's intention from the outset. In January 1953, in his first letter to the trustees of the Fellowship Church informing them of the possibility of his going to Boston, Thurman wrote, "As the result of what has been developed practically as a religious fellowship cutting across various lines in our church, President Case wants to project, through my leadership, the development of a community church at the university, membership of which would come from the university family and the community of Boston. This would be a non-creedal, non-sectarian, interracial, interfaith and intercultural religious fellowship."[97] He was convinced that his "decision was made to come to Boston, not to leave San Francisco," seeing his Boston work as a parallel to and extension of his work at the Fellowship Church.[98]

However, Thurman's plan to create a religious fellowship at Marsh Chapel foundered. There were numerous complications. Perhaps the most obvious problem was that a university chapel was not a religious congregation but a place for worship without any explicit or implicit membership requirements, whose institutional existence came not from the worshippers but from its connection to the university. Thurman was determined to make worship at Marsh Chapel as open and encompassing as possible. As he wrote in 1955, his "first and primary aim at the Chapel [was] to seek, under God, to develop the Chapel as a worship center, welcoming all men to come before God in the high act of celebration."[99] But this openness was potentially at cross purposes with the creation of a religious fellowship. As at the Fellowship Church, Thurman felt that to get the full benefit from the act of worship, those who gathered together needed to be bound together by some sort of framework that recognized their mutual relation and established collective goals. In his first annual report as dean of Marsh Chapel in June 1954, he wrote that he was working on plans "for establishing some kind of religious fellowship in connection with the chapel" and hoped that the details would be ready by the end of the summer.[100]

These details do not seem to have been forthcoming at the time, although Thurman continued to work toward those goals. In April 1956, at a meeting of the Chapel Committee, he stated, "There must be some simple, comprehensive agreement, a covenant or commitment to which the individual who wished to be a part formally of the society would accept as the things on which he personally agreed to. Work out some statement, not a creed, that will bind us together."[101] The problem for Thurman was that the members of the committee did "not know how to provide an experience of spiritual growth for people whose approach to God and religious meaning may be radically different." The wider the scope of inclusion, the more abstract and elusive common ground would become. Thurman was encouraged that in the chapel, "there are moments when a person is just himself before God" apart from any particular religious or creedal affirmation. He wrote, "Some such creative possibility may be possible within the framework of that which has a Christian orientation and inspiration. . . . Organizational[ly] [it] has to be kept close to zero. The barest minimum necessary to provide a framework for the spirit."[102]

By the following year Thurman had concluded, "The plan to organize the Chapel, either as a church or as a formal fellowship, has complications which at the moment seem insurmountable." Therefore he had "abandoned any plans which point directly to formalizing the religious experience which is a growing thing in connection with the ministry of Marsh Chapel."[103] This proved a temporary retreat, however, and he tried again. In the fall of 1959 the effort was revived, and a "Committee of Inquiry and Proposal" was formed; its members included Walter Muelder, several students, and members of the outside community. Chaired by George A. Warmer, vice president for university affairs and a onetime Methodist minister, the committee tried to shape a proposal for a chapel fellowship.[104]

In the fall of 1960 a "Statement of Affirmation" for a Boston University chapel fellowship was drafted by the committee and presented to the university's board of trustees. Although the proposal for the chapel fellowship did contain Christian elements—probably a reluctant concession on Thurman's part—a promise was made not to undermine or challenge the religious beliefs of any participant in the fellowship while seeking to enhance and deepen the "quest for spiritual reality" for all members of the fellowship. The proposal affirmed nine propositions, a belief in one God, and a belief "in Jesus Christ and in his specific witness of God" for "our culture and faith," although it also included the statement that God "has not left himself without specific witness in all cultures and faiths." Other affirmations included the belief in the Holy Spirit, the Bible as a source "containing insights useful for our faith and practice," the Kingdom of God, "life everlasting," "the inescapable necessity for social responsibility," and the belief that "experiences of spiritual unity wherever they occur, are more compelling than the creeds, the ways of life and the ideologies that divide men."[105]

The precise history and sequence of events of the chapel fellowship proposal are somewhat unclear. The proposal was submitted to the board of trustees in the spring of 1960.[106] The "Statement of Affirmation" (c. October 1960) stated that it had been "approved by the President and Board of Trustees of the University," although there is no evidence of the existence of a chapel fellowship or its approval by the trustees outside of this statement. Possibly it was drafted in optimistic anticipation of a future approval.[107] In any event, by June 1961 Thurman in his annual report had written that the proposal had been submitted "to the Trustees of the University and was rejected by them."[108]

According to Thurman, there were two main reasons for the decision of the board of trustees. One problem was the need for the chapel fellowship to be autonomous and to shape its own direction if it were to be effective. The trustees were unclear how an autonomous religious fellowship could function under the aegis and imprimatur of Boston University. The problem was heightened because most churchgoing faculty members usually worshipped near their homes and therefore the core of regular attendees at Marsh Chapel largely consisted of students—whose membership would be inherently temporary—and members of the larger Boston community who had fallen under Thurman's spell and who often had little or no connection to the university. How the fellowship would reflect and represent Boston University, some felt, was unclear.[109]

The other problem was the ambiguous relation of the proposed chapel fellowship to Protestantism. Thurman's refusal to tie his chapel ministry to official Protestantism was a problem from the beginning of his time in Boston. As he stated in his first annual report, "In many people's minds, the chapel is the formal representative of Protestant Christianity on the campus." Given that the chapel's services had always been Methodist, this was a natural assumption. To change this, to create the chapel as "a center for religious worship in the heart of the university to which any and all members of the university may come for spiritual renewal," would always be a challenge. On one side, no doubt many non-Protestants felt that the chapel service even after Thurman's careful pruning still betrayed its Protestant origins. However, on the other side, there were many on campus who, Thurman wrote, felt that "the ministry of the chapel should become the official Protestant mouthpiece and hold its own on equal footing with the Jewish and the Catholic positions." Thurman clearly stated, "The present Dean of the Chapel has no interest in that alternative."[110]

Thurman's relationships with the official representatives of Protestantism on the Boston University campus were strained. In his annual report for the 1955–56 academic year, he complained of the "obvious discourtesies extended to him" by the Protestant chaplain on campus, Dr. William Overholt, the one time they met, and he was "ambivalent in regard to the measure of responsibility he should carry for the development of the Student Christian Association."[111] Relations between the two men were subsequently patched up, but they were never close, and Thurman frequently felt that he was being maneuvered into an avowal of an official Protestantism for Marsh Chapel. The ambivalence was never entirely clarified. As the chapel fellowship committee stated, the services at Marsh Chapel "are rooted in the Protestant tradition of the University, while experiments continue to find ways to become increasingly inclusive of the total community within and without the university."[112] If some officials at Boston University applauded these efforts, others, it is clear, were made uneasy by Thurman's efforts, in his Marsh Chapel services and in the proposed chapel fellowship, to extend and elide the boundaries of Protestantism. Remarks by Dean Walter Muelder at Thurman's retirement celebration in spring 1965 are insightful: "I may note in passing that it is no secret to historians and sociologists of the church that mystical devotion is a very dangerous phenomenon. Mysticism is generally verging on heresy and the mystic is seldom an organization man. Those who avoid the securities of mediated grace, whether in doctrine or sacrament or institution—and insist on speaking in public—give uneasy hours to the ecclesiastical bureaucrat."[113]

After the chapel fellowship was rejected, plans were made for a new Protestant ministry on campus, which seemed to have as one of its purposes to rein in Thurman's free-floating spirituality. A proposal sent to him in July 1961 stated, "The Dean of the Chapel, as principal administrative officer for the religious life of the campus shall serve as chairman of the Council for the Protestant ministry."[114] With the final rejection of the chapel fellowship proposal, Thurman determined to leave Boston University as soon as that was practicable. In his autobiography he wrote, "It was not long after this that my term of tenure at the university closed and I resigned the position as dean of the chapel and became university minister-at-large," sharply curtailing his involvement with the chapel and university affairs.[115] He attributed the loosening of his ties with the university to his desire to avoid a repeat of the "profound emotional upheaval" that had accompanied the decision to go to Boston, and to avoid "the psychic pains of withdrawal both for myself and those who felt dependent on my ministry" by a gradual and extended leave-taking.[116]

This was no doubt true, but Thurman was often reluctant to disclose his deeper, angrier feelings in *With Head and Heart*. With the final quashing of the fellowship ideal, Thurman felt that an informal agreement had been abrogated and that without a chapel fellowship to develop, his work at Boston University was done. In addition, if race did not directly enter into the consideration of the chapel fellowship, he was of course aware that he was working in a predominantly white institution in which all the members of the administrative hierarchy except him were white. As he wrote in March 1961 to J. Wendell Yeo, a university vice president whose duties included supervision of the chapel, "the only way in good conscience that I can keep from feeling that the gifts of God that is in me is not being exploited by the University, is the reassurance that it is available to be shared beyond the boundaries of Marsh Chapel and particularly to be shared with Negroes who live and work and suffer in American society."[117] With the nullification of the chapel fellowship plans, Thurman's feelings that he had neglected blacks during his Boston years grew stronger. In his first annual report on the wider ministry in 1963, he stated, "I was acutely aware of the fact that only a minor part of my availability could be put at the disposal of the Negro Community."[118]

The "wider ministry" was Thurman's way of extricating himself from Boston University without cutting all formal ties. From fall 1962 through spring 1964 he would remain dean of the chapel, but this involved few responsibilities in Boston. His ministry was elsewhere, primarily in the many appearances he made in churches and colleges across the country. Since his Boston University salary would largely cease, funds to supplement his income would come from two California friends, the San Francisco businessman Boice Gross and Lloyd Smith, a Los Angeles lawyer who oversaw the budget of the Claremore Fund.[119] Thurman saw the "wider ministry" as effectively a divorce from Boston University. As he wrote Gross in April 1962, as of that September he would be "free of all responsibility to Boston University as Dean of the Chapel and as Professor of Spiritual Disciplines." The use of his time would be exclusively his responsibility, and he would be under no obligation "to refer to the University for veto or certification of any act or function which I may wish to perform or undertake."[120]

It proved to be a relatively bitter divorce. As early as May 1962 Thurman was complaining to Yeo and President Case that "it is as if I had already left the campus," and he was being "completely ignored" in decisions made about Marsh Chapel.[121] He had to vacate his old office and complained about his new one, up five flights of stairs with no elevator. He and Sue Bailey Thurman somewhat reluctantly vacated their home at 184 Bay State Road near the campus, angrily complaining to President Case of mistreatment, and by mid-November 1962 they had relocated.[122] Their new apartment at 80 Beacon Street, overlooking the Boston Public Garden in downtown Boston, had its compensations. It provided a spatial distancing from the university that both Thurmans appreciated. As Thurman wrote to a friend shortly after the move, "It is the first time in 30 years that we have a sense of being private citizens."[123] The new location led to closer ties with Boston's black community and enabled Sue to pursue her long-standing interests in black history.[124]

Thurman's greatest grievance against Boston University was the matter of his replacement. Although Thurman undertook his leave with the understanding that no permanent replacement would be named until his retirement as dean—it is not clear that President Case and the Boston University administration had a similar understanding—Robert Hamill, who had been chaplain at the University of Wisconsin at Madison, was named dean-designate in early fall 1962, at the beginning of the wider ministry. Thurman was upset that his replacement was named so soon, and he was more upset that the new dean-designate was advertised as implying that Thurman had already retired.[125]

Most upsetting to Thurman was that Hamill, a liberal Methodist but without Thurman's commitment to an interreligious spirituality, had changed the order of service. Thurman was outraged, and he refused to preach under the new order of service.[126] Thurman was not the only person upset by the changes. His friend Dean George Makechnie, who had regularly worshipped in Marsh Chapel since Thurman's arrival, complained to Case that the new order of service was inappropriate "for a university chapel in a community so pluralistic in character as Boston University" and that it was "not one with which my own spirit and that of my family can find union."[127] When in April 1963 Thurman finally attended a service under Hamill's leadership, he afterward described it in a letter to Case as "a traditional orthodox trinitarian Protestant Christian service of worship." Thurman wrote, "Now the campus has the three Faiths functioning in spiritual isolation, with the university Chapel deeply committed to one as over against the other two." He despaired that "in the public worship of God we are back where we were in the 18th century."[128]

Case replied that Thurman too had made substantial changes to the order of service when he arrived at Boston University and that Hamill was merely exercising his prerogative to do the same. In response Thurman argued that when he had come to Boston, the chapel was moribund and that "the constituency of the Chapel was almost negligible." Moreover there was no parallel to the current situation, in which the order of service was changed against the wishes of the current dean of the chapel. Thurman's anger would eventually subside, and he agreed to preach in the chapel during the summer—when he had more control over the order of service; eventually he preached during the academic year as well.[129] This did not mean, however, that he had forgotten what he regarded as a deep personal insult.

Thurman spent the two years of the wider ministry much as he had promised: speaking, preaching, and writing, with minimal connection to Boston University. He indeed concentrated extensively, though by no means exclusively, on southern black schools, colleges, and congregations at an exciting time when, as he wrote a friend in July 1963, America was "in the throes of a mighty revolution."[130] Certainly the highlight of the wider ministry occurred in the fall of 1963, when he spent a semester at the University of Ibadan in Nigeria, his only extensive stay in Africa, followed by a fortnight in Israel.[131]

By agreement the 1964–65 academic year would be Thurman's last before his formal retirement from Boston University, but he needed a new title since he would retire as dean of the chapel as of 1 July 1964. He very much wanted to be named dean of the chapel emeritus, but this would only come later, and he instead received the title "minister-at-large."[132] When his friend Rabbi Zalman Schachter heard the new title, he responded, "I am greatly pleased with one thing. I've finally found out what you are. You have been, all the time, a minister at large, and no matter how wonderful and flexible the institution was, it could not quite contain you. I suppose this is what is meant to be in the image of one's Maker, whom the heavens can't contain."[133]

Thurman's years in Boston brought him new professional renown and visibility. During his years at Boston University he published ten books—eight of them in the years covered in the present volume.[134] He was also awarded eight honorary degrees—five from historically black colleges and universities.[135] In June 1959 he was elected as a fellow of the American Academy of Arts and Sciences. The prominent Harlem Renaissance poet and playwright Georgia Douglas Johnson (1880–1966), on reading of this honor, wrote to Thurman, "It isn't often that one achieves such splendid recognition as you have during one lifetime. I salute you!"[136]

Thurman had been preaching sermon series since the earliest days of his ministry; these were linked sermons around common themes.[137] They dominated his preaching at both the Fellowship Church and Marsh Chapel during the years covered in this volume. Each series comprised two or more sermons structured, sometimes loosely and sometimes more tightly, around a common topic, enabling Thurman to explore a theme in greater depth than was possible in a single sermon. Thurman's engagements as a guest speaker often employed the sermon series format as he spoke several times over the course of a few days around a shared theme. However, the sermon series that Thurman gave when speaking to his home congregation differed in that these sermons were often longer and more elaborate, sometimes stretching over a number of months. The sermons in a series were usually given consecutively, but on some occasions they were broken up with sermons on other topics. Thurman's sermon series will be included in a volume of *The Papers of Howard Washington Thurman* exclusively dedicated to them, and so they are not included in this volume. However, since Thurman devoted so much of his preaching at Fellowship Church and Marsh Chapel to sermon series, the following brief overview of the sermon series topics and titles provides a sense of his interests during the years covered in this volume.

Thurman offered his first sermon series at the Fellowship Church in his first summer in San Francisco, and over the course of his years in that city they would become increasingly prominent. The time period covered in this volume begins in June 1949. From July to December of that year Thurman gave eleven sermons on the theme of "Man and the Moral Struggle," speaking on prominent individuals, biblical figures, and literary texts.[138] From April to October 1950 he gave the first of two sermon series he would offer at the Fellowship Church that were loosely derived from Sheldon Cheney's overview of the history of mysticism, *Men Who Have Walked with God*.[139] In his remaining years at the Fellowship Church, he gave sermon series titled "The Fruits of the Spirit,"[140] "The Meaning of Commitment,"[141] "The Meaning of Loyalty,"[142] "The Declaration of Independence,"[143] "The Parables of Jesus,"[144] "An Objective Basis of Hope,"[145] "Pain,"[146] "The Message of the Hebrew Prophets,"[147] "A Faith to Live By,"[148] "The Creative Imagination,"[149] and "The Divine Encounter"[150] before concluding his years at Fellowship Church with a return to "Men Who Walked with God," a series comprised of thirteen sermons.[151]

After he moved to Boston, Thurman continued to offer sermon series, although with a few exceptions they tended to be shorter than those delivered in the Fellowship Church. He also reused some of the sermon series titles he had used at Fellowship Church, although the choice of subtopics and the contents of individual sermons differed. Starting in October 1953 he gave sermon series at Marsh Chapel on "Barren or Fruitful?" (two sermons, October 1953), "The Quest for Peace" (two sermons, November 1953), "A Faith for Living" (three sermons, December 1953), "The Quest for Stability" (two sermons, March 1954), and "Love Your Enemies" (two sermons, April and May 1954). Returning to the Fellowship Church as a guest preacher in July 1954, he delivered two sermons on "The Outwardness of Religion." Back in Boston he delivered several sermons —probably more than the two that are extant—in the fall of 1954 on the theme of "Your Life's Working Paper."

Thurman's first long sermon series at Marsh Chapel comprised the nine sermons in "Man and the Moral Struggle," given from November 1954 to March 1955.[152] This was followed by "Love Your Enemy" (three sermons, September–October 1955) and "The Search for Life's Meaning" (two sermons, November

and December 1955). In 1956 and 1957 Thurman delivered "Prayer and Meditation,"[153] "Not Peace—A Sword" (two sermons, March 1956), "The Other Cheek"
(two sermons, May 1956), "The Quest for Maturity,"[154] "The Religion of Jesus,"[155]
"Pain,"[156] and "Seeking and Finding."[157] Over the following four years Thurman preached on "The Moment of Truth" (two sermons, January 1958), "The
Moment of Crisis" (six sermons, February–March 1958), "Modern Challenges
to Religion" (two sermons, April 1958), "The Single Mind" (two sermons, July
1958), "The Creative Encounter,"[158] "Jesus and the Disinherited,"[159] "The Fundamental Ends of Life" (three sermons, June 1959), "The Meaning of Tradition,"[160]
"The Meaning of Freedom,"[161] "Disciplines of the Spirit,"[162] "Community and
the Will of God" (three sermons, May 1961), and "The Inward Journey."[163] In
1962, the final year of his active tenure as dean of the chapel at Boston University, Thurman delivered "Quests of the Human Spirit"[164] and "The Dilemma of
Jesus."[165]

Thurman's preaching and teaching introduced a generation of students to
his ideas about spirituality and created, as he always did, large numbers of disciples and acolytes. As for Marsh Chapel, although his struggle to define his role
there was challenging, it was also quite rewarding. In March 1963 in a letter to his
successor Robert Hamill, he wrote, "It took 9 years of impossible effort, under
God, to develop a congregation in Marsh Chapel. It is, perhaps, the most dramatic work of the Holy Spirit in my experience."[166] The unsatisfying conclusion
of his efforts and the failure of the chapel fellowship idea were probably his most
disappointing professional experiences. He would go back to San Francisco,
but only as a private citizen, free and unaffiliated, returning to the Fellowship
Church as a member and without any ministerial responsibilities. The pattern
of the wider ministry in his last years in Boston would persist for the rest of his
life; he would remain unaffiliated, preaching, lecturing, and teaching without a
fixed academic or ministerial home. In many ways Schachter was right that no
institution could easily contain him. If the search for religious community and
the search for common ground were at the core of Thurman's spiritual life, the
years in Boston were a demonstration of the centrality and importance of this
quest as well as the difficulty and elusiveness in its realization.

NOTES
   1. To the Board of Trustees of Fellowship Church, 31 January 1953, printed in the current volume.
   2. For a more extended discussion of Thurman's reasons for leaving the Fellowship
Church, see "Biographical Essay," PHWT, 3: xvii–liii.
   3. To the Board of Trustees of Fellowship Church, 31 January 1953, printed in the current volume. Not until 1977 would Boston University hire another African American dean,
Hubert E. Jones (a Thurman admirer), who was appointed dean of the School of Social
Work.

4. "Negro Educator at B.U.," *Boston Globe*, 10 March 1933. Thurman's address was delivered at the School of Education, not the School of Theology, as reported in the article.

5. Reprinted in *PHWT*, 1:263–70. For the background to the talk, see Quinton Dixie and Peter Eisenstadt, *Visions of a Better World: Howard Thurman's Pilgrimage to India and the Origins of African American Nonviolence* (Boston: Beacon Press, 2011), 183–88.

6. John Wesley Edward Bowen (1855–1933) was born into slavery in New Orleans but was manumitted before the Civil War. He graduated from New Orleans University in 1878 and undertook graduate studies at Boston University, becoming in 1887 the second African American to be awarded a Ph.D. He pastored congregations in Baltimore and Washington, D.C., prior to joining the previously all-white faculty at Gammon Theological Seminary in Atlanta in 1893. He remained at historically black Gammon in different capacities, including a term as president, until his retirement in 1932. Other early African American Ph.D. recipients from the Boston University School of Theology included Leonard J. Farmer, Sr. (1886–1961), the father of the civil rights leader, in 1918; and in 1921 Willis J. King (1886–1976), who became an exponent of Boston personalism. See n. 17, infra.

7. Kathleen Kilgore, *Transformations: A History of Boston University* (Boston: Boston University, 1991), 251–52. In addition to Martin Luther King, Jr., other prominent African American graduates of this era included Samuel DeWitt Proctor (School of Theology, 1950) and Barbara Jordan (School of Law, 1959).

8. Among his other political involvements after becoming dean of the School of Theology in 1945, Muelder called for the internationalization of atomic energy in 1946, called for a "day of mourning" to protest the commencement of the peace-time draft in 1948, and was an early critic of McCarthyism.

9. Stanley High, "Methodism's Pink Fringe," *Reader's Digest* (February 1950): 134–38. See also Kilgore, *Transformations*, 229–30.

10. Kilgore, *Transformations*, 144–46, 223.

11. Daniel L. Marsh, *The Charm of the Chapel* (Boston: Boston University Press, 1950), 2. The chapel was not named for Marsh until his 1951 retirement.

12. From Daniel L. Marsh, 8 January 1961. Marsh was quoting from "Windbreak . . . . Against Existence," *Bostonia* (Fall 1960): 7–9, printed in the current volume.

13. Kilgore, *Transformations*, 247.

14. Gary J. Dorrien, *The Making of American Liberal Theology: Idealism, Realism, and Modernity, 1900–1950* (Louisville, Ky.: Westminster John Knox Press, 2003), 286.

15. From Jannette E. Newhall, 23 March 1953, printed in the current volume. Brightman, before his untimely death, was the primary dissertation adviser of Martin Luther King, Jr.

16. Dorrien, *The Making of American Liberal Theology*, 300, citing Edgar S. Brightman, "The Unpopularity of Personalism," *Methodist Review* 104 (January 1921): 13.

17. See Willis J. King, "Personalism and Race," in *Personalism in Theology: A Symposium in Honor of Albert Cornelius Knudson*, ed. Edgar Sheffield Brightman (Boston: Boston University Press, 1943), 204–24. King (1886–1976) was an African American Methodist, and at the time he wrote the essay, he was president of Gammon Theological Seminary in Atlanta.

18. *PHWT*, 1:39, 44.

19. *PHWT*, 2:163.

20. *PHWT*, 2:250.

21. Howard Thurman (hereafter HT), *Disciplines of the Spirit* (New York: Harper & Row, 1963), 67.

22. To Walter G. Borchers, Jr., 20 March 1946.

23. *WHAH*, 166–67. See also Dixie and Eisenstadt, *Visions of a Better World*, 138–44.

24. *WHAH*, 170.

25. Kilgore, *Transformations*, 251.

26. To the Board of Trustees of Fellowship Church, 31 January 1953, printed in the current volume.

27. Ibid.

28. For Brightman, see From Jannette E. Newhall, 23 March 1953, printed in the current volume.

29. See To Walter G. Muelder, 1 August 1952, printed in the current volume.

30. From Allan Knight Chalmers, 25 March 1953.

31. *WHAH*, 174. Beyond Thurman's statement in his autobiography, little is known about the extent and nature of the opposition to his appointment at Boston University.

32. Ibid., 173.

33. Ibid., 169.

34. G. James Fleming, "Noted Preacher to Head Boston U's Chapel Staff," *New York Amsterdam News*, 28 March 1953.

35. "Baptist Pastor Is Named Preacher by Boston U," *New York Times*, 22 March 1953.

36. "Great Preachers: These 12—and Others—Bring America Back to the Churches," *Life*, 6 April 1953, 126.

37. Jean Burden (1914–2008) was a journalist and editor. She was the longtime poetry editor of *Yankee* magazine and the West Coast editor for *Faith Today*. She wrote extensively on religious themes and authored a number of well-regarded volumes of poetry, including *Taking Light from Each Other* (Gainesville: University of Florida Press, 1992). Under the penname Felicia Ames she wrote a number of books on cat and animal care and lore. She and Thurman remained good friends and frequent correspondents until the end of his life. See To Jean Burden, 23 September 1975, printed in *PHWT*, vol. 5 (forthcoming).

38. Jean Burden, "Howard Thurman," *Atlantic Monthly*, October 1953, 39–44.

39. "Annual Report, Dean of Chapel [1953–54]," 21 June 1954, printed in the current volume.

40. "All University Religious Services, Daniel L. Marsh Chapel, Boston University," 20 September 1953.

41. George K. Makechnie, *Howard Thurman: His Enduring Dream* (Boston: Howard Thurman Center, Boston University, 1988), 69.

42. Attendance figures are available in Thurman's annual reports as dean of the chapel, which estimate an average attendance of 226 in "Annual Report, Dean of Chapel [1953–54]"; 286 in "Annual Report, Dean of Chapel [1955–56]"; 225 in "Annual Report, Dean of Chapel [1960–61]"; and 300 in "Annual Report, Dean of Chapel [1961–62]." George Makechnie's estimate of an average attendance of 500 seems inflated; see Makechnie, *Howard Thurman*, 41.

43. Makechnie, *Howard Thurman*, 41.

44. Ibid., 55.

45. Ibid., 82.

46. From Henry Bollman, 7 January 1956, printed in the current volume.

47. See "We Believe [Love Its Own Reward]," 20 November 1959, printed in the current volume.

48. Makechnie, *Howard Thurman*, 38–39 (brackets in original).

49. HT, Martin Luther King Lecture #2, 10 April 1975.

50. Ibid. For an extended discussion of King's and Thurman's early contacts and the impact of *Jesus and the Disinherited* on King, see Dixie and Eisenstadt, *Visions of a Better World*, 183–94.

51. HT, Martin Luther King Lecture #2, 10 April 1975. See also Walter Earl Fluker, *They Looked for a City: A Comparative Analysis of the Ideal of Community in the Thought of Howard Thurman and Martin Luther King, Jr.* (Lanham, Md.: University Press of America, 1988), 111–13. In an interview that Fluker conducted with Coretta Scott King for *They Looked for a City*, King told him that her husband sometimes heard Thurman preach at Marsh Chapel and that he and his fellow black theology and philosophy students at Boston University would sometimes imitate and affectionately mock Thurman's distinctive slow and deliberate preaching style.

52. From A. W. Dent, 1 December 1954; To A. W. Dent, 14 December 1954, both printed in the current volume. Even if Thurman had strongly recommended King for the position at Dillard, it is unlikely that King, who by this time had commenced his ministry at Dexter Avenue Baptist Church in Montgomery, Alabama, would have changed jobs prior to the beginning of the Montgomery bus boycott in December 1955. Both King's and Thurman's preferred candidate, Major Jones, subsequently interviewed for the Dillard position.

53. *WHAH*, 254.

54. Lewis V. Baldwin, *There Is a Balm in Gilead: The Cultural Roots of Martin Luther King, Jr.* (Minneapolis: Fortress Press, 1991), 300–301.

55. For details on King's allusions to Thurman, see Dixie and Eisenstadt, *Visions of a Better World*, 192–93, 226n31. See also Fluker, *They Looked for a City*, 112.

56. The sermons that Thurman preached on those occasions were as follows (extant sermons are starred): "The Quest for Fulfillment" (20 September 1953); "What Shall I Do with My Life?" (27 September 1953); "The Single Mind" (4 October 1953); "Barren or Fruitful? I" (11 October 1953); "Barren or Fruitful? II" (18 October 1953); "Deep River" (15 October 1953); "The Quest for Peace I" (8 November 1953)*; "The Quest for Peace II" (15 November 1953)*; "Faith for Living III" (20 December 1953)*; "The Gift of Memory" (31 January 1954)*; "The High Priest of Truth" (14 February 1954)*; "The Quest for Stability I" (21 March 1954); "The Quest for Stability II" (28 March 1954); "The Gathering in Gethsemane" (3 April 1954); "The Quest for Life Eternal" (18 April 1954)*; "Love Your Enemies II" (9 May 1954)*; "Be Ye Not Overcome by Evil" (16 May 1954)*; and "Vignettes of Life" (20 June 1954). On 11 April 1954, "The Seven Last Words of Christ," an Easter performance-recitation of Haydn's cantata, was presented.

57. Harold C. Case, *"Harvest from the Seed": Boston University in Mid-Century* (New York: Newcomen Society in North America, 1957), 15–16. Thurman was the only faculty member mentioned by name in Case's essay.

58. Makechnie, *Howard Thurman*, 57–58.

59. "Annual Report, Dean of Chapel [1953–54]."

60. "Annual Report, Dean of Chapel [1954–55]."

61. "Annual Report, Dean of Chapel [1955–56]."

62. "Annual Report, Dean of Chapel [1954–55]."

63. Makechnie, *Howard Thurman*, 25.

64. *WHAH*, 178.

65. Thurman's approach to the Bible has affinities with the move away from historical-critical exegesis in much recent African American biblical scholarship toward more

imaginative readings that interrogate "the silences within the texts" to find new frames of meaning and calls to agency and prophetic speech. Examples of this approach can be found in Cain Hope Felder, *Troubling Biblical Waters: Race, Class, and Family* (Maryknoll, N.Y.: Orbis Books, 1989); Vincent Wimbush, ed., *African Americans and the Bible: Sacred Texts and Social Textures* (New York: Continuum, 2000); Randall C. Bailey, *Yet with a Steady Beat: Contemporary U.S. Afrocentric Biblical Interpretation* (Atlanta: Society of Biblical Literature, 2003); Michael Brown, *Blackening the Bible: The Aims of African American Biblical Scholarship* (Harrisburg, Pa.: Trinity Press International, 2004); Brian Blount, *Can I Get a Witness? Reading Revelation through African American Culture* (Louisville, Ky.: Westminster John Knox Press, 2005); Brian K. Blount et al., eds., *True to Our Native Land: An African American New Testament Commentary* (Minneapolis.: Fortress Press, 2007); Dwight Callahan, *The Talking Book: African Americans and the Bible* (New Haven, Conn.: Yale University Press, 2006); and Hugh Page et al., eds., *The Africana Bible: Reading Israel's Scriptures from Africa and the African Diaspora* (Minneapolis: Fortress Press, 2010). For Thurman's own Bible interpretation during his Boston University years, see his Habakkuk commentary, printed in the current volume, and "Zephaniah: Text, Exegesis, and Exposition," in *The Interpreter's Bible*, vol. 6 (New York: Abingdon, 1956).

66. HT, *Disciplines of the Spirit*, 9; "Course Material, 1955–1971."

67. HT, *Disciplines of the Spirit*, 9.

68. Ibid., 9–10.

69. Ibid., 127.

70. Ibid., 96.

71. "March 1, 1955" in "Course Material, 1955–71"; Rabbi Zalman M. Schachter-Shalomi, with Edward Hoffman, *My Life in Jewish Renewal: A Memoir* (Lanham, Md.: Rowman and Littlefield, 2012), 91. Thurman described his first course on Spiritual Disciplines and Resources at Boston University to his friend Lloyd Smith: "Twice each week the forty-six students spend one-half hour of the class meditating around a central theme. Then they write a page giving glimpses of their inner stirrings. This is the most exciting experiment I have ever conducted" (To Lloyd Smith, 6 October 1953).

72. "March 1, 1955" in "Course Material, 1955–71."

73. Schachter-Shalomi, *My Life in Jewish Renewal*, 91.

74. Ibid., 90–91. See also To Zalman Schachter, 3 March 1959, printed in the current volume.

75. For Pahnke, see From Walter N. Pahnke, 6 September 1957, printed in the current volume. For a general overview of the Good Friday Experiment, see Robert Greenfield, *Timothy Leary: A Biography* (New York: Harcourt, 2006); Don Lattin, *The Harvard Psychedelic Club* (New York: HarperCollins, 2010).

76. Aldous Huxley, *The Doors of Perception* (New York: Harper, 1954).

77. From Coleman Jennings, 14 November 1959.

78. Timothy Leary, *Your Brain Is God* (Berkeley, Calif.: Ronin, 1988), 8. See also Timothy Leary, *Changing My Mind, among Others: Lifetime Writings* (Englewood Cliffs, N.J.: Prentice-Hall, 1982), 88; Huston Smith, *Cleansing the Doors of Perception: The Religious Significance of Entheogenic Plants and Chemicals* (New York: Tarcher/Putnam, 2000), 15–16. Smith dedicated *Cleansing the Doors of Perception* "To the memory of Walter Pahnke."

79. Walter Pahnke, "Drugs and Mysticism: An Analysis of the Relationship between Psychedelic Drugs and the Mystical Consciousness" (Ph.D. diss., Harvard University, 1963).

80. Greenfield, *Timothy Leary*, 180.

81. Timothy Leary, *Flashbacks: An Autobiography* (Los Angeles: J. P. Tarcher, 1983), 102. Leary's misspelling of Thurman's name has, unfortunately, been repeated in much of the subsequent literature on the Good Friday Experiment.

82. Most of the students had been recruited from a seminar taught by Walter Huston Clark at Andover-Newton Theological Seminary. See Huston Smith, *Cleansing the Doors of Perception*, 99–103. There is no evidence that Thurman suggested that any of his own students at Boston University participate.

83. Pahnke, "Drugs and Mysticism," 100.

84. Michael Hollingshead, *The Man Who Turned the World On* (New York: Abelard-Schuman, 1974), 55. Leary wrote that Thurman "visited our subjects a few minutes before the start of the noon service and gave a brief 'inspirational' talk" (Leary, *Changing My Mind*, 89).

85. Thurman preached similar sermons for each of his Good Friday services. The 1959 sermon is available at the Howard Thurman Virtual Listening Room at http://hgar-srv3.bu.edu/web/howard-thurman/virtual-listening-room/detail?id=371901, accessed 2 November 2016.

86. Jeanne Malgren, "Tune In, Turn On, Drop Out: The Good Friday Experiment," *St. Petersburg Times*, 27 November 1994.

87. Lattin, *The Harvard Psychedelic Club*, 80.

88. Ibid., 75–76; Huston Smith, *Cleansing the Doors of Perception*, 105.

89. Lattin, *The Harvard Psychedelic Club*, 77.

90. Greenfield, *Timothy Leary*, 182.

91. Lattin, *The Harvard Psychedelic Club*, 81.

92. Pahnke, "Drugs and Mysticism," 234.

93. Rick Doblin, "Pahnke's 'Good Friday Experiment': A Long-Term Follow-up and Methodological Critique," *Journal of Transpersonal Psychology* 23, no. 1 (1991): 1–28. See also Richard Elliot Doblin, "Regulation of the Medical Use of Psychedelics and Marijuana" (Ph.D. diss., Harvard University, 2000). The Good Friday Experiment was re-created many years later, with results similar to those of the original experiment. See R. R. Griffiths et al., "Psilocybin Can Occasion Mystical-Type Experiences Having Substantial and Sustained Personal Meaning and Spiritual Significance," *Psychopharmacology* 187 (August 2006): 1–16.

94. To Shirley Katzander, 8 August 1963, printed in the current volume.

95. From Timothy Leary, 29 October 1962, printed in the current volume.

96. Communication with Luther Smith, July 2007.

97. To the Board of Trustees of Fellowship Church, 31 January 1953, printed in the current volume.

98. HT, "Untitled" [On the relation between Marsh Chapel and the Fellowship Church], 1955.

99. Ibid.

100. "Annual Report, Dean of Chapel [1954–55]."

101. Chapel Committee Meeting, 29 April 1956.

102. Ibid.

103. "Annual Report, Dean of Chapel [1956–57]."

104. "Annual Report, Dean of Chapel [1960–61]."

105. Statement of Affirmation (undated, c. October 1960).

106. From George Warmer, 10 June 1960; George Warmer to Jean Hodge, 28 October 1960; "Annual Report, Dean of Chapel [1960–61]."

107. Statement of Affirmation (undated, c. October 1960).

108. "Annual Report, Dean of Chapel [1960–61]."

109. *WHAH*, 180–81.

110. "Annual Report, Dean of Chapel [1953–54]."

111. "Annual Report, Dean of Chapel [1955–56]."

112. Statement of Affirmation (undated, c. October 1960).

113. "Apostles of Growth," salutary remarks made on the occasion of Thurman's retirement by Dean Walter G. Muelder, Howard Thurman Collection, Howard Gotlieb Archival Research Center, Boston University; quoted in Fluker, *They Looked for a City*, 19.

114. From J. Wendell Yeo, 11 July 1961.

115. *WHAH*, 181.

116. Ibid., 187.

117. To J. Wendell Yeo, 16 March 1961, printed in the current volume.

118. "The Annual Report on the Wider Ministry of Dr. Howard Thurman, Dean of Marsh Chapel (on leave) September 1, 1962 to July 31, 1963."

119. See "Thurman Fund Budget, 27 December 1962."

120. To Boice Gross, 24 April 1962.

121. To J. Wendell Yeo, cc'd to Harold Case and William Overholt, 10 May 1962.

122. To Harold Case, 4 October 1962; To Harold Case, 17 November 1962. In a memo to President Case on 6 March 1962, Thurman proposed remaining at 184 Bay State Road until the fall of 1964.

123. To W. Stuart MacLeod, 21 December 1962.

124. *WHAH*, 188.

125. To Harold Case, 29 April 1963.

126. From Robert Hamill, 15 February 1963.

127. George Makechnie to Harold Case, 6 February 1962.

128. To Harold Case, 29 April 1963.

129. From Harold Case, 17 February 1963; To Harold Case, 17 February 1963.

130. To Coleman Jennings, 11 July 1963.

131. These trips will be treated in the forthcoming vol. 5 of *The Papers of Howard Washington Thurman*.

132. To Boice Gross, 19 March 1963.

133. From Zalman Schachter, 9 November 1964.

134. All of these books were published in New York by Harper & Brothers or Harper & Row unless otherwise noted. They are *Meditations of the Heart* (1953); *The Creative Encounter* (1954); *Deep River* (1955); *The Growing Edge* (1956); *Footprints of a Dream: The Story of the Fellowship Church of All Peoples* (1959); *Mysticism and the Experience of Love* (Wallingford, Pa.: Pendle Hill, 1961); *The Inward Journey* (Richmond, Ind.: Friends United Press, 1961); *The Temptations of Jesus: Five Sermons* (San Francisco: Lawton Kennedy, 1962); *Disciplines of the Spirit* (1963); and *The Luminous Darkness* (1965).

135. The degrees were awarded by Ohio Wesleyan University (1954); Lincoln University (Pennsylvania, 1954); Tuskegee Institute (1954); Washington University (1955); Howard University (1955); Oberlin College (1958); Virginia State University (1959); and Florida Normal and Industrial Memorial College (1963).

136. From Georgia Douglas Johnson, 4 June 1959.

137. Thurman wrote in his autobiography that during his first ministerial position, at the Mount Zion Baptist Church in Oberlin, Ohio, from 1926 to 1928, he discovered that his "most creative method" of preaching was through a sermon series (*WHAH*, 67).

138. The topics in "Man and the Moral Struggle" were "Albert Schweitzer, Spiritual Genius," "The Prophet of Deutero-Isaiah," Jesus, Paul, Job, Prometheus, Goethe's *Faust,* George Bernard Shaw's *St. Joan,* "Tolstoy—The Power of Darkness," and Johann Boger's novel *The Great Hunger.*

139. Sheldon Cheney, *Men Who Have Walked with God: Being the Story of Mysticism through the Ages Told in the Biographies of Representative Seers and Saints* (New York: Knopf, 1945). After two introductory sermons on "The Religion of the Inner Life," Thurman spoke on Lao Tse, Jacob Boehme, and Gandhi.

140. "The Fruits of the Spirit" comprised five sermons delivered in December 1950. The only extant sermon titles are the first, "Love," and the last, "Goodness."

141. "The Meaning of Commitment" comprised five sermons delivered from January to April 1951. The topics included "Spiritual Awareness," "A Vital Experience of God," and "The Bond that Unites."

142. "The Meaning of Loyalty" comprised at least six sermons in May and June 1951. Some were not further titled, but the series included one sermon titled "Job's Dilemma" and two on Deutero-Isaiah.

143. "The Declaration of Independence" comprised three sermons delivered in July and August 1951.

144. "The Parables of Jesus" comprised at least seven sermons delivered in the fall of 1951. Extant titles are "The Prodigal Son" and "The Possessions."

145. "An Objective Basis of Hope" comprised three sermons delivered in January 1952.

146. Thurman gave at least four sermons on pain in April and May 1952, speaking on "The Mystery of Pain" and "Pain and Failure" and delivering two sermons on "Pain and Misunderstanding."

147. "The Message of the Hebrew Prophets" comprised nine sermons delivered from May to August 1952 on Amos, Hosea, First Isaiah (two sermons), Second Isaiah, Jeremiah (two sermons), Ezekiel, and Micah.

148. "A Faith to Live By" comprised seven sermons given in September and October 1952. The topics included "God," "Jesus Christ," "Man" (two sermons), and "Democracy" (two sermons.)

149. "The Creative Imagination" comprised two sermons given in December 1952.

150. "The Divine Encounter" comprised three sermons given in March 1953. Topics included "In the Common Place" and "In Human Need."

151. Thurman delivered the sermons in the "Men Who Walked with God" series from April to July 1952. After an introductory sermon, the topics were Lao Tse, the Brahman mystics, the Buddha, Plotinus, St. Augustine, Gandhi, St. Francis, Jane Steger, Fra Angelico, Meister Eckhart, Jacob Boehme, and Thomas à Kempis.

152. The sermon topics, after an introductory sermon, were Second Isaiah, Job, Paul, Prometheus, Goethe's *Faust,* Shakespeare's *King Lear,* Henrik Ibsen's *Brand,* and Herman Melville's *Moby-Dick.*

153. "Prayer and Meditation" comprised three sermons delivered in January and February 1956. Sermon topics included "Prayer and Silence" and "Prayer and Pressure."

154. "The Quest for Maturity" comprised four sermons delivered in September and October 1956. After an introduction, the topics were "Increasing in Stature," "In Favor with God," and "In Favor with Man."

155. "The Religion of Jesus" comprised thirteen sermons given from November 1956 to March 1957. The extant sermon titles are "Who Is My Neighbor?," "Forgiveness," "Freedom,"

"Equality," "The Lost," "Poverty and Riches," "The Kingdom of God," "The Judgment," "The Great Feast," "The Great Moment," and "Jesus Prays."

156. "Pain" comprised six sermons delivered in March and April 1957 on "The Conquest of Pain," "Through a Glass Darkly" (two sermons), "Affliction," "Life and Death," and "Pain and Crisis."

157. "Seeking and Finding" comprised nine sermons given between September and December 1957: an introductory sermon, "Seeking and Finding God" (two sermons), "Seeking and Finding Forgiveness" (two sermons), and "Seeking and Finding the Self" (four sermons).

158. "The Creative Encounter" comprised six sermons delivered in November and December 1958. After an introductory sermon, Thurman spoke on "Integrity," "Habakkuk," "Amos," "Hosea," and "Isaiah."

159. "Jesus and the Disinherited" comprised twelve sermons delivered from January to May 1959. The five surviving sermons lack individual titles.

160. "The Meaning of Tradition" comprised five sermons given in September and October 1959 on "The Sense of Tradition" and "The Source of Tradition" (four sermons).

161. "The Meaning of Freedom" comprised four sermons given in November 1959 on "Freedom and Failure," "Freedom and Grace," and "Freedom and Suffering" (two sermons).

162. "Disciplines of the Spirit" comprised seven sermons given from October to December 1960 on "Growth," "Personal Stability," "The Single Mind," "When Commitment Becomes Idolatrous," "The Disciplined Act," "Suffering," and "Job."

163. "The Inward Journey" comprised nine sermons given from October to December 1961. After an introductory sermon, Thurman spoke on "The Mystic Will—Jacob Boehme," "Meister Eckhart," "The Inner Light" (two sermons), "St. Francis," "Plotinus: The Inner Journey," and "St. Augustine: Architect of a New Faith" (two sermons).

164. "Quests of the Human Spirit" comprised seven sermons given from February to May 1962. After an introductory sermon, Thurman spoke on "The Quest for Freedom," "The Quest for Truth," "The Quest for Security," "The Quest for Integrity," "The Quest for Identity," and "The Quest for God."

165. The "Dilemma of Jesus" comprised four sermons given in July 1962: an introductory sermon, "The Dilemma in the Wilderness," "The Dilemma of the Crossroad," and "The Dilemma in the Garden."

166. To Robert Hamill, 7 March 1963.

Editorial Statement

Document Selection

Spanning the years 1918 to 1981, *The Papers of Howard Washington Thurman* covers Thurman's formative period and tenure at Howard University, his founding of the Fellowship Church in San Francisco, and his tenure at Boston University, and it ends with his work as director of the Howard Thurman Educational Trust. The volumes are arranged chronologically, and each includes a biographical essay, a chronology, a selection of photographs, and an index. The array of Howard Thurman materials from which documents have been chosen for publication in this documentary edition is considerable. The Howard Thurman Papers Project had access to approximately seventy-four hundred documents generated during the period covered in this volume. This includes incoming and outgoing correspondence; public statements; published and unpublished lectures, sermons, and essays; articles; book reviews; public comments; and interviews. This volume includes about 2 percent of this universe of documents. Covering the period from June 1949 to December 1962, this volume treats Thurman's last years at the Fellowship Church, his decision to move to Boston University, and all of his active years as dean of the chapel at Boston University and as a professor at the Boston University School of Theology, which ended in spring 1962, although Thurman's formal retirement from Boston University was not until 1965. Because of space limitations, several documents relating to the last phase of Thurman's career at Boston University will be published in volume 5.

The documents selected for publication are those that the editors have determined best represent Thurman's thoughts and activities. Some published writings have been included if they are not included in Thurman's later collections of sermons and essays. In the current volume, such writings are "Habakkuk Exposition," "The Christian Minister and the Desegregation Decision," and "Two Options." Most of the writings in the current volume are published here for the first time; especially notable are an excerpt from Thurman's personal journal, Thurman's first annual report as dean of the chapel at Boston University, and sermons preached by Thurman at Fellowship Church and Boston University.

Each sermon given by Thurman at Boston University is presented here with the meditation that Thurman read in conjunction with the sermon.

Correspondence to Thurman is included if it was written by prominent individuals, relates to significant events in Thurman's life or the lives of his prominent associates, provides important historical context, or gives insight into Thurman's personality or interactions with other persons.

The editors of the Howard Thurman Papers Project had access to audiotapes of most of the sermons that Thurman preached at Boston University as well as the eulogy for Mary McLeod Bethune. The transcriptions for these sermons and for the eulogy were prepared by the editors and are indicated by "At." in the source notes. All of the remaining transcriptions of Thurman's sermons, addresses, and lectures that are published in this volume were based on transcripts that, evidence indicates, were prepared in the 1970s by the Howard Thurman Educational Trust. The editors are confident that all of the transcriptions accurately convey the substance and style of the orations.

The editors have excluded the lengthy sermon series that Thurman preached at the Fellowship Church and Boston University; as part of each series Thurman presented multiple sermons on one theme. These will be included in a volume of *The Papers of Howard Washington Thurman* exclusively dedicated to Thurman's sermon series. This was done to allow each of the later volumes of *The Papers of Howard Washington Thurman* to correspond roughly to a major phase in Thurman's life—one volume each for the years at Fellowship Church, the Boston University period, and the years of retirement.

ANNOTATION

The editors of *The Papers of Howard Washington Thurman* have, in keeping with current documentary editing practice, followed a policy of parsimony in annotations, with the expectation that the documents speak well enough for themselves. Annotations for prominent persons are kept to a minimum, and well-known political events and institutions are not described. We have left without annotation those persons, places, and things that, despite extensive research, we were unable to identify. Annotations focus on Thurman's biography, and discussions of theology are limited to what is necessary to evoke Thurman's intellectual and religious world at the time of the document's composition.

However, ample annotations have been provided where they are necessary to treat some aspects of Thurman's life and career adequately. No comprehensive biography of Thurman has been written. Therefore it was necessary for the editors to perform a great deal of original research into many aspects of Thurman's life. Such research is reflected in the biographical essay that precedes the documents and in many of the annotations.

The best account of Thurman's life remains his autobiography, *With Head and Heart*. This will remain *the* essential source on Thurman's life, but like many autobiographies, it recounts many events that took place decades before its writing, lacks footnotes and other documentation, is selective in its choice of topics, and on some subjects—especially Thurman's relations with his close associates—is at times less than fully candid. *The Papers of Howard Washington Thurman* provides an alternative account of Thurman's life, at various points confirming, amplifying, modifying, and challenging the narrative in *With Head and Heart*.

EDITORIAL PRINCIPLES

In preparing transcriptions and annotations, general editorial principles established in other documentary editing projects have been followed. The editors were particularly influenced by the principles followed by the editors of *The Papers of Martin Luther King, Jr.*, and we acknowledge a special debt to the project's senior editor, Clayborne Carson. For questions of editorial style, we have been guided by *The Chicago Manual of Style*.

Most of the primary documents that have been consulted for the annotations are from the Howard Thurman Papers, which are housed at the Howard Gotlieb Archival Research Center at Boston University. Where documents are from the Howard Thurman Papers, no source is indicated. When cited documents are from other collections or repositories, these are indicated in the annotations.

In all documents silent editorial corrections were made in cases of malformed letters, words that were misspelled due to a one-letter mistake, and the transposing of two characters.

In all documents periods were silently added at the ends of sentences if missing.

Unless otherwise indicated, words in brackets ([ ]) have been added by the editors.

In typescripts of sermons and other writings, all misspellings have been silently corrected, the editors have made corrections where it was apparent that errors were made by the transcriptionist, and the editors have filled in lacunae where they were certain about the missing word or words; such was particularly the case where names of individuals and places were missing.

Hyphens and dashes in the documents have been modified by the editors in the following manner: end-of-line dashes were silently deleted unless the usage was ambiguous; hyphens between numbers were changed to en dashes (–); and long dashes were changed to em dashes (—).

Strikeovers and insertions in such minor cases as correcting a misspelling or adding an overlooked connective word were not reproduced. When significant, insertions (usually handwritten) are indicated by placement in curly braces ({ }) and positioned to replicate their locations in the original documents as closely as possible.

Words of theological significance that are customarily capitalized, such as Christian and Lent, have been capitalized by the editors whether or not they are capitalized in the original text.

Line breaks, pagination, and vertical and horizontal spacing in the original documents were not replicated.

In typescripts, the underlining of book titles, court cases, and other words and phrases has been reproduced by the editors.

Indiscernible words—or segments of words—in a document or recording are indicated by the terms "illegible" and "inaudible," respectively; these terms appear in italic type and have been placed within brackets: [*illegible*] and [*inaudible*]. Conjectures of unclear text or audiotape are indicated in the same manner, with question marks preceding the closing brackets. If the number of illegible words is known, it is noted, such as [2 *words illegible*].

Illegible crossed-out words are indicated in the following manner: [*strike-over illegible*].

If the last part of a document is missing or unintelligible, this is noted as [*remainder missing*] or [*remainder unintelligible*], respectively.

Printed letterheads have not been reproduced. Significant information in the letterhead is noted in the headnote or in an endnote.

Signed, original documents were selected in preference to copies. Signatures in both original documents and copies have been reproduced in the following manner: [*signed*] name. For example:

Sincerely,
[*signed*] Mordecai Johnson
Mordecai W. Johnson

Most of the transcriptions of letters written by Howard Thurman were transcribed from carbon copies. Although the carbon copies are unsigned, the originals would have been signed. Unsigned documents, including unsigned carbon copies, are indicated in the following manner:

Sincerely,
Howard Thurman

If the closing includes neither a signature nor a typed name, and based on surrounding correspondence the editors have determined the letter's author, the name is placed in square brackets.

The date of the document is reproduced on the line below the title, and the place of origin is indicated on the line immediately below the date.

If a document does not contain a date and the editors have speculated on the date, it appears italicized in brackets. If a document does not contain a place of origin and the editors have speculated on the place of origin, it appears italicized in brackets.

If a document has been previously published, information about the previous publication—such as its name, date of publication, and publisher—is given immediately following the document.

Places in the United States are identified by state, and places in Canada are identified by province. For places located elsewhere, country identifiers are provided. Well-known cities, wherever located, are not further identified.

Places are identified by their historically appropriate names and orthography. Current names are indicated by, for example, [now Sri Lanka].

References to secondary works follow *The Chicago Manual of Style* format.

Source Notes

The source of the majority of documents in the current volume is the Howard Thurman Papers, which are housed at the Howard Gotlieb Archival Research Center at Boston University. Where documents are from the Howard Thurman Papers, no source is indicated. For documents obtained from sources other than the Howard Thurman Papers, the sources are indicated in source notes. Source notes are in two parts—separated by a period and a space—at the end of each document. The first part is an abbreviated description of the document's script, format, version, and signature, as applicable—all categories do not pertain to all documents. The second part of the source note indicates the location of the original document. Thus the source note for a typed letter that is signed by Thurman, the original of which is held in the John Swomley Papers of Swarthmore College, will look like this:

TLS. JSP-SWA

The *T* stands for typed, the *L* for letter or memo, and the *S* for signed.

Where no document format is given, the document is the original.

Note

1. The tapes are held by the Howard Gotlieb Archival Research Center at Boston University and are available at http://hgar-srv3.bu.edu/web/howard-thurman/virtual-listening-room, last accessed 2 November 2016.

Howard Thurman Chronology

The following chronology lists Thurman's appearances as a visiting preacher and lecturer, his published books, and a few major life events from 1 June 1949 through 31 December 1962. It has been compiled from Thurman's correspondence and writings, subject files, and from secondary accounts of his engagements in newspapers. Unless otherwise noted, all of the locations set forth below are the sites of speaking engagements. This abbreviated version of the chronology does not include any sermons preached at Fellowship Church except those delivered when Thurman was no longer its minister; nor does it include, with one exception, those preached at Marsh Chapel or Boston University, or the titles of the sermons he preached as a guest lecturer. A more comprehensive version of the chronology containing these omitted elements can be accessed at the Web site of the Howard Thurman Papers Project, http://www.bu.edu/htpp/.

1949

12–13 June
Baccalaureate Address, Wellesley College, Wellesley, Massachusetts

15 June
Northfield Prep Conference, East Northfield, Massachusetts

June (dates uncertain)
Visits Alice Sams, Thurman's mother (who is ailing), in Daytona Beach, Florida

3–10 August
Christian Training Camp, Leadership Training School, Naramata, British Columbia

September (dates uncertain)
Fellowship Church of All Peoples Delegation to UNESCO Conference in Paris, France; Thurman does not accompany the delegation

19–20 November
Canadian Memorial Church, Vancouver, British Columbia
Victoria, British Columbia

28 November–1 December
Campus Religious Council, Oregon State College, Corvallis

December
"I Will Light Three Candles," *Parents* magazine (article)

26 December–1 January 1950
National Intercollegiate Christian Council Conference, Asilomar, California

1950

12 February
Race Relations Sunday, Houston, Texas

13 February
Texas State University, Houston

19 February
Sunday Evening Forum, Tucson, Arizona (radio broadcast)

3 March
Garrison Forest School, Garrison, Maryland

5 March
Vassar College, Poughkeepsie, New York

6–8 March
Wesleyan University, Middletown, Connecticut

9–10 March
Kalamazoo College, Kalamazoo, Michigan

12 March
Rockefeller Memorial Chapel, University of Chicago

13–17 March
Lenten Services, Detroit Council of Churches

19 March
Fellowship House, Philadelphia
Unitarian Church of Germantown, Germantown, Pennsylvania

5 April
California Elementary School Administrators Association, Hollywood High
   School, Los Angeles

25 April
Jefferson School, San Diego

7 May
Death of Alice Sams, Thurman's mother, in San Francisco

6 June
Commencement Address, Morehouse College, Atlanta, Georgia

16 July
Mt. Hollywood Congregational Church, Los Angeles

15 October
Phillips Academy, Andover, Massachusetts

19–22 October
National Preparatory School Committee Conference, Atlantic City, New Jersey

22 October
Wesleyan University Chapel

23 October
King's Chapel, Boston
Dana Hall School, Wellesley, Massachusetts

24–25 October
Memorial Church, Harvard University, Cambridge, Massachusetts

26 October
Choate School, Wallingford, Connecticut

27 October
National Preparatory School Committee Conference, Atlantic City, New Jersey

28 October
McGill YWCA, Chicago
Friends of Fellowship Church, Chicago
Chicago Sunday Evening Club (radio broadcast)

30 October
Public Affairs Forum, YMCA, St. Louis, Missouri

5 November
The Masters School, Dobbs Ferry, New York

13 November
St. Agnes School, Alexandria, Virginia

14–16 November
Annual Convocation, Howard University School of Religion, Washington, D.C.

December
"'Our Father' and My Brother," *Adult Student* (Methodist Church, U.S.A., article)

1951

Deep Is the Hunger: Meditations for Apostles of Sensitiveness (New York: Harper & Brothers)

14 January
Stanford University Memorial Church, Stanford, California

15 January
Leadership Institute, Community Welfare Council, San Jose, California

19 January
Congregation Beth Shalom, San Francisco

14–15 February
YWCA, Long Beach, California

15 February
NBC Studios, Burbank, California (roundtable radio discussion)

16 February
Convocation Address, Negro History Week, University of California, Los
    Angeles

18 February
Sunday Evening Forum, Tucson, Arizona (radio broadcast)

23 February
Congregation Emanu-El, San Francisco

12–16 March
Religion in Life Institute at the First Methodist and First Presbyterian
    Churches, Portland, Oregon

16 March
Portland City Club, Portland, Oregon

26 March
Big Ten Alumni Association, San Francisco

2 April
San Jose State College, San Jose, California

16 April
Dana Hall School

17 April
Union Theological Seminary, New York City
Fellowship Church Dinner, Riverside Church, New York City

8–9 May
Hollywood Congregational Church, Los Angeles

3 June
Baccalaureate Sermon, Katharine Branson School, Ross, California

22 June
Annual Conference of the Church of the Brethren, San Jose, California

15 July
Yosemite National Park Church, California

3–6, 8–9 August
Christian Leadership Training School, Naramata, British Columbia

21 September
Invocation, American Federation of Labor Conference, Civic Center, San
Francisco

11–12 October
Canadian Memorial Chapel, Vancouver, British Columbia

12 October
Taylor Union College, Vancouver, British Columbia

9 November
Emma Willard School, Troy, New York

11 November
Phillips Academy

12–17 November
YWCA, Montreal, Quebec

18 November
Memorial Church, Harvard University

1952

28 January
Dedication of Interracial Community House, Santa Barbara, California

29–31 January
Ministers' Convocation, University of Southern California, Los Angeles

2 February
Conference on Civil Rights, American Friends Service Committee, San
Francisco

5 February
University of Iowa, Iowa City

6–7 February
Lawrence College, Appleton, Wisconsin

8 February
Washington University, St. Louis, Missouri

10 February
Denison University, Granville, Ohio

11–12 February
Oberlin College, Oberlin, Ohio

13–18 February
Religious Emphasis Week, College of Wooster, Wooster, Ohio

19 February
Wooster Methodist Church, Wooster, Ohio

20 February
Ohio Wesleyan University, Delaware, Ohio

24 February
Community Church of New York, New York City

23 March
Pomona College, Claremont, California
Inter-congregational Union Church Service, Pasadena, California

27 March
Mills College, Oakland, California

3 May
First Unitarian Church, San Francisco

24 August
Hennepin Avenue Methodist Church, Minneapolis, Minnesota

26 August
Camp Miniwanca (American Youth Foundation), Shelby, Michigan

2 November
Rockefeller Memorial Chapel, University of Chicago

5 November
Howard University School of Religion (Annual Convocation), Washington,
   D.C.

7–8 November
Choate School

7 December
California State Prison, San Quentin

12 December
Congregation Emanu-El, San Francisco

28 December–2 January 1953
Student YMCA and YWCA, Pacific Southwest Region, Asilomar Conference
   Center, Pacific Grove, California

1953

Meditations of the Heart (New York: Harper & Brothers)

8–12 February
Religious Emphasis Week, University of Washington, Seattle

1–3 March
Religious Emphasis Week, Wellesley College

18 March
First Methodist Church, Palo Alto, California

22 March
First Presbyterian Church, Oakland, California

29 March–2 April
Holy Week, Westminster United Presbyterian Church, Des Moines, Iowa

19 April
KNBC, San Francisco (radio broadcast)

5–6 May
Caltech YMCA, Pasadena, California

27 May
Commencement Address, Dillard University, New Orleans, Louisiana

31 May
Baccalaureate Sermon, Florida Agricultural and Mechanical College,
  Tallahassee

2 June
Commencement Address, Barber-Scotia College, Concord, North Carolina

27 June
Grace Cathedral, San Francisco

11 July
California State Prison, San Quentin

6 September
Hennepin Avenue Methodist Church, Minneapolis, Minnesota

8–11 September
The School of the Prophets (Indiana Methodist Convention), De Pauw
  University, Greencastle, Indiana

20 September
Marsh Chapel, Boston University (Thurman's first service as dean of the
  chapel)

30 October
Virginia Teachers Association, Virginia Union University, Richmond

1 November
Tuskegee Institute, Tuskegee, Alabama

13 November
Temple Ohabei Shalom, Brookline, Massachusetts

22 November
Dana Hall School

25 November
Wheelock College, Boston

14 December
McMillan Theater, Columbia University, New York City

1954

The Creative Encounter (New York: Harper & Brothers)

10 January
Sweetbriar College, Sweetbriar, Virginia
Hollins College, Roanoke, Virginia

17 January
Unitarian Church of Germantown
The Masters School

24 January
Church of Christ, Wesleyan University

25 January
Choate School

31 January
Phillips Academy

7 February
Memorial Church, Harvard University

8–9 February
Morning Prayers, Memorial Church, Harvard University

19 February
First Presbyterian Church, Bristol, Tennessee

1 March
Trinity Church, Boston

3 March
St. George's Church, New York City

14–17 March
Merrick Lectures, Ohio Wesleyan University (awarded doctor of humanities
   degree)

17 March
Columbus Interracial Church Fellowship, Columbus, Ohio

19 March
Boston Authors Club

30–31 March
King's Chapel, Boston

5–9 April
Lenten Week Sermons, Grace Methodist Church, Metropolitan Church
Federation of Greater St. Louis

7 April
Graham Memorial Chapel, Washington University, St. Louis, Missouri

25 April
Walnut Hill School, Natick, Massachusetts

27 April
Keynote Address, National Association of Foreign Student Advisors, Boston
YWCA, Worcester, Massachusetts

2 May
Connecticut College, New London

14 May
Emma Willard School

16 May
Tabor Academy, Marion, Massachusetts

19 May
Mayor's Council on Human Relations, Milwaukee, Wisconsin

23 May
Commencement Address, Western College for Women, Oxford, Ohio

27 May
Commencement Address, Allen University, Columbia, South Carolina

30 May
Baccalaureate Sermon, Bennett College, Greensboro, North Carolina

8 June
Commencement Address, Lincoln University, Oxford, Pennsylvania (awarded
doctor of divinity degree)

13 June
Baccalaureate Sermon, Vassar College

2 July
Pacific Coast Festival, Santa Barbara, California

15 August
Canadian Memorial Church, Vancouver, British Columbia

29–30 September
Westminster Theological Seminary, Westminster, Maryland

October
"Litany of Thanksgiving," *Braille Magazine* (article)

4 October
Regional Meeting of Council for State Leagues for Nursing, Boston

6 October
Graduation Address, School of Nursing, Massachusetts Memorial Hospitals, Boston

8 October
Essex County Teachers' Association, Boston

16 October
Massachusetts Schoolmasters' Club, Boston

24 October
Twelfth Baptist Church, Roxbury, Massachusetts

26 October
Federation of Protestant Welfare Agencies, New York City

26–27 October
Massachusetts State Baptist Convention, Framingham

3 November
Howard University School of Religion, Washington, D.C.

6 November
Dana Hall School

9 November
Women's Association, Wellesley Hills Congregational Church, Wellesley Hills, Massachusetts

11 November
National Council of Negro Women, Washington, D.C.

12 November
University of Vermont, Burlington

17 November
Annual Brotherhood Award Luncheon, Junior Chamber of Commerce of Philadelphia

24 November
Thanksgiving Eve Annual Union Service, United Congregational Church, Boston

13 December
Christmas Convocation, Massachusetts Institute of Technology, Cambridge, Massachusetts

15 December
Alpha Lambda Chapter, Phi Delta Kappa (fraternity for educators), Boston

19 December
Annual Goodwill Dinner for Temple Brotherhood, Temple Ohabei Shalom, Brookline, Massachusetts

1955
Deep River: Reflections on the Insights of Certain of the Negro Spirituals (New York: Harper & Brothers)

7–8 January
University of Vermont

10 January
Winchester Unitarian Society, Winchester, Massachusetts

14 January
Community-Wide Preaching Mission, Norfolk, Virginia

16 January
Rollins Chapel, Dartmouth College, Hanover, New Hampshire

24–26 January
Minnesota Pastors Conference, Minneapolis

30 January–1 February
Keuka College, Keuka Park, New York

6 February
Memorial Church, Harvard University
Annual Dwight L. Moody Memorial Vespers Service, Boston Northfield Club, Boston

14–16 February
Tri-City Preaching Mission to Kingsport, Johnson City, and Bristol, Tennessee

20 February
Second Century Convocation, Washington University, St. Louis, Missouri (awarded doctor of laws degree)

23 February
Union Theological Seminary, New York City

27 February
Boston Northfield Club
Eastern Division Music Educators National Conference, Boston

2 March
Asbury First Methodist Church, Rochester, New York

3 March
First Baptist Church, Syracuse, New York

4 March
Richmond Avenue Methodist Church, Buffalo, New York

6 March
Wheaton College, Norton, Massachusetts
First Baptist Church, Fall River, Massachusetts

16 March
Choate School

17 March
Church of the Redeemer, New Haven, Connecticut

23 March
Lenten Service, Darien Congregational Church, Darien, Connecticut

28 March–1 April
Christ Church, Cincinnati, Ohio

11–13 April
Convocation Chaplain and Alumni Banquet Address, Colgate-Rochester
   Divinity School, Rochester, New York

27 April
Phillips Academy

8 May
Princeton University Chapel, Princeton, New Jersey

12 May
Denison University

15 May
Memorial Church, Harvard University

23 May
Eulogy for Mary McLeod Bethune, Bethune-Cookman College, Daytona
   Beach, Florida

30 May
Commencement Address, Knoxville College, Knoxville, Tennessee

2 June
Asbury First Methodist Church, Rochester, New York

3 June
Awarded doctor of divinity degree, Howard University

6 June
Commencement Address, Wheelock College

12 June
Baccalaureate Sermon, Connecticut College

19, 26 June, 3 July
Fellowship Church

19 June
Festival of Faith, Cow Palace, San Francisco

24 July
Central Methodist Church, Detroit, Michigan

14 August
Wellfleet Methodist Church, Wellfleet, Massachusetts

20 August
Eulogy for John B. Chambers, Community Church of New York

11 September
Unitarian Church of Germantown

25 September
Dana Hall School

14 October
Harriet Tubman Memorial Foundation, AME Zion Church, Auburn, New
    York

16 October
Twelfth Baptist Church, Roxbury, Massachusetts
Dana Hall School

23 October
Dedicatory Sermon for Chapel, Dillard University, New Orleans, Louisiana

27 October
Dana Hall School

4 November
Women's Association, Hancock Church, Lexington, Massachusetts

10 November
Jefferson County Education Association, Birmingham, Alabama

12 November
Morehouse College

13 November
Friendship Baptist Church, Atlanta, Georgia

17 November
Ministers' Club, Cambridge, Massachusetts

19 November
Lambda Kappa Mu (sorority of African American professional women and
businesswomen), Boston

22 November
Argo Club, Harvard Medical School

27–28 November
Dana Hall School

5–6 December
Antioch College, Yellow Springs, Ohio

19 December
Christmas Convocation, Massachusetts Institute of Technology

29 December
Mid-Winter Unitarian-Universalist Ministers' Institute, Exeter, New
Hampshire

1956

The Growing Edge (New York: Harper & Brothers)
Apostles of Sensitiveness: The Ware Lecture (Boston: American Unitarian
Association)
"Habakkuk: Text, Exegesis, and Exposition" and "Zephaniah: Text, Exegesis,
and Exposition" in *The Interpreter's Bible,* vol. 6 (New York: Abingdon Press)

3 January
Haverford College, Haverford, Pennsylvania

8 January
The Masters School

12 January
Hartford Seminary, Hartford, Connecticut

15 January
Bowdoin College, Brunswick, Maine

20 January
Norfolk United Preaching Mission, Norfolk, Virginia

4 February
Massachusetts Schoolmasters' Club

5 February
Phillips Academy

6 February
Brookline First Parish Branch of the Women's Alliance, Brookline,
Massachusetts

12 February
Community Church of New York

13 February
The Hill School, Pottstown, Pennsylvania

14 February
South End House, Boston

19 February
Asylum Hill Congregational Church, Hartford, Connecticut

22 February
St. James Presbyterian Church, Harlem, New York City

23 February
Asbury First Methodist Church, Rochester, New York

24 February
Mills College of Education, New York City

2 March
Asbury-Delaware Methodist Church, Buffalo, New York

4 March
Founder's Day Sermon, Virginia State College, Petersburg

18 March
First Baptist Church, Fall River, Massachusetts

22–23 March
Morgan State College, Baltimore, Maryland

24 March
Tuskegee Institute (awarded honorary degree)

29 March
Emmanuel Church, Boston

3 April
Second Baptist Church, Detroit, Michigan

17 April
Williams College, Williamstown, Massachusetts

18 April
Emma Willard School

21 April
Massachusetts Association of the New Jerusalem, Boston

22 April
Tabor Academy

29 April
Connecticut College

6 May
Boston University Alumni Club of Greater Springfield, Springfield,
   Massachusetts

7 May
Thayer Academy, Braintree, Massachusetts

9 May
Lesley College, Cambridge, Massachusetts

14 May
Commencement Address, Colgate-Rochester Divinity School

15 May
Emma Willard School

17 May
Akron Community Service Center, Akron, Ohio

18 May
Ware Lecture, Annual Meeting, American Unitarian Association, Boston

21 May
Commencement Address, Virginia State School, Hampton

29 May
Commencement Address, Theological Seminary of the Reformed and
   Evangelical Church, Lancaster, Pennsylvania

27 June
Chicago Inter-Alumni Council of the United Negro College Fund

1, 8, 15, 22 July
Fellowship Church

15 July
First Methodist Church, Pasadena, California

21 July
Spiritual Life Retreat (Fellowship Church), Stonetree Ranch, Sonoma County,
   California

5 August
Central Methodist Church, Detroit, Michigan

7 September
Annual Meeting, National Baptist Convention, U.S.A., Inc., Denver, Colorado

9 September
Unitarian Church of Germantown

7 October
House in the Pines School, Norton, Massachusetts

21 October
Milton Academy, Milton, Massachusetts

11 November
Helen Eakin Eisenhower Chapel, Pennsylvania State University, University Park

15 November
Preaching Institute, Arlington Street Church, Boston

26–27 November
Five Oaks Christian Worker Center, Paris, Ontario

16 December
Unitarian Church of Sanford, Sanford, Maine

1957

2–3 January
New England Unitarian-Universalist Mid-Winter Institute, Phillips Exeter
   Academy, Exeter, New Hampshire

9 January
Riverside Church, New York City

11 January
Emma Willard School

17 January
Florida Open Forum, Palm Beach

20 January
Riverside Church, New York City

21–23 January
Michigan Pastors Conference, Ann Arbor

27 January
Phillips Academy

5 February
Wesleyan University

10 February
The Hill School

12 February
Franklin and Marshall College, Lancaster, Pennsylvania

25–26 February
Pastors' Study Conference, Board of Home Missions of the Congregational
   and Christian Churches, New York City

6 March
St. James Presbyterian Church, Harlem, New York City

13–14 March
Institute on Successful Marriage and Family Living, Morehouse College

17 March
Asylum Hill Congregational Church, Hartford, Connecticut

18–19 March
Convocation for Preaching for the Philadelphia Area, Buck Hill Falls, Pennsylvania

25–26 March
Crozier Theological Seminary, Chester, Pennsylvania

1–5, 8–12 April
Christ Church, Cincinnati, Ohio

29 April
Connecticut College

6 May
National League for Nursing Convention, Chicago

7 May
Lake Forest College, Lake Forest, Illinois

16–17 May
Maine Conference of the Methodist Church, Augusta

4 June
Commencement Address, North Carolina State College at Durham

18–22 June
Northeast Ohio Annual Methodist Ministers' Conference, Lakeside, Ohio

25 June–1 August
Vacation with Sue Bailey Thurman in Edinburgh, Scotland; guests of Coleman Jennings

5 August
Canadian Memorial Chapel, Vancouver, British Columbia

11, 18 August
Fellowship Church

17 August
Spiritual Life Retreat (Fellowship Church), Stonetree Ranch

8 September
Unitarian Church of Germantown

20 October
Vassar College

3 November
First Baptist Church, Worcester, Massachusetts

10 November
University of Michigan, Ann Arbor

12 November
Virginia Union University, Richmond

1958

12 January
Connecticut College

13 January
Choate School

20 January
Emma Willard School

27–29 January
Bangor Theological Seminary, Bangor, Maine

10 February
Syracuse Ministers' Association, Syracuse, New York

14–15 February
Tri-State Preaching Mission, Ashland, Kentucky; Huntington, West Virginia

16–17 February
Hampton Institute, Hampton, Virginia

26 February
St. James Presbyterian Church, Harlem, New York City

27 February
Dwight School, Englewood, New Jersey

4 March
Temple Emanu-El B'Ne Jeshurun, Milwaukee, Wisconsin

5 March
Religious Forum Lecture, University of Wisconsin, Madison

6 March
Lake Forest College

13 March
University of Rochester, Rochester, New York

20 March
Lincoln University, Oxford, Pennsylvania

23 March
Asylum Hill Congregational Church, Hartford, Connecticut

13 April
University of Rochester

16 April
Princeton Theological Seminary, Princeton, New Jersey

19 April
Wellesley Congregational Church, Wellesley, Massachusetts

27 April
Providence Ministers' Seminar, The First Baptist Church in America,
 Providence, Rhode Island

4 May
House in the Pines School

8–9 May
Lutheran Theological Seminary, Gettysburg, Pennsylvania

25 May
Phillips Exeter Academy

27 May
Commencement Speaker, Virginia State College, Norfolk

1 June
Baccalaureate Speaker, Atlanta University-Morehouse and Spelman
 Colleges

15 June
All Soul's Church, Washington, D.C.

16 June
Southern Baptist Theological Seminary, Louisville, Kentucky

23–27 June
American Alumni Council, Lake Placid, New York

10 August
Fellowship Church

24, 31 August
Canadian Memorial Church, Vancouver, British Columbia

14 September
Unitarian Church of Germantown

28 September
Graduation Address, Leominster Hospital School of Nursing, Leominster,
 Massachusetts

8 October
Wesleyan University

18–19 October
Anniversary Convocation, Oberlin College (awarded doctor of divinity degree)

8 November
Wheaton College, Norton, Massachusetts

9 November
St. George's School, Newport, Rhode Island

23 November
Lawrenceville School, Lawrenceville, New Jersey

29 December–1 January
University of Redlands, Redlands, California

1959

Footprints of a Dream: The Story of the Fellowship Church of All Peoples (New York: Harper & Brothers)

3 January
San Jose Branch NAACP, San Jose, California

18 January
The Masters School

8–12 February
Texas Southern University, Houston

19 February
St. Paul's Church, Niagara Falls, New York

20 February
Woodside Methodist Church, Buffalo, New York

1 March
Council of Churches, Fall River, Massachusetts

11 March
St. John the Evangelist, Hingham, Massachusetts

13 March
Temple Emanu-El B'Ne Jeshurun, Milwaukee, Wisconsin

15 March
Chicago Sunday Evening Club, Orchestra Hall, Chicago

16 March
Ohio Wesleyan University

5 April
Bowdoin College

3 May
Milton Academy

14 May
South Presbyterian Church, Dobbs Ferry, New York

25 May
Virginia State College, Petersburg (awarded doctor of humanities degree)

30 May
Baccalaureate Service, Milton Academy

June
Elected Fellow of American Academy of Arts and Sciences

2 June
Commencement Address, Savannah State College, Savannah, Georgia

4 June
Commencement Address, Beaver County Day School, Chestnut Hill, Massachusetts

16 June
Memorial Service for Oswald W. McCall, Marsh Chapel

10 July
Retreat Leader (Fellowship Church), Stonetree Ranch

11 July
First Methodist Church, Oakland, California

13 July
Pacific School of Religion, Berkeley, California

13–31 July
Taught at Pacific School of Religion

19 July
First Methodist Church, Oakland, California

25 July
Retreat Leader (Fellowship Church), Stonetree Ranch

26 July
First Methodist Church, Oakland, California

8 September
First Unitarian Church, San Francisco

13 September
First Unitarian Church of Germantown

4 October
The Hill School

25 October
Central Square Ministers' Association, Cambridge, Massachusetts

28 October
First Unitarian Church, Portland, Oregon

1960 (ON SABBATICAL UNTIL SEPTEMBER)

11–13 January
Hampton Institute

14–16 January
Bennett College, Greensboro, North Carolina

19–22 January
Tuskegee Institute

30 January–5 February
Arkansas Agricultural, Mechanical and Normal College, Pine Bluff

9 February–4 March
In Los Angeles

6 March
Narrator, "Queen Esther" (Oratorio), by Marc Lavry, San Francisco War Memorial
    Opera House (in honor of 100th anniversary of Congregation Beth Israel)

8 March–15 September
Round-the-world tour

24 July
St. Martin's-in-the-Fields, Trafalgar Square, London, England

26 July
Manchester and Salford Methodist Mission, England

31 July
Bristol Methodist Mission, England

25 September
Cathedral of the Pines, Rindge, New Hampshire

9–11 November
Smith-Willson Lectures, Southwestern College, Winfield, Kansas

11 November
Langston University, Langston, Oklahoma

22 November
Andover Newton Theological School, Newton Centre, Massachusetts

1961

The Inward Journey (New York: Harper & Brothers)
Mysticism and the Experience of Love (Wallingford, Pa.: Pendle Hill
    Publications (pamphlet))
"Two Options," in *God and the H-Bomb*, ed. Donald Keys (New York:
    Bellmeadows Press and Bernard Geis Associates)

6–8 February
Mendenhall Lecturer, DePauw University, Greencastle, Indiana

22–24 February
Ministerial Conference, Board of Church Extension, Presbyterian Church in
    the United States, Atlanta, Georgia

27 February
Friends General Conference, Baltimore, Maryland

19 March
Emma Willard School

20–24 March
Lenten Services, Christ Church, Cincinnati, Ohio

20–22 April
Halifax Area Council of Human Relations, Daytona Beach, Florida

26 April
Tourist Church, Daytona Beach, Florida

28 April
Temple Shalom of Newton, West Newton, Massachusetts

27 May
Commencement Address, E. J. Hayes School, Williamston, North Carolina

28 May
Commencement Address, Barber-Scotia College, Concord, North Carolina

29 May
Commencement Address, St. Paul's School, Lawrenceville, Virginia

27–30 June
Hampton Institute

10 July
Pasadena Methodist Church, Pasadena, California

26 July
First AME Church, Oakland, California

12–19 August
Christian Leadership Training School, Naramata, British Columbia

10 September
Unitarian Church of Germantown

9–11 October
Nebraska Wesleyan University, Lincoln

23 October
Invocation at Plenary Session, United States National Commission
    for UNESCO, Boston University

5–10 November
Metropolitan United Church, Toronto, Ontario

19 November
Mount Holyoke College, South Hadley, Massachusetts
Amherst Unitarian Church, Amherst, Massachusetts

4–5 December
Deer Hill Retreat Center, Hughsonville, New York

11 December
Fisher Junior College, Boston

17 December
Chicago Sunday Evening Club, Orchestra Hall, Chicago

18 December
McCormick Theological Seminary, Chicago

1962

The Temptations of Jesus: Five Sermons (San Francisco: Lawton
    Kennedy)

19 January
The Hill School

25–28 February
Spelman College, Atlanta, Georgia

2 March
Charter Day Lecture, Howard University

5 March
Mothers' Council of West Newton, West Newton, Massachusetts

8–9 March
Church of the Redeemer, Washington, D.C.

15 March
Scarsdale Community Baptist Church, Scarsdale, New York

19–20 March
Emma Willard School

25 March
Asylum Hill Congregational Church, Hartford, Connecticut

27 March
Frontiers of America (fraternal organization), Tampa, Florida

8 April
Wellesley College

25 April
Forrest City Hospital Lecture, Cleveland, Ohio

29 April
Detroit Chapter NAACP

1–3 May
Earlham College, Richmond, Indiana

8 May
Wainwright House, Rye, New York

11 May
Tilton School, Tilton, New Hampshire

20–21 May
Baccalaureate Sermon and Commencement Address, Florida Normal and
    Industrial Memorial College, St. Augustine (awarded doctor of letters
    degree)

26–29 June
Devotional Leader, Ministers' Conference, Hampton Institute

3–11 August
International Christian Writers Conference, Green Lake, Wisconsin

12–19 September
Theme Worship Leader, General Council, United Church of Canada, London,
    Ontario

16–18 October
Federation of Indian Chiefs, Fort Qu'applle, Saskatchewan, Canada

22–25 October
YWCA, Montreal, Quebec

1 November
Morris Harvey College, Charleston, West Virginia

11 November
Smithfield Street Methodist Church, Pittsburgh, Pennsylvania

13 November
Convocation Speaker, Payne Theological Seminary, Wilberforce, Ohio

25 November
World Fellowship Service Conference, YWCA, Los Angeles

27–30 November
La Verne College, La Verne, California

November–December
"The Search for God in Religion," *Layman's Retreat Review* (article)

The Papers of
Howard Washington Thurman

Volume 4

*Emily Worthy,[1] the younger sister of Alice Sams, writes Thurman with the
devastating news that his mother had suffered a major stroke. Although Worthy
described the event as a "light stroke," it was incapacitating, and Alice Sams's
health would never recover; she died less than a year later.[2]*

Dear Howard

Please do not be alarmed at this letter—but read it first.

This is to say that Fri. of last wk June 17th Sis. Alice had a light stroke. They
called me around 12 and when I got there, she was quite ill, but Dr St_[3] instructed
me to wait 2 or 3 days before calling to see how she would respond to treatment.
Well, she had steadily improved, and when I left yesterday, she had been sitting
up ate her dinner Mon, sitting in a chair. She had lost the use of left hand [&]
foot, but is using both again, so I can truthfully say she is coming on fine. Dr
St—has been very attentive. He left the city Sun. & left Evelyn, his daughter in
charge. I felt myself going down + blood pressure rising as you know I have the
ailment she has, only not in such an advanced stage as hers. The lady with her
& myself carried on until yesterday. The Dr. said she had to have real nursing,
& would trust no one but me. Well, I was giving out, so, she (S. Alice) and I
decided to get a Nurse. We got Audrey Jones, a cousin of ours, who takes care
of her in the day—She is no trouble at night only to give her medicine, & Mrs.
(her Companion) does that. I called over there just before writing this letter, and
Audrey says she is doing fine. I'll go back in a day or 2—.

Now, you are not to worry, as Dr. St says he is doing all that can be done, and
she should out of trouble in a few days. If not we will notify you. Of course he
does not know I am writing to you—but I feel that it is time you should know
what has happened. Don't get upset or come back, unless he tells you—as he is
in charge, and I am acting on his orders. I can check on her daily since she has
her telephone. I am so glad she has it. Carrie Lawrence and Louise Ambrose
from Ormond[4] comes in, Carrie comes every day & help in many ways—Lou is
very faithful too, for doing errands, and helping me with her. Also the lady in
the house is faithful too—and her neighbors also.

Now, ~~she~~ I read your instructions about the money I hold for her. She asked me to hold it a little longer, and see what happens, as she may need it here—But, if you say so, I will send you a cashier's check immediately. Audrey is charging $20.00 per wk. for day service, and seems to take a personal interest in her.

Now, when you write <u>please</u> take a little pains, so I can read your letter correctly, as I have to read her letters for her—she is not able to try to decipher them, and I can't make them out without study of signs + content (smile).[5]

All of the family and friends are doing what is to be done—Love to Sue & the children & to you—

[*signed*] Aunt Emily

ALS.

NOTES

1. Emily Ambrose Worthy, a sibling of Gilbert Ambrose and Alice Thurman Sams, lived much of her life in DeLand, Florida. She was married to C. A. Worthy.
2. See To Fellowship Church Family, 3 May 1950, printed in the current volume.
3. John T. Stocking. See *PHWT*, 2:284.
4. Ormond Beach is about six miles from Daytona Beach.
5. Worthy is apparently familiar with Thurman's sometimes indecipherable handwriting.

"THE QUEST FOR PEACE"
[*21 August 1949*][1]
SAN FRANCISCO, CALIF.

In this sermon given at the Fellowship Church, Thurman speaks to the question of peace and pacifism, and how easily even pacifism can become coercive.[2] For Thurman, the search for peace is the quest for creating a social climate in which "every man can sit under his own fig tree and be unafraid," maximizing both individual autonomy and social harmony. He feels that the task of pacifism is "the tremendous business of trying to get a world in which an ordinary human being can keep his self-respect and be alive."

May I refresh your minds with two or three of the stanzas read as a part of our responsive reading this morning. "But they shall sit every man under his vine and under his fig tree and none shall make them afraid."[3] "Speak ye every man the truth to his neighbor; execute the judgment of truth and peace in your gates and let none of you imagine evil in your hearts against his neighbor. Violence shall no more be heard in thy land, wasting or destruction within thy borders, and all thy children shall be taught of the Lord and great shall be the peace of thy children—peace to him that is afar off and to him that is near, saith the Lord. The work of righteousness shall be peace, and the effect of righteousness, quietness and assurance forever. For the fruit of righteousness is sown in peace to them that make peace. Therefore, Blessed are the peacemakers for they shall be called the children of God."[4]

We are all interested in peace, and it is a rather interesting paradox—this interest in peace, and we have never experienced it in the world. When I was a high school boy I studied a course in Ancient History and the man who wrote that book had a rather striking preamble to his discussion of certain phases of the Roman Empire. He said that all the world was at peace for the first time in the history of the world and at that breathlessly tranquil moment, Jesus was born.[5] Well—it was very wonderful, this. I read about it in that far off time in the past but subsequent study revealed very clearly that either the man who wrote the book had no sense of history or felt that he had to fix this up in a broken dose so that high school youngsters' minds would not be contaminated. There wasn't any peace.[6] There hasn't been any peace; and yet we long for it. We think about it and talk about it and we work for it here and there, but we haven't experienced it. And it's a curious thing—puzzling. Either the concept itself is so fundamental—so intimately part of the very structure of the creative process that we call "life," and therefore the urge for peace, the reaching for peace, the quest for peace is native to the human spirit; or—there is something so utterly demonic about the nature of life, something so demonic that if peoples, the brains and the emotions of men with an insatiable longing which has no basis in fact, in order that this demonic force that presides over the destiny of man may chortle and chuckle as generation after generation rises and falls in the midst of the torment. And I don't think the latter.

There are two observations that I want to make before I say the other things that are in my mind about the quest for peace—and the first observation is this: wherever man thinks seriously about peace and its meaning; wherever men work for it either professionally or privately (thinking of peace at the moment in terms of the relationship between nations, those impersonal things—conflicts and areas of relationships that are outside of the immediate control of the individual), wherever men work at peace, they are always exposed to the critical judgment that they are never consistent. Now, I hope that will not be misunderstood; and what I want to say, at this point, is that as far as my knowledge of human nature is concerned, the only people who are consistent are the people who are dead or not yet born. So it is no judgment against them to say that they are inconsistent. That doesn't mean anything, altogether. That's the first observation I want to make.

The second observation is that there has always moved in upon the monotony of daily living with a new kind of enthusiasm, war that always confronts the individual with a great irrationality. Nobody can really make a rational case for the destruction of his fellows, and no person who is interested either in peace or war knows that he can deal with the issue of war on a basis of rationality. War is a great irrationality. That is precisely its insidious and its curious hold on the imagination and the mind; for it causes the rational pattern of daily living to be faced at once with a tremendous irrationality and as it faces that irrationality it throws the rational pattern of living out of line and men begin to become aware of aspects of their existence of which they were not aware as long as they were submerged under the rational pattern of daily life. It is for this reason, I think, that it is as important for those of us who are concerned about peace to seek for aesthetic equivalents to war as well as moral equivalents,[7] for life has to have some poetry in it, you know. There must be something that tingles—something that gives a lift—something that— Some years ago, a man wrote a song and it was a failure. And then a collaborator, cooperator, or some other man took the song, kept the same music, but he added this—"<u>Hooray</u>!" Do you see what I mean? "My Wife Has Gone to the Country, Hooray!"[8] Now it is that little thing that he put on there that life must have. The analogy may have been unfortunate, but the point's clear. So that men who often find themselves deeply opposed to war and to the war-machine; they know that it brutalizes life and does all sorts of things: but when the nation is at war, some tremendous thing takes possession of the common life so that all of the monotonous chores of ordinary living are <u>quickened</u>. And we have to <u>deal</u> with that if we want to quarantine the formal manipulators—political and economic, who finally set the stage for war. Now I am not competent to discuss the great political and economic questions that are involved in a treatment of this sort nor perhaps is this the place. Now I want to call your attention to several things which have to do with what seems to me to be the fallacy in the methods by which we have sought for peace and what I think is the line along which we should go. The other evening down at the Shriners' place where Dr. Ralph Bunche,[9] who was making his presentation on behalf of the United Nations, and using his experience in the Palestinian affair as a for-instance of a certain method and process. The thing that kept going through my mind as he talked and spelled out the mechanism there, was not something that was involved in the great issues at stake, because I don't know enough about that—but the thing that interested me, impressed me tremendously was the fact that the technique that was used was the simple technique that you use when you are trying to work out something with somebody who won't see eye to eye with <u>you</u>. The mechanism is essentially the same. Now I thought about it very definitely because during the years, or part of the time that Dr. Bunche was at Howard University, he was the chairman of what was called "The Faculty Committee on Student Activities,"[10] and it was a committee that stood in the midst of the fraternity and sorority battle—in the midst of all of the pressures of undergraduate life and then finally it spread out to the medical school and the dental school and the law school and many times this faculty committee sat up most of the night trying to solve certain problems in a situation in which for the most part they had the power of the state; and no technique that was used in that infighting relationship, if I may call it that, was fundamentally different from the things that were talked about in this wider relationship between these two groups. Now the method that we use to bring about peace is almost always involved in some form of violence. I wish someone some day would get a clear and definitive insight as to the meaning and the significance of violence. There are many discussions about it. One of the most suggestive ones is the analysis that appears in Ortega y Gasset's book, "The Revolt of the Masses,"[11] in which he says that violence always remains on the horizon in any relationship between individuals, that there is no relationship between you and any other human being that does not have hovering around the edges violence in some form. Now, he says that the civilized man is the man who postpones any appeal to it until he has exhausted every other possibility, says Gasset. Now the barbarian, says the philosopher, is the man who as soon as his will is challenged or frustrated, resorts to violence. Violence is the first thing he does when he is frustrated. If he is a civilized man, says Gasset, violence is the last thing. Now, violence usually means in our ordinary thinking, physical violence. Ordinarily we do not think of violence in any other terms, but I suggest that as important as physical violence is, again and again our objection to physical violence is apt to be an aesthetic objection rather than a moral one. Let's think of that a minute. For there is a violence that is not physical, that belongs in the category of coercion, that is pressure, that is force. Now the problem, you see, is that if I use force—moral force, spiritual force, physical force in order to bring to effect in you an obedience to my will, the presupposition that I have is that my will is a righteous will, that my will is inviolate. And it is to your best interest that you yield to my will. If I can ever decide that. Then I have the inquisition, I have all sorts of things, because I am trying to save your soul. Now, the assumption that I make in my use of the term violence—and I hope you will not find this too dreary—but we will have to think it through—the distinction that I make in my use of the term of violence is this: that I think that there is a violence, force, coercion (I use all three of those together)—when violence, coercion, force is what I would call "creative," when it elicits in the other person a response not to me, but a response to the ideal that dominates me, then a basis of mutuality is at last established between me and him. If the violence does not operate that way, it succeeds merely, however benevolent and beneficent and holy and all the rest of it it may be, it merely succeeds in further alienating me from the other person. And that is one of the curious difficulties that is involved always in any commitment of the human spirit or the human heart, for in the fulfillment of that commitment—whether it be for peace or for violence—in the fulfillment of that commitment, often I am immunized against the simple, normal feelings of warmth and tenderness and kindness and graciousness that possessed me before I was laid hold upon by this commitment. And even though I am deeply committed to war or to peace, I am still a human being who wants love and kindness, understanding, and who must give it. Now, if I may illustrate how this works negatively for a moment, years ago—so many years that the person who is involved does not remember, when this person was five years old, I was reading a few pages in a book and I had to finish it before the taxi came to take me to the railway station, and this little 5-year old came rushing into my room and said, "I want you to do something with me." And I said, "I can't do it because I've got to finish reading this and you know I'm going away and the cab's coming. It's already ordered," but that didn't make any difference. There was this insistence that I do it, and I thundered a little—I just put a rumble in my voice; and she bristled—and stood her ground, because she was her mother's daughter. And then presently I closed my book and then the atmosphere became very, very tense and so she turned around and slammed the door—and went away to another part of the house. Now, I could have taken her by the hand with my mind, and stooping to the five-year-old frame of reference, have her see through my eyes what my predicament was and how I was working against this deadline; and then in that sort of exchange, she would have helped me see through her eyes, and we would have effected some kind of shift even if it meant cancelling the cab and getting the next train or something and that would have taken maybe two or three hours and I had only about twenty minutes. Now that's a very crude illustration of what I am talking about. But that is the temptation—that is the thing that blocks us in this quest for peace at the level we can reach because it is so much more a clearing of the air immediately, to threaten—either to threaten with silence, just close up, or to threaten with loose talk or pointed talk, but to get it out of the system—and that is healthy, they tell us—and to pour it upon the other person. Now what happens is that violence, using violence in the sense in which I am using it this morning, simply results in the stiffening of resistance and if the stiffening of resistance is impossible because its manifestation may mean sudden catastrophe, then the stiffening of resistance goes on apace, but it goes on underground. And the whole relationship becomes amoral.

Now there is one other aspect here and that is that we try to bring peace in the world—men try to bring peace in the world by what seems to me to be by a radically false focusing of values. We think that power that enables us to do for people what they most tragically need to have done lest they die, we think that the show of power that may serve notice upon other people that we are strong and mighty—we do it as individuals, we do it as groups, we do it as a nation, and we are involved in that now. Power, when it is in our hands—the fact of power in our hands—presupposes that we have enough maturity to handle it, and we don't. Do you know anybody, anybody, into whose hands you will without reluctance place your life? Do you? Do you know anybody who has the kind of integrity, the maturity of character that can stand, even stand emotionally, absolute power over you? Anybody you trust? Now, in all the work for peace, the assumption is that there will be on the part of the people in whom the peace motive is at work a moral sensitiveness that will enable them to respond to the good intent, to the goodwill, to the righteous thing for which we work, and in our effort in that direction we forget that even though the ideal of peace is a worthy, a righteous, and many people feel the supreme ideal, it is still contingent upon the kind of stamina and courage and body of the human beings who are manipulating it. I may give just this personal reference: I asked Mr. Gandhi, the time that we had those few hours with him, why—in his opinion—why was it that his movement of non-violence had failed its objective in India, namely to get the British out of the country. And he made a striking observation. He said that the ideal of Ahimsa[12] of this positive, cooperative, outgoing, redemptive mood was dependent upon the masses of the peoples' being able to grasp it and use it. It presupposes discipline. Now, he said it broke down because the masses of the Indians were unable to sustain this creative ideal over a time-interval of sufficient duration to be effective because they did not have enough vitality. And they lacked vitality for two reasons. The first reason was that the masses of the Indians were hungry. And so he stopped his politics and began working on the spinning-wheel and reviving the cottage industries so as to build up physical reserve in order that there would be a strong bulwark that would sustain this thing in terms of sheer physical vitality and physical energy. And the second reason they had lost their vitality was because their self-respect was lost, and here the leaking of vitality was a psychological and spiritual thing. On the one hand it was a physical thing—lack of food and a good diet; and on the other, they had lost their self-respect and in the losing of their self-respect, he said, their vital recreative and creative powers wasted, and so—as I expected him to say—they had lost their self-respect because of the presence of the British in their country over this long time; and he said, "Oh no, they have lost their self-respect because of the presence of untouchability in Hinduism, and therefore the second thing that I did when I withdrew from politics was to begin working on the redemption of Hinduism by attacking untouchability and in doing that the first step was, as a caste Hindu, to adopt into my own family an outcast, and announce to all cast Hindus, 'This is what I mean,' and the second thing that I did was to change their name from sutras or outcasts or pariahs to Harijans, and the word Harijan means Child of God." And Mr. Gandhi said, "If I can make a caste Hindu call an outcaste a Child of God, every day, I will create finally the kind of moral problem deep within his spirit that cannot be resolved until he changes his attitude towards him." This vitality.

Now in the quest for peace, it is the notion of religion that peace is the byproduct of righteousness, of social and economic justice, and it is this insight that Mr. Gandhi saw. And if I work for social righteousness so that every man can sit under his own fig tree and be unafraid—if I work to provide the kind of climate in which it is a reasonable thing that man may trust each other, then—then there will be the kind of atmosphere in which it becomes a possibility for nations to beat their swords into ploughshares and their spears into pruning-hooks. And if I sit down to wait until somebody else creates that atmosphere because I don't want to be accused of being a pacifist, then I ask others to run my risks, in the tremendous business, not of getting rid of war—that's negative—but in the tremendous business of trying to get a world in which an ordinary human being can keep his self-respect and be alive. The kind of world in which the smoking flax will not be quenched, nor the bruised reed crushed.[13] A world in which little children can grow up without fear. And men and women can live without bitterness and hatred. And that kind of peace starts on my street and your street.

TD.

NOTES

1. The typescript of this sermon has a handwritten date of 24 July 1949. However, internal and external evidence indicates that the sermon was given shortly after Ralph Bunche spoke at the Shrine Auditorium in Los Angeles on Thursday, 18 August 1949, probably on the following Sunday, 21 August. The Fellowship Quintet provided entertainment at the event. See "Dr. Bunche Assails Senate Committee," *Los Angeles Times*, 19 August 1949. Thurman speaks of his presence at the event in this sermon.

2. For earlier reflections on the connection between pacifism and coercion, see "The Significance of Jesus V: The Cross of Jesus," "The Sources of Power for Christian Action," and "Christian, Who Calls Me Christian?," *PHWT*, 2:74–81, 93–101, 106–13.

3. Mic. 4:4.

4. Isa. 32:17; Isa. 60:18; James 3:18; Matt. 5:9.

5. That Jesus was born into a world at peace, at the beginning of the so-called Pax Romana, was a commonplace in scholarly and apologetic writing in the early twentieth century. For one example, see Harris Franklin Rall, *The Life of Jesus* (New York: Abingdon, 1917), 31–32.

6. This is a point that Thurman had recently made in *Jesus and the Disinherited* (New York: Abingdon-Cokesbury, 1949).

7. This is a reference to William James's essay "The Moral Equivalent of War," in *Memories and Studies* (New York: Longmans, Green, 1911).

8. Irving Berlin, George Whiting, and Ted Snyder, "My Wife's Gone to the Country; Hurrah!, Hurrah!" (1909). This was the first big hit for the fledgling songwriter Irving Berlin, although unlike almost all of his later songs, only its lyrics were written by Berlin, with Ted Snyder generally given credit for the music. The creation of the song was collaborative, but Thurman's account of the addition of the song's tag, "hurrah or hooray" appears to be apocryphal.

9. Bunche, who had been Thurman's good friend and colleague at Howard, was chief UN negotiator for the armistice accords between Israel and neighboring Arab nations in the aftermath of the 1948 Arab-Israeli War. The four separate armistices between Israel and

the four nations on its borders were concluded in the first half of 1949. For his negotiating efforts, Bunche was awarded the 1950 Nobel Prize for Peace.

10. In late 1938, after student protests against the administration for the university's supervision of permitted off-campus activities, its prohibition against jitterbugging at dances on campus, and a female dress code viewed as too restrictive, and for kindred complaints, Howard University established a Collegiate Advisory Council, with Bunche as a member. See "New Governing Body Organized at Howard Univ.," *Afro-American*, 24 December 1938.

11. José Ortega y Gasset, *The Revolt of the Masses* (New York: W. W. Norton, 1932).

12. Ahimsa is a Sanskrit term meaning "the avoidance of injury." This religious concept is the core of Gandhian nonviolence.

13. Isa. 42:3; Matt. 12:20.

✎ FROM SUE BAILEY THURMAN TO HOWARD, MADALINE, AND OLIVE
[*NOVEMBER 1949*]
DAYTONA BEACH, FLORIDA

This undated letter from Sue Bailey Thurman to her family, written around 12 November 1949, reports on the deteriorating condition of Thurman's mother, Alice Sams, following her stroke the previous June.[1] *After attending to her duties at the annual conference of the National Council of Negro Women (NCNW), Sue returned to Daytona Beach to arrange Alice's affairs and to accompany her that December on a trip to San Francisco, where Alice would spend the last months of her life.*

Howard, Madaline and Olive—Angels:

I arrived this morning, was impressed with Mama Alice's appearance, saw Dr Stocking[2] this afternoon and am hastening this message off to report to you by tonight's airplane.

She looks fine—but all say that the improvement took place only after she received word that I was coming. Up to Friday of last week, she was quite far down the scale.

Dr Stocking says that she may be able to leave in 3 or 4 weeks. That means that I shall attend the conference, see Anne, and return for the time it takes longer to get her ready for the trip.

I think the precipitous move we made saved her life, without question. The thing that pushed her overboard was Mr Sams'[3] leaving. He has gone to his daughter and to all intents and purposes this is the end of their journey together. But the joy of coming to California and being with us has cheered her into a completely new awareness of how wonderful life can be after all the hardships—so we start getting ready today to come out.

Thornton[4] will help me arrange about the house. We think that it can be rented for a good sum and he can collect and keep the same until we pay him the $500 which is due.[5] Thornton will write you next week. Shall send a long letter as the week end unfolds. It was a thrill to enter Florida early this morning. The state fascinates me as no other! I shall write paeans about it for your enjoyment if you would like it done.

I leave Monday for D.C. Dr Stocking says that if Mama A. is anxious to get better and leave, she will do every thing required of her in my absence. I hope it goes off all right as I am to give a citation to Madame Pandit[6] during the session in D.C.[7]

With reference to the Conference, Howard, there is a wonderful surprise in store for you—but I am not to tell you as Mrs B. wants it to be a surprise. You will be delighted![8] Write me to 1318 Vermont Ave, N.W. after Sunday and until I serve notice to send mail here again.

Shall see Anne, but cannot use week end of 19–20, because conference is in full swing. However something will be arranged.

Worry none of you—for anything. All goes more than well—with all of us. Just, get on your knees—you heathen—and pray for your souls that your sins may be forgiven and your unrepentant selves washed in the blood of the Lamb! ☺[9] There now!

I love each of you—deeply, greatly, truly, muchly, thoroughly et al. Just be sure that you love us the same on the east coast.

A la Anne— XXXX ————— hugs

Kisses XXX

[*signed*] Sue

ALS.

NOTES

    1. Alice had what was described as a "light stroke" on 17 June, though she "was quite ill," with the left side of her body partially incapacitated. She required constant in-home nursing care thereafter. See From Emily Worthy, 22 June 1949, printed in the current volume. Thurman had visited his mother just before her stroke, writing a friend on 21 May 1949, "Within ten days I am going to Florida to visit my mother and to see if I cannot [get] certain improvements made in her living conditions. She is alone and is about 75 or 76 years old and is not well. For seven months I have tried to get a telephone in her house but the social situation is of such in Florida that we can not get a telephone in our house until the white citizens that want telephones get theirs. I think if I go down in person something can be done" (To John Overholt, 21 May 1949).

    2. Dr. John Stocking.

    3. James Sams, Alice's husband.

    4. Thornton L. Smith was a Daytona Beach businessman and Thurman's lifelong friend. He was active in local politics and played an important role in the mayoral election of Edward H. Armstrong (1880–1937), a five-term mayor of Daytona Beach who was

Write me to 1318 Vermont Ave. n.w. after
Sunday and until I serve
notice to send mail here again.
Shall see Anne, but cannot
rise week end of 19–20, because
conference is in full swing.
However something will be
arranged.
　　　　Worry none of you – for anything.
All goes more than well – with all of
us. Just get on your knees – you
heathen – and pray for your
souls that your sins may be
forgiven and your unrepentant
selves washed in the blood of the
Lamb! (:o) There now.
　　　I love each of you – deeply,
greatly, truly, muchly,
thoroughly et al. Just be sure
that you love us, on the east coast.
a la
anne →　xxxx
　　　Kisses　　　　xxx!　hugs　Sue.

Letter from Sue Bailey Thurman to Howard, Madaline, and Olive. From the Howard Thurman Collection, Howard Gotlieb Archival Research Center at Boston University.

elected with strong support from black voters. For many years Smith was Thurman's surrogate in Daytona Beach: "Whenever Mamma needed personal advice, she turned to Thornton. Once or twice a month, he would come by on his bicycle just to have a few words with her" (*WHAH*, 21). See also From Alice Sams, 9 January 1937, *PHWT*, 2:37.

5. This money was possibly for medical expenses and the accumulated weekly nursing costs of twenty dollars per week since June.

6. Vijay Lakshmi Pandit (1900–1990) was the sister of Jawaharlal Nehru, the first prime minister of India, and was a leader of the Congress Party with her own impressive political career, the highlights of which included positions as the first Indian ambassador to the Soviet Union (1947–49), Indian ambassador to the United States (1949–51), and the first female president of the UN General Assembly (1953). In late January 1936 Thurman and the other members of the Negro Delegation in India met her during their public meeting in Allahabad. A striking beauty, Thurman remembers her "unforgettable face—second only to [Rabindranath] Tagore's, full of agony and yearning for India's independence, yet radiant with the aura of a vast compassion, transcending all barriers of time and space" (*WHAH*, 135).

7. Sue Bailey Thurman awarded Ambassador Pandit the National Council of Negro Women's Citation of Honor at their annual meeting.

8. Thurman was awarded a "citation of merit" by the NCNW, although he was not in attendance. See "Truman Renews Rights Vow at NCNW Confab," *Chicago Defender,* 26 November 1949.

9. The drawing in the letter is not a classic 1970s smiley face or its emoticon successor, but with its smirk and its upturned eyes, it was clearly intended as a bit of ironic punctuation. The image is reproduced on page 11 in the current volume.

➴ TO FRIEND
[*JANUARY 1950*]
SAN FRANCISCO, CALIF.

In this annual letter to his friends, Thurman reviews the events of the past year: the new sanctuary for the Fellowship Church and the work of the church; his recent publications; his upcoming speaking engagements; and the recent accomplishments of his wife and daughters.

Dear Friend,

These greetings and good wishes for your happiness and well being during the second half of the century should have reached you by January 6th, in time for the traditional "Twelfth Night" celebration of the Wise Men's arrival at Bethlehem. But this has been an unusually long, full and strenuous holiday for the Thurmans. So our personal greetings come now for the gala Chinese New Year festival which we shall observe in San Francisco on February seventeenth, and the week following.

You will want to know first about affairs at Fellowship Church. On the last Sunday in January, 1949, we dedicated the new home of the Church for the Fellowship of All Peoples, at 2041 Larkin Street, between Broadway and Vallejo in San Francisco. Negotiating the purchase of this strategic location climaxes five years of work here. Arrangements have been made for payment for the same in three years, ending 1952.[1] During the past year the resident congregation has increased commensurately with the enlarged facilities so that we have now an active, participating membership of four hundred.

It was our good fortune to begin the fall program with the services of Adena Joy,[2] a gifted young woman, who graduating from the University of Chicago, held a teaching position at Lewis and Clarke College, and a parish in Oregon, before coming to resume work as Assistant Minister of Fellowship Church. She brings rich experience in the field of creative communications and editorial assignments, and will take over as Managing-editor of the year-old quarterly publication, "The Growing Edge."

You will remember Gene Walker,[3] (Marketing Counselor and Industrial Motion Picture Producer), the chairman of the Board of Directors of the church, under whose leadership so many significant things have happened, among them the securing of the Larkin Street property and reorganization of church Board and committee functions. With the new plan, Donald Glover,[4] Industrial Secretary of the San Francisco Urban League, becomes chairman of the important committee responsible for the entire program of the church. Arnold Nakajima[5] (candidate for Dth[6] degree at Pacific School of Religion, and a member of the Fellowship UNESCO[7] Delegation in Paris) is chairman of the newly created Religious Education Committee working on special curriculum for the church school. Lynn Buchanan,[8] the Executive Secretary and business manager, is a valuable asset with his special training in office management and public relations.

The Intercultural Workshop, of which Sue Thurman is Director, presents regular lecture series, exhibits, recitals and symposiums in this field, and sponsored the Fellowship Delegation of twelve (1 Chinese, 1 Mexican, 3 Negroes, 1 Japanese, and 6 Caucasians) who attended the Fourth Plenary UNESCO Conference in Paris last September. Included in the group was the professional singing unit, "The Fellowship Quintet," in charge of Corrine Barrow Williams (Music Director of Fellowship Church) who opened the well known Atelier Concert Series at the American Church in Paris, and appeared also in recital at the University of Paris, the International Club in London and in full concert on board the Queen Mary, en route to the Conference.[9]

The delegation to UNESCO was warmly received in Europe and from all indications its unique venture became a challenge as the group pioneered into new fields of interest hitherto untouched by a designated church unit. It was a great pleasure for them to meet at UNESCO House, Dr. Reinhold Niebuhr, one of the American Consultants at the conference who has long been interested in the work of the Fellowship Church.

Now a word about us. You will see H. T. in certain sections of the country in March and again in June. He goes East in the spring for preaching engagements at the University of Chicago, Princeton, Vassar, Wesleyan,[10] University in Connecticut and Morgan College, Baltimore. He looks forward with keen anticipation to visiting the latter campus because he will again live in the thought world of Negro students as he gives the closing lectures for the Religious Convocation at Morgan College. He will have a week in Detroit again as Lenten speaker for the Detroit Council of Churches.

The Ministry of Fellowship Church is and has always been an all-consuming process, but he has found time to publish writings most of which are incident to the regular lectures or sermon-series presented from his own pulpit. "Jesus and the Disinherited" which established the Mary L. Smith Lectureship, was chosen by the "Religious Pulpit," as the Book of the Month for May, 1949. He contributed the chapter on Religion to the anthology of Essays, "In Defense of Democracy."[11] Harpers will publish soon, an enlarged national edition of "Meditations for Apostles of Sensitiveness," formerly issued by the Eucalyptus Press, at Mills College. For National Associates over the country, there will be released the most recent sermon series on "Man and the Moral Struggle," presented for the last 14 Sunday mornings from the Fellowship pulpit.

Those of you who have heard the various interpretations of Honneger's Symphonic Psalm, "King David," will be interested to know that the San Francisco Symphony Orchestra, and Municipal Chorus presented this unusual modern work at the War Memorial Opera House, (birthplace of United Nations) in March, 1949, with Dimitri Mitropoulos; as guest conductor and again in January, 1950, with Artur Rodzinski, guest conductor. Howard Thurman was narrator for both of these occasions.[12]

Sue Thurman, returning from the UNESCO Paris Conference in October, travelled across the country with the fellowship Quintet stopping at Philadelphia for an appearance with the "Friends of Fellowship Church" of which Arthur Crosby of that city, is National Chairman. Engagements were presented en route in New York City and Cleveland. Once home, the workshop representatives began planning for the seven weeks' symposium on the "Indian in American Life," to be offered as a part of the Intercultural program this spring. S. B. T. contributed eight articles to the San Francisco Sun Reporter during the Gold Rush Centennial, on Pioneers of Negro Origin in California.[13] As Historian and National Chairman of the Archives and Museum Department of the NCNW, she will undertake to assemble historical materials for the Council's Museum in Washington. Libraries in Arkansas named in memory of her mother, Mrs. Susie Ford Bailey, will continue to claim the attention of all the Thurmans.

Olive, the elder daughter who graduated from Vassar in 1948, returns to Iowa University in March to complete work on a masters in dramatics, with a major in play writing. Her play which is to be performed there, is based on the China Poblana legend of 17th century Mexico.[14] She hopes eventually to have a Little Theatre of her own. Anne, the younger, is in her senior year at Emma Willard School, Troy, New York.[15] When she graduates in June, it will be the first time that this, the oldest of the girls' prep schools in the country, will have graduated a colored girl in its 135 years' history. Anne has had a fine experience, made even more meaningful by the National Associates and Friends of Fellowship Church found among faculty and students at Emma Willard School.

Madaline, our gracious aunt and sister, has joined us in San Francisco, to establish her music studio here, using methods of the Dalcroze School. We wish you had been with us at Christmas when her studio was formally opened with an evening of Chopin music and the reading of Chopin's personal letters. There was wassail at 10 o'clock, (served as usual with H. T.'s mysterious blend of Oriental spices!)

We think of you often as life deepens for us here. If one of the innumerable national conventions will bring some of our friends from the east to the City, accept a warm invitation to worship at Fellowship Church. If you were here in March, you would hear the four sermons of Dr. Charles Gilkey,[16] Dean

Emeritus of the Chapel of Chicago University, who will be guest preacher in H. T.'s absence. Or for National Associates, we wish you might have been with us for the coming of Alan Paton, (author of "Cry, the Beloved Country"), whose famous book was dedicated to the Aubrey Burns' (he, a member of our Board). Mr. Paton, an International Associate of Fellowship Church was guest speaker at a special congregation meeting on February fourth.[17]

We send the Candles of Joy, Hope and Fellowship with an abiding faith that they will burn for you the whole year long.

Sincerely,

The Howard Thurmans

TL.

Notes

1. The church building cost $30,000.00 with an additional $6,000.00 needed for repairs and refurbishings. Because no local lending institution was willing to provide a mortgage, in large part because of the interracial and nondenominational nature of the Fellowship Church—and despite the willingness of wealthier members of the congregation to sign a promissory note guaranteeing payment—the church was obliged to pay cash for the property. The money for purchasing the property was obtained in an interest-free loan from wealthy friends of Thurman and the Fellowship Church in Southern California, with the church promising to repay the loan in three years. This was accomplished as promised, and in January 1952, with much ceremony at a special service, the paperwork for the loan was burnt. See HT, *Footprints of a Dream: The Story of the Fellowship Church of All Peoples* (New York: Harper & Brothers), 105–8.

2. A native of Ashland, Oregon, Adena Joy graduated from Oregon State Agricultural College in 1933 with a degree in education, and received an M.A. from the Chicago Theological Seminary in 1940 for a thesis on rural education. She later worked as a human relations and human life counselor and received a Ph.D. in criminology from the University of California at Berkeley in 1968.

3. Gene K. Walker (1903–97) was chief executive of Gene K. Walker Productions, an industrial and documentary film company based in San Francisco.

4. D. Donald Glover, a native of Huntington, West Virginia, was educated at West Virginia State College, Ohio State University, and Dayton College. During World War II he worked for the War Manpower Commission in Ohio, and he moved to San Francisco in 1946 to become industrial secretary of the San Francisco Urban League. From 1959 to 1963 he worked for the California State Department of Urban Relations; in 1963 he was named as assistant for employment opportunities for minority affairs in the U.S. Department of Labor; and in 1967 he was named chief administrator of the department's Bureau of Employment in Chicago. He said of his involvement in the Fellowship Church that "at long last I have found a church where creed and practice require no apologetic explanations" ("Silhouettes: Donald Glover," *The Growing Edge* (Spring 1951): 11).

5. Katsuo Arnold Nakajima (1917–75) was a Presbyterian minister who after the war worked at Pilgrim House, a social service community organization for African Americans in Los Angeles's Little Tokyo. He was later the eastern area secretary for campus Christian life of the United Presbyterian Church.

6. Doctor of Theology.

7. United Nations Educational, Scientific, and Cultural Organization, headquartered in Paris since its inception in 1945.

8. Lynn Buchanan worked in advertising and public relations in the San Francisco area and had worked as executive secretary of a theater school in Beverly Hills.

9. The Fellowship Quintet was, to Thurman, "an ambulatory example of the basic concept upon which our church was built: experiences of spiritual unity were more compelling than the things that divide" (HT, *Footprints of a Dream,* 69). The quintet's existence went back to 1945, when, much to Thurman's delight, Corrine Barrow Williams, an experienced choral director, agreed to become the church's music director. The choir was soon performing ambitious works, such as Rossini's "Stabat Mater" and the African American composer R. Nathaniel Dett's "The Ordering of Moses." A quartet of the best male voices was established, to which was added the soprano of Corrine Barrow Williams herself. By 1946 the group was appearing regularly at civic events and at its own recitals. Much was made of the racial mix of the quintet, which consisted of two whites, Williams and first tenor Joseph Van Pelt; an African American, Emory Mellon, bass; a Mexican American, Rokee Acevedo, second tenor; and a Chinese American, Raymond K. Fong, baritone. Fong was Williams's protégé. He accompanied her to the church and would succeed her as music director. In 1948 the Fellowship Quintet made a transcontinental tour with stops in Washington, D.C.; Philadelphia; Chicago; Denver; and other large cities, and the group released an album of spirituals. In 1949 twelve members of the Fellowship Church, paying their own way and traveling in a caravan of station wagons—and encountering some discrimination along the way—crossed the country to New York City and then went on board the RMS *Queen Mary* to Paris, with appearances in Cleveland and New York (at the Community Church) on their return. The travelers to Paris in addition to the members of the quintet and Sue Bailey Thurman included Lynn Buchanan, Arnold Nakajima, Sylvia Nichols, Ruth Acty, and Carolyn Threlkeld. See HT, *Footprints of a Dream,* 67–69; and Corrine Barrow Williams, "Song of All Peoples," *The Growing Edge* (Spring 1950): 14–15.

10. Wesleyan University.

11. HT, "The Religion of Jesus and the Disinherited," in *In Defense of Democracy,* ed. Thomas H. Johnson (New York: Putnam, 1949), 125–35.

12. "Le Roi David" (1921), an oratorio, was the first great international success of the Swiss composer Arthur Honegger (1892–1955). Dmitri Mitropoulous (1896–1960), a Greek conductor, spent most of his career in the United States and was principal conductor of the Minneapolis Symphony (1937–49) and the New York Philharmonic (1951–57). Arthur Rodzinski (1892–1958) was principal conductor of the Los Angeles Philharmonic (1929–33), the Cleveland Symphony (1933–43), and the New York Philharmonic (1943–47).

13. Later revised and published as Sue Bailey Thurman, *Pioneers of Negro Origin in California* (San Francisco: Acme, 1952).

14. "La China Poblana" ("The Asian Woman of Puebla") is a familiar Mexican folktale set in the city of Puebla. In the early seventeenth century, the international dimensions of the Spanish Empire led to extensive Mexican trade with Spain's Asian possessions—most significantly with the Philippines—through the port of Acapulco. This included a small but significant trade in slaves and servants, although the Pacific slave trade was dwarfed by the dimensions of the Atlantic slave trade. The legend of La China Poblana, the historicity of which is uncertain, concerns a woman, supposedly of Asian Indian origins, who was captured by pirates, taken to the Philippines, and from there taken to Mexico either as a

slave or a servant. She later married a Chinese slave of a local priest. She was baptized a Christian under the name Catarina de San Juan and was known for her piety, good works, and exotic beauty. In time "la china poblana" became the name of a distinctive Mexican female costume, an embroidered white blouse and a long green and red sequined dress.

15. The Emma Willard School was founded by Emma Willard (1787–1870) in Middlebury, Vermont, in 1814 and was moved to Troy, New York, in 1821. As the Troy Female Seminary, it was one of the first schools for girls in the United States that offered a rigorous academic curriculum. It was renamed the Emma Willard School in 1895.

16. Charles Whitney Gilkey (1882–1968), Thurman's longtime friend, was a graduate of Harvard University and Union Theological Seminary and served as pastor at the Hyde Park Baptist Church in Chicago (1910–27) and as dean of the chapel at the University of Chicago (1928–47). His books include *Jesus and Our Generation* (Chicago: University of Chicago Press, 1925) and *Present- Day Dilemmas in Religion* (Nashville, Tenn.: Cokesbury, 1928).

17. Alan Paton spoke at the church on several occasions. His two-part article "Crosscurrents in South Africa" was published in the spring and summer 1950 issues of *The Growing Edge*.

To Fellowship Church Family
3 May 1950
[*San Francisco, Calif.*]

Thurman had been concerned with the health of his semi-invalid mother, Alice Sams, for many years. After Sams suffered a serious stroke in June 1949, Howard and Sue Bailey Thurman made the decision to move Sams to San Francisco. With Sue's assistance, Sams's affairs in Daytona Beach were concluded, and Sams arrived in California in December. During her months in San Francisco, in addition to the problem of her declining health, Sams, who had lived her life within the segregated confines of Daytona Beach, was challenged by a very different cultural environment from the one she had known. In his autobiography Thurman writes that his mother was not well enough to attend services at the Fellowship Church, and "the interracial church was outside the experience of her seventy-six years. She did not understand what I was doing, but she trusted me. There were people of all races and life-styles coming and going in our house. This, too, she could not credit in her own emotions, but she accepted it all with quiet grace."[1]

Dear Members of the Fellowship Church Family:

Some of you have known that last December we brought our Mother, Mrs. Alice Thurman Sams, from Florida to California, to make her home with us here in San Francisco. She had been an invalid for some time, but we felt that coming out to the west coast to be with her two remaining children, would be a wonderful thing for her.

She improved for a while, but in January sustained a fall, fracturing a hip, and twelve days ago suffered a second stroke. She never regained consciousness from the latter, and the end came quietly on the afternoon of May second. We have not wanted to burden the membership with our own personal grief and distress but we have known that we had the love and deep comradeship of all of you. We have asked the past and present board members, committee chairmen and staff, to represent the church at the brief funeral services which will be held on Thursday afternoon, May fourth. If you have the gracious wish to send flowers, we prefer that you make this expression in favor of the Alice Ambrose Fellowship Children's Fund (our Mother's maiden name), to benefit the department of the Church School (which needs so many facilities), and which would cause our mother's death to be the occasion for aiding the younger ones, whom she loved and cherished so deeply.
Sincerely yours,
Howard Thurman
Madaline Thurman
Sue Bailey Thurman
Olive Thurman
Anne Thurman

                                                              TL.

NOTE

1. *WHAH*, 156. At the same place in his autobiography, Thurman tells the sad story of his mother's hospitalization. She was admitted to Stanford University Medical Center, where the Thurmans' family physician, Carleton Goodlett, had attending privileges. Thurman writes that "one day she said, 'Howard, you've got to take me home.' [He] said, 'Mamma, you need to be here.' [She replied,] 'No, if I've got to die, I want to die at home. Everybody here at the hospital is a "Buckra" [a somewhat derogatory southern black term for whites]. . . . The first chance they get, you don't know what they will do to you. I'm scared to go to sleep at night, and you just have to take me out of this place", (ibid.). Thurman obeyed his mother and took her home, where she soon passed away.

🖎 TO MARY MCLEOD BETHUNE
28 SEPTEMBER 1950
[*SAN FRANCISCO, CALIF.*]

Thurman writes to his old friend Mary McLeod Bethune updating her on matters in his personal life and on developments in the Fellowship Church. He is particularly upset that Eleanor Roosevelt, who originally was a strong backer of the church, seems to have lost interest in supporting the endeavor. Thurman suggests that Bethune set up a meeting where the two of them could speak to

Mrs. Roosevelt about the Fellowship Church, and he also asks Bethune to set up a
fund-raising dinner in Washington, D.C., for the church.

Dear Mrs. Bethune:

I have wanted to write to you for a long time to bring you up to date about many things personal and having to do with the life of the church.

I shall begin personally because I want you to know how very grateful we all were for the message which you sent when Mama died. It was a long, difficult siege and in the end death was a gracious and merciful friend. At first we were concerned about the effect on Madaline's health, but that anxiety was needless; for she has ridden out the storm and is doing better than ever. She has established her own music studio on the basement floor of our home and is laying a careful foundation for a new professional career in San Francisco. The children are in Cleveland and in Oberlin. Anne is a freshman at Oberlin and Olive is director of children's theatre at Karamou House in Cleveland.[1] If you are there any time during the winter, I hope you will let them know.

Sue is making plans to go East as usual for the National Council meeting in November. En route she hopes to do some work on the Archives Project which work will take her to Florida so as to get some things done on Whitehall Street.[2]

As for me, I am in good health and working as hard as usual. I have a new book that will be published in February by Harper's.[3] You will get your copy when the issue is ready.

I shall now turn to the church. I am enclosing a copy of our annual report which will speak for itself. There are several matters on my mind; one of them is concerning Mrs. Roosevelt and her attitude toward the Church. In a letter which she sent to Mr. Crosby,[4] chairman of the Friends of Fellowship Church for underwriting our building, she said that she could not make any contribution to something that was not closer to home, that is, in the East. I cannot understand that, but the point of my concern is the fact that she does not seem to have any understanding or appreciation of the precise nature of our undertaking. When it was in the dream stage, she was very greatly interested and enthusiastic and became one of our first National Members. Her attitude puzzles me somewhat because the things for which she stands in the United Nations,[5] and the things upon which she is working as far as their spiritual implications are concerned, we are doing at the grass roots level. It seems to me that some awareness of our experience here would enormously strengthen her spirit as she undertakes the same kind of work project on an international and world-wide scale. I wish that you and she and I could sit down and have an hour's talk about the whole thing.

This leads me to another idea about the church. I am going East, leaving here in mid-October. I shall be preaching at Harvard and doing some religious lectures for the Preparatory Schoolmasters' Conference in Atlantic City, and in addition to this I shall be preaching at Howard University November 12,[6] and remaining to do some Convocation lectures there for Tuesday and Wednesday of that week. In the past occasionally Coleman Jennings has arranged for friends and associates of Fellowship Church to meet at his home for me to discuss the Church and the whole idea with them. I am wondering whether you would be interested in arranging a meeting perhaps in cooperation with Coleman, at which time I could do the same thing but with a larger group of people. It may be that some kind of dinner meeting could be worked out. The office would very gladly send you immediately, our complete list of members and friends in the District of Columbia, if you would be interested in working out something like this. For reasons which I am sure you will understand, I do not want the thing arranged by Howard University whose guest I will be for four days. It could be a very significant thing if a meeting such as the one I have in mind could be done in the Nation's Capitol. I would talk about the spiritual significance of our undertaking and answer questions and who knows but what the real core group could come out of such a meeting that would work in a concentrated manner toward having a Church like Fellowship Church in Washington, D.C. Would you think this through and let me know your reaction. I leave here October 11. If necessary, some time before I am due in Washington I could run down and have a conversation with you about the plan.

It may be interesting to know that Dr. Tobias[7] has agreed to become chairman of a New York City group which will have a Fellowship Church dinner in the Spring, the purpose of which is to help to underwrite our present building cost.

Thank you very much for taking the time to read this lengthy document. Sue joins me in love to you. Our prayers are for your continued health and gracious living.

Sincerely,

Howard Thurman

Dr. Mary Bethune
1318 Vermont Avenue
Washington, D.C.

                                                                              TLc.

NOTES

    1. Founded in 1915 by Russell and Rowena Jelliffe, who would remain its directors through the 1960s, to provide an interracial venue for presenting drama and originally named Settlement Playhouse, the theater would acquire its own building in 1927 and be renamed Karamu House (from the Swahili for "a place of joyful meeting") in 1941. It soon became one of the best-known progressive theaters for African American playwrights and authors in the United States. Between 1936 and 1939 Langston Hughes premiered five plays

at Karamu House. In 1949, thanks in part to contributions from the Rockefeller Foundation, Karamu House opened a new complex with two theaters, a visual arts studio, and a dance studio.

2. This was the former residence of Alice Sams in Daytona Beach.

3. *Deep Is the Hunger: Meditations for Apostles of Sensitiveness* (New York: Harper & Brothers, 1951).

4. Arthur U. Crosby.

5. Eleanor Roosevelt was appointed as a delegate to the United Nations General Assembly by President Truman in December 1945 and became the chair of the UN Preliminary Commission on Human Rights in April 1946 and chair of its permanent successor from 1947 to 1951. As chair, she played a major role in drafting the Universal Declaration of Human Rights, adopted by the General Assembly in December 1948.

6. See "The Power of the Spirit and the Powers of This World," printed in the current volume.

7. Channing Tobias.

"The Power of the Spirit and the Powers of This World"
14 November 1950
Washington, D.C.

On 14 November 1950 Thurman returned to the Howard University School of Religion to speak at its thirty-fourth annual convocation.[1] The theme of the convocation was "The Church, the State and Human Welfare." Thurman's talk was on a familiar theme in his work, the dilemmas faced by individuals when external political and social obligations impinge on their freedom.

Although the fig tree shall not blossom, neither shall fruit be in the vines; the labour of the olive shall fail, and the fields shall yield no meat; the flock shall be cut off from the fold, and there shall be no herd in the stalls:

"Yet I will rejoice in the Lord, I will joy in the God of my salvation."[2]

There is but one way for thee; but one. Inform thyself of it, and pursue it. One way each soul hath by which the infinite in reach lieth before him.

Seek, and ye shall find. To each the way is plain. That way the wind points all the trees along; that way run down loud, singing streams; that way pour on and on; a thousand headlands lift their cataracts with toppling flowers. That way the sun enacts his travel, and the moon, and all the stars soar; and the tides move towards it. Nothing bars the man who goes the way that he should go.

A thousand light shells in the rippling sand joy the true soul; the waves along the strand whiten beyond his eyes. The trees talk back, show him the sky; or, heaped upon his track in a black wave, wind-heaped, point onward still his one, one way.

Go thy way, all things say. Thou hast thy way to go; thou hast thy day to live; thou hast thy need of thee to make in the hearts of others. Do thy thing. And be sure of this: no other can do for thee that appointed thing of God. Not any light shall shine upon thy road. Thee the angel calls, as he calls others; and thy life to thee is precious as the greatest life can be to him. So live thy life, and go thy way.[3]

THE CONTRADICTIONS OF LIFE

I want to think with you for a little while tonight about certain aspects that are inherent in this very wide open and almost timeless topic, "The Power of the Spirit and the Powers of This World." The lectures that we are having every day, by men who are very skilled and competent and experienced, are dealing with certain significant for-instances of the general idea. So tonight I would like to think about certain of the basic principles that are here; and I would like to begin with the generalization that one of the basic assumptions about the human spirit in its encounter both with the Spirit of God and with the spirits of this world is this: that the contradictions of life, however important and thoroughgoing or even devastating they may be, are not ultimate and final contradictions.

I think everyone of us is aware of how his particular life is trapped again and again by the contradictions of his experience. We are aware that in each one of us there are impulses, desires, outreaches that are good, that are positive and creative; and we know too how we wrestle with those desires and impulses and outreaches of the human spirit that are positive but destructive.

Any sensitive man who looks out upon the world is mindful of the fact that it does seem true again and again that there is so much that stings and casts down, and often so little that uplifts and inspires. Yet one of the curious things about the human spirit in this connection is that it always insists that these contradictions are not ultimate or final contradictions; that the contradictions themselves do not indicate what is the quality of experience that bottoms all of the thinking and working and feeling of individuals.

For instance (this is a simple illustration), there has never been a time in the world when there was peace. We have no really authentic records of a time when there was peace in the world; the most that you can say is that we have records of those moments of treacherous quiet between armistices. Yet the human spirit constantly affirms its interest in, and the necessity of the logic of, peace. Even at the times of the most terrifying wars—right in the midst of them—there are individuals, there are movements, there are broodings, stirrings, that have to do with a dream, a way of living, feeling, thinking, that presupposes that the human spirit ultimately is made for peace.

At the time that the world was wrestling with Napoleon Bonaparte in the early part of the nineteenth century, everywhere there was Napoleon. Any time you thought about tomorrow, you could not think of it aside from the Napoleon encounter. He was like some mighty Colossus straddling the horizon; and many sensitive men during that time were very certain that he represented one of the final moments of the civilization of Europe. And at that very time, in that very period, at least three important babies were born! (Many babies were born, but at least three important babies.) One was Mendelssohn—an interesting answer of life to the Napoleon predicament. Another baby born at that time was Charles Darwin—life's answer. And another baby born at that time was Abraham Lincoln.[4]

It's very interesting that there is a deeper consideration always, that finally settles down in the very lees of the human spirit, that the contradictions of life are not ultimate contradictions.

THE DESIRE FOR EMPIRICAL VALIDATION

There is another generalization, and that is that the integrity of the religious experience and the ethic which it inspires are never finally dependent upon empirical validation. (I want you to think about that very carefully before you disagree with it.) And yet, even as I say that, I recognize at once that the human spirit is never relieved from the urgency to seek to establish the validity of the religious experience empirically. "By their fruits ye shall know them" is one way by which this is said. Yet every religious spirit knows that the integrity of his religious experience does not finally rest on the degree to which he can validate it empirically.

The urge to give it empirical validation—to give it for-instance validation—arises out of the desire, the bias, on the part of the human spirit to protect itself (if it can) from self-deception. For if I have—as indeed I do—my own personal religious experience, my own moment when I turn and face the divine scrutiny and there seems to be naught else except my quivering spirit and the eyes of God, how do I know that I am not being deceived in that experience? The answer to that insistence is the determination—it's more than a determination—the urge to prove it, to check it. At last we say, "I know that my Redeemer lives."[5] It is interesting that the quotation is, "I know that my Redeemer lives"—not because I have proved it in this way or that way or the other way; but, "I know that my Redeemer lives" because he lives in my soul.

But suppose I was mistaken. I'm never sure that I'm not mistaken because the margin of error does not ever leave the periphery of human awareness. I can always be mistaken. As a matter of fact, most of the fundamental decisions I make that involve the commitment of my life must of necessity be made on the basis of evidence that is never conclusive. If I waited until all the evidence were in, I would never act. So I wait as long as I can, and then there comes a moment when I can't wait any longer, and I pull the curtain down, and lock the door, and take my leap. And I hope that tomorrow and tomorrow and tomorrow will validate this. I insist upon that validation, even though I know that in the last analysis I can never validate it. For if I could validate it, something would spill over that would require additional validation.

OUR SENSE OF LIFE'S MALLEABILITY

There's a third generalization, and that is that every individual, deep within himself, is convinced that life in its very structure is fixed, finished, rounded out, complete, whole; or that life in its very structure is incomplete, unfinished, dynamic. If I am convinced that life in its very structure is finished, complete, rounded out, then I know that in the last analysis all effort on my part cancels out. There isn't anything I can do about anything; and I'm caught in the agonizing grapples of a hard determinism.

That is wonderful, if it happens that I am an advantaged person in life. If the thing is frozen, and I am fixed, then it's wonderful. But if it happens that the thing is frozen and I am unfixed, then it means that forever and forever all alternatives are denied me. And if I am stripped of any sense of alternatives, then freedom has no meaning, for freedom in its structure means a sense of alternatives.

That attitude creeps into our thinking without our knowing it. Have you ever felt (with reference to somebody else) that there wasn't anything that anybody could do to help that person—he's just out beyond the pale? Of course you know that there's always something (maybe) that can be done about you; but that other man—you feel sorry, and you try to reach him, but you can't touch him—he's out there.

There are a few who feel that way about the social order, even. "You can't do anything with it; it's fixed." A man who for a long time developed that philosophy in a rather interesting way—a man who just received the Nobel Prize—is Bertrand Russell. All of my old students here (and I feel like an old man, looking at you, because you look so young—you needn't laugh! I guess I've got to take a second look at myself!) will recall it, because you had to read it. Bertrand Russell says that we are surrounded by what he calls rather poetically "the steady march of unconscious power, meaningless, purposeless,"[6] and that human life is but an isthmus between two continents of darkness. As we walk on that isthmus for a little while, we know that there isn't anything we can do, so we say to each other, "Cheer up! We'll soon be dead." The only thing that can help you is what he calls "an attitude of unyielding despair."[7] And right in the midst of this, as you hear the steady, relentless marching of unconscious power, Bertrand Russell places something in the mind. The mind has a world—a world of dreams; it's an unreal world; it has nothing to do with all these things out here. But a wise man can take refuge in that world; and the order that he experiences there he may try to project upon the impersonal, meaningless aspects of his environment. And he leaves it there.

But on the other hand, if you take the position that life is dynamic, creative, then it becomes reasonable to assume that the human spirit, brooding over the impersonal aspects, or the diseased and disorderly aspects, of the environment, can so operate upon this stuff until, as a result of its imperious insistence, order appears where there was chaos.

Whenever we wrestle with the powers of this world, the basic assumption must be that life isn't yet made, and that it will respond, it will yield, it can be shaped.

THE MEANS OF SOCIAL CHANGE

There is one other generalization; then I have two more things to say, and that'll be it. The spiritually minded man who deals with the powers of this world on the assumption that there are real alternatives in his hand undertakes to achieve ends that may be regarded as worldly ends because they have to do with the traffic of human life, with social change; he assumes that it is possible to effect social changes having to do with the world of men and things by the use of methods that are ethical and spiritual in character.

If it happens that such a man is dealing with the kind of social situation which defines his position in a manner that places him out of the reach of what may be regarded normally as due process, then his problem becomes a very acute problem. For if I am trying to effect social change, and the social situation or predicament in which I find myself is one that provides no due processes—no legal or political processes—that I can manipulate so as to effect, within the context of the experience of the people and myself, the changes that are desired on behalf of human welfare, then it becomes more rational for me either to rely completely upon ethical and spiritual means, or to deny thoroughly the validity of ethical and spiritual ends and to take refuge only in catastrophic upheaval, revolution. (A very simple case in point, of course, is the one with which we are all familiar, that of Mr. Gandhi in India.)

But if my situation is one in which I function in a society that provides due process, then the very existence of the possibility of orderly change through due process tends to vitiate the radical character of my insistence upon ethical and spiritual means.

The curiously marvelous thing about using ethical means to effect changes (if you can hold out) is that the means are derivative from the ethical insight and the ethical experience. The means move out from that center to attack the society, rather than letting the means be determined by the stubborn character of the thing one is trying to shift or change.

THE MEANING OF RELIGION

There are two or three more specific things that I want to say. Religion, as it seems to me, fulfills always a dual demand in human life. The first is something that is personal and private and intimate. It is the whisper of God in the human heart, to which I respond, that gives to my life a sense of transcendent security and strength and vitality. It is the religion that has to do with devotion, with piety, with the inner bearings of life.

The second dimension is of another character entirely, but it is still religion; and it is in this second character that the religious experience, as expressed in the first part of the topic, "The Power of the Spirit," has bearing on the second part, "The Powers of This World."

The Touchstone[8]

Religion in the second dimension provides three things for us. First, it gives to the individual a basis for integrated action. It provides a guarantee for action; it provides a touchstone; it provides an ultimate point of referral in the light of which everything I do takes on its meaning. It provides a riding judgment upon my life and the things that I think and do; it is a source of strength to me.

Curiously enough, anything that provides this qualifies. I would like to ask you, as you think about your own life, what is it that gives to you your basis for your behavior pattern? What is the thing to which you refer, basically, when you want to convince yourself that you are somebody? What do you think? What determines whether you do this or that when you face your options? What is the thing with reference to which you do not ever want your life to do violence? What is it?

Whatever it is, that's your religion. What is it? (We need not make haste over this part of it.) What is it that provides for you the mainspring of your functioning, so that when you are trying to make up your mind with reference to what you shall do, before what altar do you kneel? That's the first thing.

The Demand

The second thing that religion in the second category provides is the thing that inspires in the individual an authentic willingness to surrender his life or anything else he has—a willingness to surrender. What is it? Think about your own selves, even as I am thinking about myself. What is it that, when I face its imperious demand, makes me willing to surrender everything?

That's what Jesus means when he asks, "What would a man give in exchange for his soul?"[9] What? What is it that is capable of inspiring in you a willingness to surrender anything? Your family? Your position? Your economic security? Your profession? What is it that, when it faces you, you say, "Here! And I wish I had more to give." Whatever that is, that is your religion.

The Unity

The third thing is a little more difficult and a little more subtle. It is that which gives to me a sense of participation, of sharing, in what to me is a collective destiny; that which gives me a sense of not being cut off, of not being isolated. When the powers of this world, however we may define them in our own thinking, impinge upon our religion in the second sense, it is then that they have us to deal with.

We can always beat a retreat if they impinge upon us in religion in the first sense, for I can always withdraw into myself, because one of the interesting psychological aspects of religion is the insistence upon detachment. I can always withdraw from my involvements, and deep within my own self commune with my own spirit and my God, and no one can invade me there. The powers of this world can cut off this, cut off that, cut off the other—but they can't touch me there. That's mine—that's way inside; they can kill me, they can do all those things, but this is mine. And I won't struggle with them very much. I'll give, give, give, because I know that the boundary that determines how far they can go is set by the very structure of the intimacy of my own personality. So I won't fight.

THE HOUSE OF RIMMON

But—when the powers of this world move in on religion in the second sense, then I put up a fight. If they tell you that they are the thing to which you must give your ultimate loyalty, and in the light of which all of the judgments that you pass upon your life must be determined, then I say, "Well, I don't know. I don't know." So the prophet said to God, "When I walk into the House of Rimmon, doing my duty as a servant of the king, do not deal harshly with me if I must genuflect before an altar in which I don't believe. I'm just carrying out my assignment as a servant of the king."[10]

I got a letter since I've been here from a schoolteacher in my church. She says, "What shall I do? Because I have only one more week now before I must sign the oath, or lose my job. What must I do? What is the religious meaning of this thing?"[11] When the powers of this world begin to move in to take over the citadel of my loyalty, and insist what my primary loyalty must be, then I fight—maybe. Or I recognize that in yielding I betray my gods. If I begin to deal realistically with all of the ethical implications of compromise, where shall I draw the line? What is crucial and what is not crucial? How much can I yield without doing violence to my overmastering loyalty? Where is the line beyond which I can't go without destruction? Those are the questions you deal with.

If the powers of this world try to determine for me what it is to which I must make a final surrender, then I challenge—perhaps. Now I must hold back; I can't give; I can't surrender everything. I'll give my money—maybe. Do you remember when during the war Rickenbacker's plane sank, and they were on a raft? The thing that interests me about the story is this: They were flying along, the plane was overloaded, and they saw that they would have to do something to make it lighter. The process through which they went in eliminating is most interesting. First they threw the extra gas out, because it was very heavy. Then they threw some other things over; then they threw all their clothes over; and then they said, "Well now, we have important State documents, in those pouches," and with great agony they finally decided to throw those over. One by one they eliminated everything but their own lives.[12]

When the powers of this world begin to make demands of surrender, what do you do? Of course, if you have no thing, no transcendent Person that has already inspired in you a willingness to surrender, then you give yourself to the highest bidder. That's simple! That is one of the difficulties of the intellectual, if I may say so in passing, because one of the characteristics of the intellectual is that he can't make up his mind. He lives in the midst of "on the other hand," of "that is right, but there is an extenuating circumstance that needs to be examined . . ." The intellectual can't make up his mind. And that is why, when the powers of this world move in to capture a society, usually the first people they capture are the intellectuals, because there's a vacuum there. They move in and possess it, and then they take over the mind. All the training and the brain, and all the discipline—all of that becomes at once vehicular for a will that is powerful enough to command.

OUR JOB

No one can decide what you will do. I can hardly decide what I will do. But there is a story that Jesus told, and it is on that note I want to stop. Jesus said that there was a man who owned a great estate, and who decided that he was going to go away on a journey. He called his prime movers to him and said, "I am going to give you $100; I am going to give you $50; I am going to give you $25; and I am going to give you $1.00. I will be back some time—I don't know when. And when I come back I want you to see me and tell me what you have done. I will hold you responsible."

So the man who had the $100 went off and put it to work; so did the man with $50 and the man with $25. The man who had $1.00 went home and told his wife, let's say, all about what had happened up at the house when the owner left. And she said, "What are you going to do?" He said, "Well, you know how hard he is. I've already picked out the place; I'm going to have a place to which I will always have free and easy access, and always in general view. I'm going to hide the $1.00 there. I won't even tell you where it is." And he did that.

Then the great day came. She saw him with it, and she said, "What are you doing with that?" "I have a feeling that he is going to come back tomorrow, so I want to have it all ready; I want to be sure; I'm going to sleep with it tonight."

Next day they all went up—the man with the $100, the man with $50, the man with $25; and finally the man with $1.00. And when his turn came he said, "I don't know whether you know this about yourself or not, but you have a very hard reputation. You collect where you haven't deposited, and you reap where you haven't sown; and knowing that characteristic of yours I put this dollar away, and here it is." And the owner had his strong men come, and he said, "Take him out." Why? Because he hadn't anything to show for it? No! He put the man in outer darkness because he hadn't worked at it.[13]

That's our job—that's our job—that's our job: we've got to work at it. And you can trust God beyond that point.

　　　　　　　　　　　　　　　　　　　　　　　　　　　　　TD.

NOTES

1. HT, "The Power of the Spirit and the Powers of This World," in *The School of Religion, Howard University, Washington, D.C., The Thirty-Fourth Annual Convocation, November 14–16, 1950, Theme: "The Church, the State and Human Welfare"* (Washington, D.C.: Howard University School of Religion, 1950), 1–7. In addition to the address by Thurman, the mimeographed volume contained three addresses by John C. Bennett, professor of Christian Ethics at Union Theological Seminary: "The Church's Responsibility for Social Welfare"; "A Christian View of the State"; and "Church and State in the United States." Thurman's former boss, Mordecai Wyatt Johnson, addressed the convocation banquet.

2. Hab. 3:17–18.

3. From "Love's Consolations," in Richard Watson Dickson, *Christ's Company and Other Poems* (London: Smith, Elder, 1861), 97–98. Thurman modified the poem; he rearranged aspects of it and did not follow the original line breaks.

4. The composer Felix Mendelssohn (1809–47) was born on 3 February, and the naturalist Charles Darwin (1809–82) and President Abraham Lincoln (1809–65) were both born on 12 February.

5. Job 19:25. The original context probably refers not to a divine power but to a kinsman who would vindicate Job in a potential future legal proceeding. See Robert Alter, *The Wisdom Books: Job, Proverbs, and Ecclesiastes* (New York: W. W. Norton, 2010), 83–84.

6. In the original, "brief and powerless is man's life" facing the "trampling march of unconscious power," from Bertrand Russell, "A Free Man's Worship" (originally written in 1903), in *Mysticism and Logic and Other Essays* (London: Longmans, Green, 1919), 57. Russell (1872–1970) won the Nobel Prize in Literature in 1950.

7. Russell, *Mysticism and Logic and Other Essays*, 48.

8. As printed in the typescript, the subheads in this section are flush left on the same line as the beginning of the paragraph text, and they are not underlined.

9. Mark 8:37.

10. 2 Kings 5:18. These words were spoken *to* a prophet, not *by* a prophet. Naaman, the commander of the army of the king of Aram, having just been cured of a skin disease (commonly translated as leprosy) by the prophet Elisha, acknowledges that "there is no God in the world except in Israel" but states that when he returns to the temple of Rimmon he will pray to its gods. Elisha tells him to "go in peace" (2 Kings 5:1–19).

11. On 3 October 1950 California governor Earl Warren signed a law requiring that all state employees within thirty days avow under oath that they were not—and had not been for five years prior—a member of any organization that "advocates the overthrow of the government by force, violence, or other unlawful means." The Board of Regents had required employees of the University of California to sign a similar oath the year previously.

Although it did not explicitly state such, the law was widely understood to ban members of the Communist Party from working for the state. Progressive liberals, including many members of the Fellowship Church, were outraged by the oath.

12. On 20 October 1943 Eddie Rickenbacker (1890–1973), America's most celebrated World War I air ace, was on a mission for the secretary of war when he was forced to ditch his B-17 in the middle of the Pacific, and he and his crewmates drifted for twenty-four days until they were rescued on 13 November.

13. Parable of the Talents, Matt. 25:14–30.

🐟 From Roland Hayes
1 March 1951

Roland Hayes responds to an invitation to worship at the Fellowship Church. Thurman had long admired Roland Hayes, the first African American concert singer to have a notable international career, writing about him as early as 1927.[1] In his autobiography Thurman writes about his frustration at a Roland Hayes concert in Atlanta at which the concert hall was segregated vertically (right and left), rather than horizontally (back and front); this was seen as a significant concession to local blacks.[2] In this letter Hayes informs Thurman that they may not have an opportunity to see each other while he is on the West Coast, but that being in touch with Thurman by letter is still spiritually rewarding. He also seeks Thurman's help in securing scholarship funding for a promising young tenor and a letter of recommendation to a local draft board on behalf of the young man. After Thurman moved to Boston in 1953, he and Hayes became good friends.

Dear Dr. Thurman:

Yours of the 24th February I have now before me and I am happy to have it.

Elmer Dickey[3] came to me yesterday (feb. 28th) to tell me that his bill for lodging at the Miles Standish for this Semester was really due at the beginning of this school term but that he had hoped to have received some funds from California before now. He said—and showed me—a promissory note he had signed to pay his lodging account today. All day I have been trying to reach proper authorities there to obtain a deferment of his obligation for a week or so and I hope to have got it all arranged satisfactory. But he will have to find a way to meet this bill of $128.00 before too long. I hasten to tell you this so that if you should know of such a person from whom he could reasonably expect this immediate help to urge you to acquaint them with his situation at the earliest moment possible.

I had entered his name with a Textile firm in Maine for a job during the summer months, but that will do him no good just now. Then, there is another terrific hurdle over which he needs very much to have his influential friends in

San Francisco to help him over and that is to reach important members of the draft {Board} there and to impress the importance of his being placed on deferment where the draft into the U.S. Army is concerned. His gift of intrinsic value as a great concert Artist of the future—to humanity—is far more important to protect from the rigors of army life than anything [*strikethrough illegible*] that he might be able to do as a soldier. THIS IS OF IMMINENT IMPORTANCE.

I shall be arriving at Hotel Green in Pasadena, California on March 31st and shall be glad to see such of the Foundation as you mention who may desire to see me. I sing there on April 1st. The day you are in Portland I shall be singing in San Francisco and the day you are back in San Francisco I shall be singing in Portland. But on March 29 I shall appear at the University of California in Berkeley—arriving in Oakland on the 28th. I do hope that our paths may meet before I leave those parts.

How gracious of you to invite me to worship with you if I found myself there and all convenient on a Sunday when you should be there. Nothing would give me greater satisfaction—and, I know, benefit—than such a rich experience. Thank you for the invitation, and I do deeply appreciate your reference to that spiritual quality that characterize both the work you are doing there and as I endeavor to reach for in my own work.

If we do not actually meet in person while on this tour of mine, it is indeed rewarding to have been able to embrace your spirit over the miles and through space as the exchange of letters has afforded.

With kind best wishes,

Sincerely yours,

[*signed*] Roland Hayes

Roland Hayes.

Dr. Howard Thurman

Fellowship Church

2041 Larkin Street

San Francisco, California.

                                                                                    TLS.

NOTES

1. *PHWT,* 1:111. See also *PHWT,* 2:210.

2. *WHAH,* 36. Thurman states that the discussion about segregated seating for Hayes's concert occurred during his senior year at Morehouse (1922–23), although Hayes's first appearance in Atlanta seems to have been in late 1925, when Thurman was studying at Rochester Theological Seminary ("Famous Negro Tenor Given Ovation by Big Audience," *Atlanta Constitution,* 19 December 1925). See also Patricia Sullivan, *Days of Hope: Race and Democracy in the New Deal Era* (Chapel Hill: University of North Carolina Press, 1996), 33–34.

3. Elmer Dickey (1927–94) was born in Weimar, Texas. He attended Fisk University and also earned a degree in music from Boston University. An army veteran, he was the 1955 winner of the Marian Anderson Award.

To Dr. and Mrs. George Collins
27 April 1951
[San Francisco, Calif.]

Few individuals had the powerful impact on Thurman's life and thought that George L. "Shorty" Collins did.[1] They first met when Thurman was an undergraduate at Morehouse and Collins was a field representative for the Fellowship of Reconciliation. Collins introduced Thurman to pacifism, and Thurman said of Collins that "[he gave me] a place to stand in my own spirit" amid Atlanta's disfiguring racism.[2] A few years later, in 1925, at a retreat in Pawling, New York, Collins introduced Thurman to the works of Olive Schreiner, beginning for Thurman what would be a lifelong passion for Schreiner's work.[3] Meetings between Thurman and Collins thereafter were infrequent—when their paths crossed at a conference in early 1938, they had not seen one another for many years.[4] Leading a life dedicated to interracial understanding, Collins was probably the first white person to become Thurman's close friend, and he was a model for Thurman of what interracial friendship could mean.

Dear Shorty and Evelyn:

How sorry I am that it is not my good fortune to be present tonight.

Many generations of students and young people have been inspired and dedicated to the highest values of Christian morality by the sustained influence which you have exerted over the years. I shall always remember the times when you "invaded" the South and established little islands of understanding and fellowship in a very stormy and turbulent sea of racial tension. And you did these things without seeming to try, with a smile and a winsomeness and great directness. You defined in person the meaning of brotherhood and wholesome human relations.[5]

The thing that I appreciated so much, and all the Negro students of my generation appreciated so much, was that you did not seem to us to be conscious of the fact that you were acting in a manner unlike the average American white person whom we knew. It is for this reason that you inspired confidence in us, and that confidence laid the foundation for many creative expressions of good will in later years. Of all the persons whose lives have touched mine in this area of human relations, you stand out in uniqueness and in simple naturalness.

I rejoice to know that our friendship has extended over so long a period, and it is my desire that the rest of your way shall be even more significant than those days that are behind you. Of course, all the things I am saying apply to both of you.

With affectionate remembrance

Sincerely,

Howard Thurman

HT:ff

Dr. and Mrs. George Collins
c/o Mr. Edward F. Burrows
The University Club
803 State Street
Madison 5, Wisconsin

TLc.

NOTES

1. George L. "Shorty" Collins (1892–1991)—lean and 6'5"—was born in Southern California and attended the University of California at Berkeley, graduating in 1915. After the horrors of serving in World War I as a member of a machine gun battalion, Collins became a pacifist, and after theological training he became the interchurch student pastor at the Denver Labor College, teaching there as well as at the Farmer Labor Summer School of Colorado and Wyoming. In 1919 he joined the Fellowship of Reconciliation (FOR), and by 1923 he was its southern field secretary. He spoke at over 250 colleges before becoming a Baptist campus minister at the University of Wisconsin at Madison in 1929. In 1957 he took a similar position at San Jose State College, also working as the Northern California field representative for the FOR. He founded the San Jose Peace Center, now known as the Collins Center. In 1964 Collins was awarded an honorary degree from Kalamazoo College, and in 1971 he received the Edward Dahlberg Peace Award from the American Baptist Convention. He was not a prolific writer, but see his "Pacifism and Social Injustice," in *Pacifism in the Modern World*, ed. Devere Allen (Garden City, N.Y.: Doubleday, Doran, 1929), 104–14.

2. *WHAH*, 265.

3. Ibid., 59.

4. *PHWT*, 2:107. The two men met again in April 1944. See To Alice Sams, 2 April 1944, printed in the current volume.

5. Collins seems to have had an extraordinary ability for making friends, eliciting conversation, and introducing people to new books and ideas. Roy Stryker, who knew Collins in Colorado and later achieved fame at the Farm Security Administration, remembered Collins running an open house, a "kind of crazy workshop," in which workers and students would gather almost every night to discuss matters of interest and concern. Stryker credited Collins for introducing him to the *New Republic*, the *Nation*, and the work of Walter Rauschebusch. See Colleen McDannell, *Picturing Faith: Photography and the Great Depression* (New Haven, Conn.: Yale University Press, 2004), 12, 280.

✒ To Dr. WILLARD JOHNSON
19 MAY 1951
[SAN FRANCISCO, CALIF.]

The Green Pastures, *written by Marc Connelly,*[1] *was a highly stylized*
depiction of African American folk religion; it was extremely popular
in its initial 1930 Broadway production, running for a year and a half and
winning that year's Pulitzer Prize for Drama. Its 1951 revival prompted
AME bishop D. Ward Nichols to denounce the play as "stupid and irreligious,"
an "Amos 'n' Andy"[2] *show that "perpetuated outmoded stereotypes of Negro*
people and their religion."[3] *As early as 1937 Thurman had used an incident*
in the play to illustrate a point about the nature of God's relation to humanity,
but he did so with the disclaimer that "the author is giving no true or factual
description or interpretation of the religious life of Negroes in his portrayal."[4]
When asked about the play in 1951, Thurman continued to express an ambi-
valent attitude, finding the mood of the drama to be "overwhelmingly impres-
sive" but noting its "relentless hammering" of stereotypes and observing that the
play's folk simplicity could be mistaken as an accurate account of the complexity
of contemporary black religion and life in the South, thus making it unsuitable
for revival.

Dr. Willard Johnson[5]
National Program Director
The National Conference of
Christians and Jews, Inc.
381 Fourth Avenue
New York 16, New York
Dear Dr. Johnson:
   Your letter of April 16 arrived while I was away in the east.
   I am very sympathetic with the position taken by Bishop Nichols[6] relative to
the way in which "The Green Pastures" underscores the stereotype as touching
the concept in many peoples' minds about Negro religious life and experience.
During its long run on Broadway when it first appeared, I was constantly ques-
tioned by student groups, particularly concerning the validity of the portrayal
so far as contemporary Negro life is concerned.
   For many people it is not possible to distinguish between the overwhelmingly impressive mood of the drama and the relentless hammering
of the stereotype. Because I feel deeply that it is possible to get the mood
in some other way, by using vehicles that do not confirm stereotypes, it is

my considered judgment that a revival of "The Green Pastures" cannot be justified.

Sincerely,

Howard Thurman

HT:ff

TLc.

NOTES

1. Marc Connelly (1890–1980).

2. "Amos 'n' Andy" was an immensely popular radio comedy depicting the various misadventures of its two African American title characters, in different formats, from 1928 to 1960. Its two creators and lead performers were white actors, and throughout its long run there were critics who thought that the show presented a risibly stereotyped view of African American life. A short-lived television version (1951–53) used black performers.

3. "'Pastures' Boycott Is Urged by Bishop," *New York Times*, 26 March 1951.

4. "The Significance of Jesus: VI," in *PHWT*, 2:88.

5. Willard Lyon Johnson (1905–86) was vice president and national program director of the National Conference of Christians and Jews from 1942 to 1951. He thereafter served as general secretary of World Brotherhood (1951–55), president of the Committee on International Economic Growth (1958–60), executive director of the Unitarian Universalist Service Committee (1960–66), and executive director of Planned Parenthood in San Diego (1966–70).

6. Decatur Ward Nichols (1900–2005), a native of Georgetown, South Carolina, attended Howard and Drew Universities. He was ordained an AME minister in 1926 and elected bishop in 1940. He served as bishop in a number of districts before his retirement in 1976, although he continued to preach actively until after his one-hundredth birthday.

📨 TO JOHN OVERHOLT

21 MAY 1951

[*SAN FRANCISCO, CALIF.*]

Thurman writes to his friend John Overholt[1] about recent developments in the church and in his life, including the rehospitalization of his sister Madaline for depression and other ailments. He expresses concern about the impact on his youngest daughter, Anne, of growing up in the Fellowship Church. Thurman notes that Sue plans to take Anne to Fisk University for three weeks to gain a more visceral sense of black life in the South.

Mr. John Overholt

P.O. Box 326

Wooster, Ohio

Dear John:

After arriving here from my visit with you I have been extremely busy. I was home one week, and then off to Los Angeles for a week of lecturing and preaching, largely for Fellowship Church. My institute down there was very successful in terms of interest and enthusiasm.

I telephoned Mrs. Nott[2] and had a good visit with her at that distance. She was very glad to hear concerning you and was happy that I could assure her you were very much improved in health and seemed to be in excellent form. She certainly is a good friend of yours. She wonders why you have not come out this winter, and expects you sometime during the year. She did not seem very enthusiastic about the prospect of coming up for a weekend when we would have the exhibit of her husband's work. I did not press her but will write her again later. My present plan is to have the exhibit in late September and early October, extending it over a period of two weeks. {* -asterisk}

I am having my two wonderful dry-points framed, but before I got to it I exhibited them at the church and talked a little about the artist. It would have warmed your heart to have felt the response of the people at the Coffee Hour when they saw them.

I have not had time to check on the other part of the tape recording. Now that I'm at home for a definite period, I shall do this within the next week. If there is any additional information to it, I shall make a note of it and pass it on to you directly.

Last week I spent most of a day visiting my sister.[3] Her general state is about the same. There is some indication that the chest picture is beginning to look a little better. What this means in the long pull the doctors do not know. It is encouraging, however, to know that for the first time since November, they are permitting her to get out a bit {of bed}. The emotional picture remains very much as it was when I talked with you in Louisville {Wooster}. In my conversations with her there were new signs of interest being manifested. What this indicates, we do not know at this time. It continues to be a very difficult period for me, but one that is not utterly impossible, for which I am very grateful to God.

The financial report from the New York meeting last weekend was $2800.[4] We hope to make it $3000 by the end of the month when the remaining outstanding commitments have been met. Thus far, we are one-third of our way toward the goal of $12,500 which we must have by January 30. I am relaxing on the whole matter because I have put as much of my strength into this part of our need as I dare. It is very important that I do not become so involved in the problems of underwriting our work that my most significant contribution to its prophetic and spiritual significance will be vitiated.

We are in the throes of trying to work out a plan by which it will be possible for Mrs. Thurman to come east to her 25th reunion at Oberlin during the first week in June, and if it can be done she will also take our daughter Anne, whom you met, with her to Fisk University in Nashville, Tennessee, to spend two or three weeks in a seminar on Negro life. One of the peculiar costs of the kind of undertaking in which Mrs. Thurman and I are engaged is that unless we plan it carefully, our younger daughter will find it difficult to develop a sense of group roots. You see, John, her experiences in the atmosphere that we have been creating in Fellowship Church cover the most crucial part of her adolescent development. It would be tragic if she is not emotionally equipped to deal with the vicissitudes of American life that have not been informed by the idealism of Fellowship Church. This land of ours is still a bitter place for a sensitive Negro man or woman. The experience at Fisk, if we can arrange it, will supplement what we have been doing in our family life with Anne in terms of giving her a deep sense of group security, without which her unfolding life will be vulnerable to the poison arrows of a socially sick environment that expresses itself in gross and refined hostilities. If Mrs. Thurman comes to Oberlin, I hope there will be time for her to come up to Wooster for an afternoon. This will depend upon how exhausting are the responsibilities of her reunion.

I want you to know how wonderful it was for me to be with you and have time for the unhurried talk and rich and rare communion of mind and spirit. You are a wonderful man, and I can understand now why so remarkable a person as Jessie was so deeply in love with you.

Please say my warm greetings to the gracious young lady who added so much thoughtfulness to the comfort of my day there.

Sincerely,

[Howard Thurman]

(*) P.S. Any time during the summer that it is convenient for you, I hope you will arrange to ship me the pictures which you will let me use as a loan for the exhibit. I will see that they are properly insured so that they will be protected.—ht

TLc.

NOTES

1. John Overholt (1886–1973), a lifetime resident of Wooster, Ohio, was a graduate of the College of Wooster (1907) and Princeton University (1909.) He married his wife, Jessie Wickwire Overholt, in 1914. A successful businessman, bank director, and inventor, he was related to the prominent industrialist Henry Clay Frick (1849–1919.) He and his wife were good friends of the Thurmans and financial supporters of the Fellowship Church.

2. Probably the widow of Raymond Nott (1888–1948), a well-known California landscape painter, who lived for many years in San Diego.

3. Madaline was hospitalized at California State Mental Hospital at Camarillo, in Southern California.

4. Probably the fund-raising event at Riverside Church in New York City on 17 April 1951.

🐦 GENE K. WALKER TO SPINGARN MEDAL CO.
29 JANUARY 1952
SAN FRANCISCO, CALIF.

Gene K. Walker, chairman of the board of trustees of the Fellowship Church, writes to the Spingarn Medal Committee recommending Thurman for the honor. Thurman was never awarded the Spingarn Medal,[1] although a number of his friends and associates were, among them Mordecai Wyatt Johnson (1929), Max Yergan (1933), Mary McLeod Bethune (1935), John Hope (1936), Channing Tobias (1948), and Benjamin Mays (1982). In 1952 the Spingarn Medal was given to Harry T. Moore (1905–51), an organizer for the Florida NAACP, who was murdered along with his wife, Harriette, when a bomb that had been planted in their bedroom exploded on Christmas Eve in 1951. The crime has never been solved, but the bomb was presumably planted by the Ku Klux Klan or some similar organization. It was the first time the Spingarn Medal was awarded posthumously.

The Spingarn Medal Committee
20 West 40th Street
New York 18, N.Y.

Gentlemen:

As you consider that significant man or woman who is to receive the Spingarn Medal for 1952, may I suggest as a most deserving candidate a man perhaps well known to you already: Dr. Howard R.[2] Thurman.

Such a recommendation would find its justification in many aspects of Dr. Thurman's many achievements. The particular one I call to your attention, however, is his outstanding accomplishment as Minister of The Church for the Fellowship of All Peoples, here in San Francisco.

When Dr. Thurman resigned his post as Dean of the Chapel at Howard University, Washington, D.C., to assume the leadership of "Fellowship Church," the congregation was a disorganized group of 25 to 30 people.

Today, as the result of Dr. Thurman's ministry, the congregation includes some 400 resident members in the San Francisco Bay Area (Fellowship Church is not an isolated neighborhood church); and nearly 1000 members-at-large, from all over North America and countless foreign countries.

This steadily increasing membership represents the greatest variety in credal, national and ethnic background engaged in religious worship anywhere in the world.

Dr. Thurman's influence, and through him the influence of the Fellowship Church movement, extend to hundreds of schools and colleges, for whose students and teachers he has become a regular visiting minister.

In 1947 the Board of Regents at the University of California signally honored Dr. Thurman by designating him as "minister of the day" for the June commencement. I know of no instance, anywhere in the United States, in which a Negro clergyman has been so honored.

As the direct result of Dr. Thurman's leadership, the financial support for Fellowship Church has come from all parts of the world, and has made it possible, within a 3-year period, to invest a sum of more than $40,000 in the purchase of a church building. As of January 1, 1952, title to the property is clear and unencumbered.

These are but scattered instances of the effect of Dr. Thurman's work. His fundamental achievement, however, is in what he has done to break down prejudice in the hearts of men. . . . to create in its place a deep faith in man's capacity to live upon the earth in bonds of brotherhood. The testament to this truth may be found in the thousands of lives he has touched inwardly, as few other men have done.

It is my understanding that the Spingarn Medal has never yet been awarded for achievement in the field of religion and the church.[3] Would it not be fitting, therefore, for the first and foremost pioneer in that field to receive your distinguished recognition?

I speak as a friend of Dr. Thurman and as a citizen of San Francisco. I have not discussed my act in writing this letter with Dr. Thurman.

Sincerely,
[*signed*]
Gene K. Walker

GKW:cb
Encls.
bc: Mrs. Sue Bailey Thurman

TLS.

NOTES

1. On the Spingarn Medal, see *PHWT,* 3:124n1.

2. Thurman's rarely used middle name was Washington.

3. Prior to 1952 the Spingarn Medal had been awarded to Mordecai Wyatt Johnson and Channing Tobias, though it is probably the case that ministers were underrepresented among award recipients. Since 1952 the award has gone to clergymen noted for their general contributions to black America and not for denominational leadership; award recipients have included Martin Luther King, Jr. (1957), Andrew Young (1978), Jesse Jackson (1989), and Benjamin Mays.

֎ To Carleton E. Byrne
26 April 1952
[*San Francisco, Calif.*]

Thurman writes to Fellowship Church supporter and benefactor Carleton E.
Byrne[1] about church matters. He outlines a plan for creating a series of books
for use in schools on the contributions of different racial and ethnic groups to
the history of California, along the lines of Sue Bailey Thurman's work on black
pioneers in California.[2] As Thurman later wrote, "missionaries taught others to
understand our culture, but failed to teach us the cultures they had met."[3] This
reversal of the missionary impulse was always, for Thurman, a key facet of the
Fellowship Church.

Mr. Carleton E. Byrne
633 South Shatto Place
Los Angeles 5, California

Dear Carleton:

I need not say how happy I was to have a good healthy visit with you when I
was down in Los Angeles a few days ago. There are several things on my mind—
and here they are:

First, I am enclosing a letter, the contents of which are clear. I am wondering
whether or not you would be interested in doing anything about this. If you are,
I would suggest that it be done through the agency of the church and we could
work out an arrangement by which this student would spend some time at Fellowship Church before and after his experience at Fisk.

This may be a very significant opportunity to make a far-reaching contribution to East-West race relations, and to goodwill in Japan. I have not answered
the letter, and I do not know what your reaction would be. It may not appeal
to you, and it may not be as significant as I think it is. At any rate, please let me
know how you feel about it.

I have given considerable thought to the larger plan concerning the publishing of a series on Pioneers. The main outline of the plan is as follows:

(1) The Intercultural Workshop of Fellowship Church and the International
Institute of San Francisco would sponsor jointly a committee brought into
being for the purpose of developing this project, to wit, the publishing of
a series of comprehensive books dealing with the contribution of several
non-Caucasian members to the life and the culture of California in its
earlier history. The general plan would follow that of Mrs. Thurman's
book, "Pioneers of Negro Ancestry."

(2) The committee would seek to get the books published by a standard press such as Stanford or the University of California. If this could not be arranged, then they would seek to get them privately published as Mrs. Thurman's book was.

(3) The plan would be to seek the adoption of these books for use in the public schools of California. The procedure for this has not at the moment been determined. I assume that they would have to receive the approval of the State Board of Education or some such State authority.

(4) An individual Japanese-American and a Chinese-American would be employed to do the writing of the respective volumes. For this service a suitable fee would be paid which would include the cost of research, time for writing, etc. The contracting author would be paid out-right for the job and the manuscript would become the property of the committee.

(5) The committee would have to select an editor who is equipped to see the literary angle of the project through to the end.

I do not now know what would be a sound estimate of the cost of such a venture. The steps that are being taken at the moment are the setting up of the committee. The idea has been approved in principle by our Board, and is being considered by the Board of the International Institute. A Japanese writer has already been located, and I am talking with him informally within the next ten days or two weeks. The secretary of International Institute assures me that she knows a Chinese woman who is equipped to do the job we have in mind.

While I was in Los Angeles, I had a conference with a representative of the Golden State Life Insurance Company[4] about the possibility of their making a contribution to this venture. There was a manifest interest, but the complications seem almost insurmountable. At any rate, I was advised to submit the detailed proposal when it is ready and they would see if the insurance commissioners would approve any contribution from them. This seems to be a requirement for any mutual insurance company licensed by the State of California. Beyond this, I have sought no other help. I am wondering if you have thought of any interested group or foundation outside of your own connections.

I do not write this letter for the purpose of involving you personally in the matter. You will remember my point made when we talked several weeks ago.

The plans for reorganizing our staff are temporarily held up because they involve commitments for at least 12 months, and I am unwilling to engage new people if we are not assured that their salaries can be guaranteed. I would not be hesitant if our congregation to date had absorbed our monthly deficit. We are having a special pledge campaign during the month of May with the hope that the monthly ante can be raised and guaranteed. Our central financial problem hovers around the fact that the "necessitous" program which we must develop in keeping with the genius of our church requires more funds to sustain it than it is reasonable to expect from a congregation our size, however sacrificial may be the spirit and mood.

This has been our dilemma from the beginning, and will be until our congregation is twice its present size. If it becomes twice its present size, then our present quarters which are cramp[ed] now will be utterly impossible. Thus the dilemma becomes more involved and complicated as we grow. Frankly, I do not know what the answer to this problem might be. I am happy, however, that the burden of it does not rest exclusively on my shoulders, but is the increasing concern of the Board and Finance Committee and the congregation. I have been informed that the Finance Committee is organizing a small nucleus called The Friends of Fellowship Church for the purpose of getting more financial support from the community of San Francisco than has been forthcoming in the past. This is very encouraging, and I am giving as much inspiration to the idea as possible. I am determined, however, that I shall not become deeply involved in it personally. When you come up for the arts festival, I hope it will be possible for you, Fred Cromwell, Gene and a few of the other men to have a good session on this whole problem.

Thank you for all the time it has taken you to read through this.

You are one of my favorite human beings.

Sincerely,

[unsigned]

HT:f

TLc.

NOTES

1. Carleton E. Byrne was a California businessman. His wife, Esther Smith Byrne, and his brother-in-law, Lloyd M. Smith, were children of Eleanor Lloyd Smith, to whom Thurman dedicated *Meditations of the Heart* (New York: Harper & Brothers, 1953): "To Eleanor Lloyd Smith, in whom the inner and the outer are one," 5. Eleanor Lloyd Smith, whom Thurman usually addressed as Mrs. Ralph M. Smith, was the brother of Ralph B. Lloyd (1875–1953), who developed the Ventura Avenue oil lease in Southern California into one of the most valuable oil fields in the United States; it produced over a billion barrels of oil after its discovery in 1919. Ralph M. Smith was an associate of Lloyd in the oil lease. Byrne was an executive of the West Shore Company, a family-owned holding company that had an interest in the Ventura oil lease, among other businesses, including a tuna cannery.

The Byrnes, Lloyd M. Smith, and Eleanor Lloyd Smith were benefactors of a number of liberal Christian and progressive causes, including the ACLU, Pacifica Radio, and the YWCA. They were generous supporters of Thurman and the Fellowship Church, and all became good friends with Thurman. In 1960 Byrne and Lloyd M. Smith, a lawyer, were two of the original three trustees of the Howard Thurman Trust Fund, later the Howard Thurman Educational Trust. For Byrne, see Austin H. Peck, Jr., *Bold Beginnings: A Story About the First 50 Years of Latham & Watkins* (Los Angeles: Latham and Watkins, 1984), 23–24. For Byrne's family connections, see To Mrs. Ralph Smith, 10 March 1953; and *WHAH*, 261.

2. Sue Bailey Thurman, *Pioneers of Negro Origin in California* (San Francisco: Acme, 1952). It does not appear that any of these books on California ethnic groups were published.

3. HT, *Footprints of a Dream*, 66.

4. The Golden State Mutual Life Insurance Company, founded by William Nickerson, Jr., in 1925, was the largest black-owned life insurance company in the western United States.

✎ To GAIL HUDSON
26 JUNE 1952
[*SAN FRANCISCO, CALIF.*]

Thurman cautions a contributor to the Fellowship Church against involvement in the Civil Rights Congress, an organization closely allied with the American Communist Party. Despite some pressure from members of the congregation, Thurman was careful during his years at the Fellowship Church to keep the church free from any entanglements with the Communist Party.[1] Although he acknowledged that the Civil Rights Congress's "goals are those towards which my own beliefs operate," he was reluctant to have connections to the organization, choosing to associate only with organizations in which he had "abiding confidence."

Mrs. Gail Hudson
Box 56—Murray Hill Station
New York 16, N.Y.

Dear Friend:

I am sending a line to you just before I leave town for a two or three weeks' vacation.

I do not know very much about the Civil Rights Congress.[2] I have not been identified with it myself. The general impression is, in various parts of the country, that it is some kind of "front" organization. What the facts are I do not know, nor have I had time to look into them. My own theory is that the channels through which I work must be channels in which I have abiding confidence. I do not work through a channel merely because its goals are those towards which my own beliefs operate. If I select the channel through which to work, then I seek to satisfy the demands of my own mind about what its purposes, its methods, its supports are.

If there is any question in your mind about the Civil Rights Congress, I would deal with the matter merely by letting my energies be used in some organization about which I do not have any fundamental reservations.

Thank you for the dollar and it goes into the kitty for the church. You will enjoy receiving one of the souvenir programs of the Arts Festival. I wish you could have been here.
Sincerely yours,
Howard Thurman

HT:r
Sent separately—Arts Festival Program

TLc.

NOTES
1. There were aspects of the American Communist Party that Thurman admired, such as its courage in supporting civil rights efforts in the South. He also admired the official Soviet constitutional ban on racism, anti-Semitism, and all forms of ethnic discrimination. See "USSR Constitution: no form of discrimination on the basis of race or nationality. Any person who shows prejudice (hatred) will be punished by the state," Thurman's handwritten notes in "The Protestant Dilemma Concerning Race," October 1947. Thurman was not alone among educated, non-Communist African Americans of his time in giving these provisions far more credence and credit than they deserved, an attitude that is perhaps understandable given the utter lack of any similar statutory or constitutional language in U.S. federal law. For another example, see a letter from Thurman's protégé Melvin H. Watson: Watson to Martin Luther King, Jr. [14 August 1952], in Clayborne Carson, ed., *The Papers of Martin Luther King, Jr.*, vol. 1: *Called to Serve, January 1929–June 1951* (Berkeley: University of California Press, 1992), 156–57. However, in practical matters Thurman tried to keep the church from involvement with Communist-backed organizations, such as the California Labor School (*WHAH*, 145). Thurman was worried about the frequent talk about the presence of FBI agents in the church and did not want to give them a pretext for investigating the church further (From Robert Meyners, 9 April 1948; HT to Marion and Gilbert Banfield, 3 August 1948). In one of his infrequent discussions of communism, Thurman told the Fellowship Church in a 1948 sermon that "any public statement about the Communist development at once classes the individual as either a baiter of that which is Red or a believer of that which is Red, so that we find our tongues tied" ("Modern Challenges to Religion: Secular Radicalism," 7 November 1948). In the end, Thurman was neither pro-Communist nor anti-Communist but an interested, skeptical observer.
2. The Civil Rights Congress (CRC) was formed in 1946 by the merger of the International Labor Defense and the National Federation for Constitutional Liberties. The National Negro Congress merged into the CRC the following year. All three organizations had ties to the American Communist Party. The CRC led several well-publicized campaigns against egregious cases of unjust incarceration of blacks and is probably best remembered for its 1951 petition to the United Nations, "We Charge Genocide: The Crime of Government against the Negro People." In 1956, largely as a result of debilitating legal and tax bills brought about by determined government action against the organization, the CRC voted to dissolve. Throughout its history the CRC was led by the prominent African American Communist William Patterson (1891–1980), the husband of Sue Bailey Thurman's close friend Louise Thompson Patterson (1901–99). See Gerald Horne, *Communist Front? The Civil Rights Congress, 1946–1956* (Rutherford, N.J.: Fairleigh Dickinson University Press, 1988).

🐟 To WALTER G. MUELDER
1 AUGUST 1952
[*SAN FRANCISCO, CALIF.*]

Walter G. Muelder,[1] dean of the Boston University School of Theology, wrote to Thurman on 25 July 1952 requesting that Thurman speak at a conference on preaching. Muelder closed his letter with the following: "Have you given any thought to the possibility of return to academic life? Could I possibly interest you in considering a position here at Boston University School of Theology? I think you have a great deal to give to theological students in many ways. I shall be glad to write you more fully about this if you would care to consider it."[2] In his auto-biography Thurman writes that he "had declined" Muelder's proposal, although his initial response was hardly an outright rejection and might have spurred subsequent efforts on the part of Boston University to hire him.[3]

Dean Walter G. Muelder
School of Theology
Boston University
745 Commonwealth Avenue
Boston 15, Massachusetts

Dear Walter:

It was very wonderful to get your good letter under date of July 25.

Unfortunately, the dates of your Annual Conference on Preaching are impossible for me. I shall be coming to Wellesley for their religion emphasis lectures February 28 to March 3. I cannot come east earlier in February because of the limitations in my schedule. Perhaps, I could be with you on Friday, February 27, to do a chapel or the like. Would you be interested in that possibility?

I am deeply honored by your suggestion about the possibility of my joining your staff. That is all that I can say at this writing. You will be hearing from me a little later.

Thank you for your letter, and I look forward to seeing you.
Sincerely yours,
Howard Thurman
HT: r

TLc.

NOTES
1. Walter George Muelder (1907–2004), a native of Illinois, graduated from Knox College and earned an S.T.B. at Boston University School of Theology in 1930 and a Ph.D. at Boston University's Graduate School in 1933. After teaching at Berea College and the University of Southern California, he returned to the Boston University School of Theology in

1945 as dean and remained in that position until 1972 and on the faculty until 1993. He was active in the postwar ecumenical movement and served as chairman of the Commission of Institutions of the World Council of Churches from 1955 to 1961 and chairman of the board of the Ecumenical Institute of the World Council of Churches in Bossey, Switzerland, from 1961 to 1968. His books include *Religion and Economic Responsibility* (New York: Scribner, 1959); *Foundations of a Responsible Society* (New York: Abingdon, 1959); and *Moral Law in Christian Social Ethics* (Lewiston, N.Y.: Edwin Mellen, 1966).

2. From Walter G. Muelder, 25 July 1952.

3. *WHAH*, 166. If there is a further response by Thurman to Muelder's suggestion, it is not extant.

ᴥᴥ To Harold C. Case
20 December 1952
[*San Francisco, Calif.*]

When Thurman turned down Dean Walter Muelder's August 1952 suggestion that he consider joining the faculty of the Boston University School of Theology, his resolve was evidently quite firm, as he told someone who inquired about his interest in a pastorate in Chicago in October that "my commitment and satisfaction in the work here are of such that I would have no interest in considering any change."[1] But when the effort to bring Thurman to Boston University was taken up by its president, Harold Case[2] (evidently in a December phone conversation), Thurman sensed that the proposal "would be very different,"[3] probably because it involved not merely joining the faculty but also having the opportunity, as dean of the chapel, to create a new religious community.

Dr. Harold J. Case, President
Boston University
Boston, Massachusetts

Dear Dr. Case:

I have delayed confirming the possibility of our getting together for a conference in early January when you will be on the Coast, because of the complications in my own schedule.

The most practical thing for me is to meet you in Los Angeles Friday evening, January 9. I could come down on the Friday morning "Daylight."[4] If this fits in to your schedule, please advise me and state also where I may meet you.

The plan which you sketched in broad outline on the telephone is significantly challenging to me. It seems to be another dimension of the direction along which I have been working at Fellowship Church from its beginning. It is very stirring to think that any academic institution that is church related would be daring enough to move experimentally in the direction of a religious concept that is capable of floating the demands of the human spirit for a one-world community.

The crucial problem for me is the commitment which I have to develop this unique church in an environment that is not under control and to the hundreds of little people scattered all over the United States, whose hopes have been revived because of our survival up to this time. Even though I do not see at the moment any light, I am willing to discuss the whole matter with you. You can understand how impossible it is for me to make a commitment of any kind at this stage.

It would be good to see you.

Sincerely,

Howard Thurman

HT: r

TLc.

NOTES

1. To Neil House, 21 October 1952.

2. Harold C. Case (1903–72)—the middle initial used by Thurman is incorrect—was a native of Cottonwood Falls, Kansas. He graduated from Baker University in Baldwin City, Kansas, in 1923 and from the Boston University School of Theology in 1927. After serving in Methodist pastorates in Glencoe, Illinois; Topeka, Kansas; Scranton, Pennsylvania; and Pasadena, California, in 1951 he was named president of Boston University. Case served as president until 1967, overseeing a period of extensive building and expansion for the university. After his retirement he spent a year as acting president of Whittier College.

3. WHAH, 166.

4. The "Coast Daylight" ran on the Southern Pacific Railroad.

🪡 To Gene K. Walker

8 January 1953

[Boston, Mass.]

Thurman, writing a testimonial statement he probably intended to be read at a forthcoming San Francisco convocation of the United Negro College Fund, offers one of his most succinct defenses of the continued need for historically black colleges despite his abhorrence of all racially separate institutions. Presciently he looks to the likely difficulties that unfunded black colleges would face in a system of higher education without racial barriers.

Mr. Gene K. Walker[1]

Master of Ceremonies

Convocation, United Negro College Fund

Fairmont Hotel

San Francisco, California

Dear Mr. Walker:

I regret very much that it is not possible for me to be present to share in the welcome of the citizens of San Francisco to the presidents of the colleges represented by the United Negro College Fund.[2] The plans for the convocation were so late in maturing that it was impossible for me to re-arrange my own scheduled responsibilities so as to be present.

It is my considered judgment that the Fund is worthy of support on the part of our community despite the fact that all of the colleges are the product of the system of segregation by which our Democracy is disgraced. This is true also of all of the white colleges in the section of the country in which chattel slavery obtained. The fact of legal segregation in this area creates a real dilemma, particularly for Negroes. Either they must provide separate education or go without the benefits of higher education.

The colleges in the Fund are the product of one solution of the dilemma. When they are supported, it does not mean that segregation is endorsed but it does mean that a compromise is seized upon which will give to the least privileged members of the society the opportunities of higher education. Vast social forces are in operation today which will result in the eradication of segregation even in that section of the country. If these colleges are made strong and stable, they will be able to function in a non-segregated society as useful institutions of learning for all peoples. To stabilize them now is to anticipate this function in the future.

It would be very tragic if we were shortsighted enough in America to support white private institutions in the South on the theory that they are not segregated. At the moment, both institutions are segregated, but if only the white institutions are stabilized and made secure by private funds, they, and they alone, will be ready to function in a non-segregated society when the time arrives. This would mean that all of the wisdom and the strength that have made dynamic survival possible for Negro institutions in the South would be lost when the society emerges out of its present social illness.

You will pardon me for taking so much of your time to make this statement, but I feel that it is very important that my position with reference to this issue be set forth.

My best to you for a good meeting.

Sincerely,

Howard Thurman
HT:r

TLc.

NOTES

1. Gene K. Walker was chairman of the board of the Fellowship Church and a good friend of Thurman. It is likely that this letter was read in public, which probably accounts for the formality of the salutation.

2. The United Negro College Fund was founded in 1944, with Tuskegee Institute president Frederick Douglass Patterson (1901–88) as its first president, for the purpose of

streamlining and coordinating fund-raising among private historically black colleges and universities. Initially there were twenty-seven participating colleges.

🍂 From Walter G. Muelder
16 January 1953
Boston, Mass.

Dean Muelder outlines many possibilities that would be open to Thurman at Boston University.

Dr. Howard Thurman
Fellowship Church
2041 Larkin Street
San Francisco 9, California

Dear Howard:

President Case has written me of his very fine conference recently with you regarding the possibility of your coming to Boston University with a relationship both to the Marsh Chapel and to the faculty of the School of Theology. I am glad that you are finding it possible to give this serious consideration. I should like from my angle to say a few things about the situation in Boston University at this time.

You know, of course, how much it would mean to me personally if you should find it possible to come. But the more important points are the whole challenge of the opportunities which are made possible in the way of creative religious activities and the unlimited social responsibilities confronting our kind of University at this particular junction in history. With Harold Case at the helm Religion has an opportunity in Higher Education unequalled, I think, anywhere else.

The University as a whole draws students from Greater Boston and New England in large numbers. More national and international in their drawing power are Sargent College of Physical Education and the Medical School and the School of Theology. We have had fine cooperation from the Director of the Newman Clubs, Father O'Connor.[1] Rabbi Perlman[2] has just come to lead the Hillel Foundation, which is in the process of building a structure immediately adjacent to the President's House. Dr. Franklin H. Littell,[3] as Dean of the Marsh Chapel, has been the general administrative officer and been more specifically responsible for the work in the Protestant Clubs and the Christian Association. Last year before Dean Littell came we asked Rabbi Freedman[4] to be Acting University Chaplain for a period of months. This action will indicate more than many pages can the inclusive community philosophy of our whole present effort. Rabbi Abraham

Klausner[5] teaches in the School of Theology in the second semester. Before him we had the part-time services on a fairly regular basis of Rabbi Liebman.[6]

Last spring at the Founders' Day Exercises the University featured a "Brotherhood In Action" program which has led to the establishment of a Human Relations Center in the University. An Executive Director[7] has been appointed and the actual functioning of the Center is soon to be finally announced. It is my privilege to be one of the members of the Board of Governors of that Human Relations Center. This Center will, of course, relate to all the activities of the University which make for deeper understanding and interpersonal participation across all group lines, but it will also assist in relating the University more adequately to the Boston community as a whole.

I should also like to speak of the University's new step in announcing an African Area Studies Program. The Director of this Program, who has been the Chief Advisor of the State Department for Africa, Mr. Brown,[8] will officially take up his duties on July first. He is currently making a survey of the African problems on a grant from the Ford Foundation. Within the year probably five of our Boston University faculty people in Social Science will be spending at least some period in Africa. The two Methodist Bishops who are responsible for the Southern half of that whole continent are alumni of the School of Theology.[9] As we plan our own faculty expansion in the field of Missions we are keeping in mind the University's broad anthropological and social interest in African Studies. Inasmuch as there are very few centers in the United States which have really become concerned in a big way with the problems of that great revolutionary area in the world we feel that an unusually challenging opportunity presents itself to us here. We do not yet know all the ways in which the School of Theology will in the future be related to these investigations, but it is obvious that Religion will play a very important part.

The School of Theology is itself in a great period. You know how delighted we will be for you to enrich our offerings in those areas in which you feel special interest. Our needs cover a wide range in our expanding curriculum and faculty program, including such areas as Homiletics, Philosophy of Literature, Creative Arts, Worship, Social Ethics, and the like. While I should hope that your coming to us would give enrichment in the field of Homiletics I should like to have you express to me the very special areas in which at the present time you have developed an interest. This fall we had a gross of 411 men[10] in the School of Theology. They create a tremendous demand in terms of curriculum enrichment, needs for spiritual disciplines, philosophical depth, and social responsibility. The opportunity to influence the whole Church is one of the things which is constantly an inspiration here to me. Our students come from more than 230 universities and colleges all over the United States and from 15 foreign countries. The effective outreach is really quite overwhelming.

Dr. Case tells me that you will be in New England at the end of February and the first few days in March. It would be quite exciting to confer with you at that time. We are looking forward to having you in Chapel on Friday, February 27th, at 10:30 a.m., as per our correspondence last summer.

Sincerely yours,

[*signed*] Walter G. Muelder

Walter G. Muelder, Dean.

WGM: DL

TLS.

NOTES

1. Norman James O'Connor (1921–2003), a native of Detroit, was ordained as a Paulist priest in 1948 and directed the Newman Center at Boston University from 1951 to 1961. He thereafter was radio and television director for the Paulist order in New York City and director of a drug and alcohol treatment center in Patterson, New Jersey. He was on the board of the original Newport Jazz Festival from its founding in 1954, and his lifelong and passionate involvement with jazz earned him the sobriquet "the jazz priest."

2. Rabbi Samuel Perlman (1905–76) was the author of "Guiding Youth Work and Citizenship: A Study of the National Youth Administration Centers in New Jersey" (Ph.D. diss., Columbia University, 1950) and *Students versus Parents: Problems and Conflicts* (Boston: H. A. Doyle, 1969).

3. Franklin Hamlin Litell (1917–2009), a native of Syracuse, New York, graduated from Cornell, Union Theological Seminary, and Yale, where he received his Ph.D. in 1946. After spending several years as Protestant adviser to the U.S. de-Nazification program in occupied Germany, he served a year as dean of the chapel at Boston University from 1952 to 1953. After leaving Boston University, he taught at many different academic institutions, including Temple University, Richard Stockton College of New Jersey, and Emory University, where in 1959 he taught what is believed to have been the first college course in the United States on the Holocaust. One of the pioneers of academic research into the Holocaust, he was the author of many books, among them *The Crucifixion of the Jews* (New York: Harper & Row, 1975).

4. Charles S. Freedman (1907–64) graduated from Columbia University in 1931 and the Jewish Institute of Religion in 1937. After service as a chaplain in World War II, he spent seven years as Hillel director at Boston University and thereafter led congregations in Bay Shore, New York; Niagara Falls, New York; and Westbury, New York.

5. Abraham J. Klausner (1915–2007), born in Memphis, graduated from Hebrew Union College and served as a chaplain in World War II. He was one of the first Jewish chaplains to enter the Dachau concentration camp, and he worked extensively with Holocaust survivors in displaced-person camps in occupied Germany. He wrote of his experiences in *A Letter to My Children: From the Edge of the Holocaust* (San Francisco: Holocaust Center of Northern California, 2002). He was rabbi for the Reform congregation Temple Emanu-el in Yonkers, New York, from 1954 to 1989.

6. Joshua Loth Liebman (1907–48) was raised in Hamilton, Ohio, and graduated from Hebrew Union College in 1930. He was rabbi of the Reform congregations KAM Temple in Chicago (1934–39) and Temple Israel in Boston (1939–48). His best-known book, *Peace of*

Mind (New York: Simon and Schuster, 1946), became a publishing phenomenon, spending over a year in the top position on the *New York Times* best-seller list. He died suddenly in 1948.

7. Kenneth Dean Benne (1908–92) was a philosopher and educational theorist who taught at Columbia University's Teachers College and the University of Illinois before in 1953 joining the faculty of Boston University, where he would remain until 1972. His publications include *A Conception of Authority: An Introductory Study* (New York: Columbia University Teachers College, 1943).

8. William O. Brown (1900–1968) was a native of Texas and earned a Ph.D. from the University of Chicago in 1930. After teaching in several universities, in 1943 he became chief of the African section of the Office of Strategic Services. He remained in government work until joining the faculty at Boston University, where he was director of the African Area Studies Program from 1953 until his retirement in 1966.

9. Newell S. Booth (1904–68), a graduate of Boston University and Hartford Seminary Foundation, spent several decades working in Africa. In 1944 he was elected as a bishop of the Methodist Episcopal Church with responsibility for Methodist activities in southern Africa and the Belgian Congo, headquartered in the city of Elisabethville (now Lubumbashi) in the Belgian Congo (now the Democratic Republic of the Congo). In 1964 he became bishop for the diocese of Harrisburg, Pennsylvania. He was the author of *The Cross over Africa* (New York: Friendship Press, 1945) and *This Is Africa South of the Sahara* (New York: Friendship Press, 1959). Willis J. King (1886–1976), a native of Texas, was a graduate of Wiley College and the Boston University School of Theology (S.T.B., 1913; Ph.D., 1921; D.D. [honorary degree], 1933). He taught at Gammon Theological Seminary from 1918 to 1930 and was its president from 1932 to 1944. He was also president of Samuel Huston College from 1930 to 1932. In 1944 the Central Jurisdiction of the Methodist Episcopal Church elected him bishop for Liberia, where he served from 1944 to 1956, after which he served in Louisiana and Texas until his retirement. He wrote *The Negro in America: An Elective Course for Young People on Christian Race Relations* (New York: Methodist Book Concern, 1926).

10. Despite Muelder's gendered language, the School of Theology was coeducational.

ᔥ From Harold C. Case
26 January 1953
Boston, Mass.

Dr. Howard Thurman
Fellowship Church
2041 Larkin Street
San Francisco 9, California

Harold Case writes Thurman a brief follow-up letter after their meeting in Los Angeles.

My dear Howard:

Thank you very much for the visit with you in Los Angeles and for the opportunity to discuss the plan for your leadership in religion in Boston University. It was a great pleasure to renew acquaintance and to discuss matters of such deep mutual interest.

I hope you are making progress in your thinking {about Boston University}. I have conferred with Dean Muelder, and we hope to have an opportunity for luncheon with you on Friday, February 27, after your address in the School of Theology Chapel. If you have any additional questions or ideas to put before me, please feel free to send them before that date. We are more anxious than ever to have you come to the faculty of the School of Theology and to the leadership of religion in the life of Boston University.

With very kind regards in which Phyllis[1] joins me, I am

Faithfully yours,

[signed] Harold

Harold C. Case, President

HCC: hs

TLS.

NOTE

1. Phyllis Kirk Case (1906–97) spent her early years in Baldwin, Kansas, where her father was president of Baker University. A graduate of Southwestern College in Winfield, Kansas, she married Harold Case (a graduate of Baker University) in 1927. She was active in many civic causes throughout her life, and during World War II during a preacher shortage she obtained a Methodist preaching license and became minister at Bradley Memorial Church in Scranton, Pennsylvania. She served on the boards of directors of the National Board of Churchwomen of America and the Japan International Christian University.

✒ To the Board of Trustees of Fellowship Church

31 JANUARY 1953

[SAN FRANCISCO, CALIF.]

In this memorandum to the board of trustees of the Fellowship Church, Thurman discusses Harold Case's offer to appoint him dean of the chapel of Boston University and the reasons for his potential interest in the position.

MEMORANDUM

TO: Board of Trustees

FROM: Howard Thurman

RE: Boston University

PART I

As the result of a long-distance telephone conversation with President Harold Case of Boston University, I had a conference with him at the Statler Hotel in Los Angeles Friday, January 9.

At this conference, President Case formally offered me the position of Dean of the Marsh Memorial Chapel, Minister of the Boston University Community Church[1] which I would have full responsibility in shaping the organization thereof, and a professorship in the School of Theology.

There are several considerations which he presented for my reflection:

1. I would be one of the nine administrative deans of the university.
2. As dean, I would be the university preacher, carrying responsibility for special services on various occasions in the life of the community, and with the assistance of a student-faculty commission provide weekday chapel services. In addition to these duties, I would serve as the coordinator of all religious affairs at the university, assisting the deans and student councils of the several colleges and schools in planning programs and assemblies of religious nature and be the adviser to numerous interfaith, interdenominational and denominational organizations on campus.
3. The general counseling in matters of religious needs would be shared with me by the Roman Catholic Chaplain and the Jewish Chaplain of the university.
4. As the result of what has been developed practically as a religious fellowship cutting across various lines in our church, President Case wants to project, through my leadership, the development of a community church at the university, membership of which would come from the university family and the community of Boston. This would be a non-creedal, non-sectarian, interracial, interfaith and intercultural religious fellowship.
5. In addition to the university choir with a full-time director, there would be at my disposal the resources of the Sargent School of the Dance, the School of Theology, the Fine Arts and Drama Department and any other facilities in the total university life.
6. The enrollment at Boston University, as of March 15, 1952, showed a net total of 18,161 men and 11,472 women, making a grand number of 29,633. In the School of Theology, as of the fall of 1952, there were 411 men coming from more than 230 universities and colleges in the United States, and from 15 foreign countries.
7. Last Founders Day, the university introduced a Brotherhood in Action program, culminating in the establishment of a Human Relations Center. This center will relate to all the activities of the university which make for deeper understanding and interpersonal participation across all group lines.
8. On July 1, a Mr. Brown, who has been Chief Adviser of the State Department for Africa, will become the head of the newly developed African Area Studies program.

PART II

1. President Case recognized in his discussion with me the wisdom and the necessity for my maintaining some kind of continuing relationship with Fellowship Church. He had no detailed suggestion to make except to express a willingness to confer with any representatives of the church for the consideration of plans and/or proposals for the continuation of the tremendous undertaking which has taken root in this place.

2. On Saturday, February 28, when I am at Wellesley for the Religious Forum lectures, I shall spend most of the day visiting the campus and talking with the President and the Dean of Theology and various other people. I did not want to do this without having the Board share with me the fateful decision which some time between now and the middle of the summer I shall be called upon to make.

3. I may add that of the various opportunities that have come to me during the past eight and one-half years, this is the first one to which I have given any serious consideration. And for the following reasons:

a. To develop a church somewhat like this in a university community is to touch at every step of the way hundreds of young people who themselves will be going to the ends of the earth to take up their responsibilities as members of communities. Conceivably, this means the widest possible dissemination of the ideas in which I believe, in the very nature of the operation itself.

b. The fact that one of America's great universities takes the completely unprecedented step in American education to invite a Negro to become one of its administrative deans, on behalf of a development in religious meaning and experience, in itself makes a limitless contribution to intergroup relations at this fateful moment in the history of America and the world.

c. At the moment, and I emphasize the words at the moment, it seems to be in line with the vision which first sent me forth from Howard University to live and work in the church here.

d. I am 52 years old, which means that according to the classical American timetable, I have 13 years of active work. This gives me no sense of urgency but it does point up the fact that if my life is to be spent to the fullest advantage on behalf of what seems to me to be the great hope for mankind, it is important to work on its behalf where there is the maximum possibility of contagion.

4. I would like it clearly understood that I have made no decision nor have I made any commitment of any kind with reference to this matter. I present it to you primarily for your information and if you have any discussion that may be suggestive to me as I come to rest in a decision, as my friends

and colleagues committed to the same adventure, I would want you to share it.

I would appreciate it if this memorandum which I am reading to you be regarded as confidential matter for the Board.

I shall share with you the results of my discussion in Boston when I return from Wellesley.

HT:r

TLc.

Note
    1. This probably was the prospective name of the religious fellowship that Case encouraged Thurman to form at Boston University; there is no evidence that it was ever organized under this title.

✎ To Harold C. Case
6 February 1953
[*San Francisco, Calif.*]

Thurman writes to Case that he is continuing to mull over the offer from Boston University and that he has informed the board of the Fellowship Church about the possibility of his leaving.

President Harold C. Case
Boston University
755 Commonwealth Avenue
Boston 15, Massachusetts

Dear Harold:
    Last Monday night, I discussed the possibility of my coming to Boston with the Board of the church. It was an exploratory conversation because I wanted them to know that I was giving careful and prayerful consideration to the tremendous opportunity which your invitation opens up for the things to which we are committed.
    We are in the midst of plans for the tenth anniversary of the church, which is October, 1954. I am working on a manuscript covering the history of the organization and development of this church, which manuscript I have promised to deliver to Harpers some time before the end of the year.[1]
    I have written Walter to see if we cannot have lunch together on Saturday, February 28, because it will not be possible for me to speak in chapel on Friday, the 27th. Thursday and Friday of that week I shall be working in Washington,

D.C. with the Unitarian Commission on the integration of non-Caucasians into the functioning membership of the socalled liberal churches. I am one of the two non-Unitarians on the commission of five. Would it be possible for you to have lunch with us on Saturday? I shall have the afternoon free until about 4:00 o'clock when I go out to Wellesley.

It was wonderful to see you and Phyllis and to have had the privilege of sharing somewhat in your enthusiasm for the tremendous work in which you are engaged.

With every good wish.

Sincerely,

Howard Thurman

HT: r

TLc.

NOTE
1. This would eventually be published as HT, *Footprints of a Dream* (1959).

➤ To HAROLD C. CASE
7 MARCH 1953
[*SAN FRANCISCO, CALIF.*]

Thurman met with Boston University president Harold Case and School of Theology dean Walter Muelder to discuss the dean of the chapel position at Boston University on Saturday, 28 February, in Boston. After several speaking engagements in the East, he returned to San Francisco on Friday, 6 March. Having spent much of the long train trip home "meditating" on the offer, he tells Harold Case that his "inclination" is to "consider your invitation favorably." Although he wanted clarification on the issue raised in this letter—and some of the matters raised in the letter would bedevil him throughout the Boston University years— he had already made his decision. Before receiving a response just two days later, he wrote to the members of the Fellowship Church asking for a leave of absence.

President Harold C. Case
Boston University
755 Commonwealth Avenue
Boston 15, Massachusetts

Dear Harold:

It was very good to see you on Saturday and to have the opportunity of thinking aloud with you and Walter about our common dream.

My inclination, after spending much time on the train meditating upon it, is to consider your invitation favorably. In order for me to get a more accurate picture of what is involved, I would like to raise the following questions from notes which I made on the train yesterday at the end of my meditation:

1. What is the budget of the chapel, how is it determined and from what sources does it come—general funds or special funds of the university? What share of the budget must come from chapel offerings, if any? Once the budget is adopted, whose authority is it to certify expenditures from it? Is the salary of the dean included in the chapel budget and/or what part of the salary is paid by the School of Theology, inasmuch as he is a member also of the faculty of the school?

2. Precisely, what is the relation of the Dean of the Chapel to the School of Theology? I raise this question because the School of Theology is directly related by tradition and financial support to the Methodist Church. The general impression is, as far as I have been able to ascertain it, that the university chapel is a part of the same arrangement. You can appreciate how important it is that the proposed church, sponsored by the chapel, should not be regarded as a Methodist church.

3. Am I right in assuming that the pulpit is free, the assumption being that the preacher is thoughtful and committed but that no limitations are placed upon the range of his thinking so long as sensitive courtesies and reverences are maintained.

4. What would be the technical steps involved in organizing a church in the chapel? I am thinking here of the channels through which the proposals would move before the authority is granted. Would the line of responsibility move from the minister and the board of the church directly to you as the representative of the trustees of the university, or would they move from the minister and the board through the faculty of the School of Theology to you? I am trying to see where the lines of authority are and where they rest finally.

5. Does the dean inherit a secretary or does he name his own? Is the secretary's salary scale fixed by university policy or is it determined by the Dean of the Chapel? I assume that such a salary is included in the budget of the chapel. Are there regularly assigned student assistants from the School of Theology who work with the chapel?

6. Is there a Sunday chapel bulletin? If so, is it mimeographed or printed now?

7. Does the chapel equipment include a good tape recorder? In the event that I come, such a machine is a necessity for me because I do not preach from notes or manuscript and a recording device is essential. If there are no provisions made for such, I would have to make my own arrangements.

8. How flexible would the arrangement be as far as outside preaching is concerned? I would want to do at least three-fourths of the preaching on Sunday for very obvious reasons, certainly at the beginning. For many years now, I have preached and lectured at a large number of institutions in the United States and Canada and would want to maintain some of these services. My schedule for next January, for instance, includes Harvard, Wesleyan, Choate, Andover, with the possibility of the University of Chicago, The Chicago Sunday Evening Club, Sweetbriar and Hollins Colleges in Virginia. These are all blanketed on one trip east. I am sure that arrangements could be worked out to spread them through the entire year. In September, I am scheduled to do the lectures on preaching for Dick Raines[1] at Purdue University. I recognize that details of this sort can be worked out but I am concerned about the principle of flexibility and its limitations.

9. What is the salary that goes with the position? What is the nature of the deductions, other than Federal Income Tax; what are the tenure arrangements? Would I come for a specified period, subject to joint review and consideration at the end of that time, or what?

The problems of the transfer of direct leadership from my shoulders to someone else here at the church are very difficult. Somehow, I must enlist the moral support and the enthusiasm of the congregation for this venture in which, through me, they would share. I have given nine of very productive years to the launching of this church. Into it has gone the kind of sustained work unlike anything I have ever given to any commitment. This church is as much of my life as any dream or its projection could possibly be. There must be, for me as for them, a clearly defined tie between 2041 Larkin Street and Marsh Chapel in Boston. How to do this will take all of the help that your own wisdom and spiritual sensitiveness can share.

After I hear from you, I will then present the matter here. When that is cleared, we will be in a position to make whatever formal announcements are in order. I want you to know, Harold, that if, with God's help, the launching of our work in Boston can be seen as the next step in the process which was undertaken here nine years ago, all the bells will ring and the sons of God will shout for joy.

This is a long letter but it is as short as I could make it.

Remember me to Phyllis.

Sincerely,

Howard Thurman

HT: r

TLc.

NOTE

1. Richard C. Raines (1889–1981), a graduate of Cornell College in Iowa and the Boston University School of Theology, was a Methodist minister in Scituate, Massachusetts; Providence, Rhode Island; and Minneapolis, Minnesota. In 1948 he was elected as a bishop of the United Methodist Church, and he headed the Indiana Conference of the church from 1948 to 1968. He also served as president of the Board of Missions and the Council of Bishops.

✒ TO THE BOARD OF TRUSTEES AND MEMBERS OF THE FELLOWSHIP CHURCH
9 MARCH 1953
[SAN FRANCISCO, CALIF.]

In this letter to the members of the Fellowship Church, Thurman indicates that he has in principle accepted the position at Boston University and requests a leave of absence from the church.

To: Board of Trustees and
        Members of the Church for the Fellowship of All Peoples
From: Howard Thurman

A few weeks ago, I presented to the Board a memorandum to the effect that I had been invited to the position of Dean of the Chapel of Boston University.[1] This request came as a result of Boston University's desire to pioneer in the field of religion and education by establishing a program for its new gothic chapel that will cut across all lines of separateness and weld university and community together in organized religious worship.

The program which we have been able to develop at Fellowship Church in the last few years was a decisive factor in the university's decision to undertake a broader but similar program in the city of Boston.

In the light of my own religious commitment, I feel compelled to give this invitation favorable consideration. The university has a student body of some 26,000, with 16 colleges in the system, including a School of Theology with 411 students from more than 200 American colleges and 15 foreign countries.

We have been distressed, all of us in Fellowship Church, that the young theologians coming out of the seminaries today have no special training in developing churches that can break through the intercultural-interracial barriers in religion. The opportunity to "pastor" the university, to take leadership in developing a church there and, at the same time, to offer courses in the School of Theology, is the most crucial challenge inherent in this invitation.

I am convinced, also, that the close relationship between our program here and the one to be developed there should make all of us feel a direct and personal connection with this larger projection of the Fellowship Dream. Whether or not the foundation of the creative adventure which we are, has been securely laid, will be determined by the way in which we rise to meet this new challenge which is presented to us.

In the light of these convictions, I am requesting that the church grant me a leave of absence, beginning August 1, 1953, that I may spend the necessary time helping Boston University develop a strategic blueprint for this most extraordinary venture that has taken place in American university life.

It would be my plan to return to San Francisco during the summer months, sharing in the work of the church in any ways that seemed useful and also to maintain as much contact with the development here as would be conducive to growth and responsibility. I would like it clearly understood that San Francisco is home, and the church, into which nine crucial years have been put, must continue to be a part of whatever I may undertake in the future.

In a few days, the Chairman of the Board will call a meeting of the congregation for the purpose of making plans that will guide us in the adjustment necessary to deal effectively with this new challenge. You will give this your best thought and personal prayers that the thing that is done may be as God wills it.

HT: r

TLc.

NOTE

1. To the Board of Trustees of Fellowship Church, 31 January 1953, printed in the current volume.

To Coleman Jennings
11 MARCH 1953
[SAN FRANCISCO, CALIF.]

Thurman tells his good friend Coleman Jennings[1] that though he has not given his formal assent, he has already made up his mind to go to Boston, despite the "emotional lacerations" the decision is causing. In his response Jennings wrote, "Here I am, at your side, identifying myself with another momentous made decision in your life. Knowing the processes through which it was reached, the weighing, the dissecting, the prayer, I know that it was RIGHT." He added, "But that does not remove the pain. I have a full realization of what that will be, the pathetic look from the eyes of those who will have to face life without you, the haunting questions of how your years of work will stand up in your absence."[2]

Mr. Coleman Jennings
The Anchorage
1900 Que Street
Washington 6, D.C.

Dear Coleman:

It is good to know that you are on the same planet where I am.

I have made up my mind that I must go to Boston. The opportunity to develop in that center a church along the lines of our church here is a challenge which, in the light of my commitment, leaves me no alternative. This city and 2660 California Street will remain my home and Fellowship Church will remain my church, and I will regard myself as its minister-at-large, taking on an outpost assignment for a limited time. I have not given my final word to the university but I have asked the congregation here for a leave of absence to do this job.

You can imagine the emotional lacerations that are involved in arriving at this decision. I am in the curiously torturous position of feeling the hand of God on my shoulder while, at the same time, much of me is in rebellion against the insistence. I am sure that between now and the end of the summer all of me will be reconciled to what I must do. In your quiet time, I hope you will remember me.

I am excited about the new Growing Edge and I hope you like the way your article was done.[3]

The love of the family is yours.

Sincerely,

Howard Thurman

HT: r

TLc.

NOTES

1. Coleman Jennings (1890–1978) was born in Johannesburg, Transvaal Republic (Zud-Afrikaansche Republiek; now in the Republic of South Africa), where his father was a successful mining engineer. He moved to Washington, D.C., with his family and lived there for the remainder of his life. A graduate of Harvard College, he worked as an investment banker before retiring in 1928, thereafter making a reputation as a philanthropist and prominent Episcopal layperson. He was a member of the chapter (similar to a board of trustees) for Washington Cathedral. He became a devoted friend of the Thurmans during their time at Howard University and sponsored their farewell dinner when they moved to San Francisco. See "Testimonial dinner for Howard Thurman, 30 May 1944" (photograph), *PHWT*, 3:59; and To Alfred G. Fisk, 19 May 1944, printed in ibid., 65. Jennings and Thurman would stay good friends and frequent correspondents for the remainder of their days. Jennings usually spent his summers in Edinburgh, and in 1957 and 1960 the Thurmans

spent most of their summer in Scotland as his guest. See To Friends of the International Fellowship Committee, 15 August 1960, printed in the current volume.

    2. From Coleman Jennings, 16 March 1953.

    3. Coleman Jennings, "'A Growing Edge'—in Scotland," *The Growing Edge* 5, no. 1 (Winter 1952–53): 1–8.

༞ From Joseph Van Pelt
12 March 1953
[*San Francisco, Calif.*]

There was a wide range of responses to the news of Thurman's departure from the Fellowship Church. Some active church members, such as Joseph Van Pelt, who had been a member of the Fellowship Quintet[1] when it traveled and performed at UNESCO in Paris in 1949, were deeply disappointed and angered by Thurman's decision. Van Pelt's anger at Thurman would subside, however. In 1960, when Van Pelt was living in Japan, he was excited by the news that Thurman was coming for a visit and offered to meet his ship, writing "we are so eager to see you."[2]

Dear Dr. Thurman,

    Although I should be contemplating the ways and means of repairing the damage instead of bemoaning our lot, I feel that too few of us in Fellowship Church have expressed our true feelings regarding your leaving, Dr. Thurman.

    Naturally, your decision is made, and anything I say can only add a heavier burden to your already overloaded mind, but at the same time, I must live with my conscience, and I do not wish to add hypocrisy to my other mortal sins by wishing you God-speed in your new venture.

    Personally, I feel tremendously let down by your leaving, and keep asking myself if it would have made any difference had the progress of Fellowship Church been more rapid and dramatic, but I think not.

    For almost six years I have been listening to Reverend Thurman on Sundays, without ever realizing that Howard Thurman the man might not be the same person. Of course, that was my error, not yours, and I do not regret my mistake. It's just that in my mind, I can't reconcile the two.

    Perhaps if I had known Howard Thurman the man better, I wouldn't feel so let down, but you see, Dr. Thurman, I have used you as the very cornerstone of my faith, and now I must clear the debris and start again.

    May God forgive me if I am doing you an injustice.

Sincerely,

[*signed*] Joseph Van Pelt

                                                                    ALS.

NOTES
1. For the Fellowship Quintet, see To Friend [January 1950], printed in the current volume.
2. From Joseph Van Pelt, 18 February 1960.

❧ To ARTHUR U. CROSBY
21 MARCH 1953
[*SAN FRANCISCO, CALIF.*]

Thurman writes to a friend, Philadelphia business executive Arthur U. Crosby,[1] about another reason contributing to his decision to leave the Fellowship Church: his conviction that the church needs "to find its own feet," something it could not do while he remained in its pulpit.

Mr. Arthur U. Crosby
12 South 12th Street
Philadelphia 7, Pennsylvania

Dear Art:
I have made my decision to go to Boston on a leave of absence from the church. After a series of various kinds of meetings, we are all slowly becoming reconciled to the fact that one of the surest ways for the church to find its own feet is for me to be out of the picture for a while. At the end of a year at Boston, I will be in the position to have some idea about the possibilities of that situation as an extension of this dream, and the university will have some idea about me; also, there will be rather strong indications of the stamina or lack of stamina of the church.
I had a long talk with Ted Ferris,[2] who was very helpful and suggestive. He pointed out several of the problems that are unique in some ways there but was as enthusiastic as an Episcopal clergyman can be, I suppose.
Thank you very much, Art, for the work on the manuscript which you made possible. I sent the typist a check last week. The manuscript should leave the end of the week for Harper's, and I shall be greatly relieved.[3]
It does not seem likely that I shall be coming as far east as Philadelphia when I am in Des Moines during Holy Week.
Everything else here seems to be moving along with its usual ups and downs. I hope all goes well with you.
Sincerely,
Howard Thurman
HT:r

TLc.

NOTES

1. Arthur U. Crosby, a 1917 graduate of Yale and a decorated veteran of World War I, was a Philadelphia-area businessman, a longtime friend of Thurman, and a supporter of the Fellowship Church.

2. Possibly Theodore Parker Ferris (1908–72), pastor of Emmanuel Church (1937–42) in Baltimore and Trinity Church (1942–72) in Boston.

3. Probably *Meditations of the Heart*.

✌➣ From Jannette E. Newhall
23 March 1953
Boston, Mass.

Edgar S. Brightman (1884–1953), who passed away on 26 February 1953, had been a friend and acquaintance of Thurman for many years and in 1946 had become a national member of the Fellowship Church, calling it "one of the most important projects in American religion."[1] Jannette Newhall[2] was Brightman's colleague at the Boston University School of Theology.

Dear Howard,

It is a matter of great personal satisfaction to know that you have accepted the invitation to come to Boston University. There are great opportunities and great needs here. You will bring us much that we need.

I well remember your Ingersoll Lecture[3] and also the photographers afterwards taking pictures of you and Dr. Brightman and some of the rest of us. Dr. Brightman knew of the hopes for your coming and was very happy over the idea. I wish he might have lived to greet you and give you his sturdy support. These last weeks since his death have been difficult ones for me since I have been practically a member of the family for thirty years. I have been rereading your Deep is the Hunger and have found much in it to "speak to my condition." In warm friendship,

[*signed*] Jannette (E. Newhall)

TLS.

NOTES

1. From Edgar S. Brightman, 9 October 1946. Before his death Brightman was the primary dissertation adviser of Martin Luther King, Jr.

2. Jannette Elthina Newhall (1898–1979) received her Ph.D. in religion from Boston University in 1931 and taught at several colleges and seminaries before becoming librarian and professor of research methods in 1949 at the Boston University School of Theology, where she remained until her retirement in1964. She was the author of several books, including *A Theological Library Manual* (London: Theological Education Fund, 1970). She was president of the American Theological Library Association from 1948 to 1950.

3. Published as *The Negro Spiritual Speaks of Life and Death* (New York: Harper & Brothers, 1948).

᠅ To A. J. Muste
18 April 1953
San Francisco, Calif.

With this letter Thurman severs his connection to the leadership of the Fellowship of Reconciliation, ending three decades of close involvement in the Christian pacifist organization.[1] *He continued to remain active in causes associated with world peace and disarmament.*[2]

Mr. A. J. Muste
Fellowship of Reconciliation
21 Audubon Avenue
New York 32, N.Y.

Dear A. J.:
This is a letter formally to offer my resignation as a member of the National Council of the FOR.

For a long time, I have been deeply embarrassed by the fact that the peace witness which my kind of work and life give does not make it easy for me to participate actively in the work of the FOR. I think, therefore, that someone should take my place on the Council who can be of significant service specifically to the Council.

This letter of resignation must not indicate to you any relaxation of my concern for peace in all of the dimensions to which the FOR is dedicated. It is the result of a deliberate and considered judgment on my part.

With every kind regard,
Sincerely yours,
[*signed*] Howard Thurman
Howard Thurman

TLS. JSP-SWA

Notes
1. Not all involvement with the FOR ended. See Thurman's account of the importance of the FOR in one of its publications, "[Untitled Testimonial for the Fellowship of Reconciliation]," 8 October 1957.

2. See "Letter in Support of United World Federalists" (1960) and "Two Options" (1961), both printed in the current volume.

🦋 From Cardella Clifton and Family
23 April 1953
San Francisco, Calif.

Like many other members of the Fellowship Church, Cardella Clifton[1] had mixed emotions about Thurman's decision to go to Boston; she was excited about the possibilities of the new position but saddened by the thought of his absence.

Rev. Howard Thurman
2660 California St
San Francisco, Calif.

Dear Dr. Thurman:
Congratulations to you in your new field and I pray Divine guidance that you may be able to carry on the great work.

We are very grateful to you and proud to have in our race such an able and capable man. We are happy to have had the association with you and learned the true way to worship and live with our fellow men.

In our house we feel that you were chosen as Moses to lead the people in this new era. As for Fellowship Church we will miss you but we feel that you will do a greater work; with the youth coming out of Boston University it will establish that fellowship all over the world.

Please do not forget us (my family) and if you and my cousin Sue want to steal away to relax quietly my door stands ajar, the latch is on the outside make our home your home at any time. My one request is—if you are near when I "pass on" will you please take charge.

May God bless and sustain you and your family and remember we are your friends.
Yours for a greater fellowship,
[*signed*] Cardella Clifton & Family

TLS.

Note
1. Cardella Clifton (1894–1974) lived in San Francisco.

🦋 To the Board of Trustees of Fellowship Church
19 May 1953
[*San Francisco, Calif.*]

In this memo to the board of trustees of the Fellowship Church, Thurman outlines his thoughts about the future of the church after his departure from San

Francisco. It is important, he believes, that the church find able black leadership after his departure, and one of his main concerns is the difficulty of recruiting an African American minister.

MEMORANDUM

TO: The Board of Trustees
FROM: Howard Thurman

In accordance with my promise at the time of the granting of the request for an indefinite leave of absence, I am herewith submitting a series of comprehensive suggestions concerning the immediate future of Fellowship Church.

1. In my conference with the Leadership Committee and subsequently in my letter to the congregation, I stated my interpretation of the significance of the leave of absence. The matter of how I would be related to Fellowship Church formally after August 1st is open and undecided. As long as I am on leave of absence, I am technically the minister of the church and it should be so listed. I have expressed my willingness to come back to the church next summer if in the program of the church there is a normal natural way in which my services may be useful. I do not want to be cut adrift from the church nor do I want the church to be cut adrift from me. It is my desire that as far as the philosophy and the overall resource responsibility which I feel for Fellowship Church are concerned, it be understood that I am always available to be used on behalf of our commitment.

   I would like it clearly understood that the church is under no obligation whatsoever to have me come back. Now, then and always, what is for the best interest of the church is my major concern. It is in full recognition of the meaning of this that I repeat now what I have said before—if in the judgment of the Board and the congregation the whole atmosphere is cleared by my changing my leave of absence into a resignation, this I am willing to do at any moment, now or a year from now. If it is best that I resign, then I would work on behalf of Fellowship Church and its ideal as a Member at Large, with the peculiar advantage of my historic connection with it. With the status of leave of absence, I would be regarded as a spiritual and psychological source, which would give to the congregation free access to whatever resources I have that would be useful to them in the on-the-spot fulfillment of the dream. Such an arrangement would relate the work of Boston University directly to Fellowship Church and vice versa. If the present status of the leave of absence is to remain, then I suggest that I be listed as Minister on Leave, with no technical or specifically advisory responsibility with reference to local problem, decision or program.

2. It is necessary that the program structure, the organizational machinery and the pastoral needs of the congregation be guaranteed in ways that will assure morale, efficiency and growth. This means that after August 1st when technically my formal responsibility ends as Resident Minister, someone step immediately into the leadership position of the congregation and its activities. I am, therefore, suggesting that Dr. Dryden Phelps[1] who is now functioning as Assistant Minister be given this responsibility until such time as the congregation is able to make a permanent arrangement— whether such a permanent arrangement involves Dr. Phelps or some other designated individual. I suggest Dr. Phelps for the following reasons: (a) He is intelligent; (b) he is religiously committed to the goals of the church; (c) he has a wide intercultural experience, background and history; (d) he knows how to give to the individual a feeling of being cared for, which makes him an excellent pastor of the flock; (e) he has a sense of worship and will move easily into our worship tradition; (f) he is civic-minded and will bring to the resident leadership of the church a fresh dimension of the moral responsibility of the church for the welfare of the community in which the church resides.

As you have already been informed, Dr. Phelps holds a Ph.D. degree from the University of California, a graduate degree in divinity from the Union Theological Seminary in New York City[2] and has had extensive training as a counselor. For 30 years he was a professor and Dean of the Chapel at Yenching University in China and is regarded as one of the American authorities not only on Chinese life and culture but also in Zen-Buddhism.

In the light of this suggestion, Dr. Phelps would enter into a new relationship with Fellowship Church when he returns from the Pendle Hill lectures about August 15. Such arrangements as necessary should be made with him before he leaves June 20.

3. Francis Geddes[3] as Assistant Minister was Director of the Intercultural Workshop for Children. Under ordinary circumstances Dr. Phelps, who has come in as Assistant Minister, would take over that responsibility but, due to the Pendle Hill lectures to which Dr. Phelps was committed more than a year ago, he will not be available to us from June 20 to August 15. I have therefore, after conferring with the Chairman of the Board, invited Dwight Harwell[4] to become director of the workshop and to serve as Assistant Minister for the rest of the summer until Dr. Phelps returns in mid-August.

The salary for Dwight should be that which Dr. Phelps would be receiving if he were here from June 20 to August 15. I am trying to raise from other sources some special compensation to him as director of the workshop. This is necessary, as I see it, because, beginning immediately, he will have to put in many hours in working with the Workshop Committee prior to the opening of the school in late June. When the workshop is over, Dwight would take over the full responsibility of Assistant Minister, which would include sharing in the worship service, giving leadership to any functioning groups that may need it, sick calling and as much counseling as his experience would indicate.

4. It seems to me to be important that at least for the next nine or ten months the congregation would not be under the necessity for making a quick or hasty choice of a resident minister. It is out of a consideration of that sort that I have made the above suggestion concerning Dr. Phelps as Resident Minister in charge of the religious life and nurture.

With this breather as far as the pulpit is concerned, several exciting possibilities emerge (these may be carried out without creating any new machinery):

a. We may have a series of guest ministers who would be chosen not as candidates for the pulpit but because of the unique contribution which their thinking would make to our growth, development and stimulation. We might decide on certain areas of religious thought and experience that we would like to explore under such an arrangement. Possibilities that occur to me immediately are: (1) world religions, (2) religious values and social change, (3) the bearing of religious experience on personal stability, (4) religion and personal and social convictions.

b. A regular preaching schedule for three months may be outlined somewhat as follows: Dr. Phelps, Dwight Harwell, Daniel Falcon,[5] and a person who conceivably might be regarded as a candidate.

c. We might experiment with an occasional Sunday service that would be radically different from the conventional service even for us. To illustrate: the Verse Speaking Choir of our church could take the entire period for the sermon in sharing with the congregation some of the great timeless poetic insights of world religions, or of Christianity. This would mean that we would be generating some measure of our own inspiration for deepening our morale; for morale is, in essence, a belief in one's own cause. We have experimented already with having the choral choir take a Sunday morning for great music. In other words, what I am trying to say is that with a little imagination, vision and courage we could involve ourselves in providing fresh opportunities for the visitation of the spirit of God in our midst, rather than sitting back depending upon some man to preach his heart out in an effort to provide openings in us for the visitation of the spirit of God.

If we were willing to experiment in these directions as outlined, or others that may occur to you, at the end of the year we would know so much more about ourselves, what deep down we want to have for the church, and would be in a favorable position for offering some kind of challenge to an able minister.

5. It is important that I share, almost as a supplement to the above suggestions what my experience has been in trying to secure an able minority person, primarily Negro, to consider coming out here as the leader of Fellowship Church. There are three men with whom I have made direct contact:

   a. Dr. Melvin Watson, whom many of you know. He is completely involved in a position in Georgia with tenure and rank. He is not interested in making a change.

   b. Dr. Richard I. McKinney, head of the Department of Philosophy, Morgan College. Dr. McKinney is interested but is unable to get even a temporary release from his college appointment without the necessity of resigning. On my own initiative, I have invited Dr. McKinney to come by San Francisco en route from Texas, where he will be teaching in summer school, to Wisconsin, where he will be lecturing during the last two weeks in August. In the event that he accepts the invitation, he would take the pulpit on the first Sunday in August and the congregation would have a chance to meet him and he to meet them, without any of the urgencies that would be present if either was called upon to make a decision immediately. Under no circumstances would he be available, if we wanted him, until twelve months from now.

   c. Reverend Maynard Catchings of Washington, D.C. was not available because he had just signed a three-year contract as a national secretary of the Student Division of the YMCA, with an office in New York City.

There are certain elementary considerations to which I feel honor bound to call your attention.

   a. We need not be surprised if we have special difficulties in finding an able Negro minister to share in our leadership. This will be due to at least one important factor: if he is able and mature enough to move into this kind of situation, he is already well established in some other position in which he feels that he is making a contribution as significant as this one. Therefore, we must be able to offer to him a challenge which can only come if we ourselves know what it is that we are about. He would want to know how do we conceive of our goals; to what extent are we willing to put ourselves at the disposal of these goals? He would have no interest in coming to be the minister of 375 people who were just interested in a church. If he is able and wanted a church, there would be at his disposal a large church with equipment and the kind of income that goes with it. It is for this reason that Fellowship Church needs the next twelve months to get itself defined so that it could be in a position to offer something challenging to a new minister.

b. Whatever decision we make about our future leader or leaders, the question has to be raised as to whether or not we are far enough along to run the risk of having less than two groups represented in our ministry. This poses the question of working out an organizational structure capable of handling a dual or triple ministry. Will there be a minister, Negro or white or what have you, with the other groups represented as associate minister? Or, will we try to define the responsibilities of a co-ministry; or, will we find the ablest man we can and let him work out the way in which ministers representing groups other than his should share in the leadership?

c. There are available very few men in the United States who are equipped emotionally and psychologically to be the leader of a congregation such as ours. In some ways despite the fabulous growth that has taken place in the church with reference to certain levels of integration, our church is the only one like it in the United States. A minister must learn how to minister to a congregation like ours. Therefore, in the final analysis, we may have the responsibility of taking unto ourselves one or two able young men, like Dwight, Dan Falcon, Francis Geddes, and develop them into the leaders of our congregation and the spearhead of the great dream to which we are committed.

Dwight Harwell at the end of the next academic year will receive his Master's Degree and his Graduate Divinity Degree from the Pacific School of Religion. He has served not only as a member of the Board of the church and its secretary but has been student assistant for the past two years. His denominational affiliation is Congregational.

Daniel Falcon, who was guest minister last Sunday, made a very positive impression on all who heard him. He is a graduate of the San Francisco Theological Seminary and is a candidate for the Ph.D. degree in religious counseling at the University of Southern California. At present he is serving as Protestant Chaplain at the large Los Angeles County Hospital. His denominational affiliation is Presbyterian.

We know about Francis Geddes.

How exciting a prospect to create in our own womb the redeemers of the dream! While we are doing that we may secure our position by having the lines held by certain old-timers for whom the sun is already on their backs.

                                                                    TLc.

Notes

1. Dryden Linsley Phelps (1892–1977), a graduate of Yale College and Yale Divinity School, was a military chaplain in World War I and received his doctorate in oriental languages from the University of California at Berkeley in 1929 for a dissertation on Zen Buddhism. He spent three decades teaching at West China Union University in Chengdu, Sichuan Provence, in Southwest China until the Communist Revolution. In a 1950 article that appeared in *Soviet Russia Today* (a missive intended as a private communication to a friend), Phelps said that the Chinese revolution of the previous year had been "the most dynamic change in human history" and that "God is working alongside these Communists," comments that led the State Department to confiscate his passport and that forced his resignation from the American Baptist Foreign Mission Society in early 1952. See "Red Letter Causes Missionary Recall," *New York Times,* 20 December 1950; "Accused Missionary Back," *New York Times,* 23 November 1951; "Missionary Quits: Lauded Red China," *New York Times,* 23 January 1952. He served two years as interim minister of the Fellowship Church and was the author of *Exploring the Mind of Jesus* (New York: Friendship Press, 1974) and the translator of several works from Chinese. He also translated several works into Chinese, including an edition of the poetry of Robert Browning. He was a nephew of the well-known literary critic William Lyon Phelps.

2. Thurman was mistaken about this.

3. Francis Geddes (b. 1923), a United Church of Christ minister, is a graduate of Stanford University and Yale Divinity School. He was an assistant minister at the Fellowship Church in the early 1950s and minister there from 1957 through 1964. He thereafter served a number of congregations in the Bay Area until his retirement in 1995. He is an expert in Christian healing, the subject of his 1981 D.Min. dissertation at the San Francisco Theological Seminary, "Healing Training in the Church."

4. Dwight Wesley Harwell (1926–72) was a native of Chicago and a graduate of the University of Illinois at Chicago. In 1948–49 he was the student president of the YMCA chapter at the University of California at Berkeley, the first African American to hold this position. He received his Ph.D. from Berkeley in 1953.

5. The Reverend Daniel Falcon was a Presbyterian minister of Mexican descent who worked in the San Francisco Bay Area.

🐦 To Benjamin E. Mays

21 September 1953

[*Boston, Mass.*]

On 15 September, Benjamin Mays wrote to Thurman suggesting that Charles M. Jones[1] *might be a good replacement for him at the Fellowship Church. Jones was a white Presbyterian minister in Chapel Hill who recently had been forced to resign his ministerial position because of his outspoken support for civil rights. Thurman appreciated the suggestion but replied that for the church to survive as an interracial institution, a "non-Caucasian" minister was necessary.*[2]

Dr. Benjamin E. Mays
Morehouse College
Atlanta, Georgia

Dear Bennie:

Thank you very much for your letter of greeting on the date of September 15. I am sending the copy of the letter which you mailed me to the Committee at Fellowship Church. I do not know what their plans will be at the end of this year. It is my judgment, however, that it is crucial that the minister should be a representative of one of the minorities in American life. We are not far enough out of the woods in our society for any considerable number of non-Caucasians to cast their lot with confidence in an enterprise led predominantly by a Caucasian. There may be holes in my thinking, but my remark comes out of ten years on the firing line. At any rate, there is no hurry.

Thank you for your letter.

Sincerely,

Howard Thurman

HT/ sh

TLc.

NOTES

1. Charles Miles Jones (1906–93), a native of Nashville, was a 1932 graduate of Union Theological Seminary. After pulpits in Keswick, Virginia; and Brevard, North Carolina, he in 1941 became minister of the First Presbyterian Church in Chapel Hill, where his liberal political and theological views led to tensions with some of the congregants. After the local Presbytery initiated an investigation, he resigned in 1953 and started a new congregation, the Community Church of Chapel Hill, which he pastored until 1967. Mays had recently written an article about Jones's forced resignation: Benjamin E. Mays, "The Presbyterian Church Loses a True Prophet, the Rev. Charles Jones," *Pittsburgh Courier*, 5 September 1953. In 1943 Thurman had appeared as the main speaker at an interfaith and interracial service at the First Presbyterian Church that was arranged by Jones; it was one of Thurman's first appearances at a white church in the South. See "N.C. Pastor Has Unique Service," *Pittsburgh Courier*, 13 February 1943.

2. However, Thurman's next two long-term successors, Dryden Phelps and Francis Geddes, were both white.

☙ TO DRYDEN PHELPS

19 JANUARY 1954
[*BOSTON, MASS.*]

Having been in Boston for several months, Thurman tried to stay active in the affairs of the Fellowship Church, but he worried about appearing too involved;

he did not want to interfere with "the creative processes" of the church as it developed after his departure.

Dr. Dryden Phelps
Fellowship Church
2041 Larkin Street
San Francisco, California

Dear Dryden:

I think it would be a fatal blunder even to consider employing Bob Smith to take Lynn's[1] position. I say this, of course, in confidence. My reasons are as follows: 1. He is a very integral part of the Pines group.[2] I have not said anything about them before to you but they have taken on some of the characteristics of a cult and during the past I have had some difficulty in preventing them from making of Fellowship Church an annex to or laboratory for the Pines and Jungians. 2. He is an arrogant young fellow, full of self-confidence, which is in essence the positive expression of his sense of insecurity and inferiority. I have seen him work with groups in the church and he antagonizes. You have your hands full of problem children and I certainly would not take on another one.

With reference to the children's participation, last Sunday I was at the Germantown Unitarian Church for the morning service. They have the children into the service an average of twice a month only. As soon as the processional hymn, call to worship or invocation and responsive reading are over, the children's talk is given and then they recess to their quarters. This gives to them a sense of participation in worship with their elders but it does not put them under the strain of stretching the attention span beyond its possibility. It may be that some such plan as this could be followed. I make this suggestion in response to your letter but I do not wish to do more than suggest.

I have not been able to make any definite plans about my calendar for next summer. I know that I am free of responsibilities here from the last of June until after Labor Day. I am working so very hard with such long hours that I must have a vacation during the summer. I would like to take the service at the church for three Sundays perhaps. We must be careful so that my presence in the pulpit for a limited interval will not interfere with the creative processes which you have helped to set in motion during this year. We must be hardheaded about this. The future of the church is importantly involved in how we have handled my returning into the situation for a short interval. As soon as possible, I shall write a letter about my thoughts for the tenth anniversary.

Is the committee at work on the Children's Workshop for next summer? I hope you will discuss with Harold Case the possibility of a student from the School of Theology working in the church next summer.[3]

I suppose I ought to be present at Evanston[4] next August, in accordance with the suggestion which you are making. It is much more important that you be there than that I attend.

I shall arrange to see Dean Bartlett[5] if I know when he arrives.

Thank you for the enclosures from the Smith family. Will you please communicate directly with Carleton Byrne[6] about further help for Corrinne.[7] I told him that when the money gave out you would let him know. I am not sure that they will be able to continue assistance but they will tell you. Please write him, giving him an overall progress report. You do not have to break it down in detail.

The days continue full and again and again Sue and I bring you and Margaret vividly to mind. God keep you.

Sincerely,

Howard Thurman

Dean

TLc.

NOTES

1. Lynn Buchanan was leaving the position of church secretary.

2. The Guild for Psychological Studies, founded in San Francisco in 1942 by Elizabeth Boyden Hewes and Fritz Kunkel, had a retreat in the San Bernardino mountains called The Pines from 1942 to 1956. The group was particularly interested in exploring the Gospels from the perspective of Jungian psychology.

3. Harold Case was scheduled to preach at the Fellowship Church on 7 February; see From Dryden Phelps, 8 January 1954. Particularly during his first years in Boston, Thurman tried to develop a strong connection between the School of Theology and the Fellowship Church. For his first two summers in Boston, students from the School of Theology interned at the Fellowship Church and served the church in other capacities. For a summary of Thurman's endeavors in this area, see HT, "[Untitled: On the Relation between Boston University and Fellowship Church]," c. autumn 1955.

4. The Second Assembly of the World Council of Churches was held in Evanston, Illinois, 15–31 August 1954. Thurman did not attend.

5. Josiah Reed Bartlett (1913–97) was dean of Starr King School for the Ministry in Berkeley, California, from 1949 to 1957, after filling Unitarian pulpits in Flatbush, New York; and Seattle, Washington. He served as president of Starr King from 1957 to 1968. Raised in the suburbs of Philadelphia, Bartlett graduated from Amherst College (1934), the University of Michigan (1937), and Union Theological Seminary (1940). He and his wife, Laile E. Bartlett, coauthored *Moment of Truth: Our Next Four Hundred Years, an Analysis of Unitarian Universalism* (Berkeley, Calif.: Josiah R. and Laile E. Bartlett, 1968). See From Josiah R. Bartlett, 22 January 1953.

6. Byrne was a longtime supporter of the Fellowship Church and a trustee of the Claremore Fund; he helped organize the Howard Thurman Educational Trust.

7. Corrine Barrow Williams was the former music director of the Fellowship Church and had suffered a disabling stroke.

ᴗ⸲ "Horn of the Wild Oxen"
28 February 1954
Boston, Mass.

In this sermon Thurman speaks of the personal burdens that every individual carries, here called the "tragic fact of life," and the ways by which—especially by seeking "the limitless energy of God"— life's burdens can be shared and lightened.

Meditation:
As we sit together in the quietness, may we lay bare before God the prides of our lives. Pride of family, of name, and all the circling series of conceits that nourish it and keep it alive. Pride of achievement, and all the blindness which causes us to take complete and full credit for that which can never be ours and ours alone. Pride in beauty of face, of body, of apparel and decoration. Pride of knowledge, as if our little minds could contain the vastness of the reaches of wisdom and disciplines to which we are heirs. Pride in our goodness, with all the smugness that makes us feel that our characters are superior to other characters, that we are better in deed than another. Pride of nation, that fills us with the harsh discords of vaunting nationalism. Pride, pride, pride. Pride. Arrogance. Conceits.

O God, our Father, we make to Thee the offering of our prides. Hold them in Thy hand until naught is left to bedevil our days and trap our souls. This, this is our prayer, O God who loves us and trusts us, even our Father.

Sermon:
About twenty-five years ago, these lines were written by a man who may not be living now, but he was a prisoner in this state doing a life sentence. And I want to read these lines as a background for our thinking together.

> Life, you have beaten me
> Still with stinging wounds, I kiss your hands
> Though you have tortured me until
> My joy was crushed, my hopes, my will
> For things I do not understand.
> Though I have trembled at your power
> And wept in terror, hour by hour,
> For all your struggling, hate, and strife,
> I love you, Life.
> Though what I build, you will destroy,
> Though what I seek and hoard, you take,
> Though you have snatched joy after joy
> From my weak hands, and though you break

My heart, and all my dreams dispel,
And silence every drum and fife
That makes my march less terrible . . .
I love you, Life.
And Life, for all your cruel powers,
For all your proud brutality:
How wonderful the few brief hours,
When you are kind to me.[1]

From the horns of the oxen I cried unto Him, and He will answer me.[2] We are involved, all of us, in what has been aptly called, "the tragic fact of life."[3] Soon or late, and sometimes soon and late, we are visited by the tragic fact. What do you do with your tragic fact? Not what can you do with it, what may you do with it, but what *do* you do with it? As we look at our suffering or the sufferings of others, we are struck by the fact that so much of human suffering is involved in the ordinary logic of events—reaping and sowing. This has been deeply imbedded in our minds.

I remember when I was a boy, I broke this right arm in one or two little places in the wrist, and I amused myself during the days that my arm was in [*inaudible*] sticks, and I couldn't play baseball, couldn't go fishing—I amused myself by trying to remember what was it that I had done that merited that kind of discomfort. I know that something must have happened. I must have done something, but all the things of which I was capable didn't seem to me to rate that kind of disorder.

It's in the very way we think about our experiences—antecedent, consequence; reaping, sowing; always on the hunt for the logic of the event, and that's right. But there is an aspect of the tragic fact that seems to be other than the logic of the event, other than reaping and sowing as such. And the psalmist —and I repeat after him—calls that dimension of the tragic fact being on the horns of the wild oxen.

What do you do with that tragic fact? Let's think about it unhurriedly for a few minutes. The moment when it seems as if the events of your life are so terrible that in your wildest moments of hostility, you would not pass those events on into the life of your worst enemy. There is something about suffering in that dimension that seems to be degrading, that seems to insult the human spirit. Something about it that is unclean. Something about it that is demonic.

Now there are three simple observations that I would make and they in no sense are regarded as answers to the problem of suffering because I would not be so stupid to try and answer. But I want to think about it in terms of how far in my own thinking and feeling I have come along, no further. It's a sort of witness, a kind of testimony, that's all.

The first is this, that the tragic fact must be placed in some kind of causal context. One of the things that is so disturbing about the tragic fact as it invades our lives is this, that it seems to be unable to take our private concerns into account. But there is a causal context in which my tragic fact may be put. For instance, suppose I am wrestling with a disease, and because I am thus afflicted, one by one my duties must end, one by one my lights go out. All the dreams, many of the dreams of my life that are contingent upon robust health must now be abandoned. But it seems as if I am involved in a dimension of life that deals with me in a manner that is ruthless because it ignores my own private world of concerns, ambitions, hopes, desires. And out of that mood I personalize my tragic fact, as a little boy when he runs along and stubs his toe on a root that protrudes from the ground; he turns around and kicks the root, and hurts his foot all over again, as if the root had it in for him, as if the root knew he was coming along and protruded itself in order to trip him. We tend to pull our tragic fact out of any context whatsoever and let it be the active agent of a demonic dimension of life.

Now I am suggesting that one of the first things that we must do with our tragic fact is to put it in a causal context. There is a logic, that I can put this in the words that I want. There is a logic in the disease, not a logic in the disease in relation to me. No, I didn't say that. There is a logic in the disease. For instance, why are we wrestling now trying to, with great hope that we can do something with cancer? All of the work, all of the research that is being done in this area says what about cancer? That there is inherent in cancer, in this malignancy, an order, a structure of dependability, a logic; and if the rational principle that is at work in this disease can be grasped by the rational principle in my mind, then as this rational principle relates to that, I may be able either to reduce the disease to a manageable unit of control, or create out of another dimension of my mind a specific that will neutralize its effect. Now that says, you see, that there is in the disease a logic, a causal portal. Now I must see that it doesn't make me have the disease any less, but it does enable me to do this, to recognize it as not being an irrationality in the presence of which I am completely paralyzed. I establish some level of relatedness when I see it in a context of order, and it does not then undermine my confidence in the integrity of the rational grounding of the universe.

The second thing that I do with my tragic fact is to learn how to carry it and then to put it down. And that's very difficult. I think I mentioned to you once the conversation I had with a lady on the train about prayer. I needn't go into the detail except to suggest a point. She asked me did I believe in prayer, and I said, "Well, yes, I believe in prayer." But I didn't say it hurriedly like that. I said, "Y-e-s, I do." And she said, "I do, too. Before I left home this morning, I had my prayer time, and do you know what I did? I took all of my troubles, did them up in one bundle"—and then she took about twenty-five minutes' detour to tell me about some more of these troubles—"in one bundle" she said, "tied them neatly, handed them to God. But before He could get the bundle opened, I snatched it back again. I didn't want to trust Him with it." Now what I am suggesting that I must do with my tragic fact; I must carry it and then I must put it down. I must not let my tragic fact become the total and thorough-going preoccupation of my mind and my energies and my enthusiasm. For if I do, it chokes to death all of the margins that will give to me momentary release, detachment, from the intensity of the involvement. And the part of the discipline of my life, and your life, is involved in learning how to put things down and do something else, and then pick them up again. There is nothing new in the idea. But it is to remind us that I can't become preoccupied with my tragic fact. If I do, then I become my tragic fact. And I am destroyed by it.

Now there is a third thing that I must do. I must recognize that this is a kind of world in which that which cannot be borne must still be borne anyway. That my tragic fact, because of its perennial dynamics, its power, its changeless character, seems to me to be infinite in its energies. And therefore, I must somehow learn how to put at the disposal of the limitless energies of my tragic fact the limitless energy of God. Not that God might change my tragic fact, but rather that I may discover in my own soul, through prayer, through inner exploration, through the deepening of my inward parts, through meditation—all the disciplines—I must learn through them how I can make available in me at the point of my tragic fact the limitless resources of God to the end that what I must bear, because I have no alternative, instead of enduring it, I can float it. Float it.

And this is the word of religion. And when it is said in this context, it is no mere sentimentality. I must be surer of God than I am of my tragic fact. Thus, my life then becomes the channel through which the energies of God are focused upon the threat which for me may be inescapable, and it is then that I discover that what I know of myself I cannot possibly endure, I will endure.

From the horns of the wild oxen I cried unto Him, not through panic, not through fear, but through courage. And He answered me! He answered me . . . me . . . me.

Give to Thy children Thy spirit, our Father, as we separate one from the other to take up our own tragic fact.

                      At.

NOTES

 1. The probable author of this poem was Mary Carolyn Davies (1888–1940?), a popular poet, playwright, and novelist who was raised in Oregon and spent her professional life in New York City and who does not appear to have done hard time in Massachusetts penitentiaries. Under the title "I Love You, Life" the poem appeared, with minor differences in lineation and punctuation from Thurman's version, in *Everybody's Magazine* (June 1920):

109. However, it also appeared in a publication of the Illinois Department of Public Welfare as "Meditation," attributed to "J.F.B.," and reprinted from the *Mentor,* a publication of the Massachusetts State Prison at Charlestown, in the magazine *Welfare* 19 (March 1928): 308. It seems likely that Thurman came across the poem with the latter attribution. Thurman quotes the same poem in the sermon "The Grace of God," reprinted in HT, *The Growing Edge* (New York: Harper & Brothers, 1956), 71–72.

2. Ps. 22:21.

3. Thurman here combines a favorite term—"the tragic sense of life"—with his notion that every person has a fact, here called a "tragic fact," that is unique and irreducibly personal; this view was derived from his reading of T. S. Eliot's essay "The Function of Criticism"; see *PWHT,* 2:191. The phrase "the tragic sense of life" was used by Thurman on several occasions as the title of a sermon, including one given on 14 November 1954; it was derived from Miguel de Unamuno's well-known book of philosophical reflections, *The Tragic Sense of Life in Men and Peoples* (London: Macmillan, 1926).

🦅 "Be Ye Not Overcome by Evil"
16 May 1954
Boston, Mass.

In this sermon delivered in Marsh Chapel in May 1954, Thurman speaks on a theme familiar from his earlier work: how an individual can maintain his integrity amid an evil world, and how to use that integrity to challenge some of the surrounding evil.

Meditation:

I seek the strength to overcome evil, to overcome the tendency to evil in my own heart.
I recognize the tendency to do the unkind thing when the mood of retaliation or revenge rides high in my spirit;
I recognize the tendency to make of others a means to my own ends, the tendency to yield to fear and cowardice when fearlessness and courage seem to fit easily into the pattern of my security.
I seek the strength to overcome the tendency to evil in my own heart.
I seek the strength to overcome the evil that is present about me.
I recognize the evil in much of the organized life about me;
The evil in the will to power as found in groups and institutions and individuals;
I recognize the terrible havoc of hate and bitterness which makes for fear and panic in the common life.
I seek the strength to overcome the evil that is present all about me.
I seek the strength to overcome evil for I must not myself be overcome by evil.
I seek the purification of my own heart, the purging of my own motives;

I seek the strength to withstand the logic of bitterness, the terrible divisiveness
of hate, the demonic triumph of the conquest of others.
What I seek for myself, O God, I desire with all my heart for friend and for foe
alike.
Together we seek the strength to overcome evil.[1]

Sermon:
"As long as a man has a dream in his heart, he cannot lose the significance of
living."[2]
"The dream in the heart is the outlet. It is one with the living water well-
ing up from the very springs of Being, nourishing and sustaining all of life.
Where there is no dream, the life becomes a swamp, a dreary dead place and,
deep within, a man's heart begins to rot. The dream need not be some great and
overwhelming plan; it need not be a dramatic picture of what might or must be
someday; it need not be a concrete outpouring of a world-shaking possibility
of sure fulfillment. Such may be important for some; such may be crucial for
a particular moment of human history. But it is not in these grand ways that
the dream nourishes life. The dream is the quiet persistence in the heart that
enables a man to ride out the storms of his churning experiences. It is the exciting whisper moving through the aisles of his spirit answering the monotony of
limitless days of dull routine. It is the ever-recurring melody in the midst of the
broken harmony and harsh discords of human conflict. It is the touch of significance which highlights the ordinary experience, the common event. The dream
is no outward thing. It does not take its rise from the environment in which one
moves or functions. The dream lives in the inward parts, it is deep within, where
the issues of life and death are ultimately determined. Keep alive the dream; for
as long as a man has a dream in his heart, he cannot lose the significance of living." And to be overcome by evil is to permit the dream in the heart to be killed.
    What does it mean, really, to be overcome by evil? What does it mean for
you, for me? You may have your own list, as doubtless you do, but there are two
or three things that are moving in my own mind and spirit that I want to share
with you about the meaning of this, and the first has to do with sin. That is not a
very dignified word now, it's—particularly in an intellectual community. There's
error, there's blindness, there's stupidity, there is immaturity, you know, all of
those wonderful blessings from the discipline of psychology. But there is also
sin. Sin. If I am adding up a column of figures and I make a mistake, that's an
error and I can erase it. But if I see you in need by the roadside and I look the
other way pretending that you are not there, that is also a mistake. But there is
a desert and a sea dividing those two, for sin means, finally, that in some crucial
moral issue I have been weighed and I am wanting; that some quality irradiates
the totality of my spirit—dulling it. And somehow as a result of it, I am not quite

able to be present and accounted for in the face of the imperious demand that is ethical in quality and moral in tone. And to be overcome by evil is to have one's inner awarenesses of rightness and wrongness so dulled, so worked over, that slowly, here a little and there a little, for me there is no right and wrong. When moral dullness and then deadness so irradiates my life that I can hurt you, I can be involved in a series of activities and actions, the results of which are destructive to moral values and to human needs without ever realizing that I am rotting on the inside. And therefore, keep alive your sense of sin! Keep it alive. Don't let it die for the day that it dies you move out into the darkness. Now in talking that way I don't want to depress you on a gloomy day like this one, but you must remember.

The second thing I want to say about it is that I am overcome by evil when I permit the factors or the elements in my environment, the situation, however you wish to say it, by which I am surrounded, the context in which I am living at a particular moment in my life or in human history, that I permit any of these things to make me scale down the ideals to which I am committed because as I look at the facts of my life I do not now see that my ideals have any chance for fulfillment. And because they seem to be so utterly out of range of the possibility of living as I must live life because of these factors by which I am surrounded, I may be tempted to say of my ideals that they are of no significance. And that is a terribly urgent word for our time. We are surrounded by so much brutality in life, so much mass slaughter, so much organized brutality to which there is dedicated the most far-reaching powers of the mind of man that we are tempted to say to ourselves, "Why should I be decent? Why should I be sensitive? It really doesn't matter." Now I'm not wise enough, nor inspired enough, or anything to answer that. But the only word that I can say about it is this, that the ultimate word that can be said about a good thing is that it is good; that precisely if all around me (this may sound very arrogant to you to feel enough for me to feel it, but it is important for me to say it), if all around me, there is this blindness to human worth, let us say as an illustration, it is all the more important that I be sensitive to human worth. If at no point my ideal seems to have a chance for fulfillment because of the vicissitudes of fortune by which I am surrounded, it is all the more important then that my ideal shall have a chance to fulfill itself in me. Though all around me right is conquered, though all around me I see quite clearly that this is the kind of world in which the wicked do prosper, then it is all the more crucial for me that at least in my own soul, evil will not conquer. This I can do! That's the second.

First I must not let the sense of sin get dull and then second I must, I must see to it that my ideal will triumph in me even though it may not be possible for me to preside over its triumph in the environment. It *may* not be possible, but at least in me it will triumph. And in as much as I am a part of life, you see, to the extent to which it triumphs in me, it triumphs in the world. And that is important to remember. Important to remember!

And now the third. I must not permit—all these things are negative things—I must not permit my life to be destroyed by inner bitterness, by the inner spirit of retaliation, by hate.

I recognize how hard these words are and how they sound like Pollyanna.[3] I remember years ago reading the autobiography of Tolstoy and how I came to a certain description that I will tell you about. I chuckled and thought that it was a very superficial kind of optimism; it was ridiculous. And this was the thing, you may remember it, he describes how he was being attacked by a bear. Do you remember that? And this huge beast had him down on the ground—yes, that's right. He was on the ground in one of these bear hugs and this bear was trying to maneuver Tolstoy in a position so that he could bite him. And Tolstoy looked up just, oh four or five inches his head was from the slavering jaws of this tremendous creature, with all the drooling that went on, and as the bear opened his mouth and began moving around in this direction where Tolstoy's head was located, Tolstoy looked at the sky between the opening in the jaws of the bear and said to himself, "What a beautiful blue."[4] Now that sounds ridiculous, you know, ridiculous. But what he is talking about is the very heart of the secret, for the moment the fear I fight against, the moment the evil against which I struggle is able to shift its center of operation from outside of me to inside of me, I have been overcome.

Now, when I hate as an answer to hatred, when I retaliate in the august fulfillment of my right to [*inaudible*], what happens? Something worse than the evil that I fight against begins to take place inside of me. And what is that? The disintegration of my own soul so that inside I begin to go to pieces; inside I begin to disintegrate; inside the world and its meaning falls apart and turns to ashes in my hands, to mix the figure. And then I become what I fight against and evil has won and my soul has lost. What would a man give, give, give, in exchange for his soul? The slaying of his enemies? Is that worth it? What would he give? Be ye not overcome by evil says the strange, wandering, homeless teacher of Galilee, but overcome evil with good. And to do that is madness but it is that kind of madness that will redeem our world.

Leave us not deserted, O God, our Father, but walk the long way with us that in the darkness and in the light. Dismiss us with Thy Spirit and inspire our steps in the way that they take. O God, who loves us and has trusted us with Thy Spirit.

At.

NOTES

 1. This is a paraphrase of "To Overcome Evil," in HT, *Meditations of the Heart* (1953), 164–65.

 2. This is the opening sentence of "Keep Alive the Dream in the Heart," in *Meditations of the Heart* (1953), 36–37. Thurman did not recite the remainder of the opening paragraph

of the meditation in this sermon. The second paragraph, which he did recite, is in the transcription.

3. "Pollyanna" is a term for unrealistic cheeriness and optimism, from the title character in Eleanor H. Porter's popular 1913 novel, *Pollyanna*.

4. The Russian novelist Leo Tolstoy (1828–1910) told the story of his near fatal encounter with a bear during a hunt in 1858 on numerous occasions, in the story "The Bear Hunt," and in his autobiographical reminiscences.

☙ ANNUAL REPORT, DEAN OF THE CHAPEL
21 JUNE 1954
BOSTON, MASS.

Thurman's first annual report as dean of the chapel at Boston University highlights the hectic nature of his schedule and his roles as preacher, coordinator of activities at Marsh Chapel, and host for numerous student and faculty gatherings. It also shows that he was a guest speaker who was much in demand at both on-campus and off-campus events. The report provided Thurman his first opportunity to expound at length on his ideas for a chapel-based religious fellowship that would transcend the usual confessional boundaries of Protestant, Catholic, and Jew. Thurman's efforts to create a chapel fellowship would be unstinting. His failure to get the trustees to agree to the plan would be his greatest and gravest disappointment from his years at Boston University.

President Harold Case
Dean Howard Thurman

Dear Mr. President:
    It is a pleasure for me to submit to you, as my first annual report as Dean of the Chapel, a summary of the year's work and certain basic recommendations as we look to the future.
Sincerely yours,
Howard Thurman
Dean

enc.

PUBLIC WORSHIP SERVICES

The first chapel service for the academic year 1953–54 was held on Sunday, September 20. This service marked the beginning of a new order of service, based upon the religious theory upon which the chapel would proceed under my leadership. I enclose as Exhibit A a sample of the order of service, with a copy of the previous order of service that the differences may be clearly seen.[1]

The chapel has sought to provide an opportunity to the university community for the public worship of God and to create a climate in which such worship may take place without doing violence either to the intellectual integrity or to the personal religious context in which the individual worshiper finds meaning for his own life. In the development of this idea, the major insights inherent in the Judeo-Christian religion and the varied fruits of the disciplines of mind, spirit and character are made manifest through music, the spoken word and inspiring or sacred records.

The response to this approach during the first year was deeply gratifying. The average Sunday attendance throughout the academic year was 226. This figure covers a period from July 1953 through May, 1954. Services were held during all of the regular university holidays, despite the fact that dormitories were closed and students had gone home. The average attendance at these services was 125.

In addition to the regular Sunday morning services, there were held a Christmas vesper service on December 13, a Masonic service on May 9 and a Spring vesper service, when the choir, augmented by the Choral Arts Society, rendered Nathaniel Dett's "The Ordering of Moses."[2] In addition to these services, an experimental mid-week meditation service was held in the little chapel for three weeks, on Wednesday evening of each week. My experience with these three meditation services was sufficiently encouraging to suggest that a regular service of that kind should be inaugurated during the next academic year.

The following persons occupied the pulpit of March Chapel during the regular school term:

November 1-President Harold Case
January 10-Rev. Thomas Trotter[3]
   " 17-Dr. Harold Ehrensperger[4]
February 7-Rabbi Samuel Perlman
   " 21-Bishop Lewis Hartman[5]
March 14-Chancellor Daniel L. Marsh[6]
May 2-Muriel Lester[7]
   " 23-Dr. Edwin Booth[8]
   " 30-Dr. Amaya Chakravarty[9]

This means that on a total of nine Sundays there were guest preachers and at all of the other services, beginning in September through Commencement, 1954, the Dean of the Chapel has been the preacher.

The collection from September 20 through June 20 is $2,979.67 as contrasted with $1,489.56 for the same period last year.

MUSIC

Professor Samuel Walter,[10] University Organist, has rendered creative service as organist for all of the public worship. He set to music a special call to worship which was written by the Dean of the Chapel. The Dean of the Chapel has prepared several texts for music which will be written during the summer, so that at the beginning of the school year all of the choral responses in the Sunday services will be original music and texts. In addition to this, two anthems are being prepared, one of which is a special Thanksgiving anthem and will be sung by the choir during the Thanksgiving season.

The chapel choir, under the leadership of Professor Lannom,[11] has rendered enthusiastic and intelligent support for the Sunday service. Words of commendation cannot be too strong for the loyalty and devotion of both the choir and its director. It is no ordinary thing to be supported by a choir and its director. It is no ordinary thing to be supported by a choir that shares in the worship service as active participants as well as a choir that sings at a certain point in the service. It is our hope that next year the choir will be enlarged so that we will have a wider range of good voices.

The achievement in "The Ordering of Moses"[12] was outstanding. It is of interest to note that there were four solo parts in that oratorio. One was taken by a guest soloist, a Chinese baritone from San Francisco, a Negro tenor, a Jewish contralto and a Protestant soprano.[13] It is our plan next winter to have four music vespers given by the choir.

A plan is being developed for making an hour of music available in the late afternoon once a week in the chapel all during the school term.

COUNSELING

Perhaps the most significant opportunity available to the Dean of the Chapel is found in the privilege of personal counseling. From mid September until the end of June, the average counseling load was eleven per week. Some of these were of longer than one hour's duration. There were undergraduates, faculty members, graduate students and persons from the wider university community. The demand was greater than time and energy to meet.

INTER-UNIVERSITY SERVICES

From the sixth of January to June 10, the Dean of the Chapel spoke for the following University groups:
Congregational Club
College of General Education
P.A.L.[14]
School of Nursing Convocation
B.U. Women's Council
Sargent College[15]—twice
School of Education
S.C.A. of C.B.A.[16]
Charlesgate[17]
Hillel
Medical School

The engagements outside the university, beginning January 1, I am submitting as Exhibit B.

GIFTS TO THE CHAPEL

In October the Claremore Fund[18] of California made a gift of a professional Concertone tape recorder for the purpose of making a permanent tape record of all of the Sunday services. In addition to giving the recorder, a year's supply of tapes was also included. This gift has been a great blessing in the spirit of the ministry of the chapel because copies of the tapes have been sent regularly to southern California. Various ministers have been able to secure them for their own churches and occasionally opportunity has been provided for those persons who wanted to hear a service which they had missed or to get a repeat on a service which they had attended.

In addition to this gift, Mrs. Ralph Smith[19] of Los Angeles contributed during the year an average of $65.00 a month to the Discretionary Fund for the Dean of the Chapel's use in any special ways to enhance the work. There is a conditional promise that this amount will be given during the next academic year.

Under Exhibit C there will be a listing to indicate the wide use to which the chapel has been put.

RECOGNITIONS

The Dean of the Chapel gave the Merrick Lectures at Ohio Wesleyan University March 14–16 on the general topic "Religious Experience and the Social Witness."

These lectures will be published by Harper and Brothers of New York City on November 15 in a volume titled "The Creative Encounter."[20] On the occasion of the lectures, Ohio Wesleyan awarded the Dean of the Chapel the honorary degree Doctor of Humanities. On May 27, Allen University of Columbia, South Carolina awarded him the honorary degree of Doctor of Letters. On June 8, Lincoln University[21] awarded him the honorary degree Doctor of Divinity as a part of its centennial celebration.

Two of the most significant commencement activities were the delivery of the Baccalaureate sermon as a part of the centennial celebration of the Western College for Women at Oxford, Ohio, and the Baccalaureate sermon for Vassar College. On July 2, the Dean of the Chapel gives one of the lectures in the celebration of the 200th anniversary of the founding of Columbia University, as it will be observed in Santa Barbara, California.

On November 26 the Abingdon-Cokesbury Book Store held an Author's Tea in honor of the publishing of "Meditations of the Heart" by Harper and Brothers.

USE OF 184 BAY STATE ROAD

We have no record of the number of groups and the size of them that were guests at the residence of the Dean and Mrs. Thurman. It is a fair estimate to say that the average has been one group each week and often as many as three groups in a single week. Most of these were dinner or supper meetings. There has been a steady stream of traffic in the house which gave to the facilities very hard use. It will be necessary for reconditioning to be done, but this will appear as a separate memorandum. It is my considered judgment that the home at 184 Bay State Road is an indispensible and integral part of the fulfillment of Marsh Chapel.

RECOMMENDATIONS

1. That plans be perfected for establishing some kind of religious fellowship in connection with the chapel, the details concerning which will be ready the first of September.
2. That some means be perfected for giving a sense of belonging and participating to the increasingly wide radio audience on Sunday morning.
3. That provisions be made and equipment secured for furnishing a parlor for informal meetings and discussions as a part of the ministry of the chapel. Details concerning this have already been submitted.
4. That suitable office space be devised for the Director of the United Ministry within the chapel building, inasmuch as this is an important aspect of the total religious program for students.

THE RELIGIOUS LIFE OF THE UNIVERSITY

It is recognized generally that we have not yet found a formula for integrating the religious life of the university. At the present time, work among Roman Catholic students, Jewish students and Orthodox students is the best organized and most effective. The denominational clubs touch only a very few students and, for the most part, are ineffective. The Student Christian Association, during the present year, involved about 300 students, which merely scratched the surface. The Brotherhood Council, which was created as an agent of cooperation at a student level among Protestants, Catholics and Jews, has limped along during the year.

The present plans for next year hold a great deal of promise. At the level of staff, the relations between the Catholic and Jewish chaplains, the Executive of the S.C.A., the Director of United Ministry and the Dean of the Chapel have been very congenial. In no sense that is fundamental are Protestants, Catholics and Jews close together. The position of the chapel and the very nature of the case continues to be ambivalent.

In many people's minds, the chapel is the formal representative of Protestant Christianity on the campus. As such, it symbolizes a sectarian emphasis. The position of the Dean of the Chapel, however, continues to be, as it has been, that the ministry of the chapel, because it represents the formal intent of the university, with reference to the religious life of its constituency, should be devoted to developing a center for religious worship in the heart of the university to which any and all members of the university may come for spiritual renewal and regeneration. It remains to be seen whether such a position can survive in this climate. If it cannot survive, then the ministry of the chapel should become the official Protestant mouthpiece and hold its own on equal footing with the Jewish and the Catholic positions. The present Dean of the Chapel has no interest in that alternative.

With the coming of a matured and older person as the Director of the S.C.A.[22] and with Dr. Deats[23] continuing another year as Director of the United Ministry, it may be possible to evolve a plan and a strategy of integrating all of the religious activity among the students of the university. The ideal arrangement, perhaps, would be for the university to sponsor a single religious association open to all students. Within that association, ample provisions would be made for the denominational interests to be recognized and channeled to the local churches in the community to which the student groups would be officially related.[24]

This would mean that, as far as work on the campus is concerned, during the week there would be a single united student religious organization exclusive of the Catholic and Jewish. On weekends, the various denominational groups will meet in the local church that has the residence sponsorship.

George Makechnie and Howard and Sue Bailey Thurman at an event honoring
Howard Thurman on his retirement from Boston University, 1965. From the Bailey
Thurman Family Papers; the Stuart A. Rose Manuscript, Archives, and Rare Book
Library, Emory University.

It is good to know that the climate is sufficiently yeasty and dynamic to make
possible the widest possible experimentation on behalf of the creative ideal that
is the gift of God to all of His children without regard to faith or creed, class or
race.

A final word of appreciation to the administration and to the university community for the outstanding spirit of cooperation which has enveloped the chapel
and its program on every hand.

TD.

NOTES

1. When Thurman arrived at Boston University, he dramatically changed the service
by eliminating many of its overtly Christian elements, including the recitation of the Prayer
of Confession, the Lord's Prayer, the Affirmation of Faith, and the Act of Common Prayer.

2. "The Ordering of Moses" (1937) was an oratorio by the prominent African American composer R. Nathaniel Dett (1882–1943). It drew on Negro spirituals to tell the story of
the exodus and was a work much favored by Thurman.

3. Frederick Thomas Trotter (1926–) received his S.T.B. (1953) and Ph.D. (1958) from the Boston University School of Theology. He had a distinguished career in Methodist education and taught at the Southern California School of Theology (1957–73). In addition he served as general secretary of the Board of Higher Education and Ministry of the United Methodist Church (1973–87) and as president of Alaska Pacific University (1987–93) in Anchorage. He later wrote of Thurman that he was "an extraordinary boss in the Chapel. I was the Protestant chaplain and had worked for three other supervisors over a very short time. When Howard arrived, the tempo picked up. Marsh Chapel became a church." He also said that Thurman's piety was in touch with many things: "He loved sports and good food and friends and books and music. He loved the world, and his piety was what drew him into that world." See George K. Makechnie, *Howard Thurman: His Enduring Dream,* 69–70. Trotter also mentioned that after a fire in Trotter's apartment, Trotter and his wife lived with the Thurmans for several months.

4. Harold Adam Ehrensperger (1897–1973) headed the program on the creative arts and religion at the Boston University School of Theology. He was one of the founders of the discipline, and his books include *Conscience of Stage* (New York: Abingdon-Cokesbury, 1947) and *Religious Drama: Ends and Means* (New York: Abingdon, 1962).

5. Lewis Oliver Hartman (1876–1955), a native of La Grange, Indiana, and a graduate of the Boston University School of Theology, held numerous positions with the United Methodist Church. He was editor of *Zion's Herald* from 1920 to 1944 and bishop for New England from 1944 to 1948. He was noted for socially progressive views and his opposition to segregation and militarism.

6. Daniel L. Marsh (1880–1968), president of Boston University from 1926 to 1951, was a native of West Newton, Pennsylvania, and a graduate of Northwestern University (1907) and the Boston University School of Theology (1908). He assumed the presidency of Boston University after several Pennsylvania pastorates and positions in the Methodist Church. Marsh Chapel was named in his honor after his retirement. He devoted considerable attention to its construction. See Daniel L. Marsh, *The Charm of the Chapel* (Boston: Boston University Press, 1950).

7. For Muriel Lester, see *PHWT,* 1:233.

8. Edwin Prince Booth (1898–1969), a graduate of Allegany College, received his S.T.B. (1922) and Ph.D. (1929) from the Boston University School of Theology, where he taught after 1924, becoming professor of church history. His best-known book is *Martin Luther: Oak of Saxony* (New York: Roundtable, 1933).

9. Amaya Chandra Chakravarty (1901–86), a native of Bengal, was educated in Calcutta and became a close associate of Rabindranath Tagore and Mahatma Gandhi. In his later years he was a good friend of Thomas Merton. He taught at Boston University from 1953 to 1966. He was a poet, journalist, and critic, and his publications include several edited volumes of the works of Tagore and *The Dynasts and the Post-War Age in Poetry* (Oxford: Oxford University Press, 1938).

10. Samuel Walter (1916–87) received a doctorate in music from Boston University, where he was university organist. He later taught at Rutgers University. His compositions, primarily of a religious nature, include those collected in *Six Hymn-Tune Preludes* (New York: Abingdon, 1962). He wrote *Basic Principles of Service Playing* (New York: Abingdon, 1963) and *Music Composition and Arranging* (New York: Abingdon, 1965).

11. Allen C. Lannom (1917–2006) was a graduate of Occidental College and the Juilliard School. He was director of choral activities at Boston University from 1951 to 1982 and

then taught and conducted at the Boston Conservatory for nearly twenty years. From 1952 to 2005 he was director of the Boston-area Masterworks Chorale.

12. "The Ordering of Moses," by R. Nathaniel Dett, was performed at the Marsh Chapel Vespers on 9 May 1954.

13. Raymond Fong, member of the Fellowship Church Quintet, was the baritone; Elmer Dickey was the tenor; Joan Caplan was the contralto; and Marilyn Zoller was the soprano.

14. Boston University's College of Practical Arts and Letters opened in 1919 and closed in 1955; it accepted only women until 1950.

15. This is now Boston University's Sargent College of Health and Rehabilitation Sciences, offering degrees in physical therapy and allied subjects; it became a unit of the university in 1929.

16. This was the Student Christian Association of the College of Business Administration. The College of Business Administration, founded in 1913, became the Boston University School of Management before being renamed the Boston University Questrom School of Business in March 2015.

17. The Charlesgate Hotel was built in 1901 and used by Boston University as a women's dormitory from 1947 to 1973.

18. The Claremore Fund, a Los Angeles–based philanthropy founded around 1946, supported grants in the areas of higher education, scholarship, intercultural relations, liberal Protestantism, and youth. In 1951 it had assets of $115,590 and made disbursements of $9,990. Its trustees (all good friends of Thurman) included Lloyd Melvin Smith, Eleanor Lloyd Smith, and Carleton E. Byrne. See *American Philanthropies and Their Fields* (American Foundation Information Service, 1955). Lloyd Melvin Smith would later serve as the lawyer who assisted Thurman in establishing the Howard Thurman Educational Trust.

19. A close friend and benefactor of Thurman.

20. HT, *The Creative Encounter: An Interpretation of Religion and the Social Witness* (New York: Harper & Brothers, 1954).

21. Lincoln University in Pennsylvania.

22. William A. Overholt (1917–96) was a Methodist minister who became Protestant minister of the Student Christian Association in 1954 and subsequently associate dean of student affairs and assistant professor of religion. In 1973 he was named dean of student affairs at the University of Illinois medical center in Chicago. His books include *Christian Responsibility for World Development with Economic Justice: A Stimulus to Dialogue* (New York: University Christian Movement, 1967) and *Religion in American Colleges and Universities* (Washington, D.C.: American College Personnel Association, 1970). From 1947 to 1950, before entering the ministry full-time, he served as the secretary of state for West Virginia. He and Thurman had a tense relationship. In his next annual report, Thurman would complain of the "obvious discourtesies extended to him" by Dr. Overholt; see HT, "Annual Report, Dean of Chapel, [1955–56]."

23. Paul Deats (1919–2009), a native of Texas, was a graduate of Southern Methodist University and Union Theological Seminary, and he received his Ph.D. from Boston University in 1954. He taught at the Boston University School of Theology from 1953 to 1986 and in 1979 became the Walter G. Muelder Professor of Social Ethics. His books include, with Herbert E. Stotts, *Methodism and Society: Guidelines for Strategy* (New York: Abingdon, 1962); and, edited with Carol Robb, *The Boston Personalist Tradition in Philosophy, Social Ethics, and Theology* (Macon, Ga.: Mercer University Press, 1986).

24. Thurman's opposition to limiting campus access to Protestant denominational groups was of long standing; he had fought a similar battle as dean of the chapel at Howard University. See *PHWT*, 2:267–68.

🎵 FROM ROLAND HAYES
25 AUGUST 1954
BROOKLINE, MASS.

Roland Hayes invites Thurman to provide the narration to an upcoming record-ing of Negro spirituals. However, Vanguard Recordings ultimately decided to record only Hayes because including Thurman "would delay the production of the records for too great a time."¹ Hayes occasionally worshipped in Marsh Chapel and was honored by the chapel on the occasion of the 175th anniversary of the death of the Boston African American poet Phillis Wheatley in 1784.²

Dear Dr. Thurman:

Many thanks for your good letter. Although I know you to be overwhelmed with duties which your great work imposes, I, nevertheless, am hoping you can find a possible moment to do this vastly important item with me both for the sake of its spiritual message and that of our forefathers of the ministry whose profound religious convictions saved the millions of our race through their religious teachings, who, otherwise, might have become completely lost in its absence. You, my dear friend, <u>understand</u> and have <u>inherited</u> their <u>understand-ing</u> and <u>power</u>, and, in an <u>extraordinary way</u>, have fused that with your mastery of the here and now, so-called, advance posts of scholarly accomplishments of the times.

In the enclosed song setup of items on the life of Christ, you will note that I have been able to find scriptural readings out of which the songs came into being. In the matter of your own commentary in connection with the record-ing session, if indeed you can join me, I leave you to make your own summary and abridgements of Biblical matter and inject your own philosophical under-standing of what our fathers saw{, meant to convey,} and projected. I have not heard how long the VANGUARD recording session for this recording will take, but my guess is that they would wish to do the whole recording of songs and commentary within one hour's duration of time for actual time-running of the record. As I have observed, the clocking time for performing all of the songs in my cycle takes around 40 minutes or less. This I shall work out again this week. I do not think that it would take more than 4 or 5 hours of one day to make the recording. The time I have offered Vanguard for the recording of the life of Christ record, and, a Christmas Carol recording of several nations, which they are asking me to do in addition, is from September 16 through September the

19th. I expect to be in Boston from now until it is time for me to go to New York for the recordings—except for the 11th when my wife and I expect to motor Afrika[3] back to Princeton to school.

I have given your name and address to Vanguard Recording Society, Inc. who will contact you with respect to this recording session and I am so hoping that we can do it together.

My family joins in warm wishes to you and yours,
With kind regards,
Sincerely yours,
[*signed*] Roland Hayes
Roland Hayes.

TLS.

NOTES

    1. From Maynard Solomon, 16 November 1954. The album was released as *The Life of Christ: As Told through Aframerican Folksong,* Vanguard Recordings VRS-462, 1955, vinyl LP.
    2. *WHAH,* 188.
    3. Afrika Hayes (b. 1933), Roland Hayes's daughter.

   FROM SIDNEY DIMOND
28 NOVEMBER 1954
BOSTON, MASS.

The weekly radio broadcasts of Thurman's services from Marsh Chapel spread his message beyond the chapel audience and acquired a bevy of devoted listeners. Sidney Dimond,[1] one of the broadcasts' facilitators, was one of their number.

BOSTON UNIVERSITY
To: Dr. Howard Thurman
From: Associate Professor Sid Dimond, SPRC[2]
Subject: You, Me, and the Chapel

I came in early this morning to check on the WBUR crew which was handling the Chapel broadcast, and decided to stay here at the Station to follow through on this end. We have a new student handling things at that end; one who is more competent than the one previously. We now need checking at this end of the line to get the Chapel on and off the air satisfactorily.

    I want you to know how very grateful those of us at the Station are for your cooperation and sympathy with our problem. The station is vastly over-extended, and I'm afraid sometimes we expect too much from our students, who tend often to be immature and to lack judgement. The past two weeks we have had many, many problems, including two major equipment breakdowns.

Jim Bonney has been busy trying to just keep us on the air. I have instructed him to get to the technical work at the Chapel as soon as he can overcome the emergencies here. Our equipment is now six years old, and showing it. Please be assured we will do all we can to make the broadcast from the Chapel the very best we can make it.

Aside from considerations dealing with my work at B.U. as Chairman of the Radio Department here, I want you to know how very much you have done for me personally in the strengthening and development of my faith. I never meet you, nor hear you preach, but that I feel the impact of the deep spiritual you represent and live, coming into my life. I'm deeply grateful to you for this. When you're teaching, there's a tendency for much to be taken from you, day in and day out. The question becomes then: Where do I get what I give? Your spiritual leadership here at the University is answering this question for many of us. Thanks.

Congratulations on your new book![3]

[signed] Sid Dimond

TLS.

NOTES

1. Sidney Allen Dimond (1921–2007) was a professor of broadcasting and chair of the broadcasting department at Boston University from 1947 to 1963. In 1948 he was instrumental in the creation of the public radio station WBUR. After leaving Boston University he was president of a public relations and communications firm, Sid Dimond Associates, Inc., until 1976.

2. The School of Public Relations and Communications. The school changed its name several times; since 1984 it has been the College of Communication.

3. HT, *The Creative Encounter.*

✎ From Albert W. Dent

1 December 1954

New Orleans, Louisiana

Looking for a new dean of the chapel for Dillard University, Albert W. Dent,[1] president of Dillard University, writes that he has "heard some good things about M. L. King, Jr." and wants the opinion of his friend Howard Thurman.

Dear Howard:

We were all sorry that you could not come down for the State Teachers' Association,[2] but hope that you can come to visit with us in the near future.

Ground was broken for the new chapel on November 23 and we expect to have the building completed within a year.[3] This means that I must hurry in the finding of a person for this work.[4] The other day I heard some good things about M. L. King, Jr.,[5] whose father is at Ebenezer[6] at Atlanta. I understand that King after finishing Morehouse, went to Boston University where he has about completed his work for the doctorate.[7] Do you know anything about his record, and do you think him to be the type of person into whom I should take a good look? It is important that we get a good person started in the new building. With best wishes, I am

Sincerely yours,

[*signed*] Albert

A. W. Dent
President

Dr. Howard Thurman, Dean
Daniel L. Marsh Chapel
Boston University
300 Bay State Road
Boston 15, Massachusetts

AWD: db

TLS.

NOTES

1. Albert W. Dent (1907–84), a 1926 graduate of Morehouse College, was chief administrator of Flint-Goodridge Hospital in New Orleans before becoming associated with Dillard University in 1932. He served as president of Dillard from 1941 to 1968. See Joe Richardson, "Albert W. Dent: A Black New Orleans Hospital and University Administrator," *Louisiana History* 37, no. 3 (Summer 1996): 309–23.

2. The Louisiana State Colored Teachers Association was founded in 1902, and its name was changed to the Louisiana Education Association in 1947. It was a major force for racial equality in the state in the 1950s and 1960s. In 1977 Louisiana became the last state in the country to end racially segregated state teacher associations, when the Louisiana Education Association merged with its white counterpart, the Louisiana Teachers Association.

3. The Lawless Memorial Chapel at Dillard University was dedicated on 23 October 1955, with Thurman giving the dedicatory sermon. See "Sermon Delivered at the Dedication of the Lawless Memorial Chapel," 23 October 1955.

4. The position went to Samuel L. Gandy (1917–88), a 1938 graduate of the Howard University School of Religion, where he was a student and protégé of Thurman. He received his Ph.D. from the University of Chicago in 1952. Gandy taught at a number of historically black colleges and universities during his career, among them Fisk and Virginia Union Universities, and was dean of the Howard University School of Religion from 1965 to 1974.

5. Martin Luther King, Jr. (1929–68), a native of Atlanta, was a 1948 graduate of Morehouse College and a 1951 graduate of Crozer Theological Seminary. He entered Boston University in 1951, graduating with a Ph.D. in 1955. King became pastor of the Dexter Avenue Baptist Church in Montgomery, Alabama, in the fall of 1954 and president of the Montgomery Improvement Association in December 1955. As the spokesperson for the

Montgomery bus boycott, he soon became the most prominent national leader of the civil rights movement throughout its most turbulent years in the late 1950s and early 1960s. In 1964 he was awarded the Nobel Prize for Peace. In April 1968 he was assassinated in Memphis, Tennessee, and since 1987 his birthday has been celebrated in the United States as a national holiday.

     6. Ebenezer Baptist Church in Atlanta.

     7. By the fall of 1954 King had finished his course work at Boston University; he graduated with a Ph.D. in systematic theology in the spring of 1955.

To Albert W. Dent

14 December 1954

[*Boston, Mass.*]

In his response to Dent,[1] *Thurman strongly favors another Boston University graduate student, Major Jones, over Dent's original subject of inquiry, Martin Luther King, Jr.*

Dr. Albert W. Dent
Dillard University
New Orleans, Louisiana

Dear Albert:

     It was good to hear from you as always.

     With reference to M. L. King, Jr., I know him casually. He has made a good record here in the university and I understand that he is a good preacher. I do not know anything about his experience with students. But, of course, a man has to start some time. Sue has had some conversations with King and is very much impressed with him.

     I have a man to whom I wish you would give consideration. His name is Major Jones.[2] He is a graduate of Clark, Gammon, with a masters from Oberlin, and is finishing up his Ph.D. at Boston University in religious education. He has served as pastor of a Methodist church in Atlanta and for several years was a director of youth activities for the Methodist church in the state of Georgia, and until he came here to work for his Ph.D. he was chaplain at Wiley and Professor of Philosophy.

     I think, Albert, he is the kind of man for whom you are looking. He is relaxed, very competent, and I understand is a good preacher. In a conversation with him the other day, I asked rather casually if he were obligated to return to Wiley. I find that he is not. He is the sort of man who is very much in demand by the Methodist church and, therefore, at the present time is considering several things. If you are interested in him, I would suggest that you write an exploratory letter, addressing him in care of the School of Theology, Boston University.

It may be that during the spring recess he may come down for a weekend to preach at Dillard and you can hear him and talk to him.

I hope all goes well with you and Jessie.

I am sending a gift to the two of you under separate cover.

Sincerely,

Howard Thurman

TLc.

NOTES

1. From Albert Dent, 1 December 1954, printed in the current volume.

2. Major J. Jones (1919–93), a native of Rome, Georgia, received an A.B. from Clark College in 1941, a B.D. from Gammon Theological Seminary in 1944, and an S.T.M. from Oberlin's Graduate School of Theology in 1950. He received a Th.D. from the Boston University School of Theology in 1957 for his dissertation on "The Place of God in the Educative Process According to George A. Coe, William C. Bower, and Harrison S. Elliot." Jones served as a pastor in eastern Tennessee from 1956 to 1967, when he became president of the Gammon Theological Seminary in Atlanta. He served as Gammon's president until 1985, when he became chaplain of the Atlanta University Center. His publications include *Black Awareness: A Theology of Hope* (Nashville, Tenn.: Abingdon, 1971) and *The Color of God: The Concept of God in Afro-American Thought* (Macon, Ga.: Mercer University Press, 1987).

"LIMITATION OF INTAKE"

[*1955*]

This sermon, its place and date of delivery unknown but probably dating from 1955, is on a familiar Thurman theme: the need to focus intently on what is important in one's personal and spiritual life. In the language of this sermon, it is a call to limit one's intake, to uncover one's true self.[1]

I'm reading a poem that comes from another culture and another faith:[2]

"Thou hast to churn the milk, O Disciple, if thou desirest to taste the butter.
And it serveth not thy purpose, if, sitting in idleness, thou sayest,
'Lo, the butter is in the milk. Yes, the butter is in the milk.'
Even so, how canst thou find the Lord, my son, by merely uttering, 'God is'
Be thou then up and doing in right earnest and ply thy task.
Thou hast to churn the milk, O Disciple, if thou desirest the taste of butter."

And there is a strange paradox in religion—many strange paradoxes, perhaps; but I am thinking of one in particular. There is in all great religious experience, a recognition of the fact that God speaks and becomes articulate in the inward parts of the human spirit and the human heart. God is to be found within, and in the language of Jesus, the Kingdom of God is within. Someone else expresses it in another faith: "I laugh when you say that the fish in the water is thirsty. Do you seek the real truth? Go where you will, from Benares to --------- if you have not found your own soul, the world is unreal to you."[3] That's in the same vein. In the railway station in Washington, D.C., there is cut in one of the facades the quotation: "He who seeks the wealth of the Indies, must carry the wealth of the Indies with him."[4] It is the same notion, that the reality of life—that the deeply moving significance of human experience—is at last revalidated within the confines of the human spirit and within the human heart, within the human mind.

And that's one end of it. And yet there is always the insistence as expressed again in the word of Jesus: "By their fruits ye shall know them." There is the insistence upon deeds, upon actions, and the test of the inward part is often interpreted in terms of the degree to which this inner experience is able to become articulate in deeds. The inward part. That is where God is. In your deeds—that's where God is. Now it is with an aspect of that paragraph that I am going to deal this morning. And the subject is not original. It is borrowed from an experience that I shall always remember.

Some years ago when I lived in Washington and was in Howard University, Dr. Cabot of Harvard came down to the University to speak at the Sunday morning chapel.[5] He came early Saturday morning because he was having one of the famous Cabot Pathological Conferences down at the medical school. Before that, he came over to my little hole in the wall which was my office; and he and I sat there trying to engage in conversation. About every two minutes or three, there would be a buzz and I would answer the telephone and then as soon as that was over, he would begin a sentence and get half through it and someone would knock at the door, and I'd go to the door and talk to a student and come back in order to get myself comfortable to answer the telephone again and then; and that went on for some fifteen minutes. Then he got together, with great composure and dignity he said, "Will you do me a favor?" I said, "Yes." "Please buzz and tell whoever it is on the other end of that buzzer that buzzer that constantly asks you to answer the telephone—tell that person not to disturb you for ten minutes." I did that. "Now will you please lock the door? And do not answer it for ten minutes." I did that. "Now sir, I will tell you something." And this is what he told me. And this of course is the essence of my sermon. He said, "Some years ago the National Council of Social Workers invited me to give their annual lecture there at ----, and I decided that I would give them a lecture on the 'Limitation of Intake.'"[6] And I didn't quite understand, and I expressed it in my face and he said, 'Just wait a minute, and you'll see. I told them that the number 25 bears the same relation to infinity that the number 2,000,000 bears—that it is impossible to make a quantitative impression on infinity. Human need represents that which is infinite and if a man worked a thousand years, 24 hours a day, without eating or sleeping; when he finished, the amount of human need remaining to be met would still be infinite. Therefore, the wise man learns how to limit his intake so that he can increase the quality of his quality as he decreases the quantity of his quantity. Now,' said he, 'you may unlock the door and you may answer the telephone.'"

We are involved in a very special demand in our time, a demand to do things—to function. A part of our heritage in America is a heritage of function. Any time one enters into a discussion with people who come from, let us say, Europe, who are a part of the whole Christian Church in Europe—and one of the things that impresses them when they are brought into contact with Americans is that we tend to be activistic—we do things—we specialize in technics[7] and know-how, of methodology,—and that has become a part of the very climate of our lives. We want always to be busy. I wonder, sitting here this morning, can you sit down at the end of the day or during the day—any time, assuming that you have the leisure to do it, can [you] sit down for 20 or 25 minutes doing nothing, and at the same time still awake? If we go to visit someone, just to visit and if somebody isn't talking all the time, then we think the person is bored. We must— Now that has created a very interesting moral and ethical problem for us. And what is it? In order to guarantee some measure of inner integrity, even at the level of our particular demands—however limited those demands may be—we have devised increasingly skillful means by which we separate ourselves from the things that we do so that we actually find ourselves at one point while we are functioning over there. And we learn how to get the operations going, and then withdraw, and leave them over there, functioning—now and then we tamper with them to keep up the tempo, but increasingly we find that in order to survive we must withdraw ourselves from many of the things that we are doing which fact causes us to increase the aspect of our pretensions. Now that's a very terrifying thing. How many things in which you are involved, activities in which you share,—think about it for a moment—have very much to do, either with where you are in your own mind, with what you believe, which you recognize as being true and honest and valuable and relevant—Think over your own week—aside from the things you've done to earn your bread—how many other things in which you have participated with all the pretensions of earnestness, of believing—and inside you will say to those who shared with you in the participation, "If you only knew." Does that happen to you? Don't think about someone with reference to whom you are sure it is happening. That's too easy. But has it happened to you? Now, let us push it just a step further—It is a part of the price of becoming mature—that's the thing that creates the moral problem for us—for as we become adult, one of the things by which we measure our maturity is our ability to hang out in front of us one kind of sign while the operations that are going on in the place where that sign is hung up are of another character. One of the interesting things about children is that a child is so direct, so honest, so inside-outy; and so the children must be conditioned by adults in order to make it possible for adults not to become embarrassed by the simple, direct honesty of the child. The child, you see, hasn't learned how to hang out the sign which says X, while only G is there. Now there is a straight line you see between the kind of moral responsibility that is involved is the integrity of intent, as that intent is related to what is expressed, and the insight that makes it possible for the individual increasingly to have his motives and his deeds so illumined by the Mind of God as reflected in his truest insight, that what he does, he will be. Now, one reason why we must limit our intake, if we are not to become involved increasingly in activities that destroy our sense of direction and goal; if we do not limit our intake, then we have no alternative except the grossest kind of hypocrisy and dishonesty. Either we participate actively within, in terms of the confirmation of our own spirits in the things that we do so that we will be present and accounted for in our deeds; or, we must work constantly with our creative minds and devoted spirits, brooding over all of the extensions of our personalities in terms of acts and deeds until at last we are able to reduce the things that we do and for which we are responsible to manageable units. And then there will be increasingly some striking relationship between the inner and the outer. For if this doesn't happen, then we begin to lose our confidence in the integrity of our own hearts and minds—lose our confidence in the integrity of our own ideals; for if I day after day do the things that are not increasingly [a] direct expression of my level of intent, then I will become so involved in the doing end of it that my confidence in the intent itself will be undermined. You will recall, doubtless, an old story that was written years ago by H. G. Wells about an oriental king whose wife died in childbirth. And he wanted to build a wonderful memorial to her and he had such a memorial built and after it was built he had it torn down because he said, "She was so wonderful that this can't express my love for her." And then he had another one built with the same story and finally his wise men came to him and said, "Inasmuch as you enjoy the sea so very much and your favorite palace is down along the seashore, your favorite act is to stand at the door of the palace in the early morning and the sun is coming out, and watch the rainbows created by the spray as the sunlight plays on them; why not build a corridor from the door of the palace to the sea and then put in that corridor, deep within it on a pedestal, your wife's bier so that as you look morning after morning out through that corridor at your favorite sight for inspiration, there will be mixed and mingled with the glory of that moment her bier which will be a constant reminder that as wonderful as the spray and the sunlight is, she was even more wonderful." So it was done and he enjoyed it. Years passed and he enjoyed it over and over again; and then one morning when he was looking out he wanted to catch a particular aspect of radiation that came from that combination of sun and spray, but every time his eyes were focused on it, something stood in the way; and he clapped his hands and had his servant come and he said, "Something is obscuring my view. Will you have it moved." And it was his wife's coffin—the thing that was the center—the thing that caused him in the first place to build it that had somehow got lost in other things so that it became his stumbling block.[8]

How about your intake? As you sit here this morning, are there some dreams, some ideals, some great stirrings which sent you on your way long ago, ten years ago, fifteen years ago, twenty years ago—and under the push of the glory of this great awakening that was yours, you moved out on the highway of your adventure—and the years have passed and somewhere along the way, something happened and you lost it—because as you went along you didn't limit your intake; so that more raw material came in than you could handle and keep somehow before you the glory of the thing that sent you out. And you have become more and more involved in activities until at last the (live?) center of your consent has been taken over by the tyranny of details. And in the words of Sara Teasdale, "I wanted to see the glory of the hills, the top of the hills, the wonder; and I said when I get up there it will be so wonderful to stand at the top of the world and take in the glory not only of the view but the fresh mountain air—just think how far I can see in every direction; but the briars are always pulling on my gown. I don't know. I must have crossed the brow of the hill some time ago, but the briars are always pulling at my gown. I crossed it and I didn't know it. And now," says she, "All the rest of the way will be only going down."[9] Of course I don't believe all of that, you see, but there is enough in there to give you a chill. There is something that can be done about it. It is never too late to limit the intake, even at the price of complete withdrawal until at last one's inner resources can be reorganized and refocused and reestablished and resensitized, and then moved back into participation again. For the butter is in the milk, but if I do not have deep within me a stillness and a sense of togetherness and wholeness, I'll be churning skimmed milk, trying to get butter. And I didn't even know it was skimmed milk.

"Thou must churn the milk, O Disciple, if thou desirest the taste of butter." Action—making the thing articulate—but I must have something to make articulate if I am to be, in what I do; or if I am to taste the butter, I must churn milk that has some butter fat content. This is our responsibility, our opportunity, and our challenge—and in our effort to do that we can draw upon the ever-present guiding hand of God, our Father in whom always dwells the fullness and the riches of life.

TD.

NOTES

1. Thurman had preached a sermon on this topic, no longer extant, in the summer of 1949, presumably at the Fellowship Church. See From Francis Geddes, 12 March 1959.

2. Thurman had quoted the poem, from a Hindu source, in *Meditations for the Apostles of Sensitiveness* (Mills College, Oakland, Calif.: Eucalyptus Press, 1947), 34, repr. in *Deep Is the Hunger* (New York: Harper & Brothers, 1951), 27–28. The notion that one's deeper self, to quote the Śvetāśvalara Upaniṣad, "is contained [in the body] like butter in milk" is a commonplace in Hindu thought. See Patrick Olivelle, *The Early Upanisads: Annotated Text and Translation* (Oxford: Oxford University Press, 1998), 423.

3. From Kabir, a sixteenth-century Hindu poet, in the translation of Rabindranath Tagore. Thurman had previously quoted this poem in a 1925 article. See *PHWT*, 1:51–52. In that article Thurman had substituted, for the missing word in the transcription, "Malthurs" for Tagore's original "Mathura."

4. The quotation, inscribed on a wall of Union Station in Washington, D.C., is from James Boswell's *Life of Johnson*. See *PHWT*, 1:166.

5. Cabot, the source of Thurman's favored phrase "the growing edge," visited Howard University several times in the mid-1930s. See *PHWT*, 1:246–48.

6. Cabot had spoken about "limitation of intake" for many years, probably starting with his 1911 address to the National Conference of Charities and Corrections, "The Health of Social Workers." The address included as its final subsection "The Limitation of In-Take," in which Cabot advised his fellow social workers to understand their limits and not try to do more than was physically or psychologically possible, lest we "do poor work owing to the clogging of our minds and energies"; see Richard C. Cabot, "The Health of Social Workers," in *Proceedings of the National Conference of Charities and Corrections,* ed. Alexander Know (Fort Wayne, Ind.: Fort Wayne Printing Company, 1911), 333–40.

7. Lewis Mumford, one of Thurman's favorite writers, is associated with the term "technics," as in *Technics and Civilization* (New York: Harcourt, Brace, 1934) and other works. For Mumford, "technics" is a broader term than "technology," encompassing not only technology itself but also the associated mental and social attitudes it creates.

8. This story is probably from "The Pearl of Love" (1925), supposedly a Persian tale set in North India, in which a young Indian prince, bereft after the death of his wife, spends his life building an ever more elaborate and beautiful mausoleum to house his wife's remains but decides at the end that her sarcophagus disturbs the design and the perfect proportions of the building and his view of the distant mountains, and so he orders it removed. See H. G. Wells, *The Complete Short Stories of H. G. Wells* (London: Ernest Benn, 1927), 162–66.

9. This is Thurman's paraphrase of Sara Teasdale's "The Long Hill," which reads, "I must have passed the crest a while ago / And now I am going down— / Strange to have crossed the crest and not to know, / But the brambles were always catching the hem of my gown. All the morning I thought how proud I should be / To stand there straight as a queen, / Wrapped in the wind and sun with the world under me— / But the air was dull, there was little I could see. / It was nearly level along the beaten track / And the brambles caught my gown / But it's no use now to think of turning back / The rest of the way will only be down" (Sarah Teasdale, "The Long Hill," in Sara Teasdale, *Flame and Shadow* [New York: Macmillan, 1920], 121).

ॐ "He Looked for a City"

2 January 1955
Boston, Mass.

"He Looked for a City"[1] *was a favorite sermon topic of Thurman's at the start of a new year—a time of searchings and beginnings—and he used as its text and theme the journeys of Abraham as interpreted in the Epistle to the Hebrews. For Thurman, returning to a familiar topic, the real task of those "concerned about social change," is not finding "better schemes, better utopian dreams" but opening their innermost selves to a transformation wrought by "an increasing exposure" to "the mind of God and the literal truth which it inspires."*[2]

Meditation:
For our meditation this morning, this first day in the New Year, I am reading two paragraphs from *The Hand of God*:

> The Old Year, like an exhausted arrow, was settling to rest, and, in the waiting silence, I sat watching thoughtfully a thin stream running from a glass.
> Suddenly a gun sounded, a bell began to ring, another, and another.
> "The New Year," I said, and putting out my hand I turned the glass that marked the hours. "The New Year. The years do not wait."
> And then, as must be with all time's pomp and circumstance, presently man's brief and noisy tumult of the opening year ceased. There was a listening stillness now and again; and I rose and went to a large window.

My eyes began to climb, up and up and up. Up the glittering stairways of eternity they went, past Orion and the Pleiades and all the host of them, and, from the topmost diamond height, contemplating awfully the petty triviality of years that come and go, and I murmured: "God! God! God!"

And then I communed and marvelled, and said: "What *is* man, that Thou visitest him, and the mind of man that, like Thine own self, weighteth the mountains in scales and calleth the stars by name? What *is* man, that he feels forever beyond the stars, beyond, beyond, beyond—hungrier than a wolf hunting on the white snows?"

O Eternal, who in divers portions and in divers manners
hast spoken, men say, through prophet, seer and Son,
despair not of me, the least of all Thy servants, but speak
again, even to me also, that deep may call to deep, and
voice to voice, and truth to truth, in me also, if Thou art
Father, in me also, spirit answering to Spirit![3]

Sermon:

It seems almost inappropriate and noisy to break into the movement of the spirit of God in our minds and hearts as we worship together by the use of phrases and words, weak words, weak phrases. So let us meditate for a little while about the meaning of faith in this new year.

The words of our text are taken from the book of Hebrews.[4] And they are words that describe the mood, the searching insistence and the hunger of Abraham, but they are words that describe the mood and the search and the hunger of all of us. We are looking for a city, a city which has foundations whose builder and maker is God. We are looking for something that will not deceive us; something that in the last analysis upon which we may depend with whole hearted and abiding enthusiasm knowing that it will not be altered by our weakness, it will not be betrayed by our limitations but something that will never desert us, that will keep working over the stuff of our lives and the stuff of our world, and the stuff of our experiencing, never giving up but always kneading, working. And we want that. I want it and you want it; I need it and you need it. And this quality I'm calling faith. And to me faith is the tutor, the instructor of man's life. It is not merely assumptions, it is not merely the embracing of an hypothesis, the implications of which we are trying to work out and verify. It is not something that has to do primarily with belief, belief in facts and their validity. Man doesn't have faith in facts, he has belief in facts. No I don't think faith is like that. Faith, and I'm sure when I get through in the next ten or twelve minutes I will be overwhelmed with the feeling that I didn't say it, but that does not relieve me of my immediate responsibility. Faith has to do with literal truth and the conviction that it inspires. It is the unseen model that every man uses, by which he structures the experience of his days. If I ask you, "What is it you are trying to do with your life? What kind of person are you trying to become?" Or if I ask you about the world, if I ask a patriotic American about America, "What are you trying to do through law, through order, through all of the circling series of social processes, what are you trying to do?" If he examined the roots of his movement he would see that he is trying through the manipulation of social forces, of political process, of economic order, to snare into the body of his facts, his conviction about those facts. And when he is doing that he may do violence to me, to you, to someone else. And that is why the man who is concerned about social change must not only understand the materials with which he has to do, the things which he is trying to manipulate, to reorder, to refashion but again and again he must expose the roots of his mind to the literal truth that is the tutor of the facts, the orderer and reorderer of the facts of his experience. That is why there can be no such thing as a faith, once and for all declared, because all the time the mind and the spirit must expose themselves to this literal truth which in my language is the truth of God that becomes for the individual, conviction so that the operation of his life and what he seeks to do with his life or his world are never things that conform to some external pattern but which are modeled and shaped and ordered in accordance to the innermost transformation that is constantly going on in his spirit.

So, on this New Year, my hope for you and my hope for myself and for all men is not that we find better schemes, better utopian dreams, no; but that our innermost selves, from which the integrity of all action moves, be increasingly transformed in the light of an increasing exposure of our innermost selves to the mind of God and the literal truth which it inspires. And I wish for my country that this day, not that we shall have more defenses against enemies, bigger armies and navies or more devices by which we may share in the strangulation of the human race, no not that, but that this thing that we talk about by which we weigh men as if we were God, called the American way, that it be laid bare before not merely the scrutiny which means judgment, but laid bare before the mind of God that the innermost soul of America will be more and more transformed, which transformation will tutor all of the arrangements, the formalities by which we live. Anything less than that is a delusion. And that is faith. Faith is, oh I will use a deadly word, faith is intuitive conviction brought into consciousness in the individual by his response to what to him is literal truth, literal truth. And that's why the man of faith as he works at the materials of his life, whatever they may be, does not ever despair. He may fail, he may be upset in his timetable, his heart may be broken but he does not give up because in him is the city which hath foundations whose builder and maker is God. And what more shall I say? Nothing.

Our words, our thoughts, stumble over themselves, O God, our Father. Thou dost know in ways that transcend the furthest rim of human thought and in thy knowledge is our confidence and our security. Walk with us through the long days that stretch out before us, give unto our deepest needs Thy self this day and forever more.

At.

NOTES

1. Thurman had given a similar sermon, with an identical title, five years earlier to the day: "He Looked for a City," 2 January 1949. For more on this general theme, see Walter Earl Fluker, "Dangerous Memories and Redemptive Possibilities: Howard Thurman and Black Leadership in the South," in *Black Leaders and Ideologies in the South: Resistance and Nonviolence,* ed. Preston King and Walter Earl Fluker (New York: Taylor & Francis, 2004), 167–68; and Walter E. Fluker, *They Looked for a City: A Comparative Analysis of the Ideal of Community in the Thought of Howard Thurman and Martin Luther King, Jr.* (Lanham, Md.: University Press of America, 1989).

2. For earlier examples of similar arguments, see "The Sources of Power for Christian Action" and "Christian, Who Calls Me Christian?" in *PHWT,* 2:93–101, 106–13, respectively.

3. Oswald W. S. McCall, *The Hand of God* (New York: Harper & Brothers, 1957), 50–51. Thurman made minor alterations to the text.

4. Heb. 11:10.

🐾 FROM MARY McLEOD BETHUNE
18 JANUARY 1955
DAYTONA BEACH, FLORIDA

An ailing Mary McLeod Bethune writes to Howard and Sue Bailey Thurman of their long and cherished connections. Bethune's mood is reflective; she writes of her eagerness to get started on her autobiography (which, alas, would remain largely unwritten) and of the future of the National Council of Negro Women without her leadership. Bethune died the following May, and as she had requested, Thurman delivered the major eulogy at her funeral in Daytona Beach.[1]

My dear, dear Children:

Your beautiful letter[2] and the album of Meditations of the Heart[3] came to me at a time when I needed them most. I was not well; I have not been well for some time but I am very much better.

I am so happy that both of you attended the convention. I could not realize for a long time that I really, truly could not attend. But I am very happy to know that the girls who have associated with me all of these years may not be carrying on in my way, but they are carrying on. I hope that they may be strengthened year by year to do an even greater work than I have been able to do.

I do think, Howard, that you and Sue realize just what you do mean to me and what I feel that I mean to you. I am longing to hear these records of meditations. I do not have a machine, but I will try to see if I can get one somehow that will play them. You might say to your great and admired friend, Mr. Danielson[4] that he might provide one for me. It is a great blessing, Howard, that you are leaving these meditations for those who will come after you. I think that it is marvelous that we can have some kind of provision for communing together.

My mind has been very busy in trying to carry on the task that I have undertaken, but my physical strength has not been all that it should be. I am very anxious, Sue, to get on with my autobiography. I do not know why I feel so helpless about it and why I feel that you must be with me for a while in getting it on the way.

Vivian[5] is going to help me in tying together my activities among the women. Frank Horne[6] is coming down to visit me this weekend and we are going to work together on the services rendered the government, particularly the National Youth Administration.[7] You are going to help me in tying all of it. I wish that you were with me for two or three months.

We are getting the Foundation[8] on the way. On March 17 we will be two years old. We are sending out a letter to friends getting some money for the basic work that is to be done. It will take several years, you know, to get it really formulated and put in the form that it should be, but we are doing our best.

I spent ten days recently in Washington attending the World Assembly for Moral Re-Armament.[9] It was a glorious meeting. I will talk with you and Howard about it when we see each other.

I am at home now and will not be away very much. I am trying my best to keep as quiet as I can.

I am glad that Olive is married and hope that she will be happy. Is she continuing to work in her field of art? It warms my heart to know that both of the girls are at work and prepared for life's duties.

My children here are very well. Albert[10] grows better, but he will never be the buoyant, lively Albert he once was. My little great-grandchildren[11] are very lovely and getting on very well.

Be prayerful for my work. Use any means that you can for communicating with me, but above all, Sue, try to arrange to come down and be with me a little while in trying to get the basic things started here in the Foundation and my autobiography.

I am so happy that God has opened up such a wonderful way for you and is using you in such an unusual way. Just know that He never fails us if we trust Him. Lots of love,

[*signed*] Mother Bethune

Mary McLeod Bethune

Dr. and Mrs. Howard Thurman

184 Bay State Road

Boston, Massachusetts

TLS.

NOTES

1. See the eulogy for Mary McLeod Bethune, printed in the current volume.

2. The letter is not extant.

3. Recorded in the early 1950s, the long-playing record contained two sermons: "How Good It Is to Center Down" and "The Contradictions of Life."

4. Albert V. Danielsen (1893–1986) was a Boston-area businessman who with his wife, Jessie Boyd Danielsen (1901–97), started the Danielsen Fund (later the Danielsen Institute) in 1945. The Danielsen Fund supported several projects at the Boston University School of Theology, including helping to underwrite a pastoral counseling center starting in 1952 and after Thurman's arrival in 1953 supporting his work as dean of the chapel, including the recording and dissemination of his sermons. The Danielsen Fund also gave support to several Historically Black Colleges and Universities, including Bethune-Cookman College and Clark-Atlanta University.

5. Presumably Vivian C. Mason (1900–1982), Bethune's successor as president of the National Council of Negro Women (1953–57).

6. Frank Horne (1899–1974), a native of New York City, was an acclaimed poet during the Harlem Renaissance and later trained as an ophthalmologist. From 1936 to 1938 he was Bethune's colleague in the Negro Division of the National Youth Administration. He subsequently was a member of the New York City Commission on Inter-Group Relations.

7. The National Youth Administration (NYA), charged with providing employment and educational opportunities to people between ages sixteen and twenty-three, was created in 1935. Originally part of the Works Progress Administration, it was transferred to the Federal Security Administration in 1939 and to the War Manpower Commission in 1942, a year before its dissolution. Bethune joined the NYA in 1936 and in 1939 became the director of the Division of Negro Affairs, a position she retained until the NYA was disbanded. This was at the time the most senior position in the federal government ever obtained by an African American woman.

8. The Mary McLeod Bethune Foundation was established on 17 March 1953 to perpetuate Bethune's ideals, to preserve her papers (with the intention of helping her to write her autobiography), to support scholarships to Bethune-Cookman College, to foster interracial goodwill, and to inspire young people. Since Bethune's death, the foundation has maintained her former home in Daytona Beach and supported educational projects. See Audrey Thomas McCluskey and Elaine M. Smith, eds., *Mary McLeod Bethune: Building a Better World, Essays and Selected Documents* (Bloomington: Indiana University Press, 1999), 261.

9. In the last years of her life, Bethune became an ardent supporter of Moral Re-Armament (MRA), a Christian organization founded by Frank Buchman (1878–1961), a white Lutheran minister from Pennsylvania. While working in Oxford, England, in 1921, Buchman pioneered a new form of group evangelicalism. The organization was known as the Oxford Group after 1929 and as MRA after 1938. MRA stressed personal reformation and return to the principles of faith as a basis for world peace and for resolving national problems such as racial tension. It was always strongly anticommunist, a tendency that strengthened during the Cold War. MRA's critics faulted the organization for its political naïveté and its lack of attention to social and economic issues. Bethune was involved in MRA by the late 1930s, but her involvement intensified in the last year of her life. She attended several World Assemblies of the MRA, including in Switzerland in August 1954; on Mackinac Island, Michigan, in October of that year; and in Washington, D.C., in January 1955. At the latter venue she argued that racial integration would require "a basic change of heart" among both whites and blacks ("Mrs. Bethune Calls for 'Basic Change' of Heart," *Atlanta Daily World,* 9 January 1955). Barbara Savage has argued that Bethune's interest in Moral Re-Armament reflected her interest in a "personal theological reinterpretation of Christianity to better enable it to serve as a basis for a universal worldwide religion," which directly reflected her interest in Thurman's effort to reconstruct the "religion of Jesus," rather than a "religion about Jesus," although Bethune, unlike Thurman, kept her understanding of "the religion of Jesus" within the conventional bounds of Christianity; see Barbara Dianne Savage, *Your Spirits Walk Beside Us: The Politics of Black Religion* (Cambridge, Mass.: Harvard University Press, 2008), 149–59, esp. 157. Bethune's writings on MRA include "Sees Moral Re-Armament as Means of World Salvation," *Chicago Defender,* 7 August 1954; and "A Tribute to Frank Buchman," *Atlanta Daily World,* 20 April 1955.

10. Albert M. Bethune (1899–1989), Mary McLeod Bethune's only child, was a longtime resident of Daytona Beach, where he was head of vocational services at Bethune-Cookman College and for many years operated the Bethune Funeral Home.

11. At the time of Albert Bethune's death in 1989, he had five children and twenty-three grandchildren

✐ To Melvin Watson

18 January 1955
[Boston, Mass.]

Thurman writes a hearty and jocular letter to his friend and protégé Melvin "Monk" Watson.

Dr. Melvin Watson
Morehouse College
Atlanta, Georgia

Dear Monk:

I appreciate your letter inviting me to preach at Ebenezer[1] next December. About three months ago, Sam Williams[2] telephoned me to invite me to preach at Friendship[3] some time in November. I agreed tentatively to do this and will doubtless confirm it when I am working on my schedule for next year.

This means that I cannot come to Ebenezer because it will be possible for me to make only one trip to Atlanta. I know you will understand this despite the constant fog that surrounds your brain.

We are in the midst of many things in this New England outpost. I shall be leaving on Sunday to go to California to spend some days with Madaline, helping in what may be a final desperate effort of rehabilitation. While I am out there, I will see Olive, who expects sometime in May to make me a grandfather.[4] My friend, you have made such a late start that the great possibility is that you may not look forward to being a grandfather except as you view the earth from Beulah Land.[5]

The reception of my new book, "The Creative Encounter," has been most gratifying. If you read it, it would crack your brain wide open.

Give my love to your beautiful wife[6] and tell her that a constant flood of sympathy flows from me to her as she seeks to endure the dreadful responsibility of trying to make peace out of chaos. Sue says that some day she will surprise you with a letter or a personal appearance. Until such time, my friend, keep your shirt on, even if you must tighten it with safety pins.

Sincerely,
Howard Thurman

TLc.

NOTES

1. Ebenezer Baptist Church in Atlanta, founded in 1886. Martin Luther King, Sr., Melvin Watson's classmate at Morehouse College, was pastor there from 1931 to 1974. Until he was named minister of Liberty Baptist Church in Atlanta in 1958, Watson was a member of Ebenezer Baptist Church, where his father, P. O. Watson, was the longtime clerk and superintendent of its Sunday school.

2. For Samuel W. Williams, see *PHWT*, 2:25–26.

3. Friendship Baptist Church, founded in 1862 and formally organized in 1866, is the oldest black Baptist church in Atlanta.

4. Thurman's granddaughter Emily Sue Wong was born in 1955.

5. Thurman's prediction did not prove true. Melvin Watson, who lived until 2006, had three grandchildren—Melvin Hampton Watson III (b. 1978), Clinton Rahman Fluker (b. 1985), and Hampton Sterling Fluker (b. 1990)—and got to know them well. "Beulah Land," from Isa. 62:4, is a reference to the return of the Jews from exile and became a popular synonym for heaven, as in the popular hymn "Beulah Land" (1875). The hymn was written by Edgar Page Stites and was set to music written by John R. Sweney.

6. Agnes Regina Watson. See To Agnes Robinson, 12 April 1946, in *PHWT*, 3:182–83.

"FREEDOM UNDER GOD"
FEBRUARY 1955
ST. LOUIS, MISSOURI

Washington University in St. Louis, founded in 1853, celebrated its centennial with a "Second Century Convocation" from 19 to 22 February 1955, to which were invited distinguished guests who spoke on the theme of "the Blessings of Liberty."[1] Thurman was the only African American to deliver an address. The other speakers included several university presidents,[2] foreign dignitaries,[3] and Chief Justice of the United States Supreme Court Earl Warren.[4] St. Louis in 1955 was still largely a city where Jim Crow prevailed, and Washington University had only recently been integrated.[5] Thurman told his audience that anything that "restricts the blessings of liberty to a particular class, group, or type of human being is not only against the Constitution, but also contributes directly to moral and spiritual delinquency" and limits our ability to find "freedom under God."

Washington University
Second Century Convocation
I have chosen as my subject for this occasion "Freedom under God," a discussion of the implications of the theme of this Convocation for religion and its important insights.

The Declaration of Independence and the Constitution of the Government of the United States rest upon a simple but very profound spiritual insight—"all men endowed by their Creator with certain unalienable rights." These rights are not conferred upon men by their fellows, acting individually or in formal conclave or deliberation. They are not the predicates of any human subjects. They are not contingent upon status or any social classification whatsoever. They belong to man as a child of God.

The phrase, "the Blessings of Liberty," has no meaning apart from a profound conception of the intrinsic worth of human beings and their ultimate destiny.

Either liberty has to do with the total of life of man and therefore is inclusive of all men, or it is a prerogative of "cult of Inequality."[6] Any device, social arrangement, legislation, custom, dogma, tradition, doctrine, or creed that restricts the blessings of liberty to a particular class, group, or type of human being is not only against the Constitution, but also contributes directly to moral and spiritual delinquency. Persons involved in such attitudes and responsible for such practices are at once guilty of inhumanity.[7]

In reflecting upon the significance of the theme of this celebration for the meaning of religion, I have chosen rather deliberately the subject, "Freedom under God." I begin with the insight that God is the Creator of existence. This means that not only are all living things, the world of nature, time, and space, creations of God, but also, and perhaps more importantly, life itself is so regarded. No event, no experience, no expression of life, has meaning outside of the context of the literal truth of God, conceived as Creator, Ground and Source of all that is. Thus all human history exists under the living judgment of God. Brooding over all law and order, as well as over all of the tragic manifestations of individual and collective chaos, is the creative Spirit of the Living God. Freedom, then, means the operation of individual initiative within the limitations established by an all-comprehensive Mind conceived in terms that are ethical. There is a structure, then, indigenous in life itself, that undergirds and sustains this concept. This structure defines freedom essentially as an awareness of a sense of option or alternative. This introduces at once the ethical or moral note as inherent in the nature of freedom itself. Wherever there is a margin of creativity sufficient for choice or option, the responsibility for such creativity is mandatory. I shall return to the implications of this at a later point in my discussion.

Where there is no sense of alternative, where there is no sense of option or choice, the concept of freedom has no meaning. To be stripped of all option, which would be true if freedom were absolute, is to be denied freedom itself. Therefore, I regard the sense of alternative as the basic context in which all freedoms, of whatever kind, have their significance.

I turn now to a more detailed examination of this proposition. It is my position that this conception of freedom which I am outlining is, in a sense, the rationalization of the most fundamental experience of life as manifested in the meaning of death. Suppose man's physical existence could never be terminated. In other words, let us suppose that a man could not die. This would mean, among other things, that power in the control of his fellows could establish a complete and indefinite tyranny over his life. There would be available to the individual no workable margin of genuine alternatives.

But because of the fact of death, in which all men are finally involved, a fixed point is available by which all merely human activity is defined. Such a fixed point in fact does not have a corresponding point in time. We shall die, this we know; but when, we may not know. The extent to which the point in time is unknown marks the measure of fundamental freedom characteristic of life itself. Within the limits between the time of death and all other experiences of life, the individual has the guarantee of options. As a living creature, however, he is bound by time. Any situation confronting a man which strips him of all effective alternatives is a tyranny. It is only to the Creator of life that such a prerogative is yielded; any person or system that assumes such a prerogative over the life of man is an impostor and soon or late is ultimately rejected or overthrown. This is the rock upon which all doctrines of the divine right of kings, or the divine right of the state, or even the divine right of the Church are finally overturned.

One of the most moving sermons that I heard as a boy was one preached about the meaning of hell. The preacher was a very simple, unsophisticated man, and he was talking to people whose lives moved in very hard places and whose hearts could only be satisfied with ultimate insights. With a vast poetic vitality, he described what hell was like. There was no lake of fire, no wailing, no gnashing of teeth—there was not even a devil. He drew two pictures: one was a large dance hall in which there were thousands of couples dancing, and the other was a large gaming room in which there were thousands of people playing cards. The thing that made the situation hell was the fact that the dancers could never stop dancing. They were condemned to dance, forever and ever—and with the same partner. The card players could never stop playing cards. It was hell because all options and alternatives were forfeited. It was hell because it was a tyranny. It was hell because there was no freedom.

Here we have it. To be denied any sense of alternative is to be cut off from the most fundamental prerogative of the human spirit. The sense of alternative is basic to all meaningful existence.

"Freedom under God" means the recognition of the essential dignity of the human spirit; therefore it is inherent in man's experience with life and is a basic ingredient in personality. This is so universal that it is the key to the intrinsic worthfulness which every man ascribes, at long last, to himself. There is a strange and mighty potency in the elemental knowledge that resides deep in the heart of every man that freedom under God is his birthright as a child of God. Whatever may be the temporary character of its denial, he does not ever give it up. The logic of this is that only before God, the Creator of life, must a man acknowledge a final authority. It is for this reason that men who seek an absolute power over their fellows know that unless they can somehow undermine this conviction, they cannot abide. The dictator, very astutely, seeks to capture or destroy the religious institutions which nourish the springs of this assurance and thereby sustain the freedom of the spirit of man. If the religious institution fails to nourish this assurance, even under the guise that such a position is for the good of the soul of the man, the human spirit, in defense of its own integrity, breaks out in utter and open and dramatic defiance.

If the value judgment of infinite worth is the correlative of the conception of freedom, as I believe it is, then there is available an authentic basis of equality among all men. This means that a man is of infinite worth to himself. For the individual, this is beyond debate, whatever someone else may think to the contrary. The relations that a man works out with his fellows, then, must be circumscribed by the disclosure which he derives from his self–estimate.

We are now prepared to deal with the ethical significance of this spiritual insight. This can be stated in a very simple category: no human being may become the means to ends that deny his worth. Whenever an individual becomes the tool of another human being or of the state or of any social institution whatsoever, he is to that extent degraded and violated. No tyranny, whether it is over the minds of men or over their bodies or over their institutions, can finally be tolerated. Men must be met where they are and treated there as if they were where they should be. In the language of religion, this is what it means to love. It means to deal with a man at a point in him that is beyond both the good and the evil in him. It is to deal with him in a manner or in a sense that is total and exhaustive.

Such a concept of the ethical import of freedom carries with it, by true implication, great and living responsibilities. These responsibilities break down in several important ways. There is the responsibility which the individual has for his own action. The temptation to seek a scapegoat must ever be viewed with the greatest suspicion. Men grow by assuming great responsibilities. Important among these is the responsibility for one's own action. Often it is comforting and reassuring to say that someone else is responsible for what I do. The moment I transfer responsibility for my own actions, I relinquish my own free initiative. I become an instrument in another's hands. This is the iniquity of all forms of human slavery. The slave is not a responsible person, and the result of slavery is the destruction, finally, of any sense of inner worth growing out of an estimate of one's self informed by a sense of alternatives. This observation has far-reaching bearing upon all aspects of human relations. In a family, for instance, if children are permitted to grow up without a sense of responsibility for their own actions, they become lopsided, underdeveloped, and ultimately antisocial. How to define personal responsibility in the midst of the growing complexities of modern life is one of the major tasks of the free spirit. This task is aggravated by the large-scale character of almost all social enterprises. One of the reasons for the contemporary loss of morale with reference to the democratic dogma, for instance, is the disintegration of personal morale on the part of the individual in our society. For morale, in its simplest terms, is a belief in one's own cause. In the absence of a sense of responsibility, there can be no such belief.

It is in order to raise the question: Responsibility to whom? Does it mean responsibility to one's self as if the individual existed alone in all the universe? The answer to this question has to be "yes," but within certain limitations. No man lives to himself, no man lives by himself alone. We are all of us involved in relations with our fellows. This suggests that responsibility is a shared experience. The prerogative which I ascribe to and for myself, I must make adequate provisions for in my relations with others. I am responsible to myself for my own actions; I am responsible to my society for my own actions. It follows, then, that I may never withdraw myself from my involvement with my fellows. Whenever a society takes from the individual the sense of responsibility to it and for it, the grounds of his freedom are undermined. In a highly organized social order such as ours, with its apparent necessity for a wide variety of bureaucratic structures on behalf of order and efficiency, the individual sense of responsibility for and to society is constantly threatened. The manifestation of this contemporary characteristic of our common life is expressed in the personal attitude that many of us have today, that we are not responsible to anyone or to any group, present or past. One of the substantial grounds for the phenomenal rise of crime among juveniles and adults, I believe, is that the sense of belonging somewhere, and therefore of being responsible to something more than to one's self, is disintegrating within our midst. There is a profound sense of isolation creeping through our spirits like a deadly dry rot. There is a spiritual sickness among us marked by despair, hopelessness, emptiness, and loss of nerve. Where personal and social responsibility no longer abide, the life of man turns to ashes on his sleeve. Free men must be responsible to themselves and to each other for the personal and collective life which marks their days.

But there is still another measure of responsibility with which we are involved. "Freedom under God" means that the individual is not only responsible to the society, and the society is not only responsible to the individual, but also, the individual and the society are responsible to God. Justice William Douglas,[8] in calling our attention to this fact, states the following, and I quote his lines: "Our system presupposes that there is what James Otis,[9] in 1764, called the 'higher authority' to which all laws are ultimately appealable. Laws that prick the conscience, that violate standards of decency and justice are laws that courts ameliorate or even strike down. Our civilization rests on the premise that there is a Supreme Being to whom not only man, but government, is accountable. The Declaration of Independence so states."[10]

There is a judgment that presides over the private and collective destiny of man. It is a judgment that establishes itself in human history as well as in human character. God is the Creator of life, and the ultimate responsibility of life is to God. Man's responsibility to God is personal and solitary, but it is not experience in isolation or in detachment.

The religious significance of "Freedom under God" is at once primary and fundamental. It means that a man is not free to initiate or to involve himself in the evil enterprise without serious peril and jeopardy. The value judgment by which the evil enterprise is defined is this: that which is against life in its fullest and most creative unfolding. Whatever works against life, works against God. In a man's private life, this places a limitation upon what a man is free to do, upon what options he is at liberty to elect. To sin means to do violence not only to the light that is within, but also to what conceivably is the purpose of the world. It is to create a disharmony between man and his Creator, his God. It is to be involved in the act that inspires the guilt that separates the individual from God. To state this in psychological terms, it is to undermine the meaning of life for the individual. What is true for the individual is true for the society and the nation. If there be any government or social institution, of whatever kind, that operates among men in a manner that makes for human misery, whether of the mind through fear and despair, or of the body through the freezing of the movement, such as segregation of the spirit through the destruction of any sense of the future, such a government or such a social institution, without regard to its sanctions, is evil and is a diabolical perversion. To the extent that it is so, it cannot survive, because it is against life and carries within itself the seeds of its own destruction. The moral law is binding. There is no escape from the relentless logic of antecedent and consequence. Ultimately, freedom means the ability to actualize potentials. It is to live day by day with the conviction that there is a way for man by which, if he lives, he will become increasingly human, humane, and whole, full of health and peace. To choose such a way is to put at the disposal of the individual life the boundless resources of the Creator of life.

Of such is the fateful character of our responsibility as a nation at this crucial moment in the history of man's life on the planet. It is my conviction that our nation is involved in the far-flung purpose of God to establish a world community of friendly men living beneath a friendly sky. Think of our startling history at this point just for a moment! It is not chauvinistic to affirm that our total life as a nation has been a schooling in the meaning of human freedom against a time when the only thing that saves the collective life of man is a dynamic faith in the worth of the individual and the freedom which it inspires.[11] Our national life was launched in a revolution against tyranny with its corresponding assertion of human dignity. Our emergence as a nation is a judgment against all dictatorships. From the beginning we have been made up of the widest variety of peoples from the ends of the earth. Our roots go deep into the various cultures, faiths, and heritages of the peoples of this planet. For a long time interval we were isolated by two oceans, and in this isolation we were tutored by a political, social, and religious ideal which placed the premium supreme upon the inherent worth and dignity of persons. Our response as a nation to this tutoring was to inscribe these ideals in the formal arrangements by which we pledged ourselves under God to undertake our social adventure. We were blessed with the kind of climate and the abundance of natural resources which contributed deeply to our individual and our collective emotional security—all of this social development against a time when the human race would be faced with a mass crisis created by the almost sudden emergence of such vast power over nature that both time and space are cancelled out, and for the first time in human history, men, wherever they are on the planet, are, as if they were, next-door neighbors. The world is a neighborhood, but there is no confidence in the integrity of neighborliness. For more than a century, we, as token representatives of the many peoples of the earth, have been in school, learning the meaning of human dignity and the responsibility of the freedom which it inspires. Our fateful responsibility before God is to provide the inspiration for and the confidence in the possibilities of a way of life on this planet in which no man need to be afraid and in which "the bruised reed will not be crushed or the smoking flax quenched!" No strength of arms, no might of material wealth can qualify our nation for such a role. This possibility of a life of freedom under God is the crown that He holds steadily over our heads with the hope that as a nation we may grow tall enough to wear it.

> Where the mind is without fear and the head is held high;
> Where knowledge is free;
> Where the world has not been broken up into fragments by narrow domestic walls;
> Where words come out of the depths of truth;
> Where tireless striving stretches its arms towards perfection;
> Where the clear stream of reason has not lost its way into the dreary desert sand of dead habit;
> Where the mind is led forward by Thee into everwidening thought and action—
> Into that heaven of freedom, my Father, let my country awake.[12]

In this prayer of the Hindu poet, the deepest desires of our own hearts are voiced.

                                                                    TD.

NOTES

   1. Thurman's talk was reprinted in "The Blessings of Liberty . . . " (St. Louis, Mo.: Washington University, 1955), 35–46. The title of the convocation was drawn from the preamble to the U.S. Constitution.

   2. Two of these were Grayson Kirk (1903–97), president of Columbia University from 1953 to 1968; and Abram L. Sachar (1899–1993), president of Brandeis University from 1948 to 1968.

   3. These included Carlos P. Romulo (1899–1985), a prominent Filipino politician and president of the General Assembly of the United Nations in 1949–50.

Howard Thurman in his study with the religious scholar Huston C. Smith. Behind Smith is Thurman's painting of a young boy, whom Thurman referred to as "Ben." From the Bailey Thurman Family Papers; the Stuart A. Rose Manuscript, Archives, and Rare Book Library, Emory University.

4. Earl Warren (1891–1974), a native of Los Angeles, worked as a prosecutor and district attorney before being elected attorney general of California in 1938. In 1942 he was a leading supporter of the internment of Japanese Americans who were living on the West Coast, a position he later regretted. That same year he was elected for the first of three terms as governor of California. In 1948 he was the Republican candidate for vice president, and in 1953 he became chief justice of the U.S. Supreme Court, serving until 1969. Under his leadership the Warren Court issued a number of sweeping and often controversial decisions that transformed many areas of the law, including civil rights, civil liberties, the rights of criminal defendants, and legislative apportionment. In 1964 he chaired the Warren Commission, which investigated President John F. Kennedy's assassination.

5. Washington University admitted African American graduate students for the first time in 1948 and undergraduates in 1952. It was only shortly before Thurman arrived on campus, in the fall of 1954, that residence and dining halls were desegregated.

6. This was a possible reference to Stuart Omer Landry, *The Cult of Equality: A Study of the Race Problem* (New Orleans: Pelican, 1945), a defense of racial inequality.

7. Thurman made a similar argument in "The Fascist Masquerade" (1946), repr. in *PHWT*, 3:145–62.

8. William O. Douglas (1898–1980) was associate justice of the U.S. Supreme Court from 1939 to 1975, where he was an outspoken leader of the liberal wing of the court.

9. James Otis, Jr. (1723–83), a lawyer in Massachusetts, in 1761 argued against the colonial Massachusetts government in the *Writs of Assistance* case, an early landmark in the legal struggles that led to the War of Independence. In Otis's published version of his position, *The Rights of the British Colonies Asserted and Proved* (Boston: Edes and Gill, 1764), he argued in favor of judging British laws by a standard of natural law, which he maintained was a higher authority than the British constitution—which is not written in a single document but is comprised of a number of treaties, laws, and conventions.

10. William O. Douglas, *An Almanac of Liberty* (Garden City, N.Y.: Doubleday, 1954), 184.

11. Thurman would make a similar argument in "America in Search of a Soul" (1976), reprinted in Walter Earl Fluker and Catherine Tumber, *A Strange Freedom: The Best of Howard Thurman on Religious Experience and Public Life* (Boston: Beacon Press, 1998), 265–72.

12. Rabindranath Tagore, "35," in *Gitanjali: Song Offerings* (New York: Macmillan, 1916), 27–28.

❧ To Dorothy Henderson

24 MARCH 1955
[*BOSTON, MASS.*]

In a letter to his friend Dorothy Henderson,[1] *Thurman discusses a recent session in his Boston University class Spiritual Disciplines and Resources*[2] *on the distinction between faith and belief.*

Mrs. Dorothy Henderson
R. R. #2
King, Ontario

Dear Dorothy:

The last meeting of the class was on Hebrews 11.[3] It was an experiment in the use of a hard idea as a focal point for religious experience. The substance of the idea was this: Belief is an object of proof and validation. Faith is what belief becomes when it develops into a part of the conscious thinking and feeling of the individual and is not an object of proof.

The analogy that I used was this: In learning a foreign language, a person studies grammar, produces a foreign vocabulary and sentence structure until at last there comes a time when he thinks in the language rather than going through the process of translating the foreign word into his mother tongue and then thinking the word.

The next session of the class will be April 7. The reading assignment is the 13th chapter of I Corinthians. I do not know what the procedure will be but as soon as I know, I will advise you.

I am enclosing the manuscript of the address I gave in connection with the Second Century Celebration at Washington University.[4]

Sincerely yours,

Howard Thurman

Dean

enc.

TLc.

NOTES

1. Dorothy McLaughlin Henderson (1900–1986) was a Canadian author of books on many subjects. The final chapter of her *Biographical Sketches of Six Humanitarians Whose Lives Have Been for the Greater Glory* (Toronto: Ryerson, 1958), 160–88, is on Thurman. She first met Thurman when he spoke in Toronto in 1944 and found that he "did not talk to us, rather he thought with us. Here was no sentimental emotionalism, no wordy intellectualism. Here was something deeper" (ibid., 160). The two became friends, and in 1952 she visited the Fellowship Church, of which she said that "it is a daring experiment. It is not an attempt to weaken the power of religion by adding extraneous elements, but rather an attempt to strengthen the power of religion by rediscovering its essence" (ibid., 168).

2. For an account of Thurman's course on Spiritual Disciplines and Resources, see the biographical essay in the current volume.

3. Thurman used a verse from Heb. 11 as a sermon text several months earlier in "He Looked for a City," printed in the current volume.

4. "Freedom under God," printed in the current volume.

🍃 TO DRYDEN PHELPS

23 APRIL 1955

BOSTON, MASS.

Thurman is "profoundly disturbed" about reports that the Fellowship Church is becoming predominantly African American, a trend that if it continued would choke the "genius of our church" in "the jungle growth of separateness in American life."[1]

Dr. Dryden Phelps

2041 Larkin Street

San Francisco, California

Dear Dryden:

I hope by this time word has come from Sy[2] accepting the appointment for the coming year. As I understand it, he will begin sometime in June and will take time out in the late summer to get married. I am very happy about this because I think that he has a rather important contribution to make and we have a significant one to make to him.

I talked a few minutes ago with Jack Taylor.[3] He is writing to say that it is his plan to arrive in San Francisco on Thursday, June sixteenth. The agreement which I have with him is that I will be responsible for a total of $350 which I will send to the church earmarked for him. I would suggest that when you get my check that you send him $250, the balance of $100 payable to him at the end of the summer. It is my understanding further that by the time he arrives you will have a place of residence for him and will assume responsibility for his expenses. He does not have a car and is not married. This means that if a place can be found in walking distance of the church, it would be a saving in transportation.

One of the constant words that I get from casual visitors of the church during this winter is that the congregation is largely Negro. One visitor actually made a head count as a documentation of what he was saying to me. I am profoundly disturbed about this because we have not found the answer to the intergroup fellowship problem that is created by the sense of separateness in American life. During all the years of the church we have had to face this problem and deal with it. There were times when individuals in the church and the board were inclined to look the other way and to say that the fellowship was so real that no notice should be taken of the social tendency for an inter-racial organization to become more and more dominated by one group or the other. I am very clear at one point and that is that the validity of our religious experience in the fellowship of the church turns finally {largely} on the degree to which we are able to keep the fellowship integrated as to races. If the present tendency keeps up, in another year or two, Fellowship Church will be as any one of a hundred other churches in the United States with token memberships of other racial groups. I have no suggestions to make as to what can be done because I am not there working and would not presume to tell you or the board what to do. I am simply passing on to you what has come to me from a wide variety of people who are all deeply concerned that the genius of our church will not be choked by the jungle growth of separateness in American life.

It is my plan to arrive on Friday or Saturday before June nineteenth. I wish I could come earlier but it is not possible to leave until after the fifteenth.

Thank you very much for the material that comes to me now from the church. It does give me a feeling of belonging. Sue joins me in best wishes to you and Margaret.

Sincerely,

[signed] Howard

Howard Thurman

Dean

TLS. FC

NOTES

1. This trend continued. In September 1958 Francis Geddes wrote to Thurman that the current racial makeup of the Fellowship Church was "30% Caucasian, 65% Negro, 5% other" (From Francis Geddes, 20 September 1958).

2. Dryden Phelps proved to be a controversial replacement for Thurman in the Fellowship Church pulpit. There were complaints that he was an ineffectual and uninspiring leader for the congregation. Biographical details for Sy or Cy Williams are unavailable, but he did not become pastor of Fellowship Church. See From Grace [Huntzinger]?, 20 February 1955. When Phelps left, he was replaced in the fall of 1955 by Francis Geddes. See To Francis Geddes, 1 September 1955.

3. John A. "Jack" Taylor (1931–2011) served as pastor of the Fellowship Church from 1968 to 1971. Taylor, a native of Oklahoma, graduated from Oklahoma City University (1951) and the Boston University School of Theology (M.Div., 1955), where he served as Thurman's assistant at Marsh Chapel. Originally ordained a Methodist, he switched his denominational affiliation to the Unitarian Universalist Association in 1960. He served congregations in Medford, Oregon; Amherst, Massachusetts; Madison, Wisconsin; and Urbana, Illinois, before moving to San Francisco. In 1972 he became minister of the First Unitarian Society of Ithaca in Ithaca, New York, where he remained until his retirement. For Taylor's closeness to Thurman, see From Jack Taylor, 15 October 1956, a long letter asking Thurman for advice about his career.

☙ EULOGY FOR MARY MCLEOD BETHUNE
23 MAY 1955
DAYTONA BEACH, FLORIDA

Although Mary McLeod Bethune was ailing, her sudden death from a heart attack in Daytona Beach on 18 May 1955 was unexpected. Bethune's family asked Thurman to deliver the eulogy, and Thurman, who traveled only by train, by dint of "much twisting and turning" was able to rearrange his busy schedule and journeyed from Massachusetts to Florida in time for the funeral service on 23 May 1955.[1] The service was held in the auditorium of Bethune-Cookman College.[2] Most of the estimated crowd of five thousand listened to the service on an adjacent lawn, with chairs and a public address system provided by the city of Daytona Beach, which also lowered its flags in Bethune's honor.[3]

In his eulogy, after an opening reading from The Pilgrim's Progress,[4] *Thurman spoke of Bethune's remarkable career and of the personal impact of the woman he would later call "a second mother" to him.[5] Thurman's dominant metaphor was Bethune's ability to create "shafts of light," blazing a path forward, surmounting the hardships and frustrations she faced because of her sex and her race, to become perhaps the best-known African American civic leader and educator of her generation. He spoke of her deep Christian faith, her capacity for*

leadership and problem solving, and her tenacious struggle her entire life for the
full inclusion of blacks as equals in every aspect of American life.

Thurman never published this eulogy, which survives only in a thirty-one-
minute tape recording. The quality of the recording is only fair. Some passages,
especially when Thurman was speaking rapidly, are difficult to discern or are
inaudible. Despite the problems the tape presents, the editors believe that the
importance of the eulogy warrants its inclusion in the present volume, and that
the sweep and rhetoric of Thurman's comments have been accurately conveyed.
Indecipherable passages are indicated by brackets; conjectural readings are brack-
eted with a question mark. Doubled words and false starts have been omitted.

After this I beheld until they were come unto the Land of Beulah, where the
Sun shineth Night and Day. Here, because they were weary, they betook themselves a while to Rest. And because this Country was common for Pilgrims, and
because the Orchards and Vineyards that were here belonged to the King of the
Celestial Country, therefore they were licensed to make bold with any of his
things. . . . But a little sleep refreshed them here and they were on their way.[6] . . .
Then the Pilgrims got up and walked to and fro: But how were their Ears now
filled with Heavenly Voices, and their eyes delighted with Celestial Visions![7] . . .
In this place there was a Record kept of the Names of them that had been Pilgrims of old, and a History of all the famous Acts that they had done. . . .

After this, It was noised abroad that Mr. *Valiant-for-truth* was taken with
a Summons, by the same *Post* as the others,[8] and had this for a Token that the
Summons was true, *That his Pitcher was broken at the Fountain*.[9] When he
understood it, he called for his Friends, and he[10] told them of it. Then said he, I
am going to my Fathers, and tho with great Difficulty I am got hither, yet now
do I not repent me of all the Trouble I have done[11] at arriving[12] where I am. *My
Sword* I give to him that shall succeed me in my Pilgrimage, and my *Courage*
and my[13] *Skill* I give to him that can get it. My *Marks* and my[14] *Scars* I carry
with me, to be a Witness for me, that I have fought his Battels who will be my
Rewarder.[15]

When the Day that he must go hence, was come, many accompanied him
to the River side, into which as he went, he said, . . . I am finished.[16]. . . And[17] he
passed over, and all the Trumpets sounded for him on the other side. . . . But
glorious it was, to see how the open Region was filled with Horses and Chariots,
with Trumpeters and Pipers, with Singers, and Players on stringed Instruments,
to welcome the pilgrims as they went up, and followed one another in at the
beautiful Gate of the City.[18]

I come to this moment with a deep sense of gratitude and with a profound
measure of rejoicing. Rejoicing because, it has been our good fortune in our

lifetime to be blessed by so remarkable a human being as was Mrs. Bethune. And therefore because my own sense of personal love and a certain quiet pulling of my own heart strings, because her life has been involved with my own life almost since I remember my own life.

Nevertheless, my overall feeling this afternoon is not one of sadness and depression and heaviness and anguish, but one of very great inspiration and very great courage and very great thanksgiving.

If I were to use a text, I would take the words from the prophet Jeremiah.[19]

Cursed is the man who relies upon man who depends upon mere human aid for he is like some desert scrub that never thrives set in a salt solitary place in the hills. But happy is the man who relies on God who has God for his confidence for he is like a tree planted beside a stream sending his roots down to the water. He has no fear of scorching heat, his leaves are always green, he goes on bearing fruit when all around him is barren, and he looks out on life with quiet eyes.[20]

Now those are the words for our friend.

I have two simple things to say. For this is no time for imparting many words, for her life is an open book. Her monuments are all around us everywhere,[21] so why should we waste time with words trying to say something that the words cannot express because they are listening so hard to what they see.

I have two simple things to say as I have reflected upon the meaning of the life of Mother Bethune. And the first is this. She was able under the widest possible variety of circumstances to turn all frustrations and all handicaps into shafts of burning light.[22] She turned all handicaps and frustrations into shafts of light. Think about that. I want to say again, I want you to paint the picture. She turned all handicaps, all frustrations, all the things that block the way, that cut off the light. She turned them into shafts of light. That is one of her great gifts, and that was her great genius.

Now I want to mention a few of these frustrations which happened in that way for her. In the first place she was a woman in a man-dominated society, and that under many circumstances is a frustration and is a handicap. She did not capitalize on the fact that she was a woman. Well, but she understood what it meant to be a woman and to put at the disposal of the life around her, and indeed her generation, the kind of limitless resources and resourcefulness that is the true, authentic contribution of women of every age of every period in human history. She did that. She lived as a rallying point for the hopes and the dreams, for the aspirations of women as expressed through the way in which she identified herself with the movements and causes which had as their purpose the enlarging of the life of women.

Among her very significant and committed monuments are the monuments that are a part of the foundation of the dreamings and aspirations of the women of our generation and the generations before and the generations to come after. The last great upward push of her creative genius in this regard is symbolized in the celebration that they had a few weeks ago in Washington of the 20th Anniversary of the founding of the National Council of Negro Women.[23] She was a woman [*inaudible words*] and I think, she paved what could have been a handicap, a frustration in a man-dominated society. She turned them into a shaft of light. Whatever else you think of her, she was a leader and she deepened the [demands?][24] of her life at that point.

I remember as a little boy the year that she opened this school[25] as a girls' school, my mother permitted me to wear my first long coat. That was a long time ago. And at least once a month on Sunday night, usually on the 5th Sunday night,[26] she would come out [to Waycross?],[27] to our church, and she would make a talk and she would sing. And then, our congregation would lift an offering and always she would see to it that the little children who were there would come up to the plate with their parents to put their little penny or nickel or whatever else they wanted to put in. And for each child who came up, she would put her hand on her head and saying something—the words I don't remember at all—but the thing quickened in me as through the years she would do that I find now that almost a half a century after that I am drawing on it.

She would take groups downtown to stay at the hotels. But always, the programs she offered were programs way up on the top shelf. She did not permit any clowning. She did not permit any of the things that had to do with any of the derogatory aspects of life. She did not permit that. But always she shared the depth that she had from within the context of her life as a Negro on the assumption that if she addressed herself to the deepest thing that there is in all men by offering the best that she had then that in turn would elicit from them the best that they had. And that was her genius.

Then on Sunday afternoons she had what was called during the days of my boyhood a temperance meeting. And we sang and read speeches of all sorts. But never in any of the meetings on this campus did she ever permit herself to say that there was any difference between God's children.

Almost forty years ago when people sat in the auditorium they sat as we are sitting this afternoon. Long before there was any talk much about integration, any talk—it was before World War number I and World War number II, before the earth's surface had begun shrinking as the result of the way the creative minds of man brooding over the stuff of nature has been able to reduce all of these units to [*inaudible words*],[28] all long before that, she knew, fifty years ago, as if she were living now. That was her great genius. And all the time urging without belligerency and without chauvinism, urging all of us to be proud of our race. Not obnoxious about it, not belligerent, but quietly confident that in us God had spoken. And that we should not fear but should live in anticipation of the time when all of the limitations which we knew at that time would not be. She took this, what many people had regarded as a handicap, as a frustration, and transformed it into a shaft of light.

I remember walking with her for the first time in the Sisters Chapel at Spelman College, it was the—they had just finished the chapel. She and I walked across the campus and into this beautiful chapel.[29] It was one of the first chapels that we had on any of our campuses and as she stood inside the chapel no one was there but the two of us and I was here on one side and she was walking down the aisle. I heard her say, "Thank God. Think of it. All of this for my children." No one heard her. She wasn't talking to the grandstand. She didn't even know that I heard her. But there was always this feeling that if somehow if you manage to release the best and the deepest thing in you then as that moves out into life it reproduces itself in the life and the character of those you touch. She took this frustration and transformed it into a shaft of light.

And then she had another limitation which many would regard as a frustration. You know all of her, many of her associations as an educator were with people who were well schooled and well disciplined in some of the finest institutions in America and she herself did not have all of the advantages of the kind of formal training that many of the rest of us had.[30] This was always true of her. She was a thinker. She had a brain.

And, so profound was she a thinker that in any of the problems whether they were problems in connection with situations that were developing with reference to the government in Washington or broad in fundamental education and policy. Or whether it had to do with problems related to the development of the National Council of Negro Women. Whatever may have been the context in which the problems took place always she had the uncanny ability by what seemed to be sheer reflective thinking[31] to be able to move to the center of the issue while the rest of us tended to move along the edges; she was always working at the center. And standing within the center, she was able to throw light on the meaning of the problem—not merely in terms of the immediate issue that was at stake but in terms of the meaning of that issue first as it affected Negro life and then secondarily as it affected the life of America and the world. She sensed the heart of problems, moved straight to the heart of the problem with an active, reflective, dynamic mind and standing within the issue was able to interpret the issue in terms of its ultimate significance.

And now, the third thing. And I'm through. This gift of her's. Frustration into shafts of light. We need that. And I think that is one of the great heritages that she left to her family and I'd like to say just a personal word there because even though she was a great woman honored by everybody, loved by everybody, but for those in the immediate family she was just family, just family. And you will need to remember what her spirit would say to you at a time like this. That you must take even this frustration and transform it into a shaft of light.

The second thing[32] was her faith in God. I got a letter from her just last Monday about something that I had written.[33] And as always when she tended to business at hand she talked about the real issues in life: man, God, and his relationship with God and with each other. Her faith, her faith in God taught her three very simple things. It taught her that God is, that God is. For then, if you remember ever hearing her pray as I have many times, you were sure that if you open your eyes you could see Him there. And she prayed as though she knew that she was talking to somebody and that somebody answered and spoke deeply to her own spirit. And this was communicated in her life in many ways. Her faith taught her that God is. And it taught her not only that but that God is near, so that in all of the circumstances of her life you had a sense of her presence as being lived in the presence of God and I do not say that merely for this occasion and at this time. She carried around with her a living confidence in God. And at times of greatest crisis in her life, when all the lights were out, when all the issues seemed to be moving in the wrong direction, she always affirmed her confidence in God, on the assumption that she must at least be as sure of God as God was of her. And so she would not let God down by letting her own faith waver. And she thought that God was love and that's why in all of her experiences in the social struggle—and she was in the forefront of those who were struggling in this manner for the improvement of human decency and human relations all over the United States and in her own Southland which she loved—always she leaned into the issues without bitterness of spirit. Now that is not to suggest in any sense that she was a coward. She was a strong, courageous woman who loved deeply and who discovered that her love cast out whatever fear she may have had.

And so, we gather today to express what we cannot express. To say that God has blessed us with her presence in our midst. And that we hope that we can become worthy of all that her life has meant to us and to generations yet unborn. And you may learn of her a thing that first occurred to me when I read her a letter one day that Mahatma Gandhi had written to Muriel Lester.[34] She was discouraged because she wasn't getting anywhere by—with the village people and changing their attitudes towards the freedom of India. And she wrote a very discouraging and heartbroken letter to Mr. Gandhi. And Mr. Gandhi replied with these four lines that I would like to read to you:[35] "Speak the truth," he said, "without fear and without exaggeration. And see everybody whose work is relevant to your purpose. You are on God's work, so you need not fear men's scorn. If they listen to your requests and grant them, you will be satisfied. If they reject them, then you must make their rejection your strength." And this is what she did, always.

So I close as I began, by saying that her life was summarized for me in the words of the prophet Jeremiah:

A Curse on him who relies on man, who depends upon mere human aid, for he is like some desert scrub that never thrives, set in a salt solitary place in the steps. But happy is he who relies on God, who has God for his confidence, for he is like a tree planted beside a stream sending his roots down to the water. His leaves are always green, he goes on bearing fruit when all around him is barren, and he looks out on life with quiet eyes.

This is our friend. And may God be as gracious to us in our living as He was blessed to her in her going.

At.

NOTES

1. To Jessie Danielsen, 25 May 1955. Thurman had to cancel an appearance at Bowdoin College in Brunswick, Maine, to travel to Daytona Beach. In these years Thurman's schedule was always at its busiest in late May, during college commencement season. His travels in the weeks around the Bethune funeral included, in addition to a short trip to Canada, appearances at Princeton University; Denison University in Granville, Ohio; Knoxville College in Knoxville, Tennessee; First Asbury Church in Rochester, New York; and Howard University.

2. For an account of the funeral, see "Mrs. Bethune Called Great Lady of Age," *Atlanta Daily World*, 27 May 1955. This article as well as "Mrs. Bethune Is Buried at Daytona Beach, Fla.," *Atlanta Daily World*, 24 May 1955; and "5,000 at Rites on Fla. Campus," *Chicago Defender*, 4 June 1955, contained excerpts from Thurman's eulogy.

3. This tribute to Bethune by the city government, however heartfelt, was in a city that maintained a policy of segregation in schools, public transportation, and most public establishments.

4. The reading from *The Pilgrim's Progress* was transcribed from the eulogy. The written text is based on John Bunyan, *The Pilgrim's Progress: A Norton Critical Edition*, ed. Cynthia Wall (New York: W. W. Norton, 2008), 237–44 (hereafter Wall), which reproduces the punctuation, capitalization, and italicization of the 1684 original edition. Divergences of Thurman's reading from Wall are noted below. Thurman's excerpts are from the concluding pages of *The Pilgrim's Progress*.

5. From "The House of Thurman" to "Dear Friends of the Wider Fellowship Community," January 1956. In the same letter the Thurmans mention that Sue had visited Bethune a few weeks before her death—in early April—to present to Bethune and the Mary McLeod Bethune Foundation a quilt on Harriet Tubman's life. Sue Bailey Thurman had acquired the quilt from the Historical Quilt Society of California in her capacity as chair of the Archives and Museum Committee of the National Council of Negro Women.

6. Interpolated sentence, not in *The Pilgrim's Progress*.

7. In Wall, sentence punctuated with question mark.

8. In Wall, "other."

9. Eccles. 12:6 (King James Version).

10. Interpolated word.

11. In Wall, "done" for "have done."

12. In Wall, "to arrive."

13. Interpolated word.

14. Interpolated word.

15. In Wall, "who now will be my Rewarder."

16. Interpolated phrase.

17. In Wall, "So."

18. Thurman paused twelve seconds before proceeding.

19. Jer. 17:5–8.

20. The final phrase of the text that Thurman quotes as being from Jeremiah, "and he looks out at life with quiet eyes," is not by Jeremiah, although Thurman had long associated it with Jeremiah and with this text. Thurman used Jer. 17:5–8 as a sermon text as early as 1928; see *PHWT*, 1:122–24. Four years later Thurman's conclusion of "Barren and Fruitful," another sermon using the same text, states, "Which shall it be for you—a scrawny scrub in a desert—barren—or a fruitful tree that looks on life with quiet eyes? Which?" (*PHWT*, 1:161–66). Thurman used the "quiet eyes" quotation as a coda to the Jeremiah text in a Fellowship Church sermon, "The Message of Jeremiah II," 28 July 1952, and after the Bethune eulogy, in 1957 in "The Gothic Principle," printed in the current volume. For instances of the "quiet eyes" quotation in different contexts, see "Review of Douglas Steere's *On Beginning from Within*" (October 1944), in *PHWT*, 3:94–96; and "God Is with Me," in HT, *Meditations of the Heart* (1953; repr., Boston: Beacon Press, 1983), 48. Thurman, an avid reader of poetry, no doubt borrowed the phrase "And [he] looks on life with quiet eyes" from the Chicago poet Francis Wells Shaw (1872–1937), whose poem "Who Loves the Rain" opens as follows: "Who loves the rain / And loves his home / And looks on life with quiet eyes; / Him I will follow through the storm." It was included in Harriet Monroe and Alice Corbin Henderson's well-known collection *The New Poetry: An Anthology* (New York: Macmillan, 1917), 304, and subsequently anthologized widely.

21. A paraphrase of the famous Latin epitaph for the architect Sir Christopher Wren (1632–1723), usually translated as "if you seek his monument, look around you."

22. Thurman borrowed the phrase "shafts of light" from Felix Adler; see To Lenore V. Spivey, 7 April 1964. In *An Ethical Philosophy of Life Presented in Its Main Outlines* (New York: D. Appleton, 1918), 358, Adler wrote of his "spiritual crucifixion" and how he pressed "the sharp-pointed spears of frustration into my breast to make way for spiritual liberty. For these cruel spears turn into shafts of light, radiating outward along which my spirit travels, building its final nest—the spiritual universe."

23. Bethune was honored at a luncheon at Willard's Hotel in Washington, D.C., on 25 February 1955 at a meeting of the National Council of Negro Women, with eight hundred people in attendance. Eleanor Roosevelt gave the main address, and the television personality Ed Sullivan was a featured speaker.

24. Word unclear, sounds like "distills" on recording.

25. Bethune founded the Daytona Educational and Industrial Training School for Negro Girls in 1904, when Thurman was five years old. The school later became Bethune-Cookman College and then Bethune-Cookman University.

26. In many churches the fifth Sunday of a month, occurring four or five times annually, is an occasion for a special service or collection. During Thurman's childhood, in many Baptist churches, the day was often known as "missionary Sunday."

27. The neighborhood in Daytona, Florida, where Thurman was raised.

28. Thurman seems to be referring to modern scientific achievements that have changed the world.

29. Sisters Chapel at Spelman College was dedicated on 19 May 1927. It was named in honor of Laura Spelman Rockefeller (1839–1915), the wife of John D. Rockefeller, Sr. (1839–1937) and Spelman College's primary benefactor; and her sister, Lucy Maria Spelman.

30. Bethune graduated from the Normal and Scientific Course (a teacher training course) at Scotia Seminary in Concord, North Carolina, in 1894, followed by an additional year of schooling at Dwight L. Moody's Institute for Home and Foreign Missions in Chicago before beginning her career as a teacher. Normal schools were generally considered to be postsecondary but precollegiate education.

31. Reflective thinking, a notion borrowed from John Dewey, had long been Thurman's model for creative problem solving. See "Can It Be Truly Said That the Existence of a Supreme Spirit Is a Scientific Hypothesis?" in *PHWT*, 1:54–67.

32. Thurman's points are misnumbered.

33. The letter is not in the Howard Thurman Papers Project's collection.

34. For Muriel Lester, see *PHWT*, 1:231–33.

35. This was one of Thurman's favorite quotations, from Muriel Lester, *My Host the Hindu* (London: William and Norgate, 1931), 15; see *PHWT*, 2:168.

🐦 SPEECH AT LAMBDA KAPPA MU HUMAN RELATIONS AWARD DINNER
19 NOVEMBER 1955
BOSTON, MASS.

Thurman gave this speech at the Human Relations Award Dinner of Lambda Kappa Mu,[1] a sorority of African American professional women and businesswomen. His address, typical of his appearances before black audiences, is direct in speaking of the civil rights struggle. He argues that dramatic legal decisions will not by themselves bring about racial equality, and he calls on each audience member to get personally involved and to "act as an ambassador of good will to change the attitudes of fellow citizens and reduce group hostility."

From the moment we are born we are confronted with the challenge of human relations.[2] In the intimacy of the home there are the relationships between parent and child, sisters and brothers, containing all the potentialities for warmth, affection, cooperative effort and mutual growth on the one hand, or hostility and estrangement on the other hand. Our human relationships move outward to an ever widening spiral to the school, the church, the job, contacts with friends and acquaintances, our role as citizens of the community, our relationship to our government and finally to other peoples of the world. The challenge of human relations has preoccupied the great religions of the world and the best minds among political thinkers and philosophers of every age. It has been the particular concern of governments and social institutions in every civilization.

Every Sunday School child has met up with these provocative words: "Am I my brother's keeper?" and has been taught the second great commandment, "Thou shalt love thy neighbor as thyself," precepts of human relations handed down to us by the Judeo-Christian religion which is part of our western heritage. We have incurred the same theme in the political philosophy upon which our own democracy was founded. What more eloquent interpretation of human relations can be found than in those magnificent stirring lines of the Declaration of Independence—and I think in these times they cannot be repeated too often —

" . . . We hold these truths to be self-evident, that all men are created equal, that they are endowed by their Creator with certain unalienable rights, that among them are Life, Liberty and the pursuit of Happiness; That to secure these rights, Governments are instituted among men, deriving their just powers from the consent of the governed; That whenever any form of Government becomes destructive of these ends, it is the Right of the People to alter and abolish it . . . "

It is this urge toward liberty and equality that explains the revolution now taking place among the peoples of Asia and Africa in their effort to throw off colonial rule and become equal partners in the community of nations.

Whether we take the religious or moral view which imposes responsibility of man, or whether we approach it from the political concept of equality of all men before the law, it seems to me that the essence of good human relations is a fundamental respect for human personality and a belief in the right of the individual to develop to his highest capacity.

This right has been implicit in both the teachings of Christianity and the principles of democracy, but in the history of our own nations it has taken several large wars and many generations of effort to extend it to all sections of the population. These inspiring words of the Declaration of Independence are even more remarkable against the background of the times in which they were written. Black and white servitude was an accepted part of colonial life. Universal suffrage was unheard of and the right to vote was limited to those few who could meet property qualifications; labor's rights were unrecognized and labor unions were illegal conspiracies; women had scarcely more rights than slaves and were considered the wards of their husbands; free public education was almost as revolutionary an idea as universal emancipation from slavery. Equal protection and equality of opportunity did not become part of the basic law of the nation until nearly a century later when the Fourteenth Amendment was adopted. A system of social security for the individual—which has been expanded to include such protection as maternity and child care, workmen's compensation, unemployment insurance, disability benefits, aid to the blind and handicapped, aid to dependent children and old age pensions are all recent developments of government.

Today we are beneficiaries of rights and privileges which were almost beyond the wildest dreams of our grandfathers and our grandmothers. Each succeeding generation has added to the common heritage of liberty out of its own experience and ideals and each new generation must defend this heritage in its entirety from the backward pull of ignorance, prejudice, selfishness and greed which are still prevalent in society. As literacy, suffrage, educational and employment opportunities, and the benefits of mass production and mass communication have spread throughout the population, or responsibilities as citizens have increased, the whole range of human relations has become everybody's business. Wars are now fought by a total population. We cannot shift our responsibilities as free citizens to governments, for no government can substitute for the initiative and genius of a free people acting through voluntary organizations or in their individual capacities as responsible members of the community.

The problem of men and nations in their relationships to one another are not new, but the all-embracing concept of human relations reflects our growing awareness of the interrelatedness of all human experience and the interdependency of all peoples. We have heard a great deal about the new polio vaccine in recent months, but what many of us do not know is that in spite of the millions of dollars poured into polio research, there would have been no vaccine but for the generosity of the Indian people. In order to study the effects of the deadly polio virus and develop a protective vaccine it was necessary to use the tissues of certain monkeys which most closely approximated the human system. These monkeys came from India. Not only are they expensive, but they are sacred to the Indian people. In order that American children might be protected, the Indian people had to overcome deep-rooted traditions and their genuine apprehensions over the treatment of their monkeys in experimental research. This gesture of good will on the part of the Indian people is an example of what constructive human relations in the international field can accomplish.[3]

These unprecedented leaps forward in the physical world only emphasize the appalling gap between man's scientific achievements and his social and political—and, if you please, moral—maturity. We live in constant fear of another war and of the Hydrogen Bomb, the destructive qualities of which we only dimly realize. The world is divided between two spheres of influence and two competing ways of life. At home we have not yet learned how to live together as free citizens, but must expose to the world the spectacle of the state of Georgia blacklisting Negro teachers for belonging to an organization whose only purpose is to insist that the Constitution of the United States be obeyed,[4] the state of Mississippi refusing to prosecute the kidnappers and murderers of

Emmett Till[5]—the state of South Carolina from which Rev. J. H. Delaine had to flee from injustice[6]—the state of Florida where trade unionists cannot meet to discuss union business without being fired upon.[7] Moreover, we have somehow failed to produce a healthy environment in which our children can grow into responsible citizens of tomorrow. The growing spectre of juvenile delinquency and teenage gangs is evidence of a moral breakdown for which we must bear a share of responsibility.

In plain words, while we have accepted and enjoyed the advantages of cooperative human effort in a technological sense, we have not yet fully assumed responsibility for helping to close the gap between technological and social engineering.

The recognition of this lag should not be cause for despair, but rather a challenge to us. Let me take this opportunity to pay tribute to your own organization which has concerned itself with the improvement of human relations in many areas of experience. You have performed the vital function of giving the individual a sense of belonging to something important and a feeling of personal worth not always accorded to him in the large community. Your community program reflects your keen sense of social responsibility through scholarship offers to develop trained youth and through your contributions to other civic and social endeavors.

I said a few minutes earlier that the essence of good human relations was a fundamental respect for human personality and a belief in the right of individuals to develop freely and to fulfill themselves. Its greatest challenge therefore is to the individual—the you and I. The mother or father whose five-year-old says "I don't want to play with Johnny because he's white, or he's black, or he's Jewish, or he's Catholic, or whatever" is as deeply involved in human relations as the representative of a government grappling with the international control of atomic power. In both instances the fundamental problem is that of human beings learning to overcome superficial barriers and find a common ground of mutual appreciation and respect.

I cannot overemphasize the importance of individual effort. Too often we have underestimated the power of individuals to influence the course of events. When more people bestir themselves with issues and candidates, get out and ring doorbells and fulfill their obligation of citizenship to vote, we will have a better caliber of men and women in office and better government. When citizens take the time to write their representatives in Congress, or in the State legislature, or in the local municipal government about matters of deep concern to them, these individual personal letters have far more effect than you dream.

In that complex area of human relations of immediate and personal concern to us—minority rights—each of us can act as an ambassador of good will to change the attitudes of fellow citizens and reduce group hostility. Each of us who lives in a southern community where the issue of integration of Negro children in the public schools is now hotly contested in some areas can write a courteous letter to the local editor or the local school board expressing our views on the subject. For while the dramatic legal victories in advancing human relations in the United States have made an opening wedge, the consolidation of our advances have been brought about by just such small important chores as I have mentioned—face to face contacts among individuals, forums, letters to the editor and small sincere committees thrashing out problems around a table. These are the tiny investments which add up to tremendous dividends in the long run.

TD.

NOTES

1. Lambda Kappa Mu was founded in Harlem in 1937. The Boston chapter was established in 1947.

2. The term "human relations" was popularized by the social psychologist Elton Mayo (1880–1949), who taught for many years at the Harvard Business School. At first primarily applied to management theory, by the 1950s the term was being used as a more capacious equivalent of "race relations," including not only blacks and whites but all social groups. For instance, a few weeks before Thurman's talk, Pittsburgh established a Human Relations Commission, replacing the Civic Unity Commission and Fair Employment Practices Commission. The new commission was an advocate for the participation of all persons "in the cultural and economic life of the city, free from restrictions because of race, color, religion, ancestry, national origin or place of birth" ("15 Sworn on Human Relations Commission," *Pittsburgh Courier*, 1 October 1955).

3. The production of the Salk polio vaccine required the kidney cells of Rhesus monkeys, which had to be imported from India in large numbers. Alarmed by reports that monkeys were being tortured to produce the vaccine, and responding to strong antivivisectionist sentiments among many Hindu groups, India banned the export of monkeys on 12 March 1955 but lifted the ban on 10 April after American pressure. On 12 April successful results of the massive clinical trial of the Salk vaccine were announced, and the vaccine soon became widely available. Since the early 1960s, polio vaccines have used as their medium vero cells, a self-perpetuating in vitro cell culture, originally derived from African green monkeys.

4. On 10 July 1955 the Georgia Board of Education voted to revoke the license of any Georgia teacher belonging to the NAACP. The ruling was overturned by the board in late August, but not before Thurman's good friend Benjamin Mays wrote a column on the incident, "Is Georgia Becoming a Police State?," which was published in the *Pittsburgh Courier* on 6 August 1955.

5. Emmett Till (1941–55), an African American teenager from Chicago, was visiting relatives in the Mississippi Delta when, on 21 August, he allegedly flirted with a white woman at a grocery store. On 28 August he was kidnapped from the home of his relatives and brutally murdered. The incident became a cause célèbre, attracting international media attention. By the time Thurman gave this address, Roy Bryant and J. W. Milam had already been tried for the murder of Till in a five-day trial, widely criticized for its inadequacies,

that ended on 23 September with their acquittal. The following year the two men acknowledged their responsibility for the murder in an article in *Look* magazine, and neither man
ever served time for the crime.

    6. On 10 October 1955 Joseph Armstrong De Laine (1898–1974), an AME minister, was
forced to flee his home in Lake City, South Carolina, after his house, for the second time,
was sprayed with gunfire. In 1950 he had fled his home in Summerton, South Carolina,
over death threats for his role in organizing the suit that became the landmark federal
school discrimination case *Briggs v. Elliott*, 342 U.S. 350 (1952). After leaving South Carolina, he moved to Buffalo, New York, to resume his ministerial career. See Orville Vernon
Burton, Beatrice Burton, and Simon Appleford, "Seeds in Unlikely Soil: The *Briggs v. Elliott*
School Desegregation Case," in *Toward the Meeting of the Waters: Currents in the Civil Rights
Movement of South Carolina during the Twentieth Century*, ed. Winfred B. Moore, Jr., and
Orville Vernon Burton (Columbia: University of South Carolina Press, 2008), 176–200.

    7. In Umatilla, Florida, on 19 October 1955, shotgun blasts wounded twelve black cit-
rus workers attending an organizing meeting of the United Packing Workers Union. The
Lake County sheriff, with a history of violent racist acts, was widely suspected as the likely
perpetrator of the attacks.

"HABAKKUK EXPOSITION"
1956

In 1946 George A. Buttrick recruited Thurman as an editor and annotator for
The Interpreter's Bible,[1] *which was a twelve-volume series. Among its several
dozen editors, Thurman was the only African American. The Interpreter's Bible
was one of the most significant mid-century Protestant Bible commentaries. Its
main purpose was to help preachers find material for sermons. Thurman's most
important contribution to* The Interpreter's Bible *was providing expositions of
the Books of Habakkuk and Zephaniah.[2] Although Thurman completed and submitted his commentaries in 1950, they were not published until 1956.[3] Emphases
and boldings are reprinted as in the original.*

    In The Interpreter's Bible *the commentary sections on each book were
divided into three parts: the "Introduction," the "Exegesis," and the "Exposition."
The "Introduction" provided a general guide to each book; the "Exegesis" was a
verse-by-verse commentary illuminating the historical, linguistic, and theological
meanings of the text; and the "Exposition" was intended as a more general reflection on the text's meaning. Thurman wrote to Buttrick in 1946 that "the point
of the exposition ought to be to stimulate creative thinking based upon the basic
facts, textual and historical of the text."[4]*

    *The "Expositions" for Habakkuk and Zephaniah are the only full-scale com-
mentaries that Thurman prepared on any sacred or biblical text. It is not clear
why Thurman was asked, or why he agreed, to provide the exposition for these*

two particular books, which are, respectively, eighth and ninth in the ordering of the minor prophets in both the Jewish version of the Hebrew Bible, known as the Tanakh, and the Christian version, the Old Testament. Habakkuk and Zephaniah are dense and difficult books, bringing news of God's wrath and an impending doom. Their theology, harsh and minatory, evoking a national God of a specific people, would seem to be at a great remove from Thurman's own views of God as a benevolent and universal force. Perhaps nowhere else in his work does Thurman grapple with as much empathy, and at such extended length, with the appeal of the traditional theologies of Judaism and Christianity as he does in his Habakkuk and Zephaniah commentaries.[5] Thurman ultimately aligns his vision of God with that of the prophets. As he states in the Zephaniah "Exposition," "The tendency on the part of the prophet to regard the enemies of his people as also the enemies of God is a very human one." Thurman goes on to state that this is, however, incompatible with the declaration of one God for all peoples so fervently declared by the prophets: "Of course there can be no universal worship of the true God unless all people are one. The idea of monotheism leads irrevocably to the idea of one people—one family inclusive of all peoples—under God." If, as Thurman fears, the modern world is often moving in the opposite direction, humanity must summon enough faith in the radical unity of God to counteract it: "The demand for one faith to match one world means that the concept of monotheism is the only one that provides a religious basis for modern life." Ultimately, as Thurman concludes at the end of his Zephaniah commentary, his God and that of the prophets are, perhaps, not all that different:

The time will come, so the chapter declares, when God will be his own witness.[6] He will gather together all peoples and enter into judgment against them. At such a time he will change the speech and give to all a common tongue, the purpose of which will be to enable all to worship God and serve him with one accord. The dream of seer and prophet finally comes to the same resting place. There is one God, one family, and one habitation. God is the creator of life and all that therein is. The mark of the creator is on every forehead and his signature is in every living thing. What is inherent in life will become manifest in deed. This is the destiny of man, this is the destiny of all of life. The homing instinct is given, and the time shall come when there shall be no alien lands, no strange peoples, and no expression of life outside the divine accord. Every knee shall bow and every living thing and all creation shall join in the grand paean of praise and worship of the God of life who is at once the God of faith.

HABAKKUK[7]
EXPOSITION

1:2a. *None to Help*.[8]—Habakkuk opens with a cry which reveals the prophet's mood of despair. The prayer experience must ever take into account the times of dryness, of denials, of emptiness. The reasons for this are numerous. It may be due to scattered thoughts or attachment to plans, ideas, or experiences that break the divine accord; or to bad timing, when the mood of prayer is strangely alien to the spirit; or to the movement of the spirit of God in a manner unpredictable and strange. It is instructive that the mystics, despite their insistence upon the necessity of spiritual disciplines or exercises, are careful to point out that the exercises themselves do not guarantee the "coming of the spirit" or an awareness of the Presence. Always undergirding prayer there must be an attitude of trust and confidence that submits one's total enterprise to the will and the mind of God. But sometimes the urgency is so great, the pain growing out of the need so overwhelming, that the anguish and frustration spill over into a cry which in itself becomes a judgment and a startled accusation! **How long shall I cry, and thou wilt not hear?**[9]

2b. *Finding Words for It*.—Often there is great relief in being able to put into words the quality or the very nuance of need and suffering. To suffer in dumb silence, to be able to find no word capable of voicing what is being experienced, seems degrading to the self because it pushes the individual back into a vast feeling continuum from which he has emerged into a personality, self-conscious and self-aware. Man was a feeling creature long before he was a thinking creature. The mind is younger than the body and younger than the emotions. When we are able to be articulate it means that detachment from immediate experience, however great, has been achieved. A context of objectivity has been established, from within which the individual is able to look on his experience and name it. This seems to characterize the divine act always. When the individual is thus able to voice his profoundest feelings, he sees himself quite unconsciously presenting God with a compulsion on his behalf. There is added challenge in the words if they name what is happening.

3. *The Divine Context*.—The idea that God is responsible for ills in life is a great safety valve for the spirit of man. And yet it is much more. It springs out of a deeper insight: at long last there must be no distinction between the God of life and the God of religion. All events in life take place somehow within the divine context. The tendency to fix responsibility is inescapable. If responsibility for ills can be pinned down, then the possibility of attacking and uprooting them is very real. This possibility is grounded in the profound confidence that a structure of moral integrity bottoms all of life, that such a structure is basic in the totality of all experience. Things do not merely happen; they are a part of some kind of rationale. If the rationale can be tracked down and understood, then the living experience, however terrible, makes sense. Yet even when that is not possible, one cannot down the confidence that the logic of all ills is knowable. A man traces them as far as he can, until at last he seeks no longer to understand the ills but rather to understand God's understanding. Lacking this, he rests himself in the assurance of God's presence and sovereignty in him and in life about him. He sees the travail of his own soul and is satisfied (cf. 2:20).[10]

4. *What Is the Matter?*—The plaint of the prophet that **the law is slacked**[11] has a familiar ring. The lines have an undertone of self-pity, which is one of the most natural reactions of those subjected to injustice. The orderly process seems to be ever at the mercy of the disorderly. Weeds do not have to be cultivated, but vegetables must be. Those things in life which make for disintegration seem ever alert, taking advantage of every situation to turn it to their account.

The wicked do prosper. A casual observation suggests that this is true because of sin in human life. But the basic problem remains untouched, for the crux of the issue is not merely the fact of wickedness and injustice in life, rather the supervitality which they always seem to possess. The "evilness" of evil seems to be more dynamic and energizing than the "goodness" of good. When we are ill with tonsillitis we seek to amuse ourselves by trying to remember how we felt when we did not have tonsillitis; but we cannot do it.

The behavior of the wicked discloses an intensity of loyalty which is indeed striking. One seems to discover among them the general recognition that the stakes are very high and nothing less than a binding devotion will suffice. There is an efficiency and an intelligence about deliberate injustice that yields power even though it may be short lived. Whereas the behavior of the righteous often appears to be weak, indecisive, and uncertain. They seem to find it very difficult to make up their minds and to define their terms. The assumption that there is something about goodness that is so inherently superior to evil that it is not necessary to "work at" goodness is thoroughly gratuitous.

Note, however, that the ground rules for righteousness and for unrighteousness are the same. Whatever it is that causes strawberries to grow causes poison ivy to grow, and for exactly the same reasons. When the conditions for growth have been met, then growth follows automatically. The fact that the former is a delight and the latter is a disorder is beside the point. But this is not the whole story. If both are sustained by the same energies and guaranteed by the same vitality, then we are faced with a problem that cuts deeper than the conflict between righteousness and unrighteousness. There must be a unity deeper than the area of conflict. This unity is in God, so that back of all the outcrying against evil, back of all protests, lies the conviction that rejects evil as ultimate. This assumption is present all through the utterances of Habakkuk. The deep confidence that life will not finally sustain evil is a part of the distilled wisdom of the race, and the door of hope through which the generations have passed into the city of God.

5–17. *The Dimensions of Moral Behavior.*—This entire section calls attention to a very important insight concerning human history. It was clear to the prophets of Israel that God was the creator of life, the world, and all mankind. God was also righteous will, who had expressed himself through a series of mighty acts. One of the mighty acts was the creation of a community so sensitive to his will and purpose that they were a peculiar and special people. It was a faith that recognized the fact that God was at work in all of human history, even in those aspects of human history which seemed most negative. All movements among the nations, whether they acknowledged God or not, had to be regarded as a part of the divine process. His was a sovereignty intent on making even the selfish and most antisocial ends of all the peoples of the earth serve his holy purpose.

Such a position raises a profoundly significant moral question: If the behavior of **the Chaldeans**[12] is the result of a movement of God in their midst, and not due to acts initiated by themselves for ends which they have determined, how can moral responsibility be fixed? If a nation acts as an agent of the divine purpose, the judgment of its acts belongs only to God. But does this mean that the normal operation of moral law described in terms of reaping and sowing is suspended? In the text, it is true, the Chaldeans are characterized as **that bitter and hasty nation**; further, they are **dread and terrible. They all come for violence....** **They gather captives like sand.** And finally, they are called men of guilt, **whose own might is their god!**[13]

It seems clear that the prophet is recognizing two distinct dimensions of moral behavior and ethical responsibility. One dimension involves the private end and the personal good of a nation. These may arise out of concerns and desires which are selfish and antisocial in character. The means used to fulfill such ends are determined by the ends themselves. The moral judgment of such means and ends may be measured in terms of the effect on the nation and of the suffering such behavior inflicts upon others. But there is a still wider and more comprehensive sense in which the behavior may be interpreted. The private life of a nation takes place on a world stage, and the nation itself is involved in a vast historic movement, the total significance of which can be understood only by one who sees all of life as a whole or as a single unit. In the light of this dimension not only will the Chaldeans be involved in moral judgment because of responsibility for their own actions, but they will also become, at one and the same time, instrumental in a wider moral judgment. God relates the totality of their own situation to the fate of Judah and makes them instruments in his hands to measure his judgment upon Judah for its apostasy. The struggle of the prophet is seen most accurately in the assertion:

Art thou not from everlasting,
   O Lord my God, my Holy one?

.   .   .   .   .   .

O Lord, thou hast ordained them as a judgment;
   and thou, O Rock, hast established them for chastisement.[14]

The prophet closes the chapter with a vivid picture of life as comparable to a sea, and men are thought of as fish and crawling things that have no ruler.[15] They are caught ruthlessly and indiscriminately to be destroyed. The method by which such destruction takes place guarantees the economic security of the destroyer and becomes the object of his devotion and worship. There is a wide and sweeping note of contemporaneity in all of this. Men worship the symbols of their economic security and the guarantors of their standard of life. Consequently they tend to be moral and religious as they move away from the areas of their security, and immoral and irreligious as they move toward the centers of their security. So overwhelming is the prophet's reaction to his observation that he forgets, for one breathless moment, that all human history is in God's hand, and cries out in bewilderment and confusion:

Is he then to keep on emptying his net,
   and mercilessly slaying nations for ever?[16]

How hard it is to remember that under God life is its own restraint!

2:1. *Man Challenges God*.[17]—There is something authentic and dignified about standing one's ground. This can be done in various ways. Sometimes it is the result of being directly challenged by another, whereupon the ground of one's position has to be stated. When this is done, one's own convictions become clarified and defined. What we defend, we possess—though indeed we may possess it from either the inside or the outside.

But there is another way of taking a stand. It is to wager one's own integrity on the rightness of an issue. This is to be reckoned with. The prophet sees the destruction, the evil that has befallen his people, and he refuses to accept at its face value what he sees. He recognizes the evil; but there must be a deeper meaning, some hidden clue which, if he could understand it, would fit the terrible events into a perspective that would justify his faith in God. Fundamental to the prophet's insistence is the assumption that there is a structure of dependability undergirding the universe and informing all events. There is nothing that can exist outside the divine contingency. Against the darkness of the period something wars, something struggles to break through that will give meaning and significance to all experience. The basis of such confidence may be merely the result of a steady observation of events over a time interval of sufficient duration to give an objective basis for hope. It may go deeper, and be the result of an inner testimony of the soul which informs the interpretation of experiences.

One cannot overlook the element of arrogance implicit in the demand that God answer to man for his behavior. Here is a recognition, as we would phrase it, of that autonomy in personality which must ever be respected by God, the creator of life. The audacity of the implication is startling as the insight is exhilarating. The prophet is declaring that what we call personality must be taken into account in the far-reaching plans of the divine order. Even though he may admit his powerlessness to change circumstances, he knows that evil can be overcome as long as its center does not shift from circumstances to God, from conditions to the springs of the inner life. To say "Yes" to evil, as if it were ultimate, is to be overcome by evil. It is the recognition of this fact that underwrites the integrity of the prophet's challenge.

There is also a significant suggestion of detachment in these opening words of challenge. From the watchtower it is possible to have a sense of objectivity with reference to the crucial events of the common life. It makes it possible for one to seem to be outside of, or above, the struggle; one is aware of, but not involved in, what is going on. The detachment which fulfills itself in a thoroughgoing asceticism issues too often in avoidance; but this in no way lessens the importance of detachment. We are all activated in small or great degree by what W. E. Hocking has called the principle of alternation.[18] Involvement and withdrawal, taking up our burdens and putting them down, working and resting—all are a part of the central rhythm of existence. The prophet uses the principle as a tool by which he is enabled to lift his sight above the movement of the Chaldeans and the cry of the stricken, to glimpse the design of which all these things are but for instances.

God is not only in history; he is above history. We are in history, involved in the necessity of time-space relationships, and therefore, to say no more, often find it difficult to decipher the meaning of our personal struggles, of the struggles of our times. If, however, we could be lifted out of that context even for one swirling moment of profound perspective, then we might see the whole through the eyes of God; then with quiet courage and confidence we might walk on the earth by the light in the sky. This the prophet seeks for his times.

2. *The Moving Finger Writes.*[19]—It is a matter of more than passing significance that the prophet is urged to **write the vision**, to put it down.[20] This gives to the vision more than a temporary character, the result of the prophet's response to a temporary stimulus. It will serve also as a check against being carried away by sheer drama and emotion. *Scripta littera manet.*[21] The written word establishes a point of authentic response against which unfolding events may be checked. It is in this instance a commitment, even a covenant, giving the declared counsels of God. Moreover, it is an objective manifestation, that divine and righteous intent which places the covenant out of bounds as far as rumor or denial is concerned. It is as if God were saying to the prophet, "This is my

deliberate purpose backed by my own integrity. Write it out that all may know what it is that I will do, to the end that you yourself may be protected when it seems as if my promises are not being fulfilled."

3. *Wait for It.*—The reason for this necessity is made obvious in the opening words of the verse. The **vision** may not come to pass as quickly as is expected. Here we are face to face with the ever-present problem of timing in relation to ends. The acuteness of human need at any moment may cry out for immediate release, immediate action at the point of urgency. Because the help does not come in accordance with our own timetables, we seem driven to conclude that it will not come at all—or if it does, that it will be too late. The assumption is that our own problems are completely unique and isolated from other considerations. The assurance here is that even though the vision seems **slow**, it will come; **wait for it**.[22] Life is so interwoven, so deeply unified, that there are no solitary, isolated events. Unless we can stand outside of process, outside of all time-space operations, it is impossible to know what the particular experience which is ours means in the divine schedule. And since we can never quite do that, we must be willing to wait, informing our waiting with the assurance of faith.

There are several ways by which men **wait**. There is the waiting in rebellion. It means bringing the judgment of a great impatience upon the waiting experience. There is the waiting in resignation. All the life is given out and nothing remains but a dull listlessness. There is the waiting in anticipation. Such is the waiting of the righteous, so the prophet insists. It is alert, charged with expectation. It is on tiptoe.

4. *Timetables.*—Here is a radical contrast. The just, the righteous man waits in anticipation. He is active, but his activity is from within the timetable of God's plan. Not so with the faithless oppressor, the impious man. He is arrogant, full of idle boasting, ever trying to bolster up a sagging self-respect. That he can never do by the methods he is using; but a part of his sickness is his inability to realize this fact. It is not an accident that Christianity never tires of warning against the sin of pride and inculcating the virtue of humility. Pride is never possible when a man measures his life and deeds by God's demands held steadily before him. It can be maintained only when a man measures his life and deeds by his own egocentric impulses, or the life and deeds of others seen always from the outside. Therefore the arrogant man is never satisfied; how can he be when he is both judge and juror for his own case? There is no other-than-self reference. He is God; he can do no wrong, for who is there to make it clear? On penalty of death he may conquer others; but he cannot cope with their spirits—they always elude him. This only increases his arrogance, because it eats away at his self-respect. Only **the righteous shall live**; and he shall live **by his faith**, by his patient trust and obedience (cf. Paul's use of this text in Gal. 3:11).[23]

5-20. *The Cup in the Lord's Right Hand.*[24]—The resistance against oppression often heightens perception and yields an uncanny insight into the weakness of the oppressor. The prophet spells this out by voicing the thoughts of the oppressed. They whisper among themselves words, the basic import of which is to stabilize their own morale. Since morale springs largely from belief in one's own cause, the words provide a judgment upon the life and deeds of the oppressor.

Here the prophet discusses five great woes. These woes are the judgment of God; and that judgment is in a very real sense, from our point of view, inherent in the moral structure of life. Men who act in certain ways—so we should be inclined to say—encounter them automatically. To the prophet there was nothing automatic about it. Such men encountered God (vs. 16*b*).

The first woe[25] has to do with plundering, taking by violence what does not belong to one (see Exeg. on vs. 5).[26] Those who suffer such deprivations tend to be supported by an inner assurance that retribution will redeem their losses. The very plundering itself seems to solidify the sufferers and becomes a curious confirmation of the brotherhood of man, until at length the power of the plunderer is undermined by his own voracity, and the victims seek to get back their own. When this happens, there is all too often no mercy for the plunderer, and all ethical considerations are waived. The assumption seems to be that the act of the plunderer places the whole relationship of man to man in an amoral dimension. May it not be, however, that this is an illusion? When the victims seek to overcome the oppressor and get back what was taken from them, are they not bound by the same moral law that binds the oppressor? It is an unresolved dilemma for which there is no solution. The victims become the agents of retribution; but as such, are they not also morally responsible?

The second woe has to do with another kind of dishonesty. This woe deals with economic exploitation. When a person or nation exploits the needs of others at a price which brings **evil gain for his house** (vs. 9),[27] he inspires bitterness and contempt. For it means that gain has been got out of the helplessness and desperation of others. The fact that this is done in an effort to guarantee one's self against the same kind of desperation is beside the point. The problem is not simple in a complex society, because so many operations for gain are impersonal and ethically mindless. It is natural to seek to make one's family safe from the plight of those whose predicament is exploited. Such behavior, says the prophet, actually defeats the end one seeks, for it corrodes the very fiber of those who enter into such a heritage. **The stone will cry out from the wall** (vs. 11).[28]

The third woe is still another facet of the same issue. Here the figure is one of a nation that is built upon blood, whose cities are founded upon crime. The judgment cuts deeply into the whole basis upon which men give effect to the political, social, and economic agreements by which they live. Violence and bloodshed are the means by which civilizations are built. In one sense they are a part of the procedures of cultural and economic expansion. In the long march toward orderly social living, violence has been the mentor of man. There is no civilization that has appeared in human history that does not rest upon some form of conquest. Not only is this true, but it is also true that civilizations have found it expedient to maintain themselves in the same way. As their position became more secure, they have been content to protect themselves by the threat of violence. The prophet urges that nations are bound by the same morals as individuals. Perhaps this is the reason why the seeds of decay seem ever inherent in civilizations. They rise, they fall. Always the judgment of God is upon them (vs. 13) because they make impossible the realization of God's plan for men. And what is that plan? That the knowledge of him shall cover the earth as the waters cover the sea (vs. 14).[29] It is a dreadful judgment. The prophet implies that until nations are built in a manner that makes a climate for an immediate awareness of the knowledge of God, they cannot survive.

The fourth woe shifts the ground somewhat. It has to do with another kind of exploitation, the exploitation of the person. It is an attack upon the individual's self-estimate. Here is a picture which is strangely moving: a man is goaded by the oppressor until at last he strikes out in a kind of behavior that denies the orderly ground of his own living. He is driven to act in a way that disgraces himself. He is stripped of all dignity and sees himself as one who has been laid bare by his own rage. The feeling is that he has been tricked; as indeed, the prophet suggests, was the intent of the evildoer. When he has been thus exposed, his taunter gloats over his shame. But beware! It shall surely be repaid. The "cup of God's fury" shall the oppressor himself be forced to drink and his share shall be double. He will experience the shame of his victim as well as his own (vs. 15).[30] He will say to himself: "Woe is me! What my victim experienced was wrapped in his innocence; but what I am going through is cradled in my guilt."

The fifth and final woe has to do with idolatry, which is the source of all the woes. The essence of idolatry may perhaps be said to consist in calling a good thing bad or a bad thing good. It is the delusion which causes one to impute the prerogatives and the power of God to a no-God. This is what happens when a man makes the demand of an idol that should be made only of God. Who is being fooled? The man knows that he has fashioned the idol; he knows that it is his conception and creation. Does the fact that he made it give it certain powers that are unique? This is the ultimate arrogance. One is reminded here of the words with which Jesus spelled out the meaning of the sin that shall not be forgiven.[31] A man who calls a bad thing good, or a good thing bad, over a time interval of sufficient duration, will arrive irrevocably at the point of no-discrimination in values. He becomes a person without moral judgment. No idol can act like God.

Such behavior as is set forth in the five woes presupposes the assumption on the part of men that they are outside the divine scrutiny. They suppose that they are here

> as on a darkling plain
> Swept with confused alarms of struggle and flight,
> Where ignorant armies clash by night.[32]

But this is not so. **The Lord is in his holy temple,**[33] which is the whole earth. Therefore all of life must be lived within the context of that knowledge. It is with reference to God finally that we are to live out our days, deep within the stillness of our spirit to carry with us the constant awareness of his presence. Out of that reverence let the deeds of a man's life pour forth.

3:1–7. *The Judgment Implicit in Events.*—I have heard. . . . I saw.[34] Here we come upon the empirical basis for moral judgment. Even the prophet cannot escape the necessity for seeking such a basis. There is a sense, however, in which for him moral judgments and religious experience are absolute, carrying their own sure integrity, needing no ground for validation other than in God. They are therefore on one aspect not contingent upon any data beyond themselves. It is ever so with the prophet. "Thus saith the Lord" puts for him the final stamp upon the act, the word, the deed. Standing within the enclosure of such assurance he is protected from the invasion of the urgency to prove that what he says is true.

The peril of this kind of authority is of course that there is provided no means by which the individual can be protected from the ever-present possibility of self-deception. At some point error may have entered into his judgment, error that may not be related to the judgment itself, but error which may have crept into his interpretation. That contingency never disappears from the horizon of human activity and thought. That it does not is one of the high tributes which God pays to personality. Personality is dynamic, characterized by growth, by change, by elasticity. Man is not an automaton, thanks be to God. But this very fact makes it possible for all calculations and judgments to go awry.

Suppose then that the moral judgment and the empirical experience seem to be irrelevant or contradictory. It may be that the individual is looking in the wrong places for verification. It may be that the time interval at his immediate disposal is too short. Here again we pick up the earlier note of the prophet— we must wait, we must not be hasty in our judgment. We may be overlooking the whole matter of timing and of process. It may be with the events of human history as it is with seeds. Some seeds grow, blossom, and fulfill themselves in a single short season; other take many months, or even years, before they realize themselves. The law of growth, the schedule of each, is its own secret disclosure. Thus it may be with the events of human history. But in the last analysis the imperious demand of the moral judgment is inescapable, even though we are unable to decipher its empirical involvement. Yet the attempt has to be made. Inherent in the experience of moral judgment is the insistence to establish its validity outside of one's private relationship with the judgment itself. Its relevancy must ever be sought, even though it may always escape detection. Paradox or paradoxes.

The prophet, however, is speaking from within an inclusive perspective. He is not confronted with the customary dilemma. For him the moral judgment is implicit in the event. Of this he is sure because of what he has seen and heard. On the basis of such data he confidently asks and expects God to *be* God. In this divine movement, however, despite his confidence, he wants to be sure that there will be no wide sweep of divine judgment which will include the innocent as well as the guilty. He wants God to **remember mercy.**[35] Is there a place for mercy in the concept of retributive justice? Can there be reaping and sowing without the innocent being involved? The prayer of the prophet is that God's judgment will be a discriminatory one within the context of the divine morality. And with that he leaves the final issue to God.

3–16. *The God Above History.*—In these verses the prophet reviews what he has seen and heard, the mighty manifestation which he prays may take place again: "In the midst of the years make [thyself] known" (vs. 2*b*). God is the creator of the world and all of life, and the proper response of the earth to his glory is to give him praise (vs. 3*b*). But be not mistaken by this glory; it is the light behind which his **power** rests (vs. 4). It is awful majesty, and when it operates among the works of creation, it moves in as a mighty force on the rampage (vs. 5), inspiring a deep fear where once was praise. Now the God above history, the God above nature, is on the march. And terrible things follow in his wake.

In a single question, **was thy wrath against the rivers?**[36] the prophet raises the whole problem of the involvement of creation in the judgments of God. Not only man is responsive to the mind of God, but all of nature as well. The moral judgment of God is inherent in the whole process of creation. There is nothing that is not included in the divine movement. "The Lord is in his holy temple," and his holy temple is "all the earth" (2:20).

Note that it is the moral judgment of God expressed in his concern for his people that initiates the movement in which all creation is involved. God as righteous will expressed himself in a series of mighty events of which the creation of the world was one. But another of his works was the creation of a people peculiarly responsive to his will. On their behalf he sweeps through all time and space.

We may quarrel with the way in which the prophet seems to establish squatters' rights over the divine prerogative. We may find it difficult to accept the validity of the ancient insistence of Israel that they are a peculiar people. But the fact remains that the influence of Israel on human history, growing out of that presupposition, has moved through the centuries like the Gulf Stream in the Atlantic. Why this is true remains to this day a baffling enigma. The miracle of Israel provides at least one empirical basis for the moral judgment of God on human history. So convinced is the prophet of this that with confidence he can say:

> I will quietly wait for the day of trouble
> to come upon people who invade us.[37]

17-19. What Are the Odds?—These verses are an idyl of hope and confidence. The conclusion is that paradox itself may be the ultimate validation of the moral judgment. The final resting place of the religious spirit is that the basis of hope is never ultimately to be found in the course of events. Man is not required to wait until the stubborn and unyielding facts of life justify his faith in life. The testimony of the spirit of God in man is the final testimony, the ultimate truth by which his steps must be guided. His assurance must never be at the mercy of the movement of life about him; he must find the witness of God in his own heart or he will never find it.

From "Habakkuk: Text, Exegesis, and Exposition," in *The Interpreter's Bible,* vol. 6 (New York: Abingdon, 1956), 979–1002. Copyright © 1956 by Abingdon Press. Used by permission. All rights reserved.

PD.

NOTES

1. See To George A. Buttrick, 3 May 1946, in *PHWT,* 3:190–92.

2. Because of space limitations, the Zephaniah "Exposition" is not included in this volume. See "Zephaniah: Text, Exegesis, and Exposition," in *The Interpreter's Bible,* vol. 6 (New York: Abingdon, 1956), 1013–34.

3. See From Elizabeth Stouffer [Buttrick's secretary], 14 August 1950.

4. Ibid.

5. Thurman returned to Habakkuk as part of a 1958 Marsh Chapel sermon series on the prophets ("The Creative Encounter–Habakkuk," 16 November 1958).

6. Zeph. 3:8.

7. The Book of Habakkuk, unlike most prophetic books, provides no biographical information about its author. Because of its mention of the Babylonians, also known as the Chaldeans, who came to prominence around 612 B.C.E., we know that it was written after that date. Scholars have disagreed on whether it was written before or after the destruction of the Judean kingdom in 586 B.C.E. by the Babylonian armies under King Nebuchadnezzar.

8. "O Lord, how long shall I cry for help, and thou will not hear?" (Hab. 1:2). The *Interpreter's Bible* includes the King James Version (KJV) and the Revised Standard Version (RSV), which are printed side by side. All biblical quotations and citations in Thurman's "Exposition" and the endnotes are from the RSV unless otherwise noted.

9. Thurman's quotation combines the KJV and the RSV of Hab. 1:2.

10. "But the Lord is in his holy temple; let all the earth keep silence before him" (Hab. 2:20).

11. "So the law is slacked and justice never goes forth, for the wicked surround the righteous, and justice goes perverted" (Hab. 1:4).

12. "For lo, I am rousing the Chaldeans, that bitter and hasty nation, who march through the breadth of the earth to seize habitations not their own" (Hab. 1:6).

13. Boldface text quotations are from Hab. 1:6–11.

14. Hab. 1:12 (KJV), here omitting the phrase "we shall not die" before the continuation of the verse after the elision.

15. Hab. 1:14 (KJV).

16. Hab. 1:17.

17. "I will take my stand to watch, and station myself on the tower, and look forth to see what he will say to me, and what I will answer concerning my complaint" (Hab. 2:1).

18. For Thurman's prior use of the American philosopher William Earnest Hocking's (1873–1966) principle that "God and the world . . . must be pursued in alternation," see *PHWT*, 2:221n43.

19. From Edward Fitzgerald's 1859 translation of "The Rubáiyát of Omar Khayyám," st. 51.

20. "And the Lord answered me, 'Write the vision; make it plain among tablets, so that he may run who reads it'" (Hab. 2:1).

21. Translation of the Latin is "the written word endures."

22. "For still the vision awaits its time; it hastens to the end—it will not lie. If it seems slow, wait for it; it will surely come, it will not delay" (Hab. 2:3).

23. "Behold, he whose soul is not upright in him shall fail, but the righteous shall live by his faith" (Hab. 2:4). Galatians 3:11 quotes this verse to set up the classic Pauline distinction between "the law" and "living by faith," a distinction not in Habakkuk.

24. From Hab. 2:16.

25. Hab. 2:5–8.

26. Hab. 2:5, "Moreover wine is treacherous; the arrogant man shall not abide" is notoriously obscure. The exegesis (by Charles L. Taylor, Jr.) of verse 5 follows the text of the Septuagint, the Greek translation of the Tanakh, and the Habakkuk commentary found in 1947 at Qumran, now in the West Bank, and suggests reading the reference to wine as "the oppressor"; see *The Interpreter's Bible*, 6:989–90. The Habakkuk commentary, or Pesher, one of the most celebrated of the Qumran or Dead Sea Scrolls, was in 1950 also among the first to be published.

27. "Woe to him who gets evil gain for his house, to set his nest on high, to be safe from the reach of harm!" (Hab. 2:9).

28. "For the stone will cry out from the wall, and the beam from the woodwork respond" (Hab. 2:11).

29. "For the earth will be filled with the knowledge of the glory of the Lord, as the waters cover the sea" (Hab. 2:14).

30. "Woe to him who makes his neighbor drink of the cup of his wrath, and makes them drunk to gaze on their shame!" (Hab. 2:15).

31. That is, the sin against the Holy Spirit, in Mark 3:28–30, Matt. 12:30–32, and Luke 12:8–10.

32. Matthew Arnold, "Dover Beach" (1867), lines 35–37.

33. "The Lord is in his Holy Temple; let all the earth keep silent before him" (Hab. 2:20).

34. "I have heard the report of thee, and thy work, O Lord, do I fear" (Hab. 3:7); "I saw the tents of Cushan in affliction; the curtains of the land of Midian did tremble" (Hab. 3:2).

35. "In wrath remember mercy" (Hab. 3:2).

36. "Was thy wrath against the rivers, O Lord? Was thy anger against the rivers, or thy indignation against the sea, when thou didst ride upon thy horses, upon thy chariot of victory?" (Hab. 3:8).

37. Hab. 3:16.

From Henry Bollman
7 January[1] 1956
East Gloucester, Mass.

Thurman's weekly Sunday broadcasts reached many who did not attend services in Marsh Chapel and many, such as Henry Bollman,[2] who rarely or never attended regular church services. Bollman's admiration for Thurman's preaching led to a friendship between the two men that lasted throughout Thurman's years in Boston.

Dear Dr. Thurman,

I am writing this letter immediately after hearing your very inspiring and moving sermon on the subject of Peace of God,[3] which came to me via FM radio.

Though I am 66 years old, I believe this is the first time in my life that I have been enough moved to sit down and write such a letter as this, to a speaker. Generally, radio sermons leave me cold . . . as indeed do most church services.

I wish I could convey to you my appreciation of your profound understanding of the meaning of God's peace. Perhaps you will understand better when I tell you that, for many years, I have been a student of Vedanta . . . and have heard many of the great Hindu teachers speak. Until I heard you today, I have never heard a Christian preacher who could be put on the same level of spiritual understanding as the great Swamis of India. As you spoke, it was as though I were hearing Sri Ramakrishna,[4] talking in the language of today. That, I can assure you, is as high a compliment as I can imagine.[5]

What you said about the necessity for suffering to achieve understanding came home to me forcefully. My wife was recently killed in an automobile accident, while driving with her sister. I was not in the car. We had been happily married for 33 years.

Suddenly this radiant creature was snatched from my life . . . and now I am totally alone, living in a tiny cottage on a windy hilltop in East Gloucester, with a grand view of the harbor, and the ocean beyond . . . as my only solace.

Suddenly to find yourself, ill, alone, and with very very slender means of existence; growing old . . . there you have a classic combination of the elements of suffering.

Yet, my lowest moments have, in a sense, been my highest. The sharper the pain, the deeper the ache, the more enlightenment came to me . . . as you said it would.

Since I can not hold a regular job, I amuse myself with writing a column in the Gloucester Daily Times. It brings me many friends, and provides a sort of vicarious companionship.

I mention these personal matters to give you an idea of the person whose life you have brightened; and whose soul you have strengthened.

I imagine you must feel, sometimes, that you are speaking into a vacuum . . . as far as receiving response, or seeing the fruits of your preaching. Well, at any rate, here is one soul that cries "Thank you" for your message . . . one who will benefit from it.

Very gratefully yours

[*signed*] Henry Bollman

Henry Bollman

                                                                                                        TLS.

Notes

1. Bollman misdated the letter; he wrote it the following day, Sunday, 8 January, the date of Thurman's sermon.

2. Henry Bollman had a varied career as an educational filmmaker, real estate agent, potter, and author. His wife Gladys was killed in an automobile accident in Pennsylvania in 1952. They wrote *Motion Pictures for Community Needs: A Practical Manual for Information and Suggestion for Educational, Religious, and Social Work* (New York: Holt, 1922).

3. HT, "The Peace of God," 8 January 1956.

4. Sri Ramakrishna (1836–86) was a leading Indian mystic whose disciple, Swami Vivekanda, helped popularize the Vedanta school of Hinduism in the United States.

5. In his sermon Thurman spoke about Hinduism, relating that one of the "holy men of India" once told Gandhi that to find the peace of God he ought to retreat from the world and spend his time in an ashram in the Himalayas. Gandhi responded, in Thurman's telling, "that he was finding the peace, the tranquility of God in the midst of his struggle, and that he did not need an artificial hair-shirt is the way he put it; that the struggle for freedom with the empire was his hair-shirt" (HT, "The Peace of God").

🐟 To Martin Luther King, Jr.

14 March 1956

[*Boston, Mass.*]

"Martin Luther King. I suppose I am one of the few members of the faculty of the Graduate School of Theology at Boston University that while he was there had

no influence on his life," Howard Thurman would write in 1974.[1] *The two men would come to know each other better with the start of the Montgomery bus boycott, and King's rise to national prominence would bring them closer. Although King was an admirer and careful student of Thurman and his work and the two men had known each other since King was a child, their relationship had not been particularly close and was somewhat one-sided. Thurman had yet to take a full measure of King's remarkable talents and abilities.*

By March 1956 the boycott had emerged not only as the most serious challenge to Jim Crow in the South since the 1954 Brown *decision, but also as an opportunity for the civil rights movement to test the tactics, strategy, and philosophy of nonviolence. Thurman's letter to King expresses a characteristic interest to intervene quietly behind the scenes, through intimate conversation rather than through public statements or exhortation.*

Dr. Martin Luther King
309 S. Jackson Street
Montgomery, Alabama

Dear King:[2]
 I have not communicated with you before, because I wanted to be sure of my Tuskegee dates. I shall be in Tuskegee for the weekend of March 24. I arrive Saturday morning.
 I would like very much to sit down and have two or three hours talk with you and one or two of your close associates. I prefer doing it in private at Tuskegee. Would you be interested in such a possibility and, if so, would it be possible for you to drive over to Tuskegee any time of Saturday afternoon, March 24? Please let me know as soon as possible.
 Mrs. Thurman wants you to use the enclosed to do something personal in nature for Mrs. King.
Sincerely yours,
Howard Thurman
Dean
enc.

                                                                            TLc.

NOTES
    1. HT, "Martin Luther King Lecture #2," 10 April 1974, Pacific College of Religion?
    2. This seemingly gruff greeting, using only a last name, was a term of intimacy and endearment that Thurman reserved for African American friends. This perhaps reflects the practice of black colleges such as Morehouse in referring to students by their last names, as

a response to the common white southern practice of calling blacks by their first names or by insulting terms such as "boy." See *WHAH*, 36.

🐦 From Martin Luther King, Jr.
16 March 1956[1]
Montgomery, Alabama

King writes to Thurman that because of his previously scheduled engagements, they will not be able to meet. Despite this, Thurman's name appears often in King's correspondence around this time. As King notes in his response to Thurman, his name had just come up in a letter written by the civil rights activist and author Lillian Smith.[2] In her 10 March letter to King she wrote, "I think Howard Thurmond (sic) could be of help, perhaps, to you. He is truly a great man; warm, deeply religious."[3] Homer Jack,[4] a prominent Unitarian pacifist, had visited Montgomery earlier that month, in part to size up the potential of the boycott for Gandhian nonviolence. Jack wrote to King on 16 March stating that he recently had "a good talk with Howard Thurman about your protest."[5] Events would draw King and Thurman closer. About this time Thurman sent King a copy of Deep River *and inscribed it with one of his favorite sayings: "The test of life is often found in the amount of pain we can absorb without spoiling our joy."[6]*

Dr. Howard Thurman
Boston University
Marsh Chapel
300 Bay Street Road
Boston 15, Mass.

Dear Dr. Thurman:

Thanks for your very kind letter of March 14.[7] I am very happy to know of your interest in our cause. I just received a letter from Lillian Smith, and she mentioned your name as a person who could give us real advice in this situation.

Unfortunately, I will have to be out of the city on the weekend of March 24. But for this, I would be more than happy to talk with you concerning this whole situation. I will be back in town sometime Monday morning, March 26. Do you plan to be in Tuskegee that long? If not, I hope it will be possible to talk with you some time in the near future.

Mrs. King sends her best regards and wants Mrs. Thurman to know how deeply grateful she is to her for her thoughtfulness. She plans to write soon. With warm personal regards, I am

Sincerely yours,

[*signed*] M. L.

M. L. King, Jr.

President

MLK/b

TLS.

NOTES

1. This letter was reprinted in Clayborne Carson, ed., *The Papers of Martin Luther King, Jr.*, vol. 6: *Advocate of the Social Gospel* (Berkeley: University of California Press, 2007), 173–74.

2. Lillian Eugenia Smith (1897–1966), a native of Jasper, Florida, was one of the most outspoken and controversial white southern liberals of her generation; she was forthright in her condemnation of both Jim Crow and temporizing white moderates. Her books include the best-selling novel of interracial romance *Strange Fruit* (New York: Reynal and Hitchcock, 1944) and a volume of essays and memoirs, *Killers of the Dream* (New York: W. W. Norton, 1949).

3. Clayborne Carson, ed., *The Papers of Martin Luther King, Jr.*, vol. 3: *Birth of a New Age, December 1955–December 1956* (Berkeley: University of California Press, 1997), 168–70.

4. Homer Alexander Jack (1916–93) was born in Rochester, New York, and raised as a nonpracticing Jew. He entered Cornell University in 1933 to study botany, earning his Ph.D. Attracted to the Unitarian ministry, he attended Meadville Theological Seminary in Chicago (B.D., 1944). He served in a number of Unitarian pulpits and was later executive director of SANE, the National Committee for a Sane Nuclear Policy (1960–64). He was the editor of *The Gandhi Reader: A Sourcebook of His Life and Writings* (Bloomington: Indiana University Press, 1956). Jack's article "The Emergence of the Interracial Church," *Social Action* 12, no. 1 (January 1947): 31–38, was the first comprehensive account of the interracial church movement and treated the Fellowship Church at length.

5. Carson, ed., *The Papers of Martin Luther King, Jr.*, 3:178–79.

6. The inscribed cover of *Deep River* was reproduced in ibid., 6:225.

7. To Martin Luther King, Jr., 14 March 1956, printed in the current volume.

🍃 FROM JAMES EARL MASSEY

17 APRIL 1956

DETROIT, MICHIGAN

Thurman was a role model and inspiration to several generations of young black ministers. James Earl Massey,[1] at the start of a distinguished career as a preacher, teacher, and writer, was already an ardent admirer, as he makes clear in this letter. The two would go on to enjoy a close friendship, and Massey became a distinguished commentator on Thurman's preaching and religious thought.[2]

Dr. Howard Thurman
Professor of Spiritual Disciplines and Resources
Boston University
Boston, Massachusetts

Dear Dr. Thurman:

This is not my first letter to you but it is the first from me to you that you have had the occasion to read. I turned over in my mind, for many years, the desire to write to you and tell you what a blessing you have been through your writing and speaking. While in Europe in 1952, as a soldier, I wrote to you while you were still in California at the Church for the Fellowship of All Peoples—but alas: you didn't get the letter because I sent it to Los Angeles when it should have been sent to San Francisco! However, here is another occasion.

This is quite a belated congratulation but I want you to know that I well respect your appointment there at the University. I have the clipping about it from the New York Times. It seems that by no amount of turning about could I get to hear you during your recent trip to Detroit.[3] I called Dr. Banks[4] the week before you were scheduled to arrive and when he told me that you were here but for that Sunday night I was disheartened. I just couldn't get to hear you at that time. I have read nearly everything that you have written and have in my library all of your recent books: Jesus and the Disinherited, Deep Is the Hunger, Meditations of the Heart, The Negro Spiritual Speaks of Life and Death, The Creative Encounter, Deep River. While in Atlanta some years ago I went into the library there at the University and read some from your book The Greatest of These.[5] Do you happen to know where I can secure a copy of that book at this late date? Also, during one of your trips here to Detroit in connection with the Lenten Season, I heard you quote these lines, fell in love with them, and have since tried to find them but could not: "I'm tired of sailing my little boat / Within the harbor bar / I want to get out into the deep / Where the big ships are."[6] Is that one of your original poems? I should like the complete poem, if possible.

I shall expect to see that you will one day, in the not too distant future, give the Lyman Beecher Lectures on Preaching; Dr. James H? Robinson's[7] contribution is quite noteworthy, to say the least. Perhaps we might take the words of the late Edgar DeWitt Jones as an intimation of your possible choice: see p. 402 of his The Royalty of the Pulpit.[8] Perhaps I will some day be privileged to have you speak to our interracial congregation here.

I have enclosed a booklet of mine published in 1955.[9] I must confess that I have been often stimulated by your resourcefulness. I was glad to see you

156   17 APRIL 1956

listed as one of the ten most noted Negro ministers in the United States today.[10]
During my vacation this summer, I intend to stop in Boston, if possible, and
perhaps meet you really along with your family?
May God bless your labors continually.
[*signed*] James Earl Massey
JAMES EARL MASSEY
JEM/jm

                                                                           TLS.

NOTES

    1. James Earl Massey (b. 1930) was minister of Metropolitan Church of God in Detroit
(1954–76); campus minister at Anderson University in Anderson, Indiana (1969–77); lead
preacher on the weekly radio program "Christian Brotherhood Hour" (1977–82); dean of the
chapel at Tuskegee University (1984–89); and dean of the School of Theology at Anderson
University (1989–95). Anderson University is affiliated with the Church of God (Anderson,
Indiana), a denomination in the Holiness Wesleyan tradition. Some of Massey's published
books are *The Burdensome Joy of Preaching* (Nashville, Tenn.: Abingdon, 1998), *African
Americans and the Church of God* (Anderson, Ind.: Anderson University Press, 2005), and
Stewards of the Story: The Task of Preaching (Louisville, Ky.: Westminster John Knox Press,
2006). Massey first heard Thurman preach in 1949, when he attended Thurman's Lenten
sermons at Detroit's Central Methodist Church. Massey introduced himself to Thurman
at one of these sermons. In his autobiography Massey wrote of this first encounter: "I was
moved by his preaching, very deeply moved, partly because hearing it all validated my own
spiritual quest and findings in a way that no other preacher's words or pulpit approach had
ever done, and partly because of the realization of divine presence I experienced in connection with his witness. As I listened, I understood his witness, and experienced God in
my spirit, I sensed then and there that Dr. Howard Thurman and I were inwardly kin. . . .
[He] did not preach like most of the African American preachers I had heard. There was no
stormy struggle in his manner, no loud blaring of his words; his was rather a soft-spoken,
assured and assuring witness, a statement that seemed to me more like an 'inside word'
about some treasured truth and not an outside attempt to break into the truth. His style
seemed so uniquely at one with his subject. Thurman helped me to experience spoken
truth more vividly than any preacher I had ever heard before. I took note of this as something other than the effects of a mere pulpit manner or an oratorical manner. His message
and manner made me sense again the wholeness of being which since a child I had come to
believe belongs to the experience of hearing the word of God!" (James Earl Massey, *Aspects
of My Pilgrimage: An Autobiography* [Anderson, Ind.: Anderson University Press, 2002],
65–66).
    2. James Earl Massey, "Thurman's Preaching: Style and Substance," in Henry J. Young,
God and Human Freedom: A Festschrift in Honor of Howard Thurman (Richmond, Ind.:
Friends United Press, 1983), 110–21. See also James E. Massey, "Bibliographical Essay: Howard Thurman and Rufus M. Jones, Two Mystics," *Journal of Negro History* 57 (April 1972):
190–95.
    3. Thurman spoke at the Second Baptist Church in Detroit on Sunday, 8 April 1956
(From G. Merrill Lennox, 9 April 1956).

4. Allan A. Banks, Jr. (1913–77) was a native of Texas and a graduate of Bishop College in Marshall, Texas. After receiving an M.A. in economics from Howard University, he entered its School of Religion—where he was Thurman's student—earning a B.D. and an M.A., the latter degree in 1943. That same year he became an assistant pastor at the oldest African American congregation in Michigan, Second Baptist Church in Detroit. He became senior pastor in 1947 and remained in the position until his death. During the trip to Detroit discussed in this letter, Thurman stayed with Banks.

5. *The Greatest of These* (Mills College, Calif.: Eucalyptus Press, 1945) was Thurman's first book and the only one of his early books published by Eucalyptus Press that was not republished by Harper; it was the most difficult of his books to obtain. Thurman scrawled on the top of the letter, "Send Greatest of These."

6. Daisy Rinehart, "The Call of the Open Sea," *Munsey's Magazine* 34, no. 1 (October 1908): 36, repr. in John C. Lebens, ed., *Vagrant Verse* (St. Louis, Mo.: Avalon, 1926), 33. Although this was one of Thurman's favorite and most-oft-quoted (and most oft-requested) poems, he had forgotten its source, calling it in his autobiography "a poem by an unknown author I had learned many years before" (*WHAH*, 65). Thurman's version invariably skipped the second of the poem's three stanzas. Daisy Rinehart was a poet and short story writer who lived most of her life in Charlottesville, Virginia.

7. James H. Robinson (1907–72) delivered the 1954–55 Lyman Beecher Lectures on Preaching at Yale University, the first African American to do so. The lectureship was established in 1871 in memory of Lyman Beecher (1775–1863). Robinson, a graduate of Lincoln University in Pennsylvania (1935) and Union Theological Seminary (1938), pastored congregations in Cleveland before in 1958 becoming the founder and director of Operation Crossroads Africa, an aid organization. Robinson's books include *Road without Turning: The Story of Rev. James H. Robinson, an Autobiography* (New York: Farrar, Straus, 1950) and his Lyman Beecher Lecture, published as *Adventurous Preaching in a World of Change and Trouble* (Great Neck, N.Y.: Channel Press, 1956).

8. "No Negro has yet given the Beecher lectures. Perhaps this was too much to expect in the past, but what about *now*? A large section of the world of sport has lifted the color ban, and millions of devotees have approved the action. Other doors once closed to the Negro are now open. There are at least a half-dozen ministers and educators of the Negro race whose brilliance, scholarship, and consecration are such as to rate them 'markedly successful.' It is good to know that Dr. Howard Thurman recently gave *The Ingersoll Lecture on Immortality*, and that Professor Edgar Sheffield Brightman of Boston University said: 'Dr. Thurman's lecture is one of the most brilliant and satisfying, both intellectually and spiritually, in the entire Series.'" Edgar DeWitt Jones, *The Royalty of the Pulpit: A Survey and Appreciation of the Lyman Beecher Lectures on Preaching* (New York: Harper & Brothers, 1951), 402–3 (italics in original).

9. James Earl Massey, *The Growth of the Soul: Meditations on Spiritual Meaning and Behavior* (n.p., 1955).

10. Perhaps this was a reference to the 1953 article in *Life* magazine that listed Thurman (without regard to race) as one of "The Twelve Greatest Preachers of Our Time" ("Great Preachers: These 12—and Others—Bring America Back to the Churches," *Life*, 6 April 1953).

𝄞 To C. H. Winecoff
25 April 1956
[*Boston, Mass.*]

Thurman explains to a correspondent why a belief in the virgin birth and the physical resurrection of Jesus are "unnecessary" for his faith.[1]

Mr. C. H. Winecoff
1405 Brookstown Avenue, N.W.
Winston-Salem, North Carolina

Dear Mr. Winecoff:
I am in receipt of your letter under date of April 17.
For many people, their Christian faith is positive upon an active belief in the virgin birth and the physical resurrection of Jesus Christ. For many others, who are just as devout, belief in these two things is unnecessary.
As far as my own thought is concerned, I can state it very simply. For me, belief in the virgin birth is not essential. It does not add anything to the significance of the life, ministry, and teachings of Jesus.
With reference to the bodily resurrection, the same thing is true, as far as I am concerned. The important thing to me about the resurrection is the fact that it demonstrates a universal insight; namely, that death is something which takes place in life but not to life. The discovery which the disciples made after the crucifixion of Jesus was the fact that his life was not imprisoned by the event of the cross.
Sincerely yours,
Howard Thurman
Dean

                                                                        TLc.

Note
      1. These were long-standing positions of Thurman's. He wrote about the virgin birth as early as 1924; see *PHWT*, 1:24–30. He wrote about the resurrection as early as 1937; see *PHWT*, 2:81–92.

𝄞 "Chapel Committee Meeting"
29 April 1956
Boston, Mass.

Thurman's grandest—and largely unrealized—goal for his years as dean of the chapel at Boston University was the creation of a formal religious community at Marsh Chapel, a community that would transcend conventional confessional and religious boundaries. The two documents set forth below are related to this goal and to each other. The first is the minutes of the first Chapel Committee meeting, which was held on 29 April 1956. The second is Thurman's statement on the resolutions of the committee; it represents his first serious and concerted attempt to establish the community that he envisioned. It is likely that Thurman supplemented his June 1956 Report of the Dean of the Chapel[1] with one or both of the documents.

The surviving minutes seem to begin with the discussion already in progress. There is no list of the participants at the meeting, but Thurman's voice and his dominant role in the proceedings are unmistakable.[2] Thurman tells the committee members, "We do not know how to provide an experience of spiritual growth for people whose approach to God and religious meaning may be radically different." He sought to find a "creative possibility" within a "framework of that which has a Christian orientation and inspiration" to accommodate the spiritual quests of Christians and non-Christians alike.[3]

A committee to write a covenant for the Marsh Chapel religious group was appointed at the 29 April meeting. This covenant and Thurman's contextualizing of the covenant's significance constitute the second document presented here. It is undated but was probably written before Thurman's June 1956 annual report. The three-point covenant affirms a faith in God, a dedication to fulfill "God's purposes in the midst of all men," and a commitment to "undertake to learn of Jesus that the spirit that was in him may also be in me." As in much of his writing at this time, Thurman tried to separate the religious significance of Jesus from an explicitly Christian context. Thurman expresses the hope in his annual report that "by fall the society can be officially launched." This was not to be, and no religious fellowship at Marsh Chapel was created during Thurman's tenure, to his profound and lasting displeasure.[4]

The leader of the society may be a person who the society wishes to have, and the person who is in mind for the Dean of the Chapel may be someone else. What I hope is that we may think together about the possibility of doing some creative experimentation in religious and spiritual growth and development.

The Chapel, as I conceive of it, is a worship center in the university open to everybody, cutting across all lines of race, creed, etc. It is a shared experience of religious friends to the exposure of the scrutiny of God.[5]

1. Is there a need?
   Ans: There certainly is a need. I have been coming to the Chapel for four or five years, and it wasn't until I sang in the choir that I really felt a part

of it. It has made a big difference. I am not in choir this year because of classes, but I would very much like to be associated with a group that was actively engaged in Chapel work. I would also like to feel that I could raise my hand and say could you explain that?

I am in evening school, and in my own personal life I believe that there is a need for an association or organization in which I can find myself. I am a member of the university's Student Christian Association but because of my rather tenuous relationship to it, it does not have a meaning for me that it has in the past.

I am a graduate, no longer connected. Live in the area. We enjoy coming very much. It seems to be that I am an outsider to an extent, because I am not directly connected. In this organization, I could be a working part of the Chapel of the university.

I see an organization like this as an opportunity for those not in the university to contribute to the Chapel for that which we get from it each Sunday.

I am an alumnus of the university and live in the community. I would be interested in knowing about the intended function of such an organization. I find the Sunday chapel services most satisfying.

2. There must be some simple, comprehensive agreement, a covenant or commitment to which the individual who wished to be a part formally of the society would accept as the things on which he personally agreed to. Work out some statement, not a creed, that will bind us together.[6] Ans: The only analogy I can make in terms of a covenant will have to depend upon the function.

It seems to me that perhaps it has to serve the purpose for providing affiliation for students away from communities. I think it needs a very specific kind of center for persons who are closely connected with the university community and its chief commitment is here. It should relate to those persons who want to affiliate with other institutions. Some concern for persons who want to relate themselves to the medium of radio.

A thought occurred to me whether the organization could be Friends of the Boston University Chapel, so that they could be called upon by the Chapel Committee.

This is something that appeals to us very much and although we cannot contribute in committee work, we can help in interest and support.

We do not know how to provide an experience of spiritual growth for people whose approach to God and religious meaning may be radically different. One of the inspiring things about the chapel experience on Sunday is that there are moments when a person is just himself before God, and he is a Jew, and he is a

Catholic, Baptist, etc. Some such creative possibility may be possible within the framework of that which has a Christian orientation and inspiration. It is that sort of adventure we will be trying to feel our way into. Organizational[7] has to be kept close to zero. The barest minimum necessary to provide a framework for the spirit. It may be that the committee who works on the covenant will be able to make suggestions regarding this. If you would like to work on the committee, give us your name. We hope that by the end of the year, we will be able to have something fairly concrete to think about.[8]

We have not tried in the Chapel to double religious activities that are going on in the university. In the past many students who have come to see me want something to do. We have referred them to Hillel, Newman, and the Student Christian Association. There is no advantage in setting up another pattern of activities. Everybody is sure of them. The only thing that can justify it is that it is meeting a need that is not being met. One suggestion—we do a real piece of experimenting and a person who becomes a part of this will have the opportunity of becoming a part of a smaller unit that concerns itself with spiritual and religious development.

1. Working at spiritual growth through meditation and prayer
2. Explore the resources of the Bible for spiritual growth
3. Sit and share together their own quest and their own need in an intimate sense of communication. To work at this would be a genius of our fellowship.[9]

If we can grow spiritually, if somehow that can happen to us, then that is the real reason for this.

Boston is full of things to do and if you want something to do, I can give you something. If we can have little fellowships for seeking for ways by which the spiritual growth resources of God may be made available to us out of all of the known resources—prayer, study, music, Bible devotion, literature. The little group will determine what it wishes to do. The strength of our fellowship will be at that point rather than at the point of a lot of other things. The Chapel has a program which creaks and groans for help all the time.[10]

[Proposed Marsh Chapel Covenant]

Boston University recognizes the significance of religion in the life of the individual and in the development of man on this planet. It honors this significance by certain formal and informal provisions.

1. The graduate school of theology is one of the fifteen schools in the university. It is here that the individual student is technically equipped for religious leadership in the Christian church and in the wider community. In this school, men are prepared formally to teach religion in the regular curricula.

In the College of Liberal Arts, there is a regularly organized department of religions instruction open to all undergraduates.

2. Provisions are made for Jewish, Catholic and Protestant students to be guided in their graduate and undergraduate life by persons trained in the specific traditions for that purpose.

For the Jewish students there is a rabbi, who is also the director of the Hillel Foundation.

For the Catholic students there is a priest, who is the director of the Newman Club.

For the Protestant students there is a Protestant clergyman, who is the director of the Student Christian Association.

In addition to these, wherever possible, students of a particular denomination are organized into their respective groups, under the guidance of a leader of their own faith.

3. At the present moment, there are several Young Women's Christian Association groups, interfaith in character, and are sponsored by the student section of the Y.M.C.A. of Greater Boston.

4. The university expresses its official and formal intent in this regard by establishing an all-university religious service in Marsh Chapel, under the guidance of a Dean of the Chapel.

On the cover of the weekly chapel bulletin, there is a statement which expresses the purpose of this all-university religious service. It is as follows: "The Sunday morning service addresses itself to the deepest needs and aspirations of the human spirit. In so doing it does not seek to undermine whatever may be the religious context which gives meaning and richness to your particular life; but rather to deepen the authentic lines along which your quest for spiritual reality has led you. It is our hope that you will come to regard the Chapel not only as a place of stimulation, challenge and dedication, but also as a symbol of the intent of the University to recognize religion as fundamental to the human enterprise."

To give so large a place to the relevancy of religion in human experience, as expressed in the above, is in keeping not only with the genius of the university but also with the realistic demands of the human spirit.

The question is often asked me, "Are students today more concerned about religion than they were a decade or two decades ago?" Obviously, it is difficult to give an answer to this question which is completely satisfying. There are several important factors to be taken into account in considering the reply. The first is that the confidence which the academic world had in the ability of the natural sciences to create a good world and a safe community has been given a rude shock. Man's mastery over nature has expressed itself primarily in creating tools of destruction.

It is beside the point to say that this development is due to the incident of contemporary and human history. The fact remains. The threat of war and what the implementation of such a threat may mean to human life has mounted steadily through the years. We are now gripped by a sense of horror and a corresponding futility. In the face of this situation, there is a marked interest in trying to discover fresh and radical dimensions of security for the human spirit.

Inasmuch as it is the perennial insistence of religion that the ultimate security of the human spirit is in God, it is small wonder that we see all around us a fresh interest in the meaning of religious experience. Here I am not referring primarily to an increase in church attendance and in large scale religious rallies. I am thinking of the kinds of questions students and others are asking and the kind of help that they are seeking.

It is obvious that an entire volume could be written on this subject. What I have attempted to do is to make an overall interpretative statement rather than to give a tight, conclusive answer to the question.

It should be a matter of profoundest reassurance to the members of the university community that the resources of religion are formally recognized by Boston University and in this recognition provisions are made for their availability.

Howard Thurman

The Covenant as agreed upon by the members of this committee reads as follows:

1. I affirm my faith in God and seek to do His will.
2. I undertake to learn of Jesus that the spirit that was in him may also be in me.
3. I dedicate my life to the fulfillment of God's purposes in the midst of all men and through worship will discipline myself in love, in understanding, and in fellowship.

                                                                                TD.

NOTES

1. The annual report stated that "plans [are] underway for organizing a religious society of Marsh Chapel (see appendix)" ("Annual Report, Marsh Chapel," 18 June 1956).

2. The editors have indicated by endnotes those passages in the minutes that probably were spoken by Thurman.

3. Part of the context for the committee meeting and Thurman's subsequent statement were the difficulties that he was encountering with the Student Christian Association, the official representative of Protestantism on the Boston University campus. In his annual report from May 1956, Thurman stated that he was refusing to participate in meetings of the Student Christian Association because of the "obvious discourtesies" extended to him by the Protestant chaplain ("Annual Report, Marsh Chapel," 18 June 1956).

4. Ibid.
5. Thurman speaking.
6. Thurman speaking.
7. As in original.
8. Thurman speaking.
9. Thurman speaking.
10. Thurman speaking

❧ FROM HAROLD C. CASE TO MARGARET HARDING
9 JULY 1956
BOSTON, MASS.

Thurman was sensitive about slights to his institutional prerogatives, and this often led to somewhat tense relations with his superiors. President Harold Case's peremptory letter to Thurman's secretary Margaret Harding¹ when Thurman was on vacation in San Francisco prompted Thurman's first crisis with Case on the scope of the duties, responsibilities, and prerogatives of the dean of the chapel.

To: Miss Peg Harding
Marsh Chapel
From: Dr. Harold C. Case
Subject:
Dear Peg Harding:

I have discovered that we need some clarification of policy for the use of the Chapel during the summer. Let me, therefore, state the following as the policies we will follow during the summer weeks:

1. No wedding rehearsals are to be scheduled after regular Chapel hours, that is, five o'clock on week days and noon on Saturdays.
2. No overtime service is to be required of maintenance staff during the summer months.
3. A definite schedule must be made for all weddings so that there is never any question about the wedding party arriving on schedule by agreement at the appointed time. Unless it can be made definite, it cannot be scheduled at all.
4. The Chapel itself will be closed on legal holidays.
5. The Chapel will be closed at noon on August 18 and opened again on Monday, September 10.
6. No weddings shall be scheduled from August 19 to September 10 except by special arrangement with this office.
7. The Sunday morning offerings from the Chapel congregation will be placed by the ushers in a bag to be furnished by the Treasurer's Office,

locked and placed in a locked filing cabinet in the Chapel Office. On Monday morning that bag, unopened, will be brought to the Treasurer's Office where it will be counted by the staff, with memorandum of the amount returned to the Chapel Office. Henceforth, this is the plan to be followed each Sunday morning.

8. There will be no decoration or redecoration in the lounge this summer, but Buildings and Grounds will examine the lighting with a view to the removal of certain fixtures in the lounge room where there is too much illumination.

Kindly see to it that these items go into force at once.
Cordially yours,
[*signed*] Harold C. Case
Harold C. Case
cc: Dr. Oxnam,[2] Mr. Harrington,[3] Mr. Ward

TLS.

NOTES

1. Margaret "Peg" Harding was Thurman's secretary from the time of his arrival at Boston University through September 1956, prior to her marriage the following month to the Reverend Paul J. Binder, who served in a number of Methodist and United Church of Christ parishes, including the St. Andrew United Church of Christ (1982–96) in Sarasota, Florida. Margaret Harding Binder worked for many years at the Trinity United Methodist Church in Sarasota and served as president of Florida United Church of Christ Women.

2. Robert Fisher Oxnam (1915–74), son of the prominent Methodist bishop Garfield Bromley Oxnam, was born in Boston and graduated from DePauw University in 1937. After service in World War II, he received a doctorate in political science from the University of Southern California in 1948. His career as a university administrator began at Syracuse University (1948–53) and continued at Boston University (1953–58), where he was vice president for administration. In 1958 he became president of the Pratt Institute, and in 1961 he assumed a similar position at Drew University, where he remained until his death.

3. Paul Harrington, probably the chief custodian for Marsh Chapel; see To Paul Harrington, 18 September 1956.

🥢 TO HAROLD C. CASE
[*JULY 1956*]
[*BOSTON, MASS.*]

Thurman writes indignantly to President Harold Case about Case's 9 July 1956 memorandum on summer procedures for Marsh Chapel.[1] Thurman is angry that the letter was sent to his secretary and that Case did not ask him directly about the situation in the chapel. He also writes of the many obstacles he has faced in "building a feeling of fellowship and understanding within the Chapel." The handwritten letter appears to be unfinished, perhaps indicating that Thurman thought better of communicating with Case in such high dudgeon.

Dear Harold:

I have just received a copy of the letter which you sent to ~~Peg~~ my secretary covering 8 points concerning Chapel policy.

I am amazed and deeply confused that you would ~~send~~ address a directive concerning Chapel policy to my secretary. It's true that I was away but even so ~~Peg knew~~ my office knew how to reach me. The information, the basis upon which you worked out the directive, did not come from me or from the office. This means that other people in the university talked with you behind my back. This is gossip—true or false, it is still gossip. The fact that you would be influenced by this without getting in touch with the office first, leaves me completely demoralized. Please understand me, Harold, I do not question your prerogatives as chief administrator of the university. Simply I find your procedure extremely difficult for me to handle.

This memorandum makes of me a figure head. I interpret it to say that you have little confidence in my ability to function as Dean of the Chapel and that it was therefore necessary for you to take things into your hands and handle them from your office. If this is the way you want it then you do not need my services as Dean of the Chapel. ~~Even if each item~~ There is no point in discussing the items, this may come later, because I am concerned about the principle involved. It is basic.

In the three years that I have been at Boston University I have tried to have an honest, intelligent and effective ministry. I found a situation completely demoralized with all kinds of hostilities and conflicts. With God's help and much [*illegible*] I have worked quietly, slowly building a spirit of fellowship and understanding within the Chapel itself. ~~All kinds of~~ Many things have been put in my way but I have worked at it to the point that there is a fine quality of feeling among us all who carry direct responsibility. This is built upon mutual respect, courtesy and an increasing religious commitment. One directive ~~such as the one you sent~~ with all the prestige of your office, of which two janitors receive copies, transferring the responsibility for carrying out Chapel policy from the office of the dean to the office of the president destroys much of what has been built up during the first three years. The last line takes the prize—kindly see to it that these items go into force at once—and this to a secretary. How would you feel if the Chairman of the Exec Com of the Trustees, in your absence instructed your secretary to carry out a policy of which you[2]

As soon as I return to Boston about August 19th or 20th I will call your office for an appointment.

yourself were not advised.[3] ~~I am sorry but I am distraught and~~

AL.

NOTES
    1. Harold C. Case to Peg Harding, 9 July 1956, printed in the current volume.
    2. The continuation of this sentence was probably meant to be "yourself were not advised," which is the last line of the letter.
    3. See note 2.

ॐ To JOHN OVERHOLT
28 MARCH 1957
[*BOSTON, MASS.*]

John Overholt,[1] *Thurman's good friend and an Ohio businessman and philanthropist, wrote to him asking about the advisability of making a contribution to the NAACP. Thurman strongly supports the idea and suggests that the most helpful contribution would be to the NAACP Legal and Education Fund. The letter shows a side of Thurman that is sometimes difficult to discern from his sermons and writing: that of a man fully engaged in the details of the civil rights revolution in the South.*

Mr. John Overholt
665 Lombardy Lane
Laguna Beach, California

Dear John:
    It was wonderful to hear from you, particularly after so long a time. Before I get to the main question in your letter let me bring you up to date about happenings in the family.
    The word from my sister is about the same. She is in the hospital at Camerilla[2] and from all indications is not losing ground, this in itself is encouraging.
    I have just issued a new set of 12" LP records. One is a sermon as it was preached in the chapel here, and the other record is a series of shorter meditations taken from my own books. I would like for you to have a set but there is no point in sending it to you until you return to the East. I simply wanted you to know about them.
    The most exciting thing is the fact that June 12, Sue and I will celebrate our 25th wedding anniversary. I am trying to work it out so that two things can happen; one, our daughter, Olive, and her baby[3] can come East to spend a little while with us during the period covering the anniversary and that Sue and I will take a trip to Europe for the month of July. Our plan would be to go to Scotland, spending all of the time in the environs of Edinburgh, and then back to Boston from which place I will go in late July to California to visit my sister and to do some things at Fellowship Church. We are trying to secure passage on a slow boat so that much of the time will be spent on board ship.[4]

First of all I am very glad that you have been able to fulfill Jessie's desire for a gift to the Womens International League For Peace and Freedom.[5] With reference to a gift to the NAACP, I comment as follows:

A. I give to the NAACP my unqualified endorsement. Over a period of years, I have been slowly becoming a life member. I hope before the end of this year to make my last payment to that end. There is no basis in fact to the rumor that the organization is being infiltrated by subversion or Communism.[6] I know the organization very well and am personally acquainted with most of the people on the National Board and on the National Staff. The rumor is groundless.

B. During the past few years there have been such basic changes in the social situation in the country as far as the work of the NAACP is concerned that it is difficult to know the most effective way to carry out Jessie's idea. One of the most important things that has happened is that in some of the Southern states, Mississippi, Louisiana and, I think, North Carolina, the NAACP is being outlawed because of the position that it has taken in supporting the struggle toward the implementation of the Supreme Court's decision concerning the desegregation of the public school system.[7] It is necessary in various parts of the South for local organization, managed by local people, to take over much of the work of the NAACP at the local level. It would be a wonderful thing if through these local organizations it would be possible to hold institutes that would give encouragement to the people and the inspiration that comes from having more than one strategy that can be implemented in their struggle for democracy and decency. I do not know what agency could best do this at the moment the people who are carrying most of the crucial responsibility in this regard are Negro clergymen. This Jessie would find unbelievable.

C. The NAACP would be able to promote a series of institutes having to do with social and political and economic problems in connection with race, at one or two centers of learning in the South. I am not sure whether there is available within the organization, due to budgetary limitations, any leadership that would be available for promoting such a series. At any rate, this is a possibility.

My own judgment is that a gift to the local Defense Fund would be in the long run, the most significant contribution that can be made to the organization.[8] For the next fifteen years, the issues growing out of the Supreme Court's decision will be before the courts. This will take hundreds or thousands of dollars. If it is not done, the chains will not be broken for a long time. True, it is not as constructive and as educational as the thing that Jessie had in mind, but ultimately it makes possible the thing that she had in mind.

I hope you will have a wonderful holiday, and let me hear what your reaction is to my letter.
Sincerely yours,
Howard Thurman
Dean

                                                                                                TLc.

NOTES

    1. Thurman had been a good friend of Overholt's late wife, Jessie Wickwire Overholt, who had been devoted "to the far-flung testimony of the Quakers, wherever famine, pestilence, or social tragedy stalked" (from Thurman's eulogy, reprinted in a memorial pamphlet, *Jessie Wickwire Overholt, March 12, 1892–May 6, 1947* [Cleveland, Ohio?, 1947]). See also To Board of Fellowship Church, 12 July 1947; and From Pauli Murray, 5 May 1949, printed in *PHWT*, 3:239–40, 320–23, respectively. The friendship between the two men grew after Jessie Wickwire Overholt's death; see To John Overholt, 21 May 1951, printed in the currrent volume.

    2. Camarillo State Hospital, Camarillo, California.

    3. Anton Wong.

    4. The Thurmans went to Europe that summer from 25 June to 1 August, spending their time (other than travel on a suitably "slow boat") as guests of their friend Coleman Jennings in Edinburgh, Scotland.

    5. The Women's International League for Peace and Freedom (WILPF) was founded in Washington, D.C., in 1915 in an effort to find ways for nations to resolve their differences peacefully. Jane Addams was its first president, and in part because of her work for WILPF, she was awarded the Nobel Prize for Peace in 1931. WILPF remains a prominent advocate for disarmament and curbing nuclear weapons. In his eulogy for Jessie Wickwire Overholt, Thurman mentioned her dedication to WILPF. *Jessie Wickwire Overholt.*

    6. This was a common accusation at the time, especially among those hostile to the organization's civil rights agenda, and often was made out of an ignorant or intentionally malicious identification of the cause of black equality with communism. The reality was complex. The national leadership of the NAACP had long been strongly anticommunist. However, some local branches of the organization espoused a Popular Front openness to collaborating with the Communist Party or affiliated organizations during and immediately after World War II. The efforts of the national leadership to curtail communist influence in the NAACP led some historians to accuse the organization of a witch hunt against internal communist influences. For a nuanced account of this period, see Manfred Berg, "Black Civil Rights and Liberal Anti-Communism: The NAACP in the Early Cold War," *Journal of American History* 94, no. 1 (June 2007): 71–96.

    7. In 1956, as part of what white southern politicians labeled their "massive resistance" against the implementation of the U.S. Supreme Court's desegregation decision, many southern states tried to hobble the civil rights efforts of the NAACP. These efforts included outright bans of the organization in Alabama, Louisiana, and Texas; prohibitions against membership in the NAACP by public employees—with black teachers as the primary targets—in South Carolina and Mississippi; and various legal restrictions imposed on NAACP activities in Florida, Arkansas, Georgia, and Tennessee. Many of the laws remained in effect until the 1960s. As Thurman suggests, one consequence of the barriers to the NAACP in southern states was the creation of many locally led civil rights organizations.

8. The NAACP Legal and Educational Fund, Inc. was created as a separate arm of the NAACP for tax purposes in 1940. Led by Thurgood Marshall, it became a wholly separate organization in 1957. Contrary to Thurman's implication, unlike the NAACP itself, it did not have local branches.

✎ "THE CHRISTIAN MINISTER AND THE DESEGREGATION DECISION" MAY 1957

This sermon, published in Pulpit Digest *in May 1957,[1] three years after the epochal U.S. Supreme Court decision in* Brown v. Board of Education, *was delivered at a time when progress toward desegregating schools and other institutions remained slow and halting, due in large part to the determined resistance of whites to racial change. In this address Thurman explores the ways that ministers could advance or hinder the cause of desegregation. He discusses two cases. First, he argues that ministers of congregations whose doctrines of salvation tended to be fairly restrictive could make elimination of racial prejudice and bigoted behavior a requirement for personal salvation and gather around them core groups of followers who "would be under the rule of Christ, and to them all forms of anti-brotherliness would be sin." The second case is made of white ministers of typically southern mainline congregations who have largely stood on the sidelines of the racial debate. Thurman suggests that these ministers can become informed about and involved in the civil rights struggle, rebuking bigots in their own congregations and reaching out to black congregations. Working together, white and black ministers would face the challenges ahead.[2]*

The Christian minister must serve as the custodian of his own conscience and share deeply in the responsibility for the conscience of his congregation and the community. Within his interpretation of his religious commitment, he may without offense to his conscience take any of several attitudes towards the society in which he lives. It is my purpose to examine two of these attitudes, and to point out their relevance to the pressures under which a Christian minister in the South lives today due to the problems created by the tensions between the white and Negro units in his society.

Before doing this, however, I must make one important observation. I was born in the South, and was educated through college in Florida and Georgia. My first trip out of the South came in my twenty-second year. I grew up in the church. I was tutored by the love ethic as a part of the overall teaching of the church, but it did not even occur to me that the Christian demand of love included the white members of my community. For me they were ethically out of bounds. I was sure that their interpretation of the Christian demand to love did not include me. In fine, the relationship between us was fundamentally amoral. It was some time after I had finished college before the boundaries of the ethical demand extended beyond my own group. I venture to say that in many places this fundamental amorality obtains at the present moment. The insistence of my religion upon an extension of community to include men of all races and of any status has been won in a hard school, and has been made possible by the active work of the grace of God. This picture has to be held in mind as the ideas in my discussion are developed.

I.

The minister may seek to withdraw from any and all social involvements. This will mean little participation in community life, with such participation limited to the sheer necessity arising from the fact that his church is in the community and so is he. Detachment from participation is his aim.

Such a theory says that the church is the heavenly community set down in the world as a place of refuge for those who would escape from the world *into* salvation. The emphasis here is completely otherworldly. It says that the world is evil and only awaiting its final destruction as the judgment of God against sin and corruption.

Such a minister and his congregation may regard themselves as the Remnant. All that I shall do with this position is to indicate it.

II.

The minister may relate to his society as a responsible member having the advantage of a gospel to proclaim and the responsibility of a commitment to fulfill.

Such a gospel may be interpreted as being one which has important words to say about the sins of the souls and lives of men as well as the sins of the society in which men live. The mandate under which he makes his proclamation and seeks to fulfill its dedication comes from the Master to whom he gives supreme devotion. This may lead him into several paths. I shall discuss two of them.

First, he may become the defender of a particular form of redemption, personal and social. In his words and life he would offer a plan of salvation without which no man or no society may hope to be saved. All who accept, and thereby believe, participate at once in salvation and redemption.

Often this makes for a radical intolerance of all others, however genuine may be their commitment and however conscience-free they may be in the experience of the grace of God. Nevertheless, there is great power and vitality stemming from such a conviction.

What would happen if, in any community, the work of salvation were to include the redemption of the spirits of the believers from all forms of racial prejudice and anti-Negro or anti-white attitudes? The achieving of brotherhood would be at once a part of the central witness of such a church and the personal witness of the Christian in the world.

The implications of such a position are far-reaching. The most searching one is that racial prejudice, and all that flows responsively from it, would come between a man and God. The prejudice would blur the holy vision, and give to the individual a sense of profound isolation from the living spirit of the living God. The harboring of such attitudes would jeopardize a man's eternal salvation. Thus racial prejudice would be defined as mortal sin.

The purification of the life, the redemption of the spirit, the salvation of the soul, would not be possible for a man who closed his door against his fellow, whatever may be his status, color, or position in the world. Such an attitude would define for the believer the things for which he must stand with his life, and the things against which he must stand. *Social* responsibility would be the inevitable result flowing from his experience of *personal* redemption.

The important thing here is that the basis of such a man's action would not be rooted in any political or social alignment. It would not be determined by what the courts said or did not say, but rather would the source of his authority move directly out of the crucible of his religious experience and the teaching of his Master. For him the mind of Christ would be his inner symbol, and from his Christ he would draw strength and courage.

How would such a man give his witness? First of all, he would witness in his immediate family. He would be under the necessity to teach his children that racial prejudice, attitudes of hatred toward other persons, is sin.

At this point it is not beside the issue to observe that there has been a deep hesitancy, even among devout Christian believers who are also men of good will, to define racial prejudice as sin. It has been called wrong, bad, unrighteous, and even unjust—but sin? Hardly. To proclaim that prejudice and all the malpractices that flow from it will stand between a man and salvation is a step too audacious even for the church to be willing to take. It should be noted that in recent years there has emerged a disposition toward change of this basic position. Even so, it is the rare believer who is under the judgment that the harboring of racial prejudice and the practicing of segregation through which it expresses itself is sin before God.

But to return to the minister. He would teach his children that racial prejudice is sin before God. He who indulges in it, therefore, is guilty before God. It would be necessary for him to study ways for fortifying his children against the social pressure on the side of acceptance of anti-social practices in the environment. It is at such a time that the minister could understand much about the true basis of human behavior and human action. He would have to explain to his children the life around them. He would try to give to them some basis for understanding their own experiences. This would mean that he himself would be the interpreter of the background and the history of the attitudes around them. He would teach them that men do not act out of a clear conception of right and wrong, out of some inner sense of moral values clear-cut and definitive. The decisive issue for the individual is apt to be, what bearing will a particular course of action have on his own sense of belonging to some group, membership in which makes him feel at home. Above all else, he would make clear to them that a man is apt to feel that he must not do anything that would give him a sense of being cut off, of being isolated from a real sense of community.

What is the answer to such a question, or such a need?

There must be found a sense of belonging or community of which a person may feel a part, that will be more important than the one threatened by right action. There is nothing new in this process. Any man who belongs to a group under a sense of some special commitment has to deal practically with this problem. Much may be learned from such religious groups as Jehovah's Witnesses, the Seventh-Day Adventists, the Salvation Army, or even the Roman Catholic Church.

Such a minister would find himself developing a little company of the loyal to Christ, within even the larger fellowship of his church—an important nucleus of which he and his family will be a part. Their sense of being a part of the body of Christ would be more real and binding than that which was derived from being a member of any social group defined by race, or by statute, or by propaganda.

To repeat, the little company of the loyal would be under the rule of Christ, and to them all forms of anti-brotherliness would be sin, the indulgence of which would put their very souls in jeopardy.

And what would a man give in exchange for his soul? The satisfaction of hating another man, of segregating another man, or being unjust to another man? Hardly.

I turn now to a second alternative. The minister may seek deliberately to involve himself in the life of the community, and to participate responsibly in it.

Let us take a searching look at such a minister living in the South today. He is a man who feels called of God to do God's work in the world. He believes that brotherhood is a *sure* teaching of his faith. But he has not included in his definition of brotherhood the man in his community who may be of a different race. Many words have fallen from his lips about love as the chief of all the Christian virtues. In his prayers he has always included all forms of human need and suffering in his petitions before God. He has supported the missionary cause of his church. He is sincere, devout, dedicated. The question of segregation, of police brutality inflicted upon Negroes, the great inequalities in opportunities, the general social pattern of discrimination—all of these he has never confronted in terms of ethical responsibility and guilt.

He does not regard himself as being a man of deliberate race consciousness as such, or even an avowed believer in or defender of race prejudice. Vaguely he recognizes that he has made an adjustment to the social situation. As a minister he may be kind to individual Negroes, for instance. He would not willfully mistreat any man, black or white. Occasionally something happens to give the alarm signal deep within his spirit, but his inner peace is never seriously threatened nor is his conscience deeply agitated.

Occasionally in his visitations or social contacts he finds himself a part of a discussion involving the attitude of race. He does not contribute very much to the discussion, is more or less a silent listener unless his opinion is asked. At such a moment he finds himself apt to take refuge in platitudes and generalities. He does not wish to offend. If you ask him more directly he might say that he was not against Negroes but that it is not practical to go too far and too fast.

The truth is he has never thought out his own attitude and looked at it in the light of the gospel that he preaches.

Such a man wakes up one morning to discover that the Supreme Court of the land has spoken, and overnight the social pattern of the community is being challenged and threatened. For the first time in his life on such an issue he is forced to take a stand. He is the leader of his congregation, their counselor, their shepherd. His people are frightened and agitated.

What does he do?

Many possibilities may occur to him. He may be tempted to say that the church should be the church, and as such should not permit itself to be involved in the social crisis. But this is wishful thinking. Such an idea lingers in his mind for a short while only because the members of his church as well as he himself are among the responsible people of the community. For better or for worse, they are involved!

If he is a man of prayer and deep spiritual consecration, he will turn to God for wisdom and guidance. In other words he will make the crisis a matter of prayer and soul-searching in the Presence of God.

In his struggle he will get inside his own private feelings and thoughts. He may discover for the first time that his life *is* deeply colored by a profound sense of separateness, that he had never included the Negro in his field of moral and ethical responsibility. He reviews his life and discovers that he doesn't know anything about the life of the Negro who lives in his community. Until this happened, he thought he did. But the prospect of seeing his own children sitting in a classroom with Negro children day after day was something that only by the most strenuous effort could he grasp with his mind, and could not apprehend at all with his emotions.

At last, in his struggle, he is able to bring himself to say with all of his mind and heart, very quietly before God: "Search me, O God, and know my heart. Try me and know my thoughts. And see if there be any wicked way in *me*. And lead *me* in the Way everlasting."³

He emerges from his spiritual crisis deeply chastened, and a new sense of community without boundaries begins to make revolutionary demands upon his total life pattern. His task now becomes not only one of atonement as the catharsis for his guilt but also a new sense of social responsibility becomes a part of his Christian commitment.

Now he must make up his mind on a course of action which involves the leadership, primarily, of his congregation. In order to achieve this he spends long hours in preparation.

First of all he has to gather facts. He reads the decision of the Court. Whatever questions arise in his mind with reference to this document, he discusses with a well-informed and competent lawyer. This may lead him to examine the evolution of Supreme Court decisions affecting the question of segregation in the South. Next, he finds that he doesn't know anything about how Jim Crow got started, and the story of its development. By inquiry or by searching, he finds and reads a book like C. V. Woodward's *The Strange Career of Jim Crow.*⁴ He finds out whether his denomination, meeting in general conclave, has made any pronouncements on this whole question, and what these pronouncements were. He studies his main source book, the Bible, and particularly the teaching of the New Testament concerning love and the kingdom of God, and the meaning of community.

It has been his custom to share in the deliberations and the activities of the organization of ministers in his community. He discusses his findings and his resolutions with his fellow-ministers, or with the two or three within the group who have shared before in thoughtful discussion and meaningful fellowship.

He turns now to his congregation. (I am assuming all along that his wife and his family have shared in varying degrees in this process and experience.)

The word comes to him one day that one of the leaders of his church is very active in organizing a White Citizens Council.⁵ He goes to talk to him. In his conversation he draws upon every positive and creative thing he knows about this particular man through much association in the past. They have trusted each other. He tries to understand his friend's motivations, his fears, his anxieties. He seeks to displace these motivations, fears, and anxieties by having him face the question of the will of God for the man in the situation. All along, with great tenderness, he takes his stand for community inclusiveness, which puts him squarely on the side of the decision of the Court, with a recognition that what the Court has declared is what the church stands for. He may or may not succeed. His responsibility is to take his position with as much love and understanding, but firmness, as possible.

He may decide to preach about this, or he may not. It seems indicated, however, that a special meeting of his membership should be called for the purpose of discussing the whole matter under the aegis of the church and the guidance of the spirit of God. At such a meeting he would seek to give his membership an orientation into his own struggle, his crisis, and where he came out. He would offer his counsel and his help to any and all members of his congregation as they sought to find the Christian answer to the social crisis. If, out of such a meeting, his membership should decide to have him preach a series of sermons on the whole matter, it would be perfect.

The next crucial step for him would be with reference to the Negro community itself. The first thing he would discover would be that the possibility is that he may not be trusted by his fellow Negro ministers whom he now seeks to know, to understand, and with whom he must work.

Rightly or wrongly they will judge him in this situation by their interpretation of how he has functioned in the past. He may be respected but not trusted. There is no simple solution to this. The fundamental question is how can a sense of community emerge between these two ministers of God who by their traditions and their way of life live out of community, out of touch ethically?

An incident in the life of the Master may be helpful. One day a Roman captain came to him seeking help for his servant, for whom he had a profound attachment—a Roman citizen seeking help from a Jewish teacher! Deep was his anguish and distress; all other resources of help had failed. That which would have been expected in the attitude of the Roman growing out of the disjointed relationship between Romans and Jews was conspicuously lacking here. The fact that he had come to Jesus was in itself evidence that he had put aside the pride of race and status which would have caused him to regard himself as superior to Jesus. He placed his need directly and simply before Jesus, saying: "Lord, my servant lieth at home sick of the palsy, grievously tormented." By implication he says: "It is my faith that cries out. I am stripped bare of all pretense and false pride. The man in me appeals to the man in you." So great was his faith and his humility that when Jesus said he would come to his home, the captain replied: "I am not worthy that thou shouldest come under my roof; but speak the word only, and my servant shall be healed."[6]

It was the testimony of Jesus that he had found no such faith in all Israel. The Roman was confronted with an insistence that made it impossible for him to remain a Roman, or even a captain. He had to take his place alongside all the rest of humanity, and mingle his desires with the longing of all the desperate people of all the ages. When this happened, it was possible at once for him to scale with Jesus any height of understanding, fellowship, and love. The final barrier between the strong and the weak, between ruler and ruled, disappeared.

In other words the two ministers, Negro and white, must move out from underneath the burden of their separateness and relate to each other not only as two children of God, but also as two men under the same conviction to *be* the Kingdom of God.

This would lead to an active understanding of the fears, the anxieties, and the climate of pressure in which they have lived. By virtue of the social structure in the South, such a minister would for the first time in his life become a bulwark of courage, of strength, and of confidence to the Negro community.

Further, he would find the men and women, few or many, in his community outside of his church who would, with great soberness, put their resources at the disposal of the school board and the officials in searching for the best way by which shifts in the social pattern may be achieved with a minimum of disaster and trauma. It must never be forgotten that God has not left Himself without witnesses in any community, however desolate and mean the community is. The minister would find some men who are indifferent to the Negro community or to Negroes as such, but who have a fierce sense of justice and an innate decency and humaneness. There will be others who would hesitate to take a position on the side of that which to them is right because they would regard themselves as being of no particular consequence and of no prestige. But if the voice of the minister is heard, he would provide in the name of his Christ a rallying point around which positive and creative sentiment in the community could take shape, not only in terms of working out the details of the particular problem involving education, but also in the keeping of the peace, and the guaranteeing of moral integrity of the common life.

That which will sustain the minister is the categorical faith in God whose wisdom is the goal towards which the whole creation moves. Whatever others may think or believe, the minister knows that the contradictions of life are never final contradictions, and that the test of life is often found in the amount of pain a man may absorb without destroying his joy.

Published in *Pulpit Digest* 37, no. 229 (May 1957): 13–19.

PD.

NOTES

1. The date and location of the delivery of the sermon printed in *Pulpit Digest* are unknown.

2. Thurman built upon this essay, revisiting many of its themes, in HT, *Footprints of a Dream*, 141–51.

3. Ps. 139:23–24.

4. C. Vann Woodward, *The Strange Career of Jim Crow* (New York: Oxford University Press, 1955).

5. The White Citizens' Councils were groups of white southerners who after the 1954 *Brown* decision organized in many towns and communities to protect racial segregation. Often counting many prominent and influential local residents among their members, the White Citizens' Councils were fierce opponents of the civil rights movement through the 1960s.

6. Matt. 8:5–13.

🪝 "The Gothic Principle"
5 May 1957
Boston, Mass.

In this sermon Thurman introduces the notion of the Gothic principle, the inherent challenge in seeking ideals that seem to vault high above human abilities at realization, and speaks of how one can try to realize the Gothic principle within the core of one's personhood.

Meditation:[1]
A curse on him who relies on man, who depends upon mere human aid for he is like some desert scrub that never thrives, except in a salt solitary place in the hills, but happy is he who turns to God who has God for his confidence, for he is like a tree planted beside a stream sending his roots down to the water. His leaves are always green. He has no fear of scorching heat. He goes on bearing fruit when all around him is barren, and he looks out on life with quiet eyes. This, our Father, is the meaning of our striving. In our striving, make precious to us even our deepest distresses and our greatest frustration, and for our spirits and our minds and our predicaments, this will sustain and make secure, our Father.

Reading: Genesis 2:7–17, James Moffatt translation[2]
Sermon:
As an immediate background for our thinking together about the gothic principle, I am using one injunction from the lips of Jesus of Nazareth, and the other from a contemporary poet. These are the lines from the poet:

> Man born of desire
> Cometh out of the night
> A wandering spark of fire
> He striveth to know,
> To unravel the Mind . . .
> He wills to adore
> He dreameth of beauty
> He seeks to create
> Fairer and fairer
> To vanquish his Fate.[3]
>   —Robert Bridges

And from the lips of Jesus, "Be ye perfect, as your heavenly Father is perfect."[4]

The gothic principle is the fundamental process by which man seeks to realize his ideals. The gothic cathedral, as is common knowledge, is perhaps the great and significant contribution of the French mind and spirit to the culture which is our heritage. There is something very solitary and lonely about it. I remember the first time I stood in an authentic gothic cathedral, 25 years ago,[5] I felt solitary, lonely. I felt stirrings within me that lost themselves in the upper reaches of the arches, and to continue the personal note just one minute, the times that it has been my privilege to preach in that which is essentially the Gothic Cathedral, there is a moment when it seems as if the congregation is distant, far removed, uninvolved in the primary and almost terrifying encounter which the human spirit in the austerity of its isolation has with God.

The principle as it expresses itself is simple, as it manifests itself, it is simple and complicated. The picture is familiar, the great high walls, supporting the vaulting arch, the arch broken at its apex, spilling over into unfulfillment and utter reaching for a realization that cannot be contained either within the walls or within the stretch and expanse of the arches themselves. This is the principle. This is its formal manifestation.

I am suggesting for your thinking this morning that the Gothic principle is a part of the essential ingredient of the spirit of man. It is the response of a man to the pull of that which constantly tutors his spirit with the reminder that whatever may be the nature of the contradictions and the tensions which he may be experiencing at any particular moment, this tension, these contradictions are not ultimate, are not final. Caught up between the walls and the sweep of the arches is the symbol that seeks to pull together into subtle overtones of harmony and significance, God and man, life and death, the eternal and the time-bound, the universal and the particular. Wherever the individual at the level of his function seeks to make the literal truth which to him is valid and ultimate into the literal facts of his experience, he is involved in the creative manifestation of this principle. This, after all is what art, whether it is the fine art, or the industrial arts, or the art of human relations, this, after all, is what art is trying to say. The degree to which it is trying to say this, it becomes involved in the deeply moving and profound experience of the total synthesis which is the message of religion. How can I make a part of the this-ness and that-ness of my experience, how can I make the event of my life, the full-orbed manifestation of the literal truth that I see with my inward eye. When we lay bare all of the meaning of man's institutions, all that he has created in culture and civilization, when we strip it of all of its context limitation, what we see laid bare is persistent, questing of the human spirit to reduce the events of experience to authentic for instances of the dream, of the hunger, of the deep desire.

It is a matter of startling significance and awareness to me how man, at the level of his creatureliness, at the level of his body, and the way in which he is essentially a child of nature, experiences the harmony, the order which is the goal of his effort when he is trying to get rid of the barrier that separates him from the fulfillment of his dream. His body has already responded to this. He has learned, his body has learned order. There may have been a time, doubtless there was a time when his body was in the process of learning this lesson.

I remember once dedicating a little baby and as I held him in my arms, I noticed that he had something in his neck that looked like a dimple, and I remarked to his mother the next day that it was too bad that David had a dimple at a point in his neck that would be covered by his collar so that as he grew older, he could not use it as a creative expression of something significant in the fulfillment of his desires. She said that this is not a dimple. The pediatrician says that this is the vestigial remains of a gill, and the time will come when it will be removed or it would be absorbed.[6] Then my mind reached back prior to the period when man's body had committed this to memory, when he was trying to learn how to take his air neat without water, and there must have been those who buried themselves more deeply in the primeval ooze of the ocean bed saying, "No I won't do it. I can't do it. I can't, can't." Then little by little with how much labor, how much agony, how much effort, we do not know, it is hidden in the mist. At last he was able to breathe without extracting the oxygen from matter.

This is the process. The body has worked this out so that man in his rootage, in his grounding, in his essential oneness with nature, in his body, at a level perhaps more complicated or less subtle than formal reflective thinking. Man is rooted in harmony. As a creature this is the ground of his enterprise as a human animal. Now hold that there.

On the other hand, at another level there is the dream which is of the same character, whole, harmonious, integrated, whether it is the garden of Eden that keeps disturbing the moving activity of man and his function with the rumor of something that existed in the past which he is always trying to recover in the present, or whether it is something that looms large on the horizon as that which all the creative activity of man moves. The golden age of tomorrow. All of the far-reaching utopias that have harassed the horizon of men and their dreaming and their aspiring, whether it is a time when men shall beat their swords into plowshares and their spears into pruning hooks, and the lion and the lamb shall lie down together, and a little child can put his hand on an asp, and the asp will relax his self-regarding instincts and not sting the child. The dream of the time when the knowledge of God shall cover the earth as the water covers the sea. The two poles then. Man rooted in the creature experience of harmony, of order, of integration, which his body has committed to memory so that the vital functions go on apace without formal reference to mind as such. That's one pole. The other, that which tantalizes, which is always beyond the event, that is like the broken arch, that spills over, that cannot quite be contained in the vault itself, reaching for the eternal, and the eternal always trying to fulfill itself in the event, and the event always trying to come to itself in the eternal. This is the story of man, and between these two poles the struggle, the tensions are worked out. What is it that informs the struggle? It is that which the body has committed to memory and that which the mind and the spirit sense on the horizon. This is why in times of greatest disillusionment and despair, in times even of total war when everywhere on every hand, there is the stalking of death, utilizing the results of all men's most creative intent and endeavors, this is why in the midst of that kind of conflagration, right in the heart of the seething furnace of carnage, the spirit of man talks about a time when there will be no war, when the madness will be over. This is why, in your own personal moments of greatest despair, when you see your dreams whiten into ash, when one by one your doors are closed, and you are more and more and more the prisoner of the crucial event that is grinding the life out of you, something within the agony itself stirs, reaches, urges, pulls with a realization that this is not my destiny. My destiny transcends the event. So, we work. We try to make the literal truth that stirs within us about what life at its best is, or what is the dream at its best is, we try to make the literal truth become flesh and blood as literal fact. This is what the church is trying to say in its doctrine of the incarnation.

Every time at the level of my living, not way off, I am able through discipline, through skills, through techniques, through reflection, through courage to make literal fact out of the literal truth that rides deep at the core of me, I become the embodiment of the gothic principle. I become a joint creator with God, in me, being becomes fulfillment in the event. In the event which is literal fact now there is the manifestation of being. So I don't ever give myself up. I may not be as good as X or Y thinks I am. I may not be as worthy as the pretension which I have, but I don't give myself up. I cling to myself with abiding enthusiasm. Why? Because the events of my life, and of your life, are always being informed finally by something that does not exist in time and space, but lives in the soul of me, which keeps me always under its necessity and its judgment. What I am trying to do with my little world, it is my faith that God is trying to do with all of existence.

(Read[7] The Job)[8]

Walk beside us, our Father, that in our desolation and aloneness, we may be comforted and reassured. Dismiss us with Thy Spirit, and grant unto us Thy Peace, this day, O God, our Father.

TD.

Notes

1. For background to this meditation, see Thurman's "eulogy for Mary McLeod Bethune," printed in the current volume.

2. James Moffatt, *The Holy Bible, Containing the Old and New Testaments* (Garden City, N.Y.: Doubleday, Doran, 1926). Moffatt's was Thurman's favorite Bible translation.

3. The first excerpt is from "Dirge"; the second from Later Poems #3 [untitled], both in Robert S. Bridges, *The Poetical Works of Robert Bridges, Excluding the Eight Dramas* (Oxford: Oxford University Press, 1912), 399, 400. Robert S. Bridges (1844–1930) was poet laureate of England from 1913 until his death.

4. Matt. 5:48.

5. This was in the summer of 1931, during Thurman's first trip to Europe after the death of his wife the previous winter.

6. A branchial cleft cyst occurs when a branchial or gill cleft—which in fish develops into gill structures—is incompletely eliminated during human embryonic development.

7. Note by transcriber.

8. "The Job," by Badger Clark (1883–1957), was one of Thurman's favorite poems. He quoted it in "The Significance of Jesus" sermon series in 1937 and in "Christian, Who Calls Me Christian?" in early 1938. See *PHWT*, 2:58–59, 111–13.

🐟 "THE RESPONSIBILITY OF THE PROFESSIONAL TO SOCIETY"
6 MAY 1957
CHICAGO, ILLINOIS

Thurman had long been interested in the dilemmas of trained professionals, particularly those in the "helping" and "caring" professions such as teaching, health care, and the ministry. He had a special interest in speaking to health care professionals; he believed that their concern with the connections between phys-ical and spiritual well-being and with ultimate questions of life and death were much like his own. "The Responsibility of the Professional to Society" was an elaboration, with different emphases, of a talk that Thurman had been delivering at least since 1941, when he spoke on "The Three Illusions of Professionalism"[1] to the National Hospital Association.[2] If early in his career he spoke only to black professional organizations, by the 1950s he was addressing integrated groups, as when he delivered this talk to the National League for Nursing[3] at its 1957 Bien-nial Convention.

I speak to you this evening not only as a professional but also as a layman. My subject is "The Responsibility of the Professional to Society." By necessity and wisdom my address will apply to the field of nursing as one of the accepted professions in our society but I shall not deal technically with such application. This is beyond my skill and my competency. Be assured that it is a privilege for me to address you.

By simple definition a professional is one who practices a given profes-sion. Those persons who practice professions in any society do so by virtue of skills, techniques and knowledge which they have developed as a result of the disciplines peculiar to the profession. As a result of much trial and error, of distilled experience and defined need, society evolves certain prerequisites which must be met before one of its members is permitted to prepare himself for the practice of his profession. After such preparation there are certain standards of efficiency and character that must be met before one is permitted into the charmed circle of a particular profession. The older and the more established is the profession, the more classical and inflexible are the standards. As members both of society and the professions, a professional is under a social obligation to maintain high standards not only by personal efficiency but also by refraining from being a party to any activity which may undermine them.

The general tendency in society is to guarantee many considerations to the professional which are not available to the other members of society who are not thus equipped. The meaning of all this will emerge as we proceed with the discussion. Once again may you be reminded that I do not even pretend to be able to address you from within the knowledge and presuppositions of your own profession. Whatever I may say or infer about the field of nursing will be from a consideration of direct nursing care which is, after all, the point of most relevancy to the lay mind.

With this rather detailed groundwork I invite you to journey with me as I chart the course of my own thinking about the subject before us this evening.

I.

Society recognizes the necessity for making available for itself the skilled technical services of certain of its members in order to guarantee the general welfare and the maintenance of social and individual well-being. Society provides for the training of its professional by putting at the disposal of such training needs a priority on its total resources. Through many stages of growth and evaluation, a systemized plan of preparation is arrived at in order to guarantee a minimal basic equipment for the specialized services needed. Preparation of the professional is not left to chance, to whims, to panic and fear but rather it is a part of the reflective experience of the society making for increasing care in planning and providing for adequate training, adequate preparation. Such planning includes instruction given under certain controlled circumstances and by qualified persons. The planning includes the use of materials that will aid in the development of skills with reference to the use of such materials under conditions as varied as the needs in the society. Always there is the necessity for making increasingly creative combinations of theory and practice, of the academic and the clinical, under conditions of limited responsibility and critical appraisal. Then there is the time interval for study in terms of a fixed period of years and finally certain tests by which society may be assured that skills have been learned and accreditation is awarded. This is, in fine, the anatomy of the process by which society creates a professional out of a layman. Technically, this is the way that a professional group is developed.

II.

There are certain important concessions made to the individuals who are selected to be trained to carry the unique responsibilities of the professional in a given society.

1. First, there is the tacit agreement that the individuals accepted may be excused from carrying their normal share of social responsibilities that their time and thought and energy may be devoted specifically to the given ends of the professions as reflected in prescribed study. In other words, to be selected to study for a profession is a privilege. This is a most crucial concession. It means that such individuals are literally taken out of circulation temporarily. They are not required to be active, functioning members of the society. During this training period, whether they are regular students or are serving as apprentices, they are put in a special classification. The fact that the designation of student or trainee is used indicates a relationship of certain general social demands. There is a sense in which they are not required to work for a living. To this extent they are sponsored. The slack which their training creates is absorbed by other members of the society: parents, relatives and others. In some instances they are excused from political responsibilities and even at a time of universal military conscription, there are certain extenuating circumstances which relieve temporarily the individual from participating at this point in the demands of the social process. Even after the period of preparation is over the general social responsibilities are narrowed to the area in which the trained professional functions.

For the professional this kind of priority treatment can be easily accepted as something which is his due as a person rather than the tribute which is paid to his skill and training. There must be the clear recognition that preferential treatment in whatever form of social exemption is given to the professional as a professional, not as a person. If this is not clearly understood the doctor, the lawyer, the engineer, the clergyman, the nurse may regard himself as an exception to the rule. The fact of special training and equipment heightens the responsibility rather than lessens it. If the professional begins to think that life will make an exception to the rule because he is different from the layman, only trouble awaits him. Knowledge as such does not make for exceptional treatment as far as natural and social law are concerned.

I cannot emphasize too strongly. For instance a man's body does not know that he is a lawyer or a clergyman or doctor. The fact that he is a doctor does not mean that he is exempted from the human predicament or from the things by which other men are bound. Several years ago a friend of mine, a physician, connected with a certain medical school gave me a physical. I was sent to various persons for the routine tests, etc., in addition. At the appointed time I reported to his office for his findings. I sat in the familiar chair near his desk as he opened the manilla folder with the various results of the tests. Despite the fact that I felt all right, I was a bit apprehensive. He looked at each page carefully, then glanced at me until he was through. He closed the folder as he said, "You are in good health. Except . . . you are a bit overweight." Then he talked technically to me about the dangers of extra weight at my age. I found myself looking at him in the light of what he was saying to me. I chuckled because he was not quite as tall as I but he weighed easily 220 or 225 pounds. He thought that his body knew that he was a doctor. His body did not know that he was a doctor; his body knew precisely what my body knew—that he was taking in more caloric units than he was burning up—hence the bulges. The pref- erential treatment that society gives to its professionals as indeed it should and must, does not mean that such persons have any immunity against the relentless logic of so called physical laws or moral laws.

2. The second concession which society makes has to do with the highly specialized provisions for training. Institutions of learning are established for guaranteeing effective and efficient training. Such institutions represent vast investments in money, time, property—in fine, they are subsidized so that the persons in training can secure skills, develop arts, at a price less than the total cost, much less than the total cost. This is especially true for institutions whose function gives primary emphasis upon teaching and training. These subsidies vary from profession to profession depending upon many factors. In the majority of hospital schools of nursing and institutions, apprenticeship training is still the order of the day. I would hazard the guess that most of the young women in these schools earn every penny of their education. There are, of course, some hospital schools that are now making a considerable investment but they are in the distinct minority. The thing that does not vary is the fact of the general subsidy itself. This is a part of the authentic investment which society makes—in its professional.

3. In addition to this general kind of subsidy, there are special subsidies in the form of scholarships, grants, perquisites, to help insure that those of greatest promise will be relieved of maximal distractions, primarily eco- nomic in character, from the work at hand. True it is that there are far too few but the fact remains that whenever a scholarship is granted this makes a double lien in the total resources of the society granting it.

4. Then, there is the kind of concession that is primarily ego-satisfying. The gift of heightened status, of prestige that goes with the profession. Often this is subtle but very real. Prestige-bearing status is but another way by which a grateful society compensates the professional in its midst. Certain aspects of this were referred to above. I can remember even now after many years the sense of awe which I experienced the first time I ever saw a nurse in her white starched uniform, it was in the pre-nylon period. It was breath-taking—simply other! I recognize the fact that this aspect of my discussion may seem exaggerated. Nevertheless it cannot be denied that the professional is a prestige-bearing member of society and there are deeply gratifying ego-satisfactions in the fact.

III.

From this point on in my discussion I shall substitute the word nurse for the word professional. But what I shall say applies to professionals generally. Society makes certain demands of the professional—of the nurse.

1. There is little that need be said about the initial requirements of ability and intelligence. This is obvious and may be taken for granted as initial.
2. In the second place she has to be committed to her profession as the avenue along which she chooses to find the vocational fulfillment of her life as a responsible member of the community. This is particularly important. For the nurse, for instance, it says that she has made up her mind and is willing to give to the profession of nursing, the nerve center of her vocational consent. She undertakes her training under the aegis of a very definite social commitment. Such a decision is apt to be perilous because of the very nature of the case.

   Why perilous? For the simple reason that no person makes a decision involving a life-commitment on the basis of evidence that is quite conclusive and final. She may discover after the decision is made and her training has begun under the social contract as outlined above, that there were certain factors she did not take into account. In view of these the decision was a mistake. Fortunate indeed is the person who makes the discovery before it is too late, or before she has gone too far. Sometimes it is not easy to know how far is too far. Every year there are those who must be eliminated or eliminate themselves because the desire and even the commitment in and of itself may not be sufficient. It is here that the responsibility of the counselor is crucial. But even the counselor may err. The possibility of being mistaken, the possibility of effective error is ever present.
3. There must be definite character on the part of the nurse, both in training and subsequently. The word character in this context has a particular

meaning. I am not thinking primarily of character in terms of morals as
such. Character, in the sense in which I am using the term, has to do with
the integrity of the act which the individual performs. This, at the level of
training as well as at the level of the professional practice. A sense of responsibility in the acquiring of knowledge and skills, integrity in carrying out
prescribed assignments, a willingness and a disposition to honor the fact
and not to betray it because of laziness or carelessness or loss of nerve. This
is what I mean by the integrity of the act in training. This is character.

At the level of professional practice, the same thing obtains. When a
person is ill and the skilled service of the trained nurse is indicated, what
the patient wants to know above all else, is not whether the nurse is kind
to her cat, or whether she buys presents for her nieces and nephews on
their birthdays, not whether she is rearing her children well, or whether
she obeys the traffic laws in her town—all of these are important in their
place—but what the patient wants to know is this: when the nurse puts
on her uniform and takes up her duties in the sick room, can she practice
nursing—is she skilled in nursing care. This is character in this context. If
there has been little integrity of the act in the practice of her profession,
whatever may be the intent of her heart and disposition, her failure at the
crucial point of character may very easily be disastrous! Here, no alibi has
standing! As a professional it is inexcusable for her to perform as a layman.

4. There is a demand that is made with reference to compensation—compensation means the ability to pay on the part of the persons to whom
the professional service is rendered. Society seeks to protect itself and its
professionals by a series of general agreements about compensation. These
agreements represent certain stages in the evolution of the social process.
I am in no position to pass a judgment upon their validity except to say
that the principle of payment for services rendered is an accepted one.
From within the integrity of this acceptance a very important factor must
be held in mind. (I am well aware that I am treading in a danger zone.)
The factor is that due consideration must be given to the fact that there
is an original economic and social investment which society has made in
the preparation and training of the professional, which must be taken into
account. There is an original economic and personal investment that the
professional herself has made in acquiring the skill and knowledge of her
vocation. Every person who receives professional services is a member
of the society which made the training of the professional possible in the
first place. I do not wish to be misunderstood here. The principle is this: In
non-apprenticeship training institutions it is evident that the expenditure
for providing and supporting the institution is greater per capita than the
tax that is levied on the trainee by the institution. Fundamental to all that

may be said or implied at this point is a full-orbed recognition of the fact that compensation, however large or meager, is a <u>recognition</u> of services rendered rather than <u>payment</u> for services rendered.

IV.

The field of our discussion narrows markedly at this point. It is in order to raise the question as to what is involved when the professional sees herself as a person and those to whom she administers as persons. What happens when society becomes personalized in a man or woman and when the professional becomes personalized as a man or woman? It will aid us materially in the effort towards personalization to recognize initially that the terms "society" and "professional" are both abstractions. There is no such thing as society. What we mean by the term is people who eat, sleep, love, hate, die, etc. The term itself is an abstraction, a fiction—the convenient way of thinking of society as "they." But this is false. The term "professional" is the same. The professional is a person. The nurse is a person—she cares not for sick people but for a sick man, or woman, who lives somewhere and who has some kind of authentic identity as a person. The general reference breeds the general attitude—and unluckily always in the background is the threat of contempt for the person. This is the violent material out of which class and group antagonisms arise. It makes of all human relations an armed camp!

We are ready now to examine the difference that is made when the principle of concretion becomes operative. In the first place, to be specific, the nurse is a human being whose life is private, personal and unique. The professional has needs of various kinds which must be met, if, as a human being, she is to be healthy. It is as a person of emotional and physical health and well-being that she practices her profession. The responsibility is both personal and professional, private and social to maintain sound, good health. To neglect one's emotional and physical well-being because of one's professional commitment is to undermine the integrity of function and to destroy the social contract. It is very easy for institutions to become insensitive to the stark fact that the people who perform the professional functions in the institutions become weary, harassed, hostile, sick. This must be recognized and dealt with without prejudice. One of my favorite professors in college, one of whose classes met on Saturday morning at eight o'clock had a classic speech he delivered to any fellow who slept in his class. (The Friday night dances lasted until long after midnight.) This was his devastating statement: It is not dancing all night that kills the dancer, it is not praying all night that kills the prayer—but it is staying up all night. The only thing your body knows is that you have not been to bed. It does not know that you have not taken your needed rest because you have been serving your fellow man or indulging your personal whim, it only knows that you have not been to bed. The nurse must honor her obligation to herself as a person. This is crucial.

In the second place she must be intimately and progressively acquainted with the technical resources needful for carrying on her work with maximal effectiveness.

1. This means that she must be in constant touch with the resources of her profession and take advantage of them both as a nurse and as a human being. It is easy to become so absorbed in the daily routine and demands of particular assignments that there is little energy, time or disposition to keep abreast of the developments within the profession itself. The tendency to fail to read the technical journals or even to subscribe to them; the failure to attend professional meetings, lectures, demonstrations, or to adopt an attitude that reduces your exposure to the cumulative wisdom in books, monographs and studies—all of this is to betray your commitment and to let the light grow dim that long ago called you to the far horizon and the great adventure. There is no valid excuse for remaining out of touch with the major resources of your field. At the risk of seeming elementary, it is important to keep by your side the life story, the biography if you please, of certain persons whose lives are capable of stimulating and inspiring you at times when the arduous aspects of your work bear most heavily upon your spirit and your enthusiasm. There is nothing more inspiring than a life that has been deeply and well lived. You need this both as a professional and as a human being.

   There is a kind of cross-fertilization within a profession as well as outside of it. In my preparation for this address I was amazed to discover the wide range of the field of nursing, the different kinds of nurses and the highly specialized character of work and research that falls within the category. What an opportunity to have the particular area in which you are a skilled performer enriched by the fruits of all the others far removed from your operations and to feel yourself a part of a great company of women and men whose life commitment is fundamentally your own. This would add immeasurably to your own dignity both as a nurse and as a human being.

2. Again, the nurse must be alive to the resources that are available in the society outside of the areas unique to her profession. There is a vast accumulation of resources that are a part of the total development of the culture of which we are a part and the culture of the world, past and present, upon which it is our privilege to draw. This is the only way by which we can deepen our sense of belonging to life itself. As someone long ago expressed it: "I like to realize forms of life utterly unlike mine. When my own life feels small, and I am oppressed with it, I like to crush together, and see it in a picture, in an instant, a multitude of disconnected unlike

phases of human life— . . . I like to see it all; I feel it run through me, that life belongs to me; it makes my little life larger, it breaks down the narrow walls that shut me in."[4]

As a human being you are the heir to all that has gone on before in art, music, literature, the spoken word—a part of your contemporary heritage are the rich overtones that flow into the stream of our common life from all who create and dream. These are living sources which feed the springs of your life bringing to you both refreshment and inspiration.

In addition to all of these there are the resources which come from the other professions. I know all too well how easy it is to become the prisoner of your own profession, to develop a sense of exclusiveness and a false kind of pride. This is as understanding as it is corrupting. There is a very enlightening allegory about such an attitude. For many generations a colony of ants had been at work building an ant mound, a memorial to all ants. At last the memorial was complete save for one tiny spot that needed a single grain of sand to complete it. It happened that in the line of duty a solitary ant, at the end of the day, brought the single grain of sand needed for the unoccupied spot. He deposited it. As he did it, it dawned upon him like a flash of blinding light that he had just completed a thing upon which generations had been laboring, long before he was born. He could not contain himself. He lifted himself on his haunches as he exclaimed aloud—My ant heap that I have built, my mound, my memorial. Just then, the wind started moving up from the valley, over the top of the memorial and carried the vaunting ant to destruction on the other side—But the ant memorial remained. You must keep alert to the resources that are available to you from allied and separate professions that your own perspective will be a true one and your sense of sharing in a common task dedicated to the total welfare will be your constant and inspiring point of referral.

3. Then there are the resources that are within one's self. Fundamental to all else the professional must be an authentic human being. Whatever may be the degree of technical skill and proficiency that mark you as a nurse, whatever may be the depth of your specialty and your unique professional equipment and training, you must experience yourself as a human being. You must acquaint yourself with personal resources upon which in your solitariness as a human being you may draw for the renewal of your own inward parts in times of barrenness and desolation. The deepest hungers of your heart have to do with your needs as a human being. For each one of us there comes a time when we are stripped to that which is literal and irreducible in us and our lives are laid bare as one who looks steadily at himself. The major resource upon which the race has drawn through all the ages for needs of this kind is religion. Here I make no special case for

any particular kind of religion. This is a private and intensely personal matter. My insistence is that there is a hunger in the human spirit that can only be met by drawing upon a resource that is greater and more abiding than the individual life of man. Every nurse in the course of her training and/or her practice has seen this at work in the lives of many as they have faced the ultimate issues of life and death.

This is the meaning of what I am saying: The professional of whatever kind is not exempt from finding in terms of spiritual values that which will do two very simple crucial things for her.

1. Give to her a fundamental validation for her life. It is the experience of the race that the only thing capable of doing this is a supremely worthful object of adoration and worship which can be for the individual a source of strength and reassurance in the living of life—In short, God. For each of us there is the perennial necessity for having one's life undergirded, sustained by that which is not dependent upon the vicissitudes of Fortune or the incidents of Fate. Here I am not talking merely about a harbor of refuge for the weak and frightened, or a wind break for the drifting and the desolate, but more importantly, perhaps, I am talking the kind of spiritual companionship that the human spirit may experience as the ultimate immunity against the lurking sense of isolation as one encounters in the living substances, joy, sorrow, failure, success—life—death. The need for this is beyond all argument, speculation and cynicism. It is as close as breathing—as near as your hands and feet. It is the insistence of religion that this is the need that God meets in the life of man.

2. The second grows out of the first. Such a worthful object of devotion provides the life with a basis for integrated behavior. It is out of the ultimate guarantor of one's sense of values that the content of one's values, the meaning of right and wrong, is constantly being tested and redefined. So many questions which you encounter in your work as nurses have to do with your ultimate sense of values rather than your skill as a nurse. In the fulfillment of the demands of your profession you must be able in all that you do, not only to respect yourself as a nurse but to respect yourself as a person of integrity and worth. For in the pursuit of your profession as a nurse you must not put in jeopardy the moral and ethical foundation of your character as a member in good standing in the human race. Deep within you there must be a riding sense of Ethical Presence to which you are finally responsible for your life.

There is only one more thing that I would like to say in closing. I hardly know how to put this. You must take time to cultivate your inner resources as a person. Learn how to quiet your spirit in meditation and prayer. You are a part of the life of the Creator of Life and the living substance. There is a deep spirit deep within you that is as old as life and as timeless as that which has never been born. Tarry in solitude a while as you do your work and live your life. And in your heart you will hear a whisper that will give you strength and courage sufficient unto your needs whatever they may be.

TD.

NOTES

1. The reporter Sue Barnett, commenting on Thurman's address to the National Hospital Association in August 1941, noted that "in a somewhat satirical manner he discussed the illusions of routine, omnipotence, and the illusion that life will make exceptions for professional men." She continued, "In citing an example of the first illusion, he chose the profession of the ministry, pointing out that because ministers perform so many marriage ceremonies, for example, they are apt to become mere routine to them and they fail to inject the personal and peculiar to each case. This is the illusion of routine in professionalism. Dr. Thurman further pointed out that because of their proficiency, there is a danger of professional men acquiring the 'Great God I am' attitude and feeling that they are a class unto themselves. This also causes them to lose the sense of graciousness which is expected. Dr. Thurman then pointed out that it is difficult at times for ministers to be true Christians because they are professionals and are so frequently required to pray and preach at certain times rather than when they are inspired. This is the illusion of omnipotence. The third illusion is the feeling on the part of professionals that life will make exceptions. 'There is a danger,' stated Dr. Thurman, 'of professional men feeling that things which happen to them just can't happen to them.' A satirical example of this was the feeling of some doctors that the organs of their bodies know they are doctors and therefore they don't have to care for them. Dr. Thurman also felt that there was some tendency on the part of some professional men to ignore moral laws, feeling that they are made only for the masses. His very enlightening address was concluded with the hope that the professional men would beware of the three illusions of professionalism" (Sue Barnett, "Thurman Tells Doctors about Their Frailties," *Atlanta Daily World*, 26 August 1941). Thurman's handwritten notes for a talk on this topic are extant. Written on Howard University stationery, they are undated. See "The Three Illusions of Professionalism," writings, undated, Howard Gotlieb Archival Research Center.

2. The National Hospital Association, an organization of African American hospital administrators that was organized in 1923, was affiliated with the leading organization of African American physicians, the National Medical Association.

3. The National League for Nursing was organized in 1952, when three organizations—the Association of Collegiate Schools of Nursing, the National League of Nursing Organizations, and the National Organization for Public Health Nursing—merged, dividing their functions between the new organization and the older American Nurses Association. The new organization was fully integrated, in large degree through the efforts of Mabel K. Staupers (1890–1989), the longtime leader of the National Association of Colored Graduate Nurses (NACGN). Staupers had pushed the American Nurses Association to integrate in 1948, and two years later she led the members of NACGN in voting to disband their organization. In 1951 Staupers was awarded the NAACP's Spingarn Medal.

Howard Thurman with a
copy of *The Growing Edge*,
which was published in
1956. From the Howard
Thurman Collection,
Howard Gotlieb Archival
Research Center at Boston
University.

4. Olive Schreiner, *The Story of an African Farm* (Boston: Little, Brown, 1924), 259–60. Most of this quote may also be found in Thurman's Schreiner anthology, *A Track to the Water's Edge*, 6–7.

🐟 FROM WALTER N. PAHNKE
6 SEPTEMBER 1957
EN ROUTE FROM ANCHORAGE TO SEATTLE

Walter N. Pahnke[1] writes of his recent work as a rural physician in Alaska, his religious musings, and his excitement in returning to Boston, for course work at Harvard Divinity School and private study with Thurman. Pahnke, a physician and psychiatrist as well as a serious student of religious thought, packed several careers into his all-too-short life. Thurman was a key mentor and inspiration for Pahnke in his restless spiritual journeying.

Pahnke started to attend services at Marsh Chapel shortly after Thurman's arrival in Boston in the fall of 1953.[2] The two men soon started a friendship. By the end of 1954 Pahnke was reading Jesus and the Disinherited, *and the following year he was studying, with Thurman, Rufus Jones's* Studies in Mystical Religion.[3] *In the 1955–56 academic year, Pahnke probably audited Thurman's course*

on Spiritual Disciplines and Resources.[4] Thurman wrote a letter of recommendation for Pahnke for a Kent Fellowship from the National Council on Religion
in Higher Education in 1958,[5] and the following year he officiated at Pahnke's
marriage to Eva Sontum.[6] Thurman's admiration for Pahnke is evident in a letter
of recommendation he wrote in November 1956 for the Rockefeller Brothers Theological Fellowship Program: "We have had many thoughtful discussions and conferences about the meaning of religion and the demand of religion upon his own life
both personally and professionally. He is a man of authentic character and genuine
emotional stability with an excellent mind and a thoughtful approach to the meaning
of religious experience. He is concerned about exposing himself to a year of study and
discipline in a theological institution to see if it is right for him to shift his vocational
commitment from medicine to the ministry, or if some combination of these two
would seem practical and relevant. I commend him for consideration by the Theological Fellowship Program with complete confidence and abiding enthusiasm."[7]

   Pahnke is best remembered for coleading, with Timothy Leary,[8] the Good
Friday Experiment at Marsh Chapel on 20 April 1962 on the connection between
mystic experience and psychedelic substances.[9] If Thurman's own participation in
the experiment seems largely to have been limited to his granting permission to
the experimenters to use Marsh Chapel, through his protégé Pahnke the experiment reflected Thurman's commitment to the exploration of some of the most
controversial corners of mysticism and the paranormal.[10]

   Until his untimely death in a scuba-diving accident in 1971, Pahnke enjoyed
a significant career as a leading researcher into the psychological and spiritual
properties of psychedelic substances. Thurman remained in close contact with
Pahnke and his wife, Eva,[11] and visited the Pahnke family in their Maryland
home in April 1968.[12] In a prayer read at Pahnke's funeral in July 1971, Thurman
praised Pahnke's search for the "infinite reaches of the spirit in the ebb and flow
of life" and the "ancient wisdom of his spirit" that he "shared with quiet grace and
no offense," and in the only veiled reference to Pahnke's lifework, Thurman gave
thanks for "the acute restlessness of his mind that energized his steady search for
the clue to personality and the secrets locked within the quiet places of the heart."[13]

En route in a DC-4—winging my way from Anchorage to Seattle

Dear Dr. Thurman,
   It's been an exciting and interesting summer, but my hopes for the school
year ahead are for an even more stimulating and enriching experience—perhaps

the most of my life so far. This will have to be a soul searching and decisive year in my life also because it may well be the turning point in my career.

I don't yet know for sure what my schedule at HDS will be but it looks as if I will be taking 5 courses there (New Testament, Ethics, Church History, and 2 Theology courses—one from Tillich[14]). Also I want to audit as many courses at Harvard College as I have time for (3 or 4 I hope). Last but not by any means least (and to me one of the most rewarding things I will be doing all year) is the chance you offered me to take special study with you to guide my reading and thinking and personal meditation—which I hope to delve into deeply and expand greatly this year.

Last spring you mentioned that I should register my study with you as a course at a certain time so that it would be set aside in your schedule. I will consult you about this before I register at HDS. I hope you can give me 2–3 hours per week.

In my thinking and meditations this summer I have been feeling deep down inside me a growing sense that at last I am on the right track in my search for God's will for my life. When I think of the new horizons and vistas that I may open up this year as I explore the interrelationships between medicine and religion I can feel my enthusiasm and excitement growing. Although I'm afraid I will be mostly on the receiving end in our discussions, perhaps, with my medical and psychiatric background we may unearth some ideas in our thinking together which will add in some small way to your knowledge of life.

I have found my work as the only doctor on the small island of Wrangell in South Eastern Alaska for a month this summer a very worthwhile experience. One gets a little different view of people from the standpoint of private practice than from work in a charity hospital such as Denver General.[15] But I found the same thing true of the people I met. There is definitely something inside of them which is striving to be satisfied and nurtured. Some people try to satisfy this urge which they can't really understand by a blind race to accumulate material wealth. Others make some hobby, sport, or satisfaction of some desire their chief motivation and goal. But man seems happiest when he can lose himself in something greater than himself. However, he is not truly satisfied with these goals mentioned above—and some bitterly realize this when they have achieved the greatest measure of success in doing the thing they have been striving for. I have had a lot of time to think this summer—especially in the last 2 weeks since my job has been over. I have been traveling alone through Alaska with a pack on my back—hitchhiking and sleeping beneath the stars. I think this inward feeling and longing is GOD or the Creative Power of the Universe which men can best come to discover and know through prayer and quiet meditation.—More of this when we meet again!

I have gotten a great deal from reading the book you recommended to me— Rediscovering Prayer.[16] I hope we can discuss parts of it in our "class."

(Please excuse the switch in stationery, but I ran out of paper, and not what I wanted to say.)

Dr. Thurman, I must confess that I still feel rather badly about that missed appointment last February. I know how busy you always are, and it certainly looked as if I had not even appreciated the trouble you went to just to see me on your day off. You didn't have to say anything to me—I could feel how disappointed you were with me. I was quite disgusted with myself, to say the least, because seeing you was very important to me. I appreciated greatly the fact that you then did see me before I left Boston, but it was not for as long as originally planned. I have been regretting this incident ever since and I suffer a little every time I think of it. And I didn't even have a good excuse. Excuses are pretty worthless anyway, for as I have discovered in medicine—it's not excuses but RESULTS that count. So all I can do is apologize again—but I still don't feel right about it all.

I plan to arrive in Boston on Sept. 18, Wed, and registration for HDS is on Sept 19. I will call you when I get to Boston and before I must register.

Sincerely yours,

[signed] Walter N. Pahnke

ALS.

NOTES

1. Walter Norman Pahnke (1931–71) was raised in the Chicago area. He was a 1952 graduate of Carleton College and a 1956 graduate of Harvard Medical School. He received a B.D. (now the M.Div. degree) from Harvard Divinity School in 1960 and a Ph.D. from the Harvard Graduate School of Arts and Sciences in 1963 for his dissertation, "Drugs and Mysticism: An Analysis of the Relationship between Psychedelic Drugs and the Mystical Consciousness." After graduating from Harvard he did further psychiatric studies at the University of Göttingen in West Germany and completed his residency at the Massachusetts Mental Health Care Center. He subsequently was appointed director of clinical sciences at the Maryland Psychiatric Research Center and professor of psychiatry at the Johns Hopkins University School of Medicine. Pahnke wrote extensively on psychedelic drugs and in 1968 delivered the Ingersoll Lecture on Human Immortality at Harvard University; his lecture was titled "The Psychedelic Mystical Experience in the Human Encounter with Death" (Harvard Theological Review 62, no. 1 [January 1969]: 1–21). (Thurman had been the Ingersoll lecturer in 1947.)

2. In his fellowship recommendation in November 1956, Thurman wrote that he had known Pahnke "for three years, during the period of his residence at the Harvard Medical School. He was a member of my congregation in Marsh Chapel" (To the Rockefeller Brothers Theological Fellowship Program?, 26 November 1956). Pahnke wrote to Thurman that Marsh Chapel services provided "a spiritual uplift by a creative encounter with 'deepest needs and aspirations' of my own human spirit. I have felt as close to God there as when I have been all alone in a quiet forest of towering and whispering pines by the shores of a sky-blue mountain lake with majestic mountains and glaciers all around" (From Walter N. Pahnke, 13 November 1956).

3. Rufus M. Jones, *Studies in Mystical Religion* (London: Macmillan, 1909). See To Macmillan Publishing Company, 10 November 1955, in which Thurman ordered a copy of the book for Pahnke.

4. Zalman Schachter-Shalomi told an interviewer that Pahnke was his classmate in "Spiritual Disciplines and Resources in the 1955–1956 academic year" (Peter Eisenstadt, interview with Zalman Schachter-Shalomi, 28 June 2012). However, Pahnke seems to have spent at least part of the year in a hospital residency in Newfoundland, since Thurman had Jones's book sent to him at a Newfoundland hospital; see To Macmillan Publishing Company, 10 November 1955.

5. See Richard Gilman to Walter Pahnke, 23 December 1958, cc'd to Thurman, with a handwritten note to Thurman by Gilman, executive director of the National Council on Religion in Higher Education: "He [Pahnke] sounds like a good man! Thanks for suggesting he write to me."

6. From Mrs. Walter D. Pahnke [Pahnke's mother], 8 July 1959.

7. To the Rockefeller Brothers Theological Fellowship Program?, 26 November 1956.

8. See From Timothy Leary, 29 October 1962, printed in the current volume.

9. For an account of Thurman's and Pahnke's involvement in the Good Friday Experiment, see the biographical essay in the current volume.

10. At some point in their meetings, Pahnke and Thurman discussed the paranormal powers that were associated with Edgar Cayce (1877–1945), a famous American psychic. Thurman received a letter on 27 October 1960 from an organization dedicated to preserving Cayce's legacy, inquiring of Peggy Strong, an artist, and a friend of Thurman's who had received a reading from Cayce: "Walter Pahnke, who visited us here at Virginia Beach last summer, also told us that you had spoken to him about Peggy's reading" (From Gladys Davis Turner, 27 October 1960). See also To J. Goodell Schultz, 4 November 1960. For Peggy Strong, see *WHAH*, 239–40.

11. Thurman wrote several letters of recommendation for Eva Pahnke. See From Beatrix A. Park, 28 November 1961; To Harvard University Graduate School of Education, 18 May 1965. Eva wrote Thurman a long, sorrowful letter on the death of her infant daughter, in which in passing she described a recent meeting (From Eva Pahnke, 5 October 1963).

12. To Walter Pahnke, 16 April 1968.

13. "Howard Thurman Prayer, 1971," folder 5, Walter Richards Collection of Walter Pahnke Papers, 1952–71, Archives and Special Collections, Purdue University Library.

14. Paul Tillich (1886–1965) was one of the most influential theologians of the twentieth century. Tillich had a distinguished academic career in Germany before immigrating to the United States in 1933. He taught at Union Theological Seminary from 1933 to 1955, at Harvard Divinity School from 1955 to 1962, and at the University of Chicago from 1962 until his death. His works include *The Courage to Be* (New Haven, Conn.: Yale University Press, 1952) and *Systematic Theology*, 3 vols. (Chicago: University of Chicago Press, 1951–63).

15. Pahnke had a residency in Denver the previous year; see From Walter N. Pahnke, 13 November 1956.

16. John Laurence Casteel, *Rediscovering Prayer* (New York: New York Association Press, 1955).

🦅 From Harold C. Case
4 October 1957
Boston, Mass.

Harold Case upbraids Thurman for his failure to attend a meeting of the United Campus Ministry, to which belonged the heads of the campus religious groups; and a meeting of the Boston University Cabinet and Council, which was comprised of all the Boston University deans.

Dear Howard:

It was very disturbing to me yesterday that you were the only member of the United Ministry who was not present at the meeting for a full discussion of problems and policies. It was likewise a disappointment to me that at the first Cabinet and Council meeting of the academic year, all of the Deans were present, except you. I am aware of the fact that on that day you had a special Convocation in the Chapel, but of course the Council met until 12:00 noon and the Cabinet for luncheon.

I cannot over-emphasize the importance to the University councils and appropriate committees of your attendance. All of us are carrying heavy loads, and you are no exception.

I am sure that there was a reasonable excuse for your absence yesterday, but I must tell you how very disappointed I am to have the Dean of the Chapel absent when we are discussing All-University religious affairs.

Sincerely yours,
[*signed*] Harold
Harold C. Case

Dean Howard Thurman
Marsh Chapel
300 Bay State Road

                                                                                    TLS.

🦅 To Harold C. Case
15 October 1957
Boston, Mass.

In a furious response to Harold Case,[1] Thurman defends his absences from several meetings and threatens "to solve the problem" by resigning his positions at Boston University. One underlying source of tension, as Thurman's letter makes clear, is the failure of the Boston University administration and the United Campus Ministry to find a role for his proposed Marsh Chapel ministry.[2]

Howard and Sue Bailey Thurman with Harold and Phyllis Case. From the Bailey Thurman Family Papers; the Stuart A. Rose Manuscript, Archives, and Rare Book Library, Emory University.

Dear Harold:

There are three things that I must say to you in reply to your letter of reprimand to me, under date of October 4th.

1. Apparently you had forgotten that a few days prior to the meeting of the University Council, we had talked about the fact that the meeting coming up was scheduled for a Wednesday. I told you that my class met on Wednesday from 11:00 to 12:30. Often I am not through until after one o'clock. You said that you hoped that the meeting date could be changed from Wednesdays as others had expressed difficulty with the day. I did not stay away from the meeting because of the Matriculation Convocation of the School of Theology. I could not have come had there been no such meeting. Hence, I am at a loss to understand your "disappointment" because I was not at the meeting, when you knew beforehand that I could not be there.

2. It was not until your letter of October 4th, that I knew that the purpose of the luncheon meeting of the United Ministry was to have "a full discussion of problems and policies" connected with the religious life of the campus. If such was the agenda, at least I should have known beforehand,

as it would seem to me, and been given the opportunity to share with you my more intimate knowledge of the problems. Consistently, during the past four years, I have attended the meetings of the United Ministry and worked hard at the impossible ambivalence of the University in trying to fashion a satisfactory policy. I am intimately acquainted with every aspect of the work that has evidenced itself during the four years I have been a part of the University. I attended the only regularly scheduled meeting we have had this year and, with Wendell, worked on certain problems that arose incident to Freshman Orientation. At this meeting there was no announcement of any proposed meeting with you. As far as I was concerned, this was a luncheon meeting which you were calling, with no indication of the agenda, which, of course, is your privilege, but in my naivete I thought how nice it was that, inasmuch as your duties are of such that you cannot participate very much in the religious life of the University, that at the beginning of the year, you would meet the United Ministry for fellowship and for the kind of reassurance that only you can give.

I resent with every fiber of my being, the implication in your letter that I am neglecting my responsibilities as Dean of the Chapel because it was not possible for me to be present at that luncheon.

If you take it as a matter of personal affront to you, as President of the University, that I was not present, I apologize. It was an error on my part not to notify your office that I would not be there, for this I apologize.

You have problems enough in the University without my adding to them by working in the University in the only way I can work and do my job. I am genuinely sorry that I have caused you embarrassment and made your administrative problems more rugged because of my apparent lack of cooperation. I am perfectly willing, therefore, to solve the problem in any one of the following ways:

1) To advise your office, in writing, when I know beforehand that I cannot attend a meeting, so that all parties will know that I am not acting irresponsibly in fulfilling my obligation as an administrative officer; or
2) To withdraw from the Chapel and devote the time that I am at the University to the duties of a professor in the School of Theology.
3) If the above alternatives offer no solution then, in order for me to cause no further embarrassment to you as President, of the University, I am willing in all good conscience to resign from the faculty of the University and from my post as the Dean of Marsh Chapel.

Sincerely yours,
Howard Thurman

TLc.

Notes
1. See From Harold C. Case, 4 October 1957, printed in the current volume.
2. For background on Thurman's deep distress over the inability to organize a Marsh Chapel fellowship, see the biographical essay in the current volume.

❧ "The New Heaven and the New Earth"
1958

Thurman had strong feelings about both the advantages and the disadvantages of education in historically black colleges and universities, and he had written often about his own experiences as a student at Morehouse and his thoughts on the future of black higher education. He argues that black colleges could either function as "handmaiden[s] of the cult of inequality" or, alternatively, give their students the tools and the courage to challenge their subordinate status. This article in the Journal of Negro Education, *which was based on a talk he had delivered the year before,[1] contains both a summary of his long-held opinions and his tentative but optimistic reflections on the possible course of black higher education in a desegregated future.*

In reflecting upon the interpretation of certain aspects of the American Negroes' encounter with higher education, one fact stood out clearly in my mind. I could never find, see, or talk with any college-trained Negro who was not discouraged.[2] Why? Because the response to the impact of higher education was one of frustration. And frustration is what a man experiences when he is unable to achieve the thing which he seeks to achieve. This frustration, in turn, becomes tragedy when a man is convinced that he is unable to achieve something because of some weakness in himself. Or again, frustration becomes tragedy when it finds expression in terms of compromise. In other words, a man may decide that the thing which he seeks has no reality for him at the level of his living. Therefore, of necessity, he must scale down his desires and dreams so that they will come within the reach of possibility.

This is very illuminating if we look at it carefully and apply it to what is happening in higher education with us. Many times in the past, we shifted vocational aspirations for the things we really wanted to do because in our society those goals were unachievable. When I was in college, for instance, there were certain vocational goals you just didn't have. They were unrealistic despite the fact that they were like fires kindled in you as a result of your exposure to what was involved in higher education. You scaled your demands down so that they would come within reach of being achieved by one located in society as you are located. Then there was another way that we dealt with frustration. We looked at our environment and sought to operate on our environment in order to bring within our reach the goals which we have envisioned for ourselves.

It is important to point out that something also happened to higher education when it sought to communicate and to bring the full impact of its insight and resources to the minds of American Negroes. Higher education had to make an adjustment. This adjustment caused it to become a practitioner of the cult of inequality. It did not deliberately set out to be an apostle of inequality, but in its adjustment to these new demands, it began compromising in various ways. One of the things that evolved was a distinction between higher education generally and Negro higher education, in particular. For a long time, for instance, Howard University's Medical School was a class A Negro medical school. What kind of medical school is that—Class A, Negro?

Changes were wrought which made the medical school just Class A, period. But this was one of the ways in which higher education became a handmaiden of the cult of inequality. Such an emphasis invaded the curricular offering. When I was an undergraduate at Morehouse College, I wanted to study philosophy. My mind was full of questions that only this kind of discipline would help me understand. The curriculum provided for no such offering. There was logic for a half year and a wonderful course in ethics, so called, which gave the president the opportunity to become acquainted intimately with the seniors and to expose them to his working philosophy, but it didn't teach you anything about ethics as a discipline. This was not an accident, and in this regard, Morehouse was not unique. For if students are exposed to the creative process which causes them to raise profound questions about meanings and to seek answers, they may go on to raise questions about the structure of the institution which made it possible for them to get their college education. In other words, the total issue involving the segregated schools in our society would have to be dealt with.[3]

There was another element that was present in the dynamics of this situation. It was the ethical imperative growing out of the Christian commitment which established the missionary schools. These schools were segregated, of necessity, but within the ethical imperative, no category existed for the segregated schools within the missionary movement. The missionaries themselves were faced with the same problem which faced higher education. How can you put at the disposal of the students the full and boundless insight of the Christian ethic and the moral imperative which it carries, and at the same time, not become a handmaiden of the cult of inequality? Some kind of adjustment had to be made. How could the problem be counteracted so as to produce students who were emotionally healthy?

One of the first steps was to find teachers who had points of view that could not quite be contained within a segregated structure. Among them were people who had a profound sense of mission in their work and were well trained. Such

persons quietly withered as they found themselves working in a "foreign country," and unable to identify either with the Negroes to whom they ministered
or with the white persons who lived in the cities in which the institutions were
located. How to do effective work under such circumstances was the crucial
issue.[4]

One solution was to accept segregation without raising any question beyond
the fact. The profound immorality of segregation is that it limits the area of the
magnetic field of ethical and moral responsibility. To make clear my meaning:
When I was a boy in Florida, I joined the church at the age of 12. I believed in
the Kingdom of God. I was an active worker in the church and had reasonable
intelligence. But it did not ever cross even the periphery of my awareness that
I should recognize any moral responsibility to any of the white people in Daytona, Florida. They were not within the area of my ethical awareness. They were
ethically out of bounds. What was true for me was true for any young white boy
who may have belonged to the First Baptist Church, uptown. This is the immorality of segregation. He was not within the area of my ethical awareness; I was
not in the area of his ethical awareness.

I remember vividly one day when I was raking leaves in Mrs. Blochard's yard
as a part of my work in the afternoon after school, I had a traumatic experience
with her little daughter. As fast as I raked the leaves into a pile, she would go
through the pile picking out beautiful colored leaves and show them to me or
put them in another pile. This meant that I had to do my work over and over
again. Finally I said to her, "If you don't stop, I will tell your mother and she will
make you go in the house." Her reaction: She reached into her little pinafore,
found a straight pin, came over, and stuck me with it. I reacted to the pain;
whereupon she said, "Why did you do that? You can't feel." This is the graphic
and monumental godless iniquity of segregation.

It posed a crucial problem for all who came under the aegis of the profound
missionary commitment to find a way to broaden the area of ethical awareness.
They were handicapped in doing it because they themselves were rootless and
were working on a frontier far removed from the congregations in the North
which gave to them a sense of belonging.

There belongs also in this picture another important element. Gradually
young Negro teachers educated for the most part in the North came into the
schools. They were educated at Amherst, or Williams, or Mt. Holyoke, or some
other Eastern institution. They had had the experience of education in an
entirely different kind of environment. When those of us who had never been
in the kind of environment in which they had studied came into contact with
them, the ceiling of our own hopes was raised in a new way. They talked about
things that were utterly foreign to our way of life and thought. I remember the
first time I heard one of these men talk about his experience in being elected to

Phi Beta Kappa. They tended to be very exacting and were unwilling to accept extenuating circumstances as justification for poor work and bad preparation. They did not seem to be willing to take into account the kind of distorted personalities that segregation had produced in us. What the white missionary had pointed out to us as possibilities for us tended not to seem real because they were people from another world, a world that did not know segregation. When young Negro teachers began saying these same things to us, the possibilities of higher education extended now beyond the limited boundaries of self-service.

The problem that now posed itself was, can you operate within a context of segregation in a manner that will release the mind for a creative attack on the fact of segregation. If I may speak personally again, it was at this point that my understanding of Booker T. Washington was a source of great inspiration to me. It seemed to me that what Mr. Washington said in his life and work was this: You must make your hands commit to memory skills with raw materials so that they will be able to create something that has a utility value in the open market. The thing that you create can be exchanged for economic goods, thus guaranteeing the economic stability of your life and enabling you to free your mind to brood effectively and creatively over the problems inherent in segregated living.

When this concept is applied at the level of higher education, then the service motive is structured in a new way. It goes something like this. If you can acquire certain professional skills so that you can administer to certain needs of your own community, within the segregated community, then you will be able to establish economic security within this closed circuit. Hence, for a long time, the professional ceiling was established around the ministry, medicine, dentistry, and teaching. The law and social work came later. It was a simple step to broaden this concept so that the professional intent would include any person whose needs you could meet without regard to whether that person was located within or without the so called segregated world. The great contribution made to my generation by men like "Bennie" Mays, Lorimer Milton,[5] "Smokey Joe" Caroll was this: They heightened our morale. Morale by simple definition is belief in one's own cause.

While all these things were taking place, something else was happening on the broad stage of American and world life. The operation of the forces about which Dr. Cobb[6] has just spoken is a case in point. Forces that from one point of view seemed blind and mindless were undermining all established patterns and structures of subjection all over the world. In a sense these were climaxed during the second world war.

Twenty-two years ago when I was in India, as I sat in a train compartment in Calcutta, a little Indian porter staggered into the compartment with a trunk on his head and two heavy pieces of luggage in his hands. He put them down and then with great effort established them securely in the luggage rack. A British colonel was waiting. When the porter finished, the colonel gave him a coin. He looked at the coin, and then looked into the face of the colonel, and tossed the coin back so that it struck the colonel on the nose. Immediately the colonel struck the Indian across the shoulders with his bamboo stick. The Indian snatched the stick from his hand, broke it on his bony knees, and threw it out of the train window. The train started moving and the porter jumped out of the train and ran along side pouring out expletives which I could not understand but I could feel. All the way to his destination, the colonel kept muttering to himself; the only thing that I could hear was a repetition of the phrase, "it's time for me to retire and leave this blank country." The force of revolution was at work.[7]

When the Atlantic Charter was informally "formalized," and the concept of the four freedoms made manifest, the people of India wanted to know whether in the Prime Minister's judgment, these applied to India.[8] As I remember it, the expressed or implied reply was a negative one. Mr. Roosevelt, however, had to say that it applied to everybody. Now why did he have to say this? The Allied Nations were faced with a new kind of enemy, the enemy who could not be opposed by the enthusiasm which was built around a slogan like "Save The World For Democracy." The enemy this time had a hard core of purpose around which everything was oriented. The word "fascism" became the symbol of a faith. It defined man in concrete terms. It declared what was to be the nature of the new order which it would bring into being. Everything was spelled out in detail. This left no live option for the democracies. They had to match this, idea for idea, fact for fact. They could not meet psychologically or philosophically a concrete definition of fascism with broad generalizations about the meaning of democracy. This demand created for the democracies a very real problem. The degree to which they spelled out the meaning of democracy in clear cut working definitions, to that degree did they create unrest within the democracy, for now people who felt that they were denied democratic practice within the countries themselves could have this denial defined in the light of definitions created by the necessity to combat fascism. The rest of the story is recent history.[9]

The irony is that the Christian community has so often been less articulate in this regard than the state. Its members have the spiritually humiliating experience of seeing the secular forces take positions which they were unable to match even in the name of their ethical imperative. Long after the formal abolishing of segregation in the armed forces, the Christian Church remained segregated. This is what I mean.

Finally, the combination of all of these forces and many others which time will not permit me to enumerate creates a situation in which the impact of higher education on the Negro can issue in courage, enthusiasm, and hope, rather than frustration. For the forces that are at work in the environment, making for community, are at last beginning to work in him, causing him to be able to make more and more an unconditional response to the fruits of learning. To make an unconditional response to the impact of truth and to follow that truth wherever it leads, transcending all barriers and all contexts—it is into this new earth that the American Negro is catapulted in his encounter with higher education. "The new mother, when she looks at the head of the babe in her arms whispers in her heart, 'May you seek after truth. If anything I teach you be false, may you throw it from you and go on to richer knowledge and deeper truth than I have ever known. If you become a man of thought and learning, may you never fail to tear down with your right hand what your left hand has built up, through years of thought and study, if you see it at last not to be founded on that which is.

"If you become an artist may you never paint with pen or brush any picture of external life otherwise than as you see it. If you become a politician may no success for your party or even love of your nation ever lead you to tamper with reality and to play a diplomatic part.

"In all of your circumstances, my child, may you seek after truth; and cling to that as a drowning man in a stormy sea flings himself onto a plank and clings to it, knowing that whether he sink or swim with it, it is the best that he has.

"Die poor, unknown, unloved, a failure—but shut your eyes to anything that seems to them but reality."[10] —Olive Schreiner

Reprinted from "The New Heaven and the New Earth," *Journal of Negro Education* 27, no. 2 (Spring 1958): 115–19.

PD.

NOTES

    1. The talk, with the full title "The New Heaven and the New Earth: An Interpretation of Certain Aspects of the American Negroes' Encounter with Higher Education," was delivered at a special convocation commemorating the 125th anniversary of the American Baptist Home Mission Society at Virginia Union University in Richmond on 12 November 1957.

    2. Thurman had said much the same thing in 1938 while addressing the graduates of Tennessee A&I College; see *PHWT*, 2:160.

    3. See Thurman's similar comments on the reasons for the lack of serious instruction in philosophy at black colleges that were presented at a meeting of the National Association of Personnel Deans and Advisers of Men in Negro Educational Institutions in 1938 (*PHWT*, 2:151).

    4. Thurman explored the dilemma of northern whites teaching in black colleges during Jim Crow in "The Contribution of Baptist Church Schools to Negro Youth" (1938), printed in *PHWT*, 2:181–87.

    5. Lorimer Milton (1898–1971) was Thurman's adviser at Morehouse and urged him to study economics. The two remained lifelong friends. Milton became a successful banker and businessman in Atlanta and was the longtime president of the Citizen's Trust Bank.

    6. W. Montague Cobb (1904–90) was a 1929 graduate of the Howard University School of Medicine, and he taught at his alma mater from 1932 until his death. He was the author of over one thousand papers on physical anatomy, many refuting the notion of innate physical differences between the races. He was president of the NAACP (a nonexecutive position) from 1976 to 1983. His paper at the Virginia Union University conference was published

as "Not to the Swift: Progress and Prospects of the Negro in Science and the Professions," *Journal of Negro Education* 27, no. 2 (Spring 1958): 120–26.

7. See Dixie and Eisenstadt, *Visions of a Better World,* 116.

8. The Atlantic Charter was a statement of political principles for governing the post-war world issued by President Roosevelt and Prime Minister Churchill following their meeting in August 1941 off the coast of Newfoundland. Earlier that year Roosevelt, in his State of the Union Message, spoke of the four freedoms: freedom of speech, freedom of worship, freedom from want, and freedom from fear. For Thurman's earlier comments on the hypocrisy of the Atlantic Charter for its failure to address Indian independence and colonialism, see his 1943 address "Religion in a Time of Crisis," repr. in *PHWT,* 2:344–49.

9. For Thurman's most extended reflections on fascism, see "The Fascist Masquerade," repr. in *PHWT,* 3:145–62.

10. Adapted from Olive Schreiner, *From Man to Man* (New York: Harper, 1927), 158. The original is reprinted in Howard Thurman, *A Track to the Water's Edge,* 153.

🌱 TO CLARENCE R. JOHNSON
19 MARCH 1958
[*BOSTON, MASS.*]

This letter to the chairman of the board of trustees of the Fellowship Church concerns an issue that both Thurman and Francis Geddes, the current minister of the church, would find increasingly irksome: the tendency of Thurman's reputation and celebrity to inhibit the regular activities of the church.

Mr. Clarence R. Johnson
Chairman of the Board of Trustees
Fellowship Church
2041 Larkin Street
San Francisco, California

Dear Clarence:

I cannot honor you by writing a worthy answer to your overwhelming document. You ought to go into the direct mail business. Thank you very much for your letter and the warmth of heart which is expressed.

My vacation plans will bring me, and perhaps Sue, to San Francisco. I shall have to preach here in the University during the month of July, which means that I will not be getting to California until August. I am making the following proposal to the minister, board and congregation:

1) On Sunday, August 10th, which is the Sunday that I can preach at Fellowship Church, instead of having a service at 11:00 o'clock, at which I will preach at 2041 Larkin Street, that the Church present me, together with the Fellowship Church Choir, in a Sunday afternoon formal religious service in some other sanctuary that could accommodate six or seven hundred

people. Inasmuch as the inaugural service of the Church was held in the First Unitarian Church, I think that it would provide less complications if we had our public religious service there. This would be a regular religious service, presided over by the minister of Fellowship Church, Rev. Geddes. I would preach the sermon. At the close of the service we could have a very beautiful reception in the parlors of the Unitarian Church. This would solve several problems which have become increasingly urgent in my mind: (1) I am embarrassed to see dozens of people pushing and clamoring to get into Fellowship Church on Sunday morning, many of whom have not been to the Church before or have not been since I was there the previous summer. While this is going on, the faithful workers of the Church who carry the burden throughout the year are crowded out and pushed aside because they are gracious and kindly people. There is something vulgar about this and I find it increasingly difficult for me to be a part of it; (2) Despite the unbelievable graciousness of Francis, it remains a real hardship on his role as the minister of the Church, when I zoom in like a comet visiting the solar system, and zoom out again. Even though we understand each other and the Board understands, it remains true that a lot of little pieces must be picked up and painfully cemented together after I leave. If, however, my coming geared itself specifically to a service which the Church provided for the community, and this public service were held in a place that could accommodate a larger congregation, everything about it would say, this is a special circumstance and there would be fewer pieces to pick up.

2) My second proposal is that the week prior to August 10th, or immediately after, preferably prior to, we have a series of spiritual retreats out at the Ranch[1] specifically for the membership of the Church. I am perfectly willing to have as many as it will take to give the entire membership an opportunity to come. For instance, we could have retreats on Thursday and Friday afternoons and evenings, which would give one third of the congregation an opportunity to come each time. Or any other mechanical arrangement that in the wisdom of the Board would be best. This means that I would be able to have primary personal contact with the membership at the profoundest level of spiritual awareness and, after all, this is the whole point of my coming. Will you work this out and advise me?

I am enclosing my check for $100.00, to be applied to the taxation problem about which you wrote in your general letter.

This is all for now.

Sincerely,

Howard Thurman

Dean

TLc.

Howard Thurman with Anne Thurman at her graduation from Boston University
School of Law. From the Bailey Thurman Family Papers; the Stuart A. Rose Manuscript, Archives, and Rare Book Library, Emory University.

NOTE
    1. The Stone Tree Ranch in Glen Ellen, Sonoma County, California, was made avail-
able to the Fellowship Church for retreats by a wealthy benefactor.

🐟 "FAITH THE TUTOR"
18 MAY 1958
BOSTON, MASS.

*This sermon is one of Thurman's most evocative expositions of the meaning and
role of faith in religion.*

Meditation:

> O Sabbath rest by Galilee, O Calm of Hills above
> Where Jesus knelt to share with Thee, the silence of eternity.
> Interpreted by love.

Drop Thy still dews of quietness
Till all our striving cease
Take from our souls the strain and stress
And let our ordered lives confess
The beauty of Thy peace.[1]

Reading:

Thou art our peace, O Lord.
From the thousand wearinesses of our daily life,
From disillusionments and disappointments,
From nervous hurry, from breathless and senseless haste,
We turn to Thee, and are at peace.

In a moment, lo, the clamour dies,
The bonds fall off,
The clinging distractions are all shaken loose,
And our shriveled souls expand exulting
In the sunshine of Thy presence.

In a moment this earth-life is behind us,
And we tread the cool, spacious, peaceful halls of Thy eternity,
Where in quiet content our souls hold converse with Thyself.

Soon we must return to the labour and the din,
Yet on our brows, we pray Thee, set the seal of our home,
That home whence we come,
Wherein day by day we live our true lives,
Whither some day we return joyfully for ever—
That home which is Thyself.
        The Sacrament of Common Life
        —J. S. Hoyland[2]

In John Steinbeck's novel Grapes of Wrath, Casy, the preacher of magical religion struggles with a new experience of the holy unity of life:

"I ain't sayin' I'm like Jesus," the preacher went on. "But I got tired like Him,
an' I got mixed up like Him, an' I went into the wilderness like Him, without no campin' stuff. Nighttime I'd lay on my back an' look up at the stars;
morning I'd set an' watch the sun come up; midday I'd look out from a hill
at the rollin' dry country; evenin' I'd foller the sun down. Sometimes I'd pray

like I always done. On'y I couldn't figure what I was prayin' to or for. There was the hills, an' there was me, an' we wasn't separate no more. We was one thing. An' that one thing was holy.

"An' I got thinkin', on'y it wasn't thinkin', it was deeper down than thinkin'. I got thinkin' how we was holy when we was one thing, an' mankin' was holy when it was one thing. An' it on'y got unholy when one mis'able little fella got the bit in his teeth an' run off his own way, kickin' an draggin' an fightin'. Fella like that bust the holiness. But when they're all workin' together, not one fella for another fella, but one fella kind of harnessed to the whole she-bang—that's right, that's holy."

quoted in "Christian Faith and Democracy" by Gregory Vlastos (Hazen Books on Religion)[3]
Sermon:
Faith, the tutor.
When religion speaks of Faith, it has something in mind that is different from the thing that is in mind when, for instance, science speaks of faith. With the latter, faith has to do with assumptions which are used for the purpose of dis-tilling certain hypotheses about the world of nature and on the basis of these hypotheses, tests of various kinds are made, and corroboration and proofs are sometimes found. It sets up simple categories by which it confirms the validity of a hypothesis. It says that the hypothesis has to be simple. It has to cover all the facts, and on the basis of it, prediction can be within limits that are mean-ingful and significant for the interpretation of whatever the data may be. This is all right. But religion has something else in mind when it thinks of faith. Faith is something which is beyond proof, and this, of course, is one of the fingers of scorn that is pointed at religion. Faith is something that is beyond proof. It is something that is immediately apprehended. It is something that takes on the nature of that which is categorical. It is not ever involved in proof, as we under-stand it, and yet at the same time it always is subject to the demand of proof. This, of course, is one of the great and crucial demands of all religious experi-ence, and religious insight. That of which it is sure, it is sure without the necessity of establishing the basis for that assurance, in any kind of context that may be empirically defined and understood. And yet at the same time the religious man cannot ever resist the temptation, yea the necessity, for trying to prove what in the very nature of the case, he cannot ever prove. This is his dilemma. So he vacillates from confidence to a kind of despair. He is sure and he is embarrassed. What do you say when someone says to you, prove it! The moment you try to prove it you become ridiculous. This is curious. But there is a sense, of course, in which proof has relevancy to religion and to faith for proof in the religious sense must take into account not merely that which is demonstrated, and please hear

this, it must take into account the intent of the individual who is demonstrating the deed. So the Master says, "By their fruits ye shall know them."[4] The fruits would be the proof, but what does he mean by fruits? Not merely the deed that the man does. Not merely the character of the act or even the integrity of the act itself. He means also that which was the deeply lying intent, that towards which at the core of his being, the man was striving to do and to say, he may not have been able to say it. He may fail again and again and again, but always there [is] the persistent intent to do this. The intent itself has to be included in what we mean by proof in religion, whereas in this other category, intent is irrelevant. This seems to me to mark the radical difference. With that rather lengthy background, let us look at one fragmentary aspect of the meaning of faith as a tutor.

Faith, in my thinking, is the attitude that an individual takes towards the ultimate outcome. There is something that is total, all encompassing, about faith. Faith has to do with the issue of the war, not particularly the issue of the battle. It is the response of the human spirit and the human mind to the total meaning of reality, the total meaning of God, or the total meaning of another human being, or the total meaning of one's self. This is faith. So when I look at my own life, or when you look at your own life, it is from within this kind of context that you live. I know that I am not as good as my mother thought I was as long as she lived. I'm not as good as some of my friends think I am, but I don't give myself up. I don't dismiss myself because of this. I cling to myself with a kind of abiding enthusiasm knowing all the time that in this way and that way and the other way there is the persistent manifestation of the distorted view, of the corrupt mind sometimes, of the ruptured will, of the diseased heart, sometimes of the evil spirit, but always it is within a total self that I look at all these little parts. I keep saying to myself that sure at this point I didn't do it, or at that point I failed, or at this point I acted in a way of which I am ashamed. But I know that there is at work in me something that does not ever give its ultimate sanction to that which is evil, to that which is against life, and it is this total sense of the meaning of the ultimate destiny of my private life or my persona that gives the basis for my interpretation of the particular deed at a particular moment in time and space, or grappling with the particular event. I cling to myself in a totally encompassing manner. And I know that if I can live long enough, I will be able to work it out. And even when I die I say, well one lifetime isn't enough, perhaps, to do this. That which is at work in me demands a longer time interval, or more room, but the ultimate end, it is in the light of that that I do the particular thing. Now that's faith in oneself.

The same thing happens when I have faith in you. I deal with you in a sense that is total. The degree to which I am able to do this I do not ever give an ultimate and final meaning to the particular thing that you are doing. When you have faith in another person, it means that you hold over that person always, that which goes beyond the present facts. That's what I mean. It says what is your final word about the meaning of that person's life. This has a very challenging and stirring effect upon the personality. For it says that however meager may be this poor little showing that I am making now, there is held over me in a kind of brooding kind of intensity, a possibility that transcends my present achievement however good that achievement may be.

A rather crude illustration of this carries everything that is in my mind. When I was a little boy I had a sister[5] who was two years older than I was and she had a boyfriend. This boyfriend always catered to me because he knew—well, he was wise. So one day when he and his crowd of boys were playing hardball on one part of the field, the fellows my age were playing another kind of ball on another part of the field. I said to my chum, "I know that you won't believe this, but when we go up there, when Willie goes to the bat, he will let me bat in his place." So we went up on a bet, so I said to Willie, "When your turn comes, will you let me take your turn?" And Willie said, "Yes, Howard." He knew better than to deny it. This is the wonderful thing that happened. I took a bat that I could hardly hold in my hand. It was almost as big as I was. I stood there and the miracle took place because the pitcher, a big boy, threw the ball as hard to me as he threw it to the big boys. I have never forgotten it. He dealt with me there, a little nine year old boy, with a big bat, as if I had arrived where the big boys were. Now this is what faith does.

As long as your life is surrounded by an encompassing glory of that sort, you keep striving. You open up the creative resources of your mind and your imagination, and your spirit to the tutoring effect of this ultimate sense of the meaning of your life. This is why whenever Jesus touched another human being, he held before that human being this quality, and under the aegis of that quality, the sick man began to get new strength, the lame man began to walk, the man who was full of demons felt that at last he could cast them out, the man who had sinned felt that his sins could be forgiven, this is the miracle that faith creates, like a great climate. It fertilizes and irrigates the roots. It puts at the disposal of the little life the vast and infinite resources of all of life. I don't have to let myself be tutored by this. I can just decide that I will not be tutored by it, but here it is, and I'm not sure that ultimately I can resist this. But I have faith in myself, I believe in myself, and this way I have faith in you, and it is then that I begin to enter into what it means to have faith in God. Here is the ultimate categorical experience. Faith in God teaches three very simple things. It teaches that God is, that God is. Thou hast made us for Thyself. Our souls are restless till they find their rest in Thee. God is. When I swing out with the wings of my faith, and the integrity of the intimacy of my demand there is an answer, and the answer becomes its own proof. This is what religion says, and what religious men experience without regard to the kind of altar before which they kneel, or the kind of book in which they find their sanction. It teaches also that God is near, not way off on a throne high above the canopy of the heavens, with the angels standing in mid-air to obey his righteous impulses and desires, no that's all right for the imagery, but this is not what religion means. God is near, as close as the beating of my heart. As close as is the lilting music of the bird, as close as the greenness of the leaf, as close as the whisper in my heart. "Speak to him, thou, for He heareth, and Spirit with spirit may meet, closer is He than breathing, nearer than hands and feet."[6] Therefore whatever may be my predicament, however engulfed in the compounded miseries of human existence I may be, He is very close at hand, tutoring me Himself, in ancient wisdoms and eternal confidences, this is God.

It teaches me also that God is love, that God understands me totally, that He always deals with me at a point in me that is beyond all of my sins and all of my virtues, beyond all of my limitations and strengths, there is in His presence a sense of being completely and thoroughly understood, so that I am at last rid of the agonizing necessity and urgency to pretend anything. I can be myself, naked, undisguised, just me, before Him, with confidence that He will not violate me. So when I love, I find that for love's sake I will do gladly what no power in heaven or hell or on the earth could make me do if I did not love. Therefore whatever else it is that my faith teaches me about God, it insists upon this. If I want to experience a sense of the ultimate meaning of life, even as I live the limited meaning of life, love somebody. Here I am gathered up into meanings that extend beyond the furthest rim of human thought in all directions. I thank God that this is so, don't you?

Walk beside us, O God, in the way that we take. Leave us not alone, lest our footsteps stray in the darkness, and our souls perish in the night, O God, our Father, and our friend.

TD.

NOTES

1. These two stanzas from "The Brewing of Soma" (1872) by the New England poet John Greenleaf Whittier (1807–92) are probably best known from their use in the popular hymn "Dear Lord and Father of Mankind" (1884).

2. "Seventh Week: The Sacrament of Sonship," in John S. Hoyland, *The Sacrament of Common Life: A Book of Devotion* (Cambridge: W. Heffer and Sons, 1927), 21.

3. Gregory Vlastos, *Christian Faith and Democracy* (New York: Association Press, 1940), 11, quoting John Steinbeck, *The Grapes of Wrath* (1938), repr. in Steinbeck, *The Grapes of Wrath and Other Writings, 1936–1941* (New York: Library of America, 1996), 295.

4. Matt. 7:16.

5. Henrietta Thurman (1897–1917), who died of typhoid fever.

6. This quote is from Alfred Lord Tennyson (1809–92), "The Higher Pantheism" (1869), l.11–12.

🌿 "The American Dream"
6 July 1958
Boston, Mass.

In the first part of this sermon, Thurman speaks of how Americans have come from different parts of the world to a continent that once was separated from the other inhabited regions of the world by two large oceans but that now, when distance has been overcome, is a world neighborhood in which people are living without having learned how to be neighbors. Thurman suggests that one crucial reason why they have not learned this lesson is that they have not learned the meaning of equality.

Thurman then turns to the implications of this for America and the "American Dream."[1] There are, he suggests, two "basic ideas" about the meaning of this term. The first is that a good society requires a hierarchy of inequality and domination, an ideology that dates back at least to Plato. For contemporary representatives Thurman mentions Hitler and the Ku Klux Klan. He also states, as he has elsewhere, that the Christian doctrine of depravity and damnation without salvation greatly contributed to the acceptance of inequality in human relations.

As an alternative, Thurman advocates an American dream as the belief in the "dream of equality, of justice, of freedom" and in the possibility of America realizing its best and noblest ambitions.[2] He sketches a rhapsodic and almost providential view of America's possibilities, looking toward a time when every American, within themselves and in others, sees the infinite value and absolute equality of every human soul.

Meditation:
So much of the common life is lived under the shadow of the event that imprisons and encumbers the sin that opens up always dimensions of forgiveness that we have not explored, the temptations that are conquered and must be re-conquered over and over and over. The grief that silently gnaws away at all the dreams and hopes and simple plans and far-flung ambitions of the common life. Grief that finds no answer in all the ways that we have tried. The fear of tomorrow and what it may bring. The fear of disease that cripples and lays waste and despoils and outrages the dignity of the self. We live under the shadow of the event. And our hearts reach out for some measure of release and relief, hoping that our desires are not in vain. And so, our Father, it is with overwhelming relief that we come into Thy presence and expose ourselves to Thee and witness in utter amazement how Thy Spirit transcends the event, turns the shadow into light and for this we rejoice and give to Thee the emptying of our cup of

thanksgiving. This is so good, our Father, and we thank Thee for just this swirling moment of freedom, Our Father.

Sermon:
I shall read as a background for our thoughts, two selections, one from the
Psalms and one from the pen of the poet of India, Tagore.

> O Lord our Lord, how excellent is thy name in all the earth! who hast set
>   thy glory above the heavens.
> Out of the mouth of babes and sucklings hast thou ordained strength
>   because of thine enemies, that thou mightest still the enemy and the
>   avenger.
> When I consider thy heavens, the work of thy fingers, the moon and the
>   stars, which thou hast ordained;
> What is man, that thou art mindful of him? and the son of man, that thou
>   visitest him?
> For thou hast made him a little lower than the angels, and hast crowned
>   him with glory and honor.
> Thou madest him to have dominion over the works of thy hands; thou hast
>   put all things under his feet:
> All sheep and oxen, yea, and the beasts of the field;
> The foul of the air, and the fish of the sea, and whatsoever passeth through
>   the paths of the seas.
> O Lord, our Lord, how excellent is thy name in all the earth![3]

> Where the mind is without fear and the head is held high;
> Where knowledge is free;
> Where the world has not been broken up into fragments by narrow
>   domestic walls;
> Where words come out of the depths of truth;
> Where tireless striving stretches its arms towards perfection;
> Where the clear stream of reason has not lost its way into the dreary desert
>   sand of dead habit;
> Where the mind is led forward by Thee into ever-widening thought and
>   action—
> Into that heaven of freedom, my Father, let my country awake.[4]

There are many learned words that have been said and may be said even
today, by many people concerning the American Dream. My words are very
simple and direct. I would like to preface my remarks by saying something
which may seem to you to suggest that I am a rather blur-eyed believer in manifest destiny of some sort, but be that as it may, it is my considered judgment

and conviction that life is a living process. It is alive. And that life is rooted in the aliveness and the vitality of God. That life is creative and that the ends of life are more significant and valid than the private ends of the individual manifestation of life, however far reaching and significant those private ends may be. I think that there is a wisdom that cradles and sustains and informs life and that wherever any living expression of life is able to acquaint itself with this wisdom, the resources of life are at the disposal of that particular unit. Now, what do all of those words mean? It means this; that I think that it is not an accident that we in our land are here. Some of our behavior may be accidental, but I do not think that it is an accident that we are here.

Isn't it rather amazing and striking that for a long time interval we experienced a unique kind of isolation, surrounded by these two great oceans that are zero now. We also experienced the naked exposure to a good climate, good soil, rich resources. We also experienced a primary exposure to the beginning of a nation in which on the ground floor, that is, at its very beginning, there were certain formative, creative, ethical, and political, and social ideals. So that here we are, people from the ends of the earth. If each one of you stood up in here this morning and told the rest of us where you came from, I don't mean just this morning, but where you came from back just a little bit. If you kept talking, using the language that belonged with the period, it would not be long before the rest of us would not understand what you are saying. Because we are all the posterity of people who came from the ends of the earth. There is nothing new in this. So here we are. For a long time we were isolated. For a long time we were in the throes of trying to work out the implications of certain political and religious ideals within the boundaries of our limitations, our physical limitations, and in the midst of a kind of mixture of people that in itself was unique until yesterday. Now I believe that this is not incidental. I think that every opportunity and every privilege carries with it its responsibilities. It is as if life said there will come a time in the history of man on the planet when he will, with his mind, explore the heights and depths of the world that surrounds him and as a result of this exploration and the discovery of the principle of rationality in all of the stuff of nature and the stuff of life around him, he will be able to reduce time to zero, space to zero, and there will be no man anywhere on the planet that in terms of time and space who is alien to any other man on the planet. Now this will come I think, the great wisdom plus the muse, and it will come rather precipitously because man will be so involved in the process that he will not take the time to distill the meaning in terms of anything that is far reaching and in terms of the ultimate meaning of life. He is so caught by the excitement and the pressure of the immediacy that he will not know what all of this means. And so he will be a neighbor without a neighborly mind. And there ought to be people scattered all over the world who will have had some exposure to developing the fine art of neighborliness under great pressure and difficulty, and if they learn this fine art, if they are able to commit it to memory through their social processes and their collective behavior patterns and their private wills, then when mankind suddenly realizes that the world is a neighborhood, as he looks around on the horizon to see if there is anybody in the world anywhere who knows anything about how to be a neighbor, please come to the rescue because time is running out. Now, we had the chance and I ask you whether we learned the lesson. Now that's the first half of what I want to say.

Now the second half. The American Dream it seems to me, is a dream of equality, of justice, of freedom. If I may crystalize it in terms of categorical statements. Men have had two basic ideas about the meaning of the content of this kind of dream. There is the dream, the notion, that the only possible way by which mankind can live a peaceful, adjusted, and happy life on this planet is by embracing the cult of inequality. The cult of inequality.[5] When Plato talks about those who would rule, of course the philosopher will be king, he will rule, he represents the brain, the mind, and then of course there must be those who will, for instance, the ideas, who will carry it out and they, of course, will be the warriors and the merchants and people like that. And then, of course, there must be those who will supply the things that all these other two groups need. Somebody has to do that. So they will be the workers. They will do the crud things; they will wear crepe on their fingernails. Now, if you get this worked out, you will have a society that is orderly, that is beautiful, because every individual will know constitutionally where he belongs and he will not seek to move outside of that sphere. It is built upon class, you see, and the superior human being is, of course, is the human being who has the brains. Now this is the way Plato works it out in *The Republic*. It's interesting, isn't it, because it sounds like some other things I've heard; parts of it sound like Hitler's *Mein Kampf,* only the people who are at the top are not the philosophers.[6] They are those who are—well, you see, those are the ones—and the other people are broken down into their classifications. And as long as you stay where you belong, as long as you freeze yourself in the niche which is in accordance with the order of life and the sanction of the Creator of life, this will be a wonderfully peaceful world.

It is the same sort of thing that we see about those who rhapsodize about the pre–Civil War South, where you had a group here who were the owners and then you had slaves and then you had some other people and as long as everybody stayed where he belonged, there would be no trouble.

This is expressed in the doctrine of the Ku Klux Klan. If I may, let me read a little of it to you. I remember about fifteen years ago I made a study of the organization; I want to take a minute to read this to you. Because it sounds if you can substitute certain phrases of Plato—as you see—or *Mein Kampf,* or some other things that I could name, and you would have it. Now the first position about the Klan is,[7] "This of course is a White Man's Organization, exalting the Caucasian Race and teaching the Doctrine of White Supremacy. Second, it is a Gentile Organization and as such it has its mission the interpretation of the highest ideals of the White, Gentile peoples. It is an American Organization."[8] See it gets narrower and narrower. "Fourth, it is a Protestant Organization. Membership is restricted to those who accept the tenets of true Christianity, which is essentially Protestant.[9] We maintain and contend that it is the inalienable right of Protestants to have their own distinctive organization" and so forth and so on.

Then the document—and this is a photostatic copy from it—talks about the ideals.

"We stand for White Supremacy. Distinction among the races is not accidental but designed." It sounds like Plato, you see. "This is clearly brought out in the one book that tells authoritatively of the origin of the races.[10] We must keep this a White Man's Country. Only by doing this can we be faithful to the foundations laid by our forefathers. This Republic was established by White Man. It was established for White Man. Our forefathers never intended that it should fall into the hands of any inferior race. Every effort to wrest from White Man the management of its affairs in order to transfer it to the control of blacks or any other color, or to permit them to share in its control, is an invasion of our sacred constitutional prerogatives and a violation of divinely established law."

Now, I have taken more time than I should to do this because the cult of inequality is older than any of the particular forms that may be manifesting themselves at any particular moment in human history.

Now that's on the one side. Now, on the other there is the notion that the dream of equality, and many have gone at that in interesting ways. There is Rousseau for instance, who establishes it in terms of the innate goodness of everybody—you know the rest of that. And then, of course, there is the way in which it is established by John Calvin, in the total depravity of everybody. We are all together because we are all lost; we are all together because we are very good. Now the interesting thing is that any doctrine of universal depravity is very interesting because every time a man can do it, he gets out of that class and starts working his way up. Then, you see, the moment he begins working his way up, his mind begins to feel that—and his heart—that he has been plucked as a brand from the burning. He did not deserve this, he was selected by the grace of God and it is to the credit of God that this is done. Now if I suddenly become aware of the fact that I have been salvaged from the human wreckage and that the light of God breaks in me through no merit on my part, when I open my eyes and look at you and see that you have not been plucked from the burning, then I am, of course, quietly forced to say that God must see in me something that he doesn't see in you. And if God, the Creator of life, sees in me what he doesn't see in you, then of course I must be forgiven for thinking that I am better than you. So I arrive at the cult of inequality through this basis.[11]

Now what does all of this tie into? Simply this, that there is inherent in the American Dream, rooted in the insight, that there is an equality that is not built upon learning, upon training, upon status, upon wealth or lack of wealth, privilege or lack of privilege, but an equality that each man recognizes when he feels as he experiences life, that this is not life in general, this is *my* life. When a man feels that he himself, in and of himself, without reference to any pretension whatsoever, that he is of worth beyond value. And when in a society we call out from other men as we meet them, this which announces that the sense of infinite worth and value, which I know applies to myself, I affirm that it applies to you. And when that happens, the great discovery is made and that is that whatever may be the contradictions of life at any particular moment in time, in space, in circumstance, these contradictions are not final and ultimate. This is the metaphysical basis for the doctrine that in the presence of God the human soul is of value, infinite; and the only equality that will survive in the American Dream is the kind of equality that places a significance upon the infinite estimate that the individual places upon himself and this infinite estimate is constantly being transformed into terms that express social worth, hence the democratic dogma and the spiritual commitment that floats it. And when I work on behalf of that, it may be that in that activity I sense the wisdom that is greater than my particular wisdom or my country's wisdom and I feel that where I am in that act, the great God Himself becomes incarnate in a man. This is why when we look into the face of the Master, our response is of that character. Not because of anything else, and if we do not make that discovery, may God deal mercifully with our souls.

Walk beside us our Father, in the way that we take, and leave us not alone lest we stumble in the darkness and lose our way. O God, God our Father, our Father.

At.

NOTES

1. The phrase "the American dream" was popularized by the historian James Truslow Adams (1879–1949) in *The Epic of America* (Boston: Little, Brown, 1931). For a critical summary and interpretation of Thurman's American dream, see Walter Earl Fluker, "Howard Thurman's Vision of National Community," in *The Human Search: Howard Thurman and the Quest for Freedom; Proceedings of the Second Annual Thurman Convocation (Martin Luther King, Jr. Memorial)*, ed. Mozella G. Mitchell (New York: Peter Lang, 1992), 85–112.

2. Thurman's version of the American dream has affinities with Gunnar Myrdal's notion of "the American Creed" as described in his book *An American Dilemma: The Negro Problem and Modern Democracy* (New York: Harper & Brothers, 1944), 1–25. Myrdal's notion of "the American Creed" was in part shaped by his chief researcher, Ralph Bunche, Thurman's good friend and Howard colleague (ibid., 2). Bunche's commitment to an interracial America living up to its democratic promise was a view widely shared by Thurman and others at Howard in the 1930s. See Jonathan Holloway, *Confronting the Veil: Abram Harris, Jr., E. Franklin Frazier, and Ralph Bunche, 1919–1941* (Chapel Hill: University of North Carolina Press, 2002).

3. Ps. 8.

4. "Poem 35," in Rabindranath Tagore, *Gitanjali: Song Offerings* (New York: Macmillan, 1916), 27–28, usually known as "Let My Country Awake," slightly modified by Thurman.

5. This is a possible reference to Stuart O. Landry, *The Cult of Equality: A Study of the Race Problem* (New Orleans: Pelican, 1945), a defense of racial inequality.

6. There were many in the postwar period who argued that Plato was an inspiration for twentieth-century totalitarianism; the most influential was Karl Popper, *The Open Society and Its Enemies*, 2 vols. (London: Routledge, 1945). The first volume was entitled *The Spell of Plato*.

7. Here, Thurman shortens and slightly alters quotations from the Ku Klux Klan document, which can be found at greater length (though still excerpted from Thurman's source) in his earlier essay "The Fascist Masquerade," repr. in *PHWT*, 3:145–62.

8. "It is an American Organization, and we do restrict membership to native-born American citizens" (ibid.).

9. "It is a Protestant Organization. Membership is restricted to those who accept the tenets of true Christianity, which is essentially Protestant. We maintain and contend that it is the inalienable right of Protestants to have their own distinctive organization. We can say to the world without apology, and say truly, that our forefathers founded this as a Protestant country and that it is our purpose to re-establish and maintain it as such. While we will energetically maintain and proclaim the principles of Protestantism, we will also maintain the principles of religious liberty as essential to the life and progress of this nation, and we will vigorously oppose all efforts to rob the American people of this right" (ibid).

10. The "one book," if not the Bible, is possibly—to judge from the related excerpt from the Klan document in "The Fascist Masquerade"—Lothrop Stoddard, *The Rising Tide of Color: The Threat against White World Supremacy* (New York: Scribner, 1920).

11. For Thurman's critique of Christianity as a source of ideas of racial inequality, see "The Fascist Masquerade."

To Harold C. Case
23 July 1958
[*Boston, Mass.*]

Thurman writes to President Case requesting a sabbatical the following year, in part because of the intense pressures on him and the many challenges he faced and to rest his "weary" soul. Thurman was granted the sabbatical, and his itinerary closely followed the tentative plans laid out in this letter.[1]

President Harold C. Case
Boston University
Boston, Massachusetts

Dear Harold:

The first of September will mark the beginning of Sue and my sixth year here at the university. We would like very much to take a year off beginning in the fall of 1959. I do not know whether the courtesy of a sabbatical which the University extends to its faculty applies to deans or not. If I can have a sabbatical year, for the year, this would be a practical help in carrying out the plans which we have in mind. But whether the sabbatical leave is possible or not, I would still want to take the year off.

There are many reasons for this. The first and most important one is that our souls are weary and in defense of our own integrity of mind and spirit we must get away from the intense pressure of the University, not only for rest and renewal but also for taking a long look at what we are about here. If possible we would like to go around the world or at least to spend some time in certain strategic spots—the Philippines, Japan, India, Africa and the Deep South of our own United States. At the present moment we have no concrete plan, everything is in the talking stage, but I wanted to advise you first about the over-all idea so that we may have a meeting of minds about the proposal itself.

The work of the Chapel is now sufficiently stabilized and integrated into the University process so that by wise planning the basic work need not be interrupted.

I am off to California next week and will see you when I return in September. I hope you and Phyllis are having a good rest.
Sincerely,
Howard Thurman
Dean

TLc.

NOTE
    1. For more on the sabbatical voyage, see "An Imperative to Understanding" (12 October 1960), printed in the current volume.

☙ To Martin Luther King, Jr.
20 October 1958
[Boston, Mass.]

On Saturday afternoon, 20 September 1958, Martin Luther King, Jr., was in Blumstein's Department Store in Harlem signing copies of his just-published book, Stride toward Freedom, *when a deranged African American woman, Izola Ware Curry,*[1] *plunged a letter opener into his chest, narrowly missing his aorta. King was successfully operated on and remained in Harlem Hospital until 3 October.*

King's brush with death greatly affected Thurman. He writes in his autobiography, "Many times through the years I have had strange visitations in which there emerges at the center of my consciousness a face, a sense of urgency, a vibrant sensation regarding some particular person. On a certain Friday afternoon, Martin emerged in my consciousness and would not leave. When I came home I said to

*Sue, 'Tomorrow morning I am going down to New York to see Martin. I am not
sure why, but I must talk to him personally if the doctors will permit.'*[2]

*Thurman likely saw King at Harlem Hospital over the weekend of 27–28 Sep-
tember. He advised King to extend his period of convalescence by an additional
two weeks. This would "give him time away from the immediate pressure of the
movement to reassess himself in relation to the cause, to rest his body and mind
with healing detachment, and to take a long look that only solitary brooding can
provide."*[3] *The two men did not discuss in depth "the progress, success, or failure
of the movement itself." Instead they discussed King's relation to the civil rights
movement, which had "become an organism with a life of its own to which he
must relate in fresh or extraordinary ways or be swallowed up by it."*[4] *The meeting had a considerable impact on both men.*[5]

Rev. Martin Luther King, Jr.
Dexter Avenue Baptist Church
309 South Jackson Street
Montgomery, Alabama

Dear Martin:

I don't know where you are but I hope that wherever you are, you are taking
the additional four weeks to those that the doctor felt that you needed for complete recovery.

Have you been able to give any additional thought to finding a personal
male secretary who can handle your publicity and travel with you? I don't know
how you feel about it really, but I am sure that such a solution will make a radical
difference in both the quality and effectiveness of your unique ministry. Anything that I can do to help find such a person, I am yours to command.

As I told you when I saw you in New York, I was trying to juggle the date so
as to come to Montgomery. I find that I cannot be away on that Sunday. It means,
therefore, that you will have a rain check for this year. If you would like to have
me do so, I would be glad to come in the fall of next year, even though I am hoping to get a sabbatical. If you want me to plan for this, please drop me a note as
soon as possible because by January 1st, I will need to have before me whatever
invitations I am considering for next year. This I am sure you will understand.

Mrs. Thurman joins me in good wishes to you and your wife in the task to
which your hands are set.
Sincerely yours,
Howard Thurman
Dean

TLc.

NOTES

1. Izola Ware Curry (1916–2015), a native of Adrian, Georgia, was found to be a paranoid schizophrenic and was committed for an indefinite period of time to the Matteawan State Hospital for the Criminally Insane in Fishkill, New York. After leaving Matteawan in 1972, she spent a year at Manhattan Psychiatric Hospital and thereafter lived in a number of residential group homes in New York City for persons suffering from severe mental illness.

2. *WHAH*, 254–55.

3. Ibid., 255.

4. Ibid.

5. See From Martin Luther King, Jr., 8 November 1958, printed in the current volume.

ॐ "THE THIRD COMPONENT"
26 OCTOBER 1958
BOSTON, MASS.

In this sermon Thurman makes the case that when two people interact, their interaction is "the third component," or "common consciousness,"[1] separate from—and somehow transcending—each participant, opening the possibility of new and deeper connections.

Meditation:[2]
I dreamt God took my soul to Hell. Hell was a fair place and the water of the lake was blue. I said to God, "I like this place." And God said, "You do?" Birds sang, turf came to the water's edge and trees grew from it. A way off among the trees I saw beautiful women walking, their clothes were of many delicate colors and clung to them, and they were tall and graceful and had yellow hair. Their robes trailed over the grass, they glided in and out among the trees and over their heads hung yellow fruit like large pears of melted gold.

And I said to God, "This is very fair. I would go up and taste the fruit." And God said, "Wait." And after a while I noticed a very fair woman passed. She looked this way and that way and drew down a branch and it seemed that she kissed the fruit upon it softly and went on her way. And her dress made no rustle as she passed over the grass. And then I saw other and other women come, making no noise. Then I saw one woman come. She drew down the fruit and when she'd looked it over to find a place, she put her mouth to it softly and went away. And then I said to God, "What are they doing?" And God said, "They are poisoning." And I said, "How?" And God said, "They touch the fruit with their lips, when they have made a tiny wound in it with their four teeth, they set in it that which is under their tongues, they close it with their lip that no man may see the place and pass on." And I said to God, "Why do they do that?" And God said, "That another may not eat." And I said to God, "But if they poison all the fruit, no one can eat, what do they gain?" And God said, "Nothing." And

I said, "Are they not afraid that they themselves may bite where someone else has already bitten?" And God said, "Yes, they are afraid. In Hell, everybody is afraid."

And then to the right among the trees were men working. And I said to God, "I should like to go and work with those men. Hell must be a very fruitful place, the grass is so green." And God said, "Nothing grows in the garden they are making." We stood looking, and I saw the men working among the bushes, digging holes, but in the holes they set nothing; and when they had covered the holes with sticks and earth each went a way off and sat behind the bushes watching; and I noticed that as each walked he set his foot down carefully looking where he trod. And I said to God, "What are they doing?" And God said, "They are making pitfalls into which their fellows may sink." And I said to God, "Why do they do it?" And God said, "Because each man thinks that when his brother falls he will rise." And I said to God, "How will he rise?" And God said, "He will not rise." And I saw their eyes gleam from behind the bushes. And I said to God, "Are these men sane?" And God said, "No, they are not sane; there is no sane man in Hell."

Sermon:

"The third component"; I am almost self-conscious in announcing this. Someone telephoned this morning and I happened to answer the telephone at the office, and the person wanted to know what was my topic for today, a very nice gentle voice, and I said, I said, "It is the third component," and there was a long quiet moment, and then the voice recovered and said, "Thank you very much."

Many years ago a Dr. White[3] wrote these words: "When A and B are together in a relationship, if you made a sum of A and B, this would not total what A and B in a relationship amount to because, he said, there is a third component that must be included, and that component is the relationship between them."[4] This is the idea. Now I would like to do it in a different way today. I would like to call your attention to two, or three, or four moments, vignettes, and then let you work at it. And I hope I will have restraint enough to let you work at it rather than working at it on your behalf.

I had a dean in college and we affectionately called him Big Boy.[5] He was a man about six feet five inches tall, a wonderfully lumbering gait, and a great quiet face full of masculine affection. We loved him very much and I remember one day when one of the men in the college had violated one of the important laws of the college, and the Discipline Committee had met, voted that he was not a good member of the community, and that he should withdraw from the college. Everybody agreed that this was the only wise and effective or creative or even, the only option that the committee had if the college were to remain intact. They notified this fellow and I happened to meet him on the walk as he came out of the dormitory with his bag; his trunk had gone, and he was walking down to the corner to get the streetcar. We walked along together and then when we came by the administration building he bade me good-bye and said, "I've got to go in here a minute." I said, "What are you going in there to do?" He said, "I must go in to tell Big Boy good-bye because I don't want him to feel that anything has happened between me and him because as chairman of the Discipline Committee he had to send me home." That's the first one.

Now the second. Some of you are familiar with the name Kropotkin.[6] Those of you who are newcomers will not recognize the name in this connection, but Kropotkin was the name, is the name, of a dog which I had once upon a time. When Kropotkin was a puppy—well, an early adolescent—we found that he was not very obedient, he couldn't, wouldn't respond to his name when he was under pressure on Bay State Road so that it was necessary for us to send him to school. And we sent him out to, took him out to a kennel, about 12 [or] 14 miles from here, and when we walked into this little office of the kennel keeper, he said to me, "Why do you bring your dog here?" And I explained to him what I wanted. Just I wanted the dog to learn two or three simple things, how to stop when you ask him to, and how to come when you call him, and how to recognize his name even at a time of crisis. "So," he said, "all right, I have been training dogs for 16 years, and when I see a dog or when any kind of dog is exposed to me, he comes into a climate of acceptance. It doesn't matter whether he's old or young, bad, vicious, it doesn't matter what kind of dog he is. He is surrounded by this climate of acceptance." "Now," he said, "my experience is that it takes me two weeks to teach the dog to trust me. Now if I can teach the dog to trust me then after that I can teach him anything else. I can make into a vicious attack dog the most introverted dog you have ever seen. But if I cannot teach him to trust me then I can't teach him anything. So at the end of two weeks I will call you and tell you, let the dog stay or to come and get him."

The third. In 1926 one of the great teachers of religion, Dr. Edward Increase Bosworth,[7] of Oberlin College, Oberlin Graduate Divinity School, died and a few days after his death I went up on the campus. I saw a man cutting the lawn, mowing the lawn. I walked over to him and I said, "We shall certainly miss Dr. Bosworth in the village." And he said, "Oh yes, but I don't think anyone will miss him quite as much as I shall miss him because during the years that I have been the janitor in Council Hall, removing the snow in the winter and cutting the grass in the summer, I have seen Dr. Bosworth walk two blocks around out of his way just to tell me good morning. I shall miss him in a way that is perhaps a little different from the way anyone else will miss him in the village."

And now this. And I hope you will, well, feel your way into this without embarrassment. About ten years ago, I was on a train going from St. Louie to

Cheyenne, Wyoming. I was riding the, some sort of Eagle, I don't remember, either California Eagle or some; Eagle was the last name. I decided as the train pulled into the railway station in Kansas City that I would go in and have my dinner and I took advantage of this moment when the train was standing still because this was a very rough ride, the train ran so fast. I walked in the dining room, there was one seat near the door, one vacant seat and table and I sat. As I sat I noticed a very beautiful little girl just across the aisle, she was about just beyond the talking stage, and her eyes followed the waiters as they went up and down in the diner. And then presently she looked and she saw me and she said to her mother in a very high voice, "Mommy, there is a Zigaboo sitting down." And her mother said, "Shhhh." "Mommy, there *is* a Zigaboo sitting down." "Shhhh." By this time all conversation in the diner had stopped, everything was frozen and into that chaotic moment, the steward who was down at the end of the diner walked the length of the diner, came to my table, and he said into the silence, "How delighted I am to see you again. It's been a long time since you have ridden with us." He shook my hand and I shook his hand, and he went back to his place and life moved again. The steward had never seen me before; he didn't know me.

The third component, the third component. We have many contacts in the world, each one of us has, in our homes, our families, communities, but again and again there are contacts without fellowship, contacts without the third component, and contacts without fellowship tend to lead to an understanding that is unsympathetic, the sort of thing you experience when you walk into a man's office and he looks at you hard and you wonder whether the third button on your shirt is open but you dare not look. That cold, unsympathetic, hard, callous, understanding nevertheless, but hard. It isn't ignorance, no, it's understanding but it's hard, it's cold, it's impersonal, it strips you, and this profanes your personality. And unsympathetic understanding tends to express itself in the exercise of a will that's sick, a sick will, an ill will we call it, and an ill will is a very contagious thing. An ill will caught, dramatized for instance in a human being is what we mean by hate walking on the earth. And the reverse of this is true. Contacts with fellowship, whether it is within the family or out of the family, leads to an understanding that is sympathetic and this is very important to remember because sometimes we assume that because this person organically is my brother or because biologically this man is my father and this woman is my mother, that the relationship between us is a relationship of mother and child but it may not be at all if the third component is lacking.

Now, contacts with fellowship lead to an understanding that is sympathetic, that is warm, that is gracious, that surrounds you with a climate of felicity so that into that climate you may venture forth with your little life and its little secret and its little burden, its little anxiety. You may expose your life in a climate like that and know that it will not be violated. Because whatever the other person sees will be seen with sympathy, with tenderness, with understanding, with a dimension of kindness that is creative and restorative and redemptive. It follows then that the third component may be a gift, may be a gift. There are some people I think who have what may be called the gift of intimacy. Just as any other gift, they have a way of moving quietly into the life of others and watering their roots and making them blossom, it's a way they have. It's a gift that's true for some of us. But for the most part, the third component is something that we must work at, it takes imagination, it personalizes even impersonal institutions. I remember reading the other day about a doctor who was describing what he used to do in his hospital in San Francisco thirty years ago. He discovered that the people in the hospital, early in the morning was a bad time, just when you were waking up and you don't know quite where you are, and life is difficult. So he hit upon the idea of getting the trustees of the hospital to secure the services of a beautiful Chinese girl who dressed in beautiful Chinese clothing and who had the kind of memory that would make it possible for her to get each patient's name so that the first thing in the morning even before you quite were aware of your awareness, she opened the door, called you by name, and offered you a little cup of coffee. Now you may not be a coffee drinker but it didn't make any difference you see. This said to the isolated, lonely, frightened, patient that the hospital had heart, that it was exercising this third component as the institution related to the individual. Now this takes imagination, it takes discipline, it takes caring, one has to work at it.

Now it is the word of religion and I speak now in the language of our text, of the text of the Scripture that was read, that God is that way with reference to us. "Who are they that have come through great tribulation,"[8] the writer of Revelation says, "these are the people God, God," we read this hurriedly but listen to it, "God will wipe every tear from their eyes." Do you know how it feels when you weep and someone wipes the tear? This ultimately breathless moment of caring. Now, in the Revelation the writer says that this is what God will do, God Himself, the Creator of [the] world will gentle you by wiping the tears from your eyes. This is the way James Weldon Johnson describes it in his paraphrasing of the funeral sermon. I want to read a part of it to you.

> Day before yesterday morning,
> God was looking down from his great, high heaven,
> Looking down on all his children,
> And his eyes fell on Sister Caroline,
> Tossing on her bed of pain.
> And God's big heart was touched with pity,
> With the everlasting pity.

And God said: Go down, Death, go down,
To Savannah, Georgia,
Down in Yamacraw,
And find Sister Caroline.
She's borne the burden and heat of the day,
She's labored long in my vineyard,
She's tired—
She's weary—
Go down, and bring her to me.

And Death didn't say a word,
But he loosed the reins on his pale, white horse,
And he clamped the spurs to his bloodless sides,
And out and down he rode,
Through heaven's pearly gates,
Past suns and moons and stars;
On Death rode,
And the foam from his horse was like a comet in the sky;
On Death rode,
Leaving the lightning's flash behind;
Straight on down he came.

While we were watching round her bed,
She turned her eyes and looked away,
She saw what we couldn't see;
She saw Old Death. She saw Old Death
Coming like a falling star.
But Death didn't frighten Sister Caroline;
He looked to her like a welcome friend.
And she whispered to us: I'm going home.
And she smiled and closed her eyes.

And Death took her up like a baby,
And she lay in his icy arms,
But she didn't feel any chill.
And Death began to ride again—
Up beyond the evening star,
Out beyond the morning star,
Into the glittering light of glory,
On to the Great White Throne.
And there he laid Sister Caroline
On the loving breast of Jesus.

And Jesus took his own hand and wiped away her tears.
And he smoothed the furrows from her face,
And the angels sang a little song,
And Jesus rocked her in his arms,
And kept saying: Take your rest now,
Take your rest, Take your rest.

Weep not—weep not,
She is not dead;
She's resting in the bosom of Jesus.[9]

Oh, the theology may be way off, who cares. The experience of the third component is the thing we must have or we perish and die. If, if we cannot get it, we cannot find a way of life that is worth living whatever else we have. The relationship between you and another, this is the third component, what is it like? *You* know, perhaps the other person knows, and *God* knows.

Journey with us Our Father in the way that we take, leave us not alone in the desolation of our spirit but reassure us and steady us that we may walk courageously on the earth by the light in the sky. Dismiss us with Thy spirit and grant unto us Thy peace.

At.

NOTES

1. "A fundamental assumption in Thurman's thinking is what he calls *common consciousness,* which refers to the affinity between human consciousness and other forms of sentient existence evident in nature. For Thurman, the theme of the kinship of all living things extends even into the realm of communication between animals, plants, and human beings. He reasons that if life is one, then there ought to be a fundamental sense of unity at all levels of existence. Since life in any form cannot be fundamentally alien to life, then more than two forms may share the same moment in time without resistance and without threat. This understanding of common consciousness is fundamental to Thurman's understanding of mysticism and the role of imagination." Walter Earl Fluker, "Howard Thurman: Intercultural and Interreligious Leader," in *Religious Leadership: A Reference Handbook,* vol. 2, ed. Sharon Henderson Callahan (Thousand Oaks, Calif.: Sage, 2013), 575 (italics in original).

2. From the opening of Olive Schreiner, "The Sunlight Lay across My Bed—," in *Dreams* (Boston: Little, Brown, 1890), 133–37, repr. in HT, ed., *A Track to the Water's Edge: The Olive Schreiner Reader* (New York: Harper & Row, 1973), 64–66.

3. William Alanson White (1870–1937), a prominent American psychologist and psychoanalyst.

4. "There is something else that has come into the picture besides A and B—a third component, and that third component is the relationship between them. That relationship

cannot be expressed in the formula representing merely the sum of A plus B." William Alanson White, *Twentieth Century Psychiatry: Its Contribution to Man's Knowledge of Himself* (New York: W. W. Norton, 1936), 75.

5. For Samuel Howard Archer (1870–1941), see *PHWT*, 2:1.

6. Prince Pyotr Alexeyevich Kropotkin (1842–1921) was a prominent Russian anarchist theorist who lived much of his life after 1876 in exile, primarily in England, until his return to Russia in 1917. For more on Kropotkin the dog, see *WHAH*, 234–37.

7. For Edward Increase Bosworth (1861–1927), see *PHWT*, 1:6.

8. Rev. 7:14.

9. From "Go Down Death—A Funeral Sermon" (1927), in James Weldon Johnson, *Writings* (New York: Library of America, 2004), 849–51. Thurman made minor alterations in his recitation and did not recite the first, third, and fourth stanzas.

✍ From Martin Luther King, Jr.
8 November 1958
[*Montgomery, Alabama*]

Writing to Thurman about five weeks after their meeting in Harlem Hospital, Martin Luther King, Jr. tries to arrange a suitable time for Thurman to preach at Dexter Avenue Baptist Church in Montgomery, Alabama. In the end, despite the best efforts of both men, this proved futile. King also thanks Thurman for suggesting that he use his period of recovery from his wound as a time of spiritual convalescence and to take a temporary step back from the pressures of the movement. King writes, "I am following your advice on the question 'where do I go from here.'" After being released from Harlem Hospital in early October, King spent some time with a family friend in Brooklyn. After he returned home to Montgomery on 24 October, there was, in the words of his biographer Taylor Branch, "a period of relative stillness unique to his entire adult life" with a greatly reduced number of public engagements.[1]

It seems likely that the two men also discussed Thurman's trip to India, his meeting with Gandhi, and the need for spiritual pilgrimage. Gandhi's famous statement to the Negro delegation in India that "it may be through the Negroes that the unadulterated message of nonviolence will be delivered to the world"[2] is echoed in King's first public statement after the stabbing, released on 30 September, presumably only a day or two after his extended conversation with Thurman: "I am now convinced that if the Negro holds fast to the spirit of non-violence, our struggle and example will challenge and help redeem, not only America but the world."[3] King also determined during his period of rest to take a long-intended pilgrimage to India in the near future. He wrote in 1959, "After I recovered from this near-fatal encounter and was finally released by my doctors, it occurred to me that it might be better to get in the trip to India before plunging too deeply once again into the sea of the southern segregation struggle.[4] *King traveled in India from 2 February to 10 March 1959.*

Dear Dr. Thurman:

Thanks for your letter of October 20.[5] I received it just a few minutes after I sent the telegram to you. And so it came just in time.

Knowing your busy schedule and the important work that you are doing I can well understand your inability to be with us this year. I am happy to know that you can arrange to come next year. I would like to suggest two days. The first one is the second Sunday in July which is our annual Men's Day observance. The second one is the second Sunday in December which is the occasion of the 82nd Anniversary of the church. While I would prefer your coming in July for the Men's Day observance, we would be very honored to have you on the anniversary if that is the only possibility. I will look forward to hearing from you concerning this matter at your earliest convenience.

It was certainly kind of you to come by Harlem Hospital to see me. The few minutes that we spent together were rich indeed. Your encouraging words came as a great spiritual lift and were of inestimable value in giving me the strength and courage to face the ordeal of that trying period.

I am happy to report that I am feeling very well now and making steady progress toward a complete recovery. I am following your advice on the question "where do I go from here."

Please give my best regards to Mrs. Thurman. Mrs. King joins me in good wishes to you and your family.

Yours very truly,
Martin L. King, Jr.

Dr. Howard Thurman
Boston University

TL.

Notes

1. Taylor Branch, *Parting the Waters: America in the King Years, 1954–63* (New York: Simon & Schuster, 1988), 245.

2. Printed in *PHWT*, 1:337.

3. "Statement Issued from Harlem Hospital," 30 September 1958, in Clayborne Carson, ed., *The Papers of Martin Luther King, Jr.*, vol. 4: *Symbol of the Movement, January 1957–December 1958* (Berkeley: University of California Press, 2000), 502.

4. Martin Luther King, Jr., "My Trip to the Land of Gandhi," *Ebony* (July 1959), repr. in James M. Washington, ed., *A Testament of Hope: The Essential Writings and Speeches of Martin Luther King, Jr.* (New York: HarperCollins, 1986), 23.

5. To Martin Luther King, Jr., 20 October 1958, printed in the current volume.

To Martin Luther King, Jr.

19 NOVEMBER 1958

BOSTON, MASS.

In response to King's letter of 8 November,[1] Thurman writes about scheduling a time to visit Montgomery and is heartened by King's continuing physical and spiritual recuperation from the recent assassination attempt.

Dr. Martin Luther King, Jr.
Dexter Avenue Baptist Church
454 Dexter Avenue
Montgomery 4, Alabama

Dear Martin:

Thank you very much for your letter and the gracious spirit of understanding which it indicated. I am afraid that the July date is out, because it is my plan to be in California during that entire period. There is a real possibility of my coming next December. I am taking this into account when I make my plans in January for the next year. Please know that I am anxious to worship in your congregation and to share in the ferment of the spirit as manifested there.

It is wonderful to know that you are better and that plans are afoot in your own thinking for structuring your life in a way that will deepen its channel. It would be a very good thing if we could spend several hours in uninterrupted talk about these matters that are of such paramount significance for the fulfillment of the tasks to which our hands are set.

Mrs. Thurman joins me in vibrant wishes to you and Mrs. King.
Sincerely yours,
[*signed*] Howard Thurman
Howard Thurman
Dean

TLcS.

NOTE

1. From Martin Luther King, Jr., 8 November 1958, printed in the current volume.

🙰 To Harold C. Case
28 November 1958
Boston, Mass.

Thurman writes to President Case updating him on the events in his work as dean.

Dr. Harold C. Case

Dear Harold:

This is my second assessment letter for the year.

The Thanksgiving Service yesterday would have warmed your heart and delighted your spirit. We had an excellent congregation of community and University people, numbering more than 300. There were some twenty students who volunteered to provide a choir for the service. Mrs. Paukulis[1] and Julius Kaizer,[2] a Hungarian dancer who is studying at the New England Conservatory, did the dance duet of Praise and Thanksgiving, which was one of the simplest and most searching dance moments that I have ever experienced. The reaction was unanimous. As a part of the service, I read a meditation that one of the choir girls had written to be read at a dinner which she was having, to which some of the choir and other students were invited. I was so touched by the quality and the idea of it that I shared it with the entire congregation. I am enclosing it for you to see, but please return it.

When Allen[3] announced to the Choir that inasmuch as the weekend was a vacation weekend, that there would be no choir for the service on November 30th, some twenty members asked him if they may not volunteer so that for that Sunday there would be a choir. This is a spirit which makes many rough places smooth.

The Sunday attendance has kept up remarkably well. In fact, this is the first time since I have been here that the attendance on Sunday morning has been consistently a full chapel, with more than half the time an overflow downstairs in Robinson Chapel.[4]

The cooperation of WBUR[5] in broadcasting the Sunday service with its repeat in the evening, and the weekly Friday night meditations, is outstanding. A happily sensitive relation is obtaining between the chapel and those persons responsible for the work of WBUR.

At the beginning of the television series this year, I announced that we would make a new mailing list for transcriptions of the talks.[6] I did not want to have a passed list, as this represents waste and distortion. We have received in a return postal card, more than a hundred positive replies. So that, as of today, the weekly up to the minute mailing list is about 150. This has created a minor problem in paper work as far as the office is concerned, but we have worked it out by getting additional help. It is quite a chore to prepare and mail 150 transcriptions every week. The appreciation, however, is far reaching.

On Sunday afternoon, December 7th, at 4:30 o'clock, we are having the Annual Christmas Vesper Service, at which time both the choral group and the dance group will participate. Most of the material that I shall be reading is written by Allen Lannom. It is going to be a very inspiring service. It would be very gratifying, particularly to the choir, if in your crowded schedule, you could somehow manage to be present.

The participation of the various Schools and Divisions of the University, in the Sunday service as special guests, with the Deans or the heads of Departments standing with me to greet friends at the coffee hour, is all that could be desired. Thus far we have had the Dean of Men,[7] the Dean of Women[8] and their staffs; the College of Liberal Arts;[9] Sargent College;[10] School of Public Relations & Communications;[11] the School of Education;[12] the School of Fine & Applied Arts;[13] and next Sunday the Publicity Bureau. There have been some significant developments which enlarge the opportunities by which the Chapel can be of service in the separate school.

The discussion groups, as suggested in my first letter, are developing in a manner that is very satisfactory. At the present time the numbers are not large, but the groups are consistent and the development is sound.

The guest preachers for the holiday season are: Rev. John Neff,[14] Dr. Robert Treese,[15] and Dr. George A. Warmer.[16] It is my plan to journey with Sue on Thursday after the Christmas Convocation, to California, where we will spend Christmas Day with our daughter and her family. I will go on to Redlands to give the platform addresses for the Methodist Youth Convocation of California-Arizona-New Mexico Conferences.[17] I shall be returning the first of the new year at the resumption of classes.

The monthly Organ Vesper has at last found its place in the Chapel ministry. The attendance at the last Vesper was better than at any other previous vesper since we began. The participation seems to be not only more intelligent, but more enthusiastic than ever before. This leads me to say that some careful thought must be given to certain basic repairs in the organ. I am suggesting that Max[18] make an appointment with you to explain what the need is and what can be done about it. I think this is better than my trying to do it because he can answer specifically all of your questions. The organ is almost continuously in use because the demands for its service has developed tremendously over the past two years.

Sometime, when you are over in the building, I wish you would take a quick look at the bulletin boards, both in the halls outside of the Conference Lounge and in the Lounge itself. Miss Adeline Clark, of the CBA Library, volunteered to provide materials and its arrangement on the bulletin board as an act of service which she wants to give, particularly in lieu of the fact that her circumstances make it impossible for her to attend Chapel regularly, as she did once upon a time.

The ceiling of the hall on the ground floor, just outside of the offices, is peeling off. It makes a very untidy appearance. I hope that something can be done about it during the holidays. It is at the center of traffic and the impression that it makes speaks for itself. There is no cause for you to be involved in this unless when I speak to Buildings and Grounds, they feel that the matter must be referred to you for approval.

I look forward to Julia's working out a time when I can come in and see you.

Sincerely,

[*signed*] How

Howard Thurman

Dean

TLcS.

Notes

1. Shirley June Paukulis, a dance instructor at Sargent College, was an award-winning ballroom dancer and an expert in many kinds of participatory dance.

2. Julius "Gyula" Kaiser (1931–2014) was a Hungarian who arrived in the United States as a refugee after the 1956 Hungarian revolt. He became one of the foremost teachers of competitive ballroom dancing in the United States.

3. Allan C. Lannom.

4. The service in the main chapel was piped into Robinson Chapel.

5. WBUR-FM, Boston University's radio station, began broadcasting on 1 March 1950. In the 1970s it became a National Public Radio affiliate. Thurman's Sunday sermons in Marsh Chapel were broadcast on WBUR from the time of his arrival in the fall of 1953; see *WHAH*, 174. For the broadcasts' impact, see From Henry Bollman, 7 January 1956, printed in the current volume. Thurman also made separate radio broadcasts, such as cohosting a three-hour tribute to Albert Schweitzer; see "WBUR Plans Program as Schweitzer Tribute," *Christian Science Monitor*, 12 January 1955.

6. For Thurman's television broadcasts, see "We Believe," 20 November 1959, printed in the current volume. Boston television station WHDH, the local ABC affiliate, broadcast Thurman's "We Believe" talks every Friday morning from 11:15 to 11:30. In the summer of 1959, before his round-the-world tour in 1960, Thurman prerecorded thirty-two television talks (*WHAH*, 174–75).

7. John F. McKenzie.

8. Elsbeth Melville (1905–97).

9. Dean Edward K. Graham.

10. Dean George Makechnie. George Makechnie (1907–2005) was probably Thurman's closest friend at Boston University, as well as Thurman's most stalwart supporter in his administrative battles. Makechnie entered Boston University as an undergraduate in 1925 and remained closely involved in the university until his final retirement in 2003. After

earning two degrees (1929 and 1931) from the university, he became assistant dean of Sargent College in 1931 and was made dean in 1945. That year he was the moving force behind the successful integration of Boston University's residence halls. He remained dean of Sargent College until his formal retirement in 1972, although he continued to work at the university, and in 1986 he became the founding director of the Howard Thurman Center. In 2001, at the age of ninety-four, he was named university historian. He was the author of *Howard Thurman: His Enduring Dream* (Boston: Howard Thurman Center, Boston University, 1988). Makechnie and his daughter, Joan Makechnie Diver, were central figures in J. Anthony Lukas's acclaimed study of the Boston school desegregation crisis, *Common Ground: A Turbulent Decade in the Lives of Three American Families* (New York: Knopf, 1985). For Lukas on the Makechnies and Thurman, see the foreword in Thurman's *The Search for Common Ground: An Inquiry into the Basis of Man's Experience of Community* (Richmond, Ind.: Friends United Press, 1986), ix–xi.

11. Dean Melvin Brodshaug (1900–1988).

12. Dean Max R. Goodson.

13. Dean Robert A. Choate (1910–75).

14. The Rev. John Wesley Neff preached "The Carol That Was Never Sung" in Marsh Chapel on 21 December 1959.

15. Robert L. Treese (1919–2008) received his doctorate in 1958 from the Boston University School of Theology, where he taught for many decades. Among his publications is *Homosexuality: A Contemporary View of the Biblical Perspective* (San Francisco: Glide Urban Center, 1966). He preached "Jesus Is Lord" in Marsh Chapel on 28 December 1958.

16. After serving as a Methodist minister, George A. Warmer was vice president for university affairs at Boston University. From 1968 to 1976 he was president of Hawai'i Pacific University in Honolulu. He preached "Proud of Being Humble" in Marsh Chapel on 4 January 1959.

17. Thurman delivered four sermons at the University of Redlands between 29 December 1959 and 1 January 1960: "Seeking and Finding"; "The Three-Way Dialogue–The Self"; "The Three-Way Dialogue—Others"; and "The Three-Way Dialogue—God."

18. Max B. Miller (1927–2013), with appointments in both the Boston University School of Theology and the School of Music, was university organist at Marsh Chapel from 1947 to 1991.

〽 To George Britton
24 February 1959
[*Boston, Mass.*]

Thurman replies to Fellowship Church member George Britton,[1] one of his oldest and closest friends in the church, who had suggested that Francis Geddes, the church's minister, be encouraged to spend some time away from the church in order to have "a chance to develop."[2] Thurman is cool to the idea, suggesting instead that Geddes spend time visiting interracial congregations in other cities. He opposes raising funds for Geddes's travel or study from outside the church's membership, arguing that in the past such external subvention "has crippled us."

Howard Thurman and
George Makechnie at a
wedding, with unidenti-
fied participants. From the
Howard Thurman Col-
lection, Howard Gotlieb
Archival Research Center
at Boston University.

Mr. George Britton
Box 555
Kentfield, California

Dear George:

It was good to get your letter which came on the eve of my journeying to Texas for a week. Hence the rather extended delay in reply to it.

I am certainly in agreement with the idea that for the long pull ahead it would be very advantageous for Francis to have some broadening experiences. He and I have talked about this many times and, as recently as the Christmas holidays, when Sue was in San Francisco a much longer period than my two days, she and Francis talked about various aspects of the same problem which you raise. My specific reaction to your alternate proposals is as follows:

It may be unrealistic, both in the light of the immediate needs of the Church and of Francis' personal situation for him to have a long absence from the leadership of the church.

My thought would be that it would be wonderful if he could take a four or five weeks spin around the country, on the basis of an itinerary that covered cities in which inter-group churches are trying to develop and in which there are persons who at one time were on our mailing lists and had an active interest in what we are about. In my judgment, this kind of experience would do both Francis and the Church more good than an extended leave for study at this time.

Since Fellowship Church began in 1944, many denominations have become committed to development of this character. The success has varied. It would be a very [good] perspective giving experience in depth for Francis to talk with the ministers and to meet the persons who are carrying the responsibility for these local undertakings. He could accumulate in this process a variety of literature which has been developed, and make it possible for our congregation, through him, to locate itself in a growing edge that is a part of the religious movement in the United States.

Such a journey might include spending a week at the Church of the Cross-roads in Hawaii.[3]

It would do our congregation a great deal of good if individual members, by personal contributions over and above their pledge, made this possible. They would then have a stake in what he is doing, for it would be true, literally, that they are sending him to do on their behalf something that needs desperately to be done. I do not think well at all of raising the money outside of the Church. This has crippled us through the years. I am sure that there would have been far more cohesiveness in our congregation if the ownership of our present building had been the result of real sacrifice on the part of the people, but, as you recall, instead the entire cost of the building was paid for by persons who were not local members of the congregation. I would certainly be willing to carry my end of the financial stick, out of my pocket.

This is my reaction to your letter. Please let me know what the developments are. Just last week I ate the last date. My gratitude to you and Barbara.

Sincerely,

Howard Thurman

Dean

TLc.

NOTES

1. George E. Britton, a California businessman, was one of the founding members of the Fellowship Church. He met the Thurmans on their arrival in San Francisco in July 1944. See "San Francisco Journal," printed in *PHWT*, 3:84–88.

2. From George Britton, 3 February 1959.

3. The Church of the Crossroads in Honolulu was an early self-identified interracial church. See "Biographical Essay," *PHWT*, 3:xlviiin72. See also To Friends of the International Fellowship Community, 15 August 1960, printed in the current volume.

❧ To Zalman M. Schachter
3 March 1959
Boston, Mass.

In 1955 Zalman Schachter[1] was rabbi of a Chabad (Lubavitch Hasidic) congregation in New Bedford, Massachusetts. He felt the need to broaden his understanding of religion and psychology and enrolled in the Boston University School of Theology that fall.[2] Because of his long early-morning commute from New Bedford, Schachter was unable to say his morning prayers before arriving on campus. He was uncomfortable praying in the areas designated for prayers in Marsh Chapel because of the Christian symbolism and iconography there, so he started praying in a common area. Shortly thereafter a middle-aged black man, whom Schachter thought might be the janitor, came up to him and said, "I've seen you here several times. Wouldn't you like to say your prayers in the small chapel?" This chapel was downstairs from the main chapel. Schachter did not want to offend the man by telling him that he could not pray at an altar with a crucifix and so said nothing. The man again suggested that Schachter try praying in the small chapel. When Schachter arrived the next morning, the crucifix was off the altar, two candles were lit, and the Bible on the lectern was open to Psalm 139, Thurman's favorite psalm.[3]

Schachter enrolled in Thurman's class on Spiritual Resources and Disciplines but was afraid that the instructor would try to convert him. When he arrived to speak to the teacher, he was surprised to see the same black man who had given him advice about his morning prayers.[4] The course was one of the turning points in Schachter's life, a foundation of much of his later work in attempting to revive Jewish spirituality. The two men would remain in contact thereafter. Their most extended time together occurred when Thurman was on a speaking tour in western Canada in 1962 and Schachter was teaching at the University of Manitoba in Winnipeg.[5] They spent a day together, the highlights of which were a tour of a nearby Trappist monastery and a special bar mitzvah blessing that Thurman gave to Schachter's son. Schachter-Shalomi wrote that he learned from Thurman that there were "non-Jews who were wonderful, blessed souls" and that "there are ways of loving and expressing God that are so simple."[6] Thurman, he concluded, "wasn't interested in getting souls to Christ, but, like Jesus, he wanted to get souls to God."[7]

Rabbi Zalman M. Schachter
B'nai B'rith Hillel Foundation
University of Manitoba
471 Inkster Boulevard
Winnipeg, Manitoba

Dear Zalman:

Of course I remember you! It is wonderful to hear from you and particularly to receive the copy of your handbook for Spiritual Disciplines.[8] I have wanted such a book for some time. Would you be willing to send me a dozen copies, for which I will gladly pay whatever the charges are. At the moment I am counselling with a Jewish student who has very little orientation in his own religion's faith, even though culturally in this regard he is authentic. I am working with him with the hope that he will find his way into the heart of the religious experience of Israel. I want to give him a copy of your book.

I am sorry that I missed you when you were here in September, and I look forward to seeing you if you are ever this way again. Please know how exciting it is to me, personally, that you are making available to your students the spiritual insights which are not only their heritage but which they must honor the right to experience.

Thank you for your letter and for the Spiritual Guide.
Sincerely yours,
Howard Thurman
Dean

TLc.

NOTES

1. Zalman M. Schachter-Shalomi (1924–2014) was born in Poland and raised in Vienna. He came to the United States in 1941 after escaping Vichy France. He received his rabbinic ordination within the Chabad Lubavitch community in Brooklyn in 1947 and served several Chabad congregations. In 1956 he received an M.A. from the Boston University School of Theology. That same year he became a professor at the University of Manitoba in Winnipeg and the director of its Hillel program. He earned a doctorate from Hebrew Union College in 1966. After leaving Winnipeg in the late 1960s, he became one of the founders and leaders of the Havurah "Jewish Renewal" movement, which tried to reorient Judaism away from formal congregational settings and toward more personal and spiritual forms of Judaism. He was the author of many books; the one Thurman refers to in this letter was his first. He added "Shalomi," Hebrew for "of peace," to his name in the 1970s.

2. Peter Eisenstadt, interview with Zalman Schachter-Shalomi, 28 June 2012. He attended Boston University because it was the only Boston-area school of religion that would accept his *semikhah* (rabbinic ordination) from the nonaccredited Lubavitch seminary as a basis of graduate work.

3. Zalman Schachter-Shalomi, "What I Found in the Chapel," in *My Neighbor's Faith: Stories of Interreligious Encounter, Growth, and Transformation,* ed. Jennifer Howe Peace,

Or N. Rose, and Gregory Mobley (Maryknoll, N.Y.: Orbis Books, 2012), 207–10. Another version of the story is related in a volume that consists of an extended conversation with Schachter-Shalomi: Sara Davidson, *The December Project: An Extraordinary Rabbi and a Skeptical Seeker Confront Life's Greatest Mystery* (New York: HarperOne, 2014), 75–77.

4. For more on this meeting, see the biographical essay in the current volume.

5. For more on Thurman's visit with Schachter-Shalomi in Manitoba, see "Annual Report: The Wider Ministry, 1962–1963," printed in *PHWT*, vol. 5 (forthcoming).

6. Schachter-Shalomi told the story of the time he brought an Orthodox school group to meet Thurman and someone asked Thurman, "'What happens when you don't feel like praying?' Thurman said, 'think of a phrase that touched you in the past, and keep on repeating it.' One of the students thought this was foolish advice, but he tried it one day, and it opened a new world for him." Eisenstadt, interview with Zalman Schachter-Shalomi.

7. Ibid. In a letter to Thurman, Schachter-Shalomi applied an extended Talmudic metaphor, comparing a revered rabbi to a spreading tree to describe Thurman: "Tree, tree, what can I wish you? You are rooted in the confluence of rivers, you have the best climate. Sun all day, and gentle wind, bees & butterflies. I wish you that your seeds may grow as you. So others may grow as you, partake of the fruit, and rest in the shade." (From Zalman Schachter, 5 February 1961.)

8. Meshullan Zalman HaCohen [Zalman M. Schachter], *The First Step: A Primer of a Jew's Spiritual Life* (Winnipeg, Manitoba?, 1958?). This was reprinted in revised form as Zalman Schachter-Shalomi, with Donald Gropman, *The First Step: A Guide for the New Jewish Spirit* (New York: Bantam Books, 1983).

꒚ To Arthur L. James
11 March 1959
[*Boston, Mass.*]

Thurman responds in this letter to correspondence from his old mentor, the Reverend Arthur L. James.[1] Thurman's personal and professional ties to James were deep and long-standing. During his boyhood Thurman attended Mount Bethel Baptist Church in Daytona, Florida, while James was its minister. Their friendship continued when James was called to the ministry of First Baptist Church in Roanoke, Virginia, in 1919. Thurman spent the summers of 1924 and 1925 as an assistant minister in Roanoke, and it was at James's church in the summer of 1925 that Thurman was ordained into the Baptist ministry.[2]

Rev. Arthur L. James, Pastor Emeritus
First Baptist Church
923 Staunton Avenue, N.W.
Roanoke, Virginia

Dear Cousin Arthur:
    It was very wonderful to get a letter from you[3] bringing me up to date about the family. I did not know about Miss Josie's death until your letter came. I hope

that she did not suffer long. I have seen a great deal of the suffering that comes from cancer.

I am enclosing a copy of our Christmas letter which will bring you up to date about the happenings in the Thurman family.

I was not able to go to Aunt Emily's funeral because she died during the time when Sue and I were in California. I have heard from Uncle Gilbert[4] twice since then. It was wonderful that Aunt Emily was able to realize even for so short a time the fulfillment of a dream that she had had, that would bring her and Uncle Gilbert together in her own home in Deland. It may be that the strain and excitement were too much. I had not seen her for more than two years. The last time I was in Deland we had a good long visit. This I must keep and cherish.

I am in the middle of my sixth year here. The time has passed very rapidly under relatively happy circumstances. I find that the demands upon me, in the nature of my work, are greater than I can meet. This means a certain amount of pressure which takes its toll. The emotional strain on me and the family, because at many points in our life here there is reflected the general social ill health of our time. I am hoping to get a sabbatical leave next year in order that I may have some time for resting my nervous system and listening to the Voice of God without so many distractions. This week I am completing the manuscript of a book on the development of Fellowship Church.[5] It will not be ready until the fall.

I pray that you will continue in good health. It is quite wonderful to read a book which you sent and see the vigor of your mind and the depth of your spirit.[6] Through all these years you have lived a full and creative ministry unlike so many other men of your own generation you have believed profoundly in the ethicacy of the written word. Your latest book is a clear indication of the fruits of such concentration. I do not know when I will be coming that way, but I do look forward to a time when we can sit down and have a good heart to heart visit about many things.

May the Lord bless you and keep you.

Sincerely,

Howard Thurman

TLc.

NOTES

1. Arthur Leonard James (1877–1968) was born in Madison, Florida, in the same county where Thurman's mother and grandmother were born and raised. When James was five, his father was murdered by a white mob. He was educated at Florida Baptist Academy in Jacksonville (also Thurman's high school). James began his ministry in Florida and was a minister at Mount Bethel Baptist Church in Daytona. During World War I he served as a YMCA secretary overseas. He was called to the First Baptist Church in Roanoke, Virginia,

in 1919 and remained there as minister until 1958. Under his direction the church grew to more than two thousand members and was the largest black Baptist congregation in Virginia west of Richmond. James was a member of the Roanoke draft board from 1940 to 1961 and was appointed to the city school board. He also served as president of the Virginia State Baptist Convention and of the Hampton Ministers' Conference. He was the author of *Sketches of My Life and Ministry* (Roanoke, Va.: First Baptist Church, 1958) and *Sermons Worth Reading* (Roanoke, Va.: Roanoke Publishing Company, 1947).

2. *WHAH*, 56–58. Thurman had wanted to be ordained without the traditional laying on of hands, but James told him that "there will be laying on of hands or there will be no ordination." For an article written by Thurman at this time for the *Roanoke Church News*, a newspaper founded by James, see *PHWT*, 1:41–42.

3. From Arthur L. James, 24 February 1959.

4. This was Gilbert Ambrose, Thurman's mother's brother; see To Gilbert Ambrose, 24 January 1962, printed in the current volume.

5. HT, *Footprints of a Dream*.

6. Arthur L. James, *Sketches of My Life and Ministry* (Roanoke, Va.: First Baptist Church, 1958).

🐟 From Richard Nixon
24 April 1959
Washington, D.C.

Vice President Richard M. Nixon,[1] chairman of the President's Committee on Government Contracts, invited Thurman to attend a meeting of the committee for clergy. Thurman replied to Nixon on 29 April that "even though the date is very late, I shall plan to attend the Conference which convenes at the Sheraton Park Hotel on May 11, 1959 at 10:00 a.m."[2] At the meeting over four hundred religious leaders gathered to hear Nixon and others speak on the moral urgency of ending employment discrimination and on the role that clergy could play in spreading the message. Speakers included Martin Luther King, Jr., A. Philip Randolph, and James M. Nabrit, Jr., dean of the Howard University School of Law.[3]

Mr. Howard Thurman
2041 Larkin Street
San Francisco, California

Dear Mr. Thurman:

On behalf of the President's Committee on Government Contracts[4] I would like to invite you to attend a Religious Leaders Conference on May 11, 1959 at 9:30 a.m. at the Sheraton Park Hotel, 2660 Connecticut Avenue, N.W., Washington, D.C.

Participants in the 1959 commemoration of Phillis Wheatley at Marsh Chapel cele-
brating African American artistic creativity (*from left:* the sculptor Meta Vaux Warrick
Fuller, Howard Thurman and Sue Bailey Thurman, Helen Alzada Mann Hayes, the
tenor Roland Hayes, the poet Georgia Douglas Johnson). From the Bailey Thurman
Family Papers; the Stuart A. Rose Manuscript, Archives, and Rare Book Library, Emory
University.

The purpose of the Conference will be to discuss the policies and program
of the President's Committee and ways in which interested religious leaders
might assist the Committee in advancing its program of elimination of discrimination in employment in government contracts, because of race, religion, color
or national origin. The counsel of the participants will be sought on specific
ways through which the moral commitment to this national policy of equal job
opportunity can be implemented.

In reviewing its activities over the past five years, the Committee has
observed progress in opening new job areas to minority groups and has concluded that in order to make these employment gains permanent, the principle
of equal job opportunity must be advanced at the community level. To that end,
the Committee believes that acquainting religious leaders with its objectives
and accomplishments will result in greater motivation of minority youth to
acquire the necessary training and skills to compete effectively in the national
labor market and to advance themselves after being hired.

We would appreciate hearing from you as to whether you will be able to
attend. A detailed agenda will be mailed to you upon receipt of your acceptance

of this invitation. We look forward with great pleasure to meeting you at this significant meeting.

Sincerely yours,

[*signed*] Richard Nixon

Richard Nixon

TLS.

NOTES

1. Richard Milhous Nixon (1913–94), a Republican politician from California, was elected to the U.S. House of Representatives in 1946 and to the U.S. Senate in 1950. In 1952 he was elected to the first of his two terms as vice president. He was the unsuccessful Republican presidential candidate in 1960 and in 1962 lost the California gubernatorial race. He was elected as president of the United States in 1968 and in 1972. The Watergate scandal forced his resignation in 1974.

2. To Richard Nixon, 29 April 1959.

3. Louis Cassels, "Nixon Urges Ministers to Build Support for Rights," *Chicago Defender*, 12 May 1959.

4. The President's Committee on Government Contracts was created by President Eisenhower in 1953 to enforce nondiscrimination by government contractors. It was succeeded in 1961 by the President's Committee for Equal Employment Opportunity.

 To HAROLD C. CASE

24 APRIL 1959

BOSTON, MASS.

Thurman's reluctance to lead the United Ministry to Students[1] at Boston University causes another crisis with university president Harold Case. Although this particular issue was resolved in Thurman's favor—his sabbatical was not contingent on his assuming the chairmanship of the United Ministry—the underlying issue remained. Thurman continued to press for the creation of a nondenominational and interreligious fellowship attached to Marsh Chapel and to resist narrowing his religious outreach to Protestants.

Dear Harold:

Your memorandum of April 23rd[2] throws me into confusion. I am enclosing a copy of a letter written January 7, 1959,[3] with the notation, "not sent," because instead I had an appointment with you to discuss these matters. There is real misunderstanding here, because I thought I made it very clear to you that I could not take the chairmanship of the United Ministry until within myself it was clear that it was the thing that I should do. One of the necessities for my leave is the fact that I must assess my six years' work, in order that I will know in what direction, within my own spirit, I am free to move, as far as whatever future religious leadership I may have in the University.

If my leave is contingent upon my accepting the Chairmanship of the United Ministry, I am in no spiritual position to agree to it. In that event, I shall make my plans to take the leave without salary from the University and without obligation for anything that I cannot conscientiously do.

I recognize the awkwardness of this position of mine as far as administrative technicalities are concerned. I thought that I made this very clear to you when we talked. And my recollection was this, that you personally would take responsibility for requesting the leave, without these strings attached, and that you and I understood the necessities under which I, myself had to labor. Now, in your letter, you hold me to Item 7, which was completely nullified in our conversation.

To indicate my concern for the problem of religion on the campus, I have been working with Bill Overholt, John Neff, and Joe Washington,[4] in a series of extended meetings on an over-all plan for the religious life of the University, without regard to the personnel of the leadership. We had hoped that our discussions would develop to the point that there would be presented to you an over-all proposal, in line with some of the personal discussions that you and I have had together. In the confused picture as far as the protestant ministry on this campus is concerned, the chairmanship of the United Ministry at this time is merely a matter of mechanics. However, if I agreed to do it, so much more is involved than mechanics that I must be sure that with my life I can back what is involved in making the chairmanship of the United Ministry dynamic and creative.

You will pardon my taking so much of your time to say all of this, but your letter of the 22nd makes it mandatory.

Sincerely yours,
Howard Thurman
Dean

Enc.

{N.B. I am mindful of the administrative problem, somewhat. My only point is that I cannot agree to do something to which I am unable to make commitment. It is not my purpose to be difficult but I am no good to you or the university if I am [in] spiritual conflict on this point. I must have time.
HT}

NOTES

1. The United Ministry to Students at Boston University was founded in the fall of 1953 to coordinate campus activities between religious groups and foster ecumenical and interreligious activities. The All-University Committee on Religious Affairs was organized at the same time, with Thurman as one of its members. See Betty Driscoll Mays, "BU Works for Unity among Religious Groups," *Christian Science Monitor*, 4 April 1955. Although this would seem to be the sort of organization in which Thurman would have wanted to participate, apparently he felt that it was too dominated by denominational divisions.

2. From Harold C. Case, 23 April 1959.

3. To Harold Case, 9 January 1959.

4. Joseph R. Washington, Jr. (1931–), a graduate of Andover-Newton Seminary, came to national attention for pastoring several white congregations in Maine. After teaching at Boston University and Dillard University, he taught religious and African American studies at the University of Virginia. He is the author of many books on black religion, among them *Black Religion: The Negro and Christianity in the United States* (Boston: Beacon Press, 1964) and *Black Sects and Cults* (Garden City, N.Y.: Doubleday, 1972). *Black Religion* contained a lengthy discussion of Thurman, in which Washington called him Negro America's "most provocative innovator in the spiritual realm" and "the leading preacher among Negroes and their most creative spiritual leader" (Washington, *Black Religion*, 105).

FROM CLARENCE PROCTOR
31 MAY 1959
NEW ORLEANS, LOUISIANA

Thurman receives this letter asking him about his positions on birth control and pacifism.

Dear Dr. Thurman:

My name is Clarence Proctor. I am 22 yrs. old and have read several of your books. I've found them very inspiring.

There are some religious issues about which I am confused. I am now in the process of asking some religious leaders—Dean Pike,[1] Dr. Lloyd Imes[2] and Prof. Reinhold Niebuhr—whom I respect as preachers and scholars to comment on these questions. It would mean so much to me if you would write me some of your views on the following issues:

1. Whether it is right for a Christian to practice birth control. If it is right— under what conditions? If it is wrong why?

2. Should a Christian participate (take up arms) in a war?

My mailing address is:

Clarence Proctor
5032½ Loyola Street
New Orleans, La.

Thank you,
[*signed*] Clarence Proctor

TLS.

NOTES

1. James Pike (1913–69), a controversial Episcopal priest, served as dean of the Cathedral of St. John the Divine until 1958, when he was elected Episcopal bishop of California.

2. William Lloyd Imes (1889–1986) graduated from Fisk University in 1910 and Union Theological Seminary in 1915. A Presbyterian minister, he served congregations in Plainfield, N.J.; Philadelphia; and Harlem, where he was minister of St. James Church from 1925 to 1943. In 1943 he became president of Knoxville College, and from 1947 until his retirement in 1955, he was director of social and adult education for the New York Council of Churches. See also *PHWT*, 1:225, 325.

🐟 To Clarence Proctor

12 June 1959
[*Boston, Mass.*]

In his response to a letter from Clarence Proctor, Thurman succinctly states his views on "whether it is right for a Christian to practice birth control" or to "participate (take up arms) in a war."[1]

Mr. Clarence Proctor
5032½ Loyola Street
New Orleans, Louisiana

Dear Mr. Proctor:
Your letter, sent to me in California, has been forwarded to me in Boston. I am sorry that my work in connection with the end of the school year makes it impossible for me to write a letter discussing the questions which you raise. I will have to give simple and categorical answers.
One: I do not think that it is wrong for a married couple to practice birth control. I do not think that under that circumstance it is a moral issue at all. It seems to me that a family should do the thing that is for the best interest of the kinds of opportunities which they will be able to give the children with which they are blessed. Anything that an individual does must reflect the quality of character which that person has.
With reference to No. 2: Christians have taken up arms and Christians have refused to take up arms. In both instances being activated by their interpretation of the meaning of their Christian commitment. I think that any attitude or deed that is not for the maintenance and furtherance of the best and highest interests of other individuals is in violation of what to me is the Christian commitment.
Sincerely yours,
Howard Thurman
Dean

TLc.

NOTE
1. See From Clarence Proctor, 31 May 1959, printed in the current volume.

250   15 June 1959

To M. H. Fleming
·15 June 1959
[*Boston, Mass.*]

Monroe H. Fleming,[1] *a frequent correspondent of Thurman's and an ardent admirer of his work, was one of the few persons of African descent in the Mormon Church in the 1950s.*[2] *Until 1978 persons of African descent were barred from the Mormon priesthood orders, ordinations that were and are nearly universal for males in the Mormon Church.*[3] *In response to a question about the bar against blacks entering the priesthood contained in a 1957 letter from Fleming, Thurman wrote, "I have only this to say: If your statement is correct, it is from my point of view a device for justifying racial prejudice and is in violation of common sense, ethics and religion. It is in the category of superstition and is unworthy of an intelligent mind."*[4] *In the letter here, in response to another query by Fleming, Thurman gives his opinion of the idea of the priesthood within Christianity in general.*[5]

Mr. M. H. Fleming
814 2nd Avenue
Salt Lake City 3, Utah

Dear Mr. Fleming:

It is very difficult for me to put in a letter very much that can be helpful to you in an interpretation of the priesthood. There is a long history that branches off in many directions. Fundamentally, the concept of the priesthood has to do with the special spiritual gifts that an individual has of God enabling him to interpret through ritual and ceremony the will of God for mankind. In Protestantism the doctrine of the priesthood of all believers is based upon the idea that any individual who gives the nerve center of his consent to the will of God will share in the revelation of that will, not only for his life, but through his life; not merely his words or his vocational functioning, but through his total life. This means that it is not necessary for a believer to go through some special office in order to get to God, but rather that God is as close as is the whisper in the heart. It is true that there is a religious vocation into which a person may enter that will give him unique facility in administering, through ritual and ceremony, to the religious needs of people, but this is a vocational function and it is not any indication that those persons whose vocation this is not, but who also are believers will be denied the wisdom and the guidance of the spirit of God. This is about all that I can say, but it indicates a bit of my thinking in this regard.

I am sending you, under separate cover, Volume 4 and also a new record recently released by Oberlin College, giving the 125th Anniversary sermon

which I preached at the time. The text[s] for volumes 1, 2, and 3 are to be found in "Meditations of the Heart" and "Deep Is the Hunger."
Sincerely yours,
Howard Thurman

Dean

TLc.

Notes
    1. Monroe H. Fleming (1894–1982), a native of Mississippi, worked for many years at the Hotel Utah in Salt Lake City and in the 1950s was a promoter for performances in Salt Lake City for Marian Anderson, Paul Robeson, and other African American musicians. He converted to Mormonism in the early 1950s and in 1978 became one of the first African Americans to enter the Mormon priesthood.
    2. In the early years of the Mormon Church after its 1830 founding, there was no ban on priesthood ordination for blacks—although only a handful of black people were church members. Their eligibility changed in the late 1840s and early 1850s with pronouncements by Brigham Young barring all persons of African descent from the Mormon priesthood ordinances. Despite this, a small number of blacks remained in the Mormon Church and pressured the church to change its policy. In June 1978 the Mormon Church opened its priesthood orders to all qualified males.
    3. There are two orders of Mormon priesthood, both open only to males: the Aaronic priesthood and the Melchizedek priesthood, the latter of which is the senior and more important of the two ordinances. Although there are no formal age requirements, the Aaronic priesthood is open to eligible candidates ages twelve to eighteen, and the Melchizedek priesthood is entered into by adults.
    4. To M. H. Fleming, 28 January 1957.
    5. Fleming was quoted as saying that "the claim that the Negro is contented as a member of the church without the priesthood is not true. I know most of the members of the Negro race in the church and know they feel that they should have the priesthood if they live a life based upon the principles of the Gospel" (Frank Owens, "Mormon Politicians Woo Negro Vote, but Find Their Doctrine a Handicap," *Chicago Defender,* 8 August 1962).

☙ From Martin Luther King, Jr.
22 June 1959
Montgomery, Alabama

Martin Luther King, Jr. writes to Thurman about their recent meeting in Boston.

Dear Dr. Thurman:
    We are eagerly awaiting your coming to the Dexter Avenue Baptist Church to preach the anniversary sermon on Sunday, December 13, 1959.[1] I would appreciate it very much if you would send me two glossy photos and an "immodest" biographical sketch for publicity purposes. At a later date I will be writing you concerning your arrival time.

It was certainly good to see you in Boston a few days ago. I hope you will have a fruitful summer. Coretta joins me in extending best regards to you and Mrs. Thurman. We are looking forward with great anticipation to your presence here in Montgomery on the second Sunday in December.

Very sincerely yours,

[*signed with representation of author*] Martin L. King, Jr.

Martin Luther King, Jr.

Dr. Howard Thurman
Boston University

(Dictated, but not personally signed by Dr. King.)

TLSr.

NOTE

1. Thurman was unable to preach at the church on that date. See To Martin Luther King, Jr., 11 September 1959, printed in the current volume.

✺ To Martin Luther King, Jr.

11 September 1959

[*Boston, Mass.*]

Thurman has to withdraw his tentative promise to Martin Luther King, Jr., to preach at Dexter Avenue Baptist Church.

Dr. Martin Luther King, Jr.
Dexter Avenue Baptist Church
454 Dexter Avenue
Montgomery, Alabama

Dear Martin:

At last I am in a position to be very definite about the December 13th date.[1] Since talking with you, two situations have arisen that work against my coming. One is it is definite now that I will be on leave from the University for about ten months beginning in January, therefore it is crucial that I stick as close to the Chapel during the fall as possible. The second thing is that President Case will be out of the country during the month of December and he is asking me to give the Christmas Convocation address on Tuesday, December 15th. This about wraps it up, my friend. I can only ask you to do the generous thing by furnishing me with another rain check which, in due course, I will redeem, I promise.

I am sorry I missed you in San Francisco, but I had to leave on September 7th. I think of you in my prayers and quiet time very often with the hope that you will continue to find all the things that are needful for your peace.
Sincerely yours,
Howard Thurman
Dean

TLc.

NOTE

1. See From Martin Luther King, Jr., 8 November 1958; and From Martin Luther King, Jr., 22 June 1959, both printed in the current volume.

⤳ FROM MARTIN LUTHER KING, JR.
30 SEPTEMBER 1959
MONTGOMERY, ALABAMA

King responds to Thurman's letter of 11 September and expresses the hope that they will be able to meet in the near future.

My dear friend Howard Thurman:
This is just a note to acknowledge receipt of your letter of September 11, stating your inability to be with our congregation on Sunday, December 13. Please know that I well understand the situations which made it necessary for you to decline this invitation.
I do hope it will be possible for us to work out something else at a later date.
I, too, am sorry that we missed each other in San Francisco.[1] I can assure you that it would have been much more lifting to spend my time there talking with you than listening to the sometimes meaningless outbursts. I hope we will be able to talk together in the not-too-distant future.
Very sincerely yours,
[*signed with representation of author*] Martin
Martin

Dr. Howard Thurman, Dean
Marsh Chapel
Boston University
Boston, Mass.

(Dictated, but not personally signed by Dr. King.)

TLSr.

NOTE

1. King had been in Oakland on 9–12 September to address the National Baptist Laymen Convention. Thurman, who had spent the summer in the Bay Area and elsewhere on the West Coast, was in San Francisco as late as 6 September, when he spoke at the First Unitarian Church, before departing shortly thereafter for Boston and the East Coast.

❧ "We Believe [Love Its Own Reward]"
Program broadcast on 20 November 1959
Boston, Mass.

In November 1957 WHDH-TV, Channel 5, in Boston began broadcasting.[1] From the beginning of its operations it featured "We Believe," a daily weekday fifteen-minute program of religious inspiration, usually broadcast from 11:15 to 11:30 A.M. Thurman soon became a regular weekly presenter on the program, scheduled in the Friday morning slot. This soon became what he called a "very important part" of his ministry.[2] It continued after Thurman ceased to preach regularly at Marsh Chapel in the spring of 1962 until May 1965, shortly before the Thurmans left Boston for San Francisco. Thurman regularly appeared on the program for seven and a half years. "We Believe" made Thurman a minor celebrity in Boston.[3] Because his face as well as his voice became familiar to his audiences, Thurman was often stopped on the street or on the train by fans of the program.[4] Many others wrote or called to thank him for his messages. Thurman's chapel staff circulated about 150 transcripts of Thurman's broadcasts weekly to interested viewers.[5] Even Thurman's round-the-world sabbatical in 1960 did not interrupt the flow of his appearances, as he prerecorded a year's worth of programming prior to his departure.[6]

Thurman was initially worried that without the physical presence of an audience his television messages would lack immediacy. As he said in his final broadcast, "I was sure that it would not be possible to do this because I need so much in my own public addresses and speaking the feel of the minds of the people to whom I am talking. And the thought of talking to two red eyes on a manmade machine was very paralyzing to my spirit."[7] However, he soon found a virtual audience in the form of approving letters and phone calls, and he found himself speaking to the studio technicians, who had minds with a "margin of availability, and here and there, there was an interested look or the feeling of a mind moving towards mine, and so that Friday after Friday I felt that I was in an encounter with many minds absent and minds present."[8]

The 20 November 1959 broadcast was typical of Thurman's "We Believe" programs. He typically arranged the broadcasts into series on specific topics. This

Liturgical dance, Marsh Chapel, c. 1960. From the Bailey Thurman Family Papers; the Stuart A. Rose Manuscript, Archives, and Rare Book Library, Emory University.

broadcast was part of an ongoing series on a familiar Thurman topic, the complexities of the meaning of true love.

Let the words of my mouth and the meditation of my heart be acceptable in Thy sight, O Lord, my strength and my redeemer.[9]

Before continuing our series on the meaning of love, because next week is Thanksgiving, I am reading "A Litany of Thanksgiving."[10]

We are continuing our thought together about the meaning of love and its implications. Our working definition is that love is the experience through which a person passes when he deals with another human being at a point in that human being that is beyond all good and beyond all evil. The experience of love is the experience of being dealt with at a point in oneself that is beyond all good and beyond all evil. The experience of being totally dealt with, significantly dealt with. Now this morning we are thinking about another aspect of this meaning. Love seeketh not its own. Love is not demanding in the sense of justice, for instance, as over against that which is more than justice, that which transcends justice. One of the rough, but important working definitions of justice in certain schools of thought is that justice is the artificial equalization of unequals. It is a balancing, always. It is expressed in the Judeo-Christian tradition in what is called the law of the lex talionis, the eye for an eye and the tooth for a tooth. This feeling in the human spirit that demands that I will get as good as I give, I will give as good as I get, life is made up essentially of reward and punishment, of a kind of balance. Now this is rooted in a certain aspect of human nature and human experience. And anyone who deals with life on a basis of that kind of rough notion of equality has much to be said on the side of the contention and on the side of the validity of the position. But love is something more than this.

Love seeketh not its own. Love does not demand eye for an eye, and tooth for a tooth. Sometimes in relationships between parents and children we see what this means in its most disastrous dimensions. When a parent feels that after all the sacrifices that I have made for my son, or my daughter, this is the thanks I get, this is the reward that I get. Or when, sometimes between friends, there is a careful balancing of gifts. I will give you something of a certain quality and I expect in return that you will give me something of the same quality. This mood will be very rampant in a few weeks from now as we begin to go over our Christmas lists and we remember that last year we gave "X" a gift that was worth twenty dollars and what we received from "X" was a gift that was worth fifty cents. Therefore when you are making up your list this year and you come to "X"'s name, you will remember this discrepancy between these two gifts and will give to "X" this year that which in your judgment "X" deserves. Or you know how you feel, for instance, when someone says to you, after all that I have done for you, all the things that I have given you, all the ways by which I have extended myself on your behalf and now the only thing that I get is this kind of treatment at your hands. Now there is a certain rationale at work here. This insistence on the part of the mind that things balance. Now this is rooted in the constitution of man's mind and his nature, for you see, the mind insists that things must make sense. This is a rational world and the mind applies the principle of rationality that seems to be inherent in it to all of the constructs of man's experience. But love is something else again. For love says that I will not give because I will be given, even though it is perfectly natural and in a sense normal, whatever we mean by the word "normal," but in a sense normal that people will love and then be loved in return. The notion of requitement for love. I love and I am loved back. This is a very rational thing and sometimes a very deeply satisfying thing, but love insists—love at its best insists—that the individual will give and there is no demand placed upon the object of one's love that one shall be loved in return. The essential quality of love in the context of our thinking in this series is that there is a reward for love, a very searching and insistent reward, but it has nothing to do with the quality of the response from the other person. The reward of love is more love with which to love. So that the more I love, in the sense that I deal with the other person at a point in that person beyond all good and all evil, the more love there is with which to love. And that is why in all religions when men think about God, they think of God in terms of self-giving love that only demands of the individual an acceptance and no demand in terms of swinging back. The balance we do not seek in love as normal as it is. Love goes beyond the balance. The reward of love is to love.

Let the words of my mouth and the meditation of my heart be acceptable in Thy sight, O Lord, my rock and my redeemer.

At.

NOTES

1. WHDH was initially an ABC affiliate and became a CBS affiliate at the beginning of 1961. The station stopped broadcasting in 1972; in 1990 an unrelated station assumed the WHDH-TV call letters.

2. *WHAH*, 175.

3. To Harold C. Case, 28 November 1958, printed in the current volume.

4. "We Believe," 28 May 1965.

5. To Harold C. Case, 28 November 1958, printed in the current volume.

6. *WHAH*, 175. However, against this claim in Thurman's autobiography, a Boston University press release stated that only four of the "We Believe" meditations were prerecorded (Boston University News Release, 3 January 1960).

7. "We Believe," 28 May 1965. Thurman tells the same story, in different language, in *WHAH*, 174–75.

8. "We Believe," 28 May 1965.

9. Ps. 19:14. Thurman recited this verse at the beginning and conclusion of every "We Believe" broadcast. The verse forms part of the conclusion of the *Amidah*, one of the most important Jewish prayers, included in almost every Jewish worship service in all branches of Judaism.

10. See HT, *Meditations of the Heart* (1953), 147–49.

꒰ꉂ FROM FRANCIS GEDDES
26 DECEMBER 1959
SAN FRANCISCO, CALIF.

Geddes expresses his simmering resentments over an issue that had been unresolved since Thurman's departure for Boston in 1953: whether Thurman, as minister-at-large, overshadowed his successors to such an extent as to limit their effectiveness. Thurman was well aware that, as he had written to Clarence R. Johnson the previous year, "despite the unbelievable graciousness of Francis, it remains a real hardship on his role as the minister of the Church, when I zoom in like a comet visiting the solar system, and zoom out again."[1]

Dear Howard:

It was a good Christmas this year—overflowing in all good things to wipe away the recollections of 1958. We had an enjoyable open house Sunday and a service of Carols and Candles Christmas Eve.

I am enclosing a copy of my booklet of Lenten Devotions just off the press. As you glance through them you will find your own contribution to my spirit, the categories that I use, the figures I choose and the words that I have selected. Your mind and spirit have been more influential in my own unfolding than any living person. I shall ever carry an authentic imprint upon my ministry and being because of you. It is not enough for me to express thanks or gratitude to you, for these words simply do not cover the depth and breadth of my appreciation. I am just glad that you are what you are and that I was around to receive what I received. I do not believe that it is by accident that people of similar temperaments and purpose are drawn together.

There are of course wide differences of approach as well as similarities. These differences, by their very nature, and by reason of the situation will result in clashes from time to time. I feel that the present is such a time. We have talked about these differences and tensions in the past. I have previously expressed myself to the effect that I felt that you were crowding me in the area of leadership channels. I know that your actions were motivated by what you believed to be the highest good of the church. I have felt at times that your active participation was not fair to me.

Certain things were accomplished by your continued interest and contribution. The idea of the church continued to be stated abroad in the land. Financial help continued to come in from outside interested people because of you and spiritual leadership was provided when you were in residence. However, these things were accomplished at a cost . . . to me and to the independence of the church. There are many ways in which you have and are helping the church. There are many ways in which a parent can help his teen age adolescent, many things that can be done for the youngster, but sometimes the "help" can be a hindrance to the development of necessary independence and self-sufficiency. There are things that a young church must do for itself if it is going to find its own destiny. It is just beginning to do this. I used to feel apologetic about what I considered to be my own ego involvement. Today I do not feel apologetic and I do feel that the shadow you cast upon the scene is unfair to me. I feel that you crowded me. (The 15th Anniv. intensified this.)

I know that you are sustained, as I am, by a network of rich personal relationships in Fellowship Church. I am not in any sense objecting to them for I know that they stand on their own.

There it is . . . off my chest. I have tried to be as honest as I know how to be. I am quite certain that some of what I have said has hurt you. I do not enjoy hurting anyone, least of all you, but I feel that these are the things that I must say if I am going to communicate with you on anything but a superficial level.

I want to talk with you about these things when you come out in February, for I feel that there is a kind of barrier between us, and I want to get at it. I would like to spend a day or an afternoon with you at the ranch . . . talking, thinking, reflecting about this. I want to do this for many reasons—not the least of which is my deep affection for you and concern for our friendship.

As ever,

[*signed*] Francis

TLS.

Note

1. To Clarence R. Johnson, 19 March 1958, printed in the current volume.

🌱 Letter in Support of United World Federalists
[*1960*]
[*Boston, Mass.*]

Thurman was an infrequent lender of his name to good causes, but world federalism was an issue close to his heart. For many liberals in the postwar period, strengthening the United Nations into an effective world government was the only way to prevent a third world war. For Thurman and other pacifists who shared his opinion, such as Martin Luther King, Jr.,[1] world government was the political equivalent of their spiritual belief that humanity's unity could transcend petty nationalisms and clashing sovereignties.

COPY (on UWF letterhead)
{draft of letter}
Dear Friend:

You may recall the article by Tracy Mygatt[2] in the October issue of Motive entitled "World Federation A Must."[3]

The concept of the application of enforceable law on the world level is daily gaining wider acceptance.

Today we see news of our leaders calling for the rule of law in the world. Delegations at the United Nations are asking that that body be transformed into a world government. Heads of state are stressing the need to sacrifice sovereignty.

For some time now I have been interested in the idea of a world federation with the necessary powers to preserve the peace. United World Federalists[4] as an organization is working in this direction through both a political and an educational program. Enclosed is a folder describing the organization.

The New England Branch of the United World Federalists has speakers available to talk on such subjects as World Federation, The Disarmament Problem, Inspection for Peace, The UN its strengths and Weaknesses.

Should any of your youth . . . or for that matter any other groups . . . desire a speaker in these or related fields you may advise the Branch office by using the enclosed envelope. This will be sent immediately to the Federalist Speakers Bureau nearest you.

I cordially commend the cause and those serving it. I would be happy if the New England Branch could be of help to you in your programming by making one of their speakers available to talk on whatever aspect of the problem is of greatest importance to your group.

Very truly yours,

Howard Thurman, Dean

Marsh Chapel

Boston University

TLc.

NOTES

1. In August 1959, after Tracy Mygatt sent King a copy of the article that Thurman mentions in his letter, King replied that though he was "not unmindful of the fact that there are many practical problems" in its implementation, "world government is the ideal toward which men of goodwill should work passionately and unrelentingly"; see Clayborne Carson, ed., *The Papers of Martin Luther King, Jr.*, vol. 5: *Threshold of a New Decade, January 1959–December 1960* (Berkeley: University of California Press, 2005), 255–56.

2. Tracy D. Mygatt (1885–1973) was a 1908 graduate of Bryn Mawr College. Often working closely with her lifelong companion, Frances M. Witherspoon (1886–1973), Mygatt dedicated her career to numerous pacifist, feminist, and world government causes. Mygatt was an official at the Campaign for World Government for thirty years, starting in 1941.

3. Tracy D. Mygatt, "World Federation—A Must," *motive* 18 (October 1957): 9–11.

4. United World Federalists was formed in 1947 through a merger of six smaller world federalist organizations. After World War II ended, there was a widespread feeling among liberals that the war had been caused by the breakdown of international order following World War I and the weakness of the League of Nations, and they looked to the United Nations as the first step toward an effective world government. The influence of United World Federalists waned in the 1960s. Nonetheless the organization continued to advocate for world peace, a ban on nuclear testing, and disarmament. Since 2003 United World Federalists has been known as Citizens for Global Solutions.

🌫 To WILLIAM J. TRENT, JR.

23 JANUARY 1960

[*BOSTON, MASS.*]

After leaving Howard University in 1944, Thurman had been concerned about his lack of regular contact with students at black colleges. From time to time he made visits to remedy this, as in a tour of three historically black colleges in early 1960 at the beginning of his sabbatical.[1] *This tour, which was paid for by the United Negro College Fund (UNCF), consisted entirely of informal discussion sessions without any public appearances, which was unusual for Thurman.*

Thurman found and helped inspire a new mood of activism among students at Tuskegee,[2] *and he probably had similar experiences at the other colleges he visited as well. Two weeks after his visit to Bennett College in Greensboro, four students from neighboring North Carolina A&T College, soon joined by students from Bennett, began the famous sit-in at a downtown Greensboro Woolworth's*[3] *luncheon counter, rekindling the civil rights movement in the South and triggering kindred protests throughout the region.*

Mr. William J. Trent, Jr.[4]
Executive Director
United Negro College Fund, Inc.
22 East Fifty-fourth Street
New York 22, New York

Dear Bill:

The experience on the campuses exceeded all possible expectations as far as the Thurmans are concerned. We returned to Boston completely exhausted but profoundly exhilarated. There is no time to write a re-action letter to you and I am not sure that that would be wise anyway. When I see you we can talk.

I am enclosing tickets for which you may be able to get a refund. We were driven from Tuskegee to Atlanta, so this is the unused part of the ticket. Do not think further about any of the expenses of the trip beyond actual transportation. Someone else is taking care of this.

The only thing that I can say to you is this. There is nothing that we could have done that could have been more significant on the campuses for us, and we hope for those whom we encountered, than this kind of journey, executed in this manner. That is all I can say now. We leave Boston January 28th, but mail sent here can reach me, until the first of March.

Sincerely yours,
Howard Thurman
Dean

                                                                TLc.

NOTES

    1. The Thurmans visited Hampton Institute (Hampton, Va.) January 11–13; Bennett College (Greensboro, N.C.) January 14–18; and Tuskegee Institute (Tuskegee, Ala.) January 19–22.

2. See From Charles V. Hamilton, 18 February 1960, printed in the current volume.

3. F. W. Woolworth's, founded in 1879, was a network of "five and ten cents stores" that at its height was probably the largest chain retail company in the world, with over five thousand outlets. Woolworth's closed its last American stores in 1997.

4. William J. Trent, Jr. (1910–93) was a 1930 graduate of Livingston College (where his father was college president). After teaching at Livingston and Bennett Colleges, he worked for the federal government from 1938 to 1944, first as adviser on Negro affairs for the Department of the Interior and then as an official of the Federal Works Agency. In 1944 he became the first executive director of the United Negro College Fund, a position he held for twenty years. In 1964 he became assistant personnel director for Time, Inc.

🐦 To Francis Geddes
25 January 1960
[*Boston, Mass.*]

Thurman responds to a letter[1] from Francis Geddes in which Geddes had complained that Thurman's continued involvement in the Fellowship Church as minister-at-large left him feeling "crowded" in the church and that it was preventing the church from becoming truly self-sufficient. In response, Thurman tells Geddes that he plans to ask the board to allow him to become minister emeritus. Thereafter his relation to the church will "be merely that of any member-at-large, with all of my active participation formally relegated to the past history of the Church."

Rev. Francis Geddes
Fellowship Church
2041 Larkin Street
San Francisco, California

Dear Francis:

I was very glad to get your letter and to have you express yourself so clearly and frankly to me about the psychological and spiritual problem that my involvement in Fellowship Church creates for you and your leadership. As you know, this has been very much on my mind ever since you have been there. It is due to my own feeling about this, you may recall, that I suggested the transfer of the Sunday service from Fellowship Church to the Unitarian Church.[2]

I want you to know that I understand the difficulties in the situation and also I understand how important it is that the Church and you be free to develop in ways that will fulfill what it is that God speaks to you during these times. Naturally, so much of our lives have been deposited in the life of the Church; we have paid with irreplaceable energy and heart for the privilege of being God's servant in a hard place at a hard time in the struggle for decency in human relations.

Further, I suppose as long as we live there will be people who will want to identify us with the life and the fate of the Church. This is inescapable.

I want you to know, Francis, that whatever you may feel about the way in which my "active participation was not fair" to you, it has been without malice on my part. I have wanted to do everything to free you and the Church from being tied to me. I see that none of the things that we have done in the past have been able to achieve this result. Therefore, I am making this proposal:

(1) I am writing a letter to the Chairman of the Board of Trustees of the Church, asking them to accept my resignation as minister-at-large and to give me the designation as Minister Emeritus.

(2) With this designation my relationship to the Church will be merely that of any member-at-large, with all of my active participation formally relegated to the past history of the Church.

(3) This will mean that I will not speak on behalf of the Church in any way that is official and will take no responsibility for its leadership at any point.

When I write my letter to the Board, I will take full responsibility for this decision. As a matter of fact, I had planned to do this anyway because the developments here are of such and my responsibilities in other ways are so heavy that it is necessary for me to pull in my horses and let some of them go to pasture. This is a convenient time to do it because the book is written for the record. We expect to be out of the country next summer and this breaks the regular, annual visit quite normally. I have already stated to you and to the person representing the Christmas card committee, that the card for 1959 was my last one, and this ends a period. I hope you will hold this letter in strictest confidence because I do not wish to have any embarrassing moments for you, for me or for the Church. I am making this decision with as much honesty and integrity as I possess, with the clear conviction that the Church and its future are more important than any personal sense of fulfillment which you or I may have or need to have.

I read your book of Meditation and am quite pleased with the quality of your insights and the creative way in which the whole thing is done. It is wonderful to have the sunlight in your face and there is no way by which we can guess that which God has in store for you in the long days that stretch out before you.
Sincerely,
Howard Thurman
Dean

                                                                    TLc.

NOTES

1. From Francis Geddes, 26 December 1959, printed in the current volume.

2. The service at the First Unitarian Church of San Francisco commemorating the fifteenth anniversary of the Fellowship Church was held on 6 September 1959.

✦ FROM CHARLES V. HAMILTON
18 FEBRUARY 1960
TUSKEGEE, ALABAMA

A young political science professor, Charles V. Hamilton,¹ writes to Thurman to tell him that Thurman's recent visit to Tuskegee Institute provided "impetus and stimulation" to Hamilton's students. Hamilton also updates Thurman on recent developments in the city's civil rights efforts.

Dr. Howard Thurman
Dean of the Chapel
Boston University
Boston, Mass.

Dear Dr. Thurman:

This comes as a kind of thank-you note for the impetus and stimulation you provided when you visited my class in American National Government.

Since that time, several of the students have been active in a way previously unknown to this campus. A mass civil rights rally was held on campus three weekends ago. The focus was a strong civil rights bill with effective voting provisions.² The students have since written approximately 383 letters to congressmen. They participated in a recent weekly mass meeting of the TCA.³ On this coming Saturday, Feb. 20, 1960, some 150–200 students will stage a protest march on downtown Tuskegee protesting voting denials.⁴ Recent events in Carolina⁵ and elsewhere have helped.

They are learning more political science than I could possibly convey in lectures.

Best regards to Mrs. Thurman, and good luck.

[*signed*] Charles V. Hamilton
Charles V. Hamilton

                                                                                    TLS.

NOTES

1. Charles V. Hamilton (1929–), a native of Oklahoma, graduated from Roosevelt University (1951) and obtained an M.A. from the University of Chicago (1957). He taught political science at Tuskegee Institute from 1958 to 1960, when his contract was not renewed. He received his Ph.D. from the University of Chicago in 1964 and taught from 1969 to 1998 at Columbia University, where after 1971 he was the W. S. Sayre Professor of Government and Political Science. He is the coauthor, with Stokely Carmichael, of *Black Power: The Politics of Liberation in America* (New York: Vintage, 1967) and the author of *Adam Clayton Powell, Jr.: The Political Biography of an American Dilemma* (New York: Atheneum, 1991).

2. Hamilton drafted the voting rights bill that the Tuskegee Civic Association submitted to Congress in 1959. See Robert J. Norell, *Reaping the Whirlwind: The Civil Rights Movement in Tuskegee* (New York: Knopf, 1985), 170.

3. This referred to the Tuskegee Civic Association, founded in 1941. Under the direction of its longtime leader, Charles G. Gomillion, dean of students and chair of the social sciences faculty at Tuskegee, the association tried to secure civil rights for black residents of Tuskegee. Its success in registering blacks to vote in the city led to a 1957 redistricting of Tuskegee that redrew the city's boundaries, eliminating almost all blacks from the city's voting rolls. In November 1960 in a landmark voting rights case, the U.S. Supreme Court ruled unanimously in *Gomillion v. Lightfoot,* 364 U.S. 339 (1960) that the legislative gerrymander was unconstitutional.

4. Hamilton spurned the gradualist strategy for advancing civil rights goals advocated by the leaders of Tuskegee Institute and the Tuskegee Civic Association; they in turn opposed the protest march as too confrontational. Hamilton's differences with the administration of Tuskegee Institute over civil rights tactics probably led to his dismissal from Tuskegee in spring 1960. See Norell, *Reaping the Whirlwind,* 171.

5. This referred to the sit-ins in Greensboro, North Carolina. See To William J. Trent, Jr., 23 January 1960, printed in the current volume.

❧ To Francis Geddes
[*May 1960*]
Aboard the *Carthage*[1]

Thurman wrote this letter in May 1960, part of his increasingly irate exchanges with Francis Geddes on the direction of the Fellowship Church.[2] *Geddes felt that he was in unfair competition with Thurman's legacy, and Thurman increasingly pulled back from involvement in the church.*

Dear Francis —

How wonderful it would have been for all concerned if what you said in your letter which came to-day would have been said earlier. But I guess the time was not ripe.

I appreciate your full letter. There is nothing to be gained by dragging out the correspondence. I think we understand the position and a bit of the attitude of each of us.

In fairness to what you are trying to accomplish under God at Fellowship Church I suggest strongly the following:

1. The Chairman of the Board should read the correspondence between us as Privileged. This would forestall any embarrassment in the future as far as any request which conceivably may come to me from the Board. Neither you nor I should be put in an awkward position.

2. The church should no longer handle my books, records, etc.—because this keeps alive an image that cannot be handled emotionally without jeopardizing the present and the future status of the church as it seeks fulfillment.

3. Some creative way must be found to let the congregation (membership) understand what is happening and some effective, helpful explanation that

is in the spirit of the Fellowship. Since I would be involved I would like to have copies of whatever written material may be sent out on this matter.

I have had some experience in letting individuals and institutions move on alone, independent of me. Fellowship Church is released as far as I am concerned. My prayer to God is that it will respond increasingly to the will and the mind of God as it moves resolutely into the days that are ahead.

You should now feel free and unencumbered in your leadership of the church.

[Howard Thurman]

ALc.

NOTES

1. The Thurmans were aboard the SS *Carthage* from 12 May 1960, when they embarked in Singapore, Mayala, until 28 May, when they disembarked in Alexandria, Egypt.

2. See To Francis Geddes, 25 January 1960; and subsequent to this letter, From Francis Geddes, 3 August 1960; and To Francis Geddes, 16 August 1960, all printed in the current volume.

🐟 FROM FRANCIS GEDDES
3 AUGUST 1960
SAN FRANCISCO, CALIF.

Geddes remains unhappy with the way Thurman's resignation as minister-at-large from the Fellowship Church was handled, in part because it has caused divisions in the congregation. He is also still smarting from what he believes to be a deliberate rebuff during Thurman's last trip to San Francisco in March. He includes in his letter a copy of a sermon, distributed to the entire congregation, in which Geddes explains why he thinks the Fellowship Church has to change.

Dear Howard . . .

We have just returned from vacation during the month of July. We spent most of it at the ranch and had a very relaxing, unbending healthful time. The children were in their element. David cannot understand why we cannot live at the ranch all of the time. I had some good discussions with Mrs. Small about a fuller utilization of the ranch toward its innate capacity: i.e. use as a place of reflection, study and renewal.

The annual meeting voted unanimously for your election as Minister Emeritus. Clarence Johnson[1] will be writing to you officially in the near future. The delay in not informing the congregation sooner of your request was unfortunate. Some of the members of long standing were quite unhappy and upset about the way it was handled and they certainly have a point. The board discussed this at the meeting last Monday and were in agreement that we should learn from that experience.

There seems to be developing a division in the church between the members of long standing (about 15 or 20 people) and the rest of the congregation. The older members could not understand why you resigned as Minister-at-Large. They were blaming Clarence Johnson, you for no longer being interested in the church, and they were unaware that I had anything to do with it. This kind of misunderstanding resulting in hurt mystification runs against my grain. I shared my exact role in your resignation with one church member who suggested that the thing would never be cleared up until it came to light and people got honest answers for honest questions instead of evasive manipulative rejoinders. After thinking on that suggestion for several weeks I felt it the most healthy and reasonable approach to the whole problem. I have told several of the members of long standing exactly what happened and why you resigned and why I put pressure on you to resign. Their response was in each case forthright and understanding placing no condemnation upon me or you. I feel much freer about the whole thing now and am as close to these people as ever . . . or even closer.

It is I suppose, part of the irony of existence that you and I . . . ministers of reconciliation are estranged. I am still rubbing the bruises of rebuff from your visit here in March. I asked to see you for a talk and you would not. I have casually talked to 3 or 4 people since then who mentioned in passing that they had seen you and talked with you which removes the excuse of a "pressing schedule." I am sure that you are still rubbing the bruises of rebuff suffered from my last letter. I am sure that the enclosed sermon will cause more bruises to result. I am sorry that it wounds you but that is the way I see it and I sent this to every member of the congregation (with very positive rejoinders on the most part) as a statement of my evaluation of the past and of my vision for the future. This sermon was brought about largely by the continual lament from members of long standing that Fellowship Church is not the way it used to be. It is my way of saying to them that as far as I see & lead I do not intend that it should be. The followers of John Wesley sought and in part succeeded in institutionalizing his dream and his genius.[2] Some of the members of long standing (whether they realize it or not) want to do just that here in Fellowship Church. They judge everything by the standards and experience of the years 1944–53 and are unhappy when things change. Fellowship Church, I have told some of them, does not have 39 Articles[3] and a close definition of belief and as a consequence the direction it takes will depend a great deal upon the minister who happens to serve the church. Whatever his gifts and capacities are . . . that will reflect in the direction the church takes . . . as it was in your case. My gifts are different from yours and I see different things of importance. That is why when you return to the scene you (certainly not by intent, but nonetheless effectively) recall people to the first decade of the church's life. I am not trying to duplicate the first decade, but when you leave that is the expectation of the members of long standing. That is why I say that you have been crowding me. Your new title of Minister Emeritus clarifies the situation and I appreciate your gesture, but I have a feeling that it is difficult for you to see the reason for it and for me the reason is so clear and unmistakable and right. However such differences between people are the stuff of existence and the material of tragic conflict. I do not want this conflict to destroy our friendship for I have love for you and I feel that you also have love for me . . . and somehow by the grace of God I hope that you and I can work this thing out with integrity and self respect on both sides. For we agree so strongly on the basic purposes, we both try to "win our way through life with dignity and honor" as best we can. If I have been unfair, unjust or unseeing . . . please be candid and state what you feel and think . . . only then can we work through this thing. I want to work it through and hope very much that we can, but please say what you really think and feel . . . otherwise we are lost.

Give my best love to Sue and tell her that she is close in my heart.
As ever,
[*signed*] Francis

TLS.

NOTES
    1. Clarence Johnson was the chairman of the board of directors of the Fellowship Church.
    2. John Wesley (1703–91), the Anglican divine who founded the Methodist movement, remained within the Church of England his entire career, although his followers created separate "Wesleyan" and Methodist denominations in Great Britain and the United States.
    3. The 39 Articles of Religion, first promulgated in 1563, are the defining dogmatic principles of the Church of England and for churches in the Anglican Communion.

🦋 To FRIENDS OF THE INTERNATIONAL FELLOWSHIP COMMUNITY
15 AUGUST 1960
EDINBURGH, SCOTLAND

In the spring of 1960 Thurman took his long-hoped-for sabbatical from Boston University. The dean of the School of Theology, Walter Muelder, hoped that in Thurman's respite from his "arduous duties at Boston University" he would find "restoration of powers, renewal of creative insights, and identification with man's deepest hurts and needs." To try to accomplish this, Thurman, who had rarely been outside North America since his return from India in 1936, spent much of the time—with his wife, Sue Bailey Thurman—on a six-month, round-the-world tour. As a prelude to the trip, the Thurmans spent an extended time in December and January touring black colleges in the South, where they met with faculty and students in informal gatherings.[2]

Before leaving on the six-month excursion, the Thurmans spent a few days in San Francisco, where Howard Thurman's failure to meet with Fellowship Church minister Francis Geddes contributed to their growing feud.[3] On 8 March the Thurmans left San Francisco on the SS President Wilson. After a brief stopover in Honolulu, they traveled by ship to Japan and then on to Hong Kong, the Philippines, Thailand, Malaya and Singapore, Ceylon, Egypt, Lebanon, Greece, Italy, France, and Great Britain, where they spent much of the last two months of their journey in an apartment in Edinburgh, Scotland, provided by their good friend Coleman Jennings, time spent in quiet "recollection and creative writing."[4] A reconstruction of the itinerary of the trip follows the current document.

On this trip—unlike the one to Asia a quarter-century earlier—the Thurmans were primarily tourists, although Thurman did do a fair amount of speaking and preaching, starting with the Church of the Crossroads in Honolulu.[5] He spoke at a Presbyterian conference in Manila organized by his old friend Frank Wilson[6] and had speaking engagements in Hong Kong, Cairo, and the Lebanese cities of Beirut and Sidon. Sue thought that Beirut, after San Francisco, was the most beautiful city she had ever seen.[7] One of the highlights of the trip for Thurman was a scheduled appearance as the Sunday preacher on 24 July in the famous London church St. Martin-in-the-Fields.

Thurman traveled twice by airplane on this trip; these were probably his first—and among his few—airplane flights. The Thurmans flew from Manila to Bangkok, a flight probably made necessary by the exigency and tightness of the schedule.[8] The Thurmans flew again from London to Boston due to a stevedores' strike in Britain and to Thurman's need to return to Boston for the beginning of the fall semester. He wrote semijocularly to a friend about the latter flight: "I did not believe that I would ever consent to that kind of violation of human decency but in order to get back to begin my work on September 17th I had to fly."[9]

Perhaps the most important part of the trip for the Thurmans was the chance to meet people from so many different cultures and backgrounds. They wrote from Edinburgh in August that "it was our privilege, too, to spend long evenings in good talk, among groups crossing all lines, with local and foreign 'nationals,' and visiting international friends closely associated, brooding together over the grave condition of a 'sick' world, probing deeply for solutions in lighted hearts and minds." The topics included the international refugee problem—a subject

that was discussed "from Hong Kong to the Damascus road"—and the fraught
future of the Congo, which received its independence from Belgium while the
Thurmans were on their journey.

Dear Friends of the International Fellowship Community,

We are sharing with you the last full days of a six-month voyage around the world by sending this communication from Edinburgh. Cards, letters, telegrams, cables have been in our minds for you many times, in many places, as we came upon some "tropical" or "highland" thing we knew would be of special interest to some particular friend. We have participated vicariously with you at home in avid daily reading of English Language Editions of periodicals published in the various countries from Waikiki to the British Isles.

This is a summary in brief, to be followed before year's end by a second more inclusive one, giving a few impressions concerned primarily with certain work assignments included in an otherwise leisurely sabbatical journey. It was farthest from our minds that the first of these would take place on our very first Sunday at sea. Without ever intending to be thus involved, when we went aboard the "SS President Wilson," H.T. consented, after a rather "pressing" invitation from the ship's Purser, to take the 11 o'clock worship service for passengers on the First Class Deck. The audience was composed of Americans, for the most part, who take vacations in the spring, and Orientals on official business to their homelands, scattered throughout Southeast Asia.

It was a usual order of service—the meditation period, the sermon, the music, with the one unusual feature—the harmony of human voices blending prophetically with the rhythm of the steamer and the diapason of the sea. The offerings contributed, (a sum of some $150) was designated according to custom, by the minister-of-the-day, for one of his own welfare interests, in this case, "Meals for Millions"[10] worldwide, non-sectarian service agency with international headquarters in Los Angeles.

Amidst the beauty of cherry blossoms which flooded the Japanese Islands in April, there were rare moments to visit unique institutions, many with which we have long been deeply concerned, marking the beginning point of a round-the-world circuit of International Churches. It was not quite the beginning, however, as we had spent a most fascinating afternoon at the Church of the Crossroads in Hawaii, (the day "SS President Wilson" lay in port) having as the finest of guides, our friend, Eloise Ewing, Executive Director of the YWCA of Honolulu, who was at one time a member of the Church for the Fellowship of All Peoples in San Francisco.

"The Union Church"[11] in Tokyo, (as such internationally-interracially-interdenominally- "inclusive" churches are called) is a singular congregation, like others found in international urban communities (especially capital cities) where foreign "nationals" in residence, as teachers, diplomats, service and business personnel, join the local community in church communion. H.T. gave the Palm Sunday sermon here, followed by an informal discussion hour with members of the congregation. Then there was a Sunday Evening Supper-Meeting at the Union Church in Kobe, and Sunday morning sermons or afternoon or evening meetings at Manila, Silliman College in Dumagetta,[12] Hong Kong, Cairo, Beirut; a baccalaureate address for combined schools of Sidon,[13] ending with the long-scheduled engagement at the Royal Parish Church of "St. Martin-in-the-Fields,"[14] London.

We were happy to find that with most "fraternal workers" (the new designation given missionary teachers and ministers from abroad,) a privileged task and duty remains to interpret with insight, knowledge, vision and sympathy, the dreams, aspirations, as well [as] the most complicated perplexities and problems, of the peoples with whom they have chosen to live their daily lives. They have become in many instances, seasoned students of world affairs, religions and cultures, having mastered most difficult languages, speaking and communicating in them with the facility of natives and developing within themselves an awareness and concern for dedication to commitment, which many of us at home could never understand.

So it was our privilege too, to spend long evenings in good talk, among groups crossing all lines, with local and foreign "nationals," and visiting international friends closely associated, brooding together over the grave condition of a "sick" world, probing deeply for solutions in lighted hearts and minds. We have heard discussions carried on with reason and understanding by partisans on various sides of the Refugee question, stretching all the way from Hong Kong to the Damascus Road. We dined with touring Belgians on vacation, an early summer afternoon in Greece. Independence had not yet come to the Congo, but there was a subtle memory among them, during the meal, of the dark past going back some decades, when in violent practice, the hands of men, women and children were cut off at the wrist, as punishment for default in bringing in the specified quota of rubber for King Leopold and his Belgian company. We wondered if the grand and great grandsons of executioners and victims alike had ever had a chance to discuss together the ravages of this vague, uneasy memory, depth calling to depth, during any of the intervening years leading up to June 30, 1960.[15]

If they had ever attended the various services of St. Martin-in-the-Fields, it is certain that this fine, historic old Church would have provided for them numerous occasions with quiet, unhurried hours together, to find, each for the other, forgiveness and atonement to replace and restore the severed hands of the early Congolese, in mutual commitment to the High Cause of Love's Magnificence, today!

St. Martin's is indeed a great, heartwarming institution. Although it is the Queen's Parish Church, and the Royal Boxes, or pews for use of the Royal Family, are located on either side of the chancel, the church seems to hold the Being of the Universal Spirit which its remarkable vicar, the Rev. Austen Williams[16] heightens for each participant in the total impact of morning and evening worship. We were intrigued to read of the long record of service this church has extended to all peoples with its strategic location on Trafalgar Square, going back to the reign of Henry VIII.

It has been written of this communion:

"St Martin's is loved and famed the world over for its work of encouraging humanity—the weary and heavy laden who, in this modern world of tension and bewilderment, are legion.

"There are well over 50 organizations and activities within St. Martin's. You could 'stand in' for a day with the Social Service Unit and witness the endless stream of people with every type of problem and difficulty, or attend one of the many parties given to extend a welcome and hospitality to hundreds of colonial students and overseas visitors. You could spend an hilarious afternoon with the Darby and Joan Club, visit one of the activities for the young and old, watch the Scrub Club clean the Church, visit a group of the blind, accompany the Parish visitors, listen to the music of the Academy of St. Martin-in-the-Fields[17] or see a little of the help given towards the vast world refugee problem—and you would have experienced but a few of St. Martin's facets.

"As you have affection for this church, so you can help maintain and expand its tradition of service to mankind—heedless of race, colour or creed."

On the Sunday that H.T. preached at St. Martin's, we were delighted to have in the audience a former member of Fellowship Church, a young woman now engaged in conducting Study Groups on Religion for prisoners in an English penitentiary, as well as a present member of the Women's Committee of Marsh Chapel. This London engagement with two others in Manchester and Bristol, under auspices of a British-American Pulpit Exchange, ended the work assignments as such, for this tour.

In the communication which comes later, we shall try to describe other aspects of this journey: the "laughter learnt of friends and gentleness in hearts at peace"; the smile on the face of Joey and Phyllis Van Pelt's[18] baby daughter, as she was being dedicated in Osaka, Japan, with attending tea ceremonial and music played on the ancient "Noh" instrument; the sharing in a conference in the Philippines, with an old, old friend, Frank Wilson,[19] whose tremendous responsibility for Presbyterian Schools and Colleges overseas, takes him constantly by air to all parts of the world; and finally coming for rest and for creative activity in beloved Edinburgh, with our cherished companion of the "high road," Coleman Jennings, and the amazing "C.J. Fellowship"[20] of Scottish men, women and children, which he, an American, established in this city over 32 years ago.

A dear friend provided us with a "Rolex,"[21] and another with a petite "Sony"[22] for this journey, so that later in time, because of the eager travellers' gift of "second," "Third" and "fourth" sight, you may receive "impressions" of a thousand golden sunsets taken from ocean, land and sky.

We shall be very happy to be with you all again, at home, or on another global voyage to come.

With warmest good wishes
[*signed*] Howard and Sue Thurman
Howard and Sue Thurman

TLcS.

Itinerary for the Thurmans' Around-the-World Trip[23]

Date	Departures and Arrivals[24]
March 8	Leave San Francisco
March 24	Arrive Yokohama, Japan[25]
April 18	Leave Yokohama[26]
April 24	Arrive Hong Kong
April 28	Leave Hong Kong
May 1	Arrive Manila, Philippines
May 5	Leave Manila (by air)
May 5	Arrive Bangkok
May 10	Leave Bangkok (by train)
May 12	Arrive Singapore[27]
May 13	Arrive Penang, Malaya
May 17	Arrive Colombo, Ceylon[28]
May 28	Arrive Alexandria, Egypt
June 8	Leave Alexandria
June 9	Arrive Beirut, Lebanon
June 12	Leave Beirut
June 17	Arrive Athens[29]
June 24	Leave Athens
June 26	Arrive Naples
June 27	Leave Naples (by train)
June 27	Arrive Rome
July 1	Leave Rome (by train)
July 2	Arrive Paris
July 5	Leave Paris

July 6   Arrive Edinburgh (by ferry and train)

September 6?[30]   Leave London, Arrive Boston (by air)

SOURCES: "Itinerary for the Rev. Dr. & Mrs. Thurman" (c. 8 March 1960); To Dear Friend, 15 March 1960 [I]; To Dear Friend, 15 March 1960 [II].

NOTES

   1. From Walter Muelder, 18 November 1959.

   2. See To William J. Trent, Jr., 23 January 1960, printed in the current volume.

   3. See From Francis Geddes, 4 August 1960; To Francis Geddes, 16 August 1960, both printed in the current volume.

   4. To E. H. Hall, 19 September 1960.

   5. This was perhaps the first consciously interracial church in the United States. See "Biographical Essay," PHWT, 3:xlviiin72.

   6. Frank Theodore Wilson (1900–1988) was a native of Maxton, North Carolina, and spent his early childhood in Greensboro and Wadesboro, North Carolina. He graduated from Lincoln University, Pennsylvania, with an A.B. (1921) and an S.T.B. (1924), and from Columbia University (M.A. 1932; Ed.D, 1937). From 1924 to 1935 he was national student secretary for the YMCA. Wilson was dean of men and professor of education and psychology at Lincoln University from 1936 to 1949 and dean of the School of Religion at Howard University from 1949 to 1957. From 1957 to 1967 he was secretary for education of the Commission on Ecumenical Missions and Relations of the United Presbyterian Church, U.S.A., a position that required extensive travel in several nations in Asia, Africa, Latin America, and the Middle East, including an extended stay in South Korea. He subsequently (1968–70) was executive secretary of the Commission on Theological Education in the Southeast and later served as chairman of the board of directors of the Interdenominational Theological Center in Atlanta. He was the author of *Black Presbyterians in Ministry* (New York: United Presbyterian Church, 1978). In his autobiography Thurman called Wilson "my oldest friend" (*WHAH*, 183).

   7. Margaret Harding? to Coleman Jennings, 20 June 1960.

   8. *WHAH*, 183.

   9. To Boice Gross, 19 September 1960.

   10. The Meals for Millions Foundation was founded in California in 1946 originally to help the malnourished in Europe. In 1987 it merged into the Freedom from Hunger Foundation.

   11. The Union Church in Tokyo, in which missionaries of various Christian denominations collaborated on regular services, was organized in 1872, the year after a similar Union Church began operations in Kobe.

   12. Silliman University in Dumaguete was established by the Presbyterian Board of Foreign Missions in 1901 and was the first private American college in the country. It remains one of the premier institutions of higher learning in the Philippines.

   13. In Lebanon.

   14. Designed by James Gibbs, the current building of St. Martin-in-the-Fields on Trafalgar Square, London, opened in 1724. The parish originally dates to the thirteenth century.

15. King Leopold II of Belgium (1835–1909) established the Congo Free State in central Africa as his personal domain in 1885. The horrendous exploitation of the native population over the next two decades—which led to the death and mutilation of several million native inhabitants—was chronicled in Joseph Conrad's novella *Heart of Darkness* (1899) and other works and became a major international scandal. The colony became known as the Belgian Congo in 1908 after Leopold was forced to relinquish his personal control of the territory. Independence in 1960 brought the Congo further misery, as Cold War rivalries stoked the outbreak of a bloody and prolonged civil war.

16. Austen Williams (1907–87) was ordained in 1938. A German POW from 1940 to 1945, he was the vicar of St. Martin-in-the-Fields from 1956 to 1984. He achieved considerable acclaim for his work with the parish's Social Service Unit, organized in 1948.

17. The Academy of St. Martin in the Fields, one of the premier classical chamber orchestras in the world, gave its first concerts in November 1959.

18. For Joseph Van Pelt, see From Joseph Van Pelt, 12 March 1953, printed in the current volume.

19. For Frank Wilson, see *PHWT*, 1:194–95.

20. The C. J. Fellowship was a social club for young people, similar to a settlement house, that Jennings started in a poor neighborhood of Edinburgh in the late 1920s. See Coleman Jennings, "A Growing Edge—In Scotland," *The Growing Edge* 5, no.1 (Winter 1952–53): 1–8. Jennings adopted Edinburgh as a second home.

21. A camera manufactured by the Toko Seiko Company in Japan.

22. A small camera.

23. The available documentation for the Thurmans' trip is scarce. This table relies on an itinerary available prior to their departure, To "Dear Friend," 15 March 1960, as modified by other correspondence. The reconstructed itinerary is as precise as the evidence permits.

24. All travel was by ship unless otherwise noted.

25. With a one-day port of call in Honolulu.

26. While in Japan the Thurmans visited Yokohama, Tokyo, Osaka, Kyoto, and Kobe.

27. The details of the Thurmans' stay in the Federation of Malaya and Singapore are difficult to reconstruct. If as in "Itinerary 8 March" and "Dear Friend I" there was a stop in Indonesia, the Thurmans would have traveled from Djakarta to Singapore by ocean liner through the Straits of Malacca to Singapore and then by train to Bangkok. However, if as in "Dear Friend II" there was no stop in Indonesia, they went by sea from Manila to Bangkok and rail from Bangkok to Singapore and then traveled by steamship to the port of Penang, in northern Malaya, and then on to Ceylon.

28. Because of Thurman's aversion to air travel, the Thurmans' planned stop in India was omitted.

29. The five days allotted to travel by boat from Beirut to Athens probably included stopovers in the Greek Islands.

30. The date is conjectural. However, given Thurman's air travel phobia, the Thurmans' departure was undoubtedly delayed until it was clear that returning to Boston by air was absolutely necessary for Thurman to be on campus by the start of the semester.

❧ TO FRANCIS GEDDES
16 AUGUST 1960
EDINBURGH, SCOTLAND

In an angry response to Francis Geddes's letter on the future direction of the Fellowship Church, Thurman disputes Geddes's analysis of the situation facing the church and of his own role in several personal conflicts between the two men. In the first part of the letter, Thurman analyzes a sermon that Geddes had preached the prior April and which was subsequently printed and distributed to the congregation. The sermon, which is not extant, is described by Geddes as challenging longtime members of the church who "judge everything by the standards and experience of the years 1944–53 [that is, the years of Thurman's ministry] and are unhappy when things change."[1] Thurman disputes Geddes's charge that he has prevented the church from changing and sees in Geddes's statements about the church an attempt to reorient the church away from a concern with interracialism and racial equality. In stinging words Thurman writes that Geddes is suggesting "what white Protestant ministers in Alabama, Georgia etc. north or south have been saying since reconstruction."

Geddes's actions increased the factional divisions within the church.[2] In a letter written to Thurman in May 1961, Geddes asked for a meeting with Thurman and for an attempt at reconciliation, and he called the tension in the church "demonic," resulting from "the bad feeling between you and me. It takes first one form then another. It goes on and on and on. I am sick of seeing innocent people sucked into its down-pulling vortex."[3] It appears that Thurman did not preach at the Fellowship Church again while Geddes remained minister. When Clarence Johnson, chair of the board of trustees, asked Thurman to preach at the church in the summer of 1961, it came as a "complete surprise" to Thurman because Geddes had "made it clear and unmistakable in a series of letters, that [Thurman's] coming back to the church on invitation year after year, not only violated 'ministerial ethics' but also so 'crowded' his ministry that his leadership of the church was seriously threatened and hamstrung."[4] Geddes resigned from the church in March 1963 after serving as its minister for seven years.[5] Thurman would write his good friend Herbert King the following year that "one of the poisonous bits of propaganda under the regime of Francis Geddes was the rumor that I kept the church from settling down with him in anticipation of the time when I would return and become the pastor. It was aided and abetted by certain delusions of grandeur which many people had with reference to the almighty significance of the Fellowship Church."[6] The deterioration of the relationship between Geddes and Thurman was

a sad one, as two men similar in many respects and who shared a common minis-
try of reconciliation, as Geddes noted in earlier correspondence, became estranged.

Dear Francis

Your amazing letter passed mine to you somewhere over the North Pole. I was glad to hear from you. You ask me to say to you how all this that has come to pass seems to me.

I begin with your sermon. Rarely do I permit myself the indulgence of thinking critically about another man's sermon—when I hear it, either it reaches me or it does not. However I want to say something about the implications of what you said on April 24, 1960.

I. Your insistence that the church should walk into the future with the face in the same direction—that the church should not <u>back</u> into the future facing the past—this is obvious and true. That is why I said at the fateful meeting last fall at the Unitarian Church that as soon as we get our altars built we must tear them down and build new ones out of what has come to us during the previous process.

II. When you interpret the above point to mean that the past has to be renounced, then I am of the mind that this is simply suicidal. A part of <u>your</u> leadership must be in teaching the people <u>how</u> to relate to the past, and to draw upon the past for inspiration for the future, and for wisdom that will keep them from making in the present whatever mistakes were made in the past.

III. On page 2 at the top you say that the fact that an integrated church can work and maintain itself has been demonstrated. I wonder, in the context of your sermon, what on earth that sentence means. If you are talking about the demonstration at a particular moment in time <u>yes</u>—but as long as America is prejudice ridden, as long as there is as much sheer religious, class and racial prejudice with basic discrimination, as there is even in our beloved San Francisco, such a demonstration has to be continuous. Whatever tradition it has developed has to be a <u>living</u> tradition. Fellowship Church has not been able to maintain even an authentic interracial character or quality. At this point the Jungle Growth of our society has closed in upon it. At the present time the church lags behind the tradition. There can be no escape from the past by an attitude of hostility toward the past.

IV. Further on that page you state that the need to-day is to make an impact on one another as over against (the inference is yours) the community. What on earth are you talking about? The impact needs to be made in the community now as never before—15 years ago things were fluid but to-day the social patterns are set and it is a far tougher job to make a community impact. Of course fundamental to the total enterprise of the Church is the necessity to witness among one another to what God has done in the life. To make the Church a probing instrument in group therapy without keeping the context in which such probing takes place crackling with a challenge that makes such probing instrumental to the Kingdom of God, is a very dreadful procedure. To forsake the community is to become a <u>swamp</u> where the water of life rots and all living things die, except that which thrives on decay. The witness in the community is needed, even the interracial emphasis. For the past 4 years I have had more trouble trying to find a* suitable place to live than in 1943.[7] My present real estate man asked permission even to use my name in the hope that this may make it simpler or easier. One member of Fellowship Church who dabbles in real estate had to admit to me that when this person talked to their regular agent, the agent refused to try because the racial situation is so touchy. <u>How</u> to make a 1960 impact in the community requires new insight, wisdom and courage—new techniques must be found but to say that it is no longer true to the commitment in the present to make such an impact in the community, is sheer nonsense. This is what white Protestant ministers in Alabama, Georgia etc. north or south have been saying since reconstruction. This was the basis of opposition to us in 1943—this was the real basis of the withdrawal of the support and sanction of the Presbyterian Church.

V. You do not say <u>what</u> the new approach is that you are suggesting. What is it—that money be sent to Africa or to the Freedom Groups in the South? That there should be a new way to regard the past? If so, how must the past be regarded by your parishioners—since most of them have no way, at present, of relating to the past? Or is the new approach the fact that the Commitment Explorers are at work? Of course it may be that I would know the answer to this if I were a part of the pastoral parish.

VI. Finally for the sermon—Your existential insistence upon the NOW is very important. There is no sense of crisis and collapse in the midst of which comfortable middle class Americans are trying to find answers of resolution. There is certainly no such sense of crisis in Fellowship Church. So the only sense in which the NOW has meaning is in the original way that it was used by Carlyle, who in a remote sense may have clued the present group. There is no NOW apart from the past and the future![8] To deny the validity of either, is to escape the demands and the responsibility for one's reaction <u>to</u> the present or <u>to</u> the past or <u>to</u> the future. No, Francis, what the Church needs desperately is a <u>sense of Cause</u>. Something has to be at <u>stake</u>. Where this is not present the people must take it out on each other in ways that are positive and destructive rather than positive and constructive.

Now I come to a few comments on your letter to me. Francis, what do you mean when you say that <u>you</u> put pressure on me to resign? When you wrote me saying that I was "crowding you," is that what you mean by 'putting pressure' on

*(A place with a view and the location advantageous for creative writing and creative retirement.)

me? What are the facts? (1) Several years ago I suggested that I should not come back to the church in the summer to preach but that there should be the public meeting at the Unitarian Church etc. As two men we talked this out—but I took the responsibility. (2) At the Retreats it was my insistence from the very first that you take charge and relate what I was doing to your program in the church. (3) At no time would I ever take the Meditation Period on Sunday. (4) Not once did I ever ask you how you were doing because I did not want you to feel that in any sense you were reporting to me. (5) Any matters involving my work as minister at large, I dealt were handled directly and openly with you & the Board. All of this you know. But what you do not know is the vast amount of time and painstaking care that I have used in doing, what at certain times I was uniquely able to do, on your behalf, in the congregation, which in the nature of the case you could not do for your self.

Now I think if you are going to tell a few key people, or anyone else, about the circumstances surrounding the voluntary decision on my part to resign, you ought in fairness to the facts and the truth give the complete picture. You should know me well enough to be assured that you could not pressure me into withdrawing from involvement with Fellowship Church, into which a lifetime of dreaming and commitment are deposited. Only my love for the Church and my love for you would make me do it.

In my previous letter I said that I was too involved to put the time and energy into a long talk with you. Yes, I saw several people for casual visits and in two or three instances some business or counseling concerns and several others for the sheer joy of seeing them. When I spoke to you on the phone I meant it when I said that I hoped that we could get together. Subsequently this was not possible in terms of the thing that I felt we would need to do.

Your letters and your sermon do not bruise me. They bring to me a very great sadness because of their hostility. I wonder what you are really fighting, Francis. What is there that is being so threatened by what I symbolized that you must strike out against it? What is the real enemy or who is the real antagonist of your spirit? To flare out against me is fighting windmills. You have insight surely to see what is happening to your own spirit. I want you to know that I am making no pretense at generosity or arrogant piety when I say that my love for you is undimmed. I think that you are up against a tough situation which makes demands of energy and strength which then must keep you hard put to it. I know somewhat of the problems of Fellowship Church which you inherited plus those that have emerged in more recent years.

When the congregation and I went through the months of preparation for my leaving to go to Boston to test the idea of an inclusive religious fellowship in a metropolitan university setting, it was the collective judgment that a line of continuity would should be maintained between the local congregation and me as well as between the national [and] international members and me. The idea was new that such a church could in various ways give a ministry of inspiration and some guidance to members-at-large scattered over the world. The church felt a real responsibility to do more than keep its hand out for financial support from these members. It must be remembered as a matter of record, that with the exception of $500– given by Alice Fahey, every dime of the $30,000– for the present building and $2500– of the $5000 spent for refurbishing, came from members-at-large. Even the $500 referred to was given before Alice became a member of the Church. Now with the new emphasis of concentration on the "we-group" urgencies of the Church, there is no need for the emphasis that would envision a wider service. The office of Minister-at-large was functional when the emphasis was different—There really is no place for it now. Had your letter which you claim, precipitated the present developments, never been written (as I think I intimated earlier some months ago) a change of status for me in relation to the Church would have been forthcoming. In due course I will be replying to Clarence and the Board with reference to the good letter which came from him yesterday.

The Purpose of God is greater than our purposes and I [*illegible*] you [*illegible*] together may continue to search.

Sincerely,

[*signed*] Howard

ALcS.

NOTES

1. From Francis Geddes, 3 August 1960, printed in the current volume.

2. The following November, Thurman received a letter from a member of the congregation who refused to go to dinner with Geddes and wrote about the necessary "unpleasantness of getting rid of Mr. Geddes" (From Coffee Henderson, 14 November 1960).

3. From Francis Geddes, 12 May 1961.

4. To Clarence Johnson, 5 April 1961.

5. Francis Geddes to John Sergeant, 4 February 1963. Geddes resigned, effective 31 March 1963, and became director of the Religious Research Foundation in San Francisco.

6. To Herbert King, 3 April 1964.

7. That is, Thurman was beginning to look for a suitable place to live in San Francisco after his retirement from Boston University.

8. Thomas Carlyle wrote, "The Present time, youngest-born of Eternity, child and heir of all the Past Times with their good and evil, and parent of all the Future . . . ," in "The Present Time," in *Latter-Day Pamphlets* (London: Chapman and Hall, 1850), 1. Thomas Carlyle (1795–1881) was a Scottish philosopher and essayist.

ॐ "WINDBREAK . . . AGAINST EXISTENCE"
FALL 1960

In this article in Bostonia, the alumni magazine of Boston University, Thurman discusses the significance of his recently completed around-the-world trip and its relevance to his work at Marsh Chapel.[1]

Dr. Thurman, Dean of Marsh Chapel, has just returned from a global tour, where he studied world conditions. *Bostonia* asked for his observations on the problems that most plague the world.

During my life I found that I received great spiritual strength from an oak tree. That oak tree was my windbreak against existence.

How many people the world over have their oak trees? How many people have something, a symbol, from which they gain spiritual strength?

Somewhere in man's journey, certainly my own journeys, I had to learn how to honor cultural and theological barriers, without making them roadblocks to communication and understanding. The basis for this in my life was rooted in the things that happened to me in early childhood in Florida.

My response to these events turned me to religion and determined my ultimate vocational choice. This choice with its unique emphasis led successively from Howard University, as Dean of Rankin Chapel, to the organizing of the Church for the Fellowship of All Peoples in San Francisco. And then to Boston University as Dean of Marsh Chapel.

What I had to find, as a growing boy, was some inner resource that could give me enough immunity to the violence of my environment to enable me to have a sense of normalcy and worthwhileness in being a human being.

There were many violences in my earlier life. Perhaps the one that left its profoundest mark was the funeral service of my father. It was conducted by an itinerant evangelist. Here was a man, knowing nothing about my father, condemning his soul to hell because he was not a member of the church.[2]

Of course, at the early age of seven, this did not seem too serious at first. But as I grew older, this trauma became more meaningful. As a result, I felt that I had to find something that could meet the devastations of this experience in a creative and sustaining manner.

I can remember in the backyard of our home there was a huge oak tree—to the small boy, the "canopy of God"—my windbreak against existence. Whenever life was rough I would go to my sacred oak tree, and with my back against it, would talk things over. It was the one thing in our yard that did not give when the seasonal hurricanes came.[3]

Again and again during these years I turned to my oak tree which became more and more not only a windbreak against existence, but also a trysting place where I met and communed with God.

Symbolically, my whole universe apparently turned on whether or not the tree would give in to the storm. Always it stood.

Throughout my career, I have had a great deal of interest in other people, other races, and other creeds. While I was at Howard University in 1935, I was chairman of the Pilgrimage of Friendship from America to Students of India, Burma, and Ceylon. It was in this connection that Mrs. Thurman and I went to India to speak to student groups in nearly one hundred educational centers in these three countries.

It was during this trip that I became aware of other people in the other countries of the world. What could we do to bring about a better understanding of all people of different races and religion?

Organizing the Church for the Fellowship of All Peoples in San Francisco pointed the way to a partial answer to this searching question.

The ministry of Marsh Chapel here at Boston University is a fundamental religious undertaking seeking still additional answers within the framework of an urban University whose roots go deep into the soil of a Protestant Christian tradition, but whose constituency is made up of many races, cultures, and religions.

It is important to have a sense of the other person's fact—whatever it may be. This is a never-ending quest upon which all communications between peoples rest.

Two months ago, Mrs. Thurman and I returned from a trip around the world. On our journey we read scores of books in an unhurried atmosphere of the sea voyage. These books deepened our own knowledge of the peoples and the struggles in which they were engaged in the major countries along our way.

You have asked me to make some observations on the problems that face mankind, particularly those that were so conspicuous during our trip.

In Japan, the people we met and with whom we talked were anxious that we understand those student-friends of democracy and the American people who were opposed to any treaties which did violence to the great creative expression for peace found in the original Japanese constitution to which we gave our blessing.[4]

They were opposed to anything that might portend a future Hiroshima for themselves, or mankind anywhere.

In Hong Kong, the vast problems of dislocation, hunger, deprivation of dwelling place—the utter loss of a sense of "home"—was overwhelming. The story was the same wherever refugees were found, from Hong Kong to Europe.

In the Philippines, there were many American fraternal workers in schools, colleges, and churches who shared deeply in the journey of that nation from the status of a ward of America, to subsequently being captives of the Japanese, to all the full-blown glory and responsibility of national freedom.

It was arresting in Egypt to see the enormity of the task of finding a way to communication between peoples who are finding their roots watered afresh by a rebirth of an ancient faith. It is a faith with vast overtones of nationalism. Here also are people of the West with all the burden of the guilt of a necessitous imperialism.

Herein is the great challenge which Marsh Chapel represents to me. Any Sunday morning there are present in the congregation men and women from the ends of the earth, often of varied creeds, faiths, and cultures. Here is a service addressed to the deepest needs and aspirations of the human spirit.

When I conducted religious services on board ship crossing the Pacific, or preached at the Union Church in Tokyo, or lectured at the American University[5] in Beirut, or gave the sermon at Saint Martin's in the Field, the Royal Parish Church of London—there was but an extension of the ministry of the Chapel itself, the same challenge, the same cross-section, the same timeless urgencies.

Now, there can be no peace in the world as long as you have hunger, desperation, poverty, and insecurity among so large a number of people. And I do not have a sense of being able to do very much about this.

As long as there are situations such as these in the world, we must remember that whenever the people themselves are ripe to be exploited of any way of life, to them it is a means to an out.

In the competition between ideologies and ways of life between East and West, one of the elements that we are trying to capture in such a struggle is not merely the minds of men, but it is their stomachs as well. This to me is very important.

There is an old Zulu adage which says: "Full belly child says to empty belly child, 'Be of good cheer.' Only the empty belly child has the right to say to the empty belly child, 'Be of good cheer.' A full belly child cannot tell the empty belly child to be of good cheer."

What can we do, individually and collectively?

First, we must find the way by which we can confirm our own faith in the values which are important, and at the same time, include in the confirmation of those values the redemption of the stomachs of people.

Next, I am convinced that whatever moral, spiritual, and political leadership we will be able to give to the world will be hampered by, or helped by, what we do in our own country in the areas of anti-Semitism, anti-Negroism, and the other anti-isms that contradict the philosophy of our way of life.

This is axiomatic to me. Therefore, I feel that it is important in an entirely fresh dimension for me to deepen my own sense of urgency about the mission which I have felt all of my life. My trip confirmed this urgency.

It is with profound sincerity that I say I wish I were five hundred people with an experience such as I have had. This is the way I feel about it and these are the things which I am willing to do in connection with them, rather than being just one person who puts his pants on, one leg at a time, like everybody else.

The feeling is just that urgent, and I think that we have a wonderful opportunity in this country to spread this feeling. Almost everywhere in the world we have foreign students who have been in this country. Mrs. Thurman and I encountered in most every country and city someone we had known, or who knew us in our work in San Francisco and university campuses, or who had studied, visited, or lectured in the United States.

Alumni of Boston University extended warm and gracious courtesies to us in all places. Mrs. Thurman, as chairman of the first Hostess Committee for International Students at Boston University, was given "art tokens" by several distinguished and beloved graduates in the Far East to bring back to the Campus. Several of these will be added to the art collection and will grace the serving tables during our Marsh Chapel Sunday morning coffee hours.

It seems to me that the opportunity to be influential in any of these countries is at our doorstep.

Here in our own Boston University, where we have some eight hundred students from all over the world, we have an opportunity that should not be neglected. Some of these students will later make policies by which our children will be profoundly affected.

But of extreme importance is for us to be aware of this without being pompous.

Another factor which certainly does not aid the world situation is that of exclusiveness. This was portrayed so vividly to me in London. There I learned that the high-turbaned Sikhs from India, many of whom live in London, were denied jobs as conductors on the trams. The rules called for standard conductor hats.

Any kind of exclusiveness is not a luxury, but a death potion. And I say that with joy, for it is this insight which has been a part of my life, most of my life.

Such insight hasn't been developed because of the threatening things I see in the environment. Rather, it is fundamental in my thoughts to the very meaning of life. I do not think that I can ever be what I ought to be as long as there is any single human being anywhere in the world who is being held up because of conditions over which he is unable to exercise any control.

I think that my freedom is locked up in his.

The final earthly security for any man is in another man's heart; the heart must be a swinging door.

One of the things that has been a watchword of mine all through these years is a phrase from Eugene Debs. He said before his death, "While there is a lower class, I am in it; while there is a criminal element, I am of it; and while there is a man in jail, I am not free."

As a religious man, I feel that God cannot be what God is destined to be in the world as long as any man is being held back and held down.

I think that wherever a man is in prison, God is in prison. And in the things that work for his release, life is on their side. The things that work to hold them there, life is against. That is why I will never become discouraged.

It doesn't matter how high the odds are, because the things that work for bigotry and discrimination—all of these things—life is against and they cannot abide.

With absolute confidence I work, and knowing that my responsibility is to do everything I can not to be one to keep the key in the lock of the prison house. That is my job.

Reprinted with permission from *Bostonia* (Fall 1960): 7–9.

PD.

NOTES

1. A marginal note accompanying the article states, "as told to Bradford Evans and Waldo Hart."

2. See *WHAH*, 4–6.

3. See *WHAH*, 8–9. As of 2016 the same live oak tree still stood in the backyard of Thurman's childhood home at 614 Whitehall Street in Daytona.

4. Clause 9 of the 1947 Japanese Constitution, adopted when Japan was under American military occupation, states that "the Japanese people forever renounce war as a sovereign right of the nation and the threat or use of force as a means of settling international disputes." The peace clause, though controversial, remains in effect. The Japanese Self-Defense Forces serve as a de facto military force for Japan.

5. American University in Beirut was founded in 1866 by American missionaries as Syrian Protestant College. It has been known under its current name since 1920.

🌱 To the Chairman and Board of Directors of Fellowship Church
29 September 1960
Boston, Mass.

Writing to the board of trustees of Fellowship Church, Thurman provides a more complete explanation for his decision to resign as minister-at-large. As Francis Geddes explained to Thurman,[1] some congregation members viewed Thurman's resignation as a rejection of the Fellowship Church. Geddes, however, saw Thurman's resignation as largely a response to Geddes's request that Thurman lower his profile in the church. In this letter Thurman makes clear that his decision to resign was based in part on his considerable responsibilities in Boston and in part on the lack of a national dimension to Fellowship Church, which made the position of minister-at-large superfluous.

To the Chairman and Board of Directors
of the Church for the Fellowship of All Peoples

Dear Friends:

I have returned to Boston and to my work in the University at Marsh Chapel. This is being written to you in response to the very gracious letter received from the Board Chairman[2] while we were in Scotland ending the six months journey around the world. I was happy to hear from him and from you through him, for I had wanted since early last summer to send you just such an interpretative communication as this letter purports to be.

I am sorry that it was not possible for me to present in person to the Board and the membership my resignation as minister-at-large of Fellowship Church. But, with this an impossibility, in the very nature of the case, its presentation occasioned discussion, conjecture and mystery which I deeply regret. I want in this communication to throw as much light on the whole situation as my point of view might make possible.

You know much of the history of the Church, both written and unwritten, but perhaps I should state its concept in my mind, as the manifestation of a movement having its beginning in a more or less ideal setting, such as San Francisco, and then as a movement, not as an organization, spreading to other regions in which it was more difficult to form community. I left my post at Howard University with the idea of associating in the creating of such a movement. I would never have left the broad field of service in Washington for any other reason.

The Church was inaugurated, Sunday, October 8, 1944, with "national associate" members signing commitment cards at the same time as the group of local personnel who joined the Fellowship during those crucial days. Mrs. Franklin D. Roosevelt, Mrs. Mary McLeod Bethune, Dr. Channing Tobias, and others became members during this period. And why did we have national associate members? Because many people were living in communities that had no "inclusive" religious fellowship of any kind, north, south, east and west; and they wanted to share, even if only to be "present in spirit," with the all-inclusiveness of the worship of God, which took place at Fellowship Church in San Francisco.

They wanted also to help with the burden of financial support that such an "inclusive" church would be compelled to sustain: the salaries of co-ministers, later the minister and well paid assistant minister, the executive director in charge of program activities, the organist, choir director, etc. The local congregation gave generously to the support of their local program with many member "tithers" among them. It was for this reason that national associates and friends at large, were eager to contribute their part in absentia, by paying with their offerings in large and small amounts, for the property at 2041 Larkin, thus leaving the local members free to carry on an extensive program that elicited from all, their individual gifts with personal dedication. In terms of the independence of the local congregation, under the judgment of our total commitment, this made possible the growing experience of a sense of the working out of God's purpose here in our midst.

When after nine years at Fellowship Church I made the decision following long formal and informal discussion with the Board and the congregation, to convey the Fellowship dream to Boston University, and into a yet more difficult environment, it seemed only wise and just that we not disturb the national-member-at-large program, but maintain a relationship even with summer and winter internes from the East in residence at Fellowship Church representing various denominations, who would take the spirit of the dream back into the churches awaiting them. Some of you will remember Jim Brewer, an interne from Harvard Divinity School, who as current pastor of a prominent church in Norfolk, Virginia, led his congregation to join in the struggle for integration in the schools and opened the doors of his church (located in an exclusive residential area) to Negro membership. There are examples among previous internes and "assistants" of similar dedication.

With the national program held intact, the position of minister-at-large was created after much discussion on the part of the Board, so that my coming to Boston would not serve to tear down the structure of members-at-large who had come to rely upon the guidance and inspiration which they had received from Fellowship Church. Since I was granted only an 'indefinite leave,' this seemed a happy solution. The intervening seven years have passed, which brought forth the written story of Fellowship Church involving local and national members, and the observance of its Fifteenth Anniversary last fall.

During recent years the local church has not had the facilities nor the inclination to continue its services in nationwide relationships. The reasons for this I understand. In the light of the fact, however, and in the light of the increasing responsibilities of my work in the East, I felt that I could no longer carry a "sense of responsibility" as minister-at-large, with its implication that I was the national representative of the local program. For throughout the entire time I have felt a deep sense of urgency to extend and deepen such a service in the widespread relationship of the Church through these fateful years in the world's history. It is for this reason that I have given in every way possible of time and means to witness in this regard. Here is the basic reason for continuing to write the Christmas card each year, distributed nationally under the auspices of the local Church; it is for this reason, basically, that I made all of my writing of every kind, and records, available, the latter without cost to the Church; and I was one of the first contributors to the initial payment for securing Stonetree Ranch. I was sure that the Ranch, for instance, would serve uniquely the resident members, the members-at-large and friends of the Church in a new and significant dimension of social and spiritual community.

All of this is to say simply that without national members-at-large and with no form of national program that makes some effort to recognize or take cognizance of this important group, there is no necessity for the functioning of a minister-at-large. This consideration, I would wish you to understand formed the basic reason, plus additional responsibilities in my work in the East, for my resignation as an active participant in the extended functioning of the Church.

We shall be living in San Francisco one day, after retirement from Boston University. You will be happy to know that we think we have found the home there for which we have been searching a long time. Until then, we welcome you as honored guests at "184" any time you may come to Boston.

My prayers and best wishes to you as you continue to share and to serve the immortal Fellowship Dream.

Sincerely,

Howard Thurman

TLc.

NOTES
1. See From Francis Geddes, 3 August 1960, printed in the current volume.
2. Clarence Johnson.

𝕾 "AN IMPERATIVE TO UNDERSTANDING"
23 OCTOBER 1960
BOSTON, MASS.

In this sermon delivered at Marsh Chapel during a vespers service for international students, Thurman tries to summarize his impressions from his recent trip around the world. He believes that the world's problems, such as "disease, poverty, and ignorance," can be addressed by developing authentic democratic responses to these challenges. He also feels that those who seek to do this work should not be frightened of their task when the ill-informed or malevolent label them as "communist."

Readings:
From the Hindu Scriptures:[1]
Who is He? He is the fire in the flame, He is the shining in the sun. He is the blowing of the wind, the silver in the moon. He is the stars reeling with light, He is Brahma the Lord Supreme. Thou art the one truth to whom men have given many names. Thou art the sanctity that is in woman and the manliness in man.

Thou art the young virgin and the little brother that stands beside her. Thou art age the staff leaner. Thou art the thousand faces born in every child, the blue trembling of the dragonfly, the startled light in the ruby eyes of the dove. Thou art the dancer whose footsteps beat out the seasons, and Thou art the lightning-wombed cloud that drags its heavy side over the tumult of the blue-black sea. Beginning, baffling, and eluding. Yet You exist and the universe spills out of You. He is the maker of many forms, the fashioner of nature and worshiper of that which has been fashioned, then having worshipped nature he slips out of his own creation. Who is He? He is the fire in the flame. He is the shining in the sun.

And this from the Islamic Scriptures:[2]

He who is Lord is also the holy, the peaceful, the faithful, the guardian over His servants, the shelterer of the orphan, the guide of the erring, the deliverer from every affliction, the friend of the bereaved, the consoler of the afflicted. In His hand is good and He is the generous Lord, the gracious, the healer, the hearer, the near at hand, the compassionate, the merciful, the very forgiving whose love for man is more tender than that of the mother bird for her young. Praise belongs to God, Lord of the worlds, the compassionate, the merciful. King of the day of judgement 'tis Thee we worship and Thee we ask for help. Guide us in the straight path, the path of those whom Thou hast favored, not the path of those who incur Thine anger nor of those who go astray.

And then from the Buddhist:[3]

By ourselves is evil done, by ourselves we pain endure, by ourselves we cease from wrong, by ourselves become we pure. No one saves us but ourselves, no one can and no one may. We ourselves must tread the path, buddhas only show the way. May I be a balm to the sick, their healer and servitor until sickness come never again. May I quench with rains of food and drink the anguish of hunger and thirst. May I be in the famine of the ages' end their drink and meat. May I become an unfailing store for the poor and serve them with manifold things for their need. My own being and my pleasures, all my righteousness in the past, present and future I surrender indifferently, that all creatures may win through to their end.

If any would procure the kingdom for himself by his own action, he will not succeed. The kingdom is a spirit-like thing, and cannot be got by active doing. He who would so win it, doth destroy it; he who would hold it in his grasp, doth lose it.[4]

Wherewith shall I come before the Lord, and bow myself before the high God? Shall I come before Him with burnt offerings, with calves of a year old? Will the

Lord be pleased with thousands of rams, or with ten thousands of rivers of oil? Shall I give my firstborn for my transgression, the fruit of my body for the sin of my soul? He hath shewed thee, O man, what is good; and what doth the Lord require of thee, but to do justly, and to love mercy, and to walk humbly with thy God?[5]

Ye have heard that it hath been said, "Thou shalt love thy neighbor, and hate thine enemy." But I say unto you, love your enemies, bless them that curse you, do good to them that hate you, and pray for them which despitefully use you, and persecute you, that ye may be the children of your Father which is in heaven: for He maketh his sun to rise on the evil and the good, and sendeth rain on the just and on the unjust.[6]

Love suffereth long, and is kind; love envieth not; love vaunteth not itself, is not puffed up, doth not behave itself unseemly, seeketh not her own, is not easily provoked, thinketh no evil, rejoiceth not in iniquity, but rejoiceth in the truth; beareth all things, believeth all things, hopeth all things, endureth all things.[7]

Sermon:

It is Tagore who has written these lines that I would have you hold as a background for our discussion:

> Where the mind is without fear and the head is held high;
> Where knowledge is free;
> Where the world has not been broken up into fragments by narrow
>   domestic walls;
> Where words come out from the depth of truth;
> Where tireless striving stretches its arms towards perfection;
> Where the clear stream of reason has not lost its way into the dreary
>   desert sand
> of dead habit;
> Where the mind is led forward by Thee into ever-widening thought and
>   action—
> Into that heaven of freedom, my Father, let my country awake.[8]

I wish it were possible this afternoon to take you vicariously on the journey which Mrs. Thurman and I completed early in September, a journey that took us around the world, visiting some twenty countries and meeting and having some primary contacts and relations with a wide variety of people against the backgrounds of their own lands and cultures and faiths. But this cannot be done for two reasons. The first reason is it would take longer than the period that is at my disposal, and the second reason [is] this is not the time nor the occasion.

I have chosen to think with you about certain imperatives to understanding in our world. We are living in a very grim world. This need not be underscored by any remarks that I may make. I think each of us is aware of that fact. The imperative has to do with the kind of urgencies which face us in our world and which must be dealt with at the level of the average individual in our society if there is to be even a modicum of balance and sanity in the common life.

The three great internationalists in our period in history are not persons at all. They are disease, poverty, and ignorance. These three internationalists do not know any race or any culture, any religion. They are not involved in all of the refinements of discrimination by which men seek to develop in one way or another the kind of communal life that speaks to their condition and that inspires them into tranquility and peaceful living. They move with authority all over the world. They provide important openings for those persons who have either concerns for human weal and human betterment or for those persons who wish on behalf of their own faith to conquer the minds and the spirits and the stomachs of the vast population of the earth. We are in America the inheritors of three very great beliefs, beliefs which in my judgement are profoundly spiritual, religious beliefs. The roots are not to be found in our own soil but they are part of our immediate heritage.

The first is a belief in the universality of order in existence, a belief that all of the world external to man and all of the world interior to man is so fundamentally structured, is so manifest with inherent orderedness that the degree to which the order in the mind is able to correspond directly and primarily with the order in the world of nature, to that degree will there be understanding, usefulness, and even control of the world of nature. It is out of this broad generalization about the nature of the external existence by which we are surrounded that all of the presuppositions and the vast activities of modern science find their place, their validity, and their foundation. It is because we affirm a belief in order that we assume with reference to any particular unit or conglomerate of nature that even though we do not understand it now it is understandable. And the creative mind of man brooding over the stubborn and unyielding and recalcitrant stuff of nature can at last find the clue to its understanding and its control.

There is another belief, a belief in the absolute worth of the individual soul before God. It is out of a belief such as that, that a simple transfer has been made to the assumption or to the affirmation which has to do with the social worth of the individual. And it is on the basis of the doctrine of the social worth of the individual that all of the concerns by which we are surrounded having to do with decency of life, with the so-called democratic order, or with the fulfillment of the democratic dogma. It is out of this basic underlying belief that all of the social concerns arise. And there is still another belief, a belief which has to do with the perfection, how to say this, the perfectibility of the human spirit in time and space. And it is out of this belief that all of the dreams of utopias arise. Over and over again there are these little experimental units within the very womb of our society, which units try in themselves to anticipate a time when the disorder, when the disorientation, will be resolved and men are living—seek to live—in these little experiments, as in accordance with their dream all men will be able to live tomorrow or tomorrow or tomorrow. And this sort of thing is rooted deep in the whole stream not only of our life, but in the common life of man.

Now it is against the background of these beliefs and the involvement, sometimes quite unconscious involvement in the resultants that flow from these beliefs in determining the behavior patterns by which we are surrounded, that many of the enormous conflicts by which we are faced today come to pass. It is no accident, for instance, that in much of the discussion that we hear today that the enemy, the archenemy, has a name and we give a certain political term to the name, the blanket name by which the enemy is recognized is communism. This is the blanket enemy. And it's a convenient enemy because whenever there is any necessity to escape from dealing with the ethical responsibility derivative from these three underlying affirmations of our common life we have a convenient scapegoat.

I remember some years ago when I lived in San Francisco, twelve people from my congregation decided that they wanted to attend the United Nations meeting, the UNESCO meeting in Paris. The church, of course, had no money, so each one of these persons decided to pay his and her own way. So they got together, pooled their money and they set out in a caravan from San Francisco to New York, an automobile caravan, and as they moved across the country they encountered various inconveniences. The party was made up of two or three American Negroes, an American Indian, one or two persons of Chinese and Japanese background, one or two persons of Jewish background. And as they moved across the country they found it rather difficult to experience community at the same motel and restaurants. And they wrote, one of the men wrote a letter back about it to a friend of his and this friend gave the letter to someone on one of the local newspapers of San Francisco and this man called me and he said, "The rumor that is going around the city has now found validation. Your church *is* a communist inspired organization, to wit because only a communist inspired organization would do what you are trying to do, or what this group of people are trying to do namely, experience community as they move from San Francisco to New York by a caravan of cars."⁹

Now, it is so simple to say, when we wish either to escape the facts or to call the facts by some other name, to pay to a group, to an institution or a philosophy such as communism the high tribute that it is only they who are concerned about the hungry; it is only they who are concerned about raising standards of living; it is only they who are concerned about brotherhood. Now what I'm saying is that if we are to experience understanding, we must first of all have a sense of root in the stream of thought and idealism and faith which is our own background, our own life, our own culture. And standing within that stream, we must not be so preoccupied with it that we are willing to close our eyes to the tragic deeds and the tragic consequences of the behavior of modern man in the world.

Now this means developing a sense of fact with reference to what democracy is and what it is not; what its roots are and what its roots are not. It means also having a sense of fact with reference to other people's facts and other people's sense of fact. I was very much interested in many of the discussions that we had when we were in Japan a few months before all of the difficulties arose and the marching and the things that finally resulted in the fact that the President of the United States did not go to Japan.[10] And over and over again as I talked with Japanese students and others and with American fraternal workers[11] who had spent a lifetime living in that land, one of the central concerns that appeared again and again was the anxiety that this people had that the registration of their national life on the side of peace as written into their constitution and blessed by us would not even on behalf of certain historical and extenuating circumstances be wiped out and obliterated lest they then would be forced to renounce that which to them had become of paramount order and significance. Now I do not pretend to suggest that wherever there is disturbance, the disturbance is of the kind that I mentioned, but I am suggesting to you that we must on behalf of the democratic dogma which we embrace and all that it implies about sympathetic and sensitive understanding, we must not give to any other philosophy, any other ideology, any other faith, a monopoly on concern for human need, hunger, disease.

Now one other thing. It is important that we feed our facts, how to say this, that we emulsify our facts with not only a concern but with the kind of imagination that enables us to move vicariously into the lives and the thoughts of other peoples whose backgrounds and whose cultures are different from ours in order that we may understand them and in that understanding of them be understood by them. For the essence of all communication at last is only possible as a living experience in human life when people are talking from the same agendas. And if the agendas are different, then there can be no meeting of mind and no meeting of purpose and no meeting of dream. So that a part of the hard job that is ours as citizens in our communities, as members of our own faith, as believers in our own fundamental political and ethical doctrine, our responsibility is to seek ways by which it will be increasingly possible for us to take[12]

At.

NOTES

1. Dhan Gopal Mukerji, *Devotional Passages from the Hindu Bible* (New York: E. P. Dutton, 1929), 41. This is a free rendering of the opening of Śvetāśvatara Upanisad, chap. 4. See Patrick Olivelle, ed., *Upanisads* (New York: Oxford University Press, 1996), 259.

2. The beginning of the quotation, through "mother bird for her young," is from Syed Ameer Ali, *The Spirit of Islam* (1891; repr., London: Christophers, 1923), 150. The remainder of the quotation is the al-fatiha, the first surah and opening exordium of the Koran. Thurman probably found both quotations in Huston Smith, *The Religions of Man* (New York: Harper, 1958), 206, 209.

3. Two quotes, slightly modified, which Thurman probably found on adjacent pages in Huston Smith, *The Religions of Man*, 120–21. The first quotation, which ends with "others only show the way," is from an unsourced Theravada Buddhist text; the second quotation is from the Bodhicharyavatara, written by Shantideva, an eighth-century Indian Buddhist.

4. From section 29 of the James Legge translation of the *Tao Te Ching* of Lao Tzu, originally published in 1891 as part of Oxford University Press's *Sacred Books of the East* series.

5. Mic. 6:6–8.

6. Matt. 5:43–45.

7. Cor. 13:4–7.

8. Rabindranath Tagore, "Poem 35," in *Gitangali* (New York: Macmillan, 1927), 27–28.

9. For the UNESCO trip, see "To Friend" [January 1950], printed in the current volume.

10. In January 1960 President Eisenhower announced that he would make the first presidential visit to Japan. However, the ratification on 31 May of a new defense treaty between Japan and the United States provoked demonstrations and rioting by its opponents, and on 16 June the Eisenhower administration announced that Japan would be omitted from the president's Far East tour.

11. "Fraternal workers" is "the new designation given missionary teachers and ministers from abroad"; see To Friends of the International Fellowship Community, 15 August 1960, printed in the current volume.

12. The audiotape ends here, apparently cutting off the end of the sermon.

❧ To LLOYD SMITH
31 OCTOBER 1960
[*BOSTON, MASS.*]

Thurman's letter to his friend and benefactor Lloyd M. Smith, a Los Angeles lawyer, initiates the project that would become the Howard Thurman Educational Trust, originally called the Howard Thurman Trust Fund. After Thurman's retirement from Boston University in 1965, the trust was the institution with which he was most closely identified. It became, he wrote in his autobiography, his "focus."[1] The trust was organized under Lloyd Smith's direction and began operations on 1 July 1961.[2] Its initial trustees were Howard and Sue Bailey Thurman and Gene Walker, who also served as the trust's first treasurer. Walker had been a chairman of the board of trustees and a financial backer of the Fellowship Church.[3]

Mr. Lloyd M. Smith
The Claremore Fund
633 South Shatto Place
Los Angeles 5, California

Dear Lloyd:
It may seem to you after reading this letter that I think that you do not have enough work to do.

During the past several years an increasing number of individuals have privileged me by putting varying sums of money at my disposal to be given to people, sometimes for assistance in education, sometimes for help [in] indigencies and emergencies of various kinds. The sums have been nominal all along. Whenever the sums are large I have accepted the funds through the discretionary fund of Marsh Chapel, which facilitates the matter of tax deductions for the donor. There is a limitation on this method because only under extraordinary circumstances is it possible for Marsh Chapel to dispense funds to persons who are not directly or indirectly involved in the constituency of the University.

In addition to these funds, to my knowledge there are two people who have made arrangements in their wills for some considerable money to be dispensed by me in accordance with prearranged agreements, when the wills are probated.

In addition to these considerations, I have a profound sense of urgency to pool all resources that are available to me, including the money that I earn that is not directly involved in my own or my family's survival. Therefore, in the light of these facts, I would like to establish a Howard Thurman Trust Fund, incorporated under the laws of California, which trust fund would have as its purpose: providing scholarship aid to students generally, on the basis of need; fellowships to young men and women who wish to do special study in the field of religion and human relations; and to make emergency grants to individuals whose life has fallen upon evil times.

Now I come to my request of you. Would it be possible for you to draw up the necessary papers to achieve these things under the laws of California. Is there such a thing as a one man trust fund, or must there be officers, or what? I do not know. The only thing that I want to do as quickly as possible is to get this established so that various people who are interested can contribute to the fund directly and have the matter of tax exemption covered. I hope you have time to give thought to this. I believe so completely in the sensitiveness of your imagination and heart in matters of this kind that I would like for your legal mind to structure this for me.

It seems that I shall have to come out to Los Angeles to visit Madaline and to take her on a little trip for two or three days during the Christmas holidays. It would be wonderful if all the preliminary work can be done on this prior to that time so that when I come in December I can sign the papers.

Always my best to you and Edie.

Sincerely,

Howard Thurman

Dean

TLc.

NOTES

　　1. *WHAH*, 259.

　　2. To John Overholt, 7 July 1961.

　　3. For a more comprehensive account of the Howard Thurman Educational Trust, see "Biographical Essay," *PWHT*, vol. 5 (forthcoming).

🦭 To E. B. THOMPSON

17 NOVEMBER 1960

[*BOSTON, MASS.*]

Thurman answers a query from Ebony *magazine on the meaning of heaven and hell.*[1]

Miss E. B. Thompson[2]

Managing Editor, EBONY

1820 South Michigan Street

Chicago, Illinois

Dear Miss Thompson:

　　Here in brief is my reply to the three questions which you raised.

　　1. Do you believe in a literal hell and heaven after death?
　　Ans. No. I believe that hell and heaven that are depicted in the Bible are descriptive of a condition of the human spirit. Hell is to be cut off from God and His presence.
　　　Heaven is to be with God.

　　2. Do you believe in punishment and reward after death?
　　Ans. I believe in sowing and reaping, and reward and punishment in life. The extent to which the moral law operates beyond death is not ours to know. Because I believe that death is something that is experienced <u>in</u> life and not <u>to</u> life, I do not think that the matter of death as such has any bearing on the moral law whatsoever.

3. Do you believe in the fear of hell as a deterrent to sinning?
Ans. No.

Sincerely yours,
Howard Thurman
Dean

TLc.

NOTES
    1. Thurman's contribution was published as part of "What Happened to Hell: Views of Negro Ministers," *Ebony* 16, no. 1 (January 1961): 47–48, 50–52.
    2. Era Bell Thompson (1907–87), a native of Iowa, was a graduate of Morningside College in Sioux City, Iowa. She worked for many years as an international reporter and editor for Johnson Publications in Chicago, including a stint as managing editor of *Ebony*. Her books include *American Daughter* (Chicago: University of Chicago Press, 1946) and *Africa, Land of My Fathers* (Garden City, N.Y.: Doubleday, 1954).

✒ "Two Options"
1961

On 19 January 1961 Thurman received a letter from Donald Keys,[1] program director of the National Committee for a Sane Nuclear Policy,[2] better known as SANE, asking for his advice on a forthcoming volume he was editing on the "religious response to the issue of nuclear warfare."[3] Although Keys did not ask Thurman to contribute to the volume, Thurman eventually did so, writing a short essay entitled "Two Options."[4] The essay presented a stark dichotomy: either the United States and the Soviet Union agree to a ban on nuclear tests and a plan for nuclear disarmament or "the weapons of death become the custodians of our consciences and the vehicles of extinction."

As early as late 1945, a few months after the bombing of Hiroshima and Nagasaki, Thurman wrote that preservation of life on the planet in the wake of atomic bombs and other war-generated weapons required a "profound revolution in the basic structures of our thought about human life and destiny."[5] Nuclear weapons raised the stakes for the consequences of warfare and in many ways reinforced Thurman's pacifist convictions, which had been a central component of his thinking for decades. If Thurman during his years at Boston University curtailed his ties to the Fellowship of Reconciliation,[6] the Christian pacifist organization he had been active in since his undergraduate years at Morehouse, he added new commitments in the area of world peace, among them the United World Federalists[7] and SANE. In 1961 Thurman appeared on SANE's masthead as a "sponsor" along with such luminaries as Steve Allen,[8] Martin Luther King, Jr., and Lewis Mumford.[9] Thurman concluded this essay by suggesting that if the United States and the Soviet Union must engage in some sort of struggle, it ought to be a peaceful one— a struggle for the goodwill of the newly independent nations of Asia and Africa.

For the first time in human history, the possibility of the biological discontinuity of the human race is a factor with which mankind has to deal. Always, in the past, the possibility of a surviving remnant to any armed conflict between nations has provided a ground of optimism concerning the future and its possibilities for human weal. In the Judeo-Christian tradition, the concept of the remnant has persisted as a door of hope for the human race and as a reminder of the grace of God that cushions human weakness, error and sin. Whatever the destruction called down upon mankind because of war, the notion of a surviving remnant remained.

This notion is no longer relevant. There is within the power of at least two of the great nations of the earth, the Soviet Union and the United States, the ability to destroy all living things on the planet. Thus we are faced with the real possibility of the discontinuity not merely of civilization but of man as a biological animal. In the light of this situation, arms competition is an exercise in alternative ways to commit suicide—and a profound exercise in both stupidity and futility. No nation can win.

The stark and terrifying fact which we face then is this: Only two options are available to us. One, all further developments along the lines of nuclear testings and bomb refinements must be banned, discontinued, and a systematic method developed for disarmament. This would mean that the complete and total resources of our national life are available for bringing into being an ethical conscience providing us as a nation with the will to exploit all possible means for involving the Soviet Union and other nations in the ways and means for the preservation of peace. To say that such an option is not practical is to beg the question. The argument for war as an instrument of national policy is that it is the only realistic way to guarantee peace in the world. Following such a policy, our planet has been visited by two world wars within a single century, plus a wide variety of wars on a more or less limited scale. It would seem, therefore, that the way in which nations have been functioning is not very practical. The resources of our national life, economic and human, put at the disposal of some such option as is suggested above, will at least kindle the imagination of the masses of people with the hope that it will be reasonable to expect mankind to experience the arts and the fulfillment of peace. The other option is to continue our present course in the world. This means living in a climate of mounting fear, until at least the weapons of death become the custodians of our consciences and the vehicles of extinction.

It is a matter of interest to me that as the awareness of what may be considered a draw or tie in lethal weapons on the part of the two major powers on this planet becomes focal in the minds of the nations, they are being forced to wage war in an entirely new dimension for human history. The battlefield more and more now is the poverty, the hunger, and the economic needs of the masses of the earth. It is ironical and yet of amazing significance that the Soviet Union and the United States are battling to see which of them can give the most aid to the so-called underprivileged countries, and in turn receive a vote of confidence and good will. For to the nation that gets the vote of confidence and good will from the "new" countries of the world, the future belongs. In such a new dimension of struggle, even men of good will may participate.

Howard Thurman, "Two Options," in Donald Keys, ed., *God and the H-Bomb* (New York: Bellmeadows Press and Bernard Geis Associates, 1961), 107–9. Copyright © 1961 by Bellmeadows Press and Bernard Geis Associates.

PD.

NOTES

1. Donald F. Keys (1924–), program director of the National Committee for a Sane Nuclear Policy (SANE) and later its executive director, was subsequently the UN representative of the World Association of World Federalists. He is the author of *Earth at Omega: Passage to Planetization* (Boston: Branden Press, 1982).

2. The National Committee for a Sane Nuclear Policy was organized in 1957, and it soon became a leading voice for liberals seeking to curb the nuclear arms race between the United States and the Soviet Union. In 1993 it was renamed Peace Action.

3. From Donald Keys, 19 January 1961.

4. On 7 July 1961 Beth Ballard, Thurman's secretary, wrote to Bernard Geis Associates, one of the publishers of *God and the H-Bomb*, telling them that Thurman wished to expand his essay and provide some additional copy (Beth Ballard to Bernard Geis Associates, 7 July 1961). Thurman's original submission probably survives in his papers as "Comments [on H-Bomb]," a short, undated statement related to "Two Options."

5. HT, "The Inner Life and World-Mindedness" (1945), repr. in *PHWT*, 3:108–13 .

6. Thurman resigned from the National Council of FOR in April 1953, claiming that he was unable to give the organization the attention it deserved; see To A. J. Muste, 18 April 1953, printed in the current volume. However, he continued his ties with the organization, writing a testimonial for a promotional folder, "Why We Belong to F.O.R.," in 1957; see From William Robert Miller, 30 September 1957; and HT, "[Fellowship of Reconciliation Testimonial]," 8 October 1957.

7. See "Letter in Support of United World Federalists," probably written in 1960, printed in the current volume.

8. Steve Allen (1921–2000), an entertainer and the original host of "The Tonight Show" (1954–57), was a supporter of numerous liberal causes. He contributed the foreword to *God and the H-Bomb*.

9. Lewis Mumford (1895–1990) was an author of numerous books on many subjects, with notable work in the areas of sociology, urban planning and cities, literary criticism, and the history of technology. See *PHWT*, 1:40n2.

᠅ To J. Wendell Yeo
16 March 1961
[*Boston, Mass.*]

Following a meeting with Dean J. Wendell Yeo,[1] vice president for student affairs at Boston University and Thurman's immediate supervisor, Thurman writes about his understanding of the scope of his duties as dean of the chapel. Thurman feels that his need to explain and justify his work to Yeo is "profoundly humiliating." He discusses the evolution of his preaching schedule at Marsh Chapel and argues that when he is working, he has a seven-day work week, so comparisons of his absences to those of other faculty members are unfair and inappropriate. In the second half of the letter, Thurman states that the administration's failure to allow him to develop a religious fellowship connected with Marsh Chapel has limited his effectiveness at Boston University. He insists that he will not be "exploited by the University" and that his ministry will continue to be shared "beyond the boundaries of Marsh Chapel and particularly . . . with Negroes who live and work and suffer in American society."

Dr. J. Wendell Yeo
Vice President for Student Affairs
755 Commonwealth Avenue

Dear Wendell:

As I promised you in conversation during our last conference, I am putting into words the working understanding that I have concerning my responsibilities in the University as Dean of Marsh Chapel.

I have said over my signature to the President that it is impossible for me to carry full responsibility for the program of the chapel during the academic year and also be involved in the program of the chapel during the summer period from commencement to the end of summer school. Ever since I have been here, I have operated on this basis. Only once have I participated in the preaching during the summer. The summer arrangement which I have followed for eight years is as follows: a special person has been designated to be the presiding officer for the Sunday chapels during June, July and two Sundays in August. This person has been compensated, usually to an amount of approximately $250. Usually the designated presiding officer preaches one Sunday. The other

Left to right: Daniel Marsh, former Boston University chancellor; Howard and Sue Bailey Thurman; and George Makechnie, 1965. From the Howard Thurman Collection, Howard Gotlieb Archival Research Center at Boston University.

preachers are guests most of whom are off-campus guests. I have set this program up during the academic year. President Case and I have had several conversations about the summer schedule [and] we have even in the earlier period of my incumbency discussed the advisability of discontinuing the service altogether or inviting one person, like Henry Hitt Crane,[2] to be the preacher in residence during the period. I have felt that it was my responsibility to provide an inspiring and significant schedule of summer preachers. I have never regarded it as my responsibility to do the preaching.

The President and I have discussed several times in the course of these eight years, my preaching schedule in the chapel during the academic year. We have agreed that there should be authentic continuity in this preaching, which is interpreted by me as meaning that I would do a large part of the preaching myself. The first year or two I was here, I did most of the preaching in order that there might be established a structure of significance for the Sunday service. Once such a structure was established, then it would be possible to bring into the Sunday schedule of preachers other voices, most of whom were a part of the University faculty or administration. This is the basis of operation at the present time. In my own thoughts I have not been bound by a mathematical precision in this matter. Rather have I made decisions about absences from the pulpit on the basis of the dynamics of the program as I sensed them and understand them.

Concerning the times when someone else preaches in the chapel. I have not used such occasions exclusively for the purpose of going somewhere else to preach. Sometimes I have. Sometimes I have not.

In this connection let me state that the normal working pattern of persons carrying administrative responsibility is a five day week. This means that every academic dean in the University may presume to have at his personal disposal, Saturday and Sunday of each week, unless some special situation arises. On the other hand, if I am in residence in the University, seven days of any given week, I am involved in responsible work seven days of any given week. The only way that I can get the normal days off in a given week is to go out of town or stay in doors. President Case and I have talked about this problem and at one time he even suggested that in order to relieve this situation Mrs. Thurman and I might consider going up to Osgood Hill[3] for a day out of every other week, or something of that sort. All of this means then that whether I am preaching or presiding on a given Sunday my involvement is still a seven day involvement. I do not state this to indicate in any sense that I think that I am being overworked, but it is material that must be taken into account when the question is raised, particularly about the use which I may make of the period from June to September.

As a matter of historic reference, I was the third dean of the chapel in the United States when I became Dean of the Chapel at Howard University.[4] There were two before me, Charlie Gilkey[5] at the University of Chicago and Dr. Weeks[6] at Princeton. At Chicago, Charlie Gilkey was always free one entire quarter out of each four. When he was in residence he preached only occasionally. The same was true with Dr. Weeks at Princeton. When I was dean of the Chapel at Howard University I had no responsibility from commencement day until my program started in the fall.

There is one other item that belongs in the picture. When Dr. Case and I discussed the possibility of my coming to Boston, he assured me that it was not his thought that the national ministry which had been mine for many years would be seriously curtailed. As a matter of fact the point was made that it would be a significant advantage to operate out of Boston University instead of the Church for the Fellowship of All Peoples in San Francisco. This appealed to me because at the same time there would be an opportunity to develop in a continuing fashion that to which I had given ten years of my life in San Francisco. A very personal word must be added here, Wendell, and that is, the only way in good conscience that I can keep from feeling that the gifts of God that is in me is not being exploited by the University, is the reassurance that it is available to be shared beyond the boundaries of Marsh Chapel and particularly to be shared with Negroes who live and work and suffer in American society.

The high hope which I had that it would be possible to develop a religious fellowship that cut across the barriers that separate men from each other in our society, once a climate could be established in Boston University, had to be abandoned.[7] This was a serious blow to me and it has been very difficult since that time for me to feel that it is possible for me to make my most significant contribution here. Now when I add to that the feeling that in the way that I am fulfilling the ministry of Marsh Chapel I am violating an agreement that I have with the University as Dean of the Chapel, the nerve center of my commitment here is seriously under siege. The fact that, after eight years of obvious development of the religious ministry of Marsh Chapel, it is necessary for me to write this kind of letter to my immediate superior, is profoundly humiliating.

Please do not misunderstand what I am saying. In my work as Dean of the Chapel I have found and am finding profound satisfaction. What I am concerned about is the insinuation that in carrying out my responsibilities I am not living up to either the agreement or the understanding that I have officially with the University.

Sincerely yours,
Howard Thurman
Dean

TLc.

NOTES

1. J. Wendell Yeo (1908–81) was a public-school teacher in Connecticut before joining the faculty of the Boston University School of Education in 1939. He remained at the university for the rest of his career, serving as dean of the School of Education from 1951 to 1953, vice president of academic affairs from 1953 to 1959, and vice president of student affairs from 1959 to 1969.

2. Henry Hitt Crane (1890–1977) was a 1916 graduate of the Boston University School of Theology and served in Methodist pulpits in Malden, Massachusetts (1919–28); Scranton, Pennsylvania (1928–38); and most prominently, the Central Methodist Church of Detroit (1938–58). He was a well-known supporter of many liberal causes and an outspoken pacifist during both world wars.

3. Osgood Hill is a conference center in North Andover, Massachusetts, that was owned by Boston University from 1951 until 1995, when it was purchased by the town of North Andover.

4. For Thurman's position as dean of the chapel at Howard University, see *PHWT*, 2:xxxi.

5. Charles W. Gilkey (1882–1968) was dean of the chapel at the University of Chicago from 1928 to 1947. He was a good friend of Thurman. See To Charles Gilkey, 19 February 1946, printed in *PHWT*, 3:174–75.

6. Robert Russell Wicks (1882–1963) was dean of the chapel at Princeton University from 1928 to 1947.

7. For a discussion of Thurman's attempt to create a Marsh Chapel fellowship, see the biographical essay in the current volume.

✒ From William Holmes Borders
25 May 1961
Atlanta, Georgia

The prominent Atlanta minister William Holmes Borders[1] wants Thurman to preach at his twenty-fifth anniversary celebration and sends Thurman a blank check for his honorarium, telling him to name his own price.

Dr. Howard Thurman
Boston University
Boston, Massachusetts

Dear Dr. Thurman:

On December 9, 1962, we will climax my twenty-fifth anniversary as pastor of Wheat Street Baptist Church. I am extending you an invitation to do the morning message on that Sunday. Enclosed is a blank check; you may write your own ticket including an honorarium and expenses for you and Mrs. Thurman if she desires to come.

The preceding week will be used in dramatizing the achievements. All of the exact details of the week's activities have not been minutely worked out. I am sure, however, that the achievements may be divided under several headings:

1. Increase in church membership of some 400 members by years; members coming from surrounding towns and villages within a radius of one hundred miles.
2. Services to about 50 non-hearing members. There are 30 interpreters who make every Sunday and weekly meeting to interpret to the deaf, who do everything in the church.
3. Establishment of a Credit Union $30,000.00 strong.
4. Completion of the church edifice 19 months and one week after it had stood incomplete for 17 years.
5. Construction of a $400,000.00 Christian Education building; paid for it in five years, though bankers and economists calculated 12 years.
6. Day nursery and grade school through the fourth grade, serving 375 children with 23 full-time paid teachers and other personnel, with three red

and white buses that pick up and deliver these children, which buses are used by the church school on Sunday mornings.

7. 2-year-old weekly radio broadcast with the second highest listening audience—local or national.

8. A children's voice-speaking choir, which chants Beatitudes, etc., each Sunday morning.

9. An increase of finances from $12,000.00 a year to $130,000.00.

10. Purchase of $43,000.00 worth of real estate in the city and a 300-acre farm for $45,000.00 used for recreational purposes and camping, etc.

11. Leading the preachers of all denominations in Atlanta in desegregating the public buses and trolleys.

12. Chairman of the Adult Liaison Adult Committee guiding citizens and students in the desegregation of lunch counters and other facilities in Atlanta.

13. Developing an order of worship in which some 400 people actively participate as musicians, interpreters, ushers, deacons, chanters, pulpit assistants.

For all of these years the Wheat Street Church has been filled Sunday after Sunday. I do want you to see all of these things because some of the ideas are yours. This is the time that I would like for you to come and fellowship with us. I know your schedule is tight but I hope you can see your way clear to accept. Sincerely yours,

[*signed*] William Holmes Borders

"Doc Borders"

P.S. – 14 –Jennie Walden Chapel given by Col. A. T. Walden in memory of his mother – used for weddings, funerals, prayer and Bryant Bible Class. W. H. B.

TLS.

NOTE

1. William Holmes Borders (1905–93) was a native of Macon, Georgia, and a 1929 graduate of Morehouse College. He received a B.D. from Garrett Theological Seminary in 1932 and pastored the Second Baptist Church in Evanston, Illinois, from 1932 until 1936, when he returned to Morehouse as an instructor. The following year he was named minister of the Wheat Street Baptist Church, where he remained until his retirement in 1968. In Atlanta he was one of the most prominent black civic leaders of his generation.

✎ From Adam C. Powell, Jr.
31 August 1961
Washington, D.C.

Congressman Adam Clayton Powell, Jr.[1] *invites Thurman to preach at the Abyssinian Baptist Church*[2] *in Harlem.*

My dear Friend:
   It was good to talk with you yesterday. We would like you to preach at both the 10:00 a.m. and 12:00 noon services on any Sunday during the balance of September or during October. I had previously wired you, on August 22nd, at Boston University asking you to come, and am sorry this did not reach you.
   We have just purchased the three buildings that formerly belonged to the Harlem YWCA, housing a dormitory, a trade center, an educational center and an activity center. Adding this to our present plan gives us a complex of five buildings with 23 floors for social service work, and an operating budget of $400,000. We have set aside September and October for dedication of these new buildings.
   I am sorry we cannot offer an honorarium of more than $300.00, due to the fact that we are utilizing this occasion for fund-raising as well.
   Please come to Macedonia.[3]
Sincerely,
[*signed*] Adam
ADAM C. POWELL

Dr. Howard Thurman
Ten Park Avenue Hotel
10 Park Avenue
New York, New York

ACP:tc

                                                                                      TLS.

Notes
   1. Adam Clayton Powell, Jr. (1908–72) earned a B.A. from Colgate University in 1930 and an M.A. in religious education from Columbia University in 1932. In 1937 he succeeded his father, Adam Clayton Powell, Sr., as minister of the Abyssinian Baptist Church in Harlem. He soon sought political office and was elected to the New York City Council in 1941 and the U.S. House of Representatives in 1944 as New York State's first African American member of Congress. He remained in Congress until 1971, becoming one of the nation's most powerful, prominent, and controversial black leaders. Thurman and Powell were acquainted by 1938. See *PHWT*, 2:156.
   2. The Abyssinian Baptist Church was founded in Lower Manhattan in 1809 as a black Baptist congregation. After several relocations it moved to Harlem in 1902 and by 1930 was

one of the largest religious congregations in the world. See Genna Rae McNeil, Houston Bryan Roberson, Quinton Hosford Dixie, and Kevin McGruder, *Witness: Two Hundred Years of African-American Faith and Practice at the Abyssinian Baptist Church of Harlem, New York* (Grand Rapids, Mich.: William B. Eerdmans, 2013).

3. This is a reference to the "Macedonian Cry" in Acts 16:9: "A vision appeared to Paul in the night; there was a man of Macedonia standing, beseeching him, and saying, come over into Macedonia, and help us" (RSV).

❧ To Adam C. Powell, Jr.
8 September 1961
[*Boston, Mass.*]

Thurman writes to Powell turning down the invitation to preach at Abyssinian Baptist Church and saying that he needs more advanced notice.

Congressman Adam C. Powell
House of Representatives
429 House Office Building
Washington 25, D.C.

Dear Adam:

Why do you treat me this way? It is impossible for me to get a free Sunday morning during the current academic year on such short notice. The enclosed first semester's Preaching Schedule will indicate how it is with me. The limited time that is available for off-campus visitations has to be worked out, usually, in January for the following academic year. With your kind of full life I am sure you appreciate what all of this means.

I am very excited about your expansion of facilities to serve your tremendous congregation and the community. I am sorry that it will not be possible for me to have any part in the dedication during this fall.

It was good to talk with you on the telephone. I tried to reach you Saturday morning but was unsuccessful. The next time, give me plenty of time.
Sincerely yours,
Howard Thurman
Dean

                                                                                    TLc.

❧ To James Van Pelt
19 September 1961
[*Boston, Mass.*]

Thurman writes to a former student at the School of Theology who had written about problems he was experiencing in his first congregational position.

Rev. James Van Pelt[1]
14 South 21st Street
Terre Haute, Indiana

Dear Jim:

I have carried your letter across the United States to California and up to Canada and back to Boston. At several intervals along the way I wanted to answer you but it was not possible.

I have no great words of wisdom to offer you, but you must remember that your ministry is taking place in the great mid-west. You are preaching in a section that is sometimes known as the "Bible belt." Isolationism has been one of the dominant moods of that section. All of this you know. I refer to it only to remind you that you cannot expect to lift your congregation to your level of thinking and experiencing in twelve short months. The only word of wisdom that I have is that somehow you must teach your congregation to love you and this can be done most effectively by disciplining yourself in love for them. Once this happens you will be able to lead them anywhere.

I am concerned over your comment about the "hierarchy." I remember the first year I came to Boston I gave the lecture at the School of the Prophets[2] for Bishop Raines.[3] In a memorable address which he gave, he assured the ministers that as long as they took courageous stands as a part of their witness of the Gospel of Jesus Christ, they could depend upon their Bishop to back them. It was a very exciting moment for me to hear a Bishop of the Church make such a statement to the clergy of his diocese.

I have felt all along that you would do very well in working with students and young people. You have a breezy way and excitingly checked vests with brass buttons, and an alert mind. With this combination and a profound spiritual experience growing out of your religious dedication, there is no limit to the contagion which you could manifest. At any rate, this is worth thinking about.

The year is upon us. I need not say more. Please remember me to Marilyn.
Sincerely yours,
Howard Thurman
Dean

TLc.

NOTES

1. James E. Van Pelt, after service in the navy in the Korean War, attended Tulane University and the Boston University School of Theology. He was ordained into the Methodist ministry in 1960 and served Methodist, United Church of Christ, and Congregational churches. In 1988 he became minister of the Beacon Falls Congregational Church in Connecticut.

2. A nickname for an annual Methodist conference in Indiana.

3. For Richard Raines, see To Harold C. Case, 7 March 1953, printed in the current volume. Raines was the presiding bishop of the Indiana Methodist Conference, and by quoting him Thurman was encouraging Van Pelt not to feel constrained by the conservatism of his congregation or the local Methodist hierarchy. Thurman spoke at the Indiana Methodist convention at DePauw University from 8 to 11 September, when he was engaged in moving to San Francisco from Boston.

❧ "Albert Schweitzer"
14 January 1962
Boston, Mass.

Thurman, prompted by listening to a morning news report filled with distressing stories about deaths in Africa, Asia, and South America, decides to scrap his planned sermon and speak instead about Albert Schweitzer and his notion of "reverence for life." Thurman's attitude toward Schweitzer is complicated; he is suspicious of an underlying paternalism in Schweitzer's view of Africa and Africans, but this is outweighed by Schweitzer's commitment to life in all of its forms and his posing of questions about the relation of the individual to the natural and social world, which had long been central to Thurman's social and religious thinking.

Meditation:
It is no ordinary experience to withdraw from the traffic and involvement of our common life, to sit together in the quietness of the sanctuary, each one of us with his own world of thoughts and desires, hopes and dreams, and fears. It is good to confess in the quietness whatever there is within us that cries out for confession. And to feel in the act of confession that he who hears and judges also understands and loves. It is no ordinary thing to be free enough within to confess even to God that which cries out for confession.

It is wonderful beyond measure to be able to share the stirrings of thanksgiving which we feel and to do this, each one in his own way with the kind of confidence that makes it unnecessary to custom make the language that we use. But to be able to say thanks to God with no necessity for trying to impress Him with our thoughtfulness or to store up some form of merit that will plead our case at other times when gratitude is lacking and thanksgiving is far removed. It is no ordinary thing simply to say to Thee, O God, thank you so much. Thank you. Thank you so very much, our Father.

Reading:[1]
Three times I had seen an ox striving to pull a heavily loaded wagon up a hill, the blood and foam streaming from its mouth and nostrils as it struggled, and

I had seen it fall dead, under the lash. In the bush in the kloof below I had seen bush-bucks and little long-tailed monkeys that I loved so shot dead, not from any necessity but for the pleasure of killing, and the cock-o-veets and the honey-suckers and the wood-doves that made the bush so beautiful to me. And sometimes I had seen bands of convicts going past to work on the roads, and I've heard the chains clanking which went round their waists and passed between their legs to the irons on their feet; I had seen the terrible look in their eyes of a wild creature, when every man's hand is against it, and no one loves it, and it only hates and fears. I had gotten up early in the morning to drop small bits of tobacco at the roadside, hoping that they would find them and pick them up. I had wanted to say to them, "Someone loves you"; but the man with the gun was always there. I had wanted to say this, but I did not dare.

Once I had seen a pack of dogs set on by men to attack a strange dog, which had come among them and had done no harm to anyone. I had watched it torn to pieces, though I had done all I could to save it. Why did everyone press on everyone and try to make him do what he wanted? Why did the strong crush the weak? Why do we hate and kill and torture? Why was life as it is? Why was I ever born?

Sermon:
I had a strange experience today that has altered my plan. I had worked with a great deal of care and discipline to isolate what it was that was in my heart and spirit to say about William Blake[2] and was about ready, and I listened to the eight o'clock news. One of these things, I don't usually do it on Sunday morning, but I did this morning. And I heard first about the epidemic of smallpox in Pakistan;[3] and then the mass for the burial of the 3,000 or more people who were killed in the avalanche;[4] and then that group of Moslem men and a little child that were sitting on the sidewalk drinking coffee and were all mowed down by a machine gun from a passing automobile.[5] And suddenly all that I had been thinking about Blake seemed to disintegrate, and my mind began thinking about life and the reverence for life, and Albert Schweitzer, for some strange reason. So what I want to do in the time that I have is talk about that. I have had for a long time a very great admiration, admiration is the wrong word, but a great feeling of quiet joy in the fact of the existence of a man on our planet like Albert Schweitzer. And yet I have had my problems in thinking about him. But this morning, as my mind began touching him, I could see him walking across the square in his little town and being thunderstruck and convicted by the statues in the park of this European and the African, half naked, standing, looking up in the European's face with a certain sense of pleading and anguish and how, by the strange movement of the spirit of God in his life he gave up one aspect of fulfillment for himself and moved out into the heart of Africa with the

amazing and stupendous undertaking to try as *one* European to atone for *all* of the violence of *all* the Europeans on the African continent.[6]

And how I first heard about it. My mind went back to that. I was sitting in my college dormitory, and I was reading "On the Edge of a Primeval Forest" and I read this, and how incensed I was that over and over again, he regarded these Africans as children.[7] And the phrase occurred here and there, I didn't know what to do with this because I was living in an environment in which, even though a man was 75 years old, he was regarded as a child. And I recoiled against this. And then I began to see how it belonged to a pattern of thinking. I remembered the British bishop, Bishop Colenso[8] who was translating the Old Testament, particularly the Pentateuch into the Zulu language, and he had a rather intelligent Zulu working with him on the translation. And they came to the account of Noah and the ark. And all the animals. And this Zulu man said to Bishop Colenso, "Do you mean to tell me that there were animals from cold climates and hot climates, animals that lived in the water and animals that lived on land, all coming into this ark at the same time? How did they get along?" And then Bishop Colenso, who had been wrestling with a new theory of the origin and the composition of the Pentateuch, but had kept it under a bushel because he did not want to incur the wrath of the Anglican church. But he bowed his head, and he said, in reply to the Zulu's request, "Should the man of God tell a lie to a child?"[9] And I began to feel that this notion of the children was a cultural thing that I must not take it personally. And yet, as I watched through the years, this has been a blind spot. I think this is perhaps the reason why, in all the years of the work of this tremendous man for whom I have the kind of reverence that I have for few human beings in the world, in a sense, why at the twilight of his life there is no great group of Africans who have come up under his tutelage and who are prepared to carry on the work of healing. If I, as a father, find it so difficult for me ever to realize that my children are no longer children, how hard it must be for a man who regards men and women as children, ever to shift. But this must not blind me to the thing that stirred me this morning, and that is the insight which led him to go to Africa, that flowered finally in the phrase with which his life is identified, "reverence for life," the recognition of the will to live as manifest in all aspects of life, including the individual person who experiences it. And that life seems to be in a grim conflict with itself. That life lives by consuming itself. And this of course may be the raw material out of which the spiritual insight, which has to do with life everlasting, life eternal, may be grounded, I am not sure, that life consumes life. And therefore life does not die, individuals die, manifestations of life die. But life does not die. Because life consumes its vitality over and over again. And yet, and yet when men become conscious of this, their own experience of life in themselves, when they become aware, personally aware, of what Schweitzer calls "the will to live," then this awareness of what is moving through them tempers their attitude towards themselves and it enables them always, constantly, to be working to try to further and to develop and to make wider the levels of consciousness of this "will to live." And as it moves out with regard to other manifestations of life, then the problem becomes more acute and more terrifying. Doesn't it?

I want to revere life. I want to put my humanness at the disposal of any trapped life that is trying to extricate itself from that which threatens and destroys. And the thing that shocked me this morning, as I listened to this broadcast, was the fact that without ever realizing it, my own heart had hardened in a way that frightened me. I found that I wasn't moved, except as to my mind, by the spectacle of 1,400 people dying from smallpox, or 3,000 people buried by an avalanche, or 8 or 9 people mowed down by machine guns. This was—I had detachment with reference to this. As if, either they were no longer a part of the human race, or I was not a part of the human race. And as I began to work myself back into some area of tenderness and sensitiveness, the whole world of meaning of the thing that was threatening the very grounds of my own spiritual integrity, burst wide open.

How can I put my life at the disposal of all the life that is trapped around me? How can my will to live make common cause with the will to live of the person in my world to whose needs are exposed to me? How can I do this without drawing the line somewhere in order that I, myself, may not be destroyed? And I began to feel then that the identification of my life, my humaneness, with the needs of other forms of life and human life, may ultimately cause me to make the great decision. That the most significant thing that I can do to maintain and further life is to give up my own life. And then I began to think further, about all the other forms of life that are not human. And what right do I have to take them? All the thousands and thousands and thousands of animals, because of the far-reaching experimentations that have been done on them, I'm able to enjoy a certain amount of health now, that would not have been true if this had not been done. Is there any mood that will grow out of my own sense of reverence for life that will enable me to keep alive and not lose my mind, to keep alive a riding persistent sense of guilt, when the necessity is upon me to do the violent thing on behalf of some larger good that may be redemptive to a larger section of life? To keep alive my sense of guilt and involvement in all the trapped life, at all the levels, and perhaps in order that I may be able to respond to the trapped life at the human level.

I remember reading some years ago, a statement from Olive Schreiner's autobiography—biography, rather—in which she felt that Christianity had somehow misunderstood one of the most important insights of Jesus, that reverence for life, for human life, and the kind of imperative that comes from that, this is rooted in reverence for all of life; for the sparrow that falls by the roadside, for this or that, for the grass, the flowers, and she said, that if human beings do not have a sense of guilt for the destruction of so-called sub-human forms of life, then the way is open for them to have no guilt for the destruction of human life. For she says, if I say to myself, I will kill this rattlesnake because the rattlesnake is dangerous and is a threat to me, the only thing I need to do is to redefine a man as a rattlesnake and I can kill him in the same way as that. And all I need to do is to define him so that he is no longer in the human race, in the human family, and then I am free of guilt. How can I keep alive my sense of guilt, without bogging down so that it is always an incentive that drives me in the widest possible dimensions of my living, to seek out fresh ways by which I may participate in acts of atonement for the redemption of individual life, or group life? How can I keep myself always exercised that the life in me may not die? But that the life in me will join, through your need, to the life in you. And this little union is one very creative answer to all the aspects of life that are divisive and destructive and it may be that this joining of life, my life and your life, is an intimation of what ultimately must be the way and the meaning of life for us all.

And the dreamers have talked about this, haven't they? You have seen that ad, perhaps, those of you who look at television, you have seen the ad of some chewing gum I believe or something, of a lion walking down the streets in the town. And he walks into a store and looks around, and walks into another place, and people are going and coming. He is at home and they are at home. You know. If this isn't ultimately what life is all about, then as I feel it today, it is better that there be no life, be no life. So, the lion and the lamb together, the child putting his hand over the hole of an asp and the asp relaxing its violent intent and not stinging the child, that a man by private and collective will and decision, and as a result of what pushes up from within him, beats his sword into a plowshare, and his spear into a pruning hook. I must find at the level of my little life how I can do this, that my heart will not get hard and that I may not be indifferent to the anguish of life.

Forgive the weakness, redeem even that which we regard as good, our Father, that we may find our way into the order of life that will joy thy spirit and pleasure thy mind.

At.

NOTES

1. The following is from Olive Schreiner, "The Dawn of Civilization," *Nation and Athenaeum* 28, no. 26 (26 March 1921): 212–14, repr. in Carol Barash, ed., *An Olive Schreiner Reader* (New York: Pandora, 1987), 217. Thurman made minor changes to the text.

2. William Blake (1757–1827) was a visionary and mystic English poet and artist.

3. An outbreak of smallpox in Karachi, Pakistan, in December 1961 and January 1962 claimed over four hundred lives; about two million Pakistanis received smallpox vaccinations.

4. On 10 January there was a massive avalanche from Huascarán, an extinct volcano, that buried the Peruvian village of Huascarán. The death toll was later estimated to be between one thousand and fifteen hundred.

5. This probably referred to an incident in the Algerian civil war, then at its height, when seven persons were killed and sixteen wounded by machine guns and hand grenades in an attack on a café in an Algiers suburb by European terrorists associated with the OAS (Organisation de l'armée secrète [Organization of the Secret Army]); see Andrew Browlec, "21 Dead and 60 Wounded in New Algerian Violence," *Washington Post*, 15 January 1962.

6. Albert Schweitzer in his memoirs wrote that the statue was "a Herculean figure with a thoughtful, sad expression. This Negro gave me a great deal to think about. Whenever we went to Colmar [a few miles from Schweitzer's boyhood home in Alsace], I sought an opportunity to look at him. His face told me about the misery of the dark continent." Albert Schweitzer, *Memoirs of Childhood and Youth* (1924; retrans. by Kurt Bergel and Alice R. Bergel [Syracuse, N.Y.: Syracuse University Press, 1997], 57–58). The statue, a symbolic representation of Africa as a reclining black man in a loincloth at the foot of a French admiral who had helped lead the invasion of Algiers in 1830, was sculpted by Frédéric Auguste Bartholdi (1843–1904), best known as the sculptor of the Statue of Liberty in New York Harbor. The African figure was reproduced in Schweitzer, *Memoirs of Childhood and Youth*, 56.

7. Albert Schweitzer, *On the Edge of the Primeval Forest: Experiences and Observations of a Doctor in Equatorial Africa* (London: A. C. Black, 1922). Schweitzer in this book frequently referred to an African as a "child of nature," easygoing and irresponsible.

8. John William Colenso (1814–83) was appointed as the first Anglican bishop of Natal (now in South Africa) in 1853. He was one of the pioneers of higher criticism, a method of subjecting biblical texts to historical analysis, in Great Britain. His questioning of the Mosaic authorship of the Pentateuch created a furor and led to efforts to remove him from his bishopric and excommunicate him, efforts which in the end were unsuccessful. In his later years he was an outspoken defender of the Zulus in Natal against the expansion of the Boers.

9. "While translating the story of the Flood, I have had a simple-minded, but intelligent, native,—one with the docility of a child, but the reasoning powers of mature age,— look up, and ask, 'Is all that true?'" (The native proceeds to outline the multiple improbabilities of the story of the ark and the flood). "My heart answered in the words of the Prophet, 'Shall a man speak lies in the name of the Lord?' Zech.xiii.3. I dared not do so." John William Colenso, *The Pentateuch and Book of Joshua Critically Examined* (London: Longman, Green, Longman, Roberts & Green, 1862), vii.

❧ To Gilbert Ambrose
24 January 1962
[*Boston, Mass.*]

Thurman writes to his uncle Gilbert Ambrose,[1] his mother's brother, about plans to establish a meditation space at Bethune-Cookman College in Daytona Beach. The letter includes a striking tribute to Thurman's grandmother and Gilbert Ambrose's mother, Nancy Ambrose, as symbolizing "a kind of strength and integrity," linking her descendants to the time of slavery.

Howard and Sue Bailey Thurman with African students at Boston University viewing
Sue Bailey Thurman's international doll collection, c. 1962. From the Bailey Thurman
Family Papers; the Stuart A. Rose Manuscript, Archives, and Rare Book Library, Emory
University.

Mr. Gilbert Ambrose
P.O. Box 2054
DeLand, Florida

Dear Uncle Gilbert:
    For some time, Sue and I have been rethinking the plans for the meditation
chapel at Bethune-Cookman. When your letter came today, I realized that I
should have written earlier telling you about our latest thoughts.

  1. Our idea about the name of the chapel has not changed. It would be
     the Ambrose-Thurman Meditation Chapel. I like the idea of Ambrose-
     Thurman more because of Grandma than the family as such. Grandma
     symbolizes a kind of strength and integrity that links in time the period
     before the civil war, and, through the other part of the name, up to the
     present time. I think it would spoil the idea to have a brass plaque list-
     ing all the family as donors. This would give a meaning that is not a true
     meaning. The fact is that the family, as such, has no interest in a idea like

this and to list them would say a great deal for family pride and nothing more. The same ends can be served by having the name Ambrose-Thurman.

2. The funds for building the chapel will come from friends of mine and out of my own earnings, and this is as it should be.

3. I would like for you to be responsible for the books that may be available in there and for whatever musical instrument we may have, a little Hammond organ or something of that sort. This would carry a special monogram or label indicating the fact that they are given by Mr. and Mrs. Gilbert Ambrose.

4. I think that any money from Aunt Emily's estate that goes to her heirs should be used to memorialize her in DeLand, where she spent most of her useful life. This would make sense to the heirs and would be in fitting with her spirit. I certainly would want any money that would be coming to me to go for that purpose. If the public school is named for her, the money could be used for having a life-size portrait painted of her and placed at the entrance of the building bearing her name.

Sue will be going down, we hope, some time during the next week or ten days. She expects to see President Moore while she is there.

Please take care of that flu bug. Do not take any chances because the bug is a tricky monster.

All our love to both of you,

[Howard Thurman]

TLc.

NOTE

1. Gilbert Ambrose (1876–1965) was presumably born in Moseley Hall, Florida. He spent many years in Cleveland, Ohio, before returning to Florida in the latter years of his life.

🪀 To A. J. MUSTE
13 FEBRUARY 1962
[BOSTON, MASS.]

Thurman agrees to the addition of his name, among those of others, to "A Christian Approach to Nuclear War," a statement issued by the Church Peace Mission.[1] Over five hundred ministers and laypersons signed the statement, which called for multilateral disarmament, a pledge by the major powers never to use nuclear weapons, and the abandonment by the United States of military alliances with "imperialist and reactionary regimes" in the developing world.[2]

Mr. A. J. Muste
The Church Peace Mission
Room 249, Interchurch Center
475 Riverside Drive, New York 27

Dear A. J.:

Thank you very much for your letter with the enclosures. I am returning the slip immediately, because I do want to be included among those whose names are attached to "A Christian Approach to Nuclear War."

You must know what a real source of inspiration your continual witness is to all of the rest of us.

Sincerely yours,
Howard Thurman
Dean

TLc.

NOTES

1. The Church Peace Mission was established in 1950 as an umbrella organization for Christian pacifist groups. Muste was missioner (an executive position) for the Church Peace Mission from its founding until 1962.

2. "Churchmen Issue a Peace Program," *New York Times,* 2 April 1962.

🎐 "HOWARD UNIVERSITY AND THE FRONTIERS OF HUMAN FREEDOM"
2 MARCH 1962
ATLANTA, GEORGIA

Thurman's connection to and deep affection for historically black colleges was a crucial part of his personal and intellectual makeup, although it was a topic he only rarely discussed. In this address given at Howard University, Thurman pays tribute to the foresight and wisdom of Howard's founders and, without mentioning his name, to his onetime mentor and former president of Howard University, Mordecai Wyatt Johnson.

(The First Robin)[1]

1. A DARING AND RADICAL DREAM

The projection of a university primarily for freed men so close upon the heels of the Civil War was as daring as it was radical. It was daring because it did not seem to take into account the realities of the social climate but literally transcended them as of no hindering account. The dream was of a university, not a high school, not a trade school, not an agricultural school, not a normal or teacher training school, not a cooking academy, but a university dedicated to the education of the whole man and his fullest realization in the learning situation and in the society into which he would go. It was radical because it presupposed the grandest possibility of personal development and unfolding on the part of men and woman who a few short years before were slaves—the enormous presupposition becomes clear when it is recalled that the word for slave is body; that is, a thing without soul, or mind, a body. A living organism in the same way that a cat or a dog or a horse is a living organism. To assume the infinite possibility for development of individuals so regarded staggers the imagination even now.

Some perspective can be given to the position which was taken when it is recalled that in 1915, when I entered high school, and in 1919 when I finished high school in the state of Florida, there were only two public high schools open to Negroes in the entire state. One was located in Jacksonville and the other was in Palatka. Further, it was not until the fall of 1923 that the first public high school for Negroes was open in the city of Atlanta, Georgia, which at that time had a Negro population of some 85,000 people.

This dream was grounded in one of the great religious beliefs derived from the Judeo-Christian tradition that insisted upon the infinite worth of every individual in the presence of God. If this is held as binding, then the social worth of the individual would be a direct and distinct derivative from this affirmation and not be conditioned by birth, by origin, by status, by wealth or condition or by any context in which the individual at any particular moment found himself located. In other words, the genius of the democratic dogma stems in a straight line from this religious belief.

The founders of Howard University assumed that the freed slave was not merely a human being but a man, standing in permanent candidacy for the full actualization of all of his potentials. This was the first frontier of human freedom which the founders of the university staked out.[2]

2. A Private University Under Federal Sponsorship[3]

The second frontier had to do with the relationship between the federal government and the new University. As a result of certain developments growing out of the old Freedmen's Aid Bureau, and its dissolving, the federal government was induced to invest in land upon which would be built the private university. This step marked the initiation of a curious relationship between the federal government and private education. The constitution reserves the responsibility for education to the several states. The federal government could participate in the private education of its citizens without violating the constitution in this instance because the university was located in a federal district and not in a state. From the beginning, Howard University was a private institution with a self-perpetuating Board of Trustees—under federal patronage and support. It remained to be seen if this extraordinary arrangement could be worked out so that in the course of the years, there would be no political interference with the internal life of the university. How to keep a university sponsored in this way from becoming a tool of the government for policing and monitoring the political beliefs of faculty and students was and continues to be a real frontier of human freedom. For it must be remembered that this sponsoring has increased through the years until at the present time the lion's share of the cost of operating the university and the cost of all of its buildings come from the treasury of the United States government. There has been no loyalty oath inflicted. The recent experience with the National Educational Defense Act of 1958 with its loyalty oath will indicate how bold and imaginative has been the relationship between the federal government and Howard University.[4]

In order to document even in a fragmentary manner the nature of this evolution and struggle, some of you may remember the incident which I am now recalling from memory.

A few congressmen from the Subcommittee on Appropriations of the House of Representatives met in Rankin Chapel with the President of the University for a special convocation of faculty and students. The question for discussion was the whole matter of freedom of thought and action in the life of a university sponsored by federal funds. One congressman took the position that freedom of thought and learning in such an institution should be highly restricted so that there would be the closest scrutiny of the minds of faculty and students to the end that no political deviation would be tolerated. He felt that this would not apply to a private school financed by private money. The other congressman who spoke to the point took the reverse position. He felt that a private school supported by private funds could quite legitimately insist that only ideas that were in keeping with those held by the donors should be permitted. But a private school supported by state funds or a state school should permit the widest possible deviations guaranteed by freedom of thought and speech because the funds came from all the people among whom would be found individuals of the widest possible variation in political thought and belief. When these two speeches were made, the President of the University responded. He reviewed in a very short and terse manner his experience in seeking to guarantee for himself freedom of thought with reference to the crucial issue of the Darwinian theory of evolution and religious thought when he himself was a student. He closed his statement by saying that as long as he was President of Howard University, if the time ever came when he must chose between freedom of thought and speech for faculty and students and federal support, he would choose freedom of thought and speech for faculty and students. When I was walking out of the Chapel, one of my friends said to me, "Yes, he would make such a choice and we'd all starve."

The responsibility of the university to safeguard the integrity of the mind and the responsibility of the federal government to honor such integrity mark the second great frontier of freedom which Howard University staked out. It has far reaching significance for the problem of the private school and federal funds today.[5]

3. A Laboratory of Experimentation in Freedom

It will follow then that a close examination of the history of Howard University should reveal that here in many ways we would find a laboratory in which various aspects of responsible freedom could be developed. Let us look at the record.

First, the earliest experiments with responsible student government among students made up primarily of Negro youths were to be found. To locate what this means, it need only be pointed out that in 1932, when I came to Howard University to join the faculty, I had been working for several years at my own college—Morehouse. Despite the atmosphere of that college in which freedom of thought was encouraged, there was not even the beginning of student government. As a matter of fact, it hardly occurred to anybody to do anything about it. The recognition of the responsibility of the university to encourage the development of freedom of initiative on the part of undergraduate students was first manifest among schools primarily for freed men—at Howard University. Therefore, it is not accidental that the first student YMCA among any of our schools was located on this campus.[6] Think of what this meant. Students were permitted to have an organization under the sponsorship of persons or institutions that were not a part of the university life. Into this organization, as routine, came traveling secretaries—men from time to time bringing with them thoughts, ideas, testimonies concerning what was taking place on far flung campuses in the United States. This not only was permitted, but encouraged.

You may recall that in one of Pliny's letters to the emperor, he complained that there was much loss of property due to fires in his district in North Africa. There was no organization of citizens to combat these fires. Hence Pliny wrote the emperor requesting permission to organize a fire-fighting collegium.[7] The request was denied because the emperor said that if he permitted a collegium to discuss plans for fire-fighting, they might in the course of their discussions, discuss plans for getting rid of the emperor. Such a risk Howard University was willing to run.

2. Almost from the beginning the faculty of this university have enjoyed more than the customary autonomy. During the period of the early development of the University, most of the faculty in the schools for freedmen scattered throughout the South were appointed by Boards—Mission Boards that were located outside of the region. The Boards through their executives made the appointments. Faculty persons therefore were only partially responsible to the President. Each knew that it might be that his particular appointment was not

initiated in the first instance by the President. This made for divided loyalties, to say the least. The line of command at Howard University from the beginning was from a Board of Trustees, holding their meetings within the region, most often on the campus, to the President, to the several faculties. This gave to the faculties a kind of autonomy which in the history of the university sometimes caused the role of the President to be a stormy one. But here was the recognition of the integrity of the faculty man or woman as a responsible person.[8]

The role of religion in the university defines even more profoundly the laboratory character of the experimentation with freedom. Among the several colleges of the University from the beginning was a school of religion. Mark you, I said a school of religion, not a school of theology, and not a divinity school.[9] It seems therefore that a very deliberate effort was made to focus upon the necessity for maintaining the dialogue between religion and the other disciplines within the university, without being under the handicap of sectarian or parochial considerations. This marked a unique role for the school of religion as distinguished from other types of religious schools. From my point of view, it is to be regretted that there has been no recognizable acceptance of this peculiar role of the school of religion. It has interpreted the demands of the historical moment on the side of preparing men to become ministers in local churches, though it has been interdenominational in its faculty and student body and therefore unique, but its true mission is not at that point. Its true mission was to address itself to the religious needs and continuing aspirations of the human spirit in a university community in which the minds of its members were undergoing constant growth and development. To confirm and affirm the significance of religion in that continuing process was its chief mission. The degree to which this mission has failed is marked by the necessity for the sectarian emphasis to be brought into the life of the university community that the claims of religion might be upheld.

The kind of freedom of religion as manifest in the historic role of Andrew Rankin Memorial Chapel should be given at least passing consideration. For a long time the religious needs of the community were in the hands of a faculty committee on religious life. This committee was made up of lay people— men and women. It was they who selected the preacher for the annual religious emphasis week series; it was they who selected the Sunday preachers for Chapel. There never was the slightest feeling that the Chapel should become a church. It is not a church and was not designed to become a church. It is a free pulpit where in the open exchange of ideas under the aegis of the Holy Spirit of God, the context of worship could be encountered and assessed in terms of the good life. During the entire period of my service as Dean of the Chapel, not a single time did the administration of the university seek in any way to abridge this freedom.

What of the future? It would seem to me that the university must daily confirm its purpose to continue its right to address itself to the frontiers of human freedom. Its purpose must be redefined constantly in the light of the new demands which the events of contemporary history present. If it is true that the purpose of education is to liberate men, to increase their competency and their knowledge so that the use to which the knowledge is put will be determined not only by human need but by the clear sweeping vitality of great moral impulses, then the function of Howard University will find its significance within the range of such a purpose.

It is so easy for the trained mind to relinquish its membership in the human race, to feel that the prerogatives which are theirs through the mastery of a discipline give to them immunity from moral and natural laws which are binding upon ordinary people. If I may in closing illustrate this. I wish to appeal beforehand to all the medical doctors who are in the audience and to say to them that there isn't anything personal in what I am about to say. Some years ago I was given a regular physical examination by a doctor who was an acquaintance of mine. After he had done his part, he sent me to several other places for different kinds of tests. When these were all in, he called me into his office and sat me down in the chair. Before him he had a manila folder in which were the typewritten reports from the various tests. As he looked at each one, his eyes would glance up at me as he nodded his head with approval, with a "uh huh." He came to one page and held it up and scrutinized it and looked at me and great was my relief when he put it down and nodded his head and went on. He closed the folder and then he looked at me saying, "You are in good shape for your age—your heart, lungs, etc. are in good shape—but you are getting too heavy." He talked with me very learnedly about what the excess weight would do to my heart and lungs, etc. Then I looked at him. He wasn't any taller than I, but he weighed about 235 pounds. He thought that his body knew that he was a doctor. His body didn't know that he was a doctor. His body only knew that he was a member of the human race, just as I, and that he was storing up more caloric units than his body was burning up. Thus the storage in the form of the bulges.

To see to it that at the heart of the knowledge and the competency there is the moral demand that determines the use to which such knowledge may be put, and the recognition that there are no immunities in which all men are not involved—this is at long last the inescapable necessity to which the university as a community of seekers after truth is dedicated.

TD.

Notes
    1. Thurman's opening reading was "The First Robin," originally published in the *Pittsburgh Press*, 15 February 1934, repr. in Heywood Hale Broun, *Collected Edition of Heywood*

Broun (New York: Harcourt, Brace, 1941), 308–10. Heywood Broun (1888–1939) was a well-known newspaper columnist. "The First Robin" contained Broun's reflections on a robin found frozen to death in late winter, the "first robin" that had flown north that year. Broun wrote, "It is almost a rule that the first robin must die alone on some bleak common before mankind will agree that he was a hero. And sometimes it takes fifty years and often a hundred. . . . You were the first, and after you will come others. They will inherit the grubs and the nests and the comfort. But yours is the glory. You are the first robin."

2. Howard University was founded in 1867 by a group of Washington-area Congregationalists, including Oliver O. Howard (1830–1909), head of the Freedmen's Bureau.

3. For the history of Howard University, see Rayford W. Logan, *Howard University: The First Hundred Years, 1867–1967* (New York: New York University Press, 1969).

4. The National Educational Defense Act of 1958, passed that September, required faculty in participating institutions to sign affidavits disclaiming a belief in the overthrow of the U.S. government. Many institutions of higher learning, including Howard, refused to participate. The affidavit requirement was eliminated in the fall of 1962.

5. This probably refers to a hearing at Rankin Chapel on 18 May 1935 held by a subcommittee of the House Committee on Appropriations. It was reported that at the hearing, Howard's president, Mordecai Wyatt Johnson, stated that he "preferred 'academic freedom' to government support." See "Mitchell Asks 'Red' Quiz for Howard," *Chicago Defender*, 1 June 1935. Johnson had created something of a furor with his speech to the graduating class of 1933, in which he called communism "a new religion" and claimed that "on Russian soil today there is a movement for the first time in the history of the world to make available the national resources for the life of the common man" ("Howard University Indorses Communism," *Chicago Defender*, 10 June 1933). Although he clarified his remarks and stated that he was not a communist, there were many members of Congress who wanted Johnson fired, and the university investigated. Those hostile to Johnson included the only African American members of Congress, Oscar De Priest and his successor Arthur W. Mitchell, who both represented Chicago. De Priest called for Johnson's firing in 1933. See "Howard Univ., President Johnson, Argued in Congress," *Baltimore Afro-American*, 24 June 1933. Mitchell spearheaded the call for an investigation of communism at Howard.

6. The YMCA chapter at Howard University was established in 1869.

7. Pliny the Younger (61–c. 112 C.E.), a Roman official, wrote a letter to the Emperor Trajan asking for advice on how to deal with the Christians; see Pliny, *Epistulae* 10.96.

8. For a discussion of the autonomy of the faculties when "deans were virtually running the school" in the years between the late nineteenth century and the arrival of Mordecai Wyatt Johnson, see Dyson, "Deans in Control," in *Howard University*, 63–69.

9. The theological department at Howard University was organized in 1870. It became the School of Religion in 1918, the Divinity School in 1981, and subsequently the School of Divinity.

☙ To James M. Nabrit, Jr.
6 March 1962
[*Boston, Mass.*]

The Thurmans had long taken an interest in African American history, and Sue Bailey Thurman made this a focus of her work, publishing several books on the subject.[1] *As Thurman notes in this letter to James M. Nabrit, Jr.,*[2] *Sue was then at work on an effort to create a black history collection in Boston. In 1964 she published, with her daughter Anne Thurman Chiarenza, an annotated map to Boston's black history.*[3] *The 1960s were times of heightened interest in the creation of black-oriented museums, and the Thurmans felt that the main organization for promoting interest in African American history, the Association for the Study of Negro Life and History, was too narrow in its focus; they implied that it lacked the energetic leadership it had enjoyed in the past.*

Dr. James M. Nabrit, Jr.
President
Howard University
Washington 1, D.C.

Dear Brother:

Before I plunge into something that is uppermost in the mind of both Sue and me, about which I wanted to talk when I was there, let me say to you that last Friday was one of the significant moments in my life.[4] I am still too close to it to assess it, but the inside feeling about it is very good.

We have been wondering if you would be interested in the possibility of converting Howard Hall into a National Museum of Negro Life and History, with office space provided for the Association for the Study of Negro Life and History. It is possible even that the Mooreland Collection could be housed there also.

When Charles Wesley[5] is no longer able to hold things together as he rapidly approaches the twilight, it is possible that the Association itself, will become only a "learned" society of professors of history in Negro colleges of the South and, in rare instances, in the North, who use the annual meeting as a springboard for reading papers and publishing dissertations and other historical material, through the Negro History Journal and Bulletin.

It is not now an organization reaching into the heart of Negro life, giving a sense of dignity and appreciation for the past without which the present and the future do not have their rightful significance. It could cover every corner of the Nation with its particular message, especially in these days. I think that one of the needful things, as our young people storm the gates on the Frontiers of Freedom, is some sense of history that will enable them to share responsibly in laying out the new city. All of this you understand much better than I.

If much of the collecting and preserving of our documents, data and landmarks continues to be left to well-intentioned but unskilled women's organizations, there will soon be nothing. One small case in point is the Douglass Home in Anacostia, "restored" by the National Association of Colored Women in the

1920s, and now being "restored" again in 1962, when all of the available papers have been scattered or lost in an unattended building. The National Council of Negro Women proposes to purchase a brand new building for "archives," raising thousands of dollars for the purpose, but even a change of administration could destroy the plan of any national, social-civic organization.[6]

Sue is working with the Association of Negro Life and History trying to organize a Chapter in Boston, and collecting historical material for them during the summer and fall in connection with a travelogue of National Landmarks in Negro History, which she expects to have ready for publication some time in 1962. But if invaluable items are discovered and collected, where will they go?

Since Carter Woodson[7] taught at Howard and had the assistance of the University faculty and staff in practically all of his publications, could not Howard Hall be given to the perpetuation of his dream as a repository for vital materials, freedom papers, first diplomas, deeds of various kinds, oldest minutes, photographs, magazines, newspapers, charters, etc.?

I understand that a college in the Deep South is eager to establish such a museum on Negro history, but it would certainly seem that there is only one place for it—the Nation's capitol.

You will please keep this correspondence between us in confidence, as neither Sue nor I, however deep and continuous are our concerns, have any authority, officially speaking, to raise these vital questions, but our interest is such that we can gladly offer our personal energy, thought and means to the service of the idea. Let me hear.

Sincerely,

Howard Thurman

Dean

TLc.

NOTES

1. Sue Bailey Thurman, *Pioneers of Negro Origin in California* (San Francisco: Acme, 1952); Sue Bailey Thurman, ed., *The Historical Cookbook of the American Negro* (Washington, D.C.: Corporate Press, 1958). The cookbook, prepared by the National Council of Negro Women with Sue Bailey Thurman as the lead editor, contained a good deal of Negro history—not only the history of characteristic African American foodstuffs and foodways, but also many accounts of significant persons and events in African American history. It was reprinted by Beacon Press in 2000.

2. James Madison Nabrit, Jr. (1900–1997), a Georgia native, was a member of Thurman's class of 1923 at Morehouse College. After graduating from the Northwestern School of Law in 1927, he practiced and taught law in various locations before joining the faculty of the Howard University School of Law in 1936. He argued many important cases for the NAACP Legal Defense Fund, was dean of the Howard University School of Law from 1958 to 1960, and had two stints as president of Howard University—from 1960 to 1965 and from 1968 to 1969.

3. Anne Thurman Chiarenza and Sue Bailey Thurman, *Freedom Trails of Negro History in Boston* (Boston, 1964). The map depicted twenty-two points of African American history in Boston, with a brief description of each. See *Crisis* 71 (March 1964): 203.

4. On 2 March, Thurman was at Howard to deliver the lecture "Howard University and the Frontiers of Human Freedom," printed in the current volume.

5. For Charles Wesley (1891–1987), see *PHWT*, 2:309. Wesley was director of the Association for the Study of Negro Life and History from 1950 until 1965. The organization was renamed the Association for the Study of African American Life and History in 1972.

6. In 1900 Helen Pitts Douglass (1838–1903), the second wife of Frederick Douglass, established the Frederick Douglass Memorial and Historical Association, which upon her death assumed ownership of Cedar Hill, the Douglass home in Anacostia, Washington, D.C. In 1916 the National Association of Colored Women's Clubs became co-owner of the house. In 1962 the National Park Service acquired the home, which now is operated by the Park Service as a National Historic Site.

7. For Carter Godwin Woodson (1875–1950), see *PWHT*, 2:6–7. After teaching at Howard for only two (rather stormy) years, 1918 to 1920, Woodson was fired by Howard's president, J. Stanley Durkee. See Jacqueline Goggin, *Carter G. Woodson: A Life in Black History* (Baton Rouge: Louisiana State University Press, 1993), 48–53.

꙳ Drafts of Telegrams to John F. Kennedy, Robert F. Kennedy, and Laurie Pritchett
11 July 1962
Boston, Mass.

On 18 December 1961 Martin Luther King, Jr., was arrested in Albany, Georgia, for his participation in the antisegregation Albany Movement. He was released, but as part of the ongoing efforts of the Albany Movement he returned on 10 July to the city, where rather than pay a fine, he and Ralph Abernathy determined to serve a forty-five-day jail sentence. Thurman's three telegrams all called for King and Abernathy to be freed. On 12 July, when a mysterious third party paid for their release, King and Abernathy were upset, assuming that this was an effort by Laurie Pritchett, the canny Albany police chief, to get the Albany Movement out of the headlines. King and Abernathy remained in Albany, were rearrested on 27 July, and remained incarcerated until 10 August.

BOSTON UNIVERSITY
To:
From:
Subject: Telegrams:
President John F. Kennedy[1] White House Washington, D.C.

Earnestly and respectfully urge you to use the tremendous weight of your moral influence on behalf of Martin Luther King and Ralph Abernathy,[2] condemned

to serve 45 days jail sentence Albany, Georgia for peacefully protesting segregation as of last December in said city.
Howard Thurman
Marsh Chapel, Boston University

Attorney General[3]
Respectfully urge you to use the power of your office on behalf of Martin Luther King and Ralph Abernathy condemned to serve 45 days jail sentence Albany, Georgia for peacefully protesting segregation as of last December in said city.

Governor Vandiver,[4] Governor's Office, Atlanta, Georgia

Police Chief Laurie Pritchett,[5] Albany, Georgia
Respectfully urge you to use the strength and moral courage of your office as police chief to insure adequate safety and protection of the Reverend Doctors King and Abernathy as they carry out the work sentence on the street force in Albany under your direction.

Howard Thurman
Marsh Chapel, Boston University

TWd.

NOTES
1. John Fitzgerald Kennedy (1917–63) was a Massachusetts member of the U.S. House of Representatives (1947–53) and the U.S. Senate (1953–60) before his election as president of the United States in 1960. For Thurman's thoughts about Kennedy, see his Africa Journal and eulogy for John F. Kennedy, printed in *PHWT*, vol. 5 (forthcoming).
2. Ralph Abernathy (1926–90) was a close associate of Martin Luther King, Jr., and King's successor as head of the Southern Christian Leadership Conference.
3. Robert Francis "Bobby" Kennedy (1925–68), brother of John F. Kennedy, was attorney general of the United States (1961–64) and a U.S. senator from New York State (1965–68). He was assassinated in California in June 1968 during his campaign for the Democratic presidential nomination.
4. Ernest Vandiver, Jr. (1918–2005), was governor of Georgia from 1959 to 1963.
5. Laurie Pritchett (1926–2000) was chief of police in Albany, Georgia, from 1959 to 1966 and police chief in High Point, North Carolina, from 1966 to 1974

෴ "WORSHIP AND WORD: A VIEW OF THE LIBERAL CONGREGATION AND ITS SERMONS"
16 OCTOBER 1962[1]

Thurman prepared this paper as a member of the Commission on Religion and the Arts of the Unitarian Universalist Church.[2] Under the chairmanship of John F.

*Hayward,[3] a professor at Meadville Theological Seminary in Chicago, the com-
mission had as its task suggesting ways to bring greater variety and vividness to
worship services through imaginative use of music and dance and rethinking the
role of the sermon. It is a subject that had long been of keen interest to Thurman.[4]*

*The commission is one of six organized by the Unitarian Church in 1959 just
prior to its merger with the Universalist Church, each reevaluating an important aspect of Unitarian practice. The timetable of the work of the Commission
on Religion and the Arts is not clear. There probably were some meetings, most
likely in Boston, and evidently some subsequent exchange of papers before the
preparation of the final report, which, without incorporating Thurman's specific
language, broadly reflects his perspectives on worship.[5]*

*"Worship and Word" was one of Thurman's most extended and illuminating
reflections on the role of the sermon in religious worship. The sermon, he argues,
has a complex role in worship. It is not a lecture or a "commonplace homily" but
"must always have the smell of ammonia about it. It must be vital and contagious." To accomplish this, the sermon, while speaking to the entire congregation,
with all of their differences and their various expectations from the sermon, must
speak to each individual without confirming "prejudices or idiosyncrasies" or
"mak[ing] a sacrament of triteness and mediocrity." Instead it must touch what
each listener "recognizes as the God and Creator of his spirit. It is as if the tidal
wave of communal fellowship which he experiences in the congregation casts him
up to the surface, and he stands there alone."*

My paper is divided into two sections. The first deals with the place and significance of the sermon in the context of worship. The second deals with the
sermon in and of itself.

The sermon is a part of the total worship experience which is designed to
challenge and convict, to inspire and reassure, to illumine and guide. It is a part
of the integrated worship experience; the word "integrated" here has to do with
the structure and the order and orderliness of the worship pattern.

The structure of the worship service in the so-called free or liberal churches
is held together by its inner quality rather than by the rigidity or the inflexibility
of its form. It is addressed to the timeless needs and aspirations of the human
spirit and the assumption upon which it rests is that those who participate in
it contribute as significantly as those who lead it. It is for this reason that the
service of worship is communal and only incidentally is there a stellar role.

I would like to consider then in the first place the congregation itself and
what it is that brings them to a place of worship and what it is they seek. It is
obvious in any consideration of this kind that the place of conditioning and

habit should and must be recognized. Despite the things that are said and written about the stark individualism, independence and emancipation of the members of the liberal churches, they are creatures of habit as are all of the other members of the human family. There is a vast kind of emotional security and therefore sense of belonging that is to be found in coming together in acts of communal celebration as one's fathers did at another time and another period. Even the deliberate effort to resist the habit pattern is but another way of confirming its significance.

Those who come to worship do not come as philosophers, scientists, metaphysicians, artists, intellectuals, "brains," but they come as human beings: men, women, who eat and sleep; who are involved not merely in the human situation but also in the human predicament. They want to be understood, to be cared for, to have their spirits warmed by human fires. It is as human beings that they come to church on Sunday morning. This is the common tie that binds and holds.

They come from a wide variety of personal and private predicaments and situations. Some of them are lonely and frightened; some are tired and world weary; some are eager and vital; some are harassed and mean, and some are spontaneous and outgoing. In the service of worship, each must find his place, and for each somewhere in the service must be found a moment which claims him and speaks to his condition.

Therefore, in building or designing the service of worship, of which the sermon is a part, deliberate care must be given to the selection of any and all of the elements that go to make up the service itself. The music must be solid and beautiful. It must warm the heart without isolating the emotions so that they become an independent entity divorced from the wholeness of the person. The significance of the music as music must be subordinate to the mood and the need of worship. And what applies to the music other than hymns applies most dramatically to the hymns themselves.

The general pattern of the worship service in the liberal churches places the sermon in a climactic sequence. Often the place given to the sermon in the order of the service indicates that everything else is preliminary and is in preparation for the moment when the preacher preaches. True, the logic of the order and the place where the sermon occurs in the service would indicate that this is the design. Historically, there is precedent for this development or evolution. It is my judgment, however, that much depends upon how the preacher conceives his role. If he regards himself as the spearhead of the collective act of worship, then in his own mind the sermon is an integral part of the creative experience which is shared by all the worshippers. If, however, his interpretation of the sermon places it in a category that is in a sense independent of the so-called worship experience, the place of the sermon is of another order entirely, and the service has a sharp division between the worship which includes the music and the prayers, the readings, and the sermon, which addresses itself almost exclusively to the minds of the people who were a few minutes before a part of the collective or communal blending.

My position is the former. For me the sermon is an integral part of the total worship experience. To use an inadequate figure, the sermon is the part of the island that emerges above the sea level but it is a part of the mountain that goes down into the depths of the sea. It does not interfere with or challenge the unity of the service, but it confirms and sustains the unity. Ideally, the sermon is a lung through which the worship service breathes one breath and the worship service is the lung through which the sermon breathes one breath. When this is achieved, the worshippers sense that through the sermon, all the meaning that they had been experiencing up to that moment is made uniquely available to each as his private insight, despite the collective and binding act of the worship experience itself. I think this is what is meant when a worshipper says to the preacher, "It's as if you were speaking directly to me." What I am saying is not to indicate that the function of the sermon in the worship scheme is to confirm prejudices or idiosyncrasies and to make a sacrament of triteness and mediocrity; it is simply to insist that the sermon belongs in and to the worship service and must in many ways confirm the human spirit in its great quest for meaning, for significance, and for intentional living.

To be sure my voice may be a minority voice in the rarified company of the intellectuals who make up this commission,[6] but I am bound to give my witness. The act of worship is the highest act of celebration of the human spirit. It is the moment of all moments when the worshipper "images" himself in the presence of his God, when he has a sense of encounter with the supreme object of his devotion, where he is stripped of everything that is not literal and irreducible in himself and the ultimate grounds of his self-respect are laid bare to him. In such an experience and at such a moment, he is not a Unitarian or a Trinitarian, an American or a European, male or female, white or black, but a human spirit in vital touch with what he recognizes as the God and Creator of his spirit. It is as if the tidal wave of communal fellowship which he experiences in the congregation casts him up to the surface, and he stands there alone.

PART II

I found myself very responsive to much of what Waldemar Argow[7] had to say in his paper on Unitarian preaching. Particularly was I impressed by his words of authority as one who not only is a part of the Unitarian tradition but who stands within that tradition with the right to speak forthrightly concerning preaching within that tradition. What I have to say in this section of my paper may be repetitious or in some ways supplementary.

The sermon is the distillation of the thinking, reading, observation, brooding and meditation of the preacher. The assumption is that it is his privilege to withdraw from the traffic of life periodically and regularly in order that he may take the kind of long hard look at the world, the society, his fellows, and speak the authentic word which will stimulate the mind, inform even as he kindles the emotions, and inspire his fellows to live the good life responsibly. He is part of the company of his fellows, making the same journey along the same way which is their journey and their way, but he has a particular task and a particular responsibility. He must get bearings concerning the road ahead. He must not lose sight of the way over which they have come and how it relates to the path or the way in which they are walking and how these are related to the road ahead.

To state my meaning categorically, it would be something like this:

a) He places before his congregation and of course himself, the vision of a great ideal for mankind; the ideal is one of community for the children of men; the vision is of a collective destiny which includes more and more the entire human race.

b) He calls attention to the quality of mind, devotion, commitment, and the kinds of skills, techniques, and methods by which the literal truth of the ideal must become literal fact for the individual and the society. Whatever has been a part of the demonstration in his particular tradition must be made relevantly current and whatever may be learned from any other traditions made available in the supreme effort of the implementation of the ideal.

c) He must expose the resources upon which he and his people may draw that can be enabling in this process: the resources of individual testimony from the past or present of those who are a part of the tradition; the resources that are to be found in contemporary life whether they fall narrowly within a context regarded as religious or not; resources that lay at a deeper level or ground than the deliberate intent of the individual or the impersonal direction of the social process, resources which in my language are to be found in God.

The sermon is not a lecture; it is not merely an academic or intellectual exercise for the mind; it is not a commonplace homily that lulls into quiescence or sedation; no—the sermon must always have the smell of ammonia about it. It must be vital and contagious.

It is now in order to make a few comments about preaching itself. Preaching is a skill, a technique and an art. It requires a particular kind of discipline because the critical tool is the spoken word. The preacher must be on friendly and intimate terms with the private life and particular history of the word.

He must be familiar with their flavor so that in his use of them they will be authentic carriers of the meaning which he seeks to convey. He must know that there are words that fly and soar high above the plains and their dwelling place is the mountain peak. There are words that nestle close to the ground and fall back quivering and helpless when forced to breathe air that is high and rarified.

There are words that sing and if they are not made to be a part of a chorus, true to their nature, their sounds will be discordant and unharmonious. This does not mean that there are not solo words which come into their fullest glory when alone and unaccompanied; they make the music of their kind. There are words that struggle and stammer because they are so big with meaning that sound and form are utterly inadequate through which their meaning can be expressed. There are words that agonize and shed their travail over all the landscape of the mind. There are gentle words whose tenderness moves through to the heart bypassing all the regions hard won by the rational and reflective process. The critical tool for the preacher is the word. The preacher must speak not merely to a condition and a need but he must speak out of the struggle of his own spirit and out of the insights which sometimes he must wrest from the stubborn and often recalcitrant grip of hard idea and whole rational processes. It must never be forgotten that the preacher is a whole man in the sense that he is a person who is learning how to honor the powers of his mind and the feelings of his heart as a part of a single personality which is he. He may not be an orator or he may not be a man with some rare mystique or speech, but he must be alive with the meaning which he thinks and feels and shares. All of this means that the sermon is the vehicle through which the word becomes flesh and bone for preacher and congregation.

                                                                                        TD.

NOTES

    1. If the typed date at the bottom of the typescript is correct, Thurman evidently, and somewhat implausibly, completed this paper on a day when he was scheduled to speak to a federation of Native American chiefs in Regina, Saskatchewan, far from his office typewriter. However, it is possible that he finished it slightly earlier. See Synda Altschuler (Thurman's secretary) to John F. Hayward, 13 September 1962.

    2. Thurman was one of ten members (all male) of the commission, which included architects and musicians as well as ministers.

    3. John F. Hayward (1918–2012) was a graduate of Harvard University (1940) and Meadville Theological Seminary (1943), and he received his Ph.D. from the University of Chicago Divinity School (1949). He taught at the University of Chicago (1951–61), Meadville Theological Seminary (1961–68), and Southern Illinois University (1968–83). His books include *Existentialism and Religious Liberalism* (Boston: Beacon Press, 1962) and *Through the Rose Window: Art, Myth, and the Religious Imagination* (Boston: Skinner House, 2002).

    4. HT, *Footprints of a Dream*, 24–28.

Howard Thurman (seated).
From the Howard Thurman
Collection, Howard Gotlieb
Archival Research Center at
Boston University.

5. "Religion and the Arts," in Unitarian Universalist Association, *The Free Church in a Changing World: The Reports of the Commissions to the Churches and Fellowships of the Unitarian Universalist Association* (Boston: Unitarian Universalist Association, 1963), 77–102.

6. Commission on Religion and the Arts.

7. Waldemar Argow (1916–96) was a prominent Unitarian minister who led congregations in Cedar Rapids, Iowa; Toledo, Ohio; and Palm Beach, Florida. His many books include *What Do Religious Liberals Believe?* (Yellow Springs, Ohio: Antioch Press, 1950) and *The Case for Liberal Religion* (Yellow Springs, Ohio: Antioch Press, 1954).

🌱 FROM TIMOTHY LEARY
29 OCTOBER 1962
CAMBRIDGE, MASS.

This is the only extant letter between Timothy Leary[1] and Thurman.[2] It is also one of two documents extant in Thurman's papers that make any reference to the Good Friday Experiment.[3] Thurman remained a good friend of Walter Pahnke until the latter's untimely death in 1971, but he had little or no contact with Leary after Leary's firing from Harvard University the following spring. Whether Thurman attended this (or any) meetings of Leary's religious mysticism group is unknown.

Dean Howard Thurman
Marsh Chapel
Boston University
Boston, Massachusetts

Dear Howard Thurman:

Walter Pahnke asked if I would send you the enclosed materials which describe some of our recent activities in "experimental mysticism."

As you know the Good Friday experiment has turned out to be a ringing success—spiritually (for the subjects) and scientifically.

There will be a meeting of the religious mysticism group on Sunday, November 4th at the home of Mr. and Mrs. Robert Greenleaf,[4] 12 Frances Avenue, Cambridge. We extend welcome to you if you can join us that evening.

May I express again my admiration for your work and my gratitude for your help and counsel to Walter Pahnke.

Sincerely yours,
[signed] Timothy Leary
Timothy Leary, Ph.D.
TL/pc
enc.

                                                                  TLS.

Notes

1. See the biographical essay in the current volume.

2. For a detailed discussion of the Good Friday Experiment and Leary's and Walter Pahnke's roles in it, see the biographical essay in the current volume.

3. The other is Thurman's telegram To Shirley Katzander, 8 August 1963, discussed in the biographical essay and the appendix in the current volume.

4. Robert K. Greenleaf (1904–90) was an executive at AT&T and a lecturer at the business schools of Harvard and MIT. A management theorist, his best-known book is *Servant Leadership: A Journey into the Nature of Legitimate Power and Greatness* (New York: Paulist Press, 1977). After his retirement in 1964, he founded the Center for Applied Ethics in Westfield, Indiana, which is now the Robert K. Greenleaf Center for Servant Leadership. Esther Hargrave Greenleaf (1905–89) was a noted art historian, painter, and printmaker. Even before meeting Leary, the Greenleafs were active experimenters with psychedelic substances. See Don M. Frick, *Robert K. Greenleaf: A Life of Servant Leadership* (San Francisco: Berrett-Koehler, 2004), 212–18.

Appendix

🦋 To Shirley Katzander
8 August 1963
[Boston, Mass.]

Shirley Katzander,[1] *the director of promotion for the* Reporter,[2] *sent Thurman an advanced copy of Noah Gordon's article "The Hallucinogenic Drug Cult"*[3] *on 5 August and wrote, "If you would care to comment, we should be interested in hearing from you."*[4] *Thurman's terse, angry telegram is his only known comment on the Good Friday Experiment,*[5] *which occurred in Marsh Chapel on 20 April 1962. The article, which did not mention Thurman by name, is one of the first to bring popular attention to the experiment and helped fashion its reputation among spiritual seekers in the 1960s. Thurman objected to the rather sensational subhead, "The Miracle of Marsh Chapel," and the implication that Boston University might have played a role in procuring the psilocybin used by Walter Pahnke and Timothy Leary in the experiment.*[6]

Copy of telegram sent 8/8/63
Shirley Katzander
Director of Promotion
The Reporter
600 Madison Avenue
New York 21, New York

The caption "The Miracle of Marsh Chapel" in body of Gordon article is a gross distortion of fact. Also, in subsequent paragraph, the article states the experiment was carried on in two small rooms off the main Chapel. The fact is the rooms were on another floor and not "off the main Chapel." Furthermore, by implication, that section of the article implies and infers that Marsh Chapel and therefore Boston University were officially involved in the procuring of drugs for the experiment and/or in other ways involved beyond the use of the rooms. This is not only a distortion of what happened and a false implication, but it is in distinct violation of what I stated clearly to Noah Gordon in a telephone conversation. I stated to him in direct response to his questions concerning the degree of Marsh Chapel's involvement in the experiment that there was no involvement beyond the use of the facilities of rooms on the ground floor into which, quite regularly, services from the sanctuary are piped.

I await your reply.

(Signed) Dr. Howard Thurman

Dean of Marsh Chapel

TW.

NOTES

1. Shirley Katzander (1921–99) was director of promotion for the *Reporter* in the 1950s and 1960s and thereafter ran her own public relations firm.

2. The *Reporter* was a biweekly journal of opinion with a liberal and anticommunist orientation published from 1949 to 1969.

3. Noah Gordon, "The Good Friday Experiment," *Reporter,* 15 August 1963, 35–43.

4. From Shirley Katzander, 5 August 1963.

5. For more on the Good Friday Experiment, see the biographical essay in the current volume.

6. Philip Horton (1911–89), executive editor of the *Reporter* from 1949 until it ceased publication in 1969, replied to Thurman's telegram; he offered to print his response to the article while stating that "the passage about Marsh Chapel was intended merely to indicate that rooms in the vicinity of the main chapel were used to conduct an experiment with the drug, that your service was piped into the rooms, and that this was done with your knowledge and consent. We consider that those facts were clearly stated in the article, and that no other interpretation is possible" (From Philip Horton, 12 August 1963).

Index

Page references in **bold** refer to illustrations or photographs; page references in *italics* refer to biographical information contained in the notes.

Abernathy, Ralph, 326–27, *327n2*

Abyssinian Baptist Church (Harlem), 307–8

Acevedo, Rokee, *16n9*

Acty, Ruth, 16n9

Adams, James Truslow, *220n1*

Addams, Jane, *169n5*

Adler, Felix, 130n22

Africa, 17n16, 51, 278, 298, 309–14, 320, 327n1; African students at Boston University, **315**; Congo, 275n15; Operation Crossroads Africa, 157n7; Thurman's visit to, xl, 222; urge toward liberty and equality, 132. *See also* Schweitzer, Albert

ahimsa, 7, 9n12

Albany Movement, The, 326

"Albert Schweitzer" (Thurman), 309–14

Algeria, 310, 314n5

Ali, Syed Ameer, 289, 294n2

Alice Ambrose Fellowship Children's Fund, 18

Allahabad, 11n6

Allen, Steve, 298, *299n8*

Allen University, 89

Alpert, Richard, xxx–xxxi. *See also* Baba Ram Dass

Alter, Robert, 29n5

"America in Search of a Soul" (Thurman), 120n11

Ambrose, Gilbert (uncle), 2n1, 243, 244n4, 314–16, *316n1*

Ambrose, Louise, 1

Ambrose, Nancy, 314–15

American Communist Party, 44–45

"American Dream, The" (Thurman), 215–21

American Methodist Episcopal Church (AME), 34, 136n6

American University of Beirut, 283

Amherst College, 203

Amidah, the, 257n9

"Amos 'n' Andy" (radio comedy) 34–35

Amsterdam News, xxiii

Andover-Newton Theological Seminary, xxxi, xlviin82

anti-Catholicism, 134

anti-Negroism, 283

anti-semitism, 134, 283

apostles of sensitiveness, 13; racial minorities as, 37; in recovery from war, 22

Archer, Samuel Howard, 225, *231n5*

Argow, Waldemar, 330, *333n7*

Armstrong, Edward H., *10n4*

Arnold, Matthew, 146

Asia, urge toward liberty and equality, 132

Association for the Study of Negro Life and History, 324–26

Atlanta (Georgia), xxvi, 30–32, 97–98, 111–12, 155, 261, 304–5, 317–18

Atlantic Charter, 205, 207n8; the Four Freedoms, 205, 207n8

Atlantic Monthly, xxiv

Augustine (saint), xlixn151

Baba Ram Dass, xxx–xxxi

Bailey, Susie Ford (mother-in-law), 14

Ballard, Beth, 299n4
Banks, Allan A., 155, *157n4*
Baptist Church, 26; Abyssinian Baptist
    Church (Harlem, New York), 306–7;
    American Baptist Convention, 33n1;
    American Baptist Home Mission Society,
    206n1; Baptist church schools, 206n4;
    Dexter Avenue Baptist Church (Mont-
    gomery, Ala.), xxvi, xlvn52, 97n5, 231,
    251–52; Ebenezer Baptist Church (Atlanta,
    Ga.), 98n6, 111n1; First Baptist Church
    (Daytona, Fla.), 203; First Baptist Church
    (Roanoke, Va.), 242; Florida Baptist
    Academy, 243n1; Friendship Baptist
    Church (Atlanta, Ga.), 112n3; Hyde Park
    Baptist Church (Chicago), 17n16; and
    interdenominationalism, 161; ministers,
    33n1, 73n1, 111n1, 242; Mount Bethel
    Baptist Church (Daytona, Fla.), 242, 243n1;
    Mount Zion Baptist Church (Oberlin,
    Ohio), xlviiin137; National Baptist Laymen
    Convention, 254n1; Second Baptist Church
    (Detroit), 156n3, 157n4; Second Baptist
    Church (Evanston, Ill.), 305m1; Thurman
    ordained into ministry, 242; Wheat Street
    Baptist Church (Atlanta, Ga.), 304
Barnett, Sue, 192n1
Bartholdi, Frédéric Auguste, *314n6*
Bartlett, Josiah Reed, 76, *76n5*
Bartlett, Laile E., 76
Benne, Kenneth Dean, 50, *52n7*
Bennett College (Greensboro, N.C.), 261,
    261n1
Bennett, John C., 29n1
Berlin, Irving, *8n8*
Bethune, Albert M., 109, *110nn10–11*
Bethune, Mary McLeod, 18–19, 38, 108, *110n7*,
    130n25, 131n30, 286; and Eleanor Roosevelt,
    19–20, 130n23; Mary McLeod Bethune
    Foundation,109–10; Thurman's eulogy
    for, lxviii, 108, 123–31, 181n1
Bethune-Cookman College, 109n4, 123,
    130n25, 314–15
"Be Ye Not Overcome by Evil" (Thurman),
    81–85

Binder, Paul J., *165n1*
birth control, 248–49
Blake, William, 310, *313n2*
Blount, Brian K., *xlvn65*
Boehme, Jacob, xlixn139, xlixn151
Boger, Johann, xlixn138
Bollman, Henry, xxv, 150–51, *151n2*
Bonaparte, Napoleon, 22
Booth, Edwin Prince, 86, *92n8*
Booth, Newell S., 50, *52n9*
Borders, William Holmes, 304–5, *305n1*
Boston University, 49; African Area Studies
    Program, 50, 52n8, 54; *Bostonia*, 281;
    Brotherhood Council, 90; ceased being
    majority-Protestant institution, xix;
    Christian Association, 49; Hillel House,
    xix, xxvii, 49, 51n4, 88, 161–62, 241; Human
    Relations Center, 50, 54; Newman Club,
    49, 51n1, 161–62; Protestant Clubs, 49;
    Robinson Chapel, 234; School of Educa-
    tion, xviii; School of Law, xxv; Student
    Christian Association, xxxvii, 90, 93n16,
    93n22, 160–63; United Ministry to Stu-
    dents, xxvii, 90, 198–200, 246–47
Boston University School of Theology, 45, 50,
    54; interdenominationalism of, xx, 49–50,
    54, 90; opposition to hiring Thurman,
    xxiii; personalism among faculty, xx;
    population of black students, xviii; Thur-
    man first tenured black professor, xviii;
    Thurman named minister-at-large, xl.
    See also Marsh Chapel
Boswell, James, 104n4
Bosworth, Edward Increase, 226, *231n7*
Bowdoin College, 129n1
Bowen, John Wesley Edward, xviii, *xliiin6*
Bowne, Borden Parker, xx
Brahman mystics, the, xlixn151
Branch, Taylor, 231
Brewer, James, 287
Bridges, Robert, 178, *182n3*
Brightman, Edgar S., xx, xxii, xliiin15, 65,
    157n8
British-American Pulpit Exchange, 272
Britton, George, 237–39, *239n1*

Brodshaug, Melvin, 235, *237n11*
brotherhood, xix, 39, 50, 54, 90, 144, 172–73, 217, 290, 292–93
Broun, Heywood, 317, *322–23n1*
Brown, Michael, *xlvn65*
Brown v. Board of Education, 152, 170, 177n5
Brown, William O., 50, *52n8*
Bruch, Max, xxix
Buddhism, xlixn151, 289. *See also* Zen Buddhism
Buchanan, Lynn, 13, *16n8*, 16n9, 75, 76n1
Bunche, Ralph, 4, *8–9n9*, 9n10, 220n2
Burden, Jean, xxiv, *xlivn37*
Bunyan, John, 123
Burns, Aubrey, 15
Buttrick, George A., 136
Byrne, Carleton E., 40–42, *42n1, 76n6*, 93n18
Byrne, Esther Smith, *42n1*

Cabot, Richard C., 100, 104n5, *104n6*
California Labor School, 44n1
Calvin, John, 219
"Can It Be Truly Said That the Existence of a Supreme Spirit Is a Scientific Hypothesis?" (Thurman), 131n31
Caplan, Joan, 93n13
Carlyle, Thomas, *280n8*
Caroll, "Smokey Joe," 204
Case, Harold C., xix–xxii, xxvii, xxxviii–xxxix, 46–47, *47n2*, 52–53, 56–59, 75, 76n3, 85–86, 164–67, 198–201, **199**, 221–22, 234–37, 246–48, 301
Case, Phyllis Kirk, xxii, *53n1*, 57, 59, **199**, 222
Casteel, John Laurence, 195, 197n16
Catchings, Maynard, 71
Catholic Church and Catholicism, 173; at Boston University, 9–10; chapel services should serve Catholics as well as Protestants, 161. *See also* Boston University: Newman Club
Cayce, Edgar, *197n10*
Chakravarty, Amaya Chandra, 86, *92n9*
Chalmers, Allan Knight, *xxii–xxiii*
Cheney, Sheldon, *Men Who Have Walked with God*, xli

Chaldeans, the, 140, 142
Chiarenza, Anne Thurman, 324, 326n3. *See also* Thurman, Anne
Chicago, Thurman serves as pastor in, xxi
Choate, Robert A., 235, *237n13*
Christians and Christianity: belief in virgin birth and physical resurrection of Jesus not necessary, 158; dangers of self-deception, 146; duty to act, 28–29, 100–3, 107, 139; duty to love all one's neighbors, 171; elimination of racial prejudice and personal salvation, 170–72; holy unity of life, 210–11; keeping the dream alive, 82; on overcoming suffering (the tragic fact), 78–80; racial prejudice a sin before God, 172; redemption leads to social responsibility, 172; resistance to secular demands to surrender principles, 27–28; respect for human personality, 132, 134; reverence for life, 312; as source of ideas of racial inequality, mv; wager personal integrity on rightness of issues, 141; warnings against pride, 143
"Christian Approach to Nuclear War, A," 316–17
"Christian Minister and the Desegregation Decision, The" (Thurman), 170–82
"Christian, Who Calls Me Christian?" (Thurman), 8n2, 107n2, 182n8
Church for the Fellowship of All Peoples (San Francisco), xxiv, xvii, xxiv, 13, 281, 285–88; and acquisition of buildings and meeting space, 12, 15n1; Archives Project, 19; Arts Festival, 44; assistant pastors, 13, 69–70; children's and young adults' programs at, 69, 75; delegation to UNESCO Conference, 13, 292; and Federal Bureau of Investigation (FBI), 44n1; finances of Fellowship Church, 36, 39, 41–42; Friends of Fellowship Church, 14; Intercultural Workshop, 13, 40, 69; interdenominationalism of, 54, 70; internationalism of, 40; interracialism of, 54, 122, 276; ministry and purpose of, 39, 239; music and arts activities, 13–14, 70; publications, 40–41;

Church for the Fellowship of All Peoples (*continued*)
 relation with Boston University, 75–76; responses to Thurman's departure, 64, 67; Religious Education Committee, 13; social change, 70; staff salaries, 41, 70, 122; Stone Tree Ranch retreats, 209, 288; Thurman discusses Boston University's offer, 53–56, 60–61; Thurman disturbed by the congregation's shift to a majority of African Americans, 121–23; Thurman overshadows and disagrees with successors, 237–39, 257–59, 262–63, 266–68; Thurman's concerns for, xvii–xviii, xxii, xxxiv, 64, 68–69, 207; Thurman's departure from, xviii, xxii, xxxiv, 53–56; Thurman's hopes for similar community in Boston, xxxiv, 58–60; Thurman's resignation from, 285–88. *See also* Fellowship Quintet; *Footprints of a Dream*; Finances of Fellowship Church; Friends of Fellowship Church

Church of England, 268n3
Church of the Crossroads (Hawaii), 239, 269–70
Church of the Latter-day Saints, 250–51
Church Peace Mission, The, 316–17
Citizens for Global Solutions, 260n4
civil rights, xi, xviii, 44n1, 73, 97–98n5, 131, 134, 135n2, 152, 153, 167, 169n7, 170–77, 223, 261, 264–65
Civil Rights Congress, 43–44
Claremore Fund, the, xxxviii, 88, 93n18
Clark, Adeline, 235–36
Clark, Badger, 181, 182n8
Clark-Atlanta University, 109n4
Clark, Walter Huston, xxxi, xlviin82
Clifton, Cardella, 67, 67n11
Cobb, W. Montague, 204, 206–7n6
Colenso, John William, 311, 314n8
Collins, Evelyn, 32
Collins, George L. "Shorty," 32–33, 33n1
colonialism, 132, 207n8
Committee on International Economic Growth, 35n5
common consciousness, 224–30, 230n1
Common Ground (Lukacs), xii

communism, 292; Thurman admires commitment against discrimination, 44n1, 293; NAACP not infiltrated by, 168. *See also* American Communist Party
community in Thurman's Jesus idea; advice to ministers, 173; in Covenant for Marsh Chapel fellowship, 163; in national community of equality and justice, 220
Conrad, Joseph, 275n15
Constitution of the United States, 112–13, 118n1, 133, 265n3, 318; constitutional prerogatives, 218; 14th Amendment, 132
"contagion" (dissemination of ideas), xvii, xxii, 331
"Contribution of Baptist Church Schools to Negro Youth, The" (Thurman), 206n4
Cram, Ralph Adams, xix
Crane, Henry Hitt, 301, 303n2
Creative Encounter: An Interpretation of Religion and the Social Witness, The, xlviiin134, lxiv, 89, 96, 111, 155
"The Creative Encounter—Habbakkuk" (Thurman), 148n5
Cromwell, Fred, 42
Crosby, Arthur U., 14, 19, 64–65, 65n1
Curry, Izola Ware, 222, 224n1

Dana Hall School, xviii
Danielson, Albert V., 108, 109n4
Danielsen, Jessie, 109n4, 129n1
Darwin, Charles, 23, 29n4, 319
Davies, Mary Carolyn, 77–78, 80–81n1
Daytona Educational and Industrial Training School for Negro Girls, 130n25
Dead Sea Scrolls, 149n26
Deats, Paul, xx, 90, 93n23
Debs, Eugene, 284–85
Declaration of Independence, the, 112, 116, 132
"Declaration of Independence, The" (Thurman), xli, xlixn143
Deep Is the Hunger (Thurman), 65, 155, 251
Deep River (Thurman), 153
De Laine, Joseph Armstrong, 134, 136n6
Dent, Albert W., 96–99, 97n1
De Priest, Oscar, 323n5

desegregation, 134–35, 136n6, 305. *See also* "Christian Minister and the Desegregation Decision, The" (Thurman); segregation
despair, xxvii, 24, 107, 116–17, 134, 138, 181, 211
Detroit Council of Churches, 13
Dett, R. Nathaniel, 16n9, 86–87, *91n2*, 93n12
DeWolf, L. Harold, xx
Dewey, John, 131n31
Dexter Avenue Baptist Church (Montgomery, Ala.), xxvi, xlv, 97, 231, 251–52
Dickey, Elmer, 31, *32n3*, 93n13
Dickson, Richard Watson, 22, *29n3*
dictatorships, 117
Dillard University, xxvi, xlvn52, 96–97
Dimond, Sidney, 95–96, *96n1*
Diver, Joan Makechnie, xxv, 236–37n10
Doblin, Rick, xxxiii, xlviin93
Donahue, Patricia K., xxvii
Douglas, William O., 116, *120n8*, 120n10
Douglass, Frederick, *48–49n2*, 324–25, 326n6
Douglass, Helen Pitts, *326n6*
Durkee, J. Stanley, 326n7
Dwight L. Moody's Institute for Home and Foreign Missions, 131n30

Ebenezer Baptist Church (Atlanta), 97, 98n6, 111
Ebony (magazine), 296–97
Edinburgh (Scotland), lxxiv, 167, 169n4, 268–70, 274, 275n20
education; African American higher education and social change, 201–4; African American professionals, 204; missionary schools segregated, 202; paucity of secondary schools in the South, 318. See also *Brown v. Board of Education;* Washington, Booker T.
Egypt, 269, 271, 283
Ehrensperger, Harold Adam, 86, *92n4*
Eisenhower, Dwight D., 246n4, 294n10
Eliot, T. S., 81n3
Emma Willard School, 14, 17n15
equality among people, 39, 115, 120n6, 132, 215; the dream of, 219; experienced in individual lives, 220; hierarchy of inequality and domination, 215

Eucalyptus Press, 13, 104n2, 157n5
"Eulogy for Mary McLeod Bethune" (Thurman), lxviii, 108, 123–29, 181n1
Evans, Bradford *285n1*
Ewing, Eloise, 270

Fahey, Alice, 280
faith, 128, 176; attitude to ultimate outcome, 212; beyond proof, 211; that God is at work in all human history, 140; the nature of, 106–7, 212; vs. belief, 120
"Faith the Tutor" (Thurman), 209–14
Falcon, Daniel, 70, 72, *73n5*
Farmer, Leonard J., Sr., *xliiin6*
fascism, 205, 207n9
"Fascist Masquerade, The" (Thurman), 120n7, 207n9, 221n7, 221nn10–11
Federal Bureau of Investigation (FBI) and Fellowship Church, 44n1
Fellowship Church. *See* Church for the Fellowship of all Peoples (San Francisco, Calif.)
Fellowship of Reconciliation: 32, 33n1, 66, 297, 299n6
Fellowship Quintet, 8n1, 13–14, 16n9, 63. *See also* Acevedo, Rokee; Fong, Raymond K.; Mellon, Emory; Van Pelt, Joseph; and Williams, Corrine Barrow
Ferris, Theodore Parker, 64, *65n2*
First Baptist Church (Roanoke, Virginia), 242
Fisk University, 35–37, 40, 97n4
Fleming, Monroe H., 250–51, *251n1*
Florida Baptist Academy, 243n1
Fong, Raymond K., *16n9, 93n13*
Footprints of a Dream (Thurman), xlviiin134, 15n1, 16n9, 43n3, 56, 57n1, 177n2, 244n5, 332n4
Ford Foundation, 50
Fra Angelico, xlixn151
Freedman, Charles S., 49, *51n4*
Freedmen's Aid Bureau, 318, 323n2
Freedom Trails of Negro History in Boston (Anne Thurman Chiarenza and Sue Bailey Thurman), 326n3

"Freedom under God" (Thurman), 112–20, 121

Friendship Baptist Church (Atlanta), 111, 112n3

Gammon Theological Seminary, xliiin6, xliiin17, 52n9, 98, 99n2

Gandhi, Mohandas K. "Mahatma," xlixn139, xlixn151, 7–8, 92n9, 151n5; change through ethical means, 25; Gandhian nonviolence, 9n12, 153, 231; and letter to Muriel Lester, 128

Gandy, Samuel L., 97n4

Geddes, Francis, 69, 72, 73n3, 123n1, 123n2, 207–08, 237–39, 257–59, 262–63, 265–68, 276–80, 285

Gilkey, Charles Whitney, 14–15, 17n16, 302, 303n5

Gilman, Richard, 197n5

Glover, D. Donald, 12, 15n4

God: both in and above history, 142, 147; comforts the suffering, 228; creative spirit of, 113; discriminates mercifully, 147; divine contingency all-inclusive, 141; gives freedom as human birthright, 114; human responsibility both personal and social, 116; is near, 214; the kingdom of God is within, 99–100, 220; living in the presence of, 128; no distinction between God of life and God of religion, 138; prophets insist on one God for all people, 137; scriptural written word a covenant with God, 142. See also love

Goethe, Johann Wolfgang von, xlixn138, xlixn152

Golden State Mutual Life Insurance Company, 41, 43n4

Gomillion, Charles G., 265n3

Good Friday Experiment, the, xxx–xxxiv, xlvin75, xlviiin93, 194

Goodson, Max R., 235, 237n12

Gordon, Noah, xxxiii, 335–36

"Gothic Principle, The," 130n20, 178–82

Graham, Billy, xxiv

Graham, Edward K., 235

Grapes of Wrath, The (Steinbeck), 210–11, 214n3

Greatest of These, The (Thurman), 155, 157n5

Greenleaf, Robert K., 334, 334n4

Green Pastures, The (Connelly), 34–35

Greensboro (North Carolina), 261n1; Woolworth's lunch counter sit-in, 261, 265n5

Gross, Boice, xxxviii

Growing Edge, The (publication of Fellowship Church), 12, 15n4, 16n9, 17n17, 62, 63n3, 275n20

Growing Edge, The (Thurman), xlviiin134, **193**

Guild for Psychological Studies, 76n2

"Habakkuk Exposition" (Thurman), 136–50

Hamill, Robert, xxxix, xlii

Hamilton, Charles V., 264–65, 264n1

Hampton Institute, 261n1

Harding, Margaret "Peg," 164–65, 165n1

Harlem Renaissance, xl, 110n6

Harrington, Paul, 165

Hart, Waldo, 285n1

Hartman, Lewis Oliver, 86, 92n5

Harvard Divinity School, xxxi, 193, 194, 287

Harvard Psychedelic Project, xxxi

Harvard University: fires Timothy Leary, xxx–xxxi, 333; Ingersoll Lecture, xviii

Harwell, Dwight Wesley, 69–70, 72, 73n4

Hayes, Afrika, 95, 95n3

Hayes, Helen Alzada Mann, **245**

Hayes, Roland, 30–32, 94–95, **245**

Hayward, John F., 327–28, 332n3

"He Looked for a City" (Thurman) 105

Henderson, Coffee, 280

Henderson, Dorothy McLaughlin, 120–21, 121n1

Hinduism, xxv, 7, 104n2, 135n3, 150–51, 288–89

Hiroshima, 297

Hitler, Adolf, 215, 218

Hocking, William Earnest, 149n18

Holloway, Jonathan, 220n2

Hong Kong, 269–71, 282

Honneger, Arthur, 14

Hope, John, 38

Horne, Frank, 108, 110n6

Horne, Gerald, 44n2

"Horn of the Wild Oxen" (Thurman), 77–81
Horton, Philip, *336n6*
Hoyland, J. S., 210
Howard, Oliver O., *323n2*
Howard Thurman Center for Common
   Ground, xii
Howard Thurman Educational Trust, 42n1,
   75n6, 294–96
Howard University, xviii–xix, 4, 8n8, 38, 202,
   260, 317–23; Bunche at, 8n8; charges of
   communism, 323n5; freedom of thought
   preserved, 319; Pilgrimage of Friendship,
   282; Rankin Chapel, xxiv, 94n24, 281, 319;
   role of religion, 321; School of Law, 244;
   School of Theology, xix; Thurman at, xxvii,
   38, 55; Thurman preaching at, 20–29
"Howard University and the Frontiers of
   Human Freedom" (Thurman), 317–23
Hudson, Gail, 43–44
Hughes, Langston, 20–21
human nature; absolute worth of the individual, 281, 291, 318; innate goodness of,
   219; perfectability of the human spirit, 292;
   universal depravity of, 215, 219
[Huntzinger], Grace, *123n2*
Huxley, Aldous, *Doors of Perception, The,* xxx

Ibsen, Henrik, *xlixn152*
idolatry, 145
Imes, William Lloyd, 248, *249n2*
India, 11n6, 133, 135n3, 25, 104n8, 133, 135n3,
   204–5, 216, 282; religious wisdom, xxv,
   150–51; struggle for independence, 7–8,
   11n6, 128, 205, 207n8; Thurman's travels
   in, xxiv, *xliiin5*, 204–205, 222, 231–232,
   268, 284. *See also* Gandhi, Mohandas K.;
   Hinduism
inequality; social hierarchy of domination
   and, 215; contribution of Christian doctrine of depravity to, 215, 219
"Imperative to Understanding, An" (Thurman), 288–94
Ingersoll Lecture on the Immortality of Man,
   xviii, 65, 157n8, 195n1
integration, 287; in public schools, 135

Intercultural Workshop. *See* Church for the
   Fellowship of all Peoples (San Francisco,
   Calif.)
interdenominationalism, 321; Thurman's plan
   for Marsh Chapel fellowship, 158–64
International Institute of San Francisco, 40–41
International Labor Defense, 44n1
Interpreter's Bible, The, 136, 148n2, 148n8
interracialism, 32, 220n2, 239n3, 270
Islam, 23, 289, 94n2
Israel (modern state), xl, 8–9n9

Jack, Homer Alexander, 153, *154n4*
Jackson, Jesse, *39n3*
James, Arthur Leonard, 242–44, *243–44n1*
Japan, 40, 63, 222, 269–70, 272, 275n26, 282,
   285n4, 294n10
Jehovah's Witnesses, 173
Jeliffe, Russell and Rowena, *20n1*
Jennings, Coleman, xxx, 20, 61–63, *62–63n1,*
   269, 273, *275n20*
Jesus and the Disinherited (Thurman), xxvi,
   13, 155, 193
Jesus Christ: life of, in song cycle, 94; over-
   coming evil with good, 84; significance of
   resurrection, 158
Jim Crow, xx, 112, 152, 154n2, 175, 206n4
Johnson, Clarence R., 207–9, 266–67, 268n1,
   276, 286, 288n2
Johnson, Georgia Douglas, xl, **245**
Johnson, James Weldon, 228, *231n9*
Johnson, Mordecai Wyatt, 29n1, 38, 39n3, 317,
   323n5, 323n8
Johnson, Willard Lyon, 34–35, *35n5*
Jones, Audrey, 1
Jones, Charles Miles, 73–74, *74n1*
Jones, Edgar DeWitt, 155
Jones, Hubert E., xxv, *xliin3*
Jones, Major J., *99n2*, xlvn52, 197n3
Jones, Rufus, *156n2*, 193
Jordan, Barbara, xxv–xxvi, xliii
Journal of Negro Education, 201
Joy, Adena, 12, *15n2*
Judaism, 137–38, 257; chapel services serve
   Jews as well as Protestants, 161

justice, xxiv, 7, 116, 177, 215, 218, 255–56; racial, xx; retributive, 147, 256

Kabir, 104n3
Kaiser, Julius "Guyula," 234, 236n2
Karamu House (Cleveland), 19–20
Katzander, Shirley, 335–36, 336n1
Kennedy, John F., 326–27, 327n1
Kennedy, Robert F., 326–27, 327n3
Keys, Donald F., 297, 299n1
Kierkegaard, Søren, xxviii
Kilgore, Kathleen, xviii
King, Coretta Scott, xxvi, xlvn51
King, Herbert, 276, 280n6
King, Martin Luther, Jr., xiii, 39n3, 44n1, 96–97, 97–98n5, 98n7, 151–54, 222–24, 231–33, 244, 251–54, 259, 298, 326–27; admirer of Thurman, xxv–xxvi, 152; ministry at Dexter Avenue Baptist Church, Montgomery, xlvn52, 231; on non-violence, 231, 251; and position at Dillard University, 96–98; *Strength to Love*, xxvii; *Stride toward Freedom*, 222; Thurman believed he had no early influence on, 152; travels in India, 231–32
King, Martin Luther, Sr., xxvi, 97, 111n1
King, Willis J., xliiin6, 52n9
Kirk, Grayson, 118n2
Klausner, Abraham, 49–50, 51n5
Kropotkin (Thurman's dog), 226, 231n6
Kropotkin, Pyotr Alexeyevich (prince), 231n6
Ku Klux Klan, 38, 215, 218–219, 221nn7–10

Lambda Kappa Mu, 131–36
Landry, Stuart O., 221n5
Lannom, Allen C., 87, 92–93n11, 235, 236n3
Lao Tse, xlixn139
Lawrence, Carrie, 1
Leary, Timothy, xxx–xxxiii, xlvin75, xlvin78, xlviin81, xlviinn84, 194, 333–35. *See also* Good Friday Experiment
Legge, James, 394n4
Lenud, Philip, xxvi
Leopold II (king of Belgium), 271, 275n15
Lester, Muriel, 86, 128, 131n35

liberty, 112–20, 132–33
Liebman, Joshua Loth, 50, 51–52n6
Life (magazine), xxiii, 157n10
Life of Jesus (Rall), 8n5
Lincoln, Abraham, 23, 29n4
Lincoln University, xlviiin135, 89, 93n21, 274n6
Litell, Franklin Hamlin, 49, 51n3
love, 255–56, 290; God loves people as they are, 214; as overall teaching of the church, 170; the ultimate meaning of life, 214
loyalty oaths. *See* National Educational Defense Act
Lukacs, J. Anthony, *Common Ground*, xii
Lyman Beecher Lectures on Preaching, 155, 157nn7–8

Makechnie, George Howard, xxxix, **91**, 235–36, 236–237n10, **238**, **301**; *Howard Thurman, His Enduring Dream*, xii
"Man and the Moral Struggle" (Thurman), xli, xlixn138, 13
Manitoba (Canada), 240, 242n5
Marian Anderson, 251n1
Marshall, Thurgood, 170n8
Marsh Chapel, xix, 85–94, 193, 281, 295, 300; attendance figures, xlivn42, 234; Hamill, Robert, succeeded Thurman as chaplain, xxxix; liturgical dance, **255**; radio broadcasts of sermons, 234; Statement of Affirmation for chapel fellowship, xxxv–xxxvi; summer procedures, 164–67; Thurman named dean of, xi–xii, xxvii; Thurman plans interracial, international, interreligious chapel fellowship, xxxiv–xxxvi, 158–49, 304n7; Thurman's opposition to sectarianism , xxxvi–xvii, 90, 91n1, 94n24; Thurman's services at, xxiv–xxv; Thurman suggest formation of Friends of the Boston University Chapel, 160; trustees reject chapel fellowship proposal, xxxvi, 198. *See also* Thurman, Harold; sermon series, at Marsh Chapel
Marsh, Daniel L., xix, xliiin11, 86, 92n6, **301**
"Martin Luther King Lecture #2" (Thurman), xlvn49, xlvn51, 152n1

Mason, Vivian C., 108, *109n5*

Massey, James Earl, 154–57, *156n1*

Mayo, Elton, *135n2*

Mays, Benjamin, 38, 73–7, *135n4*, 204

Mays, Betty Driscoll, *247n1*

McCall, Oswald W. S., 108n3

McCluskey, Audrey Thomas, *110n8*

McDannell, Colleen, *33n5*

McKenzie, John F., 235

McKinney, Richard I., 71

McNeil, Genna Rae, *306n2*

"Meals for Millions," 270, 274n10

Meditations for Apostles of Sensitiveness (Thurman), 13, 21n3, 104n2

Meditations of the Heart (Thurman), xlviiin134, 42n1, 64, 65n3, 84n1, 84–85n2, 89, 108, 130n20, 155, 251, 257n10

Meister Eckhardt, *xlixn150*

Mellon, Emory, *16n9*

Melville, Elsbeth, 235

Melville, Herman, *xlixn152*

Mendelssohn, Felix, 22

"Message of Jeremiah II" (Thurman), 130n20

Methodist Church, xxii, 58

Methodist General Biblical Institute, became Boston University School of Theology, xix

Methodist Youth Convocation of California-Arizona-New Mexico, 235

Millay, Edna St. Vincent, xxxii

Miller, Max B., 235, *237n18*

Milton, Lorimer, 203, *206n5*

Mitchell, Arthur W., *323n5*

Mitropoulos, Dimitri, 14

"Modern Challenges to Religion: Secular Radicalism" (Thurman), 44n1

Moffat, James, 178, 182n2

monotheism, 137

Montgomery, Ala., bus boycott, 98n5, 152. *See also* Dexter Avenue Baptist Church

Moody, Dwight L. *See* Dwight L. Moody's Institute for Home and Foreign Missions

Moore, Harry T. and Harriette, 38

Moral Re-Armament (MRA), 109, 110n9

Morehouse College, xxvi, 31n2, 32, 152n2, 202, 206n5, 297

Morgan College (Baltimore), 13

Mormon Church. *See* Church of the Latter-day Saints

Motive (magazine), 259, 260n3

Mount Bethel Baptist Church (Daytona, Fla.), 242, 243n1

Mt. Holyoke College, 203

Mount Zion Baptist Church (Oberlin, Ohio), xlviiin137

Muelder, Walter G., xviii–xx, xxii–xxiii, xxxv, xxxvii, 45–46, *45–46n1*, 49–52, 53, 57, 268, 274n1; accused of Communist tendencies, xix; early critic of McCarthyism, xliiin8; opposed peace-time draft, xliiin8; remarks on Thurman's retirement, xlviiin113

Mukerji, Dhan Gopal, *293n1*

Mumford, Lewis, 104n7, 298, *300n9*

Muste, A. J., 66, *299n6*, 316–17

Mygatt, Tracy, 259, 260n1, *260n2*, 260n3

My Host the Hindu (Lester), 128, 131n35

Myrdahl, Gunnar, 220n2

mysticism, xxxvii, xxiv, xxviii, xxxi, xxxiii–xxxiv, xli, xlvin79, 20n6, 138, 194, 196n1, 334

Nabrit, James Madison, Jr., 244, 323–26, *325n2*

Nagasaki, 297

Nakajima, Katsuo Arnold, 13, *15n5*, 16n9

National Association for the Advancement of Colored People (NAACP), 38, 135n4, 167–70, 169n7

National Committee for a Sane Nuclear Policy (SANE), 154n4, 297, 299n2

National Conference of Christians and Jews, 34–35

National Council of Negro Women (NCNW), 9, 11nn7–8, 108, 126–127, 325; plans for museum in Washington, 14; Sue Bailey Thurmond, National Chairman of Archives and Museum Department, 14, 129n4

National Council on Religion in Higher Education, 194, 197n5

National Educational Defense Act, 323n4

National Federation for Constitutional Liberties, 44n2

National Hospital Association, 182, 192n2

National League for Nursing, 182, 192n3

National Negro Congress, 44n2

National Youth Administration, 108

nature: belief in universality of order, 29, 291; involved in divine judgment, 147; the whole earth as God's temple, 146–47

Nebuchadnezzar (king), 148n7

Neff, John Wesley, 225, 237n14, 247

Negro Delegation to India, Ceylon, and Burma, 11n6, 231

Negro History Week, lx

Negro Spiritual Speaks of Life and Death, The (Thurman), 155

Nehru, Jawaharlal, 11n6

New England Conservatory, 234

Newhall, Jannette Elthina, 65, 65n2

"New Heaven and the New Earth, The" (Thurman), 201–7

New York Times, xxiii, xlivn35, 155

Nichols, Decatur Ward, 34, 35n6

Nichols, Sylvia, 16n9

Niebuhr, Reinhold, xx

Nixon, Richard Milhous, 244–46, 246n1

Norell, Robert J., 264n2

North Carolina A & T College, 261

Nott, (Mrs.), 36, 37n1

Nott, Raymond, 37n2

nuclear weapons and disarmament, 133, 260n4, 297–99

nursing, 182–93; importance of renewal, 190; meets social need and gains social support, 183–85; professionals as members of community, 188; spiritual values for professionals, 191

Oberlin College: xlviiin135, lxi, lxxvii, 19, 36–37, 98, 99n2, 226, 250

O'Connor, Norman James, 49, 51n1

Ohio Wesleyan University, 88–89

Olivelle, Patrick, 104n2

oppression, 143–45; confirms brotherhood of man, 144; explotation of the person, 145; resistance against, 144–45

Ortega y Gasset, José, 5

Osgood Hill, 301

Otis, James, Jr., 116, 120n9

Overholt, Jessie Wickwire, 37, 168, 169n1, 169n5

Overholt, John, 35–37, 37n1, 167–70

Overholt, William A., xxxvii, 90, 93n22, 247

Oxnam, Robert Fisher, 165n2

Pacific School of Religion, 13

pacifism, 2, 32, 33n1, 66, 248–49, 297

Pahnke, Eva Sontum, xxxiii, 194, 197n11

Pahnke, Walter Norman, xxx–xxxiii, 193–97, 196n1, 333

Pakistan, 310, 313n3

Palestine (modern-day), 4

Pandit, Vijay Lakshmi, 10, 11n6; awarded National Council of Negro Women Citation of Honor, 11n7

Pasadena, Calif., xxi, 31

Paton, Alan, 15, 17n17

Patterson, Frederick Douglass, 48n2

Patterson, Louise Thompson, 44n2

Patterson, William, 44n2

Paukulis, Shirley June, 234, 236n1

Paul (saint), 144

peace: aspiration for, 180; byproduct of social and economic justice, 7; human spirit naturally affirms, 22

"Peace of God, The" (Thurman), 150–51

Peale, Norman Vincent, xxiv

Peck, Austin H., Jr., 42n1

Pendle Hill, 69

Perlman, Samuel, 49, 51n2, 86

personalism, xx–xxi

Peru, 310, 314n4

Phelps, Dryden, 69–70, 73n1, 74n2, 74–76, 121–23

Phillipines, the, 222, 269, 271–72, 282

Pike, James, 248n1

Pilgrim House (Los Angeles), 15n5

Pilgrim's Progress, The (Bunyan), 123–24, 129n4

"Pines, the." *See* Guild for Psychological Studies

Pioneers of Negro Origin in California
(S. B. Thurman), 16n13, 40, 43n2, 40
Plato, 214, 218–19, 221n6
Pliny the Younger, 320, *323n7*
Plotinus, *xlixn151*
Popper, Karl, *221n6*
Powell, Adam Clayton, Jr., 306–7, *306n1*
"Power of the Spirit and the Powers of This
World, The" (Thurman), 21–30
Prepatory Schoolmasters' Conference, 20
Presbyterian Church, 174n1, 269; withdraws
support for Fellowship Church, 278
President's Committee on Government Con-
tracts, 246n4
President's Committee for Equal Employ-
ment Opportunity, 246n4
priesthood, nature of, 250–51
Pritchett, Laurie, 326–27, *327n5*
Proctor, Clarence, 248–49
Proctor, Samuel DeWitt, *xliiin7*
Protestantism: at Boston University,
xxxvi–xxxvii, 163n3; doctrine of the
priesthood in, 250; Klan calls itself
Protestant, 219, 221n9; liberal, xx,
93n18
providence, in the making of America, 217
psychedelic drugs, spiritual potential of,
xxx–xxxi, 194
Pulpit Digest, 170, 177

Quakers and Quaker spirituality, xxvii, 169n1
"Quest for Peace, The" (Thurman), 2–9
Qumran, 149n26

race and race relations: racial prejudice, 134;
stereotypes of African Americans, 34
Raines, Richard C., 59, *60n1,* 308, 309n3
Rall, Harris Franklin, *8n5*
Ramakrishna (Sri), 150, *151n4*
Randolph, A., Philip, 244
Reader's Digest, labels Mueder and the
School of Theology communistic, xix
reflective thinking, 121, 131n31
"Religion in a Time of Crisis" (Thurman),
207n8

"The Religion of Jesus and the Disinherited"
(Thurman), 13, 16n11
religion, meaning of, 25–26
religious experience: communal fellowship
in worship, 339; faith is beyond proof but
subject to demand for proof, 211; hope and
faith, 148; human spirit defends its integ-
rity, 115; as internal touchstone, 26, 141; not
empirically based, 23, 143, 146
Religious Leaders Conference (Washington,
D. C.), 244–46
Reporter (journal), xxxiii
"Responsibility of the Professional to Society,
The" (Thurman), 182–93
Rickenbacker, Eddie, 27–28, *30n12*
Rinehart, Daisy, 155, *157n6*
Riverside Church (New York), 37n4
Robeson, Paul, *251n1*
Robinson, James H., 155, *157n7*
Rochester Theological Seminary, xxiv, 31n2
Rockefeller Brothers Theological Fellowship
Program, 194, 196n2
Rockefeller, John David, Sr., *131n29*
Rockefeller, Laura Spelman, *131n29*
Rodzinski, Artur, 14, *16n12*
Romulo, Carlos P., *118n3*
Roosevelt, Eleanor, *21n5*; and Bethune, 18–20,
130n23; civil and human rights advocacy, 19,
21n5; support for Fellowship Church, 19, 286
Roosevelt, Franklin Delano, 205, *207n8*
Rousseau, Jean-Jacques, 219
Royalty of the Pulpit, The (Jones), 155, 157n8
Rubáiyát of Omar Khayyám, The, 142, 149n19
Russell, Bertrand, 24

Sachar, Abram L., *118n2*
St. Francis, xlixn151
St. Martin-in-the-Fields (London), 269,
271–72, 274n14, 275nn16–17
Salk polio vaccine, 133, 135n3
Sams, Alice (mother), lvii, 1–2, 9–12, 17–18,
21n2. *See also* Alice Ambrose Fellowship
Children's Fund
Sams, James, 9, *10n3*
San Jose Peace Center, 33n1

Savage, Barbara Dianne, *110n9*

Schlacter-Shalomi, Zalman, 240–42, *241n1*; and Thurman, xxix–xxx, xl, xliii, xlvin71, 197n4

Schreiner, Olive, 32, 193n4, 206, 207n10, 224–25, 230n2, 312–13

Schweitzer, Albert, *xlixn138*, 236n5. *See also* "Albert Schweitzer" (Thurman)

segregation, 30, 31n2, 129n3, 326; brutality of, 173; "the cult of inequality," 202, 218–19, 221n5; and education, 48, 202; state far ahead of Christian community in opposition to, 205. *See also* desegregation

sermons, their nature and function, 328–32; the congregation, 328–29; integral part of worship, 328, 330; placement and pace, 329; preparation for, 331

Seventh-Day Adventists, 173, 250

Shaw, Francis Wells, *130n20*

Shaw, George Bernard, *xlixn138*

Sheen, Fulton J., xxiv

"Significance of Jesus, The" (Thurman), 182n8

Sikhs, 284

Silliman College (Dumagetta, Philippines), 274n12

slavery, 48, 115, 132, 218, 314, 318

Smith, Elaine M., *110n8*

Smith, Eleanor Lloyd (Mrs. Ralph M. Smith), *42n1*, 88, 93nn18–19

Smith, Huston, xxxii, *xlviin82*, **119**, *294n3*

Smith, Lillian Eugenia, 153, *154n2*

Smith, Lloyd M., xxxviii, xlvin71, *42n1*, 93n18, 294–96

Smith, Luther, xxxiii

Smith, Thornton L., 10, *10–11n4*

Snyder, Ted, *8n8*

social change: means of, 25; need to address disease, poverty, and ignorance, 291; without bitterness, 128. *See also* civil rights movement; Gandhi, Mohandas K.; war

Southern Christian Leadership Conference, 327n2

Spelman College, 127; Sisters Chapel, 127, 131n29

Spelman, Lucy Maria, *131n29*

Spelman Seminary, xxvi

Spingarn Medal, 38–39

Spiritual Disciplines and Resources (course), xxviii–xxx, xxxviii, xlvin71, 120–21

Staupers, Mabel K., *192n3*

Steger, Jane, *xlixn151*

Steere, Douglas, xxviii

Stocking, John T., 2–3, 9

Stoddard, Lothrop, *221n10*

Strong, Peggy, 197n10

Stryker, Roy, *33n3*

Studies in Mystical Religion (Rufus Jones), 193

suffering leading to understanding, xxviii, 78–89, 138, 144, 150–51

Sullivan, Ed, *130n23*

Sullivan Patricia, *31n2*

Sun-Reporter (newspaper), 14

Supreme Court. *See* United States Supreme Court

Suzuki, D. T., xxviii

Tagore, Rabindranath, 11n6, 92n9, 104n3, 118, 216, 290

Tanakh, 136–37, 149n26

Taylor, Charles L., Jr., *149n26*

Taylor, John A. ("Jack"), 122, *123n3*

Teasdale, Sara, 103, 104n9

"Third Component, The" (Thurman), 224–31

Thomas à Kempis, *xlixn151*

Thompson, Era Bell, 296–97, *297n2*

"Three Illusions of Professionalism, The" (Thurman), 182, 192n1

Threlkeld, Carolyn, *16n9*

Thurman, Anne (daughter), 14, 19, 35–37, **209**. *See also* Chiarenza, Anne Thurman

Thurman, Henrietta (sister), 213, *214n5*

Thurman, Howard, **xxi**, **91**, **119**, **193**, **199**, 207–9, **209**, **238**, **245**, 294, **301**, **315**, **333**; affinity for health-care professionals, xxvii, 182–93; approach to the Bible, xlvn65; awarded citation of merit by NCNW, 11n8; awarded honorary degrees, xl, xlviiin135; barred from hotel dining room at Methodist conference, xxii; books written by Thurman, xlviiin134; charismatic preaching of, xxi, xxxii; chronology of travel and speaking engagements, lvii–lxxxiii; as community builder, xxi; departure from Church for the Fellowship of All Peoples, xviii, xxii, xxxiv; on dull-mindedness, xviii; elected fellow of the American Academy of Arts and Sciences, xl; the Good Friday Experiment, xxx–xxxiv; at Howard University, xxvii; in India, xxiv; at Khyber Pass, xxiv; at Marsh Chapel, xi–xii, xix, xxiv–xxvii, xxxii–xxxviii; and Martin Luther King, Jr., xxvi; ministry in southern black schools, colleges, and congregations, xl, 38; moves to San Francisco, xviii; ordination, 244n2; pastor at Church for the Fellowship of All Peoples, xxiv; and personalism, xxi; preaching draws praise, xxiii–xxiv; preaching to the underprivileged, xviii; requests sabbatical, 221–22; retires from Boston University, **91;** sermon on the temptations of Jesus, xxiv; sermon series, at Marsh Chapel, on "Barren or Fruitful," "Community and the Will of God," "The Creative Encounter," "The Dilemma of Jesus," "Disciplines of the Spirit," "A Faith for Living," "The Fundamental Ends of Life," "The Inward Journey," "Jesus and the Disinherited," "Love Your Enemies," "Man and the Moral Struggle," "The Meaning of Freedom," "The Meaning of Tradition," "Modern Challenges to Religion," "The Moment of Crisis," "The Moment of Truth," "Not Peace—A Sword," "The Other Cheek," "The Outwardness of Religion," "Pain," "Prayer and Meditation," "The Quest for Maturity," "The Quest for Peace," "The Quest for Stability," "Quetsts of the Human Spirit," "The Religion of Jesus," "The Search for Life's Meaning," "Seeking and Finding," "The Single Mind," "Your Life's Working Paper," xli–xlii, xlixn138–ln165; sermon series, Fellowship Church, on "The Creative Imagination," "A Faith for Living," "The Declaration of Independence," "The Divine Encounter," "A Faith to Live By," "The Fruits of the Spirit," "Man and the Moral Struggle," "The Meaning of Commitment," "The Message of the Hebrew Prophets," "An Objective Basis of Hope," "Pain," "The Parables of Jesus," xli; sermons preached at Marsh Chapel, xlvn56; as spiritual counselor, xxvii; teaches at University of Ibadan, Nigeria, xl; teaching, xvii, xxviii–xix; televised meditations, xxv; uninterested in formal theology, xx; wishes to extend ministry to blacks in Boston, xxxviii; *With Head and Heart,* xxxviii, liii

Thurman, Madaline (sister), 9–12, 14, 17–18, 19, 35–36, 37n3, 111, 296

Thurman, Olive (daughter), 14, 19, 109, 111, 167. *See also* Wong, Emily Sue

Thurman, Sue Bailey (wife), xxvi–xxvii, xxxviii–xxxix, 9–10, **11,** 12–14, *16n13,* 17–18, 19–20, 35, 39, *44n2,* 67, 76, **91,** 98, 108–9, 111, 122, *129n5,* 167, **199,** 207, 221, 223, 235, 238, 243, **245,** 268, 273, 284, 294, **301, 315,** 315–316, 323, 324–25, 325n1; and Intercultural Workshop, 13; National Council of Negro Women (NCNW), 2, 9, 19; writings, 14, 40, *43n2*

Till, Emmett, 133–34, *135–36n5*

Tillich, Paul, 195, *197n14*

Tobias, Channing, 20–21, 38, 286

Topeka (Kans.), Thurman serves as pastor in, xxi

Tolstoy, Leo, xlixn138, 84, *85n4*

Toronto (Ontario), *121n1*

totalitarianism, Plato as inspiration for, 217–18, 221n6

total war, 181, 298

Track to the Water's Edge, A (Thurman), 189–90, 193n4, 207n10, 224–25, 230n2

Treese, Robert, 235, *237n15*

Trent, William J., Jr., 260–62, *262n4*

Trotter, Frederick Thomas, xxv, 86, *92n3*

Tubman, Harriet, 129n5

Tuskegee Institute, 48–49n2, 152–53, 156n1,
    261, 264–65
"Two Options" (Thurman), 297–300

Unamuno, Miguel de, 81n3
Underhill, Evelyn, xxviii
Union Church (Kobe), 271
Union Church (Tokyo), 270, 274n11
Union Theological Seminary, lx, lxvii, 17n16,
    29n1, 51n3, 69, 74n1, 76n5, 93n23, 157n7,
    197n14, 249n2
Unitarian Universalist Church, 35n5, 57, 75,
    123n3, 153, 208, 263, 277, 279, 327
United Nations, 4, 11n6, 14, 19, 21n5, 44n2,
    118n2; Scientific and Cultural Organization
    (UNESCO), 13, 14, 16n7, 63, 292, 294n9;
    world federalism and, 259–60
United Negro College Fund (UNCF), 47–49,
    260–62
United States Supreme Court, 168, 169n7, 170,
    174–75, 265n3
University of California, 31, 39, 41
University of Ibadan, Nigeria, Thurman
    teaches for a semester, xl
University of Redlands, 235, 237n17
United World Federalists, 259–60, 297

Vandiver, Ernest, Jr., 327, 327n4
Vanguard Recording Society, 94–95
Van Pelt, James E., 307–9, 308n1
Van Pelt, Joseph, 16n9, 63–64, 272
Van Pelt, Phyllis, 272
Vassar College, 13, 14, 89
Vedanta, 150, 151n4
violence: against civil rights activists, 134,
    136n6; against unions, 134,136n7; as means
    for founding and preserving nations, 145;
    the nature of, 5
Vivekeanda (Swami), 151n4
Vlastos, Gregory, 210–11, 214n3

Wagner, Richard, xxix
Walker, Gene K., 12, 15n3, 38–39, 47–49, 294
Wall, Cynthia, 129n5
Walter, Samuel, 87, 92n10

war, 3–4, 212; fundamentally irrational, 3–4;
    search for spiritual security against threat
    of, 163
Warmer, George A., xxxv, 235, 237n16
Warren, Earl, 29–30n11, 112, 119n4
Washington, Booker T., 204
Washington, D. C., 20, 56–57, 100, 109, 110n9,
    126–27, 244, 286
Washington, Joseph R., Jr., 247, 248n4
Washington University (St. Louis), 112, 119n5,
    121
Watson, Melvin H. "Monk," 44n1, 71, 111–12,
    111n1, 111n5
Watson, Agnes Regina, 111, 112n6
"We Believe" (television program), xxv,
    234–35, 236n6; "Love Its Own Reward,"
    254–57
Weil, Simone, xxviii
Wellesley College, xviii, 45, 55, 56, 57
Wells, H. G., 102–3, 104n8
Wesley, Charles, 324, 326n5
Wesley, John, 267, 268n2
Western College for Women, 89
Wheatley, Phyllis, commemoration of, 94,
    245
Wheat Street Baptist Church (Atlanta), 304
White Citizens Councils, 175, 177n5
white supremacy, 219, 221n10. See also White
    Citizens Councils
White, William Alanson, 225, 230n3,
    230–31n4
Whiting, George, 8n8
Whittier, John Greenleaf, 209–10, 214n1
Wicks, Robert Russell, 302, 304n6
Williams, Alberta, xxvi
Williams, Austen, 272, 275n16
Williams College, 203
Williams, Corrine Barrow, 13, 16n9, 76n7
Williams, Cy [or Sy], 121, 123n2
Williams, Samuel W., 111, 112n2
Wilson, Frank Theodore, 269, 272–73, 274n6,
    275n19
Wimbush, Vincent, xlvn65
"Windbreak . . . Against Existence" (Thur-
    man), 281–85

Winecoff, C. H., 158
Women's International League for Peace and
Freedom (WILPF), 168, 169n5
Wong, Anton (grandson), 167, 169n3
Wong, Emily Sue (granddaughter), 112n4
Woodson, Carter Godwin, 325, 326n7
Woodward, C. Vann, 175, 177n4
World Brotherhood, 35n5
world federalism, 259–60, 297, 299n1
World War I, 27–28, 30n12, 33n1, 65n1, 73n1,
126, 243n1, 260n4, 298
World War II, xi, 51n4, 51n5, 53n1, 126, 169n6,
204, 260n4, 298
"Worship and Word: A View of the Liberal
Congregation and Its Sermons" (Thur-
man), 327–33

Worthy, Emily Ambrose, 1–2, 2n1, 316
Wren, Sir Christopher, 130n21

Yeo, J. Wendell, xxxviii, 300–304, 303n1
Yergan, Max, 38
Young, Andrew, 39n3
Young, Brigham, 251n2
Young Men's Christian Association (YMCA),
162, 320, 323n6
Young Women's Christian Association
(YWCA), 162, 306

Zen Buddhism, xxviii, 69
Zoller, Marilyn, 93n13
Zulu(s); adage, 283; Bishop Colenso and, 311,
314n8